80th Annual Volume
September 1984—August 1985

TARBELL'S
Teacher's Guide
to the International Sunday School Lessons
Includes the RSV and KJV

D0735275

80th Annual Volume
September 1984—August 1985

TARBELL'S
Teacher's Guide
to the International Sunday School Lessons
Includes the RSV and KJV

Edited by WILLIAM P. BARKER

Fleming H. Revell Company
Old Tappan, New Jersey

COPYRIGHT © 1984 BY FLEMING H. REVELL COMPANY
All rights reserved—no part of
this book may be reproduced in
any form without permission
in writing from the publisher.

Printed in the United States of America
ISSN: 0730-2622

ISBN: 0-8007-1202-1

CONTENTS

A Word to the Teacher, by William P. Barker 9
The Lessons for September 1984–August 1985 13

LIST OF LESSONS
SEPTEMBER–NOVEMBER 1984
THE LETTERS OF PAUL

Lesson   Page
   I. Sept. 2. *Paul's Conversion to the*
                Way .... Acts 7:54–8:3; 9:1–19;
                              Galatians 1 13
  II. Sept. 9. *Faith—The Way to Go* . Romans 1:1–17 19
 III. Sept. 16. *Do "Good" People Sin?* . Romans 2:1–3:20 25
 IV. Sept. 23. *The Struggle to Do Right* Romans 7:4–25 31
  V. Sept. 30. *Life in the Spirit* .... Romans 8 37
 VI. Oct. 7. *Household of Faith* ..... Romans 12:9–21; Gala-
                                tians 6:1–18. 43
 VII. Oct. 14. *Motives for Moral Liv-*
                 ing .... Philippians 2:1–18 49
VIII. Oct. 21. *The Holy Spirit's Temple* 1 Corinthians 3:9–17;
                                6:12–20; Ephesians
                                5:15–20 55
 IX. Oct. 28. *Help for Family Living* . Ephesians 5:21–6:4 62
  X. Nov. 4. *Responding to God's*
                 Authority .... Romans 13; Colossians
                                3:23–25 68
 XI. Nov. 11. *The Christian's Hope* ... 1 Thessalonians 1–4 74
 XII. Nov. 18. *Getting Ready for the*
                 Lord's Return .... 1 Thessalonians 5 80
XIII. Nov. 25. *Holding on to the Truth* . 2 Thessalonians 1–3 86

DECEMBER 1984–FEBRUARY 1985
WHAT THE BIBLE IS

   I. Dec. 2. *A Source of Instruction* . Psalms 119:97–105;
                                1 Corinthians 2;
                                2 Timothy 3 92

II. Dec.   9. *A Summons to Decision* . Ezekiel 2:1–3:3;
                                          Jeremiah 1:1–12 98
III. Dec. 16. *A Witness to Good
               News* .... Luke 4:16–21;
                                          24:44–49;
                                          Acts 10:34–43 104

JOHN: THE GOSPEL OF LIFE

IV. Dec.   23. *The Word of Life.* ...... John 1. 111
V. Dec.   30. *Believe and Receive Life* John 2:1–11; 3:1–21 117
VI. Jan.   6. *Signs of New Life* ...... John 4 123
VII. Jan.   13. *The Bread of Life* ...... John 6 129
VIII. Jan. 20. *The Water of Life* ...... John 4:7–15; 7 136
IX. Jan.   27. *The Judge of Life* ...... John 5:19–24; 8:12–59 143
X. Feb.   3. *The Light of Life* .... John 9 149
XI. Feb.   10. *The Shepherd of Life* ... John 10 155
XII. Feb.   17. *The Resurrection and
                 the Life* .... John 11:1–53 161
XIII. Feb. 24. *Through Death to Life* .. John 12 168

MARCH–MAY 1985
JOHN: THE GOSPEL OF LIFE (continued)

I. Mar.   3. *Relationships in the
               New Life* .... John 13 174
II. Mar. 10. *Support for the New
               Life* .... John 14–16 180
III. Mar. 17. *Unity in the New Life* . John 17 186
IV. Mar. 24. *Brought to Trial* .... John 18:1–19:16 193
V. Mar.   31. *Nailed to the Cross* ..... John 19:17–42 199
VI. April 7. *Raised from the Dead* .. John 20:1–23 206
VII. April 14. *Acknowledged as Lord* .. John 20:24–21:25 213

STUDIES IN WISDOM LITERATURE

VIII. April 21. *Faith Encounters Suf-
                 fering* .... Job 1–4 220
IX. April 28. *Faith Wrestles with Suf-
                 fering* .... Job 20, 21 226
X. May   5. *Faith in Spite of Suf-
                 fering* .... Job 40:1–42:6 233
XI. May   12. *Coping with Futility* .... Ecclesiastes 1:1–2:11;
                                          12 239
XII. May   19. *The Value of Wisdom* .. Proverbs 3:13–18;
                                          8:1–21 244
XIII. May 26. *Two Ways of Life* ...... Proverbs 1:7–19;
                                          3:5–8; 14:1–12 250

JUNE–AUGUST 1985
THE MINOR PROPHETS

I. June 2. *Why Judgment Comes to Humanity* .... Amos 1:1–2:8 256

II. June 9. *What God Desires* ...... Amos 4, 5 262

III. June 16. *The Day of the Lord* .... Amos 3:13–15; 5:18–20; 6:1–7; 8:7–12 268

IV. June 23. *The Lord's Complaint* ... Micah 3; 6 274

V. June 30. *The Harvest of Unbelief* Micah 7 280

VI. July 7. *The Lord's Constant Love* .... Hosea 1–3 286

VII. July 14. *A Call for True Repentance* .... Hosea 4–6 292

VIII. July 21. *Where There's Love, There's Hope* .... Hosea 11; 14 298

IX. July 28. *God's Inclusive Love* ... Jonah 303

X. Aug. 4. *Faith in the Midst of Despair* .... Habakkuk 310

XI. Aug. 11. *God Will Not Forsake His Own* .... Zechariah 1:1–6; 2:1–12; 8 316

XII. Aug. 18. *Judgment, Repentance, and Hope* .... Joel 322

XIII. Aug. 25. *Prepare for God's Return* .... Malachi .... - .. 329

A WORD TO THE TEACHER

Several years ago, during the presidency of Dwight D. Eisenhower, the well-known author James A. Michener was invited to the White House for a dinner party. Michener was flattered to be asked and immediately consulted his engagement book. He found that a few days earlier he had received another invitation for the same evening and had accepted. It was to attend a testimonial dinner for an old teacher of his. Friends, hearing about the White House event, urged Michener to cancel his acceptance to the affair for the teacher and go to the gala banquet at the White House. James Michener, however, sent his regrets to Ike. His letter was as follows:

Dear Mr. President:

I received your invitation three days after I had agreed to speak a few words at a dinner honoring the wonderful high-school teacher who taught me to write. I know you will not miss me at dinner, but she might at hers.

Sincerely yours, James A. Michener

President Eisenhower immediately sent back a reply to Michener. "In a lifetime, a man can live under fifteen or sixteen presidents," Ike's answering letter stated, "but a really fine teacher comes into his life but rarely."

As a teacher, you undoubtedly ask yourself at times whether or not it's worth the effort to prepare for your class week after week. You probably don't hear many words of appreciation. When you feel discouraged about serving as a teacher, however, remember you are one of those rare persons who comes into the lives of other people in a very special way.

As a teacher and pastor, I know the frustrations which you sometimes experience. But I also know the impact that you and thousands of other teachers make. I frequently hear people remark with deep appreciation about their teachers in Sunday church-school classes. If I were in a position to strike a "Medal of Honor" or an "Award for Meritorious Service" in Church work, I would see to it that the first to receive these honors would be you and other faithful teachers!

You will be in my thoughts and prayers as you and your class study, reflect, pray, and grow during the coming year.

Your colleague in Christ's ministry always,
William P. Barker

80th Annual Volume
September 1984—August 1985

TARBELL'S
Teacher's Guide
to the International Sunday School Lessons
Includes the RSV and KJV

SEPTEMBER—NOVEMBER 1984

THE LETTERS OF PAUL

LESSON I—SEPTEMBER 2

PAUL'S CONVERSION TO THE WAY

Background Scripture: Acts 7:54–8:3; 9:1–19; Galatians 1
Devotional Reading: Acts 9:20–31

KING JAMES VERSION

ACTS 7   59 And they stoned Stephen, calling upon *God*, and saying, Lord Jesus, receive my spirit.

60 And he kneeled down, and cried with a loud voice, Lord, lay not this sin to their charge. And when he had said this, he fell asleep.

8   1 And Saul was consenting unto his death. And at that time there was a great persecution against the church which was at Jerusalem; and they were all scattered abroad throughout the regions of Judaea and Samaria, except the apostles.

9   3 And as he journeyed, he came near Damascus: and suddenly there shined round about him a light from heaven:

4 And he fell to the earth, and heard a voice saying unto him, Saul, Saul, why persecutest thou me?

5 And he said, Who art thou, Lord? And the Lord said, I am Jesus whom thou persecutest: *it is* hard for thee to kick against the pricks.

6 And he trembling and astonished said, Lord, what wilt thou have me to do? And the Lord *said* unto him, Arise, and go into the city, and it shall be told thee what thou must do.

7 And the men which journeyed with him stood speechless, hearing a voice, but seeing no man.

8 And Saul arose from the earth; and when his eyes were opened, he saw no man: but they led him by the hand, and brought *him* into Damascus.

GALATIANS 1   11 But I certify you, brethren, that the gospel which was preached of me is not after man.

12 For I neither received it of man, neither was I taught *it*, but by the revelation of Jesus Christ.

13 For ye have heard of my conversation in time past in the Jews' religion, how that beyond measure I persecuted the church of God, and wasted it:

14 And profited in the Jews' religion above many my equals in mine own nation, being more exceedingly zealous of the traditions of my fathers.

15 But when it pleased God, who separated me from my mother's womb, and called *me* by his grace,

REVISED STANDARD VERSION

ACTS 7   59 And as they were stoning Stephen, he prayed, "Lord Jesus, receive my spirit." 60 And he knelt down and cried with a loud voice, "Lord, do not hold this sin against them." And when he had said this, he fell asleep. 8   1 And Saul was consenting to his death. And on that day a great persecution arose against the church in Jerusalem; and they were all scattered throughout the region of Judea and Samaria, except the apostles.

9   3 Now as he journeyed he approached Damascus, and suddenly a light from heaven flashed about him. 4 And he fell to the ground and heard a voice saying to him, "Saul, Saul, why do you persecute me?" 5 And he said, "Who are you, Lord?" And he said, "I am Jesus, whom you are persecuting; 6 but rise and enter the city, and you will be told what you are to do." 7 The men who were traveling with him stood speechless, hearing the voice but seeing no one. 8 Saul arose from the ground; and when his eyes were opened, he could see nothing; so they led him by the hand and brought him into Damascus.

GALATIANS 1   11 For I would have you know, brethren, that the gospel which was preached by me is not man's gospel. 12 For I did not receive it from man, nor was I taught it, but it came through a revelation of Jesus Christ. 13 For you have heard of my former life in Judaism, how I persecuted the church of God violently and tried to destroy it; 14 and I advanced in Judaism beyond many of my own age among my people, so extremely zealous was I for the traditions of my fathers. 15 But when he who had set me apart before I was born, and had called me through his grace, 16 was pleased to reveal his Son to me, in order that I might preach him among the Gentiles, I did not confer with flesh and blood, 17 nor did I go up to Jerusalem to those who were apostles before me, but I went away into Arabia; and again I returned to Damascus.

16 To reveal his Son in me, that I might preach him among the heathen; immediately I conferred not with flesh and blood:

17 Neither went I up to Jerusalem to them which were apostles before me; but I went into Arabia, and returned again unto Damascus.

KEY VERSE: He who ... set me apart ... was pleased to reveal his Son to me. Galatians 1:15, 16 (RSV).

HOME DAILY BIBLE READINGS

Aug. 27. M.   *Saul Encounters the Gospel.* Acts 7:51–8:1.
Aug. 28. T.   *Persecution Made Strong Christians.* Acts 8:1–8.
Aug. 29. W. *Paul Is Converted.* Acts 9:1–9.
Aug. 30. T.   *Ananias Receives Saul.* Acts 9:10–19.
Aug. 31. F.   *Saul Witnesses to His Faith.* Acts 9:20–30.
Sept.   1. S.   *Paul the Apostle.* Galatians 1:1–10.
Sept.   2. S.   *Paul Recounts His Conversion.* Galatians 1:11–17.

BACKGROUND

For the next thirteen weeks, we will be studying some of the letters of Paul. Paul's writings occupy more of the New Testament than those of any other author, and, next to the Gospels, his letters have influenced Christians more than any other writer.

It is important to realize that Paul did not sit down and leisurely compose "great literature." In fact, nothing was farthest from his mind. Paul was writing for Christians who were facing persecution or problems in their congregations. Consequently, each of his letters has a very practical aspect.

Although Paul wrote to meet practical needs in churches, he constantly shows that he is profoundly moved by the Spirit of Jesus Christ. An underlying theme weaving the next thirteen lessons together is Paul's focus on the Spirit of Christ.

Paul's emphasis on the Spirit of Christ led him to important conclusions. These conclusions—or doctrines—are ways of applying the meaning of the Spirit of Jesus Christ to perplexing issues. The lessons for this quarter are intended to offer your class new insights into the meaning of these teachings in Paul's letters and to understand the ethical issues which his young churches confronted.

The Spirit of Jesus Christ was not a doctrine for Paul. It was an experience. It began with his conversion on the road to Damascus and his call to the ministry. It continued until he faced death in a Roman cell. You and your class will trace the significance of the Spirit of Christ in Paul's writings about the way to salvation, ethics in daily living, and encouragement about the last things and the future.

NOTES ON THE PRINTED TEXT

I. "The blood of the martyrs is the seed of the Church," wrote Tertullian, a Christian in the second century. Stephen's death was certainly the seed which the Lord planted in a furious young persecutor named Saul.

Stephen had been one of the Greek-speaking Jews (known as "Hellenists") who were part of the earliest Christian group in Jerusalem. When some had grumbled that widows and other needy persons were being neglected, Stephen had been one of "the Seven" set apart to handle the social service program in the church in Jerusalem. However, Stephen showed he was a persuasive preacher. His sermons stirred up such intense opposition in Jerusalem that he was dragged out by an angry mob, charged with blasphemy and stoned to death. He was the first Christian to die for his faith in Jesus Christ.

As they were stoning Stephen, he prayed, "Lord Jesus, receive my spirit!" And he knelt down and cried with a loud voice, "Lord, do not hold this sin against them." Stephen was praying directly to Jesus. Jesus was so real to Stephen that he could even speak with Him in the midst of his last agonizing moments.

Furthermore, Stephen forgave his tormentors, using words similar to those Jesus Himself used on the Cross ("Father, forgive them, for they know not what they do"—Luke 23:34). One of those tormentors was "a young man named Saul" (Acts 7:58). Obviously, Stephen's death had a profound effect on Saul.

But Saul laid waste the church, entering house after house, he dragged off men and women and committed them to prison. The Greek text here has a vivid word for "laid waste." It originally referred to a wild boar rampaging through a vineyard, ripping up the vines and causing total destruction. Later, it came to refer to an army destroying an area, killing and burning everything, or to a deadly disease ravaging a victim. Saul was reacting against the witness of Stephen. As so often happens when someone encounters goodness, it seems to stir up greater meanness. Obviously, however, Saul's rampaging against Christians like a wild beast was a sign of his own inner turmoil. Something was bound to give.

II. *Now as he approached Damascus, suddenly a light from heaven flashed about him. And he fell to the ground and heard a voice saying to him, "Saul, Saul, why do you persecute me?"* Acts 9 is the first of three accounts of Saul's conversion in Acts. Although the details of the other two in Acts 22 and Acts 26 vary slightly, the essentials are the same. The most famous and most dramatic turnabout in history took place that noon on the Damascus road. Jesus Christ personally encountered the persecutor Saul.

Various critics have tried to "explain" what happened to Saul. They have offered ingenious psychological theories. Saul himself and his close friend Luke (who was a well-trained physician with a clinical eye for signs of emotional illness) reported that Jesus had made Himself known to the persecutor that noon outside the gates of Damascus. Later, Luke recounted that extraordinary encounter three different times in his volume, *The Acts of the Apostles*. Saul the persecutor of Jesus Christ became Paul the Apostle of Jesus Christ!

Now there was a disciple at Damascus named Ananias. Ananias of Damascus is one of those little-known characters who steps on to center stage of the New Testament, plays a key role briefly, then quietly retires to the wings. But what an important part he played! Although frightened and hesitant when he heard in his prayer time that the fiery Saul needed him, he laid aside his reservations and obeyed Jesus. Like the other early Christians, Ananias was aware that Jesus was present. He had no proof that the report about Saul was not a trick. He had reservations about exposing himself to possible danger and to meeting Saul who probably had Ananias's name on his hit list. Nevertheless, Ananias went to Saul and welcomed him as "Brother" (Acts 9:17) in response to Jesus' command.

SUGGESTIONS FOR TEACHERS

The word *conversion* makes some people uneasy. *Conversion* conjures up images of dramatic decisions and emotional excesses. True, some conversions may seem to be spiritual spectaculars. Paul's Damascus Road seems to be in this category. Other conversions, such as those on the Emmaus Road, may be quieter and slower.

Whether conversion is of the Damascus Road or the Emmaus Road variety, however, there are events which lead up to it and which later confirm the encounter with the Lord. Conversions are something like battles. They may appear to be swift and sudden. In actuality, however, there has been extensive planning and positioning beforehand. Both victorious generals and the Lord know that the tide is turned because of careful preparation.

Your lesson today illustrates the way conversion takes place, from preparation to follow-up, by considering Paul's startling turnabout.

1. *ENRAGED.* Examine with your class the fury which Saul showed toward Christians, especially Stephen. Take enough time to point out the way Stephen's witness affected Saul. Remind your class also that Stephen's martyrdom was used by God as a means of touching Saul. The power to love overwhelmed the rage of the persecutor! Have your class reflect on the place of witnessing in these times. It would be useful to talk about some of those who have died for their faith in our century, such as Dietrich Bonhoeffer and Archbishop Romero, Nat Saint and Jim Elliott.

2. *ENCOUNTERED.* Remind your people that the Acts account states bluntly that the Living Lord met Saul on the Damascus road. The important matter is the encounter, not the details. Don't let the discussion meander into pointless debate over why Saul's companions heard the voice but saw no one. More important, stress the fact that Jesus Christ continues to encounter people, and, most important, tell your class that the Risen Lord is encountering each of them. Without putting anyone on the spot, you may wish to encourage persons in the class to share their own conversion experiences as they feel comfortable about it.

3. *ENQUIRY.* "Who are you, Lord?" Saul asks (Acts 9:5). God introduces Himself to each of us, but sometimes we are not sure of Him or His intentions. For us, the only answer to our question, "Who are you, Lord?" is found in meeting Jesus Christ. Only He meets our deepest questions. Only Jesus discloses fully the nature of God.

4. *ENJOINED.* Saul, struck blind by the event of being encountered by the Living Christ, first must learn to accept commands humbly. Before the savage Saul can complete his conversion to the Christian Paul, he first must learn humility and be commanded. He hears, "Rise and enter the city, and you will be told what you are to do," (9:6). Saul must have wondered. Couldn't the Lord be more specific? Nevertheless, Saul learns the basic lessons of faith: humility and obedience. Remind your students that conversion always entails these hard lessons.

5. *ENABLED.* Take time in your lesson to talk about the place of Ananias in Saul's faith-journey. Have your class talk over the risk that Ananias must have felt he was taking when he responded to divine orders to welcome Saul! This would be a good time to have your class consider aloud the place of those who have enabled each of them to continue the conversion process.

TOPIC FOR ADULTS
PAUL'S CONVERSION TO THE WAY

The Appearance of the Beast. Richard Wurmbrand, a Lutheran pastor, suffered terrible torture and years of imprisonment at the hands of his Communist captors because of his Christian leadership. One of his jailors was known as "The Beast." Wurmbrand and the other prisoners dreaded The Beast. They had never seen anyone so cruel. In fact, The Beast's sadism seemed to make him so much less than a human being that he was referred to by everyone simply by his animal nickname, The Beast.

The Beast took a peculiar delight in beating Pastor Wurmbrand. After each beating, he would snarl and stare at Wurmbrand. Wurmbrand, bloodied, bruised, and aching from the torture, always quietly said to The Beast, "Christ wants you to be different. Christ wants you to be different."

Then The Beast no longer showed up in the cell block to carry out his brutalities. The prisoners felt some sense of relief from the horrible beatings from The Beast.

One day, The Beast reappeared—as Richard Wurmbrand's cell mate! Wurmbrand stared with surprise and uneasiness. Soon he heard what had happened. The Beast had been imprisoned for preaching Jesus Christ on the streets!

The Transforming Presence. "Through nineteen centuries, Christians have shared in an experience which they felt they could best describe as being with a Presence which they have associated with the historic Jesus seen in the pages of the New Testament and with the Eternal God. Of their honesty in reporting that enduring and repeated experience, there can be no doubt. Nor can there be doubt that through that experience they themselves have been transformed. Through it they have been lifted out of moral defeat and impotence into victory and from despair to triumphant hope. Through it they have found power to go through suffering, disappointment, and the loss of loved ones, of health, and of worldly goods, and to face physical death, not only unafraid but also with quiet confidence and joy. Through it strength has come to them to battle, singlehanded or with a small band of kindred spirits, against enthroned wrong and age-long evils, and yet to do so in humility, without vindictiveness and in love."—Kenneth Scott Latourette, *Anno Domini,* New York: Harper, 1982.

Melted Down by Christ's Caring. "And, finally, how good to remember how in prayer one day my stiff, tight, detailed petitions were all blown aside as though they were dandelion fluff, how I stopped praying and began to be prayed in, of how I died and was literally melted down by the love of a Power that coursed through my heart sweeping away the hard claimful core, and poured through me a torrent of infinite tenderness and caring! Blind with tears, I suddenly knew and felt the very being of suffering people whom I had recently visited, gathered, and loved in the very heart of God, who drew me to care for them as I had never done in my days among them. Theresa of Avila once wrote of this death in prayer: 'Nothing seemed to satisfy my desires; every moment my heart was ready to burst. It seemed to me as if my soul was being torn from me. It was a kind of death so delightful that my soul would gladly have prolonged it forever.' "—Douglas V. Steer, *On Beginning From Within,* New York: Harper, 1943.

Questions for Pupils on the Next Lesson. 1. As children grow up and leave home, why do so many adults question their own purpose and meaning in life? 2. Where do you find the greatest opportunities to share your commitments and values with others? 3. What is your personal support system? 4. Do you value your worth in terms of how or what you have achieved, or in terms of who you really are? 5. How is salvation achieved through faith in Christ?

TOPIC FOR YOUTH
TURNING TO GOD'S WAY

What's Inside You? One of Gutzon Borglum's great works as a sculptor is the head of Lincoln in the Capitol of Washington. He cut it from a large, square block of stone in his studio. One day when the face of Lincoln had just become recognizable out of the stone, a young girl was visiting the studio with her parents. She looked at the half done face of Lincoln, her eyes registering wonder and astonishment. She stared at the piece for a moment, then ran to the sculptor.

"Is that Lincoln?" she asked.

"Yes."

"Well," said the little girl, "how in the world did you know he was inside there?"

Like a master sculptor, Jesus Christ can bring a person of incredible significance out of your life. He knows what's inside you, and He sees immense possibilities within you.

Allow Him to sculpt your life into the image He envisions. Trust Him. Respond to Him!

The Experience of Being Born Again. "Whether a person needs to be 'born again' to be a Christian has become once again a source of friction between Christians. People who have had a drastic change in the direction of their lives stress that others also must be born again. Of course this annoys people who have been faithful church members for years and who do not in many cases put all that much emphasis on a conversion experience. Those who are 'born again' feel deeply hurt when rebuffed by them.

"The way to avoid this needless friction is to recognize that all Christians agree that the crucial thing is to be devoted to God. Part of the meaning of the word *conversion* is 'to turn toward.' This redirection may be very sudden so that a person is very much aware of turning around. But it may be very slow and gradual, so that a person is never particularly aware of any motion or sudden change, just as all of us are moving at thousands of miles an hour on the earth's surface but we do not feel any motion. The main issue, then, is whether one is devoted to God, not whether one turned toward Him rapidly or imperceptibly.

"The person who insists on everyone having a conversion experience is putting the stress on the experience of turning, not on the direction toward which one is pointed. Yet the crucial thing is direction, not the presence or absence of the experience of turning toward God. Being 'born again' should not be identified with the experience of a rapid turn, but with a commitment to God. Whether such a commitment took place by a sudden redirection or not, in both cases it is because of the presence of God's Spirit, which comes 'from above,' that we have new birth.

"There are many other reasons for disagreement among Christians, but on the matter of whether it is necessary to have an experience of being converted there is room in the church for those who have as well as for those who have not, without the Gospel being compromised in any way."—Diogenes Allen, *Presbyterian Outlook*, August 10, 1981.

He Skinned My Eyes. Several years ago, a movie appeared named *The Horse's Mouth.* The movie had an interesting scene in which a famous artist was approached by a person who appreciated his paintings and asked how he happened to take up art. The artist replied, "One time I saw a painting by the artist Matisse. I was skinned. Suddenly I saw the world in color, as though for the first time. He skinned my eyes. I became a different man. It was like a conversion."

We can use the same words to describe our encounter with Jesus Christ. We see everything differently. Instead of a dreary black-and-white-and-grey world, we become aware of color and beauty and meaning. He skins our eyes!

Has He skinned your eyes so that you see yourself as a different person?

Questions for Pupils on the Next Lesson. 1. Has your faith served as an integrating factor yet in your life? If so, in what way? If not, have you examined the meaning of Jesus Christ in your life? 2. What cause have you been willing to give yourself to because you believe in it? 3. Are you aware of your own personal sin? If so, what ways are you seeking to relieve that guilt? 4. How is your self-image influenced by your peers? Who do you think you are?

LESSON II—SEPTEMBER 9

FAITH—THE WAY TO GO

Background Scripture: Romans 1:1–17
Devotional Reading: Romans 16:17–20

KING JAMES VERSION

ROMANS 1 Paul, a servant of Jesus Christ, called *to be* an apostle, separated unto the gospel of God,

2 (Which he had promised afore by his prophets in the holy Scriptures,)

3 Concerning his son Jesus Christ our Lord, which was made of the seed of David according to the flesh;

4 And declared *to be* the Son of God with power, according to the Spirit of holiness, by the resurrection from the dead:

5 By whom we have received grace and apostleship, for obedience to the faith among all nations, for his name:

6 Among whom are ye also the called of Jesus Christ:

7 To all that be in Rome, beloved of God, called *to be* saints: Grace to you, and peace, from God our Father and the Lord Jesus Christ.

8 First, I thank my God through Jesus Christ for you all, that your faith is spoken of throughout the whole world.

9 For God is my witness, whom I serve with my spirit in the gospel of his Son, that without ceasing I make mention of you always in my prayers;

10 Making request, if by any means now at length I might have a prosperous journey by the will of God to come unto you.

11 For I long to see you, that I may impart unto you some spiritual gift, to the end ye may be established;

12 That is, that I may be comforted together with you by the mutual faith both of you and me.

13 Now I would not have you ignorant, brethren, that oftentimes I purposed to come unto you, (but was let hitherto,) that I might have some fruit among you also, even as among other Gentiles.

14 I am debtor both to the Greeks, and to the Barbarians; both to the wise, and to the unwise.

15 So, as much as in me is, I am ready to preach the gospel to you that are at Rome also.

16 For I am not ashamed of the gospel of Christ: for it is the power of God unto salvation to every one that believeth; to the Jew first, and also to the Greek.

17 For therein is the righteousness of God revealed from faith to faith: as it is written, The just shall live by faith.

REVISED STANDARD VERSION

ROMANS 1 Paul, a servant of Jesus Christ, called to be an apostle, set apart for the gospel of God 2 which he promised beforehand through his prophets in the holy scriptures, 3 the gospel concerning his Son, who was descended from David according to the flesh 4 and designated Son of God in power according to the Spirit of holiness by his resurrection from the dead, Jesus Christ our Lord, 5 through whom we have received grace and apostleship to bring about the obedience of faith for the sake of his name among all the nations, 6 including yourselves who are called to belong to Jesus Christ;

7 To all God's beloved in Rome, who are called to be saints:

Grace to you and peace from God our Father and the Lord Jesus Christ.

8 First, I thank my God through Jesus Christ for all of you, because your faith is proclaimed in all the world. 9 For God is my witness, whom I serve with my spirit in the gospel of his Son, that without ceasing I mention you always in my prayers, 10 asking that somehow by God's will I may now at last succeed in coming to you. 11 For I long to see you, that I may impart to you some spiritual gift to strengthen you, 12 that is, that we may be mutually encouraged by each other's faith, both yours and mine. 13 I want you to know, brethren, that I have often intended to come to you (but thus far have been prevented), in order that I may reap some harvest among you as well as among the rest of the Gentiles. 14 I am under obligation both to Greeks and to barbarians, both to the wise and to the foolish: 15 so I am eager to preach the gospel to you also who are in Rome.

16 For I am not ashamed of the gospel: it is the power of God for salvation to every one who has faith, to the Jew first and also to the Greek. 17 For in it the righteousness of God is revealed through faith for faith; as it is written, "He who through faith is righteous shall live."

KEY VERSE: He who through faith is righteous shall live. Romans 1:17 (RSV).

HOME DAILY BIBLE READINGS

Sept. 3. M.   *A Profile of Faithful People.* Hebrews 11:1–9.
Sept. 4. T.   *Abraham Is Faithful.* Hebrews 11:8–16.
Sept. 5. W.   *Jesus the Pioneer.* Hebrews 12:1–6.
Sept. 6. T.   *The Roman Church Has Faith.* Romans 1:8–17.
Sept. 7. F.   *Some Are Weak in Faith.* Romans 14:1–10.
Sept. 8. S.   *People of Faith Are Generous.* Romans 15:25–33.
Sept. 9. S.   *Faithful Women.* Romans 16:1–5, 25–27.

BACKGROUND

Paul had never been to Rome when he wrote his great letter to the congregation in the great city. However, he hoped to visit. The reason was not to see the sights but to meet for mutual encouragement and growth in the faith.

Paul knew that the Romans had already heard about him and had undoubtedly heard some unflattering things. Consequently, he realized he would have to introduce himself and try to set the record straight about his beliefs.

More important, Paul had deep concerns about what was happening in the Christian community everywhere. Paul had one of the keenest minds in his age or any age, and he saw the dangers in the thinking of many Christians at that time. He was aware that the distortions creeping into the beliefs of these other Christians would not only pervert the meaning of Jesus Christ but would eventually destroy the Good News. Basically, there were three separate distortions of the Gospel which Paul saw. One of these, the teachings of the Judaizers—those who insisted that a Christian had to be circumcised and keep the dietary requirements of the Jewish Law as well as be baptized. The second were the moralists—those who, in effect, taught that a person saved himself by following a list of rules for moral living, thereby reducing the Gospel to Christian etiquette. The third distortion of the faith came from the "anti-Law" group (known as the antinomians)—those who said that Jesus Christ freed believers from all restraints, thereby opening the way to appalling excesses and even cases of immorality.

Paul wanted to spell out to the Christians in Rome his concerns about Jesus Christ, sin, salvation, and grace. These were not notions he had arrived at casually. These were basic, bedrock convictions flowing from his encounter with the Living Jesus Christ. Paul had hammered out most of these doctrinal issues while working with congregations, such as in Galatia or Ephesus or Colossae. But he had never written about these vital matters in detail. His letter to Romans was his attempt to present basic Christian doctrine clearly and coherently.

Romans is Paul's greatest letter and his longest. This letter to the Roman Christians is also one of the most influential pieces of literature in the world. St. Augustine, Martin Luther, John Wesley, Karl Barth, and countless others have been profoundly affected by it. Christians still turn to Romans as the basic primer in theological thinking.

NOTES ON THE PRINTED TEXT

I. *Paul, a servant of Jesus Christ, called to be an apostle, set apart for the gospel of God:* Paul opens his letter with the formula used by nearly all first-century correspondents (and by military memos today)

FROM:
TO:
SUBJECT:

Paul, however, identifies himself solely as Christ's person. He says nothing about his Roman citizenship or impressive background. He wants to be known simply as a "servant" (or literally a "slave," according to the Greek) of Jesus Christ. He also introduces himself as an "apostle," meaning one who is "sent" by Christ. In other words, as Christ's, he is under orders.

Paul's orders meant that he was sent to the Gentiles. He will discourse on this subject at length later in the letter, and let his readers know his credentials as a divinely-appointed apostle—with the same authority as Peter or any other apostle—at the opening of this letter.

II. *The Gospel of God:* Paul lays out what the Good News of Jesus Christ is to him and to all persons. It has been "promised beforehand through his prophets in the holy scriptures," and fulfills all that the Jewish writings had hoped for and hinted at. Jesus "was descended from David according to the flesh"; that is, Jesus is the long-promised Messiah. Jesus is "designated Son of God" through the mighty event of the Resurrection. And He brings "grace and apostleship to bring about obedience to the faith for the sake of his name among all peoples." Paul has a global sense of the significance of Jesus Christ that he feels every Christian should have.

III. *To all God's beloved in Rome, who are called upon to be saints.* These words are more than graceful compliments to people Paul has never met and whom he wants to visit. And these are not idle terms of flattery meant to butter up the folks in Rome. Paul is convinced that anyone who professes faith in Jesus Christ is beloved by God, and summoned to be a "saint." The word *saint* means literally one who is "holy" or "set apart" for God's use.

After the "FROM" and the "TO" parts of the formula opening of this letter, Paul moves on to "SUBJECT."

IV. *I long to see you that I may impart to you some spiritual gift to strengthen you, that is, that we may be mutually encouraged by each other's faith:* Paul is always a churchman. He does not arrogantly claim that he can set everyone straight, or that he will do all the telling and giving and that the Romans will do all the listening and receiving. Rather, it will be mutual growth and encouragement.

V. . . . *the Gospel: it is the power of God for salvation for everyone who has faith, to the Jew first, and also to the Greek.* Paul lays out for his hearers in Rome what he is going to discuss with them in greater detail later in the letter. He tells the Roman Christians that he must share with them the most basic questions confronting every human, regardless of religious tradition—matters such as God, separation from God and guilt, getting right with God, and faith.

Righteousness of God: The Greek New Testament word means what God has done through Jesus Christ to make us right with Him. Paul returns to his theme several times in the letter and frequently uses the word translated as *righteousness*.

He who through faith is righteous shall live. The Greek says literally that the person who is made right with God by trusting that through Jesus Christ he or she is truly accepted and loved by God shall live. *Faith* means more than giving assent to a set of teachings or a system of doctrine. *Faith* means trust in Jesus. Paul insists that Jesus Christ is everything we need to inspire that trust, and states flatly that such trust leads to life!

SUGGESTIONS TO TEACHERS

Huckleberry Finn said that faith is "believin' what you know ain't so." Cynics and skeptics agree and write off the Gospel and the Church.

A better definition of faith would be "believing Him whom we know is so." Faith is not agreement with a set of dubious propositions; it is acknowledgment to the Saviour. Faith is moving on with Jesus. Faith is not assent to the ridiculous; it is consent to the Redeemer.

Remembering that the focus of faith is not on facts or proofs but on Jesus Christ, use your lesson material from Romans to help each person in your class grow in faith. Let Paul be your mentor.

1. *CALLED AS COMMUNICATOR.* Point out to your class how Paul refers to himself at the start of his letter to the Romans. He states that he is a "servant of Jesus Christ" and is "called as an apostle." Research the meaning of both of these terms in the Bible. In Greek, a servant belongs as a slave to the owner, and an apostle is literally one who is sent. Do your class members consider themselves both owned by Christ and sent by Christ? Faith is understood in the New Testament in terms of being Christ's servant and communicator. Ask your class members to state how they can be Christ's slaves and apostles in the Monday-to-Friday world.

2. *COMMITTED TO CHRIST.* Take time in the Scripture for today to grasp the way Paul insists that Jesus Christ is Good News. Paul says that Christ is promised in Scripture, is descended from David, is designated Son of God, is the Risen Lord, is the bringer of grace and apostleship—and so much more! What do the folks in your class think of Jesus? Ask each one to put together his or her own list of what Jesus Christ means. How is Jesus Christ *the* Good News for your class members?

3. *CONNECTED TO COMMUNITY.* Faith is *never* a sole performance in Christianity. Faith always is given as God's gift to His community. When God blesses you with faith, He gives you that sense of trust as His way of saying that He loves you! And He intends you to share it. He means for you to use your faith for other Christians. Call attention to the ways in Romans 1 in which Paul remembers that he and his readers in Rome are part of a closely-knit community, even though they have never met. They remember each other in their prayers. They share. They strengthen each other and encourage each other. How can your class members better realize that each is connected to Christ's community?

4. *CONVINCED WITH CONVICTION.* Paul emphasizes that he is not ashamed of the Gospel because he knows that Jesus Christ is the "power of God for salvation to every one . . ." (Romans 1:16). Compare this forthright statement of who Christ is with the timid, tentative words most of us use when we talk about our faith! Ask how others would recognize that we are Christians. Discuss ways in which we Christians can demonstrate more effectively that we truly believe that Jesus Christ is the power of God for salvation for everyone.

TOPIC FOR ADULTS
FAITH—THE WAY TO GO

Partner in the Office. Alfred Stocks is the chief executive, or city manager, of Liverpool, England. He faces almost impossible obstacles. Liverpool is beset with all the urban problems afflicting many declining metropolitan areas: high unemployment, shrinking tax base, severe racial tensions (Liverpool experienced destructive riots a few summers back), Marxist troublemakers. Stocks, a Christian, is undaunted. He states, "Before I get there in the morning, Jesus Christ is already in the office, there to meet me when I open the door." Are you able to affirm your faith this way?

Faith Brings Personhood. "How does man begin to live the higher life in God? First of all, God must come down to him; the Eternal must invade human history. This is the meaning of the Incarnation. Second, man must himself surrender his lower nature. But here there appears a difference between man and all other creatures—man is a person, which sunshine, grass and cows are not. Their lower natures are destroyed by surrendering themselves to man, but since man is a person, his personality is indestructible. What man surrenders, then, is not his whole nature, but only that portion of it which is sinful, which is ungodlike. In conversion a man suffers a mortification, a kind of spiritual death, but his personality survives."—Fulton J. Sheen, *Quote*, July 15, 1982.

To Show Him His Heart. John Wesley knew better than most that faith is the way to go. Wesley also knew that faith meant persisting in sharing the Good News of Jesus Christ.

One time, Wesley was on his way to Northampton, England, on horseback and came alongside of another traveler. The two began to converse on religious matters. Wesley quickly realized that the man's views were so foreign and antagonistic to his own that they would quickly get into a heated argument. Therefore, Wesley gently suggested they avoid getting angry with one another by changing the subject. In his *Journal* for May 20, 1742, John Wesley described what happened. "And we did for two miles, till he caught me unawares, and dragged me into the dispute before I knew where I was. He then grew warmer and warmer; told me that I was rotten at heart, and supposed I was one of John Wesley's followers. I told him, 'No, I am John Wesley himself.' Upon which ... he would gladly have run away outright. But, being the better mounted of the two, I kept close to his side, and endeavored to show him his heart, till we came into the street of Northampton."

Questions for Pupils on the Next Lesson. 1. Are most of the people in your church sensitive to the evil in the world around them? 2. Why do most of us find it so difficult to deal with the evil in ourselves? 3. Have you ever known people who use religious activities as a substitute for right relationships? 4. Why do so many people suffer from guilt feelings? 5. How can you avoid harsh judgmental attitudes toward yourself and toward others?

TOPIC FOR YOUTH
FAITH IS THE WAY!

How Did You Know? A concerned mother came to talk to her minister about her small daughter's prayers. It seems that the child was having difficulty in remembering the words of the Lord's Prayer. According to the mother, the girl insisted on praying a garbled version which always came out, "Our Father, How did You know my name. . . ." In spite of repeated corrections, the youngster kept praying, "How did You know my name?" instead of "Hallowed be thy name." The mother begged for suggestions to break her daughter of the habit of praying the wrong words.

"Now, quit worrying," the minister wisely told the mother. "Little Jennifer will learn the correct wording soon enough. Besides, we all could learn to say in wonder 'How did You know my name?' as a way of praying!"

Faith is trusting in the caring God who assures us that He does remember our names!

Building for the future. Faith is living with the Lord for the future as well as the present. Faith means confidence in tomorrow because of God.

Over a century ago, many settlers developing western states had this attitude of faith. Lord Bryce, British scholar and diplomat, found it in 1883 in Bismarck in Dakota territory.

There he attended the ceremonial laying of the cornerstone for the capitol building that would be needed when the territory became a state or, as it turned out, two states. Bismarck, then five years old, was a teeming town of 7,000. Former President Ulysses S. Grant and Chief Sitting Bull were also present.

A speaker revealed that because Bismarck was the center of Dakota, and Dakota was the center of the United States, and the United States was the center of the world, Bismarck was destined to be "the metropolitan hearth of the world's civilization." But to Bryce, the most striking thing was the spot chosen for the capitol building:

"It was not in the city, nor even on the skirts of the city; it was nearly a mile off, on the top of a hill in the brown and dusty prairie. 'Why here?' we asked, 'Is it because you mean to enclose the building in a public park?' 'By no means; the capitol is intended to be in the center of the city; it is in this direction that the city is to grow.' "

Today the capitol building is surrounded by Bismarck.

Faith in Jesus Christ instills this kind of forward-looking attitude and action!

Doubt Our Doubts. "Christians are bound continually to seek the truth with persistent determination under the promised guidance of the Holy Spirit. We must take into account the belief that our fallen human minds are predisposed to doubt, through sin that separates from the God of truth: therefore we must doubt our doubts, and realize that intellectual pride leads even the most accomplished critics to err.

"We live in an age that judges everything from a human point of view and insists on practical demonstration of proof. But some leading scientists and thinkers are questioning this over-emphasis and point to the changing climate of science itself, admitting the element of ultimate mystery in human understanding.

"History requires a kind of conversation with the past: in our enquiry it is essential that Christians try to enter into fellowship with the witnesses concerned and to share their experiences. A very short time after their Lord had been crucified, and in the same district and amidst those who could challenge them, the apostles publicly proclaimed that he had risen, making him known in preaching and 'in the breaking of bread' with transformed certainty. The whole New Testament bears witness to this belief.

" 'God raised him from the dead'—that is the heart of the Christian faith; the only counter is 'God did not raise him from the dead,' in other words 'God cannot raise Jesus from the dead.' Christianity does not teach that a corpse came to life again or received an infusion of heavenly power. As God incarnate, Jesus had revealed God's love, as representative Man, Jesus had borne the whole burden of man's fall, sin, suffering and death. He had thus anticipated the condition of the redeemed after the Judgment in the new heaven and the new earth.

"This unique act of God's saving love and power meant that Jesus rose in what has been termed a 'glorified body.'

"All this divine action is beyond the power of human understanding or description but is well established in the region of faith, which indeed is the region of all ultimate truth. The great German physicist Max Planck said that over the temple gate of science is written: 'You must have faith.' Faith accepts the assurances of ultimate authority and the most reliable evidence of the real world that exists independently of ourselves. Those who were genuine disciples, knowing and loving Jesus, received the necessary assurance from God that Jesus had risen and felt called to rise with him into new life here and hereafter."—John B. Logan, "Thoughts on the Resurrection," *Life and Work,* April 1982.

Questions for Pupils on the Next Lesson. 1. Why do young persons often suffer inordinate guilt? 2. Does knowing right and wrong and doing religious acts guarantee that a person will be right with God? 3. Will keeping a set of rules save you? 4. Why do we keep making excuses and refuse to recognize our guilt before God? 5. Is God's judgment always inescapable and impartial?

LESSON III—SEPTEMBER 16

DO "GOOD" PEOPLE SIN?

Background Scripture: Romans 2:1–3:20
Devotional Reading: Romans 2:3–16

KING JAMES VERSION

ROMANS 2 Therefore thou art inexcusable, O man, whosoever thou art that judgest: for wherein thou judgest another, thou condemnest thyself; for thou that judgest doest the same things.

17 Behold, thou art called a Jew, and restest in the law, and makest thy boast of God,

18 And knowest *his* will, and approvest the things that are more excellent, being instructed out of the law;

19 And art confident that thou thyself art a guide of the blind, a light of them which are in darkness,

20 An instructor of the foolish, a teacher of babes, which hast the form of knowledge and of the truth in the law.

21 Thou therefore which teachest another, teachest thou not thyself? thou that preachest a man should not steal, dost thou steal?

22 Thou that sayest a man should not commit adultery, dost thou commit adultery? thou that abhorrest idols, dost thou commit sacrilege?

23 Thou that makest thy boast of the law, through breaking the law dishonourest thou God?

24 For the name of God is blasphemed among the Gentiles through you, as it is written.

3 9 What then? are we better *than they?* No, in no wise: for we have before proved both Jews and Gentiles, that they are all under sin;

10 As it is written, there is none righteous, no, not one:

11 There is none that understandeth, there is none that seeketh after God.

12 They are all gone out of the way, they are together become unprofitable; there is none that doeth good, no, not one.

19 Now we know that what things soever the law saith, it saith to them who are under the law: that every mouth may be stopped, and all the world may become guilty before God.

20 Therefore by the deeds of the law there shall no flesh be justified in his sight: for by the law *is* the knowledge of sin.

REVISED STANDARD VERSION

ROMANS 2 Therefore you have no excuse, O man, whoever you are, when you judge another; for in passing judgment upon him you condemn yourself, because you, the judge, are doing the very same things.

17 But if you call yourself a Jew and rely upon the law and boast of your relation to God 18 and know his will and approve what is excellent, because you are instructed in the law, 19 and if you are sure that you are a guide to the blind, a light to those who are in darkness, 20 a corrector of the foolish, a teacher of children, having in the law the embodiment of knowledge and truth— 21 you then who teach others, will you not teach yourself? While you preach against stealing, do you steal? 22 You who say that one must not commit adultery, do you commit adultery? You who abhor idols, do you rob temples? 23 You who boast in the law, do you dishonor God by breaking the law? 24 For, as it is written, "The name of God is blasphemed among the Gentiles because of you."

3 9 What then? Are we Jews any better off? No, not at all; for I have already charged that all men, both Jews and Greeks, are under the power of sin, 10 as it is written:

"None is righteous, no, not one;

11 no one understands, no one seeks for God.

12 All have turned aside, together they have gone wrong;

no one does good, not even one."

19 Now we know that whatever the law says it speaks to those who are under the law, so that every mouth may be stopped, and the whole world may be held accountable to God. 20 For no human being will be justified in his sight by works of the law, since through the law comes knowledge of sin.

KEY VERSE: All have turned aside, together they have gone wrong; no one does good, not even one. Romans 3:12 (RSV).

HOME DAILY BIBLE READINGS

Sept. 10. M. *Sin Brings Judgment.* Romans 2:1–11.
Sept. 11. T. *The Law in Nature.* Romans 2:12–16.
Sept. 12. W. *The Law Revealed at Sinai.* Romans 2:17–29.

Sept. 13. T. *The Justness of God.* Romans 3:1–8.
Sept. 14. F. *Gentiles and Jews Sin.* Romans 3:9–20.
Sept. 15. S. *God's Grace Justifies All.* Romans 3:21–26.
Sept. 16. S. *Faith Is All Important.* Romans 3:27–31.

BACKGROUND

When the news of Jesus Christ burst upon the first-century world, the two most respected religious or moral groups were the Jews and the Greek thinkers, especially the Stoics. The Jewish tradition emphasized rigid obedience to the Law. The Greeks stressed a superior-minded attitude based on human wisdom. The Jews demanded strict adherence to the system of rules laid out in the Torah (which means "Instruction"). The Greeks urged humans to attain integrity and insight through philosophical thinking. Jerusalem and Athens each produced some outstanding thinkers and upright persons.

Paul knew both viewpoints well. He had been raised in both worlds. As a Jew, he had not only been reared in the tradition of the Law but had studied under Gamaliel, one of the leading rabbinical scholars in Jerusalem, and lived as an intensely strict Pharisee. As one born and raised in Tarsus, Paul also knew the delights of the Greek-speaking world of the academy. He could quote the philosophers and poets. He had an insider's feel for the lure of both the Greek and the Hebrew mind.

Yet, Paul also knew firsthand the sense of futility which both the Jew and the Greek faced. Neither could find a complete and lasting sense of peace with God or self or others. In fact, the harder either one worked at it, the worse off he seemed to end.

Paul was writing to the Romans, but he was describing the human state. In this great letter, the apostle who knew both the Jewish and the Greek approaches to life states bluntly how completely hopeless each is. God, he says, sees each in the same sorry state.

NOTES ON THE PRINTED TEXT

I. *Therefore, you have no excuse, O man, whoever you are:* Paul "tells it like it is": neither the Jew nor the Greek can stand smugly, assuming he is God's favorite, and look down on the other condescendingly. Both are making the same mistake; both are standing under God's judgment. Both are trying to use their own little do-it-yourself salvation kits. Each has the tragically mistaken notion that he is better than others.

II. *But if you call yourself a Jew and rely on the Law and boast of your relation to God and know his will and approve what is excellent, because you are instructed in the Law, and if you are sure that you are a guide to the blind, a light to those in darkness, a corrector of the foolish, a teacher of children, having in the Law the embodiment of knowledge and truth—then you who teach others, will you not teach yourself? . . . The name of God is blasphemed because of you.*

It bothered Paul deeply that his own people, the Jews, were persisting in such a haughty, independent attitude. He writes in Romans 2 and 3 about his fellow Jews, and returns again and again to them in Romans. Paul realized that the Jews were examples of the most religious folks apart from Christ ever to live. But they were failing to live up to their own traditions and precepts. A witch doctor with quack cures may be excused if his remedies kill people, but a Harvard-trained M.D. who fails to administer proper medication can not be let off as easily. The more one knows, the heavier the responsibilities.

Are we Jews better off? No, not at all: Paul is aware of his magnificent heritage as a Jew. Nevertheless, he points out that being a Jew means no prerogatives, no special standing with God. Trying to keep the Law brings no "good conduct" points.

III. *Both Jews and Greeks are under the power of sin.* Paul states that humans of every type are more than simply sinners. They are enthralled by sin; they are overpowered by sin. The Greek text means that sin rules the lives of all persons.

The word *sin* in the New Testament is the word literally meaning "to miss the mark." It originally referred to someone throwing a javelin which went wide or fell short of the target. Taken over into the vocabulary of Christians, it meant that a person's life did not come near to how God had aimed it.

When Paul uses the word *sin* in his letters, he does not mean minor vices. We confuse sin and "sins." Paul in speaking of sin never thought of petty lapses or naughtiness such as we think of when we use the term. Paul in Romans always considers sin to be a condition in which every human is trapped. Like the infamous dungeon called the "Little Ease" in which a man could neither stand up straight, nor lie down and stretch out, sin neither allows a person to live at the height of his potential as a human being, nor to slump down comfortably in a state of contentment.

IV. *For no human being will be justified in his sight by works of the law since through the law comes knowledge of sin:* Paul returns another time to the futility of trying to make oneself irresistibly good through trying to keep all the requirements of the Torah. In Paul's time, as in Jesus' day, it was simply impossible for any person, regardless of his sincerity and effort, to keep all the minutiae of the legal system of Pharisaism. Worse, Paul points out in Romans, the Law has the nasty tendency to make a person think of sins he otherwise wouldn't have considered. It's a bit like the old story of telling someone not under any circumstances to think about purple elephants and noting with glee that the person will thereupon think of nothing but purple elephants. The Law, Paul says, has that kind of effect; it brings up a knowledge of sin which one never would have thought about!

Paul presses his argument to the fullest in order to prove to his hearer in Rome that Jesus Christ is the Good News for everyone—Jew and Greek alike!

SUGGESTIONS TO TEACHERS

John Wesley, when in the colony of Georgia, once encountered the crusty royal governor, General Oglethorpe, and talked with him on the subject of forgiveness. "Forgiveness?" snorted Oglethorpe, "I never forgive!" Wesley smiled and replied, "Then, Sir, I hope you never sin."

Wesley, of course, realized what all writers of Scripture knew: we all sin, and we all must recognize that we do in order to receive forgiveness and extend forgiveness.

Your lesson addresses this subject today. Stick to the biblical material so that you do not get off on silly tangents.

1. *THE BOOMERANG OF JUDGING.* The Bible states clearly that all are sinners. This includes the "good" people and the not-so-good, Jews and Gentiles alike. Until we are able to face up to the plain fact of what an old-time Baptist preacher used to call the "streak of cussedness" in each of us, we are deluding ourselves! In Romans, Paul takes this a step further. He points out that the same perversity we see and dislike so in others is also present within ourselves! In a sense, when we pass judgment on another person, we also pass judgment on ourselves. Have your class reflect on human nature. Do your class members agree with G. K. Chesterton's comment about the "good news of original sin"?

2. *THE VERDICT ON US ALL.* Throughout this lesson, make sure that your

class understands the difference between sin and "sins." Romans talks about Sin, the disposition of all of us—even those of us who may like to think we are "good," that is the attitude and condition of each human. Here we are not talking about "sins" as little examples of doing something naughty. God judges each person. He holds us each responsible to live up to the highest standards we know. God judges the Jew according to how the Jew fulfills his/her understanding of Judaism, and judges the Gentile by the ways that person lives up to his/her ideals. In any case, we all realize we fall short of what God expects; we all stand convicted.

3. *THE IMPOSSIBILITY OF BEING GOOD.* Remind your class that no person has a corner on God's grace. No one, according to Romans, can make claims on God's goodness by the way he or she lives. Paul, good Jew he had tried to be, finally came to realize that he could never hope to live up to the expectations of the Jewish Law. Do your class members realize that no Christian or Jew, indeed no person, can pretend to be "good" before God? Why is it so hard for Christians to acknowledge that we are not "good"?

4. *THE HOPELESSNESS OF KEEPING SCORE.* It will be useful to share with your class how some Christians try to impress the Lord and others (and themselves as well) by legalism or moralism. Legalism means keeping a list of rules (Don't do this and don't do that, and you'll be good). Moralism means imagining that the faith can be reduced to a system of morals or maxims to live by. Romans stresses how neither legalism nor moralism can make us right with God. Only our trust in God's grace through Jesus Christ can! Have your class give examples of legalism and moralism in religion from their own experience.

TOPIC FOR ADULTS
DO "GOOD" PEOPLE SIN?

Decent Church Members. "Some of my church members protested vigorously against the allegation that they were sinful. They considered themselves the good people, which indeed they were. The bad guys were thieves, robbers, murderers, et al. They did not realize that Adam and Eve were also good, declared good by their Creator, but their downfall was sins of the spirit, not of the flesh. The disciples of Jesus were good men, but Jesus said to them, 'One of you will betray me.' Dumbfounded, they wondered who it could be. They simply did not know. One of the good men denied he knew Jesus, another betrayed Him, and all refused to believe everything He said. Jesus called Peter Satan because he disbelieved, accusing him of thinking more like man than like God. No wonder that Carl Erickson said sin can traffic 'as decent society.'

"Decent society brings on political scandals. William Stringfellow wrote, 'Our men in high places are not exceptionally immoral; they are, on the contrary, quite ordinarily moral.' That is, they conform to society, are programmed and conditioned to play a role in the way of the world, which is not the way of God.

"Good and moral people usually do not object to whatever their political leaders decide. Good, moral people conceived and manufactured nuclear weapons. Good, moral people decide when and where we go to war. Decent society acquiesced in a philosophy of permissiveness and its unanticipated evil consequences in sexuality and juvenile behavior problems in home and school.

"We all claim to be moral and good, but nobody can presume to be spiritually perfect. Sinfulness is basically what one is rather than what one does. The only salvation is forgiveness, which the cross of Christ tells us is costly to God."—Joseph Mohr, *The Weekender,* March 6, 1982, *Call-Chronicle* Newspapers, Allentown, Pa.

Seen as We Are. King Christian IV of Denmark built a delightful little house in a park not far from the center of Copenhagen. Although he called it the Rosenborg Palace, it is a rather modest royal lodge with seventeenth century interests.

One of these has to do with mirrors, which seemed to fascinate King Christian IV and so many in that era. Christian, however, designed a special small room in which mirrors cover every surface. A person may stand on a mirror and see himself literally from every angle. None of the mirrors on the floor, walls, or ceiling are trick mirrors, but the effect is startling, even unsettling. King Christian wanted to see himself reflected as he truly was.

Through Jesus Christ, God discloses His truth about us. We see ourselves as we truly are. In the presence of Christ, we discover the truth about ourselves. The sides of our character that we might have been able to ignore are shown up. Christian grace is being put into the mirror-filled room so that we are shown the violence, crudity, and sensuality which are part of our character. We begin to understand who we are: not-so-good people who sin, but also people who through God's grace are forgiven!

Live Spelled Backward. "The best definition of human evil is to realize that it is *live* spelled backward. Evil is antilife; it treats people like automatons instead of individuals; it likes control instead of freedom. Evil people have six characteristics: (1) They are consistently destructive. (2) They lack a personal sense of sin. (3) they consider themselves to be perfect. (4) They are committed to scapegoat other people for their own faults. (5) Pride is most often the basis for their evil ways. (6) They are characterized by a malignant narcissism."—Scott Peck, *Quote,* May 24, 1982.

Questions for Pupils on the Next Lesson. 1. Is it ever possible to escape the bondage or power of sin by our own efforts? 2. Why does trying to do right involve so much mental, emotional, and physical struggle? 3. Is it ever possible to be free from having to struggle with the grip of selfishness? 4. When do you find the tension between knowing what is right and not being able to do it most severe? 5. What are some of the meanings of the word *law* used in Romans 7:21-23?

TOPIC FOR YOUTH
DO "GOOD" PEOPLE SIN?

Grandfather's Secret. An attorney in Scotland noticed that his doorstep was dangerously worn and hazardous to his clients. He called in a stonemason. When the attorney heard that it would cost over ninety pounds to replace the worn block, he pondered the situation for a while. Finally he asked the stonemason how much it would cost to have the doorstep turned upside down so that the worn part would be underneath. The mason studied the problem briefly and replied that turning the block would only cost fifteen pounds.

The attorney instructed the mason to reverse the stone of the doorstep. When he came home later that day he found the stonemason standing disgustedly by the front gate. Without speaking, the mason led the attorney to the front stoop of the house and pointed to the stone. The attorney's grandfather had had exactly the same idea!

We sometimes think we can hide our selfishness. We frequently imagine that "no one will ever know," or "it's my life, isn't it?" Our selfishness and shortcuts may not be seen by anyone, and we may imagine we are getting away with them. We may, like the Scottish attorney's grandfather, pose as decent persons. Ultimately, however, we are exposed for the people we actually are! We "good" people are sinners!

Warped Perceptions. A sculptor was commissioned to do a work for Kent State University commemorating the National Guard–student encounter there during the violent 1960s in which some students were killed. He chose to do a plaster cast of Abraham's willingness to sacrifice his son Isaac. It is a powerful piece, with the son kneeling before the father and Abraham's anguish etched in his face. But

Kent State rejected the work as "too violent" and suggested instead a theme more in keeping with their interpretation of the event.

Part of our sinfulness is our refusal to face the truth about ourselves. We distort the facts. We try to interpret events to make ourselves look good. As with the Kent State authorities trying to tell themselves they were not at fault in any way and that the slaughter of five students by National Guardsmen was not violent, we delude ourselves into thinking we are good people. God knows better. He strips us of our delusions about our goodness.

List of Sins. A Tennessee preacher advertised that he had catalogued eighty-six different kinds of sin and would preach on each of these. To his surprise, he was besieged with requests for his list. Most of those writing him apparently wanted to find out what his list of sins was in case they were missing something. A few others, however, wrote to tell him that they wanted a look at the list just to check to make sure that they had already avoided every sin! These good people felt quite confident that they were morally perfect! Romans 2 and 3, however, point out that no one is ever able to go down a checklist of vices and tell himself or herself that he is without sin. We all are sinners. Although particular sins may be avoided, the tendency to sin never is.

Questions for Pupils on the Next Lesson. 1. How do your peers pressure you about what is right or wrong? 2. Are there immediate, clear-cut answers to every issue? 3. Do you question the role of the Church as a moral and social force? 4. Do you often have the feeling that you are able to handle any situation alone? 5. Is it ever possible to be free from the struggle with the power of sin and the grip of selfishness?

LESSON IV—SEPTEMBER 23

THE STRUGGLE TO DO RIGHT

Background Scripture: Romans 7:4–25
Devotional Reading: Romans 6:12–23

KING JAMES VERSION

ROMANS 7 5 For when we were in the flesh, the motions of sins, which were by the law, did work in our members to bring forth fruit unto death.

6 But now we are delivered from the law, that being dead wherein we were held; that we should serve in newness of spirit, and not *in* the oldness of the letter.

13 Was then that which is good made death unto me? God forbid. But sin, that it might appear sin, working death in me by that which is good; that sin by the commandment might become exceeding sinful.

14 For we know that the law is spiritual; but I am carnal, sold under sin.

15 For that which I do, I allow not: for what I would, that do I not; but what I hate, that do I.

16 If then I do that which I would not, I consent unto the law that *it is* good.

17 Now then it is no more I that do it, but sin that dwelleth in me.

18 For I know that in me (that is, in my flesh,) dwelleth no good thing: for to will is present with me; but *how* to perform that which is good I find not.

19 For the good that I would do, I do not: but the evil which I would not, that I do.

20 Now if I do that I would not, it is no more I that do it, but sin that dwelleth in me.

21 I find then a law, that, when I would do good, evil is present with me.

22 For I delight in the law of God after the inward man:

23 But I see another law in my members, warring against the law of my mind, and bringing me into captivity to the law of sin which is in my members.

24 O wretched man that I am! who shall deliver me from the body of this death?

25 I thank God through Jesus Christ our Lord. So then with the mind I myself serve the law of God; but with the flesh the law of sin.

REVISED STANDARD VERSION

ROMANS 7 5 While we were living in the flesh, our sinful passions, aroused by the law, were at work in our members to bear fruit for death.

6 But now we are discharged from the law, dead to that which held us captive, so that we serve not under the old written code but in the new life of the Spirit.

13 Did that which is good, then, bring death to me? By no means! It was sin, working death in me through what is good, in order that sin might be shown to be sin, and through the commandment might become sinful beyond measure. 14 We know that the law is spiritual; but I am carnal, sold under sin. 15 I do not understand my own actions. For I do not do what I want, but I do the very thing I hate. 16 Now if I do what I do not want, I agree that the law is good. 17 So then it is no longer I that do it, but sin which dwells within me. 18 For I know that nothing good dwells within me, that is, in my flesh. I can will what is right, but I cannot do it. 19 For I do not do the good I want, but the evil I do not want is what I do. 20 Now if I do what I do not want, it is no longer I that do it, but sin which dwells within me.

21 So I find it to be a law that when I want to do right, evil lies close at hand. 22 For I delight in the law of God, in my inmost self, 23 but I see in my members another law at war with the law of my mind and making me captive to the law of sin which dwells in my members. 24 Wretched man that I am! Who will deliver me from this body of death? 25 Thanks be to God through Jesus Christ our Lord! So then, I of myself serve the law of God with my mind, but with my flesh I serve the law of sin.

KEY VERSE: *Who will deliver me from this body of death? Thanks be to God through Jesus Christ our Lord!* Romans 7:24b–25a (RSV).

HOME DAILY BIBLE READINGS

Sept. 17. M. *The New Way of the Spirit.* Romans 7:1–6.
Sept. 18. T. *Being Rich Toward God.* Luke 12:13–21.
Sept. 19. W. *Trusting God in All Things.* Luke 12:22–31.
Sept. 20. T. *Peter's Struggle to Do Right.* Acts 11:1–10.

Sept. 21. F. *The Spirit Is Given to the Gentiles.* Acts 11:11–15.
Sept. 22. S. *A Theological Reflection on Law.* Romans 7:7–13.
Sept. 23. S. *The Struggle Within.* Romans 7:14–25.

BACKGROUND

Paul knew from personal experience that the only hope for despairing people comes from God's marvelous act of deliverance through Jesus Christ. Paul, however, worried that this fact was not being taken seriously within the Christian community. Other intriguing ideas were abroad, which in effect said, "Jesus is fine, but you also need something more." Sometimes the "something more" was circumcision. Sometimes, the "something more" was a code of regulations. Whatever the "something more," Paul repeatedly tried to call fellow believers back to the essential: Jesus Christ is sufficient. He does this throughout his letters, particularly in Romans.

Paul dramatizes what life without Christ is by describing it in terms of the hopeless existence of a slave. Few of us can comprehend what a slave's life would be. But Paul's first-century readers and hearers knew very well how despairing a situation a slave in the Roman world faced. Although there were instances of slaves receiving kind treatment at the hands of masters, these were the exceptions. More important, everyone understood that a slave had no real freedom. A slave was the property of another. Paul painted the picture of the person living a Christless existence as one owned by evil.

In Romans 7, critics argue whether Paul describing the slavery to sin which the man without Christ knows was writing about himself or about every person. Perhaps it was both. In any case, Paul knew from his own life the life of captivity to sin. Paul's writing this section of Romans may be the autobiography of a person who tried frantically—and unsuccessfully—to escape from the chains of enslavement to destruction.

However, millions of readers also know that Romans 7 also describes them, and, indeed, the human situation everywhere.

NOTES ON THE PRINTED TEXT

I. *Living in the flesh:* These words are often misunderstood. Some have the notion that "in the flesh" means something to do with sexual desire or sexual relationships of any kind, even between husband and wife. These with this mistaken interpretation have thought that the Bible condemned or at least frowned on any expression of sexuality. Others have thought that "the flesh" referred to anything material, as opposed to spiritual. Persons holding this view have tried to turn their backs on physical needs and specifically material things such as food and drink, shelter and warmth, relief from pain, and medicines. "Living in the flesh" means much, much more than either of these two erroneous interpretations. It refers to "our human cussedness," as the old mountain preacher liked to put it.

Paul aroused by the law: Paul writes out of his own experience what this human cussedness is. It is even "aroused by the Law," as he puts it in Romans 7:5. Paul knows the streak of meanness in him which makes him rebel against the right and the good, even when he knows he shouldn't. It's something like the mule that Mark Twain once said he knew. The stubborn beast seemed to know what the driver wanted him to do and cantankerously always did exactly the opposite, just to be "ornery." Twain acknowledged the mulishness in himself. Paul says that he and every human is "ornery" in the presence of the Law. When we think God wants us to do one thing, we seem to want to do the contrary thing. This "is living in the flesh."

I do not do the good I want, but the evil I do not want is what I do: What a vivid portrait of the civil war which rages within every person! Paul has been torn in two directions, also. He has wanted to do right and serve God. Yet he also has experienced that mulish quality in his own makeup which keeps him from doing good. In spite of his best intentions, Paul has ended up resisting God! Probably Paul had in mind some of his regrettable past, but was thinking far more about the fundamental quality in his nature which has caused him to end up helpless to do what he should. Paul states that it's not enough to tell someone what he should do. The world is full of shoulds and shouldn'ts. These are interesting and perhaps even true. But they all fall into the category of good advice. And Paul has learned the hard way that good advice doesn't save anyone from the human predicament of sin.

In fact, this schizoid situation of being torn two ways, knowing what you should do and yet turning away from doing it, is so crippling and confining that it destroys your freedom to be the person God intends you to be. Paul, who knows, says that it's like being handcuffed and put into leg irons as a captive.

Sold under sin. For centuries, victorious armies had rounded up the able-bodied people in a conquered territory and marched them off as slaves. The ancient world had often witnessed the horrors of people, manacled and chained, being whipped into submission by soldiers' cruel lashes, humiliated and uprooted from family and home forever, weak from hunger, exposure, and illness, staggering through the streets of the great Roman cities. A slave was a doomed person without rights and without a future when captured. When sold at the slave mart, the slave was expected to do the bidding of the master. If the slave tried to escape or turn against the master, he would suffer harsh and swift punishment. Crucifixion, for example, was reserved for slaves and the worst kind of criminals who were not Roman citizens. Paul has the image of a human being being captured and marched away and sold as a slave, which every Roman understood at once, when he describes the effects of sin. Sin is serving a brutal slave master.

II. *Wretched man that I am! Who will deliver me from this body of death?* Perhaps Paul was thinking of a gruesome form of torture which was occasionally practiced. The victim would be chained face to face, body to body, to a corpse, and forced to exist with the ghastly, putrifying object, often until the effect of decay infected the slave. In any case, Paul tells of the utter hopelessness of the person living as a captive to sin. Destruction inevitably follows, Paul announces.

III. *Thanks be to God through Jesus Christ our Lord!* Suddenly Paul hears the bugle note of the coming of the Rescuer! In the midst of the horrors of despair, destruction, and death, the Deliverer! Jesus Christ comes as Saviour! Paul interrupts his own argument to throw in this one liner about victory!

SUGGESTIONS TO TEACHERS

Start this lesson by reflecting on the human predicament as pondered by the greatest minds in the Church. Paul, then later Augustine, Luther, Calvin, Wesley, and others recognized the fallacy in most people's thinking. That fallacy is this: If I make myself pious enough, or smart enough, or pleasant enough, I will be acceptable to God and others. (Don't you sometimes think this?) The glitch, of course, is the harder you try, the farther you seem to be from God. The struggle is futile! You finally have to give up your self-improvement campaign and throw yourself totally on God's mercy!

The great passage in today's Scripture from Romans 7 should be studied not as doctrine but as experience. It is Paul's experience. It is also the experience of every person in your class. Your lesson ultimately should help every one in your class to understand Grace not as a doctrine but as daily experience!

1. *LIMITS OF LEGALISM.* Christians tend to try to reduce the Good News of Jesus Christ to a set of rules. Help your class to understand the problem of legal-

ism—the religion of rules. Point out Paul's difficulty with such a religion. Legalism awakened Paul's awareness of evil and tempted him to do things he otherwise wouldn't have thought about. Paul, of course, knew that there is need for the Law (he said the Law is "holy, just and good" in Romans 7:12). Help your people to grow beyond a rule-book religion to a life of trust in the divine grace.

2. *SLAVERY OF SIN.* Call attention to Paul's vivid description of a life caught in sin and self as being "sold under sin" (7:14). Have your class talk over how a life of sin is a life of captivity. Modern psychology merely confirms what the New Testament has always stated. Accept that only the Gospel of Jesus Christ frees a person from such slavery.

3. *MIRROR TO MOTIVES.* Take plenty of time in this lesson to go over the problem Paul discusses in Romans 7. Human intentions, no matter how noble and sincere, are not enough to free us from our enslavement to sin and self. Paul knows this from personal experiences. He writes, "I don't do the good I want . . ." (7:18). The harder he tries to be good, the more aware he is of his separation from God. He feels torn apart over the gap between profession and performance. Isn't this the dilemma every Christian knows? How do those in your class resolve the difference between what they mean to do and what they actually do?

4. *DOXOLOGY FOR DELIVERANCE.* The mighty climax to this passage in Romans—and to your lesson today—is the work of Jesus Christ in delivering us from captivity. Paul, in fact, insists that Jesus Christ has rescued us from death! Ask each one in your class to describe what Jesus' deliverance means to him or her.

TOPIC FOR ADULTS
THE STRUGGLE TO DO RIGHT

Uncomfortable Nonbeliever. Nathaniel Hawthorne, the great American writer, described the struggle to do right which raged within his friend and fellow author, Herman Melville.

Hawthorne was American consul in Liverpool when Melville passed through the city in 1856 on his way to the Middle East. Hawthorne in his journal noted Melville's mental restlessness and religious problem—a key to much in Melville's work.

". . . we took a pretty long walk together, and sat down in a hollow among the sand hills . . . and smoked a cigar. Melville, as he always does, began to reason of Providence and futurity, and of everything that lies beyond human ken, and informed me that he had 'pretty much made up his mind to be annihilated'; but still he does not seem to rest in that anticipation; and, I think, will never rest until he gets hold of a definite belief. It is strange how he persists—and has persisted ever since I knew him and probably long before—in wandering to-and-fro over the deserts. . . . He can neither believe, nor be comfortable in his unbelief." Is this the way you sometimes feel—neither believing nor comfortable in your unbelief?

Trust in Jesus Christ's grace! He alone brings peace and wholeness to your life.

Applicable Only to Others. In our struggle to do right, we frequently remain blind to our own follies and shortcomings while able to see those of others with astonishing clarity. This is part of our human sinfulness. We are often like the one little grey-haired lady who attended worship regularly. The dear woman, long a member of her community and church, shook hands with the minister after the service one Sunday morning. "That was a wonderful sermon," she told him, "just wonderful. Everything you said applies to someone I know."

Unable to Respond. A stout, bald gentleman was discussing his tennis game with a friend. This rather awkward individual said, "My brain barks out a command to my body: Run forward speedily. Start right away. Land the ball grace-fully over the net."

"And then what happens?" asked the friend.

"And, then," the heavy-set fellow concluded wistfully, "my body says, 'Who, Me?' "

The same thing is also true when it comes to trying to respond to the call of our minds and consciences. We tell ourselves that we should do such-and-such. But nothing happens. Part of us always seems to answer, "Who, Me?"

Questions for Pupils on the Next Lesson. 1. How does Jesus Christ liberate us from trying to save ourselves by living only by rules? 2. What exactly does Paul mean by the word *flesh* in Romans 8? 3. What exactly does it mean to live a "life in the Spirit"? 4. Why do we feel the pain of separation from another we love?

TOPIC FOR YOUTH
STRUGGLING TO DO RIGHT

Bargaining With God. Goldie Goodman Brady, a seventy-two-year-old widow, was driving home from a bingo game in Nashville one Saturday night in April, 1982. She felt pleased with herself for winning $30 at the bingo game. Somehow, her car skidded on a bad curve, went into a ravine and overturned. Mrs. Brady was knocked unconscious. When she came to, two days later, she found herself trapped in the wreck. For the next three days, the elderly woman said that she talked to God about bingo. "All I do bad is play a little bingo, I don't drink or smoke or take pills," she said she told God. "All I chew is food, and I don't want to die in this position.

"If you call bingo the Devil's work, then I did it, but I told the Lord I got to do something. Otherwise, all I do is crochet and watch TV and keep my house clean."

Fortunately, Mrs. Brady was found by a man who noticed her feet sticking out of her wrecked car at the foot of the forty-foot ravine, and discovered her wedged between the front and back seats. Although she had cuts and bruises, she had not suffered serious injuries and quickly recovered.

Her words regarding her bingo playing, however, are typical of most of us. We think that if we "do right" by not playing bingo or staying away from other vices, God will smile and help us ("I don't drink or smoke or take pills"). We also justify our vices, just as Mrs. Brady tried to explain ("I got to do something, otherwise all I do is crochet and watch TV. . .").

Only God's grace can make us right with Him, not our efforts at goodness!

More About Jerome. There is a story about a young man who was proposing to a girl. Said he: "I am not wealthy and I don't have a yacht and a convertible like Jerome Green, but, my darling, I love you." The girl thought for a moment and then replied: "And I love you, too, but tell me a little more about Jerome."

Here is the common failing of most men and most women. They know the way and they know the right person, but they cannot refrain from asking to learn a little more about the not-so-right things and actions and people. Paul discovered this and describes it in Romans 7. You also learn that it is a struggle to do right because try as you may you keep finding yourself tempted to be interested in the wrong or the second-best.

Facing Who We Are. A high-school teacher in a small town in Missouri taught a course in physiology. One day, the teacher received an angry letter from a par-ent of one of the members of his class. The note concluded, "I don't want my Alice to learn no more about her insides."

We sometimes do not like to face what we are. But because He cares about us, the Lord makes us see what's really inside our hearts and minds. Only then may we receive His grace. Only then may we be healed. Only then will we grow!

Questions for Pupils on the Next Lesson. 1. Is anything ever able to separate a Christian from God's love? 2. What does it mean to you when you hear about living a "spirit-filled life"? How does the Lord help a believer to keep the spirit as well as the letter of the Law? 4. What is meant by the word *flesh* in Romans 8? 5. Do your feelings of loneliness cause you to seek God's presence?

LESSON V—SEPTEMBER 30

LIFE IN THE SPIRIT

Background Scripture: Romans 8
Devotional Reading: Romans 8:18–30

KING JAMES VERSION

ROMANS 8 There is therefore now no condemnation to them which are in Christ Jesus, who walk not after the flesh, but after the Spirit.

2 For the law of the Spirit of life in Christ Jesus hath made me free from the law of sin and death.

3 For what the law could not do, in that it was weak through the flesh, God sending his own Son in the likeness of sinful flesh, and for sin, condemned sin in the flesh:

4 That the righteousness of the law might be fulfilled in us, who walk not after the flesh, but after the Spirit.

5 For they that are after the flesh do mind the things of the flesh; but they that are after the Spirit the things of the Spirit.

6 For to be carnally minded *is* death; but to be spiritually minded *is* life and peace.

7 Because the carnal mind *is* enmity against God: for it is not subject to the law of God, neither indeed can be.

8 So then they that are in the flesh cannot please God.

31 What shall we then say to these things? If God *be* for us who *can* be against us?

32 He that spared not his own Son, but delivered him up for us all, how shall he not with him also freely give us all things?

33 Who shall lay any thing to the charge of God's elect? *It is* God that justifieth.

34 Who *is* he that condemneth? *It is* Christ that died, yea rather, that is risen again, who is even at the right hand of God, who also maketh intercession for us.

35 Who shall separate us from the love of Christ? *shall* tribulation, or distress, or persecution, or famine, or nakedness, or peril, or sword?

36 As it is written, For thy sake we are killed all the day long; we are accounted as sheep for the slaughter.

37 Nay, in all these things we are more than conquerors through him that loved us.

38 For I am persuaded, that neither death, nor life, nor angels, nor principalities, nor powers, nor things present, nor things to come,

39 Nor height, nor depth, nor any other creature, shall be able to separate us from the love of God, which is in Christ Jesus our Lord.

REVISED STANDARD VERSION

ROMANS 8 There is therefore now no condemnation for those who are in Christ Jesus. 2 For the law of the Spirit of life in Christ Jesus has set me free from the law of sin and death. 3 For God has done what the law, weakened by the flesh, could not do: sending his own Son in the likeness of sinful flesh and for sin, he condemned sin in the flesh, 4 in order that the just requirement of the law might be fulfilled in us, who walk not according to the flesh but according to the Spirit. 5 For those who live according to the flesh set their minds on the things of the flesh, but those who live according to the Spirit set their minds on the things of the Spirit. 6 To set the mind on the flesh is death, but to set the mind on the Spirit is life and peace. 7 For the mind that is set on the flesh is hostile to God; it does not submit to God's law, indeed it cannot; 8 and those who are in the flesh cannot please God.

31 What then shall we say to this? If God is for us, who is against us? 32 He who did not spare his own Son but gave him up for us all, will he not also give us all things with him? 33 Who shall bring any charge against God's elect? It is God who justifies; 34 who is to condemn? Is it Christ Jesus, who died, yes, who was raised from the dead, who is at the right hand of God, who indeed intercedes for us? 35 Who shall separate us from the love of Christ? Shall tribulation, or distress, or persecution, or famine, or nakedness, or peril, or sword? 36 As it is written,

"For thy sake we are being killed all the day long;

we are regarded as sheep to be slaughtered."

37 No, in all these things we are more than conquerors through him who loved us. 38 For I am sure that neither death, nor life, nor angels, nor principalities, nor things present, nor things to come, nor powers, 39 nor height, nor depth, nor anything else in all creation, will be able to separate us from the love of God in Christ Jesus our Lord.

KEY VERSE: For the law of the Spirit of life in Christ Jesus has set me free from the law of sin and death. Romans 8:2 (RSV).

HOME DAILY BIBLE READINGS

Sept.   24.   M.   *Jesus and the Holy Spirit.* John 14:25–31.
Sept.   25.   T.   *Part of the Vine.* John 15:1–11.
Sept.   26.   W.   *Set Free by the Spirit.* Romans 8:1–8.
Sept.   27.   T.   *Children of God.* Romans 8:9–17.
Sept.   28.   F.   *Hope for All Creation.* Romans 8:18–24.
Sept.   29.   S.   *God at Work in the World.* Romans 8:26–30.
Sept.   30.   S.   *More Than Conquerors.* Romans 8:31–39.

BACKGROUND

After the preceding seven chapters, Romans 8 soars to heights of hope. In many ways, Romans 8 is the climax of the entire letter. The chapter easily takes its place among the greatest pieces of devotional literature in the Bible.

Paul, however, was not writing it primarily for inspirational reading. Rather, he dictated these words as the conclusion to the preceding chapters about the utter hopelessness of every human's existence apart from Jesus Christ.

Paul has argued in the first parts of his letter that everyone—Jew and Greek alike—is under God's judgment for arrogantly trying to live apart from God. Paul has built his case well. He makes it clear that everyone stands convicted as a sinner; he refuses to let anyone off the hook. He goes on to describe the miserable existence of being a sinner in terms of a captured slave living without any hope of ever being delivered from captivity.

Romans 8 is the news of mighty rescue. Here, Paul announces what Jesus Christ does. Paul also states what this means to believers. As much as the announcement of Jesus Christ's deliverance, Romans 8 is also a description of life in the Spirit. Some Christians say that in all of Paul's writings there is no chapter which says more about the Spirit of Christ than this one.

Paul does not think of the Holy Spirit as a blurry "It" but as the dynamic presence of the Living Jesus Christ. The thread running throughout Romans, and indeed all of the writings of all the authors in the New Testament, is that Jesus Christ lives and empowers His people. Romans 8 calls for celebrating and singing that the Spirit of Christ makes us "more than conquerors" in every situation!

NOTES ON THE PRINTED TEXT

I. Paul, in writing Romans 8, seemed to grow so excited about the life in the Spirit of Jesus Christ that he spills out one idea after another of what that life means.

There is, therefore now, no condemnation for those who are in Christ: The power of sin is broken. Those who trust in Jesus Christ are able to live a new life. The Greek text is emphatic: the grounds for condemning a believer have been removed. A Christian may now rest in the knowledge that through Jesus Christ he is a forgiven person.

Paul, who had lived with the burden of guilt for hounding Christians to prisons, torture, and death, knew well that he did not have a shred of hope of presenting himself as blameless. He must have realized that he stood condemned by God and by fellow Christians. He also had condemned himself for not living up to the requirements of the Law. However, Paul learned personally that though he was condemned as a sinner, through Jesus Christ he was released from living on the "death's row" of condemnation.

... the Spirit of life in Jesus Christ has set me free: Paul here throws out another notion of what life in the Spirit means—*freedom!* Freedom from the hopeless task of trying to keep an impossible-to-keep set of requirements; freedom from weariness over trying and failing, trying and failing; freedom from anxiety of future failure; freedom from guilt over past failures.

. . . walk according to the Spirit: To those who are in harmony with the Spirit of Jesus Christ, life is guided and motivated by Him. The Spirit becomes the believer's "law," a walking, living *Torah* who helps in every step of life's pilgrimage.

To set the mind on the Spirit is life and peace. "Life and Peace." Aren't these the yearnings of every human? Look at the advertisements in magazines and on television. Words meaning the same as life and peace are promised when one drives a certain car, drinks this brand of beer, wears that maker's jeans, smokes a specific cigarette. As one jaded young adult, heavily in debt, sighed, "I have been led to believe that if I would buy and buy, I'd find life and peace."

Paul states unequivocally that life and peace only come when the believer sets his mind on the Spirit of Jesus Christ. Paul also bluntly says that when one does *not* set his mind on the Spirit of Christ, the opposite of life and peace come: namely death. For those living in the death-obsessed culture of the first century and the twentieth, Paul's words pleading with believers to set their minds on the Spirit of Christ have deep significance!

II. *If God is for us, who is against us?* Paul moves into the mighty climax of this chapter with words that almost call for a chorus of 300 voices with trumpet accompaniment. Christians can face anything! Because of life in the Spirit, we know that God caringly brings us victorious through the worst that life can throw at us.

God's elect. Life in the Spirit means becoming aware that one is "elected" by God, that one is chosen in love for serving. Some modern readers recoil against the thought of God choosing or electing anyone because they think that this means that God must think the elect are superior and nicer than others. Wrong! Paul has no such thought. The elect are those who have been chosen to live a life of sacrifice for others just as Jesus Himself did.

A good analogy would be those who received a draft notice ordering them to report for induction for duty. God's elect are those who have been drafted by the Spirit to get involved in His cause.

III. *Who shall separate us from the love of Christ?* Paul reels off a list of all of the imaginable causes of separation from the Spirit of Christ. Look at them, and note that he seems to have covered every possible situation or disaster which would leave one to think that he is beyond the reach of God.

Shall tribulation, or distress, or persecution, or famine, or nakedness, or peril, or sword: This series covers all the terrible occurrences that can befall any believer in the course of his life on earth.

I am sure that neither death, nor life, nor angels, nor principalities, nor things present, nor things to come, nor powers: Not even mysterious, malevolent forces we don't understand can keep the loving Spirit of Jesus Christ from being with us! In all these we are "more than conquerors" or, in the Greek word coined here by Paul, we are superovercomers with Jesus!

SUGGESTIONS TO TEACHERS

Paul was aware of Jesus Christ's nearness. Surrounded by the presence of the living Lord, he thought of life in the Spirit in terms of inhaling a sense of Jesus Christ as naturally as one breathes in air.

As teacher, your problem is that not everyone in your class is conscious of being surrounded by the Spirit. You probably already know that some of your class members frankly don't comprehend such talk. Therefore, today's lesson is a challenge to you. But it is also an opportunity to help deepen the faith of these persons. You also will find your own awareness of the Spirit strengthened!

1. *HOW WE WORK AGAINST THE SPIRIT.* Your class may have problems

with the word *flesh* as Paul uses it in Romans 8 and elsewhere. The term does not refer to material stuff as opposed to nonmaterial. Nor does it mean sex or human sexuality. Rather *flesh* means relying on your own religiosity. *Flesh* is a phony piety. To "walk according to the flesh" is to think you can pose as being a nice, upstanding person. It is piosity instead of piety, religiosity instead of religion. Any time anyone is privately proud of his or her prayers or good works or devotional practices or charity or *anything*, that person is not walking in the Spirit but in the flesh, remind your class.

2. *HOW WE WAKEN TO THE SPIRIT.* The Spirit raised Christ from the dead, and operates in the world now, Paul states. Have your class take note of the various ways the Spirit is at work according to the many references in Romans 8, including delivering believers from fear, making them aware of being God's children when they suffer with Christ, bestowing hope and strength in times of apparent futility and weakness. When Christians begin to be aware of the extraordinary activity of the Spirit in their lives, they awaken to a deeper sense of His Presence.

3. *HOW WE WALK ACCORDING TO THE SPIRIT.* Paul joyfully announces that the Spirit is bringing a new era. Let your class savor the words in Romans 8:18–25. Everything that has transpired previously to this time is merely prologue for the mighty act of new creation now taking place beginning with the Resurrection of Jesus Christ. Remind your people that walking in the Spirit means participating in God's new creation. In spite of pain and hurts and problems, your class members are meant to be partners with the Spirit in bringing the new era of Christ's rule to pass!

4. *HOW WE WATCH FOR THE SPIRIT.* Romans 8 makes startling claims for the Spirit. The Spirit, Paul says, intercedes for us in our prayers. The Spirit providentially supplies what we need and works on our behalf to bring order and good out of chaos and evil in our existence. The Spirit establishes a permanent, indissoluble bond with God. Through the Spirit, we may be assured that we have a loving relationship with the Creator—regardless! This is a splendid opportunity to explore both the topic of Providence of God and Prayer in light of these promises of the Spirit!

TOPIC FOR ADULTS
LIFE IN THE SPIRIT

Spirit's Pressure and Call. "St. Paul did not want to be an apostle to the Gentiles. He wanted to be a clever and appreciated young Jewish scholar and kicked against the pricks. St. Ambrose and St. Augustine did not want to be overworked and worried bishops. Nothing was farther from their intentions. St. Cuthbert wanted the solitude and freedom of his hermitage on the Farne; but he did not often get there. St. Francis Xavier's preference was for an ordered life close to his beloved master, St. Ignatius. At a few hours' notice he was sent out to be the Apostle of the Indies and never returned to Europe again. Henry Martyn, the fragile and exquisite scholar, was compelled to sacrifice the intellectual life to which he was so perfectly fitted for the missionary life to which he felt he was decisively called. In all these, a power beyond themselves decided the direction of life. Yet in all we recognise not frustration, but the highest of all types of achievement. Things like this—and they are constantly happening—gradually convince us that the overruling reality of life is the Will and Choice of a Spirit acting not in a mechanical but in a living and personal way; and that the spiritual life of man does not consist in mere individual betterment, or assiduous attention to his own soul, but in a free and unconditional response to that Spirit's pressure and call, whatever the cost may be.

"The first question here, then, is not, 'What is best for my soul?' nor is it even, 'What is most useful to humanity?' But—transcending both these limited aims—what function must this life fulfil in the great and secret economy of God?"—From pp. 33–34 in *The Spiritual Life* by Evelyn Underhill, Harper & Row.

Spirit Puts Baby's Babble Together. An elderly gentleman passed his grand-daughter's room one night and overheard her repeating the alphabet in an oddly reverent way. "What on earth are you up to?" he asked.

"I'm saying my prayers," explained the little girl. "But I can't think of exactly the right words tonight, so I'm just saying all the letters. God will put them together for me, because He knows what I am thinking."

Spirit Makes It His Work. "Anyone who follows Jesus in his or her daily work, whatever the occupation or vocation, will find it linked to God's purposes for the world and therefore in opposition to the powers of evil personified by Satan or the devil. Such work will always be carried on in the shadow of death, in struggle and sacrifice, and with no guarantee of success. But the eschatological meaning of work, behind and in the company of Jesus, is that it is *his* work that we perform, and since in this work he precedes us he also waits for us at the end."—Gayraud S. Wilmore, *Last Things First,* Philadelphia, Pa.: Westminster, 1982.

Questions for Pupils on the Next Lesson. 1. Is accepting help always a sign of weakness? 2. Is life governed by the law that we reap what we sow? 3. Why do those who try to be independent financially, physically, and emotionally often tend to be harsh in attitude and treatment toward others who are more dependent in these areas? 4. How does self-discipline bring freedom? 5. Why is the Church described as a "family"? Is this your experience with the Church?

TOPIC FOR YOUTH
POWER SOURCE TO A FULL LIFE

Specific Prayers. "The biggest change came to my prayer life. In Uganda I had prayed with a deep sense of urgency. I refused to leave my knees until I was certain I had been in the presence of the resurrected Christ. It was not just the gift I needed. I needed to see the Giver. I needed to know that the God of orphans and widows, the God of the helpless, heard my prayers. Now, after a year in Philadelphia, the urgency was gone. When I prayed publicly, I was more concerned to be theologically correct than to be in God's presence. Even in private my prayers were no longer the helpless cries of a child. They were spiritual tranquilizers, thoughts that made no contact with anything outside themselves. More and more I found myself coming to God with vague requests for gifts I did not expect.

"One night, I said my prayers in a routine fashion and was about to rise from my knees when I heard the convicting voice of the Holy Spirit.

" 'Kefa, who were you praying for? What is it you wanted? I used to hear the names of children in your prayers, the names of friends and relatives. You prayed for Okelo and Topista, for Dr. K. and Ali, for Nakazi and your father. Now you pray for "the orphans," for "the church" and your "fellow refugees." Which refugees, Kefa? Which believers? Which orphans? Who are these people and what is it you want for them?'

"It was a sharp rebuke. As I fell again to my knees and asked forgiveness for my sin of unbelief, I knew that it was not just my prayers that had suffered. It was not just a bad memory that caused names to vanish from my mind and turned those closest to me into abstractions. God Himself had become a distant figure. He had become a subject of debate, an abstract category. I no longer prayed to Him as a living Father but as an impersonal being who did not mind my inattention and unbelief.

"From that night on, my prayers became specific. I prayed for real people, with real needs. And it was not long before, once again, these needs became the means by which I came face to face with the living God."—*A Distant Grief* by F. Kefa Sempangi. © copyright 1979, Regal Books, Ventura, CA 93006. Used by permission.

Forget the Count! Simeon Stylites was an eccentric Syrian monk who lived between A.D. 390 and 459. He had a streak of exhibitionism and decided to prove his piety by living full-time on a pillar from 423 until his death. He kept boosting the height of his column until it towered over sixty feet in the air. In full view of everyone, he prayed, fasted, and put himself through ascetic exercises to try to get right with God. Occasionally he preached to admirers below. His simple wants were hoisted on a basket. His few hours of sleep were snatched while hunched over a parapet. One time, admiring disciples counted him touching his toes 1,244 times in bowing before God from the top of his pillar.

The sad thing about Simeon Stylites lies partly in the exertions of the man to try to be right with God. Perhaps sadder is the way other Christians stood below to count. All missed the glorious news of the Power Source to a full life!

No Stereotype. "When the Holy Spirit is poured out upon God's people their experiences will differ widely. Some will receive new vision, others will know a new liberty in soul-winning, others will proclaim the Word of God with fresh power, and yet others will be filled with heavenly joy or overflowing praise. . . . There is nothing stereotyped about God's dealings with His children.

"Therefore, we must not, by our prejudices and preconceptions, make watertight compartments for the working of His Spirit, either in our own lives or in the lives of others. . . . We must leave God free to work as He wills, and to give what evidence He pleases of the work He does. He is Lord, and it is not for us to legislate for Him."—Watchman Nee, Chinese Theologian.

Questions for Pupils on the Next Lesson. 1. Knowing that you have the capacity (and often the desire) to do as you please, what keeps you from using your freedom irresponsibly? 2. What makes you sense God's approval or disapproval of your behavior? 3. What helps you to understand some boundaries to help you know the kind of behavior expected of you by God? 4. How do you handle the feelings of loneliness, instability, and inadequacy that you sometimes have? 5. Why do you think the Church is called a "family"?

LESSON VI—OCTOBER 7

HOUSEHOLD OF FAITH

Background Scripture: Romans 12:9–21; Galatians 6:1–18
Devotional Reading: Galatians 5:16–24

KING JAMES VERSION

ROMANS 12. 9 *Let* love be without dissimulation. Abhor that which is evil; cleave to that which is good.

10 *Be* kindly affectioned one to another with brotherly love; in honour preferring one another;

11 Not slothful in business; fervent in spirit; serving the Lord;

12 Rejoicing in hope; patient in tribulation; continuing instant in prayer;

13 Distributing to the necessity of saints; given to hospitality.

GALATIANS 6 Brethren, if a man be overtaken in a fault, ye which are spiritual, restore such an one in the spirit of meekness; considering thyself, lest thou also be tempted.

2 Bear ye one another's burdens, and so fulfil the law of Christ.

3 For if a man think himself to be something, when he is nothing, he deceiveth himself.

4 But let every man prove his own work, and then shall he have rejoicing in himself alone, and not in another.

5 For every man shall bear his own burden.

6 Let him that is taught in the word communicate unto him that teacheth in all good things.

7 Be not deceived; God is not mocked: for whatsoever a man soweth, that shall he also reap.

8 For he that soweth to his flesh shall of the flesh reap corruption;, but he that soweth to the Spirit shall of the Spirit reap life everlasting.

9 And let us not be weary in well doing; for in due season we shall reap, if we faint not.

10 As we have therefore opportunity, let us do good unto all *men*, especially unto them who are of the household of faith.

REVISED STANDARD VERSION

ROMANS 12 9 Let love be genuine; hate what is evil, hold fast to what is good; 10 love one another with brotherly affection; outdo one another in showing honor. 11 Never flag in zeal, be aglow with the Spirit, serve the Lord, 12 Rejoice in your hope, be patient in tribulation, be constant in prayer. 13 Contribute to the needs of the saints, practice hospitality.

GALATIANS 6 Brethren, if a man is overtaken in any trespass, you who are spiritual should restore him in a spirit of gentleness. Look to yourself, lest you too be tempted. 2 Bear one another's burdens, and so fulfil the law of Christ. 3 For if any one thinks he is something, when he is nothing, he deceives himself. 4 But let each one test his own work, and then his reason to boast will be in himself alone and not in his neighbor. 5 For each man will have to bear his own load.

6 Let him who is taught the word share all good things with him who teaches.

7 Do not be deceived; God is not mocked, for whatever a man sows, that he will also reap. 8 For he who sows to his own flesh will from the flesh reap corruption; but he who sows to the Spirit will from the Spirit reap eternal life. 9 And let us not grow weary in well-doing, for in due season we shall reap, if we do not lose heart. 10 So then, as we have opportunity, let us do good to all men, and especially to those who are of the household of faith.

KEY VERSE: . . . *as we have opportunity, let us do good to all.* . . . Galatians 6:10 (RSV).

HOME DAILY BIBLE READINGS

Oct.	1.	M.	*Life in the Kingdom.* Matthew 5:3–12.
Oct.	2.	T.	*Life in the Spirit.* Galatians 5:16–25.
Oct.	3.	W.	*Law Versus Gospel.* Acts 15:1–5.
Oct.	4.	T.	*All Are Saved by Grace.* Acts 15:6–11.
Oct.	5.	F.	*Free From the Law.* Acts 15:12–21.
Oct.	6.	S.	*Responsible Freedom.* Acts 15:22–29.
Oct.	7.	S.	*The Limits of Freedom.* Galatians 6:1–10.

BACKGROUND

Paul was a theologian's theologian. He had one of the keenest, most creative minds in the history of the Church. But don't ever get the notion that he was an ivory-tower thinker. He was always concerned to translate doctrine into daily doing. He was never content to pen theory. He knew that it had to be tied to life. Consequently, Paul's writings always oscillate between the profession of faith and the practice of faith. He writes chapters which soar to heights of theological theory. Then, with startling abruptness, he brings the subject to down-to-earth applications.

In Romans and Galatians, as well as in every other letter he wrote, Paul injects practical ways of responding to the Spirit of Jesus Christ. Sometimes people who read the Bible by selecting little snippets here and there without any consideration for their context pick out these passages as a way of making the Christian faith into good advice instead of Good News. Paul was not writing a first century Dear Abby column. He was helping fellow believers to understand the ramifications of the Spirit of Jesus in their lives.

Furthermore, Paul's words were always written for the Christian community. Even his letters to certain individuals such as Timothy or Titus or Philemon had others in the household of faith in mind, too. As John Wesley used to say, "The Bible knows nothing of solitary religion." Paul wrote to build up the entire family of Christ.

Each of the congregations Paul sent correspondence to was different; each had unique challenges and problems. The congregation at Rome faced a different situation than the cluster of churches in Galatia. Yet all of these gatherings of Christians felt overwhelmed by the difficulties around them at times; all also found dissension within their fellowship at times. Sounds familiar, doesn't it? Paul's comments were the words of a kindly, seasoned pastor to people he cared deeply about, and may still be read as epistles addressed to every congregation, including yours!

NOTES ON THE PRINTED TEXT

Although Paul's readers in Rome had not asked him any specific questions like his parishioners had in the churches he had founded and visited, Paul knew that they would have about the same kind of problems which churches faced everywhere. After he wrote deathless paragraphs about the meaning of the Spirit of Jesus Christ bringing a new life, Paul turned to the practical situations which Roman Christians had to face. True, Paul didn't know personally these people at Rome. But he knew people and he knew churches. Therefore, he wrote confidently to the Roman congregation he had never met, offering insights and helps to these Christians for their Christian life together. Romans 12 has such appeal because Paul wrote to cover so many situations in which congregations find themselves.

Let love be genuine; hate what is evil, hold fast to what is good; love one another with . . . affection; outdo one another in showing honor: These words remind a reader of 1 Corinthians 13, and also of Jesus' words about love. The Greek word here for love is *agape*, the kind of Christ-like love of sacrificing for the other. The ancients couldn't understand this kind of self-giving concern; it was foreign to them. The Cross was foolishness to the Greek philosopher types and a scandal to the Pharisee legalists. God's love was shown through Jesus Christ's death for all persons. In turn, *agape* or Christ's sacrificial love became the force at work in the life of each individual believer and within the corporate life of every Christian congregation. This must be the case in every church. Whatever else a church may be, it *must* demonstrate love—within, among its own members, and without, toward the people around it.

Never flag in zeal, be aglow with the Spirit, serve the Lord: Rejoice in your hope, be patient in tribulation: Many articles have appeared recently on the subject of Burnout. Some have solemnly tried to deal with burnout among ministers, Sunday-school teachers, and church workers. Surprisingly, most have discussed the matter only from a psychological perspective. Paul also knew that people face burnout, although he might not have used that term. However, Paul approached the problem not from a psychological but a spiritual perspective. The cause was not so much too much stress but too little Spirit. To the household of faith at Rome, and the household of faith in every town, Paul enjoins Christians to keep the glow of the Spirit alive. How?

Be constant in prayer: Paul reminds his audience that prayer takes effort. Being "constant" in praying means working hard to maintain a habit of being with the Spirit of Jesus Christ. After all, genuine prayer as the masters of the prayer life repeatedly tell us, is "being with" the Lord.

Contribute to the needs of the saints, practice hospitality: Christians make space for others. As Henri Nouwen, the writer of many books on the Christian devotional life, states, being with Jesus Christ means passing from hostility to hospitality as one of the key movements in the Christian life.

If a man is overtaken in any trespass, you who are spiritual should restore him in a spirit of gentleness: Here, Paul gives a case history of Christian love in action in a local congregation. Act as people filled with the Spirit of Jesus Christ, not as those who go by the rule book, Paul states. Deal gently with the man because no Christian is immune to temptation!

Restore comes from the Greek word used in medical circles to describe setting a broken bone by positioning it in its proper place again. Paul wants Christians to have the sensitivity of gentle physicians in dealing with those in the church who get into trouble.

Bear ye one another's burdens . . . every man will have to bear his own burden: At first glance, these verses in Galatians look contradictory. In verse 2, however, the word literally means a weight, whereas in verse 5 the Greek word refers to a soldier's backpack. In other words, each Christian must help carry the weight of fellow church members yet shoulder his own responsibilities.

SUGGESTIONS TO TEACHERS

Quick! Answer the question: What is the Church?

Building? Institution? Organization? Collection of people on Sunday morning? All of these?

Probably something more, you're thinking. And you're right. But before you go farther, examine what the New Testament Christians considered the Church to be. Romans 12:9–21 is a good sample. Here is the meat of your lesson for today.

You will quickly note that Paul thinks that the Church is like a family or a household. On this day of World Communion, you should emphasize this family idea of the Church throughout your class time.

1. *PROMOTING HARMONY.* Throughout this passage from Romans, we Christians are described as belonging to one another in a family-like relationship. There is no thought of one being a "lone wolf" believer in Jesus Christ. The Spirit brings us together. And the Spirit means for us to build up the relationships within that family. "Live in harmony with one another . . . live peaceably with all" (Romans 12:16, 18), Paul urges. Have your class specifically discuss how the class and your congregation may live in greater harmony. Also, discuss how

greater harmony among Christ's larger family in your area and overseas can be fostered.

2. *PRACTICING HOSPITALITY.* We are meant to be concerned for the needs of others, both within the Church and without. Devote some of your class time to considering those who receive little hospitality or welcome in your church and in your community. Refugees? Members of ethnic or minority groups? Persons of lower economic means? Teenagers? Push your class members to identify who the people are who feel left out where you live. Then, of course, encourage the class to ponder what steps should be taken to practice hospitality toward these folks.

3. *PEACEMAKING IN HOSTILITIES.* You don't have to document the fact of warfare currently blazing in many parts of the world. You may have to point out, however, the danger of militaristic thinking and reliance on weapons. Christians are called to be peacemakers. Steer the talk among your class members to considering positive steps each person individually and the congregation as a whole should take as partners in peacemaking.

4. *PARDONING OF HURTERS.* This lesson must also touch on the ministry of reconciliation which each believer and every congregation must be involved in. Look particularly at Romans 12:14, 19–21, and have each person remark on what these verses suggest. Have your people state where they most often receive hurts and slights. As members of the household of faith, ask how they are "blessing those who persecute them." Remind them that God's forgiveness can be received only to the degree that forgiveness is extended to others!

TOPIC FOR ADULTS
LIFE IN THE FELLOWSHIP

Venture Into Grace. The confirmation service February 3, 1980 at Germonds Presbyterian Church in New City, New York, was a milestone for both the congregation and the nine participants. It marked the culmination of more than three years' attendance at Germonds by the nine, who are residents of Venture Inn, a nearby community hostel for the mentally disabled.

The Germonds Church has welcomed Venture Inn residents since the spring of 1976, when four of the residents first began attending services there. "Probably most of us were apprehensive at first," admits Ruth Battles, whose husband, the Reverend Robert W. Battles, Jr., was minister at Germonds. Few of Germonds' congregants had dealt previously with the mentally handicapped, she says.

But the apprehension soon passed, she adds, and "our friends from Venture Inn have been among our most regular and attentive parishioners."

The Venture Inn community consists of moderately disabled persons who can largely care for themselves. The residents live in motel-like housing units with a communal kitchen where they cook for themselves. Those attending service at Germonds were originally picked up and returned home by Germonds parishioners, who served as their hosts during their stay at the church. But the group became so large that now they are brought to the church by van.

The confirmation service was the culmination of a two-year learning process. Two years ago Germonds Church developed a special Christian education class for the Venture Inn parishioners, and a general Bible study class a year ago. The group members began to consider confirmation, and began preparation for it seven weeks before their confirmation. All were enthusiastic about learning about their faith, according to Ruth Battles.

With her help, the group wrote a joint statement of faith to be read during the worship service on Confirmation Sunday. Four of the group also wrote their own statements of faith. These were presented with the gifts of bread and wine on the communion table.

Although not all of the nine were able to present personal statements, all understood the step they were taking, the Battleses feel.

Following the service the Venture Inn group sang "Amazing Grace." The congregation agreed that indeed it was.

Take Managers Out of the Pews and Put Them to Work. "On a plane to Chicago, I sat next to a man who told me that he taught a Sunday-school class every week. I asked him what else he did in his church. 'Occasionally I am an usher for Sunday worship,' he replied.

"As we talked on, I learned that he was a systems analyst for a large corporation—in other words, an in-house management consultant. No one had ever asked him to contribute his management knowledge and experience to make his church a more effective organization.

"The resources for good church management practice are sitting in the pews every Sunday. Every congregation has some members who are in business or who participate in planning and budgeting for profit-making or non-profit institutions. But churches are not employing much of the talent available to them."—Richard Firth, *A.D.* Magazine, July/August, 1982 © *A.D.* Used by permission.

Proximity of the Two Tables. In Kingston, Jamaica, Christian church members are conducting heroic ministries in adverse settings. In one slum area with high unemployment and illness rates, the United Church of Jamaican Protestants built a combination school and church building. Directly behind the chancel of the church sanctuary where worship services are held regularly, these Jamaican Christians have established a free clinic for those who cannot secure medical care. The examining table is only a few feet from the Communion Table. No wall, only a small curtain separates the two tables. At first, visitors are shocked to see patients thronging so close to the altar while waiting to be put on the examining table. However, the proximity of the Lord's Table for Holy Communion and the medical examining table speaks of the way that congregation ministers to the spiritual and physical needs of the whole person, just as Jesus Christ Himself did!

Is this not what every congregation should be doing in its own way?

Questions for Pupils on the Next Lesson. 1. How do you answer those who say that moral teachings are unimportant? 2. Do you find any fulfillment in responding to the needs of others? 3. Remembering that people pattern their lives after others whether or not they realize it, on what people do you pattern your life? 4. Who are the persons who shape your attitudes and lifestyle? 5. What does it mean to "have the mind of Christ"?

TOPIC FOR YOUTH
A RESPONSIBLE ME

Unknown in the Dorm. "Several years ago a suicide occurred in the Notre Dame campus. This is unusual for a Catholic college whose students have been taught that suicide is not an acceptable way of exiting from this world. It is even more unusual at Notre Dame where there is excellent supervision of dormitories with priests, nuns, religious brothers, or trained lay-people in residence in each of them. The director of student affairs was troubled and decided to get at the cause of this tragedy. He called in all the students who had attended small classes with the unfortunate student and also interviewed those who lived up and down the hall in the dormitory where the student had lived. He wanted to know what kind of person this student was. What he discovered was that *no one even knew him.* It is little wonder that the young man took his life."—Morton T. Kelsey, *Caring,* New York: Paulist Press, 1981.

Chosen People. In 1969, Richard Love, a quality control engineer for the American Sterilizer Company, makers of medical equipment in Erie, Pa., spent three weeks as a Christian volunteer at the church-related hospital in Taegu, Korea. By the time he returned, Dick Love had become aware of the desperate need for medical equipment in mission hospitals throughout the world. On his first day back at work again in Erie, he noticed a large bulk sterilizer, worth about $12,000 when new, was about to be scrapped. "Give it to me," he asked vice-president B. J. Walker. American Sterilizer did. Dick Love rebuilt and fitted the sterilizer with new controls and shipped it off to Taegu. Dick continued to scrounge surgical and medical equipment for mission hospitals overseas.

In 1971 Dick Love finally decided to resign his job at American Sterilizer to devote all his time to answering the needs of Christian hospitals. He served as volunteer consultant in church hospitals in Cameroun, India, Pakistan, Thailand, the Philippines, Hong Kong, Taiwan, and again in Korea. In each place, he was begged to remain.

Dick Love went back to Erie and enlisted the help of fellow Christians. His congregation gave him a shack behind the Sunday-school building, and volunteers fixed it up as a warehouse. Offers of used but usable medical equipment began to come in. Requests meanwhile piled up. Dick and his wife, Edith, and their Christian friends organized into an outfit called CHOSEN (Christian Hospitals Overseas Secure Equipment Needs). Each of the twenty-four men and three women in CHOSEN now spends hours in the shop behind Westminster Church or behind a typewriter or in a van, volunteering to serve Christ and fellow Christians. The Catholic Medical Mission Board and Interchurch Medical Assistance began to provide on-sea shipping arrangements, and Church World Service assumed the responsibility for securing duty-free import permits in most countries.

Thanks to CHOSEN and its team of committed members of the household of faith demonstrating Christ's life within their fellowship, millions of dollars worth of medical equipment have been shared with mission hospitals in other parts of the world!

Family! The year that the Pittsburgh Pirates won the National League pennant and the World Series, the ball team members took as their theme song, "We Are Family." At each ball game, team members and fans joyfully sang, "We are famileeeeeee!" They won ball games. They became the champs.

As we Christians and denominations work together, united as "family" we will begin to win the world!

Questions for Pupils on the Next Lesson. 1. Why are you eager to be of service to others? 2. Does your church offer you many opportunities for you to serve others? 3. How do you resolve some of the conflicts you feel between what society condones and what your parents and church tell you? 4. As you become more aware that people you trust are not perfect, how may God's Word give you dependable guidance and authority? 5. What moral teachings are most important to you?

LESSON VII—OCTOBER 14

MOTIVES FOR MORAL LIVING

Background Scripture: Philippians 2:1–18
Devotional Reading: Philippians 1:19–30

KING JAMES VERSION

PHILIPPIANS 2 If *there be* therefore any consolation in Christ, if any comfort of love, if any fellowship of the Spirit, if any bowels and mercies,

2 Fulfil ye my joy, that ye be likeminded, having the same love, *being* of one accord, of one mind.

3 *Let* nothing *be done* through strife or vainglory; but in lowliness of mind let each esteem other better than themselves.

4 Look not every man on his own things, but every man also on the things of others.

5 Let this mind be in you, which was also in Christ Jesus:

6 Who, being in the form of God, thought it not robbery to be equal with God:

7 But made himself of no reputation, and took upon him the form of a servant, and was made in the likeness of men:

8 And being found in fashion as a man, he humbled himself, and became obedient unto death, even the death of the cross.

9 Wherefore God also hath highly exalted him, and given him a name which is above every name:

10 That at the name of Jesus every knee should bow, of *things* in heaven, and *things* in earth, and *things* under the earth;

11 And *that* every tongue should confess that Jesus Christ *is* Lord, to the glory of God the Father.

12 Wherefore, my beloved, as ye have always obeyed, not as in my presence only, but now much more in my absence, work out your own salvation with fear and trembling.

13 For it is God which worketh in you both to will and to do of *his* good pleasure.

REVISED STANDARD VERSION

PHILIPPIANS 2 So if there is any encouragement in Christ, any incentive of love, any participation in the Spirit, any affection and sympathy, 2 complete my joy by being of the same mind, having the same love, being in full accord and of one mind. 3 Do nothing from selfishness or conceit, but in humility count others better than yourselves. 4 Let each of you look not only to his own interests, but also to the interests of others. 5 Have this mind among yourselves, which is yours in Christ Jesus, 6 who, though he was in the form of God, did not count equality with God a thing to be grasped, 7 but emptied himself, taking the form of a servant, being born in the likeness of men. 8 And being found in human form he humbled himself and became obedient unto death, even death on a cross. 9 Therefore God has highly exalted him and bestowed on him the name which is above every name, 10 that at the name of Jesus every knee should bow, in heaven and on earth and under the earth, 11 and every tongue confess that Jesus Christ is Lord, to the glory of God the Father.

12 Therefore, my beloved, as you have always obeyed, so now, not only as in my presence but much more in my absence, work out your own salvation with fear and trembling; 13 for God is at work in you, both to will and to work for his good pleasure.

KEY VERSE: Let each of you look not only to his own interests, but also to the interests of others. Philippians 2:4 (RSV).

HOME DAILY BIBLE READINGS

Oct.	8.	M.	*Have the Mind of Christ.* Philippians 2:1–11.
Oct.	9.	T.	*God Works in Us.* Philippians 2:12–18.
Oct.	10.	W.	*The Power of the Resurrection.* Philippians 3:1–11.
Oct.	11.	T.	*The Prize of the Upward Call.* Philippians 3:12–16.
Oct.	12.	F.	*A Home in Heaven.* Philippians 3:17–4:1.
Oct.	13.	S.	*God's Love Motivates.* 1 John 2:28–3:3.
Oct.	14.	S.	*The Devil Is Defeated.* 1 John 3:4–10.

BACKGROUND

The Letter to the Philippians was written as a "thank you" note. Paul, the writer, wanted to tell the Christians in Philippi how much he appreciated the generous gift of money they had sent him. Paul, ill and alone and in prison, needed their gift. He also treasured their friendship. Paul and the Philippian Christians had a special bond of friendship between them, going back to the first time he had met Lydia and a group of women at a morning prayer meeting at the river bank and convinced them to become Christians and the nucleus of a congregation.

Paul also had experienced fierce opposition in Philippi. Acts 16 describes his illegal arrest, beating, and jailing. However, he left behind a little core of dedicated Christians who cared deeply for Paul. No letter breathes a sense of tenderness and courtesy more than this letter by Paul. Paul comes across in other letters as a person who does not always seem to have a gentle side to his nature. In this letter, his personal humility and graciousness shine forth clearly.

Philippi was not an easy place to live as a Christian. It was located in Eastern Europe, and was at the crossroads of Asian and European traffic. People from a wide variety of backgrounds poured into Philippi. The congregation represented what a differing group they were. "Lydia," the rich woman who helped found the church at Philippi, actually should be called "the woman from Lydia" or "the Lydian lady." She was upper class and wealthy. The slave girl was a native of northern Greece, merely slave class. The jailer was a Roman official.

Furthermore, Philippi prided itself on being a Roman Colony. Originally founded by ex-soldiers who were granted Roman citizenship in order to Romanize the area, Philippi grew to think of itself as a mini-Rome, with Roman dress, speech, customs, and holidays like those of the great capital in Italy. The Philippians must have had problems with accepting humility as an ideal, just as most of us also do. The big thing is to stand on your own rights, to get ahead, to promote your own interests. This may be society's way, but it must not be the Church's philosophy. Where there is not humility, Paul points out what will follow: pride, ambition, and self-interest. Nothing can wreck a congregation faster than any one of these traits on the part of a few willful members.

I. *Have this mind among yourselves which you have in Christ Jesus:* The only cure for the tendency to selfish ambitions is to have the mind of Christ or the common goal and outlook of being Christ's family. However, such humility is hard to come by. Therefore, Paul holds up the role model of Jesus Christ Himself.

II. *Who, though he was in the form of God, did not count equality with God a thing to be grasped, but emptied himself, taking the form of a servant....* Many scholars think that these verses in Philippians are from an early Christian hymn and perhaps sung at worship services. Whether written by Paul or quoted by Paul makes little difference. They are a magnificent expression of the meaning of humility as demonstrated by Jesus.

These verses describe the God who stooped to conquer. Jesus laid aside all vestiges of divine power and authority; He lived among us as a servant, or, literally, a "slave." He gave up all rights and prerogatives. He endured all the hurts and indignities which a human can possibly know.

A certain Scottish king frequently put on the rags of a beggar and roamed the streets of his realm incognito to be able to identify with the poorest subject and to experience the suffering outside the palace. No one ever suspected that it was the king in disguise. Everyone came to recognize and appreciate the humane rule of the king in the palace. It was many years before his subjects learned that their ruler had divested himself of all kingly pomp and splendor to move among them as one of them.

Christians living in such a place easily could find themselves caught up in the immorality and paganism of a Roman Colony. Paul writes to the congregation which was close to his heart to remind it that it was "a colony of heaven" or an outpost for Christ's rule. He urges the Philippians to encourage each other to live as Christ's people.

NOTES ON THE PRINTED TEXT

There is no "perfect church." Every congregation is made up of people like you and me. Sometimes, people irritate each other. Sometimes, they offend each other. Often, they fail one another. They don't listen and are not always sensitive to others. Church people can let their own feelings and their own agendas get in the way of Christ's plans. Paul knew his friends in the church at Philippi. He loved them deeply as only a caring pastor can love his people. But he also knew them well enough to know that there were some folks who, although he loved them very much, could stir up discord. My pastor father used to call these folks "problem people," and point out that every church has some—including himself! Paul had that kind of honesty and humility.

If there is any encouragement in Christ, any incentive of love, any participation in the Spirit, any affection and sympathy, complete my joy by being of the same mind: Paul makes it clear that if the Philippian believers' fellowship with the Spirit of Jesus Christ is real, they will have a sense of being Christ's family together. They will be aware of a unity among them which transcends all differences.

I. *Do nothing from selfishness or conceit, but in humility count others better than yourselves:* Humility was not considered a virtue by the Greeks or Romans In fact, they thought it was a sign of weakness.

This is the meaning of Christ "taking the form of a servant, being born in the likeness of men." It is also a reference to Isaiah 53:12. "He poured out his soul," from the Servant Songs of the suffering Messiah which Jesus took as His model.

He humbled himself and became obedient unto death, even death on a cross: Jesus accepted the ultimate in humiliation; He even voluntarily took up a cross for the sake of others. Paul holds up the death of Jesus on the cross as the model and the motive for moral living for every Christian. The cross is the reason for humility.

II. *Therefore God has exalted him:* Paul must have sung as he wrote these lines! Verses 9-11 are a great doxology, celebrating the way God has vindicated Jesus Christ. If He vindicates Jesus' humility, God will also vindicate every Christian's humility.

SUGGESTIONS TO TEACHERS

John M., age forty-six, had been a model husband, father, and church worker until about a year ago. He grew moody and stopped attending worship services at his church, complaining it was a "waste of time." He took up racquetball and jogging to get rid of his paunch and enrolled in an encounter group to free himself of his hang-ups. John next began to complain that he was tired of being married to his wife of twenty-two years. He finally moved to an apartment so he could be "free." When family and friends ask him how he can turn his back on others and forsake Christian living, John crisply dismisses them with "Don't give me all that out-dated morality nonsense!"

Your lesson today probes the motives for moral living. You and your class must ask, "What is the basis for Christian morality?" The Scripture in Philippians offers superb guidance.

1. *THE MIND OF CHRIST.* Jesus Christ is the example for us believers.

However, Jesus gives us more than a model. He also allows us to be of the same mind as He. He is to be so much part of our thinking that our thoughts take on the hue of His thoughts. We sometimes think that believing in Jesus Christ means emphasizing heart and forgetting brain. It is both. And it is also Spirit, the Spirit of the living Lord molding our planning and our doing. Nudge your class's thinking on this subject by asking if your people consciously consider what Jesus Christ wants them to do with their money and their leisure time. What about other decisions your class members have to make? Are these fashioned according to the mind of Christ?

2. *THE MOTIVE FOR CARING.* Devote substantial time on Philippians 2:6–8, describing the God who emptied Himself of all pomp and dignity to take up the form of a servant in the person of Jesus. Here is the mind of Christ: being one who lays aside considerations of self-importance in order to serve others. Here also is the motive for moral living. Christ serves us: therefore we serve others.

3. *THE MOVEMENT TO CONTINUE.* Philippians fairly sings of the way the Spirit continues to work within us to foster growth. At times, we may feel discouraged or tired. Often, we feel overwhelmed by the "crooked and perverse generation" in which we live. However, tell your class again and again that "God is at work in you, both to will and to work for his good pleasure" (2:13).

4. *THE MERRIMENT OF CHRISTIANS.* No long faces among Christians! Paul, writing this letter to the Philippians, had ample cause for gloom and pessimism. Yet he writes, "I am glad and rejoice with you all. Likewise, you also should be glad and rejoice with me" (2:17, 18). How much joy is shown in your class? Do others find there is a spontaneous gladness within your church? Christians laugh and sing because they know that God who wills moral living also does it for our happiness!

TOPIC FOR ADULTS
MOTIVES FOR MORAL LIVING

Reconciled. "I am Japanese. In 1979, ten of us for six weeks were making a deliberate attempt on behalf of my church denomination, Nippon Seikokai (Episcopal), to extend the right hand of fellowship and to show love of Christ to the Papuans.

"Most of us had gone to Papua New Guinea as nominal Christians, full of good intentions but uncertain about our faith. We came back having experienced for the first time in our lives vital Christian living. In that primitive society, we found a life-style not dominated by material things, a life-style in which true community still lived, where faith and life were one. This was Christian fellowship at a depth we had never known.

"Wonderful as being with the Papuans was, the turning point for me was an encounter with an Australian doctor. He had been through the war as a military doctor and ever since has worked in Papua New Guinea. When we met, his greeting was like a slap in the face: 'You needn't worry—I don't hold anything against you Japs personally, but the Papuans can never forget what you did in the war!'

"What had I to do with the war? I hadn't even been born then! Anyway, the fault wasn't only on the Japanese side. Excuses and retorts piled up in my mind. I suppressed them and said nothing.

"Over the next few days I had to work with this Australian, and time and again the conversation came back to the war. I became more and more angry. We Japanese are taught to control our feelings, and so I put up with it. But all the time resentment against him was boiling inside me. Why did he have to keep harping on the war? Why did I have to work with him anyway? We had come to work with the Papuans, not with the whites!

"And then one day several of us came to a famous sightseeing spot, a cross from a church. During the war the church had been shelled and destroyed by Japanese naval gunnery. By a seeming miracle the cross stood firm and is still standing today. The proud relic is a symbol of the undefeated spirit of the Papuan people. It is known as the miracle cross.

"The Australian was with us on the sightseeing tour. He and I happened to come to this landmark, and I felt like taking a picture in front of the cross as a token that I had come here. Something made me ask the Australian to stand with me, and a friend took our picture. The Australian and I even linked arms. And then it happened. Up to that point I still felt this suppressed rage. I couldn't say anything kind or loving or humble to the Australian, but an impulse to speak overwhelmed me, an almost physical stimulus coming from the cross behind me. I had to speak.

"I blurted, 'The war was terrible. And we were to blame. Forgive us!'

"All at once he was clinging to me, weeping and saying, 'No, no, it's for you to forgive me!' I could hardly believe it. This tough, seasoned Aussie was in tears!

"All the resentment that had been building inside evaporated. Hate, jealousy, rage melted away. It was a moment of total reconciliation in front of the miracle cross.

"For the first time I experienced the love of Christ in action. At last I knew what the forgiveness of sins meant. 'God was in Christ, reconciling the world unto himself'—I had known this as a doctrine, now I knew it as a reality. The love of Christ shown on the cross has power to change our lives today. I will never be the same again."—Kentaro Hatano, "Reconciled," *Decision*, October 1980.

Motive for Moral Living. The Quaker "saint," Rufus Jones, once described what motivated him for moral living. It was an encounter with Christ's grace through his mother when he was a small boy.

"My mother left me one day to do a piece of work, and she and my father went off for the day. As soon as they were out of sight the boys of the village came and told me how fine the fishing was, and I went with them, intending to return, and to be hard at work before mother got back. But I miscalculated, and when I returned mother was standing in the door. She took me by the hand and started for my room. I knew what was just, and I knew what I was likely to get, but then came the miracle. Mother got down on her knees, put her hands on me and told God all about me and what she expected me to become and interpreted my life to God; and then she bent over me and kissed me and went out and left me. What would you think of a boy who would go back on that kind of a mother? If she had taken a switch and applied it with vigor, it would not have made the least difference to me. I should have done the same thing again, but I never could after that. That turned my life. That is grace."—Christian Century *Pulpit*, November 1929. Copyright © 1929 Christian Century Foundation. Reprinted by permission from the November 29 issue of *The Pulpit.*

Joyous Life. Many persons think that living a Christian life is all gloom and doom. Thomas Carlyle, the Scottish writer, apparently thought so.

Once Carlyle was propounding his favourite view that the worship of sorrow was the highest idea of moral goodness, and that it was to be found in the New Testament. Whereat Harriet Martineau turned on him with the retort: "I think Jesus Christ lived one of the most joyous lives."

Questions for Pupils on the Next Lesson. 1. Why are all forms of immorality sins against Christ and not merely "my own business"? 2. What are the two meanings of the words "God's Temple" in 1 Corinthians 3 and 6. 3. How should Christians express joy and gratitude? 4. How highly should we regard self-discipline? 5. How does your lifestyle reveal your value system?

TOPIC FOR YOUTH
WORKING TOGETHER

Get the Message Right! In the summer of 1940, the military situation in France was extremely critical. The French section of the Student Christian Movement sent a telegram to the British Christian Movement headquarters. The telegram said simply two words: God reigns. In transmitting the message, however, somehow the message became "God resigns."

How often we botch up the Good News! How often we do not transmit God's message as we should. How often the world gets the wrong impression and the wrong message because of the way we transmit.

Save Christianity for Christians. Several years ago, Norman Cousins, then the editor of the *Saturday Review of Literature,* took a trip to India and spoke with many Indian leaders. Many had penetrating questions about the morality of Americans, especially American Christians.

Norman Cousins reported a conversation with a Hindu priest named Satis Prasad. The man said he wanted to come to our country to work as a missionary among the Americans. Cousins assumed he meant to convert Americans to the Hindu religion. "No," said Satis Prasad, "I would like to convert them to the Christian religion. Christianity cannot survive in the abstract. It needs not membership, but believers. The people of your country may claim they believe in Christianity, but from what I read at this distance, Christianity is more a custom than anything else. I would ask that either you accept the teachings of Jesus in your everyday lives and your affairs as a nation or stop invoking His name as sanction for everything you do. . . . I want to help save Christianity for the Christians."

Food for Thought and Others: Even American dogs are afflicted with weight problems! A recent survey revealed that 41 percent of dogs in the United States are overweight. Obesity among pets has become such a problem that Ralston Purina and General Foods and others have introduced special "dieters" dog foods in U.S. supermarkets.

In the face of reports that over one third of the globe's population will go to bed hungry tonight, what do these facts about the way we overfeed our pets suggest?

Dietrich Bonhoeffer offers the following insights about moral living in the world family: "To allow the hungry man to remain hungry would be blasphemy against God and one's neighbor, for what is nearest to God is precisely the need of one's neighbor."

Questions for Pupils on the Next Lesson. 1. In what specific ways do you show any self-discipline as a Christian? 2. Are humans responsible for their own actions, or are they merely pawns of fate or unknown forces? 3. Why is immorality a sin against Jesus Christ, and not simply my own private business? 4. Why do you think many youth are caught up in the use of drugs and alcohol? 5. Does your lifestyle show that you are a Christian?

LESSON VIII—OCTOBER 21

THE HOLY SPIRIT'S TEMPLE

Background Scripture: 1 Corinthians 3:9–17; 6:12–20; Ephesians 5:15–20
Devotional Reading: 1 Corinthians 4:1–5

KING JAMES VERSION

1 CORINTHIANS 3 16 Know ye not that ye are the temple of God, and *that* the Spirit of God dwelleth in you?

17 If any man defile the temple of God, him shall God destroy; for the temple of God is holy, which *temple* ye are.

6 12 All things are lawful unto me, but all things are not expedient: all things are lawful for me, but I will not be brought under the power of any.

13 Meats for the belly, and the belly for meats: but God shall destroy both it and them. Now the body *is* not for fornication, but for the Lord; and the Lord for the body.

14 And God hath both raised up the Lord, and will also raise up us by his own power.

15 Know ye not that your bodies are the members of Christ? shall I then take the members of Christ, and make *them* the members of a harlot? God forbid.

16 What? know ye not that he which is joined to a harlot is one body? for two, saith he, shall be one flesh.

17 But he that is joined unto the Lord is one spirit.

18 Flee fornication. Every sin that a man doeth is without the body; but he that committeth fornication sinneth against his own body.

19 What? know ye not that your body is the temple of the Holy Ghost *which is* in you, which ye have of God, and ye are not your own?

20 For ye are bought with a price: therefore glorify God in your body, and in your spirit, which are God's.

EPHESIANS 5 15 See then that ye walk circumspectly, not as fools, but as wise,

16 Redeeming the time, because the days are evil.

17 Wherefore be ye not unwise, but understanding what the will of the Lord *is*.

18 And be not drunk with wine, wherein is excess; but be filled with the Spirit;

19 Speaking to yourselves in psalms and hymns and spiritual songs, singing and making melody in your heart to the Lord;

20 Giving thanks always for all things unto God and the Father in the name of our Lord Jesus Christ;

REVISED STANDARD VERSION

1 CORINTHIANS 3 16 Do you not know that you are God's temple and that God's Spirit dwells in you? 17 If any one destroys God's temple, God will destroy him. For God's temple is holy, and that temple you are.

6 12 "All things are lawful for me," but not all things are helpful. "All things are lawful for me," but I will not be enslaved by anything. 13 "Food is meant for the stomach and the stomach for food"—and God will destroy both one and the other. The body is not meant for immorality, but for the Lord, and the Lord for the body. 14 And God raised the Lord and will also raise us up by his power. 15 Do you not know that your bodies are members of Christ? Shall I therefore take the members of Christ and make them members of a prostitute? Never! 16 Do you not know that he who joins himself to a prostitute becomes one body with her? For, as it is written, "The two shall become one flesh." 17 But he who is united to the Lord becomes one spirit with him. 18 Shun immorality. Every other sin which a man commits is outside the body; but the immoral man sins against his own body. 19 Do you not know that your body is a temple of the Holy Spirit within you, which you have from God? You are not your own; 20 you were bought with a price. So glorify God in your body.

EPHESIANS 5 15 Look carefully then how you walk, not as unwise men but as wise, 16 making the most of the time, because the days are evil. 17 Therefore do not be foolish, but understand what the will of the Lord is. 18 And do not get drunk with wine, for that is debauchery; but be filled with the Spirit, 19 addressing one another in psalms and hymns and spiritual songs, singing and making melody to the Lord with all your heart, 20 always and for everything giving thanks in the name of our Lord Jesus Christ to God the Father.

KEY VERSE: For God's temple is holy, and that temple you are. 1 Corinthians 3:17 (RSV).

HOME DAILY BIBLE READINGS

Oct. 15. M. *A Temple Not Made with Hands.* John 2:13–22.
Oct. 16. T. *The Church Is God's Temple.* 1 Corinthians 3:1–9.
Oct. 17. W. *Each Builds on the Foundation.* 1 Corinthians 3:10–17.
Oct. 18. T. *Don't Destroy the Temple.* 1 Corinthians 2:18–23.
Oct. 19. F. *Solve Problems in the Brotherhood.* 1 Corinthians 6:1–8.
Oct. 20. S. *A Christian Is God's Temple.* 1 Corinthians 6:12–20.
Oct. 21. S. *Pillars in God's Temple.* Revelation 3:7–13.

BACKGROUND

Most of the big cities on the eastern coast of the Mediterranean in Paul's time were famous for vice. Corinth was so notorious that even the blasé Romans blushed. To "go Corinthian" meant to indulge in wild debauchery. Likewise, Ephesus had a reputation for raunchiness. The great Temple of Diana had a fertility cult involving 1,000 prostitutes. In some ways, both cities were enormous porno-capitals.

Both the Greeks and the Romans had easy-going cultures. Neither could quite understand why Jews, and later, Christians, were so strict about refusing to go along with the playboy philosophy everyone else accepted.

This was the type of world in which Paul worked to establish congregations. In many ways, places like the sin-cities of Corinth and Ephesus would be the last ever to want to visit to start a church. But Paul went. And he patiently found a cadre of persons who responded to the Good News of Jesus Christ and pledged themselves to live as Christ's.

These little congregations never had an easy time. Corinth proved to be such a problem-filled church that Paul had to write several letters, pleading with them to be Christians. Those in the Corinthian Church and the Ephesus congregation alike faced daily temptations to slip back into the old ways of sexual permissiveness. After all, everyone else in the city went along with the "it's my body, so why shouldn't I have my kicks whenever and with whomever?" Worse, there were even some Christians who tried to excuse their immorality (and Paul never minced words about what they were doing) on the grounds of their Christian freedom. Their argument went something like this: "The Gospel means I'm liberated from having to depend on the Law or rules to save me; therefore I can please myself. And if I'm saved by God's grace, I can go ahead and have my fun because God forgives anything."

Paul states that every Christian must treat his body as the temple of the Holy Spirit, and every congregation must regard itself as the dwelling place of the Spirit of Jesus Christ. Therefore, immoral living and drunkenness have no place among Christians!

NOTES ON THE PRINTED TEXT

Paul uses the phrase "temple of the Holy Spirit" in two different ways in 1 Corinthians. In 1 Corinthians 3:16, Paul speaks of it in terms of community of Christians. In 1 Corinthians 6:9, he thinks of the temple of the Spirit as each believer's body.

I. *Do you not know that you are God's temple and that God's Spirit dwells in you?* Paul wants the Corinthians who love to indulge every appetite to remember that corporately they are where the Spirit of Jesus Christ has taken up residence. They belong to Him and to one another in a sacred and special way. If the Living Lord resides in their midst, how, Paul asks, can they permit each other to go along with promiscuity and drunkenness?

If anyone destroys God's temple, God will destroy him: Paul carries his argument even further. Such behavior is destructive. Perhaps people think they are getting away with it. But it destroys God's temple, the church fellowship. Paul will not allow his beloved but rebellious children in the faith to imagine that immorality and debauchery makes no difference. Such scandalous goings-on destroy God's temple. He adds solemn words: "If anyone destroys God's temple, God will destroy him."

II. *"All things are lawful for me," but not all things are helpful:* Paul has to deal with some Christians who have yanked some of his words out of context, twisted their meaning, and thrown them back in his face as a license to live without restraints of any kind. Paul had spoken eloquently of how impossible it is for any person to save himself through trying to keep the requirements of the Law. Furthermore, he had preached effectively on the freedom of the Christian from legalism. Some, however, had taken this to mean, "Hooray, anything goes!" Paul acknowledges that he has said words to the effect that all things are lawful, but he adds, "Not all things are helpful." And saying, "All things are lawful" as an excuse for doing as you please is merely allowing yourself to slide back into slavery again—the enslavement to self and sin.

III. *Food is meant for the stomach and the stomach for food:* This is the argument today, just as everyone heard it in the first century world. It's the familiar, "Sex is meant for my body and my body for sex," or "If I feel sexual urgings, it's only natural for me to gratify them any way I please."

Paul also demolishes the "doing what comes naturally" philosophy. He reminds every believer that he or she belongs to Jesus Christ. That means even the believer's body is Christ's property. Since *everything*—the physical body included—belongs to the Lord, a believer treats Christ's belongings with great respect. A believer regards himself as a steward or trustee of Christ's property which includes the believer's body.

Paul is not stating that sex is sin. Do not think that either he or the Bible considers sexual relationships always to be sordid and evil. Nor is either Paul or the Bible advocating celibacy for all Christians. Rather, Scripture always stresses the sanctity of the gift of sex. In these verses in 1 Corinthians 6, Paul pleads with Christ's people to remember who they are when tempted to go along with "new morality" of the times.

IV. *Look carefully how you walk:* Paul tells his beloved children in the faith to take heed, to be on guard constantly how they conduct themselves. "Look carefully" means to watch out!

... making the most of the time: Paul offers advice on how to look carefully. "Making the most of the time" in the Greek text means literally "buying up the critical times," and comes from the business world. It means to use every bit of time for good use, to purchase each minute for the work of the Spirit of Jesus Christ in both your own life and the life of your congregation.

SUGGESTIONS TO TEACHERS

The nine-year-olds were concluding a study of Solomon's Temple. They had built a model with blocks. They had read about the rituals and sung the psalms. They listened with interest as the teacher pointed out the miniature holy of holies, with its piece of flannel as the curtain. "There, boys and girls," said the teacher, "is the place they reserved for God's Holy Spirit." Fourteen little pairs of eyes solemnly examined the tiny box. Silence. Then a voice inquired, "Miss Thomas, if the Temple is all gone, where does the Holy Spirit live now?"

If you had been Miss Thomas, how would you have answered?

Your class is to ponder the same question in the light of the scriptural material from 1 Corinthians and Ephesians. The answer, you and the class will quickly discover, is not some mushy answer like "in our hearts." Rather, God's community, the Church, is the Temple of the Holy Spirit.

1. *CAREFUL CRAFTSMANSHIP.* Paul repeatedly refers to the Christian community in terms of an edifice. Therefore, he warns leaders such as Sunday-school teachers and ministers to take care how they build. These are engaged in a divinely-appointed construction project! This Temple's foundation is Jesus Christ. "Work carefully," Paul admonishes all workers in the Church because ultimately shoddy craftsmanship will be revealed. You may find it helpful to refer to the way Christians in the Middle Ages built beautiful cathedrals, each contributing time, skills, and energy on building programs which often took several centuries to complete but which demanded great care on the part of each artisan. So also with building the Christian community—God's present-day cathedral.

2. *GOD'S GROUP.* The Church, according to 1 Corinthians 3:16, 17, is the dwelling place for the Spirit today. The Church is "holy," that is belonging to God and set apart by Him for special tasks. Since it is God's, it must be looked after diligently and not allowed to fall into disrepair. In fact, God wreaks His destruction on those who seek to destroy this special Temple, His community. Help your class to acquire a new respect for Christ's Church in view of the importance God attaches to it.

3. *MORAL MINORITY.* First Corinthians 6:12–20 stresses that each Christian also has a personal responsibility. A Christian's very body is also a temple for the Holy Spirit, and a Christian's very life part of the body of Christ, the Church. Therefore, no Christian will have anything to do with immoral behavior. Christians are different from the permissive society. As a moral minority, Christ's people reject the popular clichés about "Do as I please!" Remind your class members, "You are not your own; you were bought with a price. So glorify God in your body" (6:19, 20).

TOPIC FOR ADULTS
THE HOLY SPIRIT'S TEMPLE

Without the Partition. There is an ancient church in Stirling, Scotland, not far from the old castle. This church has a rich history. King James VI of Scotland was crowned in it, and many famous events have taken place within its walls. In 1656, however, the two ministers fell to quarreling. The conflict pulled in others. Finally, the bitterness was so deep between the two sides that the Stirling Town Council formally gave authority "to build up a partition in the church for the shunning of further controversy." The partition was erected—a solid stone wall dividing the beautiful nave. Two separate congregations—the East Church and the West Church—began worshiping in the building. Each church jealously preserved its separate identity. Finally, in 1935, almost 300 years later, better sense and deeper charity prevailed. The two congregations were again united and the offensive wall of separation was torn down. Once again the beautiful nave was an unbroken architectural masterpiece, and once again the Christian people of Stirling stood together to worship.

A Christian congregation is the temple of the Holy Spirit when it exhibits the love and forgiveness of Jesus Christ. The walls of distrust and discord that sometimes separate us prevent the Spirit from dwelling among us. To realize the Spirit's presence and power, rip down the partitions shutting us off from one another!

Forty-Year Fresh Paint. A recent article tells of an attendant stationed at the foot of a stairway in the House of Commons, London. He had been at his post for something like eighteen years, but no one knew why. Investigation revealed that the job originated some forty years ago when his grandfather had been detailed to stand at the stairs to warn people of fresh paint. His family had clung to the job for three generations.

Sometimes, we in the Church also seem to stand around without being sure why we are present or merely because grandfather or family had something to do with the place some years ago. Sometimes, we church people go through empty motions like that attendant, or carry out useless work merely because "we've always done it that way."

The Church as the Holy Spirit's Temple is not the bastion of the status quo. The Church is the Temple of the Holy Spirit, the community of those filled with an awareness of the Risen Lord's nearness and goodness! No dreary standing dumbly at the same post for eighteen years simply because it's been that way for over forty years. Rather, the Church is a dynamic, living Temple still being crafted and beautified by the Master Builder, Christ.

See the Banners Flying. When the Church prays that the Holy Spirit take up residence within its fellowship, it becomes a center for power and goodness. With the Spirit, the Church becomes a Temple of the Lord with banners streaming in the wind. Without the Spirit, it degenerates into a squabbling, petty-minded human club.

Dorothy Barnard, a church leader who served as moderator for her denomination, the Presbyterian Church, U.S., recently, described her experiences vividly.

"The *Screwtape Letters* by C. S. Lewis is a favorite book of mine. In one of the letters from Screwtape (who is the devil), he gave advice to his nephew, Wormwood, the recruiter for hell working here on earth. Screwtape told him how to get recruits. 'The church is a fertile field,' he said, 'if you just keep them bickering over details, structure, organization, money, property, personal hurts, and misunderstandings. . . . One thing you must prevent—don't ever let them look up and see the banners flying, for if they ever see the banners flying you have lost them forever.'

"This year I have seen the church at home and around the world. The church is alive, real and on the move. I HAVE SEEN THE BANNERS FLYING!!!"

Questions for Pupils on the Next Lesson. 1. What does it mean to "subject" yourself to one another in Christian family life? 2. What is the motive for mutual respect and caring among the members of a Christian family? 3. How can your congregation help your church members who are married to learn to deal with hostility and anger? 4. How does the church react to the single adults who choose not to be married and therefore feel frozen out of the life of many congregations geared only to married couples? 5. Does your church help those no longer in the traditional nuclear family by finding an extended family?

TOPIC FOR YOUTH
IS IT REALLY MY BODY?

In Gratitude, Dinner for All. They came in gym shoes, tattered coats and blue jeans, old people carrying canes and young ones carrying babies. By 11 A.M., more than 100 were lined up four abreast from the door of the Chicago restaurant and into the street. There was a freezing wind, and they lifted their collars against the cold, but this Thanksgiving they did not have to shake off loneliness and hunger.

Matt Deletioglu, a thirty-four-year-old restaurant owner from Turkey who remembered what it was like to be broke and alone on Thanksgiving, opened his restaurant at no charge to the poor and lonely today.

"I'm almost one of those people, too," Mr. Deletioglu said, glancing at the line forming outside his door. "I know exactly how they're feeling. Just because I have good times now, I don't have to forget all the bad times."

Mr. Deletioglu, orphaned at the age of ten, spent a poor childhood in a Mediterranean fishing village. He hopped a cargo ship eleven years ago to come to America. He had no family here, and no friends, and no money.

For years he worked three jobs at a time, putting away pay to start a restaurant of his own. Last year, shortly after he opened the French Port restaurant in Chicago, he vowed that others would not be lonely or hungry as he had been on holidays.

Matt Deletioglu understands that it's not really his body, or his restaurant.

Do you realize that your life, including your body, is the Temple for the Holy Spirit?

What Kind of Growth? People have been getting taller at a rate of about one centimeter—about ⅖ of an inch—every decade. The reason for this growth is only partially understood. Increased calorie intake, improved nutrition are factors, but reduced incidence of childhood illness is also believed to be of importance.

Changes in size are affecting home furnishings. The once-standard seventy-five inch bed is giving way to eighty to eighty-two inch lengths. The appliance industry is making extension legs to raise ranges. Other appliances, counters and cabinets are being built higher.

Growth isn't all lengthwise, either. To be comfortable, say seating experts, the average American man now needs a seat twenty-two to twenty-four inches wide. Old-world opera houses like Milan's La Scala get along with eighteen and nineteen inch seats, but architects for New York's Lincoln Center for Performing Arts had to reckon with new proportions. To accommodate the same number of music lovers, the new opera house will have to be ⅓ larger.

The startling size increase apparently started only in the last century. If it went back unrestrictedly to earlier centuries, fifteenth century men would have been dwarfs.

Your body may be taller and wider than your grandparents' bodies were, and you have noticed you have been growing physically during the past years. Are you aware that you are also meant to be growing spiritually?

Many young persons may be mature physically at your age, but are immature spiritually. It's all right to be a giant in strength and stature, but not all right to be a pygmy in faith and Christian maturity.

Disciplined General. "Discipline" is not a popular idea in our times. However, anyone who realizes that his or her body is meant to be the Temple of the Holy Spirit understands that discipline is more than a word. It is a lifestyle. No one understood this better than the great founder of the Salvation Army, William Booth.

General Booth set forth these rules for Christian living: (1) Consider your body as the Temple of the Holy Spirit and treat it with reverence and care. (2) Keep your mind active. Stimulate it with thoughts of others that lead to doing something. (3) Take time to be holy with daily Bible reading and prayer. (4) Support the church of your faith. Mingle with others. (5) Cultivate the presence of God. He wants to enter your life and will as far as you let Him. (6) Take God into the details of your life. You naturally call upon Him in trouble and for the bigger things. (7) Pray for this troubled world and the leaders who hold the destinies of the various nations. (8) Have a thankful spirit for the blessings of God—country, friends, and numerous other blessings. (9) Work as if everything depended upon work, and pray as if everything depended upon prayer. (10) Think of death not as something to be dreaded, but as a great and new experience where loved ones are met and ambitions realized.

Questions for Pupils on the Next Lesson. 1. What are the biggest problems you have in your relationships with authority figures, especially the members of your own family? 2. Although you sometimes feel rebellious against authority, have you sought guidance and help from your church family? 3. Who has the greatest respect and love toward you? 4. How can the Church reach out to youth who are from broken homes or victims of child abuse? 5. What clues does Jesus Christ give you in your relationships with other members of your family?

LESSON IX—OCTOBER 28

HELP FOR FAMILY LIVING

Background Scripture: Ephesians 5:21–6:4
Devotional Reading: Ephesians 5:3–17

KING JAMES VERSION

EPHESIANS 5   21 Submitting yourselves one to another in the fear of God.

22 Wives, submit yourselves unto your own husbands, as unto the Lord.

23 For the husband is the head of the wife, even as Christ is the head of the church: and he is the saviour of the body.

24 Therefore as the church is subject unto Christ, so *let* the wives *be* to their own husbands in every thing.

25 Husbands, love your wives, even as Christ also loved the church, and gave himself for it;

26 That he might sanctify and cleanse it with the washing of water by the word,

27 That he might present it to himself a glorious church, not having spot, or wrinkle, or any such thing; but that it should be holy and without blemish.

28 So ought men to love their wives as their own bodies. He that loveth his wife loveth himself.

29 For no man ever yet hated his own flesh; but nourisheth and cherisheth it, even as the Lord the church:

30 For we are members of his body, and his flesh, and of his bones.

31 For this cause shall a man leave his father and mother, and shall be joined unto his wife, and they two shall be one flesh.

32 This is a great mystery: but I speak concerning Christ and the church.

33 Nevertheless, let everyone of you in particular so love his wife even as himself; and the wife *see* that she reverence *her* husband.

6   Children, obey your parents in the Lord; for this is right.

2 Honour thy father and mother; which is the first commandment with promise;

3 That it may be well with thee, and thou mayest live long on the earth.

4 And, ye fathers, provoke not your children to wrath: but bring them up in the nurture and admonition of the Lord.

REVISED STANDARD VERSION

EPHESIANS 5   21 Be subject to one another out of reverence for Christ. 22 Wives, be subject to your husbands, as to the Lord. 23 For the husband is the head of the wife as Christ is the head of the church, his body, and is himself its Savior. 24 As the church is subject to Christ, so let wives also be subject in everything to their husbands. 25 Husbands, love your wives, as Christ loved the church and gave himself up for her, 26 that he might sanctify her, having cleansed her by the washing of water with the word, 27 that he might present the church to himself in splendor, without spot or wrinkle or any such thing, that she might be holy and without blemish. 28 Even so husbands should love their wives as their own bodies. He who loves his wife loves himself. 29 For no man ever hates his own flesh, but nourishes and cherishes it, as Christ does the church, 30 because we are members of his body. 31 "For this reason a man shall leave his father and mother and be joined to his wife, and the two shall become one." 32 This mystery is a profound one, and I am saying that it refers to Christ and the church; 33 however, let each one of you love his wife as himself, and let the wife see that she respects her husband.

6   Children, obey your parents in the Lord, for this is right. 2 "Honor your father and mother" (this is the first commandment with a promise), 3 "that it may be well with you and that you may live long on the earth." 4 Fathers, do not provoke your children to anger, but bring them up in the discipline and instruction of the Lord.

KEY VERSE: Be subject to one another out of reverence for Christ. Ephesians 5:21 (RSV).

HOME DAILY BIBLE READINGS

Oct. 22.   M.   *Walk in Love's Light.* 1 John 2:1–11.
Oct. 23.   T.   *Love God and Not Evil.* 1 John 2:12–17.
Oct. 24.   W.   *Conduct to Avoid.* Ephesians 5:1–10.
Oct. 25.   T.   *Mutual Respect Among Parents.* Ephesians 5:21–33.
Oct. 26.   F.   *Respect Between Children and Parents.* Ephesians 6:1–4.

Oct. 27. S. *Conduct Between Master and Servant.* Ephesians 6:5–9.
Oct. 28. S. *Spiritual Strength for Family Living.* Ephesians 6:10–20.

BACKGROUND

Paul's letters to the Ephesians and Romans are his greatest works. Some people think that Ephesians even surpasses Romans in depth and breadth of thought. In Ephesians, for example, Paul states that Jesus Christ is God's disclosure of the divine "secret plan" for the universe. What a breath-taking idea!

The "secret plan" described in Ephesians 1:9, 10 is that God means to bring all creation together, to have everything and everyone function in perfect harmony. However, that plan has been challenged by destructive powers. These destructive forces have been trying to tear apart God's order, pitting humans against God, humans against other humans, humans against nature, and even a human against himself or herself. But God wills unity!

The mystery has been unveiled. The private master plan of the Almighty has been shown through Jesus Christ. And God's own community—the Church of Jesus Christ—is meant to embody what God has shown His purpose in the universe to be. God's intention throughout history has been shown clearly to us in Jesus Christ, and now is to be shown clearly through our life together as His special community.

In Ephesians, Paul states that one key group within the Christian community showing God's secret plan to the world is those who are married and live in family relationships. The section in Ephesians 5 and 6 we are studying today is not merely Paul's "advice to the lovelorn." Never put Paul in the category of another Ann Landers or dispenser of tips for a happier marriage. Although Paul offers practical suggestions, he does so in the context of how God wills in His secret plan for everyone to live in harmony, at one with Him and with all others.

NOTES ON THE PRINTED TEXT

At first reading, many women in particular will react negatively to the opening lines of today's Scripture. Most women today have been raised with the notion of equality of the sexes and bridle at the idea of being "subject to your husband." (Many men, likewise, don't like words which they think suggest that the husband should dominate his wife.) Therefore, it is important to read the entire passage through, and not stop after verse 22.

The key idea is *mutual* subordination. To the old question, "Who is to be subordinate, the wife or the husband?" Paul emphatically replies, "BOTH!"

I. *Be subject to one another out of reverence for Christ:* Paul spells it out: each serves the other. Neither tries to "pull rank" on the other. Neither claims to be superior; neither implies the other is inferior.

Martin Luther repeatedly stated that marriage is "the school of life," and that the Christian who is a husband or a wife will encounter Jesus in the other. He admonished every husband or wife "to be the Christ to the other." This is the doughty old German reformer's way of stating what Paul writes in Ephesians when he urges each to serve the other "out of reverence for Christ."

II. *Wives, be subject to your husbands, as to the Lord.* This verse, especially if you leave out the key words "as to the Lord," rankles in the ears of many women. "One more example of male chauvinism," sniffed one. She missed the punch line, so to speak, where Paul adds the important qualification: *as to the Lord.* And she didn't read the next verses, in which Paul lectures the husbands in greater detail and is tougher on them!

III. *Husbands, love your wives, as Christ loved the church and gave himself up for her:* Paul tells husbands that they are to sacrifice for the wife in the same spirit that Jesus Christ went to the Cross to sacrifice for us!

Note that there is not the least idea of the husband lording it over his wife, or thinking that he can boss her around. In fact, Paul puts an impossible task on the husband, namely to care so deeply for the wife that he will suffer for her. In an era which glorifies "doing your own thing," these words come like a bucket of cold water in the face!

. . . that (Christ) might sanctify her, having cleansed her by the washing of water with the word, that he might present the church to himself in splendor . . . that she might be holy and without blemish: This is the first of a couple of brief digressions in Paul's train of thought about the responsibilities of husbands. Paul is reminded of the premarriage custom in the Middle East where the bride had a ceremonial bath, then adorned herself in her bridal gown and met her husband-to-be. Baptism, in early Christian circles, often was by immersion, and was also thought of as a washing, followed by the convert putting on a clean white robe. Paul often likened the relationship of Christ to the Church to a husband taking a wife.

Husbands should love their wives as their own bodies: Paul does not mean a man should have a narcissistic fascination with himself. This line might better be translated, "love their wives as being their own bodies." The husband who is a Christian takes care of his wife, is gentle with her, and wants to nourish her physically, mentally, emotionally, and spiritually.

This is a great mystery, and I take it to mean Christ and the church: Here is another short digression in Paul's line of reasoning. He quotes Genesis 2:24, "For this reason a man shall leave his father and mother and be joined to his wife, and the two shall become one flesh," and adds that this "mystery" symbolizes the relationship to Christ and the Church. Yet, is not a beautiful human marriage a visible reminder of the mysterious unity between Christ and His people? In my own case, I cannot ever describe how mysteriously beautiful and wonderful my marriage to Jean is through nearly thirty-five years, nor can she satisfactorily define what she says I mean to her! So also is the "mystery" of the relationship between Jesus Christ and His Church.

IV. *Fathers, do not provoke your children to anger, but bring them up in the discipline and instruction of the Lord:* Christian parenting, Paul says, requires the kind of caring which never ridicules or descends to harsh scolding.

SUGGESTIONS TO TEACHERS

Today's lesson could well be a series of lessons on the family. You will find so much material in Ephesians 5, 6 that you will have to select certain emphases for discussion and concentrate on them. As teacher, you know your class better than anyone else. You may want to spend a large part of the lesson period on marriage responsibilities for Christians, or on relationships between children and parents who are Christians, depending on who is in your class. You may also have to deal with some of the unusual problems of contemporary society, such as divorce, remarriage, and the single-parent family, which some of those in your class are experiencing.

1. *RESPECT AND REVERENCE IN RELATIONSHIPS.* The key to understanding how Christians live together in human families is, "Be subject to one another out of reverence for Christ" (Ephesians 5:21). In fact, this is the secret of the way a Christian relates to all others. "Be subject to" does not mean being a doormat. It suggests a Christlike posture where you are most anxious to serve rather than be served. Urge each person in your class to reflect on how this applies in his or her own case, whether married or single, parent or child. Perhaps

you will want to have each person write himself or herself a "letter from Jesus" in which each class member would put down on paper what the Lord may expect of him or her as one called to show reverence for Christ.

2. *MUTUALITY AND MYSTERY OF MARRIAGE.* With soaring divorce rates and crumbling marriages, you must examine the Ephesians's passage with your class to gain deeper understandings of God's Word to husbands and wives. You will find that some in your class will bring in all kinds of less-than-helpful quotes and comments from marriage "experts" and popular columnists. Remember that you and the class are gathering to hear God's Word, not human advice. In Ephesians, your class will discover that both husbands and wives are called to mutual sacrifice. No woman is to be subjugated and no man is to dominate. Rather, each cares for the other in unique ways. Being subject to the other "as to the Lord" (5:21) suggests that a marriage partner will worship Christ by being caring toward the spouse. Ask your class what your congregation could do to help strengthen and deepen the understanding of Christian commitment in marriage among those in your church.

3. *FORGIVENESS AND FIRMNESS IN FAMILIES.* Children, Paul rightly points out, guarantee the continuity and well-being of the human family. In light of the discord found in so many homes, the New Testament insists that forgiveness is the only way for mutual growth and happiness for Christian families. Direct some of the discussion on Ephesians 6:4. What does it mean, practically speaking, to bring up youngsters these days "in the discipline and instruction of the Lord"?

TOPIC FOR ADULTS
HELP FOR FAMILY LIVING

A Baptism. "Once I witnessed a baptism in a small church in a Latin American village. The community of faith had gathered; they had recalled God's gracious acts, they had proclaimed the Gospel. And now they were about to make a response. The congregation began the mournful sounds of a funeral hymn as a solemn procession moved down the aisle. A father carried a child's coffin he had made from wood; a mother carried a bucket of water from the family well; a priest carried their sleeping infant wrapped only in a native blanket. As they reached the chancel, the father placed the coffin on the altar, the mother poured the water in the coffin, and the priest covered the wakening baby's skin with embalming oil. The singing softened to a whisper. The priest slowly lowered the infant into the coffin and immersed the child's head in the water. As he did so, he exclaimed, 'I kill you in the name of the Father and of the Son and of the Holy Spirit.'

" 'Amen!' shouted the parents and the congregation.

"Then quickly lifting the child into the air for all to see, the priest declared, 'And I resurrect you that you might love and serve the Lord.'

"Immediately the congregation broke into a joyous Easter hymn. But it was not yet over. The priest covered the child with the oils of birth; he dressed the child in a beautiful homemade white robe. Once again the singing quieted as the priest, anointing the child, made the sign of the cross on the child's forehead and said, 'I brand you with the sign of Christ so that you and the world will always know who you are and to whom you belong.' As the singing continued, the people came forward to share the kiss of peace with the newest member of their family.

"What more brave, radical act can parents perform than to bring their child to the church to be baptized? Acknowledging that we are all born to die that we might have life, the parents celebrate in baptism both the child's death and resurrection. Parents know that when they do this they signify their intention to give up their child for adoption into a new family, with a new day of birth and a new family name—Christian. The child will belong now to the family of God."—John H. Westerhoff III, *Bringing up Children in the Christian Faith.* Copyright © 1980 by John H. Westerhoff III. Published by Winston Press, Inc., 430 Oak Grove, Minneapolis, MN 55403. All rights reserved. Used with permission.

Resilience of the Family. "The American family has been challenged by society and consigned to eventual death by sociologists. However, those who have written the doom of the family have not given the American couples a better option.

"The alternatives to the traditional family have been disappointing and futile. Statistics from the alternative trial-runs have been embarrassing to the proponents.

"Strange that we fail so many times to learn our lessons well. Anytime man has tried to replace the biblical pattern he has failed. Our attempt to replace the biblical concept of family met with such failure.

"The traditional concept of family is having a new review by the young couples of the world. They have observed that the alternatives did not work. So, they are going back to the basics of traditional family patterns in hopes of finding stability and strength.

"God has assigned a big task to parents—and He has not changed His order."—Neil Strait, *Quote*, October 1, 1981.

The Real Hurt. A woman who had been married for many years was suddenly confronted by her husband who announced that he was leaving her to continue his affair with another woman. The wife felt the deep pain. When she talked with her pastor, she said, "What hurts me most is not that he slept with her. Nor that he gave her jewelry. But that he had something to talk about with her."

Marriages between Christians mean communication. The relationship calls for talking with each other, especially of deepest and most important matters.

God communicates with us. He has spoken His word of love through Jesus Christ. In response to His talking with us, we talk with one another as husband and wife.

Questions for Pupils on the Next Lesson. 1. What is the source of true authority? 2. What does Romans 13 teach in regard to our attitude and actions toward civil authorities? 3. Is it possible as a matter of conscience to disobey policies and authorities with which we don't agree? If so, who and under what circumstances? If not, why not? 4. Is love the fulfillment of the Law?

TOPIC FOR YOUTH
LIVING AS FAMILY

Power of Example. "An old Chinese proverb says, 'A picture is worth a thousand words.' So is example. Charlie Shedd quotes a famous psychiatrist as saying that 'no little child will think more of God than he thinks of his father.' A youngster apparently cannot contrast. He can only compare. Shedd imagines his thinking, 'God is like my father. I'm not so sure my father really cares much about me. He's always playing golf, watching television, reading the newspaper. Besides he isn't very nice to my mother. He's not even fair. I don't think I'd like God.'

"Shedd suggests a good little model speech for dad to give to the kids: 'Listen to me, troops. When I'm the kind of father I should be, that's what God is like! Where I am not so hot, I hope you'll learn the all-important process of contrast. Wherever the Bible says that God is like a father, you can understand it means that God is like a perfect father. You know I'm not perfect. But I'm going to keep on trying. And I want you to know that I know I've got a long way to go.' "—*Pulpit Helps*, June 1977.

Words for People in Love. "Keith and Polly, it is my fervent prayer that your first love will be the deep reverence, the abiding gratitude which only our God deserves. If you and I and all of us seek him in disciplined devotion—yes, in daily dedication—then his love will become more and more a part of our lives. His love will enable our love for each other.

"And by the words 'our love for each other,' I don't mean the 'just you and me, Babe' kind of love. I mean the broader human family, which God yearns to love through us. Through our God-inspired service, the 'Me Generation' can still be transformed into the 'We Generation.' It must be, before we atomize ourselves into the 'Was Generation'!"—From a wedding meditation by the Rev. Benton M. Newcomer, pastor, The Presbyterian Church, New Bethlehem, Pa. Printed in *Monday Morning.* May 17, 1982.

Changing the Forces That Victimize as Well as Helping the Victim. "Most efforts to help children and families have tried to reform the victims, not change the forces that victimize. . . .

"Children need many things in the course of their development: love, responsiveness, guidance, continuity of care, physical vitality, adequate nutrition, health care, parents with self-respect, and so on. Parental income cannot guarantee any of these. But low income makes every one of them more difficult, more problematic.

"Poverty is the most important cause of the problems of American children and families today."—Kenneth Keniston in an address to the National Conference on Children and Youth, February 2, 1976.

Questions for Pupils on the Next Lesson. 1. Why do we all tend to question authority and authorities? 2. What is the greatest authority in your life, and why? 3. Who are the authorities you consider to be most unfair or unjust to you? 4. How do you handle situations where you are asked to do different things by different authorities? 5. Do you take any responsibility in political affairs? Why or why not?

LESSON X—NOVEMBER 4

RESPONDING TO GOD'S AUTHORITY

Background Scripture: Romans 13; Colossians 3:23–25
Devotional Reading: Romans 13:8–14

KING JAMES VERSION

ROMANS 13 Let every soul be subject unto the higher powers. For there is no power but of God: the powers that be are ordained of God.

2 Whosoever therefore resisteth the power, resisteth the ordinance of God: and they that resist shall receive to themselves damnation.

3 For rulers are not a terror to good works, but to the evil. Wilt thou then not be afraid of the power? do that which is good, and thou shalt have praise of the same:

4 For he is the minister of God to thee for good. But if thou do that which is evil, be afraid; for he beareth not the sword in vain: for he is the minister of God, a revenger to *execute* wrath upon him that doeth evil.

5 Wherefore *ye* must needs be subject, not only for wrath, but also for conscience sake.

6 For, for this cause pay ye tribute also: for they are God's ministers, attending continually upon this very thing.

7 Render therefore to all their dues: tribute to whom tribute *is due;* custom to whom custom; fear to whom fear; honour to whom honour.

8 Owe no man any thing, but to love one another: for he that loveth another hath fulfilled the law.

9 For this, Thou shalt not commit adultery, Thou shalt not kill, Thou shalt not steal, Thou shalt not bear false witness, Thou shalt not covet; and if *there be* any other commandment, it is briefly comprehended in this saying, namely, Thou shalt love thy neighbour as thyself.

10 Love worketh no ill to his neighbour: therefore love *is* the fulfilling of the law.

REVISED STANDARD VERSION

ROMANS 13 Let every person be subject to the governing authorities. For there is no authority except from God, and those that exist have been instituted by God. 2 Therefore he who resists the authorities resists what God has appointed, and those who resist will incur judgment. 3 For rulers are not a terror to good conduct, but to bad. Would you have no fear of him who is in authority? Then do what is good, and you will receive his approval, 4 for he is God's servant for your good. But if you do wrong, be afraid, for he does not bear the sword in vain; he is the servant of God to execute his wrath on the wrongdoer. 5 Therefore one must be subject, not only to avoid God's wrath but also for the sake of conscience. 6 For the same reason you also pay taxes, for the authorities are ministers of God, attending to this very thing. 7 Pay all of them their dues, taxes to whom taxes are due, revenue to whom revenue is due, respect to whom respect is due, honor to whom honor is due.

8 Owe no one anything, except to love one another; for he who loves his neighbor has fulfilled the law. 9 The commandments, "You shall not commit adultery, You shall not kill, You shall not steal, You shall not covet," and any other commandment, are summed up in this sentence, "You shall love your neighbor as yourself." 10 Love does no wrong to a neighbor; therefore love is the fulfilling of the law.

KEY VERSE: *Whatever your task, work heartily, as serving the Lord and not men.* Colossians 3:23 (RSV).

HOME DAILY BIBLE READINGS

Oct.	29.	M.	*Transformed by Christ.* Romans 12:1–13.
Oct.	30.	T.	*Love Doesn't Hate.* Romans 12:14–21.
Oct.	31.	W.	*Honor God and Then the State.* Romans 13:1–7.
Nov.	1.	T.	*Our Debt to Humankind.* Romans 13:8–14.
Nov.	2.	F.	*Christianity Confronts Conflicting Values.* Acts 4:1–6.
Nov.	3.	S.	*A Powerful Proclamation.* Acts 4:7–14.
Nov.	4.	S.	*God Is Placed Before Authorities.* Acts 4:15–22.

BACKGROUND

In Paul's time, Christians and Jews were suspected of being subversives. The problem came to a head over emperor worship. After the Roman emperors were elevated to the status of gods, all good Romans were expected to take part in the emperor cult. This involved going to an imperial shrine, throwing a pinch of incense into the flame burning there, and stating that Caesar was Lord. Christians, of course, knew that Jesus is Lord, and had problems with emperor worship.

Even if Christians could dodge the loyalty oath to Caesar, they were known for being, well, "different." Roman authorities persecuted them from time to time, sometimes subtly and sometimes harshly, for not going along with the emperor cult. The Romans wanted to use the emperor cult as a means of welding a diffuse population into some kind of sense of being one. Already, cracks were appearing in the empire. Palestine, for example, continued to seethe with revolt. Wild tribes were raiding the frontiers elsewhere. A large, restless slave population within the borders of the empire caused Roman statesmen to be uneasy. Christians? Many Romans reasoned they were a threat to the security of the empire, a kind of potential fifth column.

Paul was well aware of how suspicious Roman authorities were of Christians and Jews. He also knew that Galilee and Judea bubbled with plots, guerrilla attacks on Roman garrisons, fanatic groups such as the Zealots organizing an underground, and rumors of impending full-scale revolt.

How does a Christian regard the civil authorities? Is a Christian an anarchist? What is the relation of a Christian to the state? Both Christians and non-Christian Romans alike were asking these questions. Especially in the great capital city of Rome itself were these matters seriously discussed. Paul takes them up in the thirteenth chapter of Romans.

NOTES ON THE PRINTED TEXT

I. *Let every person be subject to the governing authorities.* To *every* governing authority? This would have included Nero! Paul knew this. He also knew Nero's reputation; he had heard how this cruel, unstable maniac delighted in torching live Christians soaked in tar to illuminate his garden parties. Some people ask how Paul possibly could be so naive as to write such a sweeping statement.

Paul did not pretend that governing authorities are above sin or criticism. He certainly does not claim that Nero is an ideal ruler. He says in effect that Nero the emperor is a symbol of governing authority. Nero the man may be a brutal tyrant, but the institution of the state must be respected.

Paul wants to establish the point that government is necessary. The state keeps the peace. If it weren't for some kind of governing authority, anarchy would result.

Paul sometimes suffered injustice at the hands of the civil authorities. However, he upheld the place of government. He took pride in his own Roman citizenship. The state and civil authorities, Paul realized, provided conditions of relative calm and order so that the Gospel could be preached and the Church organized.

II. *For there is no authority except from God, and those that exist have been instituted by God:* These words of Paul have been picked up by some of the most perceptive thinkers. God, of course, is the Supreme Authority. No human authority can dare presume to supplant God's authority. These words ultimately spelled the death knell for the idea of divine right of kings. It took several centuries, but Paul's words took root. When arrogant King James I tried to put down a critical preacher named Andrew Melville in 1606 in London, Melville bluntly told everyone present including James that the king is "God's silly vassal." James was not amused, and Melville was sent packing back to Scotland, but the point had been made. Even members of royalty must remember their vassalage before God. So must Presidents, Prime Ministers, politicians—and preachers, church officers, and everyone else with any authority!

Therefore he who resists the authorities resists what God has appointed, and those who resist incur judgment: Christian theologians, pondering these verses, remind us that God THE Authority deputizes humans with certain authority. Calvin says that for the well-being of human society, God authorizes certain "orders." Bonhoeffer said about the same thing, and stated that God set up certain "mandates" or institutions such as the state and the human family, each with limited authority. Paul, Calvin, and Bonhoeffer and other Christian thinkers point out that these authorities must be taken seriously and upheld.

Sooner or later, however, someone will ask: How far does one go in tolerating a completely repressive, totalitarian government? Do these verses mean passive acquiescence in the face of dictators like Hitler, Stalin, and Idi Amin? Must Christians always under every circumstance accept the authority of the state? Is it ever patriotic not to stand up to national authority? These verses have ignited lively debate and disagreement among church people.

One help is remembering that civil government has an authority from God only as long as it remembers that it is "under God." Christians give allegiance to their state only so far as that authority fits the description of such an authority as outlined here by Paul.

Owe no one anything, except to love one another; for he who loves his neighbor has fulfilled the law. Paul continues his comments on citizenship and the respect for law. He states in effect that the Christian as a responsible citizen does more than observe the statute books but has an inner Law which impels him to *love!* The Torah, the old Jewish Law, is summed up in that great word *agape* or love. Christians, with the "Torah" of Christ written in their minds and hearts, are people who translate their love into active *doing* for neighbors. And *neighbors* means not simply the folks next door or down the road, but the brothers and sisters in Latin America or the Middle East or wherever people live without justice or hope.

SUGGESTIONS TO TEACHERS

The word *authority* conjures up pictures of someone with a big stick barking orders. Our generation has distrust and disdain for authority. When someone mentions God's authority, many react negatively.

God, however, is not the celestial Drill Sergeant. Your lesson this Sunday will have to take into consideration the wrong images and ideas of authority, including God's. It will be helpful if you can separate authority from authoritarianism. God is authoritative without being authoritarian.

Your lesson today also examines human authority. Human authority—which nearly everyone carries to some degree—derives from God's authority. Your Scripture background will offer helpful insights to discussing this important issue.

1. *MANDATE FOR AUTHORITY.* What is the ultimate authority? What authorities are relative? These basic questions are faced by Paul in Romans 13:2 and must be considered by your class. Your people will learn that God is the Source of all authority. He grants some authority to us humans. In a sense, He authorizes or deputizes us with some of His authority. However, people in authority such as civil authorities must constantly remember that they are God's servants. Their authority is not final or supreme. The danger, of course, is that human authorities tend to think that no one, not even God, has greater authority!

2. *NEED FOR AUTHORITIES.* We live in an age which sometimes teeters toward anarchy. So many in this generation have rebelled against all authority to "do their own thing" and there has been so much emphasis on being "liberated" from all authority that we are in danger of becoming a society of selfish individualists forsaking all authority. The New Testament states there is a need for au-

thorities. Authorities provide order. Authorities deter evil conduct. Have your class mull over what kind of community we would have if we had no authorities. Ask how Christians can help various authorities to carry out their duties under God more responsibly.

3. *MINISTRY OF AUTHORITIES.* Paul often suffered at the hands of civil authorities. He knew from personal experience that some of these were corrupt, cruel, and incompetent. Yet he insisted on thinking that all human authorities, including civil, had a ministry! ("The authorities are ministers of God," Romans 13:6.) The Church has a responsibility of insisting that civil authorities remember that they are ministering for God, or serving Him and not themselves. Sometimes, this means the Church must remind or warn civil authorities that God holds civil authorities accountable!

4. *MINISTERS UNDER AUTHORITY.* Every Christian is part of Christ's ministry. Tell your class that each member is therefore under divine authority. Each has a ministry to others, a responsibility to *all* neighbors. Paul offers practical examples of this ministry: paying debts, keeping the commandments, and respecting the rights of others in matters of marriages, personhood, and property. Allow enough time in your lesson to talk over the ways we must remember we are under authority to live in a larger human community.

TOPIC FOR ADULTS
RESPONDING TO GOD'S AUTHORITY

The Authority of Jesus. "When we say of a teacher, 'He is an authority on his subject,' we mean that we are prepared to accept his judgments in those spheres in which he is knowledgeable. Many of Jesus' contemporaries instinctively felt that He was such an authority on faith and life. Many who heard Him teach asked with amazement, how it was that this man, who had no credentials of study or ordination, had such learning. Jesus replied, 'The teaching that I give is not my own; it is the teaching of him who sent me' (John 7:16). Again many of the common people believed Him. Whereas the Pharisees quoted their authorities, Jesus spoke as One who possessed authority within Himself. How often He said, 'In truth, in very truth I tell you. . . .'"

" 'You have learned that our forefathers were told . . . but what I tell you is this . . .' (John 5:21, 22). Today we miss the sense of shock these words must have originally given. It is as if a young minister was to rise in the General Assembly and say, 'The Bible says . . . but I say.' Unhesitatingly Jesus pitted His judgement against the long-standing traditions and beliefs of His nation. He adopted towards the Law of Moses an authoritatively critical attitude that no rabbi would have ventured. Without apology He assumed the right to declare what was lawful on the Sabbath, and to dispense with many of the regulations governing fasting and ritual cleansing.

"The longer the disciples were with Jesus, the more convinced they became of His rightful authority over their lives. Valuing human individuality, Jesus' authority did not mean regimentation. He did not seek to make James like John, or Thomas like Peter. Nor had His authority anything to do with authoritarianism. It is almost always those, like tyrants and dictators who possess no real authority, who resort to authoritarian methods, who seek to impose patterns of behaviour and thought on other people.

"Jesus' authority is the authority of our own hearts and our deepest longings, the authority of the way things are. 'Christianity' as Pascal said, 'is knowing profoundly what you know already' that—
". . . the beatitudes are beautiful attitudes
". . . what we are is of greater significance than what we own or what we wear

"... greatness does not consist in having many servants but in being a servant

"... there is a glory about going the second mile and doing the bit over

"... every day is holy, every act of service a sacred thing

"... mankind is one family:—all men and women are God's children

"... happiness comes more through giving than getting

"... we find ourselves by responding to the challenges and demands of life, not by avoiding them

"... love is better than hate

"... hope better than despair

"... faith nobler than cynicism.

"In Jesus, we have a mind that saw truly. With the passing centuries the convictions which Jesus implanted in the world's mind, become ever more relevant."—James A. Simpson, "The Authority of Jesus," *Life and Work*, April, 1981.

Responding to Authorities. A Christian, responding to God's authority, honors other authorities. This includes the authority of the state and the law. However, millions of Americans flout the authority of the state by cheating on income tax returns. In 1982, a Congressional committee was told of large corporations using two sets of figures on the cost of prospective regulatory burdens—one set to water down the government, the other to butter up the stockholders. In a rural area of Virginia, sponsors of a fund-raising drive conducting a ten kilometer run were dismayed to find that the boy finishing third had hidden a bicycle in the woods and pedalled part of the way. And Rosie Ruiz cheated to appear to come in first in a Boston Marathon. Two coaches were indicted for faking transcripts of grades of students on their teams. Other schools granted credits to athletes for courses never attended. Cheating in exams in colleges and universities has reached awesome dimensions, according to students and administrators.

Such lack of respect to authority undermines all authority including that of God. A Christian upholds divine authority by living obediently before all authorities.

Force of Character. The basis for your authority with others will be not so much your "clout" through money, title, position, rank, address, degrees, or other human assessments of power. Ultimately, your authority will flow from the force of your moral character. Few have this kind of authority. One who did was Edward Wilson, the companion of Captain Robert Scott, the famous explorer in the Antarctic. Scott wrote of Wilson, a deeply committed Christian, "He has by sheer force of character achieved a position of authority over the others, while retaining their warmest affections." Not surprisingly, it was Wilson who held back some of his own meager rations during their final ordeal on the ice after reaching the south pole in 1912, and secretly slipped extra food to his three companions. Tragically, Wilson, Scott, and the other two perished before reaching their base ship in March, 1912.

Questions for Pupils on the Next Lesson. 1. How have you handled your grief when losing loved ones? 2. Why does it seem to help in life's difficulties to share your hurts with understanding friends? 3. What is the basis for hope when we face the deaths of loved ones? 4. How do you comfort others who are grief-stricken? 5. Is your church a support for people experiencing rough times?

TOPIC FOR YOUTH
WHO'S IN CHARGE HERE?

Serve God With Zeal. Cardinal Thomas Wolsey, the brilliant churchman and statesman who served King Henry VIII, rose to great heights in England. The arrogant and imperious priest became the virtual ruler of the realm as royal almoner and member of the Privy Council in 1511. He seemed to forget the basis of all authority lies in God, and made the mistake of forgetting that Henry VIII's authority had to be taken seriously. Shakespeare puts the following words in Wolsey's mouth after Henry VIII charged the clever prelate with treason:

> Had I but served my God with half the zeal
> I served my king, he would not in mine age
> Have left me naked to mine enemies.

No Light. Malcolm Muggeridge, who for many years in his caustic and witty way had railed against the churches and their "superstitions," a few years ago published a statement which astonished many who knew him. "All I can say as one ageing and singularly unimportant fellowman, is that I have conscientiously looked far and wide, inside and outside my own head and heart, and I have found nothing other than this man and his words which offers any answer to the dilemma of this tragic, troubled time. If his light has gone out, then as far as I am concerned, there is no light."

Under Authority. Bobby Orr has been described by *Time* magazine as "the greatest defense man, graceful and creative, in hockey history." Orr led the Bruins to two Stanley Cup titles and then, his knees already battered, went to the Black Hawks in 1976. He was still better than most, but he was not himself. His contract called for a salary of $600,000 a year, yet he had not cashed a single paycheck when he quit after seven operations had failed to save his knees. He refused to be paid unless he delivered.

What a contrast to other athletes who have greedily seized whatever they could extract! Orr's personal sense of integrity is the basis for his authority both on the ice and off.

When God is in charge of your life, you also have the authority of being a responsible, ethical person!

Questions for Pupils on the Next Lesson. 1. What did you feel when you lost someone you loved through death, and how did you handle your grief? 2. Where are you searching for answers to your difficult questions about death? 3. How do you show sympathy and concern toward those who are bereaved? 4. Who brings you your greatest encouragement and support when you are dealing with difficult questions or experiences?

LESSON XI—NOVEMBER 11

THE CHRISTIAN'S HOPE

Background Scripture: 1 Thessalonians 1–4
Devotional Reading: 1 Thessalonians 2:1–8

KING JAMES VERSION

1 THESSALONIANS 1 Paul and Silvanus, and Timotheus, unto the church of the Thessalonians *which is* in God the Father, and *in* the Lord Jesus Christ: Grace *be* unto you, and peace, from God our Father, and the Lord Jesus Christ.

2 We give thanks to God always for you all, making mention of you in our prayers;

3 Remembering without ceasing your work of faith, and labor of love, and patience of hope in our Lord Jesus Christ, in the sight of God and our Father;

4 9 But as touching brotherly love ye need not that I write unto you: for ye yourselves are taught of God to love one another.

10 And indeed ye do it toward all the brethren which are in all Macedonia: but we beseech you, brethren, that ye increase more and more;

11 And that ye study to be quiet, and to do your own business, and to work with your own hands, as we commanded you;

12 That ye may walk honestly toward them that are without, and *that* ye may have lack of nothing.

13 But I would not have you to be ignorant, brethren, concerning them which are asleep, that ye sorrow not, even as others which have no hope.

14 For if we believe that Jesus died and rose again, even so them also which sleep in Jesus will God bring with him.

15 For this we say unto you by the word of the Lord, that we which are alive *and* remain unto the coming of the Lord shall not prevent them which are asleep.

16 For the Lord himself shall descend from heaven with a shout, with the voice of the archangel, and with the trump of God: and the dead in Christ shall rise first:

17 Then we which are alive *and* remain shall be caught up together with them in the clouds, to meet the Lord in the air: and so shall we ever be with the Lord.

18 Wherefore comfort one another with these words.

REVISED STANDARD VERSION

1 THESSALONIANS 1 Paul, Silvanus, and Timothy, To the church of the Thessalonians in God the Father and the Lord Jesus Christ:
Grace to you and peace.

2 We give thanks to God always for you all, constantly mentioning you in our prayers, 3 remembering before our God and Father your work of faith and labor of love and steadfastness of hope in our Lord Jesus Christ.

4 9 But concerning love of the brethren you have no need to have any one write to you, for you yourselves have been taught by God to love one another; 10 and indeed you do love all the brethren throughout Macedonia. But we exhort you, brethren, to do so more and more, 11 to aspire to live quietly, to mind your own affairs, and to work with your hands, as we charged you; 12 so that you may command the respect of outsiders, and be dependent on nobody.

13 But we would not have you ignorant, brethren, concerning those who are asleep, that you may not grieve as others do who have no hope. 14 For since we believe that Jesus died and rose again, even so, through Jesus, God will bring with him those who have fallen asleep. 15 For this we declare to you by the word of the Lord, that we who are alive, who are left until the coming of the Lord, shall not precede those who have fallen asleep. 16 For the Lord himself will descend from heaven with a cry of command, with the archangel's call, and with the sound of the trumpet of God. And the dead in Christ will rise first; 17 then we who are alive, who are left, shall be caught up together with them in the clouds to meet the Lord in the air; and so we shall always be with the Lord. 18 Therefore comfort one another with these words.

KEY VERSE: . . . *we shall always be with the Lord. Therefore comfort one another with these words.* 1 Thessalonians 4:17, 18 (RSV).

HOME DAILY BIBLE READINGS

Nov. 5. M. *Living Faithfully in the Endtime.* 1 Thessalonians 1:1–10.
Nov. 6. T. *The Church Begins in Thessalonica.* Acts 17:1–9.
Nov. 7. W. *Paul Writes About His Thessalonian Visit.* 1 Thessalonians 2:1–12.

Nov.	8.	T.	*Paul Sent Timothy to the Church.* 1 Thessalonians 3:1–10.
Nov.	9.	F.	*A Prayer for the Church.* 1 Thessalonians 3:11–13.
Nov.	10.	S.	*Exhortation to Live a Holy Life.* 1 Thessalonians 4:1–12.
Nov.	11.	S.	*Faithfulness Is Rewarded.* 1 Thessalonians 4:13–18.

BACKGROUND

Paul had founded the church at Thessalonica after leaving Philippi. It was the second church to be established in Europe. His work was cut short by the furious opposition of some local Jewish leaders. Paul was forced to flee, go on to Berea, and eventually to Corinth. He hoped to return to Thessalonica but could not. Meanwhile, he had to rely on reports on the progress of the tiny congregation in that city through Timothy.

Paul found himself prevented from traveling north again to Thessalonica, but he did the next best thing. He wrote. Many scholars think that 1 Thessalonians was the earliest of Paul's epistles. If this is Paul's first letter, he hit upon a useful way to let his "children" in his churches know what was on his mind and heart, and he followed up this letter with the others that are included in our New Testament.

Paul, of course, did not sit down and write pious generalities. Each letter was written in response to a question or for a reason. In the case of Thessalonians, Paul wrote to allay fears and answer queries about those who died before Jesus returned. At the time when Paul preached in Thessalonica, Paul and all other Christians expected Jesus Christ to come back soon. Paul later changed his thinking on this matter, but in the early part of his ministry, including his stay among the Thessalonians, he looked forward to it in the near future. When some of the Thessalonian converts began to die before Christ had returned, others began to ask if those who had died could share in the eternal life which His coming again would bring. Still others wondered whether Christ ever would come again, and if so, when?

Paul wrote his first letter to this little group of uneasy Christians in the hostile environment of a big pagan city.

NOTES ON THE PRINTED TEXT

I. *We give thanks to God always for you all, constantly mentioning you in our prayers....* In spite of frustrations and disappointments over the Thessalonian Christians, Paul starts his letter by telling them how thankful he is for them before God. Paul also never goes into sticky, sentimental piety, but he mentions frequently how he prays for his fellow Christians.

... remembering before our God and Father your work of faith and labor of love and steadfastness of hope in our Lord Jesus Christ. Paul always found some quality to praise when he wrote to his churches. Even when they were obstreperously disobedient and disappointing to him, he graciously praised them for what they were doing right. In the case of the Thessalonian believers, Paul picked out three qualities of Christian discipleship which he held up as praiseworthy. First, was their "work of faith," or having the kind of faith which does work. Real belief means *doing.* Faith means getting your hands dirty and feeling your feet get tired. Second, the Thessalonians are praised for their "labor of love," that is having more than caring feelings but translating love into action. Mere emotion means little if not channeled and expressed. Third, Paul thanks the Thessalonians for "steadfastness of hope." Paul commends these Christians for their stamina or endurance based on their hope in Jesus. He knew that they had cause for being discouraged. Some of those dearest to them had died. Being a Christian in Thessalonica was a daily, uphill struggle. Paul knew that they must be wondering at

times if it were any use to keep going as faithful Christians. But they had persisted as Christians, and he praised them.

You will note that Paul has touched on the triad of "faith, love and hope" which he often referred to, especially in 1 Corinthians 13.

II. *We exhort you . . . to aspire to live quietly, to mind your own affairs, and to work with your own hands; so that you may command the respect of outsiders, and be dependent on nobody:* Some Thessalonians, apparently expecting the imminent return of Jesus, had quit work and were sitting by idly, waiting. Others of course had to provide food and necessities for these who had stopped working. This caused resentment within the Christian fellowship. Non-Christians sneered that Christians were nothing but a bunch of lazy drones. Paul brusquely instructs those who'd been waiting for Christ's return in idleness to get back to their old jobs at once. His own example, of earning his keep by weaving tent cloth wherever he worked as a missionary should have reminded them that Christians do not live indolent lives, thinking they can depend on handouts. Work has a place in our lives, Paul insists.

III. *But we would not have you ignorant, brethren, concerning those who are asleep, that you may not grieve as others do who have no hope:* Paul gets down to the meat of his letter, and discusses the hope Christians have in the face of death. Paul doesn't speak of "immortality of the soul." He refers to the Resurrection of Jesus. This, and nothing else, is the reason for the Christian's hope in the face of death.

We believe that . . . through Jesus, God will bring with him those who have fallen asleep: Paul tells the worried Thessalonians to stop fretting and to begin trusting. If God raised up Jesus, reaching down into the total nothingness of the grave, and conferred new life on Him, He may be trusted to effect a resurrection in His own way and in His own time for those who belong to Christ! If a person dies in Christ, that same person shall also live again in Christ.

IV. *The Coming of the Lord:* Paul picks up the poetic terms of the Old Testament when he speaks of the time when Christ will come. He does not intend his words to be taken in a crudely literal way, but as a way of trying to express what is basically inexpressible. The details actually are not that important; it's the confidence that Jesus Christ *will* return that Paul wants us to understand. He reassures the shaky survivors in the Thessalonian church that Jesus will come at some point, but not to fret over the time. He wants them to go about their daily tasks calmly and confidently.

So shall we always be with the Lord: Paul assures his readers in the first century and today that they live in a relationship with Jesus that nothing—not even death—can break!

SUGGESTIONS TO TEACHERS

Psychiatrist Karl Menninger points out that the *Encyclopedia Britannica* prints column after column on the subjects of faith and love, but does not even list the topic of hope. Perhaps this is symptomatic of our age. Hope is in desperately short supply!

Therefore, your lesson today can be of immense help to people in your church-school class. Think about your class members for a moment; remember some of the remarks they have made and recall some of the reactions to situations they had which showed how devoid of hope they apparently are. Hold up to them the hope of Jesus Christ as conveyed in 1 Thessalonians 1–4.

1. *WAITING FOR JESUS.* We Christians know that human history has a purpose and direction because of the hope that Jesus Christ will come. This does not mean that we sit around, peering into the sky or poring over Bible verses to fix a

date. To the contrary, we know that the timetable is up to God, not us. But we have a hope! We live our lives in anticipation that God will wrap up the human story in His own way in His own time because He loves us. Have your class think together on where history seems to be going. Do they think it's headed nowhere but is a "tale told by an idiot, full of sound and fury, signifying nothing"? Or do they look forward with hope because of Jesus who delivers us from the wrath to come?

2. *WORKING IN BELIEVERS.* The Word of God or God's promise spoken through Jesus Christ "is at work in you believers" (2:13), Paul announces to us. Let the significance of this statement sink in: God is at work in our lives—*now!* This means additional cause for hope. Many in the class, however, might not have thought much about the way God is at work in their lives. Therefore, devote some time to having each person comment on at least one way in which God has been working in his or her life during the past week. If the class is too large, break the class into subgroups of twos or threes.

3. *WEATHERING OPPOSITION AND AFFLICTION.* Christians do not pretend that the world has no evil. The opposite is true. Christians are realists about the force and extent of evil. They know they'll be opposed. They know they'll be persecuted. They know they'll be tempted. They know they'll be hurt. Or they should know these things if they've met Jesus Christ and read their New Testaments! Read 1 Thessalonians 2:14–16 and 3:2,3 for reminders of Paul's sufferings. But, your class should realize, Christians in times of suffering for the Gospel's sake receive renewed hope through a deeper personal association with the Risen Lord!

4. *WAKING AFTER DYING.* Death is still considered to be a forbidden topic in many circles, but everyone has thoughts of death. Help your class to gain a deeper sense of hope in Jesus Christ in the face of the "final enemy." Allow the deep and unspoken anxieties to come out. But hold up the words in 1 Thessalonians 4:13–18. Although we all "sleep" that final sleep eventually and meanwhile must leave loved ones in that sleep, we have the resurrection hope. "We believe that Jesus died and rose again, even so, through Jesus, God will bring with him those who have fallen asleep" (4:14).

TOPIC FOR ADULTS
THE CHRISTIAN'S HOPE

Dying With Hope Through Christ's Forgiveness. ". . . Men's minds are troubled by the memory of horrors that permitted them no rest. Often their screams disturbed the sleeping camp.

"I remember a fellow prisoner in my hut who was dying of cerebral malaria. As he turned and twisted on his pallet he carried on a conversation with an unseen presence. Apparently he had been ordered to kill a Malay, accused of being a spy, for security reasons. His conversation went something like this: 'Of course I had to kill him. There was nothing else to do. But before I shot him through the head, he looked at me, his eyes pleading for mercy. I gave him no mercy when he asked for mercy. He cannot forgive me; his wife cannot forgive me; nobody can forgive me.'

"He went on for hours, arguing in this vein. As he reached the darkest depths of the valley, he became quieter and then shouted out, 'But I am forgiven. You've given me peace.' He was at rest, and at rest he died.

"It was to quiet ourselves, in the face of experiences such as these, that we joined in the closing prayer of the evening: 'O Lord, support us all the day long of this troublesome life, until the shadows lengthen and the evening comes and the busy world is hushed, and the fever of life is over and our work is done. Then, Lord, in thy mercy grant us safe lodging, a holy rest, and peace at last; through

Jesus Christ our Lord.' "—From p. 63 in *Through the Valley of the Kwai* by Ernest Gordon. Copyright © 1962 by Ernest Gordon. By permission of Harper & Row, Publishers, Inc.

The People With Hope. "This seems a cheerful world, Donatus, when I view it from this fair garden, under the shadow of these vines. But if I climbed some great mountain and looked out over the wide lands, you know very well what I would see. Brigands on the high roads, pirates on the high seas, in the amphitheatres men murdered to please the applauding crowds, and under all roofs—misery and selfishness. It is really a bad world, Donatus, an incredibly bad world. Yet, in the midst of it I have found a quiet and holy people. They have discovered a joy which is a thousand times better than any pleasure of this simple life. They are despised and persecuted, but they care not. They have overcome the world. These people, Donatus, are the Christians and I am one of them."—St. Cyprian, writing to Donatus, A.D. third century.

There She Comes! Henry Van Dyke, the beloved minister and devout Christian, once described his hope in Jesus Christ in the face of death. He put it in these words:

"I am standing upon the seashore. A ship at my side spreads her white sails to the morning breeze and starts for the blue ocean. She is an object of beauty and strength and I stand and watch until at last she hangs like a speck of white cloud just where the sea and sky come down to mingle with each other. Then someone at my side says, 'There she goes!'

"Gone where? Gone from my sight . . . that is all. She is just as large in mast and hull and spar as she was when she left my side and just as able to bear her load of living freight to the place of destination. Her diminished size is in me, not in her. And just at the moment when someone at my side says, 'There she goes!' there are other eyes watching her coming and other voices ready to take up the glad shout, 'There she comes!' "—Henry Van Dyke, *A Parable of Immortality.*

Questions for Pupils on the Next Lesson. 1. Why do we face the future with such anxiety? 2. Why do some people follow religious leaders who promote false expectations? 3. Do you know persons who substitute talking about the future as substitute for doing something about present needs? 4. Do you agree with Paul that a person is a unity of "spirit and soul and body" (1 Thessalonians 5:23)?

TOPIC FOR YOUTH
FACING BAD TIMES

Another Move! Many German writers have described the sufferings of an ancient folktale character named Dr. Faust, the man who sells his soul to the devil. Artists also have portrayed the famous character. One noted painting shows Faust and the devil playing chess. Faust is seated on one side, and the devil leers across from him. Faust's expression in the picture is filled with hopelessness. He gazes in despair at the chessboard. He has only a king, a knight, and couple of pawns. The devil smirks triumphantly, waiting to conclude the game. Many persons have looked at the picture and agreed that Faust has been checked.

One time, a grand master of chess came to the museum. He looked with interest at the painting and studied Faust's face. Peering at the chessboard, the chess player became entraced with the position of the pieces on the board in the painting. Suddenly, much later, he gave a mighty shout. "It's a lie! It's a lie! The king and the knight have another move!"

God is still the King in our lives. Because of Him, we have another move. We may face bad times. But we always live with the hope that the Lord Jesus Christ brings!

On Good Terms With Hope. "Even the most casual sports fan knows the name of Casey Stengel. Many remember him because his success as manager of the

New York Yankees baseball team stamped him as one of the outstanding heroes in baseball's Hall of Fame. Yet, the years of not winning were more than the years of winning! He knew a lot of defeats. He wound up his professional career (after retirement) managing the New York Mets who set some kind of record for the number of lost ball games in a given season.

"Casual fans may fail to remember that Casey Stengel went through twenty traumatic years between his own playing days and his becoming manager of the winning Yankees. Those were the days he went from pillar to post in the baseball world. He was derided by the press. He was booed by the fans. He was repeatedly fired by the owners of teams with which he was related. In fact, BY (Before Yankees) his main claim to fame was his use of the English language—or his misuse thereof. His fractured syntax led to coining a phrase in the language known as 'Stengelese.'

"When Casey Stengel died, someone who knew him well said that 'always in defeat, Casey was hunting for victory. He was on good terms with hope.'

"Here is no effort to suggest that his being on good terms with hope for Casey had a theological dimension to it—nor is it to imply that it did not have such a dimension. The simple fact is that Casey Stengel was always looking beyond a defeat to the next game which could be a victory. And that's a good lesson for all of us—even outside the baseball field!

"Yet, there are many of us for whom hope is something mired in the halcyon days of yore. We recall those exciting days when hope was high and life was exciting and the future seemed bright. Then hope went out like an extinguished light bulb, and all around was—maybe is—gloom and darkness. Yonder in the 130th Psalm note the despair that marks its early words. Then contrast the final word which shows that this writer was on good terms with hope because he was on good terms with God. So, he said, 'O Israel, hope in the Lord.'

"That's still a good idea for today's hopefuls!"—Hoover Rupert, *Presbyterian-Outlook,* May 1, 1978.

"I Might Have Made It." In 1952, the great long-distance swimmer, Florence Chadwick, plunged into the ocean off Catalina Island to swim to the California coast. Sixteen hours later, discouraged and numb from the cold and fog, she quit. After she was pulled into the boat, she discovered that she was only a mile short of her goal. "If only I could have seen land, I might have made it," she sighed. (She later did succeed.)

Without hope, we give up. When we have evidence for hope, we find that we can make it. Our hope rests on Christ. No matter how bad the times may seem, we plunge on because of our trust in Him!

Questions for Pupils on the Next Lesson. 1. Do your concerns for the future sometimes cause you to want to look at the occult and astrology for answers? 2. How do you respond to those who claim to know exactly when Christ will return and the world will end? 3. Why are most people uneasy about the future? 4. What role does God have in the future? 5. What specific steps are you taking in planning and setting goals for your life?

LESSON XII—NOVEMBER 18

GETTING READY FOR THE LORD'S RETURN

Background Scripture: 1 Thessalonians 5
Devotional Reading: 1 Thessalonians 4:1–12

KING JAMES VERSION

1 THESSALONIANS 5 But of the times and the seasons, brethren, ye have no need that I write unto you.

2 For yourselves know perfectly that the day of the Lord so cometh as a thief in the night.

3 For when they shall say, Peace and safety; then sudden destruction cometh upon them, as travail upon a woman with child; and they shall not escape.

4 But ye, brethren, are not in darkness, that that day should overtake you as a thief.

5 Ye are all the children of light, and the children of the day: we are not of the night, nor of darkness.

6 Therefore let us not sleep, as *do* others; but let us watch and be sober.

7 For they that sleep sleep in the night; and they that be drunken are drunken in the night.

8 But let us, who are of the day, be sober, putting on the breastplate of faith and love; and for an helmet, the hope of salvation.

9 For God hath not appointed us to wrath, but to obtain salvation by our Lord Jesus Christ,

10 Who died for us, that, whether we wake or sleep, we should live together with him.

11 Wherefore comfort yourselves together, and edify one another, even as also ye do.

12 And we beseech you, brethren, to know them which labour among you, and are over you in the Lord, and admonish you;

13 And to esteem them very highly in love for their work's sake. *And* be at peace among yourselves.

14 Now we exhort you, brethren, warn them that are unruly, comfort the feebleminded, support the weak, be patient toward all *men*.

15 See that none render evil for evil unto any *man*; but ever follow that which is good, both among yourselves, and to all *men*.

16 Rejoice evermore.

17 Pray without ceasing.

18 In every thing give thanks: for this is the will of God in Christ Jesus concerning you.

19 Quench not the Spirit.

20 Despise not prophesyings.

21 Prove all things; hold fast that which is good.

22 Abstain from all appearance of evil.

23 And the very God of peace sanctify you wholly; and *I pray God* your whole spirit and soul and body be preserved blameless unto the coming of our Lord Jesus Christ.

REVISED STANDARD VERSION

1 THESSALONIANS 5 But as to the times and the seasons, brethren, you have no need to have anything written to you. 2 For you yourselves know well that the day of the Lord will come like a thief in the night. 3 When people say, "There is peace and security," then sudden destruction will come upon them as travail comes upon a woman with child, and there will be no escape. 4 But you are not in darkness, brethren, for that day to surprise you like a thief. 5 For you are all sons of light and sons of the day; we are not of the night or of darkness. 6 So then let us not sleep, as others do, but let us keep awake and be sober. 7 For those who sleep sleep at night, and those who get drunk are drunk at night. 8 But, since we belong to the day, let us be sober, and put on the breastplate of faith and love, and for a helmet the hope of salvation. 9 For God has not destined us for wrath, but to obtain salvation through our Lord Jesus Christ, 10 who died for us so that whether we wake or sleep we might live with him. 11 Therefore encourage one another and build one another up, just as you are doing.

12 But we beseech you, brethren, to respect those who labor among you and are over you in the Lord and admonish you, 13 and to esteem them very highly in love because of their work. Be at peace among yourselves. 14 And we exhort you, brethren, admonish the idle, encourage the fainthearted, help the weak, be patient with them all.

15 See that none of you repays evil for evil, but always seek to do good to one another and to all. 16 Rejoice always, 17 pray constantly, 18 give thanks in all circumstances; for this is the will of God in Christ Jesus for you. 19 Do not quench the Spirit, 20 do not despise prophesying, 21 but test everything; hold fast what is good, 22 abstain from every form of evil.

23 May the God of peace himself sanctify you wholly; and may your spirit and soul and body be kept sound and blameless at the coming of our Lord Jesus Christ.

KEY VERSE: May the God of peace himself sanctify you wholly; and may your spirit and soul and body be kept sound and blameless at the coming of our Lord Jesus Christ. 1 Thessalonians 5:23 (RSV).

HOME DAILY BIBLE READINGS

Nov.	12.	M.	*Jesus Will Be Rejected.* Luke 17:20–25.
Nov.	13.	T.	*Normal Living Interrupted.* Luke 17:26–36.
Nov.	14.	W.	*All Will See the Second Coming.* Luke 20:9–18.
Nov.	15.	T.	*The Last Judgment.* 2 Peter 3:1–10.
Nov.	16.	F.	*The Promise of a New Heaven and Earth.* 2 Peter 3:11–18.
Nov.	17.	S.	*Work and Live Diligently.* 1 Thessalonians 5:1–11.
Nov.	18.	S.	*Instructions While Waiting for the End.* 1 Thessalonians 5:12–24.

BACKGROUND

The Old Testament often speaks of the Day of the Lord. Isaiah, Jeremiah, Amos, Joel, Zephaniah, and Malachi all refer to a time when God would conclude the present wicked age and inaugurate a new glorious era of God's rule. The Day of the Lord was always said as coming without warning. Furthermore, it was described in terms of terrible natural disasters, such as shattering earthquakes, the failure of the sun's light, stars and planets plunging from the sky. A time of sifting and judgment would follow. These Old Testament passages follow a style and a language known as "apocalyptic literature." They were not intended to be taken literally but were poetic and dramatic ways of stating that God runs this universe and history has a direction and purpose.

The earliest Christians, of course, were all Jews, and took their Jewish thinking with them when they were baptized as Christ's. They also expected Jesus' return. It was natural for them to use familiar Old Testament terminology to describe Jesus' coming again. Some even spoke of His return as the "Day of the Lord." Paul did in 1 Thessalonians. These early believers also were comfortable with the rich imagery of the Day of the Lord, whereas we moderns find the language puzzling and even disconcerting. Our problem is that we try to read these passages in a flat, literalistic way, and find that they seem to be at variance with modern astronomy and physics.

The new Christians at Thessalonica had heard Paul say that Jesus would return. Apparently, some of these people didn't hear anything more, and became so excited over Jesus' return that they gave up working and upset everyone by waiting for Jesus' early coming. Most had been Jews and used their Jewish notions of the Day of the Lord to tell about what to them was the only thing about Jesus Christ that was important. Paul's first letter to the Thessalonians was directed at these people whose entire theology seemed to revolve around the imminent return of Jesus in the Day of the Lord.

NOTES ON THE PRINTED TEXT

I. *But as to the times and seasons:* The Thessalonian Christians had a near obsession with wanting to know about the hour and day of Jesus' return. Many people still do. Some insist upon announcing the date and time, although Jesus Himself had plainly warned that no one knew when that hour and day would be. Jesus stated that even He did not know, and that only God had the knowledge. Paul reminds his friends at Thessalonica that they should already know this, and "you have no need to have anything written to you" on this matter.

II. *The day of the Lord will come like a thief in the night:* Paul uses an Old Testament buzz word when he speaks of "the day of the Lord." His readers knew what he meant. Paul uses the common terms for the cataclysmic wrapup of all history immediately preceding Christ's return, based on passages familiar to Jews, especially passages such as Zephaniah 1:2–18. Paul is not concerned about the details. In fact, he regards these as minor. What he wants to get across is that Christ's coming is not to be pinpointed on the calendar. Like the unexpected intrusion of a robber, the return of Jesus will catch everyone by surprise.

III. *So then let us not sleep, as others do, but let us keep awake and be sober:* To those who are standing around peering into the sky and worrying about the day and the hour, Paul bluntly tells them to live responsibly and watchfully. Likewise to those who fall into the opposite viewpoint, imagining that life is going nowhere and there's no need ever to concern oneself about facing Christ again, Paul reminds them to stay on the alert.

For you are all sons of light . . . . Since we belong to the day, let us be sober: Jesus repeatedly spoke of His people being "in the light" and "children of light." Even baptism in the early Church was spoken of as "enlightenment." The theme of light is brought up here also. *Sober* does not refer only to avoid getting drunk but, more, be in your most sober senses, that is to be completely alert. That means being alert to the whispers of the Spirit of Jesus Christ, alert to the cries of distress from others, and alert to what God is bringing to pass in human history.

Put on the breastplate of faith and love, and for a helmet the hope of salvation: Paul obviously had watched Roman legionnaires buckle on their battle gear, and tells Christians that they must gird up for fight to be victorious as Christ's. These lines follow up the previous words about being sober or constantly alert. The only way that a believer can do this is to stand by at his or her battle station, equipped for action at a moment's notice. The equipment of a Christian means the familiar faith, love, and hope, the three greatest gifts and most powerful weapons.

IV. *For God has not destined us for wrath, but to obtain salvation through our Lord Jesus Christ:* Paul reminds his hearers that God's intentions for His people are gracious. God is not an angry cosmic despot plotting to consign His people to perpetual torture. His design for us who know Jesus is to have "wholeness"—the literal meaning of the word *salvation.*

Paul proceeds to spell out the consequences for those who realize that God's plans for us are always kindly.

Whether we wake or sleep, we might live with him: If we are alive here on earth when Jesus returns or if we have already passed into dust, we cannot be separated from His concern and presence! In life and death, Jesus continues to stand with us!

Therefore, encourage one another and build one another up: Because God has destined the Thessalonian Christians for salvation, not wrath, Paul next urges them to help each other to grow stronger in the faith. He uses a word from the construction trade when he tells them to "build one another up," meaning to help each construct a sturdy "house" or life in the faith. Every Christian has a duty to be a builder of faith for every other Christian. Each congregation is meant to foster ways whereby this mutual upbuilding can take place.

SUGGESTIONS TO TEACHERS

On the night of October 22, 1844, thousands gathered on hilltops expecting the Second Coming of Jesus Christ to occur. Many had sold or given away houses, businesses, and possessions, not expecting to need them again. Convinced by the calculations of a farmer-turned-preacher named William Miller, they eagerly waited throughout that chilly night. By morning, many had caught colds and most felt disillusioned. The date became known as "the Great Disappointment."

October 22, 1844 was only one of literally dozens of dates selected for the Lord's Return by sincere Bible readers. Dates are being put forward by zealous souls these days—1984, 1985, 1990, 2000, and many others. Many of your class members have heard these dates. Some in your class are uneasy, while others are uncertain how to react. Your lesson on getting ready for the Lord's return should prove helpful to everyone.

1. *SECRET SURPRISE.* The problem with most of the datefixers for the Lord's return is that they do not take Scripture seriously enough or don't know their Bibles well enough. Paul bluntly warns anyone who presumes to announce the hour and day of Christ's return in 1 Thessalonians 5:1–5. The times and seasons are secret information in God's files and not available to prying human minds. Paul warns his hearers to be ready for surprises. You as the class teacher may wish to give some opportunity for your people to share some of their previously unshared anxieties about the Lord's Return picked up from television revivalists or tracts. Assure them that even Paul refused to fix a date.

2. *ALERT ATTITUDE.* Paul warns us to "keep awake and be sober" (5:6). Christians must live in state of readiness for the Lord's Return without either a date on one hand or drowsiness on the other. Note the military language Paul uses. Like a Roman soldier putting on his battle gear, strapping on a breastplate and adjusting his helmet, each Christian must stand by in a state of readiness for action. It's always "Battle Stations!" for believers! Remind your class that when Christians let down their guard, evil rushes in.

3. *UNCEASING ENCOURAGEMENT.* "Encourage one another and build one another up," Paul implores (5:11). Is your church doing that? How can your class build better morale and instill deeper courage? Perhaps you may wish to divide the class into subsections, and allow members in small groups to take some time to share together areas where each needs encouragement in daily living.

4. *PERPETUAL PRAYER.* Finally, do not let the verses on praying be a minor postscript at the end of this lesson. "Pray constantly," Paul insists (5:17). Lead your folks into a discussion on the necessity of prayer, especially prayers in which you all "give thanks in all circumstances." Ask if your class members' prayers are heavily expressions of gratitude!

TOPIC FOR ADULTS
GETTING READY FOR THE LORD'S RETURN

Building to Dispel Panic. As the year A.D. 1000 approached, many people became frightened that the world would come to an end and some terrible disaster would follow. Rumors were passed from one village to another about imagined horrors as the date grew nearer. Finally, some stalwart Christians in Staffordshire, England, decided to reassure the populace that panic was not Christian, and, that even if Christ returned at the time, preparedness was better. These believers did more than talk. They built. The lovely Abbey of Burton was erected at that time, and it was built expressly to reassure people that the world was not going to end and Christ's return was a time of hopeless doom.

How are you living when rumors of a speedy end reach your ears? Are you giving way to panic, or are you living a life of positive preparedness?

Doomsday Vigil. A group of ninety people led by a preacher named Jim Ellison have concluded that times are so bad that there is no hope for them or the country. They have fled to a remote area of the Arkansas Ozarks and founded a settlement called Zaraphath-Horeb, a name taken from the Bible. They are a band of Scripture-quoting, gun-toting Christian survivalists who have set their sights on doomsday.

In the mountain hollows, cedar barrens, and underbrush, they are getting ready for the anarchic hour when society collapses and the woods are alive with looters looking for food.

They live in trailers and homes built by hand on 220 acres near Bull Shoals Lake in northern Arkansas. With faith in God and guns, they are prepared to save their way of life from the chaos they think is coming soon.

On the shoulder of a southern Missouri country road, the battered mailbox identifies them as "The Covenant, the Sword, the Arm of the Lord." An arrow points south down two winding miles of rocks and ruts past the trees, a dry riverbed, and the Arkansas border.

"God, in the beginning, told us to come here and establish a place of refuge," said Mr. Ellison.

"God set us up as an ark so when something happens we can come here."

Like the others, he stockpiles guns and bullets with his beans and peanut butter. He will not say how many weapons or how much ammunition are on hand. That would give attackers an edge. But, he said, they could hold off an army on ten minutes notice.

When the collapse comes, "We will share what we have to the best of our ability." What will happen when people come to take? "We'll kill them—it's real simple," he said. "It's us or them in that situation."

To prepare, the leaders meet twice weekly for military training.

The Queen and the Umbrella. "It is told that Victoria, the Queen of England, when staying at her summer residence, Balmoral, likes to take long walks through the woods in simple clothes, and has pleasure in remaining unknown. Some years ago, she was caught in a heavy rainstorm while on one of these trips.

"Noticing an old cottage, she ran towards it for refuge. In this cottage lived an old peasant woman alone, who left her house only to take care of her goat and tend her small garden.

"The Queen greeted her and kindly asked if she could borrow an umbrella. She added that she would take care to have it returned soon to its owner. The old woman had never seen the Queen, and so she had no idea who she could be.

"Therefore, she answered in a grudging tone, 'Well, I have two umbrellas. One is very good and almost new. I have used it very little. The other one is very worn and has had its time. You may take the old one; the new one I don't lend to anybody—for who knows whether I would ever get it back?' With these words, she gave the Queen the old umbrella, which was torn and battered with spokes sticking out on all sides.

"The Queen thought, with this kind of weather, a bad umbrella is better than nothing at all, and accepted it politely. Thanking the woman, she left smiling.

"But how great was the horror of the poor old woman, when the next morning, a servant in royal livery entered and returned to her the old umbrella in the name of Queen Victoria—with her thanks—and the assurance that Her majesty had received good service from it! How sorry she was that she had not offered to the Queen the very best she had, and over and over she cried out, 'If only I had known! Oh, if only I would have known!' "—Corrie Ten Boom, *Corrie's Christmas Memories,* New Jersey: Fleming H. Revell Company.

Questions for Pupils on the Next Lesson. 1. What are the "traditions" which Paul refers to in 2 Thessalonians 2:15 which Paul urges his readers to hold on to? 2. What are the effects of pride and arrogance in a person's life? 3. What are some recent instances of adults being led astray by authoritarian leaders? 4. What values support you in your life struggles? 5. How does a Christian cope with life's uncertainties?

TOPIC FOR YOUTH
GETTING READY

Faulty Readings. You have undoubtedly heard of some sincere Christians who try to tell you that they have figured out when the Lord is going to return by delving into Scripture. Some of these in recent times claim they have determined the date. For example, some exponents of biblical prophecy are preaching that the European Economic Community—the Common Market of Western Europe—is the beast with seven heads and ten horns prophesied in the Book of Revelation, and that Antichrist will emerge from it.

Those of similar views are preaching millenarianism, the belief that Jesus Christ will return to earth and reign for 1,000 years. This reign of peace would follow a time of wars, ending with the defeat of Antichrist.

Millenarians base this prophecy on a series of passages in the Bible, beginning with the books of Ezekiel and Daniel.

Jesus Himself as well as Paul warns against trying to set a time for Jesus' return. Furthermore, when we read the Bible, we must remember the context in which it was written, and it is not a cryptic message about the European Economic Community but an open message to Christ's people.

Near Thing. When John Hinckley opened fire in his assassination attempt on President Reagan in March, 1981, some interpreted it in apocalyptic terms. In Whitehall, Pennsylvania, a group of high-school boys in gym weight lifting room were stunned when the news was flashed over the radio. One student dropped the barbells. Mark Walsh, another one of the Whitehall weightlifters, believed the Reagan assassination attempt had religious overtones. "It may be a sign of the devil," he opined. "It's written in the Bible." Nobody thought to ask where in the Bible Mark thought this was written (it isn't anywhere) but several agreed that it must mean that the Lord was coming soon.

We must be cautious about thinking that every catastrophe is a prelude for the Lord's return. Instead of trying to read into disastrous events or misread the Bible, it would be better to live in a state of constant readiness. This is what Paul advocates in the New Testament, and what mature Christians have been doing for nearly 2,000 years.

New Denomination. Students at the university at Berkeley, California, are asked to specify their religious preferences. Recently, one filled in the card that his denomination was Frisbeterianism. The chaplains and administration puzzled over this entry. Finally, some wag suggested that Frisbeterianism is the belief that when you die, your soul goes up on the roof and no one can get it down!

Amusing, true. Yet many young persons have such a fuzzy notion of what happens when a person dies.

Examine today's Scripture for the clearly-written hope that Christians have for their loved ones and themselves when death comes.

Questions for Pupils on the Next Lesson. 1. Why are we sometimes misled by attractive, self-glorifying leaders? 2. Where do you look for positive adult models? 3. In pressing life issues, why do we sometimes make an effort to avoid reality? 4. What values support you when you are in a time of turmoil? 5. How has your faith helped you to hold on to God's truth when you've been tempted to go along with destructive ideas?

LESSON XIII—NOVEMBER 25

HOLDING ON TO THE TRUTH

Background Scripture: 2 Thessalonians 1–3
Devotional Reading: 2 Thessalonians 3:1–15

KING JAMES VERSION

2 THESSALONIANS 2 Now we beseech you, brethren, by the coming of our Lord Jesus Christ, and *by* our gathering together unto him,

2 That ye be not soon shaken in mind, or be troubled, neither by spirit, nor by word, nor by letter as from us, as that the day of Christ is at hand.

3 Let no man deceive you by any means: for *that day shall not come,* except there come a falling away first, and that man of sin be revealed, the son of perdition;

4 Who opposeth and exalteth himself above all that is called God, or that is worshipped; so that he as God sitteth in the temple of God, showing himself that he is God.

5 Remember ye not, that, when I was yet with you, I told you these things?

6 And now ye know what withholdeth that he might be revealed in his time.

7 For the mystery of iniquity doth already work: only he who now letteth *will let,* until he be taken out of the way.

8 And then shall that Wicked be revealed, whom the Lord shall consume with the spirit of his mouth, and shall destroy with the brightness of his coming:

9 *Even him,* whose coming is after the working of Satan with all power and signs and lying wonders,

10 And with all deceivableness of unrighteousness in them that perish; because they received not the love of the truth, that they might be saved.

11 And for this cause God shall send them strong delusion, that they should believe a lie:

12 That they all might be damned who believed not the truth, but had pleasure in unrighteousness.

13 But we are bound to give thanks alway to God for you, brethren beloved of the Lord, because God hath from the beginning chosen you to salvation through sanctification of the Spirit and belief of the truth:

14 Whereunto he called you by our gospel, to the obtaining of the glory of our Lord Jesus Christ.

15 Therefore, brethren, stand fast, and hold the traditions which ye have been taught, whether by word, or our epistle.

REVISED STANDARD VERSION

2 THESSALONIANS 2 Now concerning the coming of our Lord Jesus Christ and our assembling to meet him, we beg you, brethren, 2 not to be quickly shaken in mind or excited, either by spirit or by word, or by letter purporting to be from us, to the effect that the day of the Lord has come. 3 Let no one deceive you in any way; for that day will not come, unless the rebellion comes first, and the man of lawlessness is revealed, the son of perdition, 4 who opposes and exalts himself against every so-called god or object of worship, so that he takes his seat in the temple of God, proclaiming himself to be God. 5 Do you not remember that when I was still with you I told you this? 6 And you know what is restraining him now so that he may be revealed in his time. 7 For the mystery of lawlessness is already at work; only he who now restrains it will do so until he is out of the way. 8 And then the lawless one will be revealed, and the Lord Jesus will slay him with the breath of his mouth and destroy him by his appearing and his coming. 9 The coming of the lawless one by the activity of Satan will be with all power and with pretended signs and wonders, 10 and with all wicked deception for those who are to perish, because they refused to love the truth and so be saved. 11 Therefore God sends upon them a strong delusion, to make them believe what is false, 12 so that all may be condemned who did not believe the truth but had pleasure in unrighteousness.

13 But we are bound to give thanks to God always for you, brethren beloved by the Lord, because God chose you from the beginning to be saved, through sanctification by the Spirit and belief in the truth. 14 To this he called you through our gospel, so that you may obtain the glory of our Lord Jesus Christ. 15 So then, brethren, stand firm and hold to the traditions which you were taught by us, either by word of mouth or by letter.

KEY VERSE: Stand firm and hold to the traditions which you were taught by us, either by word of mouth or by letter. 2 Thessalonians 2:15 (RSV).

HOME DAILY BIBLE READINGS

Nov. 19. M. *Hope in the Living God.* 1 Timothy 4:1–10.
Nov. 20. T. *Hold to the Truth.* 1 Timothy 4:11–16.
Nov. 21. W. *Endure Hardship for Christ.* 2 Timothy 2:1–10.
Nov. 22. T. *Don't Neglect the Scriptures.* 2 Timothy 3:10–17.
Nov. 23. F. *A Warning About False Gods.* 2 Thessalonians 2:1–5.
Nov. 24. S. *Be Confident in God's Call.* 2 Thessalonians 2:13–16.
Nov. 25. S. *Parting Admonition and Prayer.* 2 Thessalonians 3:1–5.

BACKGROUND

Letter number one to the Thessalonian Christians had been carefully prepared. Paul had sent it with the hope that it would quiet the people in the Thessalonica church who were so unsettled over when Jesus would return.

To Paul's dismay, reports came back that the problems in that church continued. Some of the church members were almost hysterically upset over the question of Jesus' speedy coming. Some were even accusing Paul of saying that the Second Coming had already occurred. Apparently, the evangelistic mission of the Thessalonian congregation had almost come to a standstill because so much of their energy was given over to debating and worrying about the time of the return of Jesus.

Therefore, Paul was constrained to write a follow-up letter to his first one. He pleads with the Thessalonians to be calm, to keep busy, to remain faithful to Jesus Christ, to persist in doing good to others. He also tried to clarify his previous words about the Coming of Jesus. He denies that he stated that Jesus had already returned. In trying to clarify his position, Paul states that there still must take place the final cosmic battle between the Lord and the forces of evil, ending the warfare between God and the destructive powers once and for all. Only then, says Paul, only after this final rebellion by evil incarnate in what Paul calls "the lawless one" will the complete triumph of God prevail.

Modern readers frequently have problems understanding this passage. Some try to use it as a Guide Book for the hereafter. Others attempt to set a schedule for Christ's return from these verses and others. Throughout this letter, however, Paul is making the point that human affairs, indeed all of cosmic history, are in God's hands. The universe has not slipped from the Creator's grasp, is not rolling out of control. Although destructive, evil forces appear to be overwhelming, God will eventually check these. Then Christ's return will take place.

NOTES ON THE PRINTED TEXT

I. *Now concerning the coming of our Lord Jesus Christ and our assembling to meet him, we beg you, brethren, not to be quickly shaken in mind or excited, either by spirit or by word, or by letter purporting to be from us, to the effect that the Lord has come.* The Thessalonian church members had become so stirred up over Christ's imminent return that they were ready to believe any rumor that the great day had come. Apparently, someone had even spread a false report that Paul had said that the Lord had arrived. Paul pleads with these nervous, excitable church members to calm themselves because the Lord has not yet come. They have not missed Him.

To reassure them that the Lord has not arrived, Paul states that a lot of history has yet to be played out before Christ will come.

... for that day will not come, unless the rebellion comes first, and the man of lawlessness is revealed, the son of perdition, who opposes and exalts himself against every so-called god or object of worship, so that he takes his seat in the temple of God, proclaiming himself to be God. Do you not remember that when I was still with you I told you this? This is puzzling and difficult for us. However, it

was not for Paul's listeners. Before we get annoyed because these verses don't make much sense to us, consider what Paul and his hearers were understanding from these words.

Words are a kind of code, and must not be taken so much at face value as for what they are encoding. For example, when we speak of the four corners of the earth, we don't literally mean that the earth is a gigantic cube. Rather, when this phrase is "decoded" it means that we are merely referring to every part of this planet. Now when Paul was writing about the lawless one, he was using the code word for the power of evil which nearly everyone used. The incarnation and personification of all the terrible destructive forces in the universe was still pitted against God. The "Day of the Lord" would be the occasion when evil would finally be vanquished by God. Meanwhile, the battle was not over. Through Christ's triumph over sin and death, Christians knew the final outcome would be total victory for God over all the dark, satanic opposition.

Other New Testament writers expressed this same idea in different ways. The writer of 1 John 2:18,22, for example, refers to this personification of evil as the "Antichrist." The book of Revelation likewise humanizes these powers under the name "Satan."Regardless of the name given to the superhuman powers of evil at work in the world by various early Christians, they all agreed on the basics: (1) These forces are destructive, must be taken seriously, and are more powerful than any human or group of humans can withstand; (2) God ultimately will deal with these raging powers; (3) Jesus will come and reign as undisputed Lord.

The activity of Satan will be with all power and with pretended signs and wonders, and with all wicked deception: Early Christians sometimes spoke of the devil as "the father of lies." In Revelation 12:9, he is described as "the deceiver of the whole world." Paul wants his friends at Thessalonica not to underestimate the cleverness of the evil one in trying to persuade people to reject the truth about God and cling to falsehood. The devil still cunningly spreads his propaganda. We Christians are still apt to get taken in by his arguments and deceitful reports. Martin Luther took the lying work of the evil one so seriously that he denounced him for trying to dissuade him from trusting in the Gospel. Read Luther's, "A Mighty Fortress Is Our God!" Once, Luther even hurled an inkwell in his anger at the way the devil was trying to bait him to go along with his lies! Christians, Paul pleads, must cling to Jesus Christ, who is the way, the *truth,* and the life!

Stand firm and hold to the traditions which you were taught. Realize that, "God chose you," Paul implores. And stand firm! The Greek word means to *persevere!* Persist in holding on to the truth, Paul commands.

SUGGESTIONS TO TEACHERS

A sixteen-year-old girl had a "born again" experience, and exuberantly bubbled about how joyful her new-found faith made her feel. Six months later, she quit attending church services. Some of her Christian friends found her morose and somewhat bitter. "I thought that when I became a Christian, everything was supposed to go nicely," she muttered.

No, when we become Christians, that does not mean that God makes everything go nicely for us. Let's say it plainly. Signing up for Jesus does not mean He's signing on as our bodyguard. Taking a stand for the Lord does not mean God has contracted to protect us from hurts or harm.

Your lesson takes up the subject of holding on to the Truth in spite of rough times. Two Thessalonians 1–3 furnishes you with deep insights for this lesson.

1. *PATIENT WHEN PERSECUTED.* At first hearing, your people may think that this passage is relevant only for those in the Soviet Union or Iron Curtain countries where Christians suffer threats and imprisonment. Without denying

this fact, you should also help your class members to be aware of the subtle ways believers in our culture may feel persecuted for Christ's sake. What about the college woman who refuses to go along with the prevailing permissive ideas about premarital sex because of her Christian convictions and feels ostracized? What about the salesperson who faces loss of job because he won't fudge on his expense account to come up with funds for an expensive "gift" demanded by the boss from all the salespeople? Christians, however, may stand steadfast in such times, remembering that God ultimately settles the scores with persecutors.

2. *PRUDENT WHEN PRESSURED.* Second Thessalonians 2 deals with the times when false reports come that the "Day of the Lord has come" (2:2) and "pretended signs and wonders" and "wicked deception" (2:10,11) take place. Paul pleads with those in Thessalonica not to be "shaken in mind or excited, either by spirit or by word, or by letter . . . to the effect the day of the Lord has come" (2:2). Fake prophets and phony prophecies are around today, too. Some of those in your class probably feel pressured to take these seriously. Remind them to hold on to the truth in Jesus Christ.

3. *PERSUADED AND PERFECTED.* Take some minutes to impress on your class the claim in 2 Thessalonians 2:13,14: "God chose you . . . to be saved. . . . He called you." The Spirit, Paul insists, is sanctifying us. That is, He is persuading us and perfecting us who belong to Christ. He guards us from evil. How do your people respond to the statement that they have been chosen by the Lord to be strengthened for His work?

4. *PERSISTENT WHEN PERPLEXED.* Some in your class as well as many in the community say, "What's the use? Life's so pointless." Agreed, these are difficult times. However, Christians do not remain idle. Just because the going is hard does not mean believers have an excuse to drop out. Let your class members confess the times when they are tempted to give up and quit on the human scene. But also have them share the ways in which Christ galvanized them to keep going! He helps us to persist because we know He is the truth!

TOPIC FOR ADULTS
HOLDING ON TO THE TRUTH

Clung to God's Truth. Hugh Latimer is known as the greatest preacher of the English Reformation. He was often asked to speak before King Henry VIII and King Edward VI. He was a man who showed great courage and faith.

Latimer was made chaplain to King Henry VIII. He struggled to be faithful and uncompromising in his proclamation before the King.

Latimer resolved to declare God's truth even if it cost him his life. Latimer was direct in confronting the King. King Henry kept a large number of horses in abbeys originally founded for the support of the poor. In a sermon, Latimer said to Henry VIII:

> "A prince ought not to prefer his horses above poor men. Abbeys were ordained for the comfort of the poor, and not for the kings' horses to be kept in them."

Some were angry at Latimer. Later at a reception, a monk came up to the King and said, "Sire, your new chaplain preaches sedition." Henry turned to Latimer, "What do you say to that, sir?" Latimer said to his accuser, "Would you have me preach nothing concerning a king in a king's sermon. . . ?" Then he turned to the King and said:

> "Your Grace, I put myself in your hands: appoint other doctors to preach in my place before your majesty. There are many more worthy of the room

than I am. If it be your Grace's pleasure, I could be content to be their servant and bear their books after them. But if your Grace allows me for a preacher, I would desire you give me leave to discharge my conscience. Permit me to frame my teaching for my audience."

Henry liked Latimer and remained on his side. When Latimer left the reception, his friends came up to him with tears in their eyes saying, "We were convinced you would sleep tonight in the tower." Latimer replied, "The king's heart is . . . in the hand of the Lord" (Proverbs 21:1).

When Queen Mary came into power, Latimer was one of the first church leaders imprisoned in the tower. For two years, he remained a prisoner. During that time, he read the New Testament through seven times. Finally on October 16, 1555, Latimer was burned alive along with Bishop Ridley (perhaps the ablest scholar of that time). They were chained to the stake. When the fire was lit, Latimer said to Ridley, "Be of good comfort, Brother Ridley, and play the man; we shall this day light a candle by God's grace, in England as I trust shall never be put out."

Night Shift. "Bishop Quail, once told how, one night he stayed up late in his study; his whole life freighted with problems—seemingly unsolvable problems. By chance his eye fell on an open Bible on his desk, when these words lept out and hit him. . . 'He who keeps Israel will not slumber or sleep.' Then, the Bishop goes on to report, he imagined God spoke to him, saying, 'My dear anxious Bishop Quail, there is no need for both of us to stay up all night. I shall be on duty. Why don't you go to bed and get a good night's rest, and leave the world to me.'

"Quail reported that he strengthened to hold on to the Truth by remembering that the Lord was standing by his bedside while Quail slept.

"Thomas Merton, one of the great spiritual leaders of our time, was a monk at the Gethsemane Abbey in a rural area of Kentucky but one of the most deeply involved persons in the crises of our time after World War II. He learned many lessons from his life of disciplined prayer. Among these was how to hold on to the truth. It meant a sense of humility about himself and an awareness of his dependence on others.

" 'Coming to the monastery has been for me exactly the right kind of withdrawal. It has given me perspective. It has taught me how to live. And now I owe everyone else in the world a share in that life. My first duty is to start, for the first time, to live as a member of a human race which is no more (and no less) ridiculous than I am myself. And my first human act is the recognition of how much I owe everybody else.' "—From p. 120 in *Thomas Merton: Contemplative Critic* by Henri J. M. Nouwen. Copyright © 1972, 1981 by Henri J. M. Nouwen. By permission of Harper & Row, Publishers, Inc.

Questions for Pupils on the Next Lesson. 1. How has Scripture served to illumine your life and equip you for good works? 2. Is the Law or instruction in the Bible meant to be a burden or a source of delight? 3. Where do you turn to find valid and enduring norms in these times of change and tension? 4. How can the tradition of groups you belong to be a positive framework of meaning in life? 5. As a Christian, how do you take seriously your role of instructing others?

TOPIC FOR YOUTH
HOLD TO THE TRUTH

God Helps You Hold to the Truth. Admiral Jeremiah Denton of the USN spent several years in the hell of a communist prison in North Vietnam—much of the time being tortured and in solitary confinement. At the time, he had the rank of commander.

In his tiny cell, there was only one book, a book of communist propaganda. By code signals and tapping he could exchange a few words with fellow prisoners. A tiny window, high in the room, did not permit him to see out but it gave a little air and at times a dim light, and he could hear some of the prison activities through it. By these means, he set about making entries in the middle of the book to keep a record of new arrivals in the prison. In the book, too, he kept a precious symbol of his faith: a cross, skillfully woven from bamboo broom strips, a gift made and smuggled to him at great risk by a fellow prisoner.

One day his record of the prisoners was discovered. There was fury as he was hauled from his cell and civilian workmen were brought to brick up almost the whole of his tiny window. He says that he didn't much mind the list being discovered for it would make the communists realise that there were those who knew the names and numbers of prisoners. He was utterly devastated however when the propaganda book was searched and his little cross was discovered. With fierce anger the North Vietnamese officer flung it on the ground and pounded it to nothing with his boot. Denton said that in that moment it seemed his last tangible link with hope and faith were gone, and he felt indescribably bereft. Then he was pushed back into the cell, and the propaganda book replaced.

A little later he thumbed through its pages and there, hidden in it, was another exquisitely woven little bamboo cross! To this day he has no idea how it got there!

Example of Those Holding to the Truth. Death struck quite hard among the Mayflower crew, carrying off half of the sailors, three of the mates, the master gunner, the bosun, and the cook. Many of these, the Pilgrims felt, deserved their fate especially the bosun, a "prowd yonge man," who used to "curse and scofe at ye passengers." When Bradford was ill and pleaded for some beer, the bosun and others mocked him and swore that "if he were their owne father, he should have none." When Captain Jones heard of this, he intervened and promised "beere for them that had need of it" even though he was left with none for the voyage home. In the end, the Saints softened even the hard heart of the bosun, caring for him in his illness after he had been deserted by his "boone companions in drinking a joyllity." The villain repented and publicly acknowledged his sins, but too late!

"O!" he confessed on his deathbed, "you, I now see, show your love like Christians indeed one to another, but we let another lye and dye like doggs."

Disney World Religion. Millions of visitors crowd into Disney World each year to enjoy the magic kingdom of America's most famous theme park. Lifelike full-size figures of Presidents come alive on Lincoln Square. A ghost moves eerily in the haunted house. Partying pirates laugh and sing, and screaming monsters roll their heads. No garbage cans are found behind the restaurants, and no trash trucks ever rumble through the streets. Computers hooked into hundreds of tape machines and underground tunnels to transport food and rubbish are part of the "total fantasy" of the operation. Tony Altobelli, of the Disney World public relations staff, states, "When people come here, we don't want them reminded of the outside world. The one thing the public does not want is reminders of the outside world." The Disney World staff succeed in doing that to a remarkable degree.

Many also wish their church would not remind them of the outside world. Some church members would welcome a Disney takeover of theology and worship to banish any concerns for sacrificing for others or heeding the cries of the hungry. Lamentably, some leaders are around who offer a Disney World religion.

Christians are called to hold to the truth of Jesus Christ, even when it costs and hurts! We may not live with a fantasy faith.

Questions for Pupils on the Next Lesson. 1. Are there values to limits, restrictions, and laws in life? 2. Has learning ever been an exciting experience for you? 3. Why do you sometimes react negatively to authority figures? 4. How did God guide writers of Scripture? 5. What has the Bible meant to you?

DECEMBER, 1984—
FEBRUARY, 1985

WHAT THE BIBLE IS (3 SESSIONS)

LESSON I—DECEMBER 2

A SOURCE OF INSTRUCTION

Background Scripture: Psalms 119:97–105; 1 Corinthians 2; 2 Timothy 3
Devotional Reading: 1 Corinthians 2:6–16

KING JAMES VERSION	REVISED STANDARD VERSION
PSALMS 119 97 O how love I thy law! it *is* my meditation all the day.	PSALMS 119 97 Oh, how I love thy law! It is my meditation all the day.
98 Thou through thy commandments hast made me wiser than mine enemies: for they *are* ever with me.	98 Thy commandment makes me wiser than my enemies, for it is ever with me.
99 I have more understanding than all my teachers: for thy testimonies *are* my meditation.	99 I have more understanding than all my teachers, for thy testimonies are my meditation.
100 I understand more than the ancients, because I keep thy precepts.	100 I understand more than the aged, for I keep thy precepts.
101 I have refrained my feet from every evil way, that I might keep thy word.	101 I hold back my feet from every evil way, in order to keep thy word.
102 I have not departed from thy judgments: for thou hast taught me.	102 I do not turn aside from thy ordinances, for thou hast taught me.
103 How sweet are thy words unto my taste! *yea, sweeter* than honey to my mouth!	103 How sweet are thy words to my taste, sweeter than honey to my mouth!
104 Through thy precepts I get understanding: therefore I hate every false way.	104 Through thy precepts I get understanding; therefore I hate every false way.
105 Thy word *is* a lamp unto my feet, and a light unto my path.	105 Thy word is a lamp to my feet and a light to my path.
2 TIMOTHY 3 14 But continue thou in the things which thou hast learned and hast been assured of, knowing of whom thou hast learned *them;*	2 TIMOTHY 3 14 But as for you, continue in what you have learned and have firmly believed, knowing from whom you learned it 15 and how from childhood you have been ac-
15 And that from a child thou hast known the holy scriptures, which are able to make thee wise unto salvation through faith which is in Christ Jesus.	quainted with the sacred writings which are able to instruct you for salvation through faith in Christ Jesus. 16 All scripture is inspired by God and profitable for teaching, for reproof, for
16 All scripture *is* given by inspiration of God, and *is* profitable for doctrine, for reproof, for correction, for instruction in righteousness:	correction, and for training in righteousness, 17 that the man of God may be complete, equipped for every good work.
17 That the man of God may be perfect, throughly furnished unto all good works.	

KEY VERSE: Thy word is a lamp to my feet and a light to my path. Psalms 119:105 (RSV).

HOME DAILY BIBLE READINGS

Nov. 26. M. *Delight in God's Law.* Psalms 1.
Nov. 27. T. *God in Nature and in Law.* Psalms 19.
Nov. 28. W. *A Prayer for Guidance.* Psalms 119:33–40.
Nov. 29. T. *A Lamp to My Feet.* Psalms 119:97–105.

Nov. 30. F. *God's True Wisdom.* 1 Corinthians 2:1–8.
Dec. 1. S. *Guided by the Spirit.* 1 Corinthians 2:9–16.
Dec. 2. S. *Training in Righteousness.* 2 Timothy 2:10–17.

BACKGROUND

Many years ago in the Church, there was a collect or short prayer in the liturgy about the Scriptures that was always read during Advent. Advent, of course, celebrates the Coming of the Lord Jesus Christ to our world. Jesus Christ is the Word of God made flesh. The Scriptures as God's Word are our only source about Jesus Christ. For this reason, for many years, the third Sunday of Advent Season was called Universal Bible Sunday.

Whether this Sunday is celebrated as Bible Sunday or not in your church, it is important to recall that the Scriptures are indispensable in the life of the Church. Theologians have pointed out God's disclosure in Jesus Christ is totally unlike any other revelation and completely unlike any other religion. Hinduism, for example, is not dependent on a book, although it has its sacred writings. However, it is entirely possible that a philosophical system like Hinduism would evolve again. Not so with the Christian Gospel. If we were to lose all our records of the life, teachings, death, and Resurrection of Jesus, the news of God's self-disclosure through Jesus Christ would be lost forever. We must have the Bible. This is why we hold the Scriptures in such a high regard in the Church, and why we study what the Bible is during these next three sessions.

This series will offer you and your class an opportunity to examine the nature of the Bible as God's written Word. The selections from Psalms 119 and 2 Timothy 3 describe what God's written Word has meant to our spiritual ancestors. The 119th Psalm is the longest Psalm in the book of Psalms, and is a magnificent hymn praising God for the written record of His Law and promise. Second Timothy, one of Paul's last letters, written in prison to the young Timothy who was like a son to the old apostle, can be understood to be Paul's final communication to Timothy. It is significant that Paul implores his younger associate to persevere faithfully in growing in awareness of the message of the Bible.

NOTES ON THE PRINTED TEXT

"Oh, how I love thy Law!" sings the Psalmist in Psalms 119. He has actually penned twenty-two poems or verses of eight lines each, each of the twenty-two beginning with a different letter of the Hebrew alphabet (The Hebrew alphabet has twenty-two letters). He has written an acrostic, a complicated literary style in which the first of the twenty-two sections begins with the letter *aleph* or "A", the second *beth* or "B", and so on through the entire twenty-two letters. But the Psalmist is doing more than writing in a clever, tricky style. He uses the acrostic as his way of celebrating Scripture as a source of instruction.

In fact, the word for *law* in Hebrew—*Torah*—means "instruction." Scripture meant receiving marching orders. Sometimes we think of turning to Scripture only for comfort or encouragement. The Bible, of course, is for inspiration as well as instruction, but the Psalmist reminds us that the Scriptures are our source of learning about the Lord. The Psalm is a long prayer-hymn directed to God giving thanks for that instruction. We find different words through the prayer-hymn for instruction, including *law, commandment, testimonies, precepts, ordinances,* and *words.* To appreciate fully the depth of feeling of the Psalmist about God's gift of Scripture as a source of instruction, we really should sing these verses from Psalms 119!

... It is my meditation all the day: the person who immerses himself or herself in the Bible finds that ideas and words from Scripture will come to mind during all of the waking hours. The great mystics of the Church discovered this and

urged others to meditate on the Bible throughout the day. For example, St. Francis de Sales suggested reading the Bible and carrying away what he called a "spiritual nosegay," just as one would pick a handful of flowers to take home after a walk to continue to catch the fragrance and sight of the beautiful landscape. The Hebrews and early Christians practiced a form of meditation by memorizing and softly repeating certain phrases of Scripture frequently throughout the day—something many of us moderns have learned can be a satisfying source of continuing instruction by God.

Thy law ... *thy* commandment ... *thy* testimonies ... *thy* precepts ... *thy* ordinances ... *thy* words: Although the Bible was written in human words by human hands laboring under human limitations, the Psalmist and millions of others have learned that the Scriptures are God's own special communication to His people. As one young executive remarked after reluctantly joining a Bible study group with three other couples, "God must have had me in mind!" The Bible is God's instruction given with us in mind.

Thy word is a lamp to my feet and a light to my path: The Psalmist uses a vividly picturesque way of telling his hearers how the Scriptures are a source of instruction to him. Have you ever lived where there was no electricity? Or have you ever had to get along during a prolonged power failure? The dark makes walking hazardous, especially along paths that are unfamiliar. It is easy to stumble or trip, and it is easy to stray off the path in the night. How welcome a lantern or flashlight is! The Scriptures are such illumination on life's dark, twisting path.

Paul and the New Testament writers undoubtedly knew these words and the truths they embody. These authors, immersed in Scripture, quoted frequently from the Bible and urged believers to continue to turn to the Scriptures.

But as for you, continue in what you have learned and have firmly believed, knowing from whom you have learned it and how from childhood you have been acquainted with the sacred writings which are able to instruct you: Paul reminds his young helper Timothy that his godly mother Eunice and grandmother Lois and others in his home church at Lystra have taught him the Bible. Instruction in the Scriptures starts in childhood. And it takes place both in the home and in the congregation. The boy or girl who is introduced to the Scriptures as God's source of instruction is extraordinarily fortunate.

All scripture is inspired by God: The Bible may be a collection of sixty-six "books" of various forms of literature, including poetry, history, genealogies, laws, prophecy, and eye-witness reports written over nearly 1,000 years ago, but it remains our unique and authoritative source of instruction from God. *Inspired* means literally "in the Spirit," and when read "in the Spirit," the Bible is the very Word of God to us.

SUGGESTIONS TO TEACHERS

The Bible is one of those books which everyone may agree is great and important but which few read or understand. Every few years, someone conducts a new survey on biblical knowledge among Christians. The results are appalling. Few can name the four Gospel accounts, or list more than a couple of the Ten Commandments. We are a Church of biblical illiterates.

You may wish to open this series of three lessons with a simple quiz to test your class members on their knowledge of the Bible. You can easily make up your own by picking out such relatively simple questions as to how many books are there in the Bible, how many in the Old Testament and New Testament, who was Abraham, who was Moses, what are the names of two of the judges, who was the first king of Israel, who was the great shepherd boy-poet who became Israel's greatest king, what are the names of two of the prophets, who wrote the Gospel accounts, what are the names of four of Jesus' disciples, what is the history boom of the early Church, what are the titles of two of Paul's letters, where in the Bible are the Ten Commandments and the Lord's Prayer?

This series of lessons, however, must be more than a quickie survey of what's in the Bible. It is meant instead to be a study of what *is* the Bible.

Your scriptural material for today's lesson offers unique helps to answering that important question. Focus your discussion in this session on how the Bible is a source of instruction.

1. *ILLUMINATION IN YOUR SEARCH.* Call attention to the way in which the Psalmist describes God's Word through Scripture as a lamp to his feet and a light for his walking (Psalms 119:105). Help your class to be more aware than before that there is no other source of enlightenment like the Bible. Ask your people to mention other forms of enlightenment, especially faulty ones such as cults or current philosophies that hold out false hopes to people. Remind the class that only Scripture is the constant light that never fails!

2. *INSISTENCE ON THE SAVIOR.* Paul's words about knowing nothing except Christ crucified (1 Corinthians 2:2) point out the purpose of all Scripture: to help believers to understand the significance of Christ's death on the Cross. Sunday classes can get off into side issues when working with the Bible and need to be reminded of the direction of all preaching, teaching, and living.

3. *INSTRUCTION FOR SALVATION.* Paul reminds Timothy to remember "the sacred writings which are able to instruct you for salvation through faith in Christ Jesus" (2 Timothy 3:15). This will provide a springboard for discussing how the Bible is the written Word of God. Ask each member of your class to state why the Bible is not like any other "inspirational literature," such as great poetry or writings of popular religious authors. Help each to grasp that the Scriptures are the unique way of instructing the Church and its members to grow in wholeness through trust in Christ.

TOPIC FOR ADULTS
A SOURCE OF INSTRUCTION

Burning Words. "One of the most interesting hymns in the Revised Church Hymnary is the hymn of which the first verse runs:

One who is all unfit to count
As scholar in Thy school,
Thou of Thy love hast named a friend—
O kindness wonderful!

"The interest of that hymn lies in the fact that it is one of the very few great hymns that the younger churches have yet produced. It is the work of Narayan Vaman Tilak, and was originally composed in Marathi.

"The story of Tilak's conversion to Christianity is a very interesting and significant one. He was a well-known Marathi poet before he was converted to Christianity.

"One day he was traveling in a train with an Englishman who treated him with the most perfect courtesy, instead of resenting his presence as many a European at that time might well have done. They talked and grew to be friendly. Finally the Englishman gave Tilak a New Testament and urged him to study it. 'If you do so,' the Englishman said, 'you will be a Christian within two years.' To Tilak at the moment this seemed a quite impossible prediction.

"He had been so impressed by the courtesy of the Englishman that he began to read the New Testament. The book gripped him. 'I could not tear myself away,' he said, 'from these burning words of love and tenderness and truth.' Two years later to the day, he was baptised in the Christian Church at Bombay."—William Barclay, "Converted by Courtesy." Published by Hodder & Stoughton Ltd as *Through the Year with William Barclay* (1971), edited by Denis Duncan.

"A Licht tae me." A devout Scotswoman, beloved for her acts of kindness to many persons in her Aberdeenshire village, suddenly began to lose the sight in both her eyes. The medical diagnosis was that she had a rapidly-growing brain tumor. The doctors were pessimistic about saving her life, not to speak of her sight. Several of her neighbors dropped in shortly after she had returned from the hospital for the latest tests. They had already heard the report from the ill woman's husband. "Janet, we hear your news is nae sae guid" (not so good), began one friend. "Aye," chimed in another, "Ye maub be gey afeart" (You must be quite afraid).

"Och, no," replied Janet, squinting to look at them through eyes grown dim in the past weeks. Picking up her well-worn Bible, she stated quietly, "This buik has been a licht tae me for fifty years an' will see me tae my hame" (This book has been a light to me for fifty years and will see me to my home).

Lamp for the Path. Several years ago, we were serving briefly as Christian education consultants for rural churches in Thailand. Our eleven-year-old daughter, Ellen, accompanied us. We were asked to visit a remote congregation north of Chieng Rai, in the jungle in the extreme northern part of the country. The trip to the village took place in the rainy season and had to be made by boat because the few roads were under water or impassable because of mud. Ellen had heard many reports of the snakes flushed out by the high waters lurking on jungle paths. When we arrived in the small village where we were to stay, it was dark. There were, of course, no lights anywhere. We climbed out of the dugout boat which had brought us to the village, gripped our baggage and started to slither up the muddy path through the deepening darkness. Our daughter said nothing, but we knew that she was thinking only of cobras and poisonous vipers which she might step on. The mud was so deep that it quickly engulfed her shoes, and she had to take them off and carry them. The path wound up from the river bank into the blackness of the jungle, and we continued to move ahead. Ellen walking barefoot along the oozy slime in the darkness was trying to be as brave as she could. Suddenly, a hissing sound and brilliant light surprised us. A Christian in the village, knowing we would have difficulty finding our way, hurried up with a gasoline lantern to light our way. For Ellen and the rest of us, the words of the 119th Psalm suddenly became very personal, as we learned what a light can be for our path!

Questions for Pupils on the Next Lesson. 1. What have been your greatest struggles over the question of what God wants you to be or to do? 2. Where is the hardest area in your life to make a decision involving your basic loyalties and values? 3. What did it mean for the Prophet Ezekiel to eat the scroll? 4. What are the places in your living in which you experience conflict between your personal commitment to the Lord and the values of others? 5. Why do Christians sense a wholeness in life when they live by values they have internalized?

TOPIC FOR YOUTH
A SOURCE OF INSTRUCTION

So Much Mail, So Little Message. "The wastebasket in my study held nearly half a bushel of stuff. Every day, after the mail arrived I fed the basket with paper. Every other day I emptied the basket.

"One day I said to my wife, 'So many items of mail today, so much paper, but no significant message.' There were plenty of messages, if you mean mere words, but there were hardly any significant messages. Very little good news that affected us personally and vitally.

"If all the mimeographed and printed matters, magazines, circular letters, pamphlets, and advertisements which reached our house were put on one pile, the mass of paper would undoubtedly have exceeded, in one year, all the manuscripts ever written in that part of the world where Jesus lived. But in that huge pile of words there would be no more significant message than the one made known long ago through the Bible. Very little good news now, but the supreme Good News then.

"Today the Bible is our only authorized source dealing with the deeds of God and the beginnings of Christianity. There we learn about the nature and will of God and also about the nature and predicament of man."—Joseph Mohr, *The Morning Call/Weekender,* February 20, 1982, *Call-Chronicle* Newspapers, Allentown, Pa.

Questions. "On her deathbed, Gertrude Stein is said to have asked, 'What is the answer?' Then, after a long silence, 'What is the question?' Don't start looking in the Bible for the answers it gives. Start by listening for the questions it asks.

"We are much involved, all of us, with questions about things that matter a good deal today but will be forgotten by this time tomorrow—the immediate wheres and whens and hows that face us daily at home and at work—but at the same time we tend to lose track of the questions about things that matter always, life-and-death questions about meaning, purpose, and value. To lose track of such deep questions as these is to risk losing track of who we really are in our own depths and where we are really going. There is perhaps no stronger reason for reading the Bible than that somewhere among all those India-paper pages there awaits each reader whoever he is the one question which, though for years he may have been pretending not to hear it, is the central question of his own life."—From p. 77 in *Wishful Thinking* by Frederick Buechner. Copyright ©1973 by Frederick Buechner. By permission of Harper & Row, Publishers, Inc.

More than Reading Matter. A family visited Gettysburg. They had a knowledgeable guide who did more than point out the monuments. This guide made the battle in 1863 so vivid that the two younger members of the family, both in high school, found themselves caught up in the epic. Standing later on Little Round Top, the seventeen-year-old turned to his younger brother and remarked, "This is the first time I ever realized that the Civil War was not just reading matter."

In the same fashion, the Bible puts you into the picture and catches you up into its story. When you take the Scriptures seriously, you discover that God is not merely "reading matter" but instructing you in person.

Questions for Pupils on the Next Lesson. 1. Are you struggling with decisions about your future? 2. What do you think God has in mind for your life in the years to come? 3. Will there ever be a time when you won't have to make tough decisions involving basic loyalties and values? 4. Which of these basic loyalties and values do you think you should incorporate into your life? 5. Why does moral living lead to inner peace?

LESSON II—DECEMBER 9

A SUMMONS TO DECISION

Background Scripture: Ezekiel 2:1–3:3; Jeremiah 1:1–12
Devotional Reading: Jeremiah 7:1–15

KING JAMES VERSION

EZEKIEL 2 And he said unto me, Son of man, stand upon thy feet, and I will speak unto thee.

2 And the spirit entered into me when he spake unto me, and set me upon my feet, that I heard him that spake unto me.

3 And he said unto me, Son of man, I send thee to the children of Israel, to a rebellious nation that hath rebelled against me: they and their fathers have transgressed against me, *even* unto this very day.

4 For *they are* impudent children and stiff-hearted. I do send thee unto them; and thou shalt say unto them, Thus saith the Lord GOD.

5 And they, whether they will hear, or whether they will forbear, (for they *are* a rebellious house,) yet shall know that there hath been a prophet among them.

6 And thou, son of man, be not afraid of them, neither be afraid of their words, though briers and thorns *be* with thee, and thou dost dwell among scorpions: be not afraid of their words, nor be dismayed at their looks, though they *be* a rebellious house.

7 And thou shalt speak my words unto them, whether they will hear, or whether they will forbear: for they *are* most rebellious.

8 But thou, son of man, hear what I say unto thee; Be not thou rebellious like that rebellious house: open thy mouth, and eat that I give thee.

9 And when I looked, behold, a hand *was* sent unto me; and, lo, a roll of a book *was* therein;

10 And he spread it before me; and it *was* written within and without: and *there was* written therein lamentations, and mourning, and woe.

3 Moreover he said unto me, Son of man, eat that thou findest; eat this roll, and go speak unto the house of Israel.

2 So I opened my mouth, and he caused me to eat that roll.

3 And he said unto me, Son of man, cause thy belly to eat, and fill thy bowels with this roll that I give thee. Then did I eat *it;* and it was in my mouth as honey for sweetness.

REVISED STANDARD VERSION

EZEKIEL 2 And he said to me, "Son of man, stand upon your feet, and I will speak with you." 2 And when he spoke to me, the Spirit entered into me and set me upon my feet; and I heard him speaking to me. 3 And he said to me, "Son of man, I send you to the people of Israel, to a nation of rebels, who have rebelled against me; they and their fathers have transgressed against me to this very day. 4 The people also are impudent and stubborn: I send you to them; and you shall say to them, 'Thus says the Lord GOD.' 5 And whether they hear or refuse to hear (for they are a rebellious house) they will know that there has been a prophet among them. 6 And you, son of man, be not afraid of them, nor be afraid of their words, though briers and thorns are with you and you sit upon scorpions; be not afraid of their words, nor be dismayed at their looks, for they are a rebellious house. 7 And you shall speak my words to them, whether they hear or refuse to hear; for they are a rebellious house.

8 "But you, son of man, hear what I say to you; be not rebellious like that rebellious house; open your mouth, and eat what I give you." 9 And when I looked, behold, a hand was stretched out to me, and, lo, a written scroll was in it; 10 and he spread it before me; and it had writing on the front and on the back, and there were written on it words of lamentation and mourning and woe.

3 And he said to me, "Son of man, eat what is offered to you; eat this scroll, and go, speak to the house of Israel." 2 So I opened my mouth, and he gave me the scroll to eat. 3 And he said to me, "Son of man, eat this scroll that I give you and fill your stomach with it." Then I ate it; and it was in my mouth as sweet as honey.

KEY VERSE: *"Son of man, eat what is offered to you; eat this scroll, and go, speak to the house of Israel."* Ezekiel 3:1 (RSV).

HOME DAILY BIBLE READINGS

Dec. 3. M. *Encounter With God.* Exodus 3:1–6.
Dec. 4. T. *A Call to Service.* 1 Samuel 3:1–9.

Dec.	5.	W.	*Vision and Commission.* Isaiah 6:1–8.
Dec.	6.	T.	*Set Apart by God.* Jeremiah 1:1–10.
Dec.	7.	F.	*Called Through Christ's Grace.* Galatians 1:3–9.
Dec.	8.	S.	*Doers of the Word.* James 1:22–27.
Dec.	9.	S.	*Two Ways of Life.* Matthew 7:21–27.

BACKGROUND

The Bible might have been penned by humans in human terms, but it is God communicating to us through those human events and human words. These authors were not motivated to write for personal fame or gain. Above all, they were presenting interesting points of view. The Bible is news, not views! And the news which these biblical writers wanted to communicate had to do with God.

Ezekiel and Jeremiah are superb examples of this fact.

Ezekiel lived in Babylon during the Exile (586–536 B.C.). Jerusalem had been captured and destroyed, the nation of Judah had been conquered, and most of the population deported to Babylon. The experience devastated God's people. Some quietly gave up on God and their faith. Many questioned God's purposes in allowing Jerusalem to fall. Most existed in the foreign land of their exile without hope for the future. Ezekiel was a young priest to whom God gave a vision for His people.

His call from God, like all summons from the Lord, was to stand up and speak fearlessly to stubborn, impudent people. Ezekiel's call featured vivid imagery in regard to the Scriptures in which Ezekiel was commanded to "eat this scroll, and go to speak to the house of Israel" (3:1). Digesting the Word of God, so that it became assimilated into every thought and word, Ezekiel rallied the exiles with God's message for those bleak times.

Another prophet, Jeremiah, was called to be God's spokesman during the tumultuous days before the Babylonians invaded and conquered Israel. Israel had been on a disaster course. The nation had persisted in idolatrous religion and corrupt leadership. Jeremiah fearlessly warned that the moral bankruptcy would bring national ruin. Few wanted to listen. Even the religious hierarchy denounced him for being unpatriotic. Jeremiah lived to see the tragedy of the beginning of the Exile.

Jeremiah's call, like Ezekiel's, was a summons for decision. God's Word to Jeremiah stripped away his excuses. Every serious encounter with the Lord, whether through Scripture or through the Spirit during worship, means having a new and serious task in life. God says to everyone He meets, "Behold, I have put my words in your mouth" (Jeremiah 1:9).

NOTES ON THE PRINTED TEXT

Son of man: This is Ezekiel's way of describing himself. He uses the phrase eighty-seven times in his writings. "Son of man" is the prophet's reminding himself and his hearers that he is merely a mortal human. God is God. Ezekiel must remember his place in the universe.

... stand on your feet and I will speak with you: When the Lord has dealings with a person, that man or woman cannot sit passively. God's call is always a summons to get up and get moving. In fact, Bible reading ultimately must have the effect of mobilizing the reader to stand up and move out. The Scriptures are a summons to decision.

And when he spoke to me, the Spirit entered into me and set me upon my feet; and I heard him speaking to me: The Spirit makes the Lord's presence and voice real for the believer. Sometimes, Bible reading and praying seem like empty exercises. The words may be read or recited, but they seem to be devoid of meaning. The Spirit, the Lord Himself, eventually comes, however, and makes those words so alive that the Christian may say with Ezekiel, "I heard him speaking to me!"

I send you: Every encounter with the Living Lord ends with this command. Every believer is sent! The Bible describes the calls and meetings of many persons with God, and in *every* case it results in that person being told in effect, "I send you." God never introduces Himself to a man or woman without sending that person on a tough assignment!

I send you to the people of Israel, to a nation of rebels, who have rebelled against me . . . people also are impudent and stubborn . . . and you shall say to them, "Thus says the Lord God": Ezekiel finds that his encounter with the Lord means a summons to go to his own people, whose refusal to heed God in the past has cost them their freedom. Ezekiel knows it's a hard task. He knows that his people don't want to listen to words from the Lord. However, the word *prophet* means being God's spokesman. God lays big jobs on those He calls, including us who call ourselves His people.

Be not rebellious: God commands Ezekiel to obey, not to conform to the norms and practices of his "rebellious house." God's people feel pressures to go along with the society in which they live and join the rebellion against the Lord. However, the encounter with God means making a decision whether to obey God or the crowd.

A written scroll: A scroll was made from pieces of skin sewed together or from strips of papyrus glued together. In Bible times, all Scripture was written on scrolls. Ezekiel's call is related to the Bible. A genuine call from the Lord is always tied to Scripture. In fact, a test of whether or not a person's claim to be "called" by God is authentic is whether it conforms to Scripture. For instance, is the call such that it is a summons to serve?

It had writing on the front and on the back, and there written on it words of lamentation and mourning and woe: God had such great criticisms of His people that it filled both sides of the scroll. Ordinarily, only one side had writing on it. Ezekiel had a heavy responsibility.

Eat this scroll: Eating a scroll seems like a strange order, but was the way the biblical writers described the way God's message through Scripture gets inside you. John, the writer of the Book of Revelation, uses the same idea in Revelation 10:8–10 to tell of the way he was ordered to chew on and assimilate God's messages for him.

We sometimes speak of "digesting" the contents of a certain book. The notion is exactly what Ezekiel and John had in mind. Scripture must be taken into your life so that it becomes part of your very being.

Then I ate it, and it was in my mouth as sweet as honey: The words of Scripture are often spoken of being as sweet as honey, as in Psalms 19:10 and Psalms 119:103. Because it was sweet, it was thought to be from the Lord. The Psalmist and Ezekiel and others all remembered that the manna in the wilderness was described as tasting like wafers made from honey. Scripture was both sweet and nourishing, just as the manna was tasty and sustaining for the Hebrews in the desert.

Believers still find that the Scriptures are God's own food for their lives!

SUGGESTIONS TO TEACHERS

The Scriptures are frequently regarded as a sort of spiritual electric blanket which you can switch on for some snuggly warmth. While you will find words of comfort when you need them in the Bible, you will also discover that God jabs you with a serious challenge to make up your mind about Him.

Your lesson for today is to help your class learn this side of Scripture. Some will resist and insist that they will choose which words of Scripture they will heed. (Usually, they pick a few passages such as the Twenty-third Psalm, and let that be their entire Bible.) The Bible is more than a few treasured, emotionally-warming verses. It is like a registered letter personally addressed to each reader calling him or her to report for duty!

Your lesson for this Sunday approaches this part of Scripture by listening to two spokesmen for God tell of their "calls" to serve Him.

1. *SUMMONED TO STAND.* Although you will dissect God's call to both Ezekiel and Jeremiah, you should help each person in your class to understand that he or she also has been "called." Many of these have the idea that only characters in the Bible or preachers or missionaries ever receive a "call." As teacher, help clarify what a call is. Don't imagine that it must be literally with the audible voice of God shouting human words. These descriptions of "calls" are essentially experiences which cannot be reduced to flat prose, but use them to encourage each member to relate how the whispers of the Spirit first came in his or her life.

2. *SENT TO SPEAK.* Each person called by God must make a decision whether or not to obey. And obedience means listening to God's Words and communicating that message. Help your class members to consider the various ways of communicating God's message to each. With some, being God's spokesman or spokeswoman may mean literally preaching or teaching. For others, it may mean speaking of Christ through hands of healing or serving. How can each person communicate God's message through Scripture more effectively and eloquently as Monday Christians?

3. *STEADIED TO SAY.* A decision to serve God and share His news always means some later second thoughts. It also means some opposition. "Be not afraid of their words," God advised Ezekiel and also any other He confronts, "You shall speak my words to them" (Ezekiel 2:6, 7). It will be helpful to let your class talk frankly of the times when it is frightening to speak out for God's Word. Call attention also to God's assurance, "Be not afraid of them, for I am with you to deliver you" (Jeremiah 1:8).

4. *SPOKEN TO SATISFY.* Take sufficient time to savor the meaning of the strange but significant "vision" of Ezekiel eating the scroll. The emphasis should be on the way each believer must respond to God's summons by savoring fully Scripture. Ezekiel's experience will be that of every person who tastes and digests God's Word in Scripture: "I ate it and it was in my mouth as sweet as honey" (Ezekiel 3:3).

TOPIC FOR ADULTS
A SUMMONS TO DECISION

Caught Up in the Drama. A small boy was taking part in a Christmas pageant in his church. He had been carefully rehearsed to play the innkeeper at Bethlehem. He had learned his role carefully. At last came the day of the big performance. He spoke his lines flawlessly as he turned away Mary and Joseph from his inn. Then, noticing how dejected they were as they trudged away, the boy suddenly abandoned the script. He ran after them and called, to the consternation of the director but the delight of the congregation, "Here, you can have my bed!"

This is something like what happens when you take the Bible seriously. You find yourself caught up in the drama. You are a participant. You are part of the story. And you find yourself challenged. You must make decisions. Like the small boy playing the innkeeper, you inadvertently discover that you are called to forget yourself and make sacrifices!

Demand for Decisions. "I recall so well that powerful story from Koinonia in the 1950s when Clarence and Florence Jordan were put out of their local Baptist

Church for bringing a dark skinned visitor (a man from India) to church with them. Clarence insisted on a meeting with the deacons of the church to have them explain to him how they were wrong in bringing that man to church. He handed a Bible to the deacons with the question, 'Here is the Bible. We Baptists believe it to be the divinely inspired word of God. Show me where I erred in bringing that man to church?' The first deacon handed it to the next and he to the next and he to the next and so on until the Bible got to the last man. He juggled it in his hands momentarily and then, laying it aside, responded, 'Clarence, we're not going into the Bible; we just don't want niggers in the church!' "—Millard Fuller, "Habitat Happenings," April-May 1982, p. 2. The official newsletter of Habitat for Humanity, Inc., 419 W. Church St., Americus, GA 31709

Explosive Stuff! An older minister had a favorite copy of the New Testament which he had used for many years. Written notes were jotted in the margins, and certain lines were underlined in different colors of pencil or ink. Finally, the binding and cover gave out. The minister, hating to part with this copy which was so important to his studying and preaching, decided to have the old Bible rebound. He sent it off to a bookbinder.

Several weeks later, he unwrapped the neatly rebound volume. He felt pleased that a strong, new cover and binding held the old pages together. Then he happened to glance at the lettering that was inscribed along the spine of the book which would show from his bookshelf when the sacred volume stood in place. Instead of the words, "The New Testament" engraved in neat gold letters, the bindery had decided to abbreviate the title and put in large bold capitals the three letters T.N.T. The minister was so annoyed at first that he almost packed up the volume and sent it back to the bookbinder. After consideration, however, he left everything as it was because he could not think of anything more appropriate than T.N.T. to describe the powerful message contained in the Book. The explosive news of Jesus Christ demands a response!

Questions for Pupils on the Next Lesson. 1. What evidence do we have of Jesus using His Bible? 2. In what way did Jesus understand His ministry to be a fulfillment of Scripture? 3. What effect did the Good News have on Cornelius? 4. Is it always possible to have a fresh start? 5. What groups do you know seek liberation from oppressive conditions?

TOPIC FOR YOUTH
A SUMMONS TO DECISION

More Than Stats. Statistics about Scriptures are startling. The complete Bible is now available in 275 languages, according to the Bible Society of London. In a report collating statistics from Bible translating agencies around the world, the society said that parts of the Bible appeared in 27 more languages in 1980, making a total of 1,710 languages in which at least one book of the Bible is available. The New Testament has been published in 479 languages. According to the Guinness Book of World Records, about 2.5 billion copies of the Bible have been printed.

The Bible is more than a bestseller. Scriptures stats are senseless unless the Bible summons *you* to decision! Have you heard the call to decide for Christ through Scripture reading?

Forgotten Destination. The bishop of Exeter, William Cecil, traveling by rail to perform a confirmation ceremony, misplaced his ticket and was unable to produce it when requested by the conductor.

"It's quite all right, my Lord, we know who you are," said the conductor reassuringly.

"That's all very well," answered the bishop, "but without the ticket how am I going to know where I am going?"

Without the Bible, we don't know where we are going. We forget our real destination in life. We are confused about our direction in living.

Open your Bible and read seriously. You will hear a summons to decide where you are going.

Summons to Decision. Bernard Fergusson was the officer in charge of the Sixteenth Brigade in the Far East during World War II. Tramping through the steaming Burmese jungle in 1944, Fergusson found the campaign both boring and dangerous. The psychological strain of leadership was immense. General Fergusson used a unique means to reinforce his decision to continue the march when fatigue, fever, and threats of attack often tempted him and his troops to turn back. Fergusson remembered what he called "long wads of Psalms" and other Scripture which he had learned in Sunday School years before, and found himself reciting these to himself. As he did, he discovered these selections from Scripture were a personal summons to decision to continue the effort.

Questions for Pupils on the Next Lesson., 1. Why is there so little sense of direction and purpose in the lives of so many people your age? 2. Why is the coming of Jesus called the Good News? 3. What changes would you like to see in your life? 4. What kinds of power impress you the most? 5. When did Jesus use the Scriptures?

LESSON III—DECEMBER 16

A WITNESS TO GOOD NEWS

Background Scripture: Luke 4:16–21; 24:44–49; Acts 10:34–43
Devotional Reading: Acts 1:1–8

KING JAMES VERSION

LUKE 4 16 And he came to Nazareth, where he had been brought up: and, as his custom was, he went into the synagogue on the sabbath day, and stood up for to read.

17 And there was delivered unto him the book of the prophet Esaias. And when he had opened the book, he found the place where it was written,

18 The Spirit of the Lord *is* upon me, because he hath anointed me to preach the gospel to the poor; he hath sent me to heal the broken-hearted, to preach deliverance to the captives, and recovering of sight to the blind, to set at liberty them that are bruised,

19 To preach the acceptable year of the Lord.

ACTS 10 34 Then Peter opened *his* mouth, and said, Of a truth I perceive that God is no respecter of persons:

35 But in every nation he that feareth him, and worketh righteousness, is accepted with him.

36 The word which *God* sent unto the children of Israel, preaching peace by Jesus Christ: (he is Lord of all:)

37 That word, *I say,* ye know, which was published throughout all Judaea, and began from Galilee, after the baptism which John preached;

38 How God anointed Jesus of Nazareth with the Holy Ghost and with power: who went about doing good, and healing all that were oppressed of the devil; for God was with him.

39 And we are witnesses of all things which he did both in the land of the Jews, and in Jerusalem; whom they slew and hanged on a tree:

40 Him God raised up the third day, and shewed him openly;

41 Not to all the people, but unto witnesses chosen before of God, *even* to us, who did eat and drink with him after he rose from the dead.

42 And he commanded us to preach unto the people, and to testify that it is he which was ordained of God *to be* the Judge of quick and dead.

43 To him give all the prophets witness, that through his name whosoever believeth in him shall receive remission of sins.

REVISED STANDARD VERSION

LUKE 4 16 And he came to Nazareth, where he had been brought up; and he went to the synagogue, as his custom was, on the sabbath day. And he stood up to read; 17 and there was given to him the book of the prophet Isaiah. He opened the book and found the place where it was written,

18 "The Spirit of the Lord is upon me,
  because he has anointed me to preach good
    news to the poor.
He has sent me to proclaim release to the
    captives
and recovering of sight to the blind,
to set at liberty those who are oppressed,
19 to proclaim the acceptable year of the
    Lord."

ACTS 10 34 And Peter opened his mouth and said: "Truly I perceive that God shows no partiality, 35 but in every nation any one who fears him and does what is right is acceptable to him. 36 You know the word which he sent to Israel, preaching good news of peace by Jesus Christ (he is Lord of all), 37 the word which was proclaimed throughout all Judea, beginning from Galilee after the baptism which John preached: 38 how God anointed Jesus of Nazareth with the Holy Spirit and with power; how he went about doing good and healing all that were oppressed by the devil, for God was with him. 39 And we are witnesses to all that he did both in the country of the Jews and in Jerusalem. They put him to death by hanging him on a tree; 40 but God raised him on the third day and made him manifest; 41 not to all the people but to us who were chosen by God as witnesses, who ate and drank with him after he rose from the dead. 42 And he commanded us to preach to the people, and to testify that he is the one ordained by God to be judge of the living and the dead. 43 To him all the prophets bear witness that every one who believes in him receives forgiveness of sins through his name."

KEY VERSE: *To him all the prophets bear witness that every one who believes in him receives forgiveness of sins through his name.* Acts 10:43 (RSV).

HOME DAILY BIBLE READINGS

Dec. 10. M. *Seek What Is Best.* Isaiah 55:1–5.
Dec. 11. T. *Return to the Lord.* Isaiah 55:6–11.
Dec. 12. W. *A Word of Consolation.* Jeremiah 31:1–9.
Dec. 13. T. *The Mission of Jesus.* Luke 4:16–21.
Dec. 14. F. *Understanding the Scriptures.* Luke 24:44–53.
Dec. 15. S. *Proclaiming the Word.* Acts 10:34–43.
Dec. 16. S. *Rejoice in the Lord!* Philippians 4:4–13.

BACKGROUND

No part of Scripture would have been written if the writers had not first participated in a momentous event or experience in which God was the key Character. No Old Testament or New Testament writer had the itch to be an author. Each biblical writer, although spanning nearly a thousand years, was impelled to witness to the news of God.

Luke, the author of the third Gospel and the Book of the Acts, was such a witness. Although he never saw Jesus, Luke witnessed to the Good News in unique ways. His witness has particular value to us in the modern, Western world because Luke was like us in so many ways.

Luke was a westerner, born and raised not in the Middle East but in Europe. He brings the perspective of the only person writing in our New Testament who was not from the Orient. Luke was a physician. His carefully-trained diagnostician's eye took in details that would interest us who have been raised in a scientific age. He is precise in his use of terms. He obviously took careful notes and kept meticulous records. In other words, Luke may be accepted as an exceptionally credible witness to the Good News.

Luke wrote a two-volume story of that Good News. Volume One describes Jesus' life, death, and Resurrection. We call that *book* the Gospel of Luke. Volume Two describes the continuing work of the Risen Lord through the presence and power of the Holy Spirit. We call that piece of writing The Acts. Each was intended for a person simply called, "Theophilus."

Who was "Theophilus"? Some think he was a Roman government official whom Luke wished to convince that Jesus' coming was Good News for everybody and that Jesus' followers were not seditious or suspicious characters. Others think that *Theophilus*—which is the Greek for "one who loves God"—was either a personal friend or a kind of "everyman" who is on a pilgrimage toward God.

Regardless of who Theophilus was, Luke also writes for us. He provides a unique and authoritative witness to Jesus Christ and His continuing work as Good News in the lives of people in Asia, Europe, and everywhere.

NOTES ON THE PRINTED TEXT

Luke, the accurate reporter of the Good News, connects God's message of Jesus Christ to Israel's Scriptures. In fact, he shows how Jesus opened His public ministry with a key passage from Isaiah to illustrate this connection between the Scriptures and Himself.

This passage from Luke 4:16–19 is important also because it shows how Jesus sets us an example for worshiping and Bible reading. *And He went to the synagogue, as his custom was, on the sabbath day:* Jesus worshiped regularly with the community of faith. Although He was God's Son, the Messiah, He presented Himself at the time and place where Scripture was read and expounded. The synagogue service of worship was the model for our Sunday church services. It emphasized Scripture reading. A portion of the Torah or the Law (that is part of the first five books of the Bible) was read. A different portion of Torah was prescribed for each Sabbath, so that the entire five books would be read every three years. Lay persons usually did the readings. In addition, a selection from the prophets was also read. The person doing the reading could select his own reading from the prophets. Since the Scriptures in the synagogue service were in Hebrew, and the common language spoken in the country was Aramaic, someone translated the readings from Hebrew to Aramaic a verse at a time. It is important to note that Jesus made sure that He heard Scripture week in and week out. He went where God's people gathered to hear God's Word. He would have no use for the lame excuse of being able to worship just as well on the golf course or the beach. Although God is of course present on golf courses and beaches, His Word through Scripture is not systematically and regularly heard on the fairways or surfboards. Scripture was integral to worship for Jesus; it had better be for us, too!

And he stood up to read: Scripture readings were done standing. Preaching was done seated. At synagogue services, men who were bar mitzvah and recognized knowledgeable in the Scriptures were invited to read. Jesus obviously was known to be such a person.

. . . and there was handed to him the book of the prophet Isaiah. He opened the book and found the place where it was written: The scroll would have been about thirty feet long. Only a person who knew Hebrew well could have found the place. Jesus could sight-read Hebrew well enough to locate the passage from Isaiah 61. This indicates that Jesus was well educated in Scripture reading, and deeply familiar with His Bible.

The Spirit of the Lord is upon me because he has anointed me to preach good news to the poor, . . . to proclaim release . . . to set at liberty those who are oppressed, to proclaim the acceptable year of the Lord: This great passage from Isaiah 61:1, 2 described the year of Jubilee when slaves would be freed, debts cancelled, and confiscated property returned to the original owner. Isaiah used these words to tell his countrymen in exile in Babylon what it would be like when the Lord would arrange for them to return to Jerusalem from captivity. Isaiah stated that his people would go back to their homeland with rejoicing when the year of the Lord's favor came.

Although Isaiah's people won release from captivity and oppression in Babylon and returned to Jerusalem, there had been no arrival of a perfect age. In fact, injustice and oppression continued. The underlying problems leading to the captivity in Babylon were still present; greed, cruelty, and disobedience remained. Only the New Messianic Age would remove these.

Jesus states that the Messianic Age has come! His ministry fulfills everything promised in Scripture!

All of those in the early Christian Church were convinced that Jesus did, in fact, inaugurate the Messianic Age and fulfilled all that Scripture promised. Luke, in the book of the Acts, emphasizes this repeatedly in the excerpts of sermons by Peter and others. Acts 10:34–43 is a sample of such preaching.

The word which he sent to Israel: All that God had said to Israel had been summed up in Jesus, Peter states.

And we are witnesses to all that he did: Our Scriptures are reliable. Our Bible is not theological theory. It is not "religious writing." It is not even "Christian concepts." It is the testimony of persons who could only state humbly that they were "chosen by God as witnesses, who ate and drank with him after he rose from the dead."

SUGGESTIONS TO TEACHERS

Here we are, less than two weeks before Christmas, and we are having a third lesson on what the Bible is. You may be curious why.

The birth of Jesus is the appearance of God's Word in human flesh. For Christians, the Scriptures are the revelation of *the* Revelation of God in the person of Jesus. Starting with next week, you will be undertaking seventeen lessons on the Gospel according to John, who announced that Jesus is "the Word made flesh" (John 1:14).

Two weeks ago, your lesson centered on what the Bible is. Last week, you discussed the nature of biblical revelation as a summons for a decision. Today, you will consider how the Bible becomes the living Word of God.

This is not meant to be merely an academic subject. As teacher, you are "called" by God to help each person in your class understand that the Bible is meant to be God's living Word for him or her. You will do this through the scriptural material which specifies that Scripture witnesses to Jesus Christ to believers.

1. *COMPLETION.* The Bible fulfills its own promises. Jesus Christ is the completion of what God has assured His people would ultimately take place. The startling scene in the Nazareth synagogue when Jesus read the scroll of Isaiah 61 and stated, "Today this scripture has been fulfilled in your hearing" (Luke 4:21), should be pondered carefully. Mention again how Jesus summarizes everything God has had to say to us humans about Himself and ourselves.

2. *KEY.* Jesus is more than another great guru. His death on the Cross and Resurrection are the clues to who Jesus is. Have your class members take note of Luke 24:44–49, the account of the walk along the road to Emmaus. Help them to walk with those two sad, despondent disciples by imagining themselves also making that hike. Ask how they would feel, what they'd have been thinking. Center on the way the Risen Jesus opened their eyes to have a new understanding of the Scriptures. As disciples are encountered by the Living Lord, the Bible becomes the living Word of God for them!

3. *CONTINUATION.* "You are my witnesses . . . you are clothed with power," the Risen Lord assures believers (Luke 24:48–49). Your class members, like the earliest disciples, are meant to be a continuation of the biblical story. In a sense, your people are the 29th chapter of Luke! They and all believers are incorporated into the Scripture's great narrative!

4. *COMMANDS.* The Spirit of the Risen Lord charts bold new paths for Peter when in Acts 10:34–43 he orders the Jewish fisherman-disciple to welcome Cornelius, the Gentile Roman soldier, into the Christian community. The biblical story grips its readers. Through it, the Lord continues to order believers to do the unexpected and take up risky tasks. In fact, remind your people that unless they have experienced nudges to undertake difficult assignments, they've not really been listening to the voice through Scripture!

TOPIC FOR ADULTS
A WITNESS TO THE GOOD NEWS

Identity Through Identifying With the Story. In the summer of 1982, a group of American church people were taking a course at St. Andrews University in Scotland. The Chancellor of the University, Stephen Watson, welcomed them and described some of the rich history of Scotland's oldest University. To the amusement of some of the visitors, Dr. Watson constantly referred to events of the past in St. Andrews as if he had been a participant. However, when Watson described the coming visit of the Queen, the visitors began to understand what the rich past of the ancient seat of learning meant to those associated with it. Dr. Watson stated, "This will be our first state visit by a reigning monarch since we welcomed James VI of Scotland or James I of England when he favored us with a visit 365 years ago," Watson spoke as if he had been a participant. He identified so closely with the rich story of St. Andrews that he considered himself a part of the university in 1617! The Americans were impressed with the way the Chancellor described the visits of 365 years ago and of that week with himself as a witness.

We Christians likewise identify with the rich story of our past. Our spiritual ancestors, Abraham and Isaac and Jacob and all the Old Testament people, Peter, James, and John, and all the New Testament characters, are our people. We are participants in their stories, and they in ours. The visit of God through the coming of The Ruler who reigns as Lord of all 1985 years ago is an event that we are part of. Furthermore, like proud members of the St. Andrews traditions, we witness to that visit as participants! History is His Story. It is also ours!

What If. . . . "How is Scripture read? Too often the Scripture lessons are read with little intonation, with only slight involvement of the reader with the text (and if the reader isn't involved why should the hearer bother?), with minimal eye contact and so no interaction between reader and hearer, and with no feeling in voice or body that what is being read is worth listening to anyway! Lest you think that the preceding remarks refer to layreaders, be assured that most clergy are incapable of reading Scripture in a way that will engage the hearer. They were taught to exegete Scripture, to read it in its original language, to study the historical context and to analyze the literary structure, but no one ever suggested that all of that study was for naught if nobody listened to the text!

"What if Scripture were read for the grand adventure that it is, not the dull doctrine that it isn't? What if the story of Adam and Eve were read like our mother used to read *The Adventures of Tom Sawyer*, pausing and whispering until our eyes were big as saucers, reading as if she were as frightened of the dark as we were: What if the Psalms were chanted as the songs they are, and not the predictable verses we have made them to be? What if everyone, not just the reader, got into the act? What if Scripture were read in such a way that verses were not chosen because they came to a resolution after fourteen verses, but were cut off before the resolution so that you had to come back next week to find out what happened?

"All of the above implies that Scripture is really a story, not just a tale constructed to get a point across and not just dull history that is irrelevant to our lives. Scripture is full of characters, dramatic movement, comic (yes, comic!) moments, mysterious plots, incredible irony, marvelous punch lines. . . ."—Cynthia A. Jarvis, *Worship in the Community of Faith.*

Know Who Jesus Is. "Gandhi, the famous Indian leader, once said: 'I have never been interested in a historical Jesus. I should not care if it were proved by someone that the man called Jesus never lived, and that what was narrated in the Gospels were a figment of the writer's imagination. For the Sermon on the Mount would still be true for me.'

"Gandhi was a great man; but, by any significant definition of the word, he was not (as he himself recognized) a 'Christian.' His kind of approach to Christianity might be possible except for the fact that Jesus himself makes it impossible. Not only in the Sermon on the Mount, but throughout all his teaching, he frames the issue in such a way that the question of who he was and is cannot be avoided.

"He does not ask us simply to accept his teachings, but to accept him—even in the famous Sermon on the Mount, which is usually, as in the case of Gandhi, the pretext for claiming that who he is is unimportant. 'Blessed are you,' he says, 'When men revile you and persecute you and utter all kinds of evil against you falsely on my account' (Matthew 5:11). He even pictures himself as the judge on the Day of Judgment, standing at the gate of heaven allowing only those who can pass his judgment to 'enter the kingdom.' He says, 'On that day many will say to me, "Lord, Lord, did we not prophesy in your name, and cast out demons in your name, and do many mighty works in your name?" And then will I declare to them, "I never knew you; depart from me, you evildoers" ' (Matthew 7:22, 23)."—Robert Clyde Johnson, *Pulpit Preaching*, Copyright 1963 Christian Century Foundation. Reprinted by permission from the December 1963 issue of *The Pulpit*.

Questions for Pupils on the Next Lesson. 1. What do you regard the major source of our knowledge of God to be? 2. Exactly what is meant by the phrase, "The Word became flesh"? 3. In what ways is the Gospel according to John different from the first three Gospel accounts? 4. What concepts did the Greek word *Logos* ("Word") have for John and his readers? 5. What similarities are there between the opening words of John and Genesis?

TOPIC FOR YOUTH
A WITNESS TO GOOD NEWS

The beginning of Moravian missions 250 years ago on the island of St. Thomas was characterized by sacrifice. The Moravian missionaries suffered a thousand hardships, but nothing daunted them—imprisonment, persecution, shipwreck, plague, privation, death—"all these things only increased the zeal and fervor of our Brethren, whose firm resolution it was rather to die than to go away without fruit." Death walked with these missionaries almost every step of the way.

Their voyages across the world in their small and overcrowded ships were perilous undertakings. Tobias Leupold, who arrived on St. Thomas, June 11, 1734, with a company of fourteen brethren and four sisters took seven months to reach St. Thomas. There malaria, dysentery, and polluted water threatened them. Before they crossed over to St. Croix, three of their number had died of yellow fever. The first service on the island was the funeral of a little child. By January 1735, ten more of the company, including Leupold himself, had died. In May, eleven more brethren arrived from Herrnhut, not knowing what they would find—no news of the earlier mission had reached Europe. By July, seven more were claimed by the fever. Nine more, miserably weakened by the fever, were forced to sail home, and three of these were lost on the voyage. In all, there had been twenty-two deaths in two years. No wonder Moravian historians have christened this episode the "Great Dying." But it was by no means unique in the missionary story.

Bishop August Spangenberg wrote: "When word of the death of the missionaries on St. Thomas reached the congregation in Bethlehem, Pennsylvania, everyone burned with a desire to put his life in the venture, too. If I had called for volunteers willing to go to the pesthole of St. Thomas, I would have found twenty to thirty brethren and sisters ready to leave at once."

The Christian Church was born out of the sacrifice of Jesus Christ, whose body was broken and whose blood was shed for us. The Good News of that sacrifice has been spread over the world by those who themselves have been willing to sacrifice in order that others may know the redeeming love of Jesus Christ. Today we remember His sacrifice and their witness.

Witness to the Good News. "The experience of Christian men confirms the classic experience of the first age of Christendom, that the Man Christ Jesus has the decisive place in man's ageless relationship with God. He is what God means by 'Man.' He is what man means by 'God.' His sinless perfection is a miracle. Wherever men have been met by him . . . the vision of God and a new spiritual life have been one and the same experience."—J. S. Whale, *Pulpit Preaching*, December 1963.

Ownership. A native African convert to the Christian faith recently made an interesting and disturbing statement about witnessing to the Good News in South

Africa. One hundred years ago, he reports, the white men owned the Bible but we owned the land. Now, he says, we own the Bible but the white man owns the land. What are the implications of this statement? What are each witnessing to?

Questions for Pupils on the Next Lesson. 1. How is John's Gospel account different from Matthew, Mark, and Luke? 2. Why did John write his version of the Good News? 3. What exactly does the phrase, "The Word became flesh" mean? 4. What did the term *Logos* (which means "Word" in Greek) mean to John and his hearers? 5. Is Jesus Christ the major source of your knowledge about God, or are there other sources? What is the claim of Jesus in John's Gospel on this matter?

JOHN: THE GOSPEL OF LIFE
(17 SESSIONS)

LESSON IV—DECEMBER 23

THE WORD OF LIFE

Background Scripture: John 1
Devotional Reading: John 1:35–42

KING JAMES VERSION

JOHN 1 In the beginning was the Word, and the Word was with God, and the Word was God.

2 The same was in the beginning with God.

3 All things were made by him; and without him was not any thing made that was made.

4 In him was life; and the life was the light of men.

5 And the light shineth in darkness; and the darkness comprehended it not.

6 There was a man sent from God, whose name *was* John.

7 The same came for a witness, to bear witness of the Light, that all *men* through him might believe,

8 He was not that Light, but *was sent* to bear witness of that Light.

9 *That* was the true light, which lighteth every man that cometh into the world.

10 He was in the world, and the world was made by him, and the world knew him not.

11 He came unto his own, and his own received him not.

12 But as many as received him, to them gave he power to become the sons of God, *even* to them that believe on his name:

13 Which were born, not of blood, nor of the will of the flesh, nor of the will of man, but of God.

14 And the Word was made flesh, and dwelt among us, (and we beheld his glory, the glory as of the only begotten of the Father,) full of grace and truth.

15 John bare witness of him, and cried, saying, This was he of whom I spake, He that cometh after me is preferred before me: for he was before me.

16 And of his fulness have all we received, and grace for grace.

17 For the law was given by Moses, *but* grace and truth came by Jesus Christ.

18 No man hath seen God at any time; the only begotten Son, which is in the bosom of the Father, he hath declared *him.*

REVISED STANDARD VERSION

JOHN 1 In the beginning was the Word, and the Word was with God, and the Word was God. 2 He was in the beginning with God; 3 all things were made through him, and without him was not anything made that was made. 4 In him was life, and the life was the light of men. 5 The light shines in the darkness, and the darkness has not overcome it.

6 There was a man sent from God, whose name was John. 7 He came for testimony, to bear witness to the light, that all might believe through him. 8 He was not the light, but came to bear witness to the light.

9 The true light that enlightens every man was coming into the world. 10 He was in the world, and the world was made through him, yet the world knew him not. 11 He came to his own home, and his own people received him not. 12 But to all who received him, who believed in his name, he gave power to become children of God; 13 who were born, not of blood nor of the will of the flesh nor of the will of man, but of God.

14 And the Word became flesh and dwelt among us, full of grace and truth; we have beheld his glory, glory as of the only Son from the Father. 15 (John bore witness to him, and cried, "This was he of whom I said, 'He who comes after me ranks before me, for he was before me.' ") 16 And from his fulness have we all received, grace upon grace. 17 For the law was given through Moses; grace and truth came through Jesus Christ. 18 No one has ever seen God; the only Son, who is in the bosom of the Father, he has made him known.

KEY VERSE: The Word was made flesh and dwelt among us full of grace and truth. . . John 1:14 (RSV).

HOME DAILY BIBLE READINGS

Dec. 17. M. *In the Beginning.* John 1:1–5.
Dec. 18. T. *A Man Sent From God.* John 1:6–13.
Dec. 19. W. *The Word Became Flesh.* John 1:14–18.
Dec. 20. T. *Make Straight the Way.* John 1:19–28.
Dec. 21. F. *"Behold, the Lamb of God."* John 1:29–34.
Dec. 22. S. *"We Have Found the Messiah."* John 1:35–42.
Dec. 23. S. *"Follow Me."* John 1:43–51.

BACKGROUND

The Gospel according to John, which you will be studying for the next seventeen weeks, is completely different in outline and content from the first three Gospel accounts. In fact, Matthew, Mark, and Luke are called the "Synoptic Gospels" (from the Greek words "to see together") because they are so parallel. John's Gospel is organized from a different perspective. It is frequently called the Gospel of Life because "Life" is such a prominent and consistent theme throughout the book.

Beginning this Sunday and continuing through February, you will focus on Jesus' public ministry as presented in John's Gospel. You will note that John selects signs and words by which Jesus reveals Himself to His own people as God's Chosen One.

Today's lesson is based on the first chapter of John, called the Prologue. John begins his account of Jesus differently from Matthew or Mark or Luke. Mark, which most scholars agree was the earliest Gospel account, starts with the appearance of John the Baptist and the call of Jesus. Matthew presents a genealogy tracing Jesus as a descendant of Abraham, showing that Jesus sums up everything within the Hebrew tradition. Luke tracks Jesus' ancestry clear back to Adam; he means to say that Jesus is the universal Savior. John, however, goes back to the beginning of everything to establish that Jesus is the expression of God from the very start of Creation. In fact, the opening lines of John sound almost exactly like the opening lines of Genesis: "In the beginning. . . ."

Two terms stand out in this first chapter of John's Gospel: *Word* and *Life.* Jesus is the Word of God, that is Jesus is God telling us everything He wants us to know about Himself. A word spells out what is on someone's mind, and through Jesus, God spells out everything about Himself. The bit of theological shorthand for God's Word enfleshed is the *Incarnation.* The other term, *Life,* will keep recurring throughout John's Gospel. It is a favorite with the writer. He maintains that Jesus confers life in every sense of the word to those who trust in Him, and insists that the opposite of life results when persons turn away from Jesus. You will examine many facets of meaning to the *Life* Jesus brings as you study this magnificent account of Jesus' life.

NOTES ON THE PRINTED TEXT

I. *In the beginning:* John deliberately selects the same words used at the beginning of the Bible in Genesis 1:1. The coming of Jesus Christ means as momentous an act to the universe as the original moment of Creation! Furthermore, John considers Jesus Christ, God's Son, not merely an appendage or an after-thought to God's planning and acting in history, but inherent in the thinking of the Creator at the very start of everything. Jesus, John maintains, has been the expression of God's mind and will even before the earth or anything else was brought into existence. John starts his Gospel account by making cosmic claims for Christ!

II. *The Word:* Think how important words are. A word gives an identity to an object or to a person. In fact, we can say that something really exists for us only when we have a word for it. We "name" a person or an object into being by providing a word for it. A baby, for example, finally identifies that big, hairy, blurry object making deep sounds as "Da-da." *Da-da* is the word for that man who sometimes holds baby and makes caring noises. Saying, "Da-da," brings that other to him. And "Da-da" now has a reality in the life of baby. "Da-da" is the expression of a human father for baby.

Jesus is the Word of God. That is, Jesus is the expression of the Creator for us. In the person of Jesus, we hear God pronounced. God has a reality and an identity for us through Jesus. In the person of Jesus, God is named into our lives.

In him was life, and the life was the light of men: As a composer will sound the sequence of chords which will be repeated as a theme throughout the entire piece of music at the opening of the selection, John rings the mighty note of LIFE through Jesus in the opening lines.

III. *A man sent from God, whose name was John:* John the Baptist made a mighty impact. In fact, a group of devoted followers remained for many years. The writer of the fourth Gospel acknowledged that John the Baptist was outstanding, even the greatest next to Jesus. But the Gospel writer insists that John the Baptist's own testimony showed that he merely pointed to Jesus. Many scholars think that the fourth Gospel had as a secondary purpose the intention of bringing those in John the Baptist's movement into the Christian community. Therefore, John writes about John the Baptist: *He came for testimony, to bear witness to the light . . . He was not the light, but came to bear witness to the light . . . and cried, "He who comes after me ranks before me, for he was before me."*

IV. *And the Word became flesh and dwelt among us:* God expressed His own Self in human form! The invisible God made Himself visible; the inexpressible expressed Himself in the person of Jesus. The greatest miracle of all is the Incarnation. God came among us in human form. John emphasizes this earthy, fleshly aspect. Even in John's time, there were people who were trying to "spiritualize" the Gospel by claiming that Jesus was actually a kind of ghostly figure or wispy wraith and not truly flesh and blood. John rightly asserted that Jesus was very much a human being who ate, drank, slept, and bled the same as any other human.

Dwelt among us: The Greek word here for *dwelt* literally means "tented" or "tabernacled." It refers to the tent or tabernacle for the Lord in the years in which the Hebrews wandered in the desert after leaving Egypt. The tabernacle was the dwelling place for the presence of the Lord in the midst of the children of Israel in their pilgrimage. Likewise, John would have his readers understand that Jesus is now where the Lord is present. In Jesus Christ, God has chosen to dwell among His pilgrim people now and forever. . . .

Full of Grace and Truth: Grace means God's undeserved loving-kindness toward us. In Jesus, God communicates His boundless undeserved loving-kindness toward us. In Jesus, God communicates His boundless compassion for each of us individually. *Truth* means God tells us all we need to know about Himself and also tells us the truth about ourselves. God does not play games with us or fool us about Himself or ourselves. He is completely truthful with us.

V. *No one has ever seen God, the only Son who is in the bosom of the Father, he has made him known:* The complete disclosure of God has been made through Jesus Christ. We need not look for other secret or private "revelations." We need not take seriously other alleged "revelations," such as certain others through history have claimed. Jesus is God's clearly spoken Word about Himself and about us. Jesus is enough. We need no other!

SUGGESTIONS TO TEACHERS

You will be teaching lessons from the Gospel of John from this Sunday through the Sunday after Easter—seventeen in all. Your first reaction may be, "How can I ever find so much to teach from just one book in the Bible for so many weeks?" Seventeen weeks from now, you probably will be saying, "There's so much more to this Gospel account that I wish I had another seventeen weeks!" That has been the experience of nearly everyone who has taught a class using the fourth Gospel.

John has certain key words which he uses repeatedly. One of these is *Life.* How appropriate that you and your class take this word as the emphasis for this Christmas week! John equated Jesus' coming into his life to the gift of new life to him. Although John doesn't tell the familiar birth stories of Jesus in the manger of Bethlehem, he goes deeper and recounts the meaning of that wondrous event.

1. *THE ETERNAL WORD.* Sometimes, teachers think that they must constantly pound facts into the pupils' heads. There is of course a need to impart "head" knowledge. However, there is also a need to encourage "heart" knowledge. John wants his readers to have both. John starts his account by stating that Jesus has cosmic significance. Jesus is the complete expression of God from the beginning of Creation. Let the wonder of the first four verses of chapter 1 be sensed by your class.

2. *THE ENLIGHTENING WORD.* John flatly states that Jesus is the Light. Not a glimpse of the light, nor one pointing to the light, but the Light, John insists. To drive home the point, John makes a point of quoting John the Baptist, the powerful and popular prophet, who testified that he could only bear witness to the Light but that Jesus is the Light. Take enough time in this lesson to let the meaning of John's contrast of existence in darkness and in light take hold of your people's imagination. Have your class bring up various kinds of darkness, such as hopelessness, or ignorance, especially from their own personal experience. How has the coming of Jesus been light for them in these conditions of darkness?

3. *THE ENFLESHED WORD.* Jesus as God's complete disclosure or statement about Himself brings life! Use the stories of Andrew and Peter, Philip and Nathanael to illustrate the ways various persons recognized the way Jesus makes them come alive to the reality of God in their midst. Bring your lesson to its climax this Christmas Sunday by challenging each member to experience new life these coming weeks through Jesus' coming.

TOPIC FOR ADULTS
THE WORD OF LIFE

Friend on the Throne. There is a tale in the records of King James the First of Scotland. He made it a practice, it is said, to go in disguise to various parts of his kingdom, to acquaint himself with the needs of his people and to observe how the laws were being administered. He dressed as a farmer, and in this capacity became well known to humble friends whom he made in the course of his wanderings. There are many traditions concerning his adventures.

A poor countryman once befriended him when he was in deadly peril and then bound up his wounds and shared his scanty meal with him. Shortly after the man was summoned to appear at Stirling Castle where the king held winter court. To be sent for to appear before the king was a most serious matter in those days and the poor man was filled with terror. He wondered what crime he had been guilty of, and whether he would ever again see his own fireside. The officers who ushered him into the royal presence knew nothing of the occasion. To them he was only one more malefactor to be disposed of. Imagine the astonishment of the poor prisoner when he heard a familiar voice bidding him look up, and asking why he refrained from speaking to an old friend. Raising his eyes to the king's face he forgot for the moment where he was and, ignoring the courtiers who stood around, he called out the name by which he had known the king in his own hut in the forest. He had no fear now. The man on the throne was just the countryman's friend.

This is the glad tidings of the Incarnation. There on the throne sits One before whom we need have no fear. He is of our kindred. He is touched with the feeling of our infirmities, for He has lived our life and known its joys and sorrows from the cradle to the grave.

The Central Miracle. "The central miracle asserted by Christians is the Incarnation. They say that God became Man. Every other miracle prepares for this, or exhibits this, or results from this. Just as every natural event is the manifestation at a particular place and moment of Nature's total character, so every particular Christian miracle manifests at a particular place and moment the character and significance of the Incarnation. The fitness, and therefore credibility, of the particular miracles depends on their relation to the Grand Miracle; all discussion of them in isolation from it is futile."—C.S. Lewis.

God Become Human.

. . . he has become man
to make it possible
for us to love
as he has loved us.
He makes himself
the hungry one,
the naked one,
the homeless one,
the sick one,
the one in prison,
the lonely one,
the unwanted one,
and he says:
You did it to me.—Mother Teresa of Calcutta.

Questions for Pupils on the Next Lesson. 1. In what way are the miracles in the Gospel of John to be regarded as "signs"? 2. Why do Christians claim that the new life Jesus brings means being born anew and born from above? 3. Exactly what is meant by the phrase "eternal life"? 4. How would you describe Mary, Jesus' Mother, at the Wedding at Cana? 5. What was the symbolism of the water jars in the story of the Wedding at Cana?

TOPIC FOR YOUTH
MAKING GOD KNOWN

Understanding. "A few years ago a young seminary student chose to do some extracurricular 'field work' with a group of underprivileged boys in East Harlem. He seemed to be making little progress with them. But one night, making his way back to the seminary, he was suddenly seized from behind by two burly policemen, who roughed him up and searched his pockets evidently under the impression that he fitted the description of some lawbreaker they were seeking. His rough clothes, his lack of any credentials (he had been warned that it was dangerous to carry a billfold at night in this area) made it impossible to establish his identity, and he was hauled off to jail, where he spent the night. The next day his release was secured, and he was turned out without even an apology for the indignities he had suffered. But when the news of this event got back to the boys in his East Harlem group, their attitude toward him changed instantly. They knew that he now understood from firsthand experience the treatment they sometimes received. They also now knew that he cared enough about them to undergo some personal risk to help them. It made all the difference."—Frederick C. Maier, *Presbyterian Life*, July 15, 1961. Copyright *Presbyterian Life*. Used by permission.

Making God Known. Croesus, the richest man in the world, once asked the wisest man in the world, Thales, "What is God?" The Philosopher asked for a day to think it over. Then another day. And another, and another, and still another day. At length, Thales confessed he was not able to give an answer. The longer he deliberated, the more difficult it was for him to frame an answer regarding God's identity.

Thales was the wisest man in the world, but he couldn't tell who God is. Even the most unsophisticated, unlearned person among Christians knows who God is and is able to make Him known to others because of the Incarnation!

Real Miracle. A Greek Cypriot immigrant who won $5 million in New York's lottery said the only spending plan he has so far is a big gift to the church—in thanks for the "miracle."

"I no feel like staying home and do nothing," said Andy Tegerides, who for twenty-one years served up Coke and cheeseburgers at his Regent Coffee Shop in the borough of Queens.

What does he plan to do with the money?

"Nothing comes to my mind."

Will he buy a new house?

"Why should I move?" he shrugged. "I like it where I am."

But, he added, "I got to give something to the church . . . This is a miracle."

Andrew Tegerides may think that winning the lottery is a miracle, but he does not understand that *the* miracle is God's coming to us in the human person, Jesus. Like most of us, Andy uses the word *miracle* carelessly, and even attributes picking a winning number to divine intervention. This season, the celebration of the Incarnation, let us associate our lives, our church, and our future with that great Miracle.

Questions for Pupils on the Next Lesson. 1. What is your definition of a miracle? 2. What does the Gospel of John mean by calling Jesus' acts such as turning water into wine at the wedding feast a "sign"? 3. How would you describe the relationship between Jesus and his Mother, Mary, in John 2? 4. What does the phrase, "Born anew" or "Born from above" mean to you? 5. How would you describe Nicodemus?

LESSON V—DECEMBER 30

BELIEVE AND RECEIVE LIFE

Background Scripture: John 2:1–11; 3:1–21
Devotional Reading: John 3:1–12

KING JAMES VERSION

JOHN 2 And the third day there was a marriage in Cana of Galilee; and the mother of Jesus was there:

2 And both Jesus was called, and his disciples, to the marriage.

3 And when they wanted wine, the mother of Jesus saith unto him, They have no wine.

4 Jesus saith unto her, Woman, what have I to do with thee? mine hour is not yet come.

5 His mother saith unto the servants, Whatsoever he saith unto you, do *it.*

6 And there were set there six waterpots of stone, after the manner of the purifying of the Jews, containing two or three firkins apiece.

7 Jesus saith unto them, Fill the waterpots with water. And they filled them up to the brim.

8 And he saith unto them, Draw out now, and bear unto the governor of the feast. And they bare *it.*

9 When the ruler of the feast had tasted the water that was made wine, and knew not whence it was, (but the servants which drew the water knew,) the governor of the feast called the bridegroom,

10 And saith unto him, Every man at the beginning doth set forth good wine; and when men have well drunk, then that which is worse; *but* thou hast kept the good wine until now.

11 This beginning of miracles did Jesus in Cana of Galilee, and manifested forth his glory; and his disciples believed on him.

3 16 For God so loved the world, that he gave his only begotten Son, that whosoever believeth in him should not perish, but have everlasting life.

17 For God sent not his Son into the world to condemn the world; but that the world through him might be saved.

18 He that believeth on him is not condemned: but he that believeth not is condemned already, because he hath not believed in the name of the only begotten Son of God.

REVISED STANDARD VERSION

JOHN 2 On the third day there was a marriage at Cana in Galilee, and the mother of Jesus was there; 2 Jesus also was invited to the marriage, with his disciples. 3 When the wine failed, the mother of Jesus said to him, "They have no wine." 4 And Jesus said to her, "O woman, what have you to do with me? My hour has not yet come." 5 His mother said to the servants, "Do whatever he tells you." 6 Now six stone jars were standing there, for the Jewish rites of purification, each holding twenty or thirty gallons. 7 Jesus said to them, "Fill the jars with water." And they filled them up to the brim. 8 He said to them, "Now draw some out, and take it to the steward of the feast." So they took it. 9 When the steward of the feast tasted the water now become wine, and did not know where it came from (though servants who had drawn the water knew), the steward of the feast called the bridegroom 10 and said to him, "Every man serves the good wine first; and when men have drunk freely, then the poor wine; but you have kept the good wine until now." 11 This, the first of his signs, Jesus did at Cana in Galilee, and manifested his glory; and his disciples believed in him.

3 16 For God so loved the world that he gave his only Son, that whoever believes in him should not perish but have eternal life. 17 For God sent the Son into the world, not to condemn the world, but that the world might be saved through him. 18 He who believes in him is not condemned; he who does not believe is condemned already, because he has not believed in the name of the only Son of God.

KEY VERSE: God sent the Son into the world, not to condemn the world, but that the world might be saved through him. John 3:17 (RSV).

HOME DAILY BIBLE READINGS

Dec. 24. M. *Magnify the Lord.* Luke 1:46–55.
Dec. 25. T. *Presented in the Temple.* Luke 2:22–32.
Dec. 26. W. *The Wedding at Cana.* John 2:1–11.

Dec.	27.	T.	*Born Anew.* John 3:1–13.
Dec.	28.	F.	*The World Receives Light.* John 3:14–21.
Dec.	29.	S.	*Proclaiming Christ.* John 3:22–30.
Dec.	30.	S.	*God Sent the Son.* John 3:31–36.

BACKGROUND

A wedding has been a joyous occasion in every culture in every age. In Jesus' time and place, a wedding was a weeklong celebration.

The wedding festivities at Cana, a tiny village near Nazareth, would have been the biggest days in the lives of the young peasant couple. Everyone in the village would have been invited. The customs of that time and place dictated that plenty of refreshments would be on hand. In fact, not to have enough for the guests to eat and drink would have been indescribably disgraceful. The young couple would have been laughed at during the rest of their lives.

Mary, Jesus' mother, is in charge of the catering arrangements at the Cana wedding. A crisis arises when Jesus and His disciples arrive unexpectedly. There won't be enough wine to go around. Mary is flustered. She knows how humiliating it will be for the poor young bride and groom if people can't be served. She turns to Jesus.

Jesus handles the situation perfectly. He instructs those assisting in the serving to fill the big thirty-gallon water jars, used for Jewish purification rites, with water, then take the contents in jugs to the master of ceremonies. The day is saved when Jesus turns water into wine.

There are several words in the Greek language which are translated as "miracle." The word for *miracle* most commonly used in John, however, actually means "sign." A sign does not point to itself but to something else. For example, the sign "Airport" calls attention not to the type of lettering or the material on which the letters are inscribed but to the place where you take a plane. In the New Testament, especially in the fourth Gospel, the signs are meant to point not to themselves but to Jesus Christ and what He means to believers. This is not meant to minimize the importance of the miracles but to state why John and the other writers included them. In the case of the miracle of turning water into wine at the wedding feast at Cana, this is a sign that Jesus indicated that what He brings supersedes what was before.

NOTES ON THE PRINTED TEXT

Cana lay about eight miles north of Nazareth, but all the villagers from the area were invited to the wedding in which Jesus saved the day. It was *on the third day,* which in Scripture means "the day after tomorrow," or two days after Nathanael's call.

I. *O woman, what have you to do with me?* To our ears, Jesus' reply to His mother's plea for help sounds harsh. Even the word, *Woman,* seems stiff and formal for Jesus to use. However, in the original language, the word is not cold and impersonal, but means something roughly akin to "Mother."

"What have you to do with me?" in the Greek text can mean both a gentle reminder to Mary not to be worried and not to boss Jesus.

II. *My hour has not yet come:* Again, there are two possible meanings to this phrase. It can mean that it's not yet the time to intervene to provide more wine. Or, it can mean it's not yet the time for Jesus to show His glory. Mary apparently was pressing Jesus to disclose that He was the Messiah by handling the crisis of the wine shortage. Jesus wants Mary to understand that His "hour" will come later, at Jerusalem at the Passover. Meanwhile, however, Jesus recognizes the problem Mary and the kitchen crew have, and quietly takes steps to meet their needs.

III. *Six stone water jars:* These large crocks in front of the house were for guests to go through the hand-washing ceremonies required of good Jews. The six jars would have furnished about 120 gallons.

The steward of the feast: Middle Eastern weddings at that time had one person appointed to be a combination head waiter, food-and-wine taster, seating arranger, and proposer of toasts to the wedding couple and honored guests. This man's job, in short, was to see that everyone enjoyed himself and felt welcome.

The fact that Jesus performed this sign or miracle at a wedding feast has symbolic value. Looking back on this occasion where Jesus brought such joy, John the Gospel writer and others remembered the Old Testament symbolism of the Messiah's coming being a time of great celebration and happiness. The messianic era was described as a sumptuous wedding banquet in which everyone present felt welcome and enjoyed the party.

The water now become wine: The point is not how much alcoholic content the beverage contained—rather, the transformation of the contents of the big twenty-gallon water jars was a sign of new life Jesus brings. Jesus' arrival as compared to the old legalistic water-jar ceremonies also exhilarates. The sparkling fresh wine of the Gospel makes all the previous religious practices as flat and stale as stagnant water.

Some picture Jesus as prim-mouthed killjoy. The poet Algernon Swinburne, for example, spoke of Jesus as "the pale Galilean." Unfortunately, religious art seldom depicts Jesus as the person you'd put first on the guest list for your party. Instead of being the dreary personality that you hope won't turn up at the celebration, but felt you had to invite anyway, Jesus was the most-wanted guest for His contemporaries. He was a happy person. He radiated joy. People liked to be around Him. They enjoyed His company. He liked to share the times of happiness in others' lives. No gloomy person He!

The bridegroom: Who was this young man? We don't know his name. He and his bride were undoubtedly two neighborhood kids whom Jesus had watched grow up. They would have been in their late teens since marriage in the villages usually took place at a young age. Their marriage would have been the happiest celebration of their lives, and enjoyed by all their relatives and friends. There was nothing outstanding about the couple. They were just a typical peasant bride and groom from a tiny, obscure village. It was to two such supposedly insignificant people that Jesus chose to show His first sign. The miracle at Cana can therefore also be seen as the first miracle of divine concern for the forgotten nobodies of this world!

SUGGESTIONS TO TEACHERS

A ten-year-old boy who was weary of hearing too much syrupy talk about the baby Jesus at church and at home blurted, "I think it's time to put Santa back into Christmas." After all the sentimental stuff about the Christmas story that everyone has been subjected to during the past few days, many are almost ready to agree with that boy. You may agree. And with your busy schedule over this holiday, you probably don't have a great deal of enthusiasm for plunging into preparing another lesson.

The Gospel of John is a healthy antidote to burnout from over exposure to sentimentality at Christmas. Today's lesson also gets your class ready to face the burdens and challenges of a new year. The scriptural material from John stresses new life through Jesus to believers.

1. *SYMBOL.* Let the story of Jesus at the wedding at Cana spin its own charm for your class. This miracle, like all such in John, is meant to be understood as a "sign." In fact, that is the literal meaning of the Greek word for "miracle" which

John consistently uses. The wedding at Cana is actually several signs: the sign of the way Jesus is involved in our lives by coming to the celebration of an obscure peasant couple in a tiny hill village, the sign of the way Jesus transforms human existence from flat and ordinary into a zesty and tasty quality. Have your class pick out as many "signs" of Jesus' coming to human life as possible from this story.

2. *SUMMONS TO BELIEVE.* You may have to point out to your class that John was not writing to entertain but to convince. He carefully selected his material, like a skillful editor, to emphasize the response which Jesus demands. Ask precisely what difference Jesus makes in the daily thinking and doing of your people. Remind them that believing in Jesus means taking Him so seriously that life is organized around Him.

3. *SIGHT.* You have a second great narrative to have your class consider—the story of Nicodemus's nighttime visit to Jesus, and the conversation between the two. Look at the words, "Unless one is born anew, he cannot see the kingdom of God" (3:3). Point out that Jesus enables a person to see everything with new eyes of faith. Also have your people take note of Jesus' warning that those who reject Him and the life He brings become blinded and subject themselves to darkness. Also note that this famous passage about being "born again" is not a plea for a dramatic emotional conversion as much as a call to commitment to Jesus personally.

4. SACRIFICE. In Jesus, we see that God allows Himself to be vulnerable. He risks failure. He gives. He accepts weakness in order to save. Have your class bear the Incarnation, the Cross, and the Resurrection in mind along with the "sweet little baby in the manger" part of Jesus' story.

TOPIC FOR ADULTS
BELIEVE AND RECEIVE LIFE

The New Wine of the Gospel. What Jesus introduces to the world is fresh and new. He is in marked contrast to the old, to everything that has gone on before. With Him, all things take on a new quality.

All previous religious institutions, ceremonies, customs, and forms lose their meaning when Jesus comes along. Those old stone water jars, symbols of legalism, a ceremonialism, a tired busy-ness in religiosity, are superseded. Jesus replaces all they stood for.

He is enough! He takes in all that these forms ever tried to do or tried to stand for. Next to Jesus, all the purification business and washing ceremonies are pointless. At Cana, Jesus—God's Sign of Life among us men and women—breaks in on the old forms with a new, lively Presence.

How badly we need a sense of His enlivening Presence today in our tired, cynical churchianity!

There is a group of admirers of A. Conan Doyle's fictional figure known as "The Baker Street Irregulars," who meet, correspond, and write periodically about their fictional hero, Sherlock Holmes. They all live in a world where, in Vincent Starrett's phrase, "It is always 1895."

How similar to us in the Church! How often we seem to be a quaint, irrelevant group who treat Jesus as a sort of fictional hero, and who live in a world where it's always 1 B.C., or A.D. 1517, or 1620, or 1895.

No Place Beyond Redemption. In Robertson Davies's novel, *Fifth Business*, he writes about the townspeople of Deptford: "We were serious people, missing nothing in our community and feeling ourselves in no way inferior to larger places. We did, however, look with pitying amusement on Bowles Corners, four miles distant and with a population of one hundred and fifty. To live in Bowles Corners, we felt, was to be rustic beyond redemption."

People in Galilee and elsewhere looked down on Cana as an insignificant place beyond redemption. However, this village and all the Bowles Corners and Canas with their people regarded as rustic beyond redemption have been touched with new life by Jesus' sign at the wedding at Cana. No one was too rustic for Jesus, not even a peasant bridal couple. No one is ever beyond redemption for Him. Believe and receive His life!

How to Keep Christmas. "Are you willing to forget what you have done for other people, and to remember what other people have done for you; to ignore what the world owes you, and to think what you owe the world; to put your rights in the background, and your duties in the middle distance, and your chances to do a little more than your duty in the foreground; to see that your fellowmen are just as real as you are, and try to look behind their faces to their hearts, hungry for joy; to own that probably the only good reason for your existence is not what you are going to get out of life, but what you are going to give to life; to close your book of complaints against the management of the universe, and look around you for a place where you can sow a few seeds of happiness—are you willing to do these things even for a day? Then you can keep Christmas."—Henry Van Dyke.

Questions for Pupils on the Next Lesson. 1. Why were the Samaritans so keenly disliked by the Jews in Jesus' time? 2. How would you characterize the Samaritan woman at the Well of Sychar? 3. How would you characterize the official from Capernaum who begged Jesus to come to heal his son? 4. Why was Jesus cautious about performing signs or miracles? 5. Are you satisfied with your life patterns?

TOPIC FOR YOUTH
BELIEVE AND LIVE

New Word of Hope. The new wine of the presence of Jesus Christ in our world means hope. How much the world in His time needed hope. People lived without any word of promise. For example, Sophocles, the great Greek playwriter, stated his philosophy of life to be completely without any hope in these words:

"Not to be born at all—that is by far the best fortune. The second best is as soon as one is born with all speed to return thither whence one has come."

To a corrupt, weary, decaying society, Jesus came with the intoxicating message: *I bring life! I am life for you.* The wedding scene at Cana says that.

In our age, He continues to bring that hope through His life among us.

More Than a "Way of Life." We sometimes hear people speak of Christianity as "a philosophy" or a collection of ideals or a system of ethics, values, thought, or some such. In other words, we throw Christianity into the ring with other religions and systems of thought and philosophies as one of many man-made schemes.

Please note that those at that wedding supper, those who were the earliest Christians (and this believer) cared not one whit about believing in a "way of life" or "a scheme of thinking." Christianity then and Christianity now is basically trust in a Person, and that Person is the Person of Jesus Christ.

Wonder in the Trenches. Jesus startles us by intruding in unexpected ways and places, such as the wedding feast in Cana. His Spirit brought new words and wonders in the trenches on December 24, 1914, during the horrors of trench warfare in the first World War. Unexplicably, the big guns inflicting terrible slaughter did not open fire on Christmas morning, 1914. During the marvelous, silent dawn without the thunder of the guns, British troops heard carols being sung in the distance. Someone called out over No Man's Land, "Merry Christmas!" Before officers realized what was happening, soldiers from both the German lines and British climbed out over the parapets and began to exchange greetings, chocolates, and cigarettes, to shake hands and wish each other a Merry Christmas. In one section, men of the famous fifty-fifth Prussian Guard even brought cognac until officers on both sides, preferring slaughter to fraternizing, bellowed to the troops to return to their positions. Next morning, murderous slaughter of shellfire from the German artillery barrages opened again. But for one memorable day on the front lines, men experienced a day of the words and wonders of Christ which stayed with them as long as they lived. Jesus transforms every setting and every relationship. Let Him bring new wonders to the battlefield of your world!

Questions for Pupils on the Next Lesson. 1. Why did the Jews dislike the Samaritans? 2. What did Jesus mean by offering the woman at the Well of Sychar "living water"? 3. What kind of person was the official from Capernaum who came to Jesus for help for his son? 4. Why did Jesus commend this man? 5. Why was Jesus cautious about working miracles?

LESSON VI—JANUARY 6

SIGNS OF NEW LIFE

Background Scripture: John 4
Devotional Reading: John 4:5–24

KING JAMES VERSION

JOHN 4 39 And many of the Samaritans of that city believed on him for the saying of the woman, which testified, He told me all that ever I did.

40 So when the Samaritans were come unto him, they besought him that he would tarry with them: and he abode there two days.

41 And many more believed because of his own word;

42 And said unto the woman, Now we believe, not because of thy saying: for we have heard *him* ourselves, and know that this is indeed the Christ, the Saviour of the world.

46 So Jesus came again into Cana of Galilee, where he made the water wine. And there was a certain nobleman, whose son was sick at Capernaum.

47 When he heard that Jesus was come out of Judea into Galilee, he went unto him, and besought him that he would come down, and heal his son: for he was at the point of death.

48 Then said Jesus unto him, Except ye see signs and wonders, ye will not believe.

49 The nobleman saith unto him, Sir, come down ere my child die.

50 Jesus saith unto him, Go thy way; thy son liveth. And the man believed the word that Jesus had spoken unto him, and he went his way.

51 And as he was now going down, his servants met him, and told *him,* saying, Thy son liveth.

52 Then inquired he of them the hour when he began to amend. And they said unto him, Yesterday at the seventh hour the fever left him.

53 So the father knew that *it was* at the same hour, in the which Jesus said unto him, Thy son liveth: and himself believed, and his whole house.

54 This *is* again the second miracle *that* Jesus did, when he was come out of Judea into Galilee.

REVISED STANDARD VERSION

JOHN 4 39 Many Samaritans from that city believed in him because of the woman's testimony, "He told me all that I ever did." 40 So when the Samaritans came to him, they asked him to stay with them; and he stayed there two days. 41 And many more believed because of his word. 42 They said to the woman, "It is no longer because of your words that we believe, for we have heard for ourselves, and we know that this is indeed the Savior of the world."

46 So he came again to Cana in Galilee, where he had made the water wine. And at Capernaum there was an official whose son was ill. 47 When he heard that Jesus had come from Judea to Galilee, he went and begged him to come down and heal his son, for he was at the point of death. 48 Jesus therefore said to him, "Unless you see signs and wonders you will not believe." 49 The official said to him, "Sir, come down before my child dies." 50 Jesus said to him, "Go; your son will live." The man believed the word that Jesus spoke to him and went his way. 51 As he was going down, his servants met him and told him that his son was living. 52 So he asked them the hour when he began to mend, and they said to him, "Yesterday at the seventh hour the fever left him." 53 The father knew that was the hour when Jesus had said to him, "Your son will live"; and he himself believed, and all his household. 54 This was now the second sign that Jesus did when he had come from Judea to Galilee.

KEY VERSE: . . . we have heard for ourselves, and we know that this is indeed the Savior of the world. John 4:42 (RSV).

HOME DAILY BIBLE READINGS

Dec. 31. M. *Life-Giving Water.* John 4:1–10.
Jan. 1. T. *Spring for Eternal Life.* John 4:11–14.
Jan. 2. W. *God Is Spirit.* John 4:15–24.
Jan. 3. T. *"Can This Be the Christ?"* John 4:25–30.
Jan. 4. F. *Gather for Eternal Life.* John 4:31–38.

Jan.   5.   S.   *"We Have Heard for Ourselves."* John 4:39–42.
Jan.   6.   S.   *Jesus Heals a Son.* John 4:43–54.

BACKGROUND

Jesus had a way of breaking taboos. Nothing illustrates this more than this account in John 4, when Jesus met the woman at the Well of Sychar.

To begin with, no self-respecting rabbi ever spoke to a woman other than his wife or daughter, mother or sister, in public. Even then, many religious leaders considered it beneath their dignity to converse with a woman, since women were held in such disregard as inferior beings. Not so with Jesus.

Furthermore, no rabbi or any male Jew would have any dealings with Samaritans if at all possible. All respectable Jews looked down on Samaritans as half-breed infidels. Jesus ignored convention by starting a conversation with a Samaritan woman.

Above all, Jews with their strict moral code scrupulously avoided persons suspected of loose living. Jesus threw caution to the wind and willingly associated with people of questionable morals. In the case of the woman at the Well of Sychar, Jesus immediately would have suspected her. It was noon, the hottest part of the day, and no woman ever came to draw water at that hour if she was accepted by the rest of the village women. Jesus knew that this woman at the Sychar well at that time was ostracized by the other women, and the only cause for being shunned was because this woman broke the rules of sexual conduct.

Here in the fourth chapter of John, Jesus throws aside all the taboos by speaking not only to a woman, but a Samaritan woman, and a Samaritan woman with a bad reputation! Jesus, however, smashes through all traditions and taboos in order to announce even to disreputable and disliked outsiders that He brings new life!

NOTES ON THE PRINTED TEXT

I. The animosity between Jews and Samaritans ran deep. Dating back over 500 years to the time of the Exile, the fussing and feuding had grown more bitter with the years. Those who had returned from the Exile in Babylon after fifty years thought that they were the pure-bred faithful who had kept the requirements of the Law. They looked critically at those who had not been deported, especially because many of the stay-at-homes from the northern area of the old kingdom of Israel, Judah's rival, were not strict in observing the Law and had taken up divergent worship practices. After Ezra insisted on marriages only within the community of faith and established what came to be known as Judaism, those who returned to Jerusalem criticized those around Samaria for marrying Canaanite women. In other words, Samaritans were sneered at as half-breeds and heretics. Needless to say, the Samaritans did not appreciate these accusations and retaliated. By Jesus' time, relations were so bad between the Jews and the Samaritans that strict Jews deliberately avoided traveling through Samaritan territory both to keep from being polluted by contact with the Samaritans and to keep from being attacked by hostile Samaritan villagers.

Jesus' willingness to welcome Samaritans was something of a miracle to everyone in His time. After His astonishing disclosure of His messiahship to the Samaritan woman at the Well of Sychar, He was invited to visit Samaritans.

Many Samaritans . . . believed in him . . . So when the Samaritans came to him, they asked him to stay with them; and he stayed there two days: Jesus smashes all the ancient human barriers between peoples by deliberately associating with despised Samaritans. He brings the new life of God's reconciling love to everyone.

And many more believed because of his word . . . for we have heard for our-

selves, and we know that this is indeed the Saviour of the world: John notes the irony in the way the Samaritans of all people recognize who Jesus is, while the Jewish authorities continue to reject His claim!

Furthermore, John emphasizes the importance of personal faith. The Samaritans say to the woman, "It is no longer because of your words that we believe, for we have heard for ourselves, and we know that this is indeed the Saviour of the world." A secondhand religion means little. Eventually, commitment comes not from reports from others but from personal experience of Jesus Christ.

II. Some scholars think that John gives his version of the story reported by Matthew (Matthew 8:5–13) and Luke (Luke 7:1–10), known as the healing of the Centurion's servant. There are, of course, both similarities and differences between John's account of the healing of the Capernaum official's son and the Synoptics report of the Centurion's servant. There is no point in quibbling over the details. The important thing is to see what John was telling and why. And that is that faith in Jesus Christ is absolutely necessary.

At Capernaum there was an official: John uses the Greek word which means a "king's man"—the official in government service of either Rome or "King" Herod Antipas, the tetrarch of Galilee. In any case, the officer stationed at Capernaum was not a Jew. However, he was a human parent with a deep personal crisis. Ultimately, his faith in Jesus grew to the point where he switched allegiance from being a "king's man" to being The King's man!

It would have taken a great deal of pride-swallowing for this official to make the journey from the city of Capernaum to the village of Cana, and as a proud official to humble himself before a Jewish rabbi to ask a personal favor. It shows how desperate the official was.

Unless you see signs and wonders you will not believe: Jesus is speaking not only to the official but to the bystanders. Probably, a crowd of curiosity seekers had gathered, hoping to be entertained by a dramatic miracle. The you in this phrase is plural, meaning that Jesus was addressing more than the official. Jesus refuses to pander to those demanding spectacular "proofs" to convince them.

Go, your son will live. The man believed: The official persisted with his request. The account shows how the man's faith gradually deepened. At first, he saw Jesus as merely a miracle-worker, and came to Jesus out of human need. He wanted Jesus to come down to Capernaum with him to work a cure. He was not discouraged by Jesus' words about wanting signs and wonders. When Jesus put the official to real test of faith—to trust in Jesus' powers to heal at a distance—the man rose to the occasion and went home confident that Jesus kept His promise. Furthermore, he became a believer, "and all his household."

This was now the second sign: The first sign was the changing water to wine at Cana. This one describes how Jesus' Word bestowed life on a boy as much as dead. It is a sign of the new life Jesus brings, even to outsiders and at a distance.

SUGGESTIONS TO TEACHERS

New Years! It means a fresh beginning. Many make resolutions to take advantage of the gift of a new year, a block of days as yet unsullied by broken promises and unfulfilled hopes. On this first Sunday of 1985, you will have two splendid stories from John's Gospel to describe the new life which Jesus Christ brings.

1. *INSISTENT INQUIRY.* Have your class examine the dialogue between Jesus and the woman at the Well of Sychar. Be sure they note her shallow character which comes through in her flippant responses and glib answers. Jesus won't let her (or anyone) get away with slick slogans. He demands a thoughtful response to His comments. Some people have "Bumper Sticker" reactions to God's serious

questions; that is, they simply mouth platitudes or commonplace pat phrases. Before new life can come to anyone from Christ, a person must enter into serious dialogue with the Lord.

2. *RESISTANT REBEL.* The woman at the well plays clever little evasion games with Jesus. Have your class point out the many ways and times she tries to switch the subject or throw Jesus off the track. Use the woman at the well as a Case History of evasive tactics in the Christian life. Ask your class to discuss why most people resist Jesus and rebel against His authority. Is it because most people want to take over for God?

3. *PERSISTENT PLEA.* If you have time, look up Francis Thompson's poem, "The Hound of Heaven." In this poem, the writer reflects on the way he tried to shake Jesus from tracking him down, but found that he could not. Jesus persistently pleads for us to take Him seriously and receive His offer of new life. In the case of the woman at the well, Jesus sees through her phony poses and sneaky ploys to get Him sidetracked. He unmasks her as the unsavory person she is. He is ruthlessly frank, yet discloses Himself to her as the Deliverer! Likewise, He knows us all for the not-so-nice people we actually are, yet persistently pleads for our commitment.

4. *CONSISTENT CONCERN.* You can easily devote all of the lesson time on the episode of the woman of Sychar, so be careful to allow plenty of time also for thoroughly reviewing the healing of the nobleman's son at Capernaum. John's Gospel account places this as the second of the "signs" of new life which Jesus Christ brings. Remind your class members that this healing is more than a miraculous event as far as John was concerned. It was a "sign"; that is, it pointed to something other than itself. In this case, it placards the new life brought by Jesus.

TOPIC FOR ADULTS
SIGNS OF NEW LIFE

Going Anywhere? Charles Dickens visited the United States in the 1840s. When he arrived in Washington, D.C., the nation's capital, he was dismayed to find it a raw, half-finished town with pigs wallowing in the streets. Although architects and planners had laid out blueprints for a great city, in the early nineteenth century Washington was a disappointment to Europeans like Dickens. Dickens took in the plans and the mud, and wrote that the American capital "had spacious avenues that begin in nothing and lead nowhere."

These words describe many lives, including the woman of Samaria at the Well of Sychar. Like so many, her life had little faith and seemed to begin in nothing and lead to nothing. She had little sense of meaning in life, and no goal.

Jesus persistently and patiently brought a sense of direction to her life. He transformed her from a person with a sense of no beginning or guidance to her existence to one centered on Him as the Deliverer. He gave her new life!

For all whose lives seem to be a dreary avenue without a start or destination, Jesus changes existence from "nothing" and "nowhere" to life with the Eternal One.

Defies the Level. One evening a man finished pouring and troweling a set of concrete steps. Next morning the steps were as he had left them, with the exception of one bulging spot, which he was astonished to see. He tried to level the bulge, but it would not stay down. Intrigued, he probed into the spot in search of the reason. Below the surface he found what looked like a small, oval stone. Actually, it was a bean!

Many times, we try to level Christ and push Him and His claims away so we won't have to think about His words. This is what the woman at the Well of Sychar tried to do. Like the bean, swelling and coming to the surface in the man's concrete job, however, Jesus will not be submerged and forgotten. His truth confronts the woman—and also confronts us!

Movie Star Confession. The official from Capernaum learned that he could trust Jesus, and discovered that Jesus gave new life to the little boy back in Capernaum the instant that trust was given. Likewise, we must learn to have such faith. When we do, we discover signs of new life in our midst.

Unfortunately, however, our faith is sometimes more like that of the Hollywood actress who was asked about her religion. "Oh, I'm so religious," the starlet burbled. "I just love faith." When asked what her faith was, the woman replied with great enthusiasm, "Oh, I believe in everything—a little bit."

Is this the nature of your faith—believing in everything a little bit?

Jesus Christ is the basis of true faith. When He receives your trust, you find that He surprises you with countless signs of new life!

Questions for Pupils on the Next Lesson. 1. What nourishment do you supply your spiritual life? 2. Is belief in Jesus Christ essential for eternal life? 3. Why were Jesus' words about being the Bread of Life in conflict with the contemporary religious beliefs? 4. How is Jesus as the Living Bread like the manna in the wilderness? 5. What pressures to legalistic conformity do you find in the church?

TOPIC FOR YOUTH
NEW WORDS AND WONDERS

"Faith Gave Me a New Start at Fifty-Six." "One night late in 1931, I was convinced I would never see another dawn. I wrote farewell letters to my family. Then I waited for the end—a failure at the age of fifty-six.

"I was in a sanitarium at Battle Creek, Michigan, a nervous and physical wreck, plagued by shingles, and certain I did not have a friend on earth. I believed the whole world was against me, including my wife and children.

"As a result of the financial dislocations of the depression, I had watched the fruits of a lifetime of toil swept away in a few brief months—a fortune estimated at $40,000,000, including all of my stock in the J. C. Penney Company, an organization I had seen grow from a single, small Wyoming store in 1902 to the world's largest department-store chain, with modern merchandising centers in every state in the Union.

"From being in a position to move mountains (I thought), I was overnight transformed into just another beaten man, in late middle age, flat broke and with no apparent future. As is not unusual in such crackups, I blamed everyone except myself. My failure seemed to weigh a ton on my shoulders.

"Somehow that dreadful night passed. The next morning as I shuffled from my room I heard the sound of singing coming from the mezzanine. The song was a hymn. I will never forget the title. It was: 'God Will Take Care of You.' I was drawn to the source of the song. A group of patients were holding a prayer meeting. Wearily I joined them.

"I prayed for God to take care of me, and an amazing thing happened. Suddenly I knew that He would. A profound sense of inner release came over me. The heavy weight seemed lifted from my spirit. That moment marked a turning point in my life.

"Perhaps the feeling of imminence of death was a sign that a new man was being born in me. Or maybe at long last I was learning how to pray, by truly submitting myself to the will of God.

"In any case, a remarkable change followed that session of prayers. I rapidly regained my mental and bodily health. Within a couple of months I was well enough to return to my family. We had been living on our sixty-five-acre estate at White Plains, New York, in a manner commensurate with wealth that no longer existed. Together with my wife, I now had the strength to take the steps that were needed."—J. C. Penney, "Journal of Living," November 1952.

We All Live by Faith. "How can I get faith? Where can I find it? You don't get faith, you already have it. The only place you can find it is within yourself. And the only way you can find your faith is to look for it instead of your fears and your failures.

"People die, businesses fail, automobiles are wrecked, jobs are lost, homes are broken up, friends are betrayed, lives are ruined. When you fill your mind with that sort of thing, no wonder you lose sight of your faith and think you have lost it. But just for one day, keep a list of the times you express faith. You will be surprised.

"I step out of bed in the morning onto the floor. I believe the floor will hold me up. I take a drink of water. The water comes from a muddy river contaminated with filth. In many places in the world, a person would not dare drink water until it was boiled. But I drink the water believing it has been purified. I eat for breakfast scrambled eggs. My wife could have put arsenic into the eggs but I have faith she didn't.

"I stop at the filling station for ten gallons of gasoline. I don't have a can to measure the gas, I have faith I'll get what I pay for. I stop at the mailbox to mail a payment on my life insurance. I am depending on that insurance to mean a lot to my wife and children if I should die, to help me if I get sick, to be a friend to me if I should get old and unable to work. That insurance means a lot to me yet I mail it to an office I have never seen, to be handled by men I will never know. Yet I have faith they will do what they say. Space doesn't permit the naming of the many times I used faith that one day.

"Along with 68 other people, I got on an airplane the other day. As we were waiting for the plane to take off, I got to figuring how much 68 people weigh. Allowing 150 pounds per person, the total is more than 10,000 pounds. Their baggage would add another 2,000 pounds. Then I got to figuring on the weight of the plane. It must be as much as 50,000 pounds. Maybe twice that much. Then I began thinking. In a few moments we would be going down that runway at 150 miles per hour. Beyond the end of the runway I could see tall trees and big rocks on the ground. If we went into those trees and rocks we would all be killed. But I looked at the big motors on the plane and I believed they had the power to lift that big plane above the trees. Looking just at the weight, I was fearful. Looking at the motors, I had faith.

"So it is in life. We automatically use faith in a thousand different ways but sometimes when we come to a place when we must consciously use faith, we shrink back. But instead of thinking of your loads to lift, think of your abilities, the support of other people, and especially of the help of God. And as you think of your power instead of your problems, you will find faith comes easily and naturally. And you are not then afraid of failure."—Charles L. Allen, *The Grace Pulpit.* Atlanta, Georgia: May 1958.

Sentence Sermon to Remember: The only place outside heaven where you can be perfectly safe from all the dangers and perturbations of love is hell—C. S. Lewis.

Questions for Pupils on the Next Lesson. 1. Why is *bread* such a meaningful symbol for who Jesus is? 2. Do you feel the need for spiritual nourishment as well as physical? If so, how are you nourishing yourself spiritually? 3. Why did Jesus' words about being the Bread of Life provoke such opposition? 4. Is trust in Jesus Christ necessary for eternal life?

LESSON VII—JANUARY 13

THE BREAD OF LIFE

Background Scripture: John 6
Devotional Reading: John 6:22–29

KING JAMES VERSION

JOHN 6 35 And Jesus said unto them, I am the bread of life: he that cometh to me shall never hunger; and he that believeth on me shall never thirst.

41 The Jews then murmured at him, because he said, I am the bread which came down from heaven.

42 And they said, Is not this Jesus, the son of Joseph, whose father and mother we know? how is it then that he saith, I came down from heaven?

43 Jesus therefore answered and said unto them, Murmur not among yourselves.

44 No man can come to me, except the Father which hath sent me draw him: and I will raise him up at the last day.

45 It is written in the prophets, And they shall be all taught of God. Every man therefore that hath heard, and hath learned of the Father, cometh unto me.

46 Not that any man hath seen the Father, save he which is of God, he hath seen the Father.

47 Verily, verily, I say unto you, He that believeth on me hath everlasting life.

48 I am that bread of life.

49 Your fathers did eat manna in the wilderness and are dead.

50 This *is* the bread which cometh down from heaven, that a man may eat thereof, and not die.

51 I am the living bread which came down from heaven: if any man eat of this bread, he shall live for ever: and the bread that I will give is my flesh, which I will give for the life of the world.

52 The Jews therefore strove among themselves, saying, How can this man give us *his* flesh to eat?

53 Then Jesus said unto them, Verily, verily, I say unto you, Except ye eat the flesh of the Son of man, and drink his blood, ye have no life in you.

54 Whoso eateth my flesh, and drinketh my blood, hath eternal life; and I will raise him up at the last day.

REVISED STANDARD VERSION

JOHN 6 35 Jesus said to them, "I am the bread of life; he who comes to me shall not hunger, and he who believes in me shall never thirst."

41 The Jews then murmured at him, because he said, "I am the bread which came down from heaven." 42 They said, "Is not this Jesus, the son of Joseph, whose father and mother we know? How does he now say, 'I have come down from heaven'?" 43 Jesus answered them, "Do not murmur among yourselves. 44 No one can come to me unless the Father who sent me draws him; and I will raise him up at the last day. 45 It is written in the prophets, 'And they shall all be taught by God.' Every one who has heard and learned from the Father comes to me. 46 Not that any one has seen the Father except him who is from God; he has seen the Father. 47 Truly, truly, I say to you, he who believes has eternal life. 48 I am the bread of life. 49 Your fathers ate the manna in the wilderness, and they died. 50 This is the bread which comes down from heaven, that a man may eat of it and not die. 51 I am the living bread which came down from heaven; if any one eats of this bread, he will live for ever; and the bread which I shall give for the life of the world is my flesh."

52 The Jews then disputed among themselves, saying, "How can this man give us his flesh to eat?" 53 So Jesus said to them, "Truly, truly, I say to you, unless you eat the flesh of the Son of man and drink his blood, you have no life in you; 54 he who eats my flesh and drinks my blood has eternal life, and I will raise him up at the last day.

KEY VERSE: *I am the living bread which came down from heaven; if any one eats of this bread, he will live for ever. . . .* John 6:51 (RSV).

HOME DAILY BIBLE READINGS

Jan. 7. M. *Healing at the Pool.* John 5:5–17.
Jan. 8. T. *Five Thousand Fed.* John 6:1–15.

Jan.   9.   W.   *Jesus Walks on the Water.* John 6:16–21.
Jan.   10. T.   *"Give Us This Bread."* John 6:22–34.
Jan.   11. F.   *Believe and Have Eternal Life.* John 6:35–40.
Jan.   12. S.   *The Living Bread.* John 6:41–51.
Jan.   13. S.   *Words of Eternal Truth.* John 6:60–71.

BACKGROUND

John's Gospel, like a great symphony, has several subthemes. One of these subthemes is the series of "I am" passages. John records the references Jesus made to Himself as the Bread of Life, the Way, the Truth, the Life, the Light, the Living Water, the Door, the Shepherd, the Resurrection and the Life. Many of the "signs" or miracle stories in the fourth Gospel lead directly into one of the "I am" statements. In the sixth chapter, for example, the Feeding of the Five Thousand is recorded by John as a sign that Jesus is the Bread of life.

When Jesus used the words, "I am . . ." He was using the very words which the Lord God used to respond to Moses' question about God's name. "I AM" was the sacred Name. Jesus employs the very term God Himself chose when He disclosed Himself to Moses in Exodus 3:14. In other words, Jesus wanted His hearers to understand that He spoke with the authority of God Himself!

The "I am the Bread of Life" saying following the miraculous feeding of the multitudes described in John 6 took place at Passover Time. Passover is a sacred family feast in Jewish tradition. Furthermore, respectable Jews were extremely selective about eating with others. Breaking bread was such a sacred ceremony and symbolized such a bond with those with whom the meal was shared that one did not eat with those who either were unclean or with whom one did not want to be bound through table fellowship. Passover was regarded as a time when meal partners were very carefully chosen. Jesus welcomed the entire rabble as His "kinfolk" to share a Passover. This sidelight on the Feeding episode gives additional meaning to Jesus' saying about Himself as "The Bread."

Passover celebrated the miraculous act of deliverance from slavery and death in Egypt at the time of Moses. Later, during the forty years' desert wandering in the wilderness, God fed the Israelites with manna. Jesus and His hearers clearly understood the series of historic references and the rich symbolism of "Bread" when Jesus spoke of Himself as the Bread of Life. In fact, many of His hearers took violent offense at the way Jesus spoke. The writer of the fourth Gospel reminded his hearers that Jesus provoked opposition from the outset by His insistence on repeating, "I am the Bread of Life."

NOTES ON THE PRINTED TEXT

I. *I am the bread of life:* These words mean both "I am the life-giving bread" and "I am the living bread." Notice that Jesus does not say that He offers some bread. He announces that He is the Bread of Life. The person receiving Him will not hunger anymore. The relationship with Jesus means coming from a state of merely existing to a condition of living!

Bread, of course, is basic. Jesus chooses this word which everybody understands to emphasize how essential He is to our growth. Some dismiss the Gospel as a frivolous extra or a marginal concern. "Some day, I may get around to looking into religions," a successful manufacturer's representative told his airplane seatmate who was a clergyman. Jesus maintains that He is not offering cake, but that He is the Bread for true living.

II. *The Jews murmured at him because he said, "I am the bread which came down from heaven." They said, "Is not this Jesus, the son of Joseph, whose father and mother we know?"* Jesus' claims are sneered at by the religious leaders. They know that Jesus is a local boy from a village up in the hills, and they know His family, so they think they know all about Him. They don't expect anything from peasant carpenters. They are a bit like the New Hampshire farmer who was so convinced that he knew all about the happenings of his crossroads village and that nothing significant could ever happen there that, when he heard that an eclipse of the sun was to take place in two days, hitched up his horses and drove to Boston to witness the phenomenon. When asked why he traveled all the way to Boston when the same sight could have been seen back in his home area, he replied, "Aw, nuthin' important can happen in that place." Like the New Hampshire farmer, the Galilean Jewish authorities "knew" nothing significant could ever happen in that place.

No one can come to me unless the Father who sent me draws him, and I will raise him up at the last day. It is written in the prophets, And they shall be taught by God. Everyone who has heard and learned from the Father comes to me: Jesus refuses to argue with His hearers on such a mundane matter, and lifts the conversation from an earthly to a heavenly level. Trust in Him, Jesus says, comes not from checking out His family pedigree and human reasoning but by God's action. God takes the initiative. He "draws" or tugs the person to believing in Jesus. Jesus makes it clear that His hearers are stubbornly resisting the divine pull.

Your fathers ate manna in the wilderness, and they died. This is the bread which comes down from heaven, that a man may eat of it and not die: The manna which the Israelites ate in their wilderness wanderings could not keep them alive forever. Death eventually won out over each of them. Jesus announces that He is the new manna. However, He will provide a new life over which death does not have the final say.

III. *Truly, truly, I say to you, unless you eat the flesh of the Son of Man and drink his blood, you have no life in you:* Jesus insists that His hearers must take Him so seriously that they will assimilate His life into their own lives. They must be so united with Jesus that they will be willing to lay down their lives in service and sacrifice for others as He does.

The words in this passage at first may seem to refer to some kind of cannibal rite, or to a crude understanding of Holy Communion. Jesus' hearers in the Capernaum synagogue, however, realized that He was making claims to be the answer for deepest human hungers. Union with Jesus Christ still means life with the Eternal!

SUGGESTIONS TO TEACHERS

Shortly after World War II, relief workers in Europe were having a difficult time with orphans found in some of the refugee camps. Most of these children had been exposed to hunger for so long that they were terrified of being deprived of enough food. The relief people repeatedly assured the youngsters that they could have all they wanted, and that there would be plenty the next day. Nonetheless, nearly all of the children suffered nightmares and woke up crying because they were so uneasy about food. Finally, one worker eased the effects of the children's traumas over fear of hunger with a simple method.

Each night, just after being put to bed, each child was handed a piece of bread to hold. The children quickly dropped off to sleep, and the number of bad dreams and nighttime screams quickly stopped. The bread symbolized security for those terrified war orphans.

Jesus selected the term *Bread* to tell others that He was the Giver of New Life. As the teacher of a class, you may well begin this lesson by having your people reflect on the meaning of *bread*. It is, of course, the staple of most people's diets.

Jesus obviously wanted everyone to think of Him as being indispensible to their lives. Your lesson from John 6 about Jesus as the Bread of Life offers plenty of lesson directions. Here are a few possibilities:

1. *INVITATION FROM A LOVING JESUS.* Others were exclusive when it came to eating with strangers. Jesus never was. Even at Passover time, the occasion when families and close friends joined for the sacred celebration, Jesus generously insisted that the disciples include the horde of bystanders when He and the Twelve prepared to eat. Jesus welcomes everyone!

2. *ABUNDANCE FROM A LITTLE LUNCH.* What could five barley loaves and two small dried fish do? We always put limits on our abilities and underestimate what we have to offer Jesus. When we share with Jesus and others, so much is possible!

3. *APPEARANCE TO SOME LONELY FRIENDS.* You may wish to include in your lesson the narrative in John 6 in which Jesus drew near to the boatload of frightened friends. He stands closer to us than we can imagine, and wants to be welcomed "into the boat" with us. Have your people relate the occasions when they became aware that they were not deserted in the midst of dark and stormy times.

4. *INSISTENCE ON THE LIVING BREAD.* Devote the heaviest portion of your lesson time on the key text about Jesus being the Bread of Life. Remind those in the class that only Jesus Christ can give authentic nourishment to grow as God's person. Only Jesus brings Eternal Life. It will help your people to think about the meaning of the phrase, "Eternal Life," as referring to living with the Eternal One, and discovering that each day takes on the character of a new creation with the Creator!

TOPIC FOR ADULTS
THE BREAD OF LIFE

Out of Solitude. "When Jesus had received five loaves and two fishes, he returned them to the crowd and there was plenty for all to eat. The gift is born out of receiving. Food came forth out of kinship with the hungry, healing out of compassion, cure out of care. He or she who can cry out with those in need can give without offense.

"As long as we are occupied and preoccupied with our desire to do good but are not able to feel the crying need of those who suffer, our help remains hanging somewhere between our minds and our hands and does not descend into the heart where we can care. But in solitude, our heart can slowly take off its many protective devices, and can grow so wide and deep that nothing human is strange to it.

"Then we can become contrite, crushed and broken, not just by our own sins and failings, but also by the pain of our fellow human beings. Then we can give birth to a new awareness reaching far beyond the boundaries of our human efforts. And then we who, in our fearful narrow-mindedness, were afraid that we would not have enough food for ourselves, will have to smile. For then we will discover that after having fed more than five thousand there were still twelve baskets of bread and fish remaining. Then our care born out of solitude can become a sign of our faithful expectation of the coming day of complete joy."— Henri J. M. Nouwen, *Out of Solitude*, Ave Maria Press, 1974.

Mike Doyle's Hunger. During a steel strike in Pittsburgh, a group of workers was shut in the Jones and Laughlin strip mill on Second Avenue for several weeks. One day, a big strapping foreman, named Mike Doyle, lumbered into the Superintendent's office.

"I'm sick," said Mike.

"Have you gone to the infirmary?"

"No. I'm sick in another way. My soul's sick."

Superintendents of hot strip mills aren't in the soul business. At first this superintendent was inclined to dismiss Mike and his complaint. Mike was dead serious, however.

"Look, I've not been to Church for weeks. I miss it. Something's wrong. I'm sick and I mean it."

Finally with union approval, they brought in a priest and a minister and held worship services for the men in the mill.

Old Mike wasn't wrong. He was sick. And so are a lot of you. Sick because you are starving to death for want of God.

God sent us One to feed us. In case you have not already known Him and received Him, pray that you may take in Him who said, "I am the Bread of Life. He that believeth on me shall never hunger. Him that cometh to me I will in no wise cast out." Amen.

Condition for Knowing God. "We cannot love God unless we love each other, and to love we must know each other; we know Him in the breaking of bread, and we know each other in the breaking of bread and we are not alone anymore."—Dorothy Day.

Questions for Pupils on the Next Lesson. 1. What was the Feast of Tabernacles? 2. Are there other ways than through Jesus to satisfy humankind's spiritual thirst? 3. How did Jesus escape arrest at the Feast in John 7? 4. What can best bring reassurance and promise to troubled persons in these times? 5. How is Jesus the answer for those who are confused about spiritual reality?

TOPIC FOR YOUTH
EVERYTHING YOU NEED

Miracle of One Aspirin Bottle. One of the most heartwarming news stories a few years ago concerned a thirteen-year-old black boy named Robert Hill. Robert Hill's father at the time was an army sergeant stationed in Italy, and Robert was living with his family there.

Robert Hill had read about Albert Schweitzer and his marvelous missionary work in Lambarene, Africa. Young Robert was inspired by Dr. Schweitzer's hospital work and decided that he would contribute a bottle of aspirin to the hospital which the late Dr. Schweitzer had founded. He asked the Allied Air Force Commander in Southern Europe if an air force plane could drop the bottle at Albert Schweitzer's hospital.

An Italian radio station heard about what seemed to be an absurd-sounding request and broadcast it. Suddenly four-and-one-half tons of medical supplies poured in from all over the world. Worth over $400,000, these supplies were carried in planes furnished by the French and Italian governments.

Robert Hill's bottle of aspirin had been used to effect a miracle. Because of one seemingly unacceptable gift by a seemingly insignificant boy in a seemingly impossible way, a gift of magnificent proportions was brought about.

This reminds us of the boy that day when Jesus fed the 5,000. A youngster probably Robert Hill's age came with the lunch of plainest fare (the barley cake was the cheapest, coarsest loaf, eaten only by the poor and peasants, the fish were the inexpensive pickled common variety to add a bit of seasoning to the bread). He was an unexpected person with unexpected materials used in an unexpected way by God.

Time after time this "miracle" has been worked, where Christ uses unexpected people with unexpected materials in unexpected ways.

Taste of Bread. "We have been caught in the talons of the great American Dream.

"It's hard to identify the American Dream: it's such a cornucopia of things. So let's allow an outsider to speak to us. Paulo Francis, a Brazilian living in New York, commented on the current malaise in 'Folha de Sao Paulo,' December 3, 1978:

" 'Propound what you may, everything points to the fact that the religion, the ideology of this nation is "Consume." One hundred million Americans, every night ... faithfully watch TV, a relentless, permanent bazaar. Every possible human emotion, anxiety, fear and uncertainty is captured in the TV commercials, whose final message invariably is that if you purchase X product every problem in your life will be resolved.

" 'Some fool wrote that we live in the "Age of Me," in the generation of "I love Me." The Madness of buying for oneself has taken hold, and the ultimate object to be consumed is the individual himself.'

"Gradually, without our realizing it, much of the life of the spirit has been squeezed out of us. We don't want to hear what Scripture says about the hungry and needy. We are moved more by this week's rise in the cost of gasoline than by the titanic problem of world hunger.

"We're busy consuming ourselves. Read the titles of the flood of books skyrocketing the sales figures of Christian bookstores. The vast majority deal with self-fulfillment.

"If we make our navels the center of the spiritual universe, we are titanic failures. Even a frenetic pursuit of spiritual highs can rob us of awareness of the world we live in—and of our absurdity in it.

"True inward spiritual discipline will lead to an outward ministry of concern—and away from the great American pursuit of self-consumption.

"We live in a hungry world in which more people are unreached than ever before. We have greater things to do in our generation than to fight one another or run a treadmill of spiritual self-fulfillment. Thousands of groups of people desperately need both bread and their first taste of the Bread of Life."—Dave Fraser, *World Vision*, August 1979. Used by permission.

Everything a Tony-Winner Needs. Ben Harney received a Tony for his outstanding acting in *Dreamgirls* in 1982. Although he is proud of the award and works hard as an actor, Ben Harney is most interested in and committed to Jesus Christ. Ben Harney speaks easily and frequently of how Jesus Christ, the Bread of Life, offers everything he really needs. Mr. Harney says prayer helps him recover from the "emotional drain" he undergoes in every performance of *Dreamgirls*.

There were moments in the 1982 Tony Awards pageant that sounded a lot like an old-fashioned revival meeting. In the midst of the usual hoopla, some winners expanded the normal round of thank-you's by paying ardent tribute to God. To many onlookers, accustomed to hearing a more conventional show-business litany of gratitude, these spiritual testimonies created a surprising, even arresting, sensation.

The display of faith was in large measure a coincidence. Awards happened to be won by certain people who are particularly open about their beliefs. Ben Harney of *Dreamgirls* just said what came naturally: that God deserved credit for his accomplishments. Harney, who keeps a Bible nearby most of the time, says he reached a turning point in his life while touring with *Ain't Misbehavin'* in 1979. He was in Boston, struggling with the question of whether he really believed the Christian message as conveyed in the Bible. He decided in favor one day and has known the strength and nourishment of Jesus Christ ever since.

A serious, personable young man, he reads the Scriptures daily, prays often, takes an active role as a member of Faith Tabernacle in Brooklyn and serves as a spiritual mentor for a prayer and Bible study group made up of theater people. Every Wednesday for the past few months, the group has convened in a lounge in the Imperial Theater, between the matinees and the evening performances. The group has steadily grown to its present average attendance of slightly more than a dozen. Some are employed as dancers and actors, others are out of work, but they share strong spiritual convictions.

At a recent meeting, Mr. Harney led the discussion, exhorting, instructing, and encouraging. At the close, all joined hands and prayed long and exuberantly, while a theater employee trooped back and forth fetching ice from a machine.

"God gave me everything I have," Mr. Harney said as the group was dispersing. His words are echoed in his Playbill program note. "Mr. Harney is a Christian with a beautiful and devoted family," it reads. "He says that all he is and has is due to the grace of God."

Questions for Pupils on the Next Lesson. 1. What was the "great feast"—the Feast of Tabernacles—described in John 7? 2. Do you sometimes feel the need for a strength beyond your own which will enable you to help others? 3. Why does it sometimes seem difficult to recognize what is good or beneficial for you? 4. Why were some people confused about who Jesus was, according to John 7? 5. Do you think that Jesus is the One who can really satisfy humankind's spiritual thirst?

LESSON VIII—JANUARY 20

THE WATER OF LIFE

Background Scripture: John 4:7–15; 7
Devotional Reading: John 7:1–13

KING JAMES VERSION

JOHN 7 30 Then they sought to take him: but no man laid hands on him, because his hour was not yet come.

31 And many of the people believed on him, and said, When Christ cometh, will he do more miracles than these which this *man* hath done?

32 The Pharisees heard that the people murmured such things concerning him; and the Pharisees and the chief priests sent officers to take him.

33 Then said Jesus unto them, Yet a little while am I with you, and *then* I go unto him that sent me.

34 Ye shall seek me, and shall not find *me:* and where I am, *thither* ye cannot come.

35 Then said the Jews among themselves, Whither will he go, that we shall not find him? will he go unto the dispersed among the Gentiles, and teach the Gentiles?

36 What *manner of* saying is this that he said, Ye shall seek me, and shall not find *me:* and where I am, *thither* ye cannot come?

37 In the last day, that great *day* of the feast, Jesus stood and cried, saying, If any man thirst, let him come unto me, and drink.

38 He that believeth on me, as the Scripture hath said, out of his belly shall flow rivers of living water.

39 (But this spake he of the Spirit, which they that believe on him should receive: for the Holy Ghost was not yet *given;* because that Jesus was not yet glorified.)

40 Many of the people therefore, when they heard this saying, said, Of a truth this is the Prophet.

41 Others said, This is the Christ. But some said, Shall Christ come out of Galilee?

42 Hath not the Scripture said, That Christ cometh out of the seed of David, and out of the town of Bethlehem, where David was?

43 So there was a division among the people because of him.

44 And some of them would have taken him; but no man laid hands on him.

REVISED STANDARD VERSION

JOHN 7 30 So they sought to arrest him; but no one laid hands on him, because his hour had not yet come. 31 Yet many of the people believed in him; they said, "When the Christ appears, will he do more signs than this man has done?"

32 The Pharisees heard the crowd thus muttering about him, and the chief priests and Pharisees sent officers to arrest him. 33 Jesus then said, "I shall be with you a little longer, and then I go to him who sent me; 34 you will seek me and you will not find me; where I am you cannot come." 35 The Jews said to one another, "Where does this man intend to go that we shall not find him? Does he intend to go to the Dispersion among the Greeks and teach the Greeks? 36 What does he mean by saying, 'You will seek me and you will not find me,' and, 'Where I am you cannot come'?"

37 On the last day of the feast, the great day, Jesus stood up and proclaimed, "If any one thirst, let him come to me and drink. 38 He who believes in me, as the scripture has said, 'Out of his heart shall flow rivers of living water.' " 39 Now this he said about the Spirit, which those who believed in him were to receive; for as yet the Spirit had not been given, because Jesus was not yet glorified.

40 When they heard these words, some of the people said, "This is really the prophet." 41 Others said, "This is the Christ." But some said, "Is the Christ to come from Galilee? 42 Has not the scripture said that the Christ is descended from David, and comes from Bethlehem, the village where David was?" 43 So there was a division among the people over him. 44 Some of them wanted to arrest him, but no one laid hands on him.

KEY VERSE: "If any one thirst, let him come to me and drink." John 7:37 (RSV).

HOME DAILY BIBLE READINGS

Jan. 14. M. *Jesus and His Brothers.* John 7:1–9.
Jan. 15. T. *Teaching in the Temple.* John 7:10–24.
Jan. 16. W. *Is This the Christ?* John 7:25–31.
Jan. 17. T. *Rivers of Living Water.* John 7:32–39.
Jan. 18. F. *The People Divided.* John 7:40–44.

Jan.   19.   S.   No Prophet From Galilee. John 7:45–52. .
Jan.   20.   S.   "Do Not Sin Again." John 8:1–11.

BACKGROUND

Water is such a precious commodity in the Middle East that battles have been
fought over the rights to use certain wells. Until recently, water sellers were a
common sight in all towns. All towns and villages, in fact, were originally situated
near a source of fresh water. Stories abound of invaders forcing towns to capitu-
late by seizing the spring or water source outside the walls. Jerusalem was saved
from the Assyrians when King Hezekiah had a tunnel dug to bring the water inside the city. In an area in which water is critically short and costly, people appreciated the value of water in a way that few of us do. Furthermore, we are so
used to turning on a faucet for an immediate and ample supply of water that few
of us can imagine the toil it would take to carry every drop for drinking, cooking,
and washing—sometimes for considerable distances.

When Jesus spoke of Himself as the Water of Life, he struck an immediate re-
sponsive chord. His hearers all knew what thirst could be. They also understood
the importance of water to their lives. Nobody took water for granted!

John tells of two occasions when Jesus spoke of Himself as the Living Water.
The first was in private to the Samaritan woman at the Well of Sychar. The second was in public to His own people in Jerusalem during the Feast of Tabernacles.

The occasion in Jerusalem during the Feast of Tabernacles provoked controversy and opposition. Jerusalem was packed with religious pilgrims. Jesus, John
reports, came to Jerusalem on several occasions to celebrate important Jewish
feasts. The Feast of Tabernacles commemorated the time when the Hebrews
wandered from oasis to oasis in the desert for forty years after fleeing from Egypt,
living in "tabernacles" or make-shift shelters. The memory of how crucial water
was to their ancestors in the desert gave additional impact to Jesus' words.

In addition, and perhaps most important, Jesus selected a term which all of His
hearers understood to refer to the Lord. There are many references in the Scriptures to God being a "Fountain of Living Water" (*see* Jeremiah 2:13; 17:13).
Jesus' choice of this word left no doubt in anyone's mind who He thought Himself
to be!

NOTES ON THE PRINTED TEXT

I. *The Pharisees heard the crowd thus muttering about him:* People in Jerusalem
during the Feast of Tabernacles began to guess that Jesus was the Messiah. They
said to each other, according to John, "When the Christ appears, will he do more
signs than this man has done?" (7:31). The authorities were growing more determined to silence Jesus.

*I shall be with you a little longer, and then I shall go to him who sent me; you
will seek me and you will not find me; where I am you cannot come:* Jesus meant
that He would soon be called upon to lay down His life on the Cross and return to
the Father, but His hearers misunderstood and assumed that He would present
His case to non-Hebrew speaking Jews and to Gentiles. The proud inhabitants of
Jerusalem looked down their noses at fellow Jews who lived outside Judea and
spoke Greek as their mother tongue. Above all, the Jerusalem folks despised
Gentiles. Although their words were spoken in derision, they actually recognized
that Jesus came for all peoples!

II. On the last day of the Feast, the great day, Jesus stood up and proclaimed,
"If anyone thirst, let him come to me and drink": The Feast of the Tabernacles,
one of the three great festivals for Jews, brought thousands of visitors to the

Temple since it was a requirement for all Jewish males within twenty miles of Jerusalem to attend. The last or eighth day was known as the "Great Day" of the holy occasion and was the climax. The central ceremony on that final day was when a priest took a pitcher made of pure gold down to the Pool of Siloam, filled it and carried it through the Water Gate to the Temple Court. As the pitcher of water was paraded through the streets, the people sang the Psalms 113–118 and recited the verse from Isaiah 12:3. "With joy you will draw water from the wells of salvation, and you will say in that day: 'Give thanks to the Lord, call upon his name.' " Finally, the water from the pitcher was poured out on the Temple altar amidst more singing and shouts of Scripture. This entire ritual of the water celebrated the memory of the way the Lord had miraculously provided fresh water from the split rock during the sojourn of the Israelites in the wilderness in Moses' time.

Jesus selects this dramatic moment to announce, "If anyone thirst, let him come to me and drink" (John 7:37). He states in effect that the worshipers are giving thanks merely for water that temporarily relieves thirsty throats. He, however, presents Himself as the only One who quenches deepest thirst.

As the scripture has said, Out of my heart shall flow rivers of living water: Scholars are puzzled by the reference to Scripture cited here, but think it is probably a paraphrase of Zechariah 14:8, part of the chapter which was always read at the Feast of the Tabernacles. Probably John the Gospel writer was also thinking of Jesus as the Rock in the wilderness, who, when His side was pierced at the crucifixion, gushed forth waters.

The important thing is that Jesus promises that anyone who believes in Him shall have within him a constant source of refreshment. The heart, according to Judaism in that time, was where a person's deepest thoughts and feelings were centered. Jesus assures His hearers that He will be for them what the rock in the wilderness in old times had been, except that He provides permanent strength for those knowing a world-weariness, dissatisfaction with life, and restlessness within themselves. Jesus is the Water of Life!

III. . . . *Some of the people said, "This really is the prophet." Others said, "This is the Christ." But some said, "Is the Christ to come from Galilee?"* In spite of Jesus' astonishing claim and offer, some insisted on quibbling about His credentials as God's Chosen One. Others acknowledged that He was "the prophet" whom Moses had promised in Deuteronomy 18:15. But a number still missed the significance of Jesus' words and complained that the Messiah was supposed to be a descendant of David and born in Bethlehem. They ruled out Jesus as the Messiah because they "knew" that He was nobody but a carpenter from a minor village up in Galilee. How often people miss the significance of Jesus because of their mistaken, preconceived notions of who He is!

SUGGESTIONS TO TEACHERS

Except for an occasional emergency, such as a ruptured water main or an exceptionally severe drought causing water shortages for a brief period of time, water is relatively cheap and plentiful in most of the Western world. Few in your class will know what it is to have to live where water is scarce. And few will have had to fetch water from a distance, such as was often done a couple of generations ago in this country in rural areas. You may want to start this lesson on Jesus as the Living Water by asking people in your class to relate any stories they know describing how hard it was to get water and how precious water was. Perhaps they can even tell of a time when they experienced a real thirst and no water was available for a time. Tie these reminiscences in with Jesus' claim to be the Living Water.

1. *SOURCE.* As teacher, you will have two excellent passages from John's Gospel to work with. Begin by considering what Jesus meant when He referred to Himself as the "Living Water" in John 4:10 and 7:38. In Jewish tradition, these words referred to God. They suggest the Source. The term also means nourishment which brings life. With these thoughts in mind, urge your class to consider how Jesus wants His hearers to think of Him.

2. *SATISFACTION.* Those who come to Him, Jesus states, will "never thirst again" (John 4:13). Ask your class if any other teacher, leader, or hero can make this claim and make it stick. Remind your people that our problem is that we insist on turning to other sources of satisfaction in life. Ask your people to identify some of these. Nudge your class to examine the kind of satisfaction which Jesus brings to believers.

3. *SUPPING.* "Come to me and drink," Jesus invites (John 7:37). Note that there is no esoteric knowledge required, no elaborate ceremony. Simply, "Come and drink!" Jesus welcomes any person thirsty for hope, for mercy, for purpose, for God Himself to approach Him. He maintains that His life is the only one which assuages those deepest thirsts in life, and that He is more than willing to grant that refreshing and satisfying sense of the Eternal to anyone who asks.

4. *SHARING.* The person who receives "the Living Waters" by associating with Jesus is expected to be a source of life-giving nourishment to others. "He who believes in me," Jesus insists "out of his heart shall flow rivers of living water" (7:38). Anyone who has been with Jesus must be a conduit of care!

TOPIC FOR ADULTS
THE WATER OF LIFE

Beginning With the Word "Water." Helen Keller, who lived in the silence and darkness of being deaf and blind, was an untamed animal as a child until an inspired teacher named Anne Sullivan brought her into the world of reality with the word *water.* Miss Keller's description could also apply to the way Jesus Christ is the Water of Life.

"One day, while I was playing with my new doll, Miss Sullivan put my big rag doll into my lap also, spelled d-o-l-l and tried to make me understand that 'd-o-l-l' applied to both. Earlier in the day we had a tussle over the words m-u-g and w-a-t-e-r. . . . I became impatient at her repeated attempts and, seizing the new doll, I dashed it upon the floor. I was keenly delighted when I felt the fragments of the broken doll at my feet . . . I had not loved the doll. In the still, dark world in which I lived there was no strong sentiment or tenderness. I felt my teacher sweep the fragments to one side. . . . She brought me my hat and I knew I was going out into the warm sunshine.

"We walked down the path to the well-house. . . . Some one was drawing water and my teacher placed my hand under the spout. As the cool stream gushed over one hand she spelled into the other the word *water,* first slowly, then rapidly. . . . Suddenly I felt a misty consciousness as of something forgotten—a thrill of returning thought; and somehow the mystery of language was revealed to me. . . .

"I left the well-house eager to learn. Everything had a name, and each name gave birth to a new thought. As we returned to the house every object which I touched seemed to quiver with life."—Helen Keller, *The Story of My Life,* New York: Doubleday & Co., Inc., 1947.

No More Thirst. When T. E. Lawrence, the famous "Lawrence of Arabia," brought a group of desert warriors to England at the close of the first World War, the thing which impressed them most was the abundance of fresh water. The Arabian sheiks even asked to buy water faucets to take home with them. When

Lawrence asked why, they told him that they wanted to be able to turn the spigot and have a drink of clean, clear, cold water any time they wanted, just as they had in England. Lawrence, of course, had to point out that the faucets were attached to pipes leading to water mains. Nonetheless, it showed again how important water was to those people.

It reminds us again how vivid Jesus' words were to His hearers when He announced that He was the Living Waters! He meets humankind's deepest thirst.

Water for a Thirsty World in Christ's Name. We are asked to focus attention on the enormous suffering and deaths that occur as a result of the use of impure water and inadequate sanitation. The World Bank estimates that three out of every four people in the Third World lack safe water and sanitation. The results are clear.

According to the World Health Organization (WHO), approximately 80 percent of all sickness and disease can be attributed to inadequate water and lack of proper sanitation. Although age does not provide immunity from water-related diseases, it is the survival of the children that is most precarious; diarrhea alone kills millions every year. UNICEF estimates that infant mortality could be cut as much as 50 percent worldwide with water and sanitation needs safely met.

It is not only the quality of water that plays a major part in this tragedy, but its availability as well. When water is not readily accessible, women must endure special hardships often as debilitating as they are inescapable. Their time and strength is sapped by the never-ending routine of carrying water over long distances, sometimes several times a day. As women strive to practice better hygiene in the home, their need for water correspondingly increases, thus a greater burden must be borne.

This daily trek uses many hours women might otherwise spend on more productive educational or income-earning pursuits which could improve the quality of life for all in the community. Water portage together with agricultural work and other essential chores leaves them barely enough time to care for themselves, their children, and their homes. Hard work, poor nutrition, and high exposure to infections all combine to threaten women's chances of survival.

From its earliest years, CWS (Church World Service) has recognized the vast difference an easily accessible source of potable water can mean for women as well as the entire community; money and expertise have been given for water projects in many parts of the world.

The most comprehensive CWS water project lies in the Malagasy Republic (Madagascar), and is an example of a project based on the use of appropriate technology and community participation. It encompasses virtually all basic drinking water supply forms, from hand-dug and drilled wells to stream-fed gravity-flow water supply systems to windmill pumps and dams.

CWS Water Supply Program staff planned the systems in consultation with villagers who requested assistance. Once the planning was completed, villagers helped to dig trenches and install water storage tanks and pipes. Where wells were dug by hand, the villagers carried out most of the labor. The supply systems have tripled water consumption in the villages affected, greatly improving hygiene.

At the end of 1979, the last CWS representative, a native of Malagasy, turned the office over to Fikrifama, the CWS colleague agency there.

All this is done in the name of the One Who is the Water of Life—Jesus Christ!

Questions for Pupils on the Next Lesson. 1. Does God judge everything and everyone, or only religious matters and church people? 2. Does sin really bring death? 3. What precisely does true discipleship entail? 4. How does freedom from enslavement to sin come? 5. Must one know Jesus in order to know the Father?

TOPIC FOR YOUTH
OPEN INVITATION

Desperate Shortage. A huge, six-foot pipe bringing water to several New Jersey communities burst unexpectedly on July 15, 1982, leaving over 300,000 people without water for several days. The break released over a million gallons an hour from the rupture in the Hackensack Meadowlands. Large gates designed to stop the flow did not work properly, and the repair crews could not weld a steel plate patch at the break because of continuing flow. Lack of water pressure prevented a back-up pipe being used. The crisis quickly became acute as water supplies were completely cut off to Jersey City.

Meanwhile, people suffered. The signboard atop the Jersey City Savings Bank recorded 99 degree temperatures during the stifling heat waves.

Restaurants, bars, and all businesses that use water were ordered closed indefinitely. The manager of a Burger King restaurant was arrested on a charge of violating the emergency declaration. Residents in the city's downtown section, who were still getting some water from a subsidiary reservoir fed by the broken pipe, were warned not to drink it because of contamination.

The National Guard moved 250-gallon water tanks through the city and distributed cartons of bottled water to nursing homes and private homes of the elderly. About forty tanker trucks were stationed at firehouses and near hospitals.

The Mayor, Gerald McCann, warned downtown residents on the water line coming from the subsidiary reservoir in the city, not to drink the water or use it for cooking under any circumstances. He said health officials had found that the bacteria count was dangerously high. The mayor said a chlorinator at the reservoir was not functioning.

Marie Stannelos and her three-year-old son, Andrew, pulled a wagon filled with plastic pails and buckets up to an 8,000 gallon milk tanker that had been pressed into service and placed in Gordon Park on Kennedy Boulevard.

"It's been very difficult," she said, "We have six people in our family. We've been using plastic plates and paper cups, but there is not enough water to flush the toilet."

Other residents lined up at dozens of water distribution points to fill every manner of vessel.

Others pulled gallon after gallon of bottled water from the shelves of supermarkets, where supplies were reported running short.

"I even work at the A & P (supermarket) and the bottled water went so fast that I couldn't get any," said Deborah Walsh.

When water finally flowed again four days later after the break was mended, people had a new appreciation of the necessity for water. Christ's people, remembering how Jesus spoke of Himself as the Water of Life, realized more deeply how vital He is after experiencing life without sufficient life-giving substance.

Two-thirds of the World Lacking Adequate Water. Two-thirds of the world's population, most of them in developing countries, are without adequate water supplies, according to Yahia Abdel Mageed, a Sudanese who is a United Nations official concerned with water problems.

Think, though, how many of the world's people are also without news of the One who is Living Water—Jesus Christ. The Church, through its mission programs, often introduces Jesus Christ to people in developing countries without adequate water supplies by helping them dig better wells and get improved irrigation systems. Through clean, fresh and abundant water in villages in Africa and Asia which have not known of Jesus, the Good News of Christ is being shared.

Twenty-Five Gallons of Water! A boy reared on a farm was very fond of corn on the cob. And he learned a great deal about raising corn from helping his father. He was astonished one day when his dad told him that it took twenty-five gallons of water to produce one ear of corn!

The boy immediately tried to imagine what a great task it would be if he had to carry that much water to the field for each of the many ears of corn which would be harvested. But his father reassured him that it is the gradual day-by-day rains that add up to the amount necessary for the corn to grow. He reminded the boy of times when the rain failed to come over a long period and the corn was lost. "Even a downpour of rain would not have have helped then," he said.

That same boy eventually came to appreciate Jesus' words about being the Water of Life. Realizing the amount of water it takes to develop one ear of corn, that boy thought how much of Christ's help it must take to help each person grow to spiritual maturity.

Questions for Pupils on the Next Lesson. 1. Do you believe that God actually judges you and everyone in the world? 2. Is it true that disobeying God brings destruction? 3. How would you define true discipleship of Jesus Christ? 4. To know the Father, do you have to know Jesus? 5. How does a person get free from being enslaved to sin?

LESSON IX—JANUARY 27

THE JUDGE OF LIFE

Background Scripture: John 5:19–24; 8:12–59
Devotional Reading: John 8:31–35

KING JAMES VERSION

JOHN 8   12 Then spake Jesus again unto them, saying, I am the light of the world: he that followeth me shall not walk in darkness, but shall have the light of life.

13 The Pharisees therefore said unto him, Thou bearest record of thyself; thy record is not true.

14 Jesus answered and said unto them, Though I bear record of myself, *yet* my record is true: for I know whence I came, and whither I go; but ye cannot tell whence I come, and whither I go.

15 Ye judge after the flesh; I judge no man.

16 And yet if I judge, my judgment is true: for I am not alone, but I and the Father that sent me.

17 It is also written in your law, that the testimony of two men is true.

18 I am one that bear witness of myself, and the Father that sent me beareth witness of me.

19 Then said they unto him, Where is thy Father? Jesus answered, Ye neither know me, nor my father: if ye had known me, ye should have known my Father also.

20 These words spake Jesus in the treasury, as he taught in the temple: and no man laid hands on him; for his hour was not yet come.

21 Then said Jesus again unto them, I go my way, and ye shall seek me, and shall die in your sins: whither I go, ye cannot come.

22 Then said the Jews, Will he kill himself? because he saith, Whither I go, ye cannot come.

23 And he said unto them, Ye are from beneath; I am from above: ye are of this world; I am not of this world.

24 I said therefore unto you, that ye shall die in your sins: for if ye believe not that I am *he*, ye shall die in your sins.

25 Then said they unto him, Who art thou? And Jesus saith unto them, Even *the same* that I said unto you from the beginning.

26 I have many things to say and to judge of you: but he that sent me is true; and I speak to the world those things which I have heard of him.

27 They understood not that he spake to them of the Father.

REVISED STANDARD VERSION

JOHN 8   12 Again Jesus spoke to them, saying, "I am the light of the world; he who follows me will not walk in darkness, but will have the light of life." 13 The Pharisees then said to him, "You are bearing witness to yourself; your testimony is not true." 14 Jesus answered, "Even if I do bear witness to myself, my testimony is true, for I know whence I have come and whither I am going, but you do not know whence I come or whither I am going. 15 You judge according to the flesh, I judge no one. 16 Yet even if I do judge, my judgment is true, for it is not I alone that judge, but I and he who sent me. 17 In your law it is written that the testimony of two men is true; 18 I bear witness to myself, and the Father who sent me bears witness to me." 19 They said to him therefore, "Where is your Father?" Jesus answered, "You know neither me nor my Father; if you knew me, you would know my Father also." 20 These words he spoke in the treasury, as he taught in the temple; but no one arrested him, because his hour had not yet come.

21 Again he said to them, "I go away, and you will seek me and die in your sin; where I am going, you cannot come." 22 Then said the Jews, "Will he kill himself, since he says, 'Where I am going, you cannot come'?" 23 He said to them, "You are from below, I am from above; you are of this world, I am not of this world. 24 I told you that you would die in your sins, for you will die in your sins unless you believe that I am he." 25 They said to him, "Who are you?" Jesus said to them, "Even what I have told you from the beginning. 26 I have much to say about you and much to judge; but he who sent me is true, and I declare to the world what I have heard from him." 27 They did not understand that he spoke to them of the Father.

KEY VERSE: *I bear witness to myself, and the Father who sent me bears witness to me.* John 8:18 (RSV).

HOME DAILY BIBLE READINGS

Jan. 21. M.   *From Death to Life.* John 5:19–24.
Jan. 22. T.   *Testimony to Jesus.* John 5:30–40.
Jan. 23. W.   *The Light of Life.* John 8:12–20.
Jan. 24. T.   *"I Am He."* John 8:21–30.
Jan. 25. F.   *"Truth Will Make You Free."* John 8:31–38.
Jan. 26. S.   *Jesus and Abraham.* John 8:39–47.
Jan. 27. S.   *God Will Judge.* John 8:48–59.

BACKGROUND

Darkness and Light are favorite themes throughout the Bible. The word *Light*, however, has a deeper meaning. It is also a term for God. "The Lord is my light and my salvation," sings the Psalmist (Psalms 27:1). "Arise, shine; for your light has come. . . . The Lord will be your everlasting light," cried Isaiah (Isaiah 60:1, 19). "The Lord will be a light to me," stated Micah (Micah 7:8). When Jesus announced that He was the Light, He shocked many of His hearers. He was deliberately selecting a word freighted with associations with God Himself. Jesus claimed to take on the authority of God.

The reaction was swift. The scribes and the Pharisees accused Him of (1) bearing witness to Himself and (2) presuming to know the truth. They tried to put Him in His place by asserting that He didn't have the necessary witnesses to make His claim stand up in a Jewish court (as in Deuteronomy 19:15). They also tried to belittle His claims by suggesting that He meant that He'd kill Himself, or would be guilty of the worst kind of blasphemy.

Jesus asserts that He has the right to judge because He had been given the same knowledge to pass judgment which God has. Jesus claims to have all the facts to judge. He states that He is one with God.

He goes further. In this passage in John 8, Jesus denounces the authorities for refusing to heed Him. Since He can make divine judgments, Jesus warns His hearers that they are in mortal danger. They reject Him at their own peril. In doing so, Jesus says, they show how little they know God! The religious authorities had become so self-righteous and self-confident that they were blind to the presence of God's authority in the person of Jesus!

NOTES ON THE PRINTED TEXT

The confrontation between Jesus and the authorities in the Temple during the Feast of Tabernacles is continued in John 8:12–27. Jesus challenges His hearers to consider who He is and what His unique relationship to God is. Those rejecting His claims, Jesus warns, bring judgment on themselves for their stubborn blindness.

I. *I am the light of the world; he who follows me will not walk in darkness, but will have the light of life:* During the Feast of the Tabernacles, four enormous candelabra were lighted in the Court of the Women in the Temple in Jerusalem. The light was said to be so great that every courtyard in the city was illuminated. During the night, the religious leaders sang and danced joyfully before a huge audience. This part of the festival was called the Illumination of the Temple, and commemorated the great pillar of fire that led the Israelites each night in their trek through the wilderness in the days of Moses. Jesus seizes this opportunity—a high point in Temple ceremonies—to make His claim as Messiah again. "I am the light," is a vivid way of announcing He is the Anointed One. *Light* was one of the traditional names for the Messiah. Isaiah, for example, had stated that the Servant of the Lord would be sent as "a light to the nations that my salvation may reach to the ends of the earth" (Isaiah 49:6).

His hearers, especially the Pharisees and other leaders, got His message. And they did not like it.

II. *The Pharisees then said to him, "You are bearing witness to yourself; your testimony is not true"*: Here is another example of Jesus' listeners refusing to try to consider who He is. The Pharisees are stuck in their rule books and insist on examining every word of Jesus from a legalistic standpoint. When He asserts His claims to be the Messiah, they trot out the requirement from the courts declaring a person's testimony about himself is not heard without the support of at least two witnesses (Deuteronomy 19:15).

Jesus tells them that only He knows where He came from and what His destiny will be, but that His testimony has the support of the One who sent Him—the Father. The authorities' retort is, in effect, "Bring in your witness" when they demand, "Where is your Father?" (John 8:19).

Where is your Father? The religious leaders try to put down Jesus both by using legal tactics, and challenging Him to produce an appearance of the invisible God immediately for them. They think that they have Him nicely boxed in a corner with this clever question. Obviously, these Temple authorities and Pharisees assume that they have the right to judge Jesus and His claims. They superciliously dismiss Him and His assertions of being the Messiah.

Jesus refuses to whip up little miracles to establish His claims before the Pharisees—or before anyone setting himself or herself above Him as judge. Jesus insists that only He is given the divine mandate to be the judge of life. "If you knew me," he asserts, "you would know my Father also" (8:19).

These words he spoke in the treasury: This exchange took place in the section of the Court of the Women of the Temple where the thirteen large trumpet-shaped receptacles stood for offerings. This was the area where Jesus watched the widow drop in her mite (Mark 12:42). It was also adjacent to the meeting place of the Sanhedrin, the Council of the Seventy or Supreme Court. John, who was familiar with the layout of the Temple, mentions this to show that Jesus' words were undoubtedly overheard by His most severe critics and bitter enemies.

Will he kill himself? Jesus announces that He is going away where they cannot come, and the religious authorities misunderstand His words to mean that Jesus is considering suicide. They persist in their refusal to recognize the divine claims Jesus makes to the point that they imagine He will destroy Himself. Instead, of course, their stubbornness will result in their destruction. The irony of the situation is that the most religious group in the world misses the vision of God when it is presented to them!

III. *Who are you?* Unwittingly, these Temple leaders ask the most basic question anyone can ever ask in life. Unfortunately, however, they will not listen to Jesus' answer.

SUGGESTIONS TO TEACHERS

You as a teacher may be put off by the idea of a lesson on Jesus as Judge. Judgment is not a popular thought. "Don't be judgmental," counselors warn. God's judgment is frequently dismissed in many church circles as a relic of an earlier day of hell-fire preaching. Sunday-School lessons and sermons in main-line Protestant congregations soft-pedal the idea of judgment. Consequently, you and your class might have been led to think that the idea is Jeeves, not Jesus, and to want God to be a pleasant, accommodating heavenly butler.

You will quickly become aware that Jesus insists on passing judgment on everyone—you, your class, your church, your community, your nation, your family—*everyone* and *every* set of values! This is the subject of this lesson; Jesus is the Judge of life.

1. *DEPUTY*. You as teacher will probably have to correct some misconceptions about divine judgment. Tell the folks in your class to skip the silly details about God as a sort of celestial Bookkeeper, scrutinizing each person's credits and debits. These passages from John 5 and 8 suggest that each person pronounces sentence on himself or herself by his or her response to the Gospel. The person who "hears my word and believes," Jesus states, "has eternal life; he does not come into judgment, but is passed from death to life" (5:24).

2. *DELIVERANCE*. Take enough time to have a long, hard look at the words, "If you continue in my word, you are truly my disciples, and you will know the truth, and the truth will make you free" (8:31, 32). You may wish to call attention to the way some educational institutions have chopped out the last words, "And the truth will make you free," from the rest of the verse and made this into a kind of motto for academic freedom. You could profitably discuss what damage this does to Jesus' claim. He is the Deliverer, not the pursuit of the philosophical concept called "truth."

3. *DESTRUCTION*. Jesus' truth threatens. He asks, "Why do you not understand what I say?" then answers His own question, "It is because you cannot bear to hear my word" (8:43). We prefer our lies. Point out to the class how unwilling we are to face the truth of Jesus. Discuss with your class our inability to understand Jesus is often because of our refusal to respect Him as the Judge of our lives.

4. *DRAMA*. Stress with your class the mighty words of Jesus: "Before Abraham was, I AM" (8:58). Make certain that they understand why these words aroused such violent opposition among certain hearers.

TOPIC FOR ADULTS
THE JUDGE OF LIFE

Lost Without the Light. J. A. Davidson as a boy in Canada describes how Jesus means a choice between hope and despair, direction and destruction, light and darkness. Once, as a small boy, he spent part of a summer with his grandfather on a small island in the Lake of the Woods. The island was about half a mile from a much larger one on which a summer camp was located. Once a week motion pictures were shown at the camp. They rowed over to see them. The first week it was rather late when the pictures finished. When they came out of the hall in which they were shown, young Davidson became very frightened; for it was a very dark night and the lake was rough. "I had terrifying visions, as only a small boy can, of our becoming lost on the lake, rowing aimlessly all the night long. But when we got down to the pier and began to untie the boat, I noticed a light in the direction of our island. My grandfather told me that when leaving the island at night he always put a lantern in the window of the cabin. The light served to guide us back to the island; it gave us our direction."

J. A. Davidson reflected on how they could have chosen to steer away from that light and have encouraged disaster. The light was not only a beacon but also the arbiter between survival and lostness. Had Davidson and his grandfather not rowed toward that light, they would have spent a long, frightening—possibly fatal—night on that enormous body of water.

Jesus as the Light is the Judge of Life. If we decide to accept Him as the Arbiter for all our values and goals, we will discover a sense of purpose leading to hope and joy in our lives. If we refuse to accept His Lordship as Judge of our lives, we risk destruction!

Closer to the Light. "One rainy night after a prayer service in a mountain mission church, part of the congregation was wending its way home over a narrow trail made dangerous by the recent downpour. One man carried a lantern, and advised the others to "watch the light" so that the dangerous places might be avoided. Another in the group neglected to heed the warning and stepped suddenly into a deep rivulet which had been cut across the trail. Struggling out of the mud and water into which he had fallen, he heard the man who carried the lantern utter an unforgettable sentence: 'Maybe you had better walk closer to the light.' "—*SS TIMES*, January 1, 1961.

The Light in the World. "Each morning as I enter my office, the first thing I do is flick the light switch illuminating all the rooms. Next I turn on a world globe that sits on our reception table.

"The other day as I twisted the knob on this global sphere, there was a flash, then darkness. The light bulb inside had burned out. Colorful countries and oceanic regions faded into opacity. Hemispheric lines became obscure. The darkened globe appeared dismal in our foyer. The light in the world had gone out.

"Looking at it, I thought how often the light has been extinguished in our earthly domain. Countries and leaders have darkened the lives of people. Disasters have come crushing down upon humanity. In many areas people are destitute of moral light; evil and wickedness have overcome goodness and righteousness, and the light in our world seems to have gone out!

"I replaced the bulb and now the world looked radiant.

"I know the problems of our universe are not that simple to solve. But if all of us worked a little harder at some humanitarian cause, gave a little more of this world's goods, sacrificed and prayed with greater enthusiasm, this darkened world might become illuminated with positive and spiritual power."—Allan W. Lee, *Sunshine Magazine,* December 1972.

Questions for Pupils on the Next Lesson. 1. Why did the Pharisees try to discredit Jesus' healing of the blind man? 2. What are some of the forms of spiritual blindness you can think of? 3. Why are many persons apparently unable to accept their need to change? 4. How has Jesus been the "Light of Life" in your personal life? 5. Does every person have to continue to learn and grow throughout his or her life, or is there a point where one may stop?

TOPIC FOR YOUTH
JUDGED FAIRLY

Staying in the Light. We do not always like the idea that Jesus also comes as Judge. Friendly teacher? That's okay. But not Judge of life. However, we have to take His claim seriously in John's Gospel. We are faced with stern choices between light and darkness.

Think of it in this simple way. Clarence Showalter once told of living in the dense Wisconsin woods for a time. Only a narrow patch of sunlight could penetrate the thick foliage. On cold days, the shaft of sunshine would come through the cabin window on to the floor. Showalter's old dog, Blackie, found that spot and basked in the warmth. However, as the morning progressed, the patch of warm sunlight would move across the chilly cabin floor. Old Blackie learned that he had to move with it. Otherwise, he would find himself out of the comfortable sunlit place and would experience the cold and shade.

So with us. If we do not recognize that we must move according to the leadings and directions of Jesus Christ, the Light of the World, we soon find ourselves in the cold darkness.

Is the Super Bowl a Roman Holiday? How does Jesus judge our society? Take Super Bowl, for example. Is the extravagance, self-indulgence and violence walking according to His light? Many wonder.

Joseph Mohr, for example, writes:

"It's estimated that merchants poured $17,570,000 into the coffers of the TV network which broadcast the spectacle. The network paid $6 million for the right to broadcast the event. The sale of food and beverages brought the hucksters a mere $1 million. All that in a time of so-called recession. The fans spent an aggregate fortune on tickets, transportation, lodging, meals and entertainment unrelated to the game itself. The extracurricular doings were, to some, more important than the game—like a Roman holiday.

"Thinking in terms of a 'Roman holiday,' we do well to review what that term implies. The parallel between ancient Rome and our civilization is disturbing. It's said that Rome wasn't built in a day, but neither did the empire collapse in a day. For a couple of centuries the mills of the 'gods' ground exceedingly fine and slow, but relentlessly the disintegration took place.

"Then, as today, political intrigue, power politics and the struggle between rich and poor were commonplace. Wealthy landowners lent money at ruinous interest rates, reducing the little man to slavery if he couldn't pay. Warfare gave the little farmer no time to tend his business when military duty called upon him to defend his freedom. Prosperity for the fortunate brought on corruption, selfishness and greed, which became the first laws of life. All people coveted but only a few could enjoy luxury. The poor had to be content with free bread and free entertainment.

"Burton S. Easton, a theological seminary professor, once said: 'Perhaps nothing shows the gulf between the prevailing standards and our own more clearly than the amusements provided for the public, the theatrical performances called "spectacles" and the gladiatorial shows. Lovers of the drama had the means to organize private presentations, but the poor had to be satisfied with the amphitheater. No holiday-maker felt happy until he had seen man after man slain before his eyes.' "—Joseph Mohr, *The Morning Call/Weekender,* Call-Chronicle Newspapers, Allentown, Pa.: January 31, 1981.

The Light That Judges Fairly. A soldier was severely injured in a training accident. Someone called for the Chaplain. As the Chaplain leaned over the gasping boy, he heard, "Give me a light, Chaplain."

The Chaplain reached into his pocket and pulled out a cigarette. As he was putting it between the boy's lips and about to strike a match, the young trooper whispered, "No, no, Chaplain. The other kind of light."

The Chaplain reached into his other pocket and took out his pocket New Testament and began to read, "I am the light of the world; he who follows me will not walk in darkness, but will have the light of life . . ." (John 8:12).

"That's it. Yes, that's it," sighed the soldier as he lapsed into unconsciousness and death.

Questions for Pupils on the Next Lesson. 1. Why is it often difficult to accept authority? 2. Are you searching for a relationship you can trust? 3. Do you sometimes find that it is hard to get a new idea heard by some established leaders? 4. Are you confused by the claims of faith-healing ministries? 5. Why is it difficult to be an independent thinker in the midst of peer pressure?

LESSON X—FEBRUARY 3

THE LIGHT OF LIFE

Background Scripture: John 9
Devotional Reading: John 8:48–59

KING JAMES VERSION

JOHN 9 24 Then again called they the man that was blind, and said unto him, Give God the praise: we know that this man is a sinner.

25 He answered and said, Whether he be a sinner *or no,* I know not: one thing I know, that, whereas I was blind, now I see.

26 Then said they to him again, What did he to thee? how opened he thine eyes?

27 He answered them, I have told you already, and ye did not hear: wherefore would ye hear *it* again? will ye also be his disciples?

28 Then they reviled him, and said, Thou art his disciple; but we are Moses' disciples.

29 We know that God spake unto Moses: as *for* this *fellow,* we know not from whence he is.

30 The man answered and said unto them, Why herein is a marvelous thing, that ye know not from whence he is, and *yet* he hath opened mine eyes.

31 Now we know that God heareth not sinners: but if any man be a worshipper of God, and doeth his will, him he heareth.

32 Since the world began was it not heard that any man opened the eyes of one that was born blind.

33 If this man were not of God, he could do nothing.

34 They answered and said unto him, Thou wast altogether born in sins, and dost thou teach us? And they cast him out.

35 Jesus heard that they had cast him out; and when he had found him, he said unto him, Dost thou believe on the Son of God?

36 He answered and said, Who is he, Lord, that I might believe on him?

37 And Jesus said unto him, Thou hast both seen him, and it is he that talketh with thee.

38 And he said, Lord, I believe. And he worshipped him.

39 And Jesus said, For judgment I am come into this world, that they which see not might see; and that they which see might be made blind.

40 And *some* of the Pharisees which were with him heard these words, and said unto him, Are we blind also?

41 Jesus said unto them, If ye were blind, ye should have no sin: but now ye say, We see; therefore your sin remaineth.

REVISED STANDARD VERSION

JOHN 9 24 So for the second time they called the man who had been blind, and said to him, "Give God the praise; we know that this man is a sinner." 25 He answered, "Whether he is a sinner, I do not know; one thing I know, that though I was blind, now I see." 26 They said to him, "What did he do to you? How did he open your eyes?" 27 He answered them, "I have told you already, and you would not listen. Why do you want to hear it again? Do you too want to become his disciples?" 28 And they reviled him, saying, "You are his disciple, but we are disciples of Moses. 29 We know that God has spoken to Moses, but as for this man, we do not know where he comes from." 30 The man answered, "Why, this is a marvel! You do not know where he comes from, and yet he opened my eyes. 31 We know that God does not listen to sinners, but if any one is a worshiper of God and does his will, God listens to him. 32 Never since the world began has it been heard that any one opened the eyes of a man born blind. 33 If this man were not from God, he could do nothing." 34 They answered him, "You were born in utter sin, and would you teach us?" And they cast him out.

35 Jesus heard that they had cast him out, and having found him he said, "Do you believe in the Son of man?" 36 He answered, "And who is he, sir, that I may believe in him?" 37 Jesus said to him, "You have seen him, and it is he who speaks to you." 38 He said, "Lord, I believe"; and he worshiped him. 39 Jesus said, "For judgment I came into this world, that those who do not see may see, and that those who see may become blind." 40 Some of the Pharisees near him heard this, and they said to him, "Are we also blind?" 41 Jesus said to them, "If you were blind, you would have no guilt; but now that you say, 'We see,' your guilt remains."

KEY VERSE: "*As long as I am in the world, I am the light of the world.*" John 9:5 (RSV).

HOME DAILY BIBLE READINGS

Jan.	28.	M.	*The Blind Man Healed.* John 9:1–12.
Jan.	29.	T.	*"He Is a Prophet."* John 9:13–17.
Jan.	30.	W.	*Parents Questioned.* John 9:18–23.
Jan.	31.	T.	*"Now I See."* John 9:24–28.
Feb.	1.	F.	*Blind Man's Testimony.* John 9:29–34.
Feb.	2.	S.	*"Lord, I Believe."* John 9:35–41.
Feb.	3.	S.	*Moses Will Accuse.* John 5:41–47.

BACKGROUND

Here is another of those "Signs" followed by a "I am" passage which are unique to John's Gospel. As you have undoubtedly noticed, what seems at first glance to be a simple story takes on astounding depth under John's editorship. It's like touring a magnificent cathedral with an expert guide and seeing details which the casual visitor overlooks.

In the case of the blind man whom Jesus gave sight, John wants his readers to comprehend that Jesus who put light into this helpless man's darkness is the Light of Life. It is important to note that John sandwiches in this miraculous healing between the sayings about being the Light of the world in chapter 8 and the comments about enabling the blind to see at the close of chapter 9. Originally, of course, there were no chapter markings, and the entire section about the Light would have flowed as a unit. Healing the blind man illustrated how Jesus is the Light.

Jesus spoke these words during the Feast of Tabernacles and brought sight to the man born blind. This great festival commemorated the forty years in the desert. You will recall that the Israelites were led from Egypt to Sinai by the pillar of fire by night and the column of smoke by day. The memory of God's light in those times was part of the Feast. Also, in the Jerusalem Temple on the first evening of the Feast, four huge firepots or flares were lighted. These blazing lights illuminated the enormous area of the Temple and shone out across the city. Jesus' listeners would have made the connection between His words and the ancient ceremonies. It was as if He was saying, "I am the light which will never flicker and die. The Temple torches burn brilliantly for a night, then sputter out. The ones who turn to Me will discover I am the Light which burns constantly!"

NOTES ON THE PRINTED TEXT

You would have thought that the Temple authorities would have been pleased that a man who had been blind from birth had been given his sight. Instead of rejoicing with the man and his family and congratulating Jesus for His compassion and cure, these religious leaders were angry. They saw only that Jesus had broken a rule about the Sabbath by making clay and anointing eyes. First, they cross-examined the man whose sight had just been restored. Then they quizzed the man's parents. Unable to get enough evidence to convict Jesus, they called the man born blind in a second time.

I. *Give God the praise:* This was the equivalent of our ceremony of swearing in a witness by asking, "Do you swear to tell the truth, the whole truth and nothing but the truth, so help me God?" The phrase in the Bible which is used here comes from Joshua 7:19, where Joshua demanded Achan swear before God after being confronted with theft, and was the courtroom oath administered in Jewish legal hearings.

One thing I know, that though I was blind, now I see: The man once blind doesn't care to get involved in theological arguments about Jesus. He does know, however, that he had been in hopeless darkness as a blind man for his entire life, and now has the light of a man with sight. He knows what Jesus has done for him.

The testimony of personal experience means more than doctrinal debates! When you share what Jesus has done for you personally, you present an irrefutable case.

The authorities however, continue to hound the man. The man formerly blind recognizes that the leaders cannot escape facing the extraordinary claims of Jesus.

Why do you want to hear it again? Do you too want to become his disciples? The man cannot help getting bolder and even sarcastic. If these people before me are supposed to be so wise in religiouᵉ matters, he reasons, why are they asking me so much about Jesus?

Needless to say, the Temple leaders are not amused. In fact, they become abusive. They accuse the man born blind of being Jesus' disciple—the worst insult they can think of—then vigorously protest they are Moses' disciples.

You are his disciple: The authorities thought this accusation would sting the man into silence and a quick retreat. Later, that same comment from the servant girl in the High Priest's courtyard cowed Simon Peter. Instead, in the case of the man given his sight, the insult goaded him to a deeper faith in Jesus.

We know that God spoke to Moses, but as for this man, we do not know where he comes from: The Temple authorities speak so belittlingly of Jesus that the blind man gets further aroused. He accuses these entrusted with the spiritual guidance of the nation of being blind to the obvious. "This is a marvel," he cries; "You do not know where he comes from, and yet he opened my eyes. We know that God does not listen to sinners, but if anyone is a worshipper of God and does his will, God listens to him. Never since the world began has it been heard that anyone opened the eyes of a man born blind. If this man were not from God, he could do nothing" (9:30–33).

And they cast him out: This speech is too much for the religious brass. They are not used to being lectured to by an unlettered layman from the streets. They are furious because his claims cannot be denied. The man born blind has beat them at their own game. They know it, and he knows it. They cannot answer his statements on scriptural or doctrinal grounds, so they resort to the threat of force. They excommunicate him.

II. *Jesus heard that they had cast him out:* Jesus knew that anyone who had been cast out was in effect a nonperson. A person who had been excommunicated could not take part in any of the ceremonies which were so important to the entire community. Jesus appreciated the sense of loneliness and exclusion that this man would feel. He refused to allow this man to be cut off from His friendship, however, and sought him out. As John Chrysostom, the great preacher of the third century said, "The Jews cast him out of the Temple but the Lord of the Temple found him."

Do you believe in the Son of Man? Jesus gently leads the man born blind to a fuller understanding of who the Man who healed and brought him light is. However, Jesus doesn't force the man to acknowledge Him as the Messiah. He helps the man to mature in his faith in Jesus as Lord. Jesus does the same with all of us. Jesus' claims are compelling, but He will not compel us to acknowledge those claims. The man states, "Lord, I believe" (9:38).

Are we also blind? The Pharisees's question remains. Do we respond to the meaning of Jesus' presence among us by receiving enlightenment? Or, do we refuse to obey Him, and blind ourselves?

The Pharisees claimed to "see." Jesus tells them that they can be excused for almost anything except the arrogance of insisting that they have light when, in fact, they are in darkness.

SUGGESTIONS TO TEACHERS

Many elementary-school teachers use a simple technique to help young children to understand the problems of those who have no sight and must live in darkness. The teacher explains the purpose of the experiment, then asks for a volunteer to be blindfolded for the day. The other children must learn to assist the "blind" child, and the blindfolded youngster learns what it is like to try to exist without light or sight. Usually, the kids take turns being the "blind person" for a day until each has a chance to experience the darkness.

You may wish to adapt this simple sensitizing experiment to get your class off to a fast start as long as you don't take too much time with it. The point you will be making, of course, is that Jesus is the Light of Life, and sight to the blind of every description. Your scriptural reading in John 9 offers beautiful material for a lesson.

1. *MIGHT.* Jesus' power always astonished His contemporaries. He was able to bestow sight on a man blind from birth. John wants his readers to understand that there is no darkness too hopeless for Jesus' light to penetrate. This can give you a good opportunity to have your class consider what some of the various forms of darkness there are for persons in these times, such as despair, doubt, anxiety, prejudice, and anger.

2. *SIGHT.* Point out to the class how the blind man was transformed from being a dependent beggar to a useful member of the community. Jesus brought him a new life. Jesus enabled the man to see. Reflect with your class on the ways in which Jesus helps persons to "see" others, the world, themselves, and above all God in new ways. Ask how each person is aware of "seeing" in new ways because of Jesus' gift of new sight.

3. *FIGHT.* Don't lose the thread of the narrative of mounting opposition to Jesus which culminated in the Crucifixion. John carefully notes the opposition which Jesus encountered from the Pharisees and the questions He faced from His own disciples. Do your pupils understand that Jesus was not ever regarded as merely a harmless eccentric who helped people?

4. *LIGHT.* Jesus Christ is the Light of Life, the Scriptures maintain. "I came into this world that those who do not see may see and that those who see may become blind" (9:39). This may seem like a paradoxical statement or a Zen riddle at first glance, but the truth of Jesus' claim needs to be pondered by everyone in your class!

TOPIC FOR ADULTS
THE LIGHT OF LIFE

Light Brings Life. We never appreciate how chilling the absence of light is. A survivor of a torpedoing during the war once told what it was like to go through a night alone in the water. His ship had gone down in the Gulf Stream. Many of the crew had been able to jump to safety even though there had not been time to launch lifeboats. The survivors clung to pieces of wreckage, during the daylight, holding on, waiting for rescue. Then came the darkness. As the hours of night dragged on, the men began to suffer. It was not from hunger or thirst or sharks, although these were all present; nor was it from numbing cold, for they were in the Gulf Stream. They suffered from a lack of will to go on in the darkness. Without light, they seemed to lose their grip and give up. There were a few brave attempts where men tried to link up or call encouragement to one another in the darkness. But gradually they all gave up and allowed themselves to drift apart. The survivor graphically described the numbing effect of the dark so that strong men were not able to hold on to life. When daylight finally came, only a few heads were visible. The coming of light meant the rebirth of hope and strength for living for these survivors.

Jesus' Coming means God's gifts of hope and strength for living for us! With Him, we will survive!

Lighting the Day with Jesus. "For Christians the beginning of the day should not be burdened and oppressed with besetting concerns for the day's work. At the threshold of the new day stands the Lord who made it. All the darkness and distraction of the dreams of night retreat before the clear light of Jesus Christ and his wakening Word. All unrest, all impurity, all care and anxiety flee before him. Therefore, at the beginning of the day let all distraction and empty talk be silenced and let the first thought and the first word belong to him to whom our whole life belongs. 'Awake thou that sleepest, and arise from the dead, and Christ shall give thee light' (Ephesians 5:14)."—Dietrich Bonhoeffer, *Life Together,* Harper & Brothers.

Light for Blind Eyes. Sir John Wilson heads the Royal Commonwealth Society for the Blind and the International Agency for the Prevention of Blindness. Although blind himself, Wilson travels over 50,000 miles each year setting up centers to restore sight to the estimated 42 million blind people in the world and to prevent the diseases which cause most of the blindness in developing countries. In one year, Wilson's programs restored the sight of over 140,000 people. Determined to bring light in every way to villagers forced to live in the darkness of the sightless, Wilson has been lobbying for funds to help eradicate the diseases which account for two-thirds of the blindness in the world. He also founded and supervises temporary eye camps which go to remote villages in Asia and the Indian subcontinent where cataracts, the clouding of the eye's lens, have blinded millions. In these village eye camps, surgeons perform more than 100 cataract operations per day on patients from the surrounding area. Wilson notes that when a blind person's relatives bring him in, they are usually leading him and bossing him around. "They are bored with having to care for this useless invalid. After the operation, when the family leaves the camp, he is a man transformed, his status restored."

How similar to the light that Jesus brought the blind man! How typical also of the way Christ's agents today are bringing light—literally—in His name!

Questions for Pupils on the Next Lesson. 1. How does Jesus use the figure of the Good Shepherd to indicate the difference between Himself and false leaders? 2. What does Jesus mean when He speaks of Himself as "the Door"? 3. Around what value system do you build your life? 4. Do you ever reflect on your life and wonder, "Is this all there is?" 5. On what basis do you make your major decisions?

TOPIC FOR YOUTH
SEEING CLEARLY

Lighting the Way. In Rochester, N.Y., a few years ago during a Leighton Ford Crusade, the offering plate one night contained a crumpled piece of paper wrapped around a small aluminum-foil-wrapped packet containing a powdery substance. The crumpled piece of paper around the packet also had a few lines of handwritten message. "Dear God, this may sound impertinent, but I won't need this hash anymore. Thank You for lighting my way through Jesus."

More Than a Light, but The Light. "All light comes from the sun, whether we get it out of the sky or out of a coalpit. Jesus did not say He was a light; He said He was *the* Light. In Him are all the treasures of wisdom and knowledge. The teaching of Jesus Christ has been before the world for two thousand years, and He has yet to be convicted of the first error. He never made any mistakes. The people who have interpreted Him have made plenty. He was the only man who ever lived who never said 'perhaps,' never balanced probabilities. Jesus Christ is God's last word. He is never a back number. He is never out of date. When we have solved our last problem He will still be ahead of us. At the midnight hour of the world all sorts and conditions of men are at the door of the Church asking for the Christian interpretation of life. The men whose brains are best worth trusting tell us there is no answer but in Jesus. There is no problem in the world that would not be solved were it in His hands."—*The Speaker's Bible,* Ephesians.

Despair and Suffering Dropped Away. In his book *Alone,* Richard Byrd tells of the despair which engulfed him in his long, lonely vigil in the icy fastness of Antarctica while he awaited the arrival of needed medical help. "I blinked my eyes and peered north." This he had done for several nights without avail. Then it happened. "The fingering beam of the searchlight . . . against the horizon. . . . When I stood up and looked again . . . the beam was fanning up and down . . . all despair and suffering dropped away."

What a perfect description of what happens when Jesus Christ lights our dark lives! Despair and suffering drop away with His coming.

Questions for Pupils on the Next Lesson. 1. What does Jesus mean when He calls Himself the "Good Shepherd"? 2. What does Jesus mean when He refers to Himself as "the Door"? 3. How did Jesus distinguish between Himself and false leaders? 4. Do you think that anyone would be willing to lay down his or her life for you? 5. How do you decide which church leaders to follow?

LESSON XI—FEBRUARY 10

THE SHEPHERD OF LIFE

Background Scripture: John 10
Devotional Reading: John 10:22–39

KING JAMES VERSION

JOHN 10   Verily, verily, I say unto you, He that entereth not by the door into the sheepfold, but climbeth up some other way, the same is a thief and a robber.

2 But he that entereth in by the door is the shepherd of the sheep.

3 To him the porter openeth; and the sheep hear his voice: and he calleth his own sheep by name, and leadeth them out.

4 And when he putteth forth his own sheep, he goeth before them, and the sheep follow him: for they know his voice.

5 And a stranger will they not follow, but will flee from him; for they know not the voice of strangers.

6 This parable spake Jesus unto them; but they understood not what things they were which he spake unto them.

7 Then said Jesus unto them again, Verily, verily, I say unto you, I am the door of the sheep.

8 All that ever came before me are thieves and robbers: but the sheep did not hear them.

9 I am the door: by me if any man enter in, he shall be saved, and shall go in and out, and find pasture.

10 The thief cometh not, but for to steal, and to kill, and to destroy: I am come that they might have life, and that they might have *it* more abundantly.

11 I am the good shepherd: the good shepherd giveth his life for the sheep.

12 But he that is a hireling, and not the shepherd, whose own the sheep are not, seeth the wolf coming, and leaveth the sheep, and fleeth; and the wolf catcheth them, and scattereth the sheep.

13 The hireling fleeth, because he is a hireling, and careth not for the sheep.

14 I am the good shepherd, and know my *sheep*, and am known of mine.

15 As the Father knoweth me, even so know I the Father: and I lay down my life for the sheep.

16 And other sheep I have, which are not of this fold: them also I must bring, and they shall hear my voice; and there shall be one fold, *and* one shepherd.

REVISED STANDARD VERSION

JOHN 10   "Truly, truly, I say to you, he who does not enter the sheepfold by the door but climbs in by another way, that man is a thief and a robber; 2 but he who enters by the door is the shepherd of the sheep. 3 To him the gatekeeper opens; the sheep hear his voice, and he calls his own sheep by name and leads them out. 4 When he has brought out all his own, he goes before them, and the sheep follow him, for they know his voice. 5 A stranger they will not follow, but they will flee from him, for they do not know the voice of strangers." 6 This figure Jesus used with them, but they did not understand what he was saying to them.

7 So Jesus again said to them, "Truly, truly, I say to you, I am the door of the sheep. 8 All who came before me are thieves and robbers; but the sheep did not heed them. 9 I am the door; if any one enters by me, he will be saved, and will go in and out and find pasture. 10 The thief comes only to steal and kill and destroy; I came that they may have life, and have it abundantly. 11 I am the good shepherd. The good shepherd lays down his life for the sheep. 12 He who is a hireling and not a shepherd, whose own the sheep are not, sees the wolf coming and leaves the sheep and flees; and the wolf snatches them and scatters them. 13 He flees because he is a hireling and cares nothing for the sheep. 14 I am the good shepherd; I know my own and my own know me, 15 as the Father knows me and I know the Father; and I lay down my life for the sheep. 16 And I have other sheep, that are not of this fold; I must bring them also, and they will heed my voice. So there shall be one flock, one shepherd.

KEY VERSE: *I am the good shepherd. The good shepherd lays down his life for the sheep.* John 10:11 (RSV).

HOME DAILY BIBLE READINGS

Feb.   4.   M.   *Parable of the Shepherd.* John 10:1–6.
Feb.   5.   T.   *Jesus the Good Shepherd.* John 10:7–16.
Feb.   6.   W.   *Divided Response.* John 10:17–21.
Feb.   7.   T.   *One With the Father.* John 10:22–30.
Feb.   8.   F.   *Jesus Rejected.* John 10:31–42.
Feb.   9.   S.   *"Come to Me."* Matthew 11:25–30.
Feb.   10. S.   *Question of Authority.* Mark 11:27–33.

BACKGROUND

Shepherd in the Bible is one of those code words for God. "The Lord is my Shepherd," (Psalms 23:1) is only one of many examples. Everyone who heard Jesus use the term *Shepherd* would make the connection with God.

In addition, the word *Shepherd* stood for the Messiah. God's promised Anointed One was often described in terms of a good and faithful shepherd, such as in Isaiah 40:11: "He will feed his flock like a shepherd; he will gather the lambs in his arms, he will carry them in his bosom, and gently lead those that are with young." Jesus' hearers also would quickly understand the reference to the Messiah.

Jesus' audience likewise would readily understand that the figure of the shepherd could also mean any religious leader. In fact, we still speak of the "shepherd of the flock" to refer to a pastor of a congregation. Old Testament prophets saved some of their fiercest words for leaders who led the flock astray. " 'Woe to the shepherds who destroy and scatter the sheep of my pasture!' says the Lord. Therefore thus says the Lord, the God of Israel, concerning the shepherds who care for my people: 'You have scattered my flock, and have driven them away, and you have not attended to them' " (Jeremiah 23:1, 2). "Ho, shepherds of Israel who have been feeding yourselves! Should not shepherds feed the sheep?" (Ezekiel 34:2).

Jesus undoubtedly had all of these metaphors in mind when He chose to speak of Himself as the Shepherd of Life. He intended that His audience of Pharisees, priests, and scribes, the "shepherds" or religious leaders, should understand that they had turned into mere hirelings who were scattering the flock. Most important, Jesus made it clear to everyone that He knew that He was the Messiah and on an equal footing with God. His claim was understood by His hearers, but the religious leaders were furious. John the Gospel writer comments that their opposition was intensifying against Jesus: "Again they tried to arrest him, but he escaped from their hands" (10:39).

NOTES ON THE PRINTED TEXT

The previous chapter of John closes with Jesus denouncing the religious leaders, especially the Pharisees, for their blindness. They have excommunicated the man born blind. To Jesus, this was an example of the way they were abusing their authority. Furthermore, Jesus saw that the man born blind and many others were dissatisfied with the Pharisees and the Temple clique, and were ready to follow Him. The scene reminded Jesus of shepherding sheep.

I. *Truly, truly, I say to you, he who does not enter the sheepfold by the door but climbs in another way is a thief and a robber:* Jesus refers to the religious rulers as thieves and robbers. They had not gained their power by entering by "the door" of doing the will of the Father as Jesus had. Instead, they had gained their authority through lies and threats. Jesus therefore compares the Pharisees and Temple authorities to those who sneak into a sheepfold at night to steal. On the other hand, Jesus asserts that He has a God-sent mission as Messiah; He is the real Shepherd of Israel.

Jesus most certainly knew His Bible, and remembered the famous 34th chapter of Ezekiel in which the prophet denounces the religious authorities as false shepherds. Jesus also knew that His hearers would remember the same oft-quoted passage.

II. *The sheep hear his voice, and he calls his own sheep by name and leads them out. When he has brought out all his own, he goes before them and the sheep follow him, for they know his voice:* Jesus describes a faithful shepherd. He also gives a true picture of sheep-raising in His area. The shepherd in the Middle East always stayed with his flock day and night, season in and season out. He didn't leave them to graze unattended, such as farmers put sheep out to pasture in North America or allow them to wander over the moors in parts of Western Europe. A Judean or Galilean shepherd not only remained with the flock constantly but got to know each sheep individually. To most outsiders, all sheep look exactly the same. The shepherd in Jesus' home area recognized each member of his flock. Furthermore, he usually gave a name to each sheep. The bond between shepherd and sheep was so close that the sheep learned to trust the shepherd and to respond to his voice. There are many eye-witness reports of how several shepherds' flocks would be gathered into one large collection of sheep and each shepherd would easily and quickly identify his own sheep and each sheep would come to the call of its own shepherd. Furthermore, unlike the practice of sheep herders in the Western world, the shepherds in the Middle East always go ahead of the flock, leading the sheep and never driving them.

Jesus related this parable to illustrate how He truly cares for His own. In complete contrast to the Pharisees and the Temple leaders, the "hirelings" and "strangers" whom the sheep cannot trust, Jesus cares. He does not exploit the people. He serves them.

III. *I am the door of the sheep:* A sheepfold in the Middle East was usually a circle of stones with an entrance. The shepherd would lead the sheep into the sheepfold for the night for safety. Then, the shepherd would lie down across the entrance way as a sort of human door. Anyone trying to enter the sheepfold (except by climbing over the wall) had to clamber over the shepherd acting as a shield or door. Jesus states that He is the way or entrance to the true community of faith, the new Israel. He offers security and safety and nurture. John bluntly wants His readers to understand that Jesus is saying that only by trust in Him as Lord and by membership in the Church can anyone be saved.

IV. *The good shepherd lays down his life for the sheep . . . I lay down my life for the sheep:* There are many tales of heroism in which Middle Eastern shepherds sacrificed their own lives to defend their flock from wild animals or bandits. Jesus announces that He will even sacrifice His life for the new community of God's own.

V. *And I have other sheep, that are not of this fold; I must bring them also, and they will heed my voice. So there shall be one flock, one shepherd:* Jesus states that He will include more than Jews in His new Israel. His shepherding will welcome Gentiles. He has a vision of the time when His flock will reach out to embrace those who may be thought to be beyond the fold. Eventually, all who believe in Jesus will consider themselves one flock and will respond to Him as the one Shepherd.

SUGGESTIONS TO TEACHERS

In this lesson on Jesus the Good Shepherd, you will have to push beyond several barricades that exist in the minds of your class members. One is the barricade of familiarity, the picture of Jesus cradling a cuddly lamb in His arms. Another is the barricade of ignorance. Few of your class are sheep farmers or knowledgeable about sheep, especially in the Middle East. Still another barricade is that of biblical illiteracy. Don't be daunted by these barricades, however, but use the lesson material in John 10 as the basis for a helpful learning experience.

1. *CHRIST'S CREDENTIALS.* Use the Notes on the Printed Text for background details on the ways of shepherds in Galilee and Judea. Jesus knew His subject and so did His hearers. When He spoke about entering by the door of the sheepfold and not crawling over the wall, Jesus stated that He was not an imposter but the authentic Leader. He wanted His hearers to understand that He would be recognized by His flock. Impress on your class that Jesus may be trusted.

2. *FLOCK'S FAITH.* A Middle East shepherd always leads his sheep; he never drives them. Furthermore, he can identify each sheep. Jesus knows each of us. We are never merely part of a flock, never an insignificant fraction, never a nameless statistic to Him. He also deals gently with us by going on ahead of us as leader. Our relationship with Jesus is one where we are known and can know He treats us with concern. Spend some time on the fact of modern life being so impersonal. Your class will appreciate discussing the way people are often treated as cyphers. Move the conversation to having the class also note that no one is anonymous to Jesus.

3. *BELIEVER'S PASSAGEWAY.* Jesus' description of Himself as the door to the sheepfold meant that He was the human barricade at the opening of the enclosure, offering protection to the flock. It also meant Jesus is the gateway to Life. As the doorway to both safety and nourishment or pasture, He assures His flock that He has their needs at heart. Believers may rest at night with a sense of security and rise in the morning with a feeling of hope! You may find that this could be an occasion to talk about the way faith means being able to receive calm and confidence instead of sleepless tossing in bed because of worry.

4. *SHEPHERD'S SACRIFICE.* Devote plenty of time on John 10:11–15 which refers to the way Jesus announces His willingness to lay down His life for us. His sacrificial death on the Cross must be held up weekly for your class to remember, and here is the place in this lesson for this vital emphasis.

5. *TRUTH'S TEST.* Jesus speaks in John 10:16 about "Other sheep that are not of this fold" who eventually will heed His voice and become part of His flock. Sometimes, church folks want to determine who is "Christian" and who isn't. Jesus rules this out. No sheep may take over for Him, the Shepherd! The true test of any member of the flock is how well he or she responds to His commands and obeys.

TOPIC FOR ADULTS
THE SHEPHERD OF LIFE

No Christmas Card Romantics. "Shepherding is romantic at a distance. It looks lovely on Christmas cards. Only those who do it know how costly it is. There are wolves to be fought off, there are precipices to climb, there are storms to brave. Hirelings flee danger to protect themselves. A true shepherd hazards his life to save his sheep. 'I am the good shepherd,' said Jesus, 'I lay down my life for the sheep.' Those who 'see' in Jesus' death the costly action of God 'for us men and for our salvation' are the sheep who 'hear' his voice and 'know' him—not with the abstract, intellectual knowledge which understands the mystery of his Person, but with the intuitive, experimental knowledge of his love.

"Who could not ask for a kinder shepherd? And what life would be more 'abundant' than being a member of his flock?"—Donald G. Miller, *Presbyterian Life*, March 1, 1963. Copyright *Presbyterian Life.* Used by permission.

Shepherd's Call. In a Scottish Highland village, there was a shepherd who was left with a small daughter to raise. He would take her with him when he went to tend and fold the sheep. The little girl loved to hear the old man sound his sheep with the shepherd's call, echoing free and beautiful down the wind over the moors and glens.

The little girl grew up. She became an attractive young woman and went off to Glasgow to work. For a while, letters came regularly every week. Then the intervals lengthened. Finally, they stopped altogether. There were rumors the girl was being seen in bad company and in questionable places.

One day a lad from her village saw her in the city and spoke to her. But she pretended she'd never seen him before. When the old shepherd heard this, he gathered a few things together, took his staff and set off for the city to find his lost daughter.

Day after day, the big highlander was seen trudging up the avenues, down through the slums and closes of the huge city. But in vain. He couldn't locate her. Then he remembered how his daughter loved to hear him give the shepherd's call. Again he set out on his mission of sorrow and love. This time, he gave his call for sheep, loud and clear. Passersby turned with astonishment. For weeks, he tramped the dusty pavements of Glasgow calling the shepherd's call.

One day in a house in a degraded section, his daughter was sitting with some companions. She looked up with astonishment on her face. There was no doubt about it. It was her father's voice, the shepherd's call. She rushed out the door to the street. There was her father, who took her back with him to the Highland home and loved her back to decency and to God.

"I Am the Door." "In the old days of heartless tyranny it seemed as though the rulers vied with each other to see who could think up the most terrible and cruel means of torture. One of the royal houses of an European country put their victims in a well furnished and comfortable room. The prisoner might think all was well, but in a few days the victim would notice that the room had contracted, that the walls were coming nearer together and his horrible fate all at once flashed through his mind. In oiled and silent grooves the metal walls were drawing closer and closer together. At last he could no longer lie down; the next day he had room only to stand erect. Frantic, he would put his hands against the iron walls to hold them, but silently, remorselessly, they closed and crushed him to death.

"What a picture this is of the world and the person in it who has no Christian hope for the world to come. The years such a person lives are the walls of his prison, and every day they are contracting about him.

"Things may seem pleasant for a time, but with every pulse beat the iron walls draw closer and closer about his soul. But for the Christian there is hope. There is the opened door through which he knows he can pass when the time comes."— *Pulpit Preaching,* March 1955. Copyright 1955 Christian Century Foundation. Reprinted by permission from the March 1955 issue of *The Pulpit.*

Questions for Pupils on the Next Lesson. 1. What do we mean by "eternal life"? 2. Did Jesus ever grieve? 3. Why do some people think they must have visible proofs before they will believe? 4. Why are some people intrigued by reports of the supernatural and stories of those clinically dead who have returned? 5. How exactly is Jesus the Resurrection and the Life?

TOPIC FOR YOUTH
A LEADER WORTH FOLLOWING

Jesus Cheer. A large group of young people were attending a church-sponsored youth rally in a midwestern city. One of the leaders on the platform delighted in leading what he called "the Jesus Cheer."

"Give me a 'J,' " he called.

The audience shouted, "JAY"
"Give me an 'E,' " he yelled.
"EEEEEEEE"
"Give me an 'S.' "
Then, the cheerleader and youth chanted the letters of the complete name: J-E-S-U-S. Several times during the program, the leader took to the platform and urged greater and greater volume as they shouted their way through the Jesus Cheer.

Later, on the way home, two of the more thoughtful senior high students who attended the rally got to talking. One asked the other, "What does J-E-S-U-S really spell for you? What do you make of Jesus?"

That's the key question for you, also. What does it spell for *you?* "Jesus" is more than a yell.

Working With the Shepherd. There is no neutrality with Jesus Christ. He came as a Shepherd. If you refuse to work with Him in gathering the sheep, you're scattering the flock. You cannot run around as you wish, because you'll only impede His work as good Shepherd.

Known by Name. Do you often feel that you are just a number? Whenever I look in my billfold, I am made to feel like a group of digits. To the government, I'm Social Security Number 280-22-5342. To the state, I'm Vehicle Operator Number W0738. To the library, to places where I have a charge account, to my insurance company, to nearly everyone, I am merely a series of numerals. Recently, waiting to conduct a funeral in a large funeral home, I happened to notice the mortician's file for the funeral service. Beside the name of the deceased were various sets of numbers, including social security number and number of the case from the coroner's files. Below, the details of the funeral itself were listed. I learned that the funeral was to be an event in parlor *B*, with organ selections 77, 83, and 192, casket 619-D, decorations C-6. It seemed that the individuality of the person whose funeral I was to conduct had all been squeezed out, and that she was merely a set of squiggles on a printout.

Jesus stated that as the good Shepherd He knows each of us by name. We are never merely a list of letters and numbers on a card filed in a huge, impersonal set of files. He knows us. He loves us. He calls us each by name!

Questions for Pupils on the Next Lesson. 1. What do you think will happen to you when you die? 2. What does Jesus mean when He says that He is the Resurrection and the Life? 3. Why are many people hooked on looking for signs of the supernatural and investigating psychic phenomena? 4. Do stories of people returning to life after being clinically dead help our faith or is the story of Jesus' Resurrection what really counts?

LESSON XII—FEBRUARY 17

THE RESURRECTION AND THE LIFE

Background Scripture: John 11:1–53
Devotional Reading: John 11:45–54

KING JAMES VERSION

JOHN 11 20 Then Martha, as soon as she heard that Jesus was coming, went and met him: but Mary sat *still* in the house.

21 Then said Martha unto Jesus, Lord, if thou hadst been here, my brother had not died.

22 But I know, that even now, whatsoever thou wilt ask of God, God will give *it* thee.

23 Jesus said unto her, Thy brother shall rise again.

24 Martha saith unto him, I know that he shall rise again in resurrection at the last day.

25 Jesus said unto her, I am the resurrection, and the life: he that believeth in me, though he were dead, yet shall he live:

26 And whosoever liveth and believeth in me shall never die. Believest thou this?

27 She saith unto him, Yea, Lord: I believe that thou art the Christ, the Son of God, which should come into the world.

38 Jesus therefore again groaning in himself cometh to the grave. It was a cave, and a stone lay upon it.

39 Jesus said, Take ye away the stone. Martha, the sister of him that was dead, saith unto him, Lord, by this time he stinketh: for he hath been *dead* four days.

40 Jesus saith unto her, Said I not unto thee, that, if thou wouldest believe, thou shouldest see the glory of God?

41 Then they took away the stone *from the place* where the dead was laid. And Jesus lifted up *his* eyes, and said, Father, I thank thee that thou hast heard me.

42 And I knew that thou hearest me always: but because of the people which stand by I said *it,* that they may believe that thou hast sent me.

43 And when he thus had spoken, he cried with a loud voice, Lazarus, come forth.

44 And he that was dead came forth, bound hand and foot with graveclothes; and his face was bound about with a napkin. Jesus saith unto them, Loose him, and let him go.

REVISED STANDARD VERSION

JOHN 11 20 When Martha heard that Jesus was coming, she went and met him, while Mary sat in the house. 21 Martha said to Jesus, "Lord, if you had been here, my brother would not have died. 22 And even now I know that whatever you ask from God, God will give you." 23 Jesus said to her, "Your brother will rise again." 24 Martha said to him, "I know that he will rise again in the resurrection at the last day." 25 Jesus said to her, "I am the resurrection and the life; he who believes in me, though he die, yet shall he live, 26 and whoever lives and believes in me shall never die. Do you believe this?" 27 She said to him, "Yes, Lord; I believe that you are the Christ, the Son of God, he who is coming into the world."

38 Then Jesus, deeply moved again, came to the tomb; it was a cave, and a stone lay upon it. 39 Jesus said, "Take away the stone." Martha, the sister of the dead man, said to him, "Lord, by this time there will be an odor, for he has been dead four days." 40 Jesus said to her, "Did I not tell you that if you would believe you would see the glory of God?" 41 So they took away the stone. And Jesus lifted up his eyes and said, "Father, I thank thee that thou hast heard me. 42 I knew that thou hearest me always, but I have said this on account of the people standing by, that they may believe that thou didst send me." 43 When he had said this, he cried with a loud voice, "Lazarus, come out." 44 The dead man came out, his hands and feet bound with bandages, and his face wrapped with a cloth. Jesus said to them, "Unbind him, and let him go."

KEY VERSE: I am the resurrection and the life; he who believes in me, though he die, yet shall he live. John 11:25 (RSV).

HOME DAILY BIBLE READINGS

Feb. 11. M. *Lazarus's Death.* John 11:1–16.
Feb. 12. T. *Jesus: Resurrection and Life.* John 11:17–22.
Feb. 13. W. *Jesus Deeply Moved.* John 11:28–37.
Feb. 14. T. *Lazarus Raised.* John 11:38–44.
Feb. 15. F. *Plot Against Jesus.* John 11:45–53.

Feb.   16.   S.   Jesus' Arrest Planned. John 11:54–57.
Feb.   17.   S.   Jesus Predicts Arrest. Matthew 26:1–5.

BACKGROUND

Everyone needs an intimate group where he can take his shoes off in the livingroom, say what he feels, eat his peas with a knife, and raid the refrigerator. Jesus found that group with two sisters and their brother, Mary and Martha and Lazarus. His own family back in Nazareth couldn't understand Him and was embarrassed by Him. Jesus found warmth and companionship in the Bethany home of this trio. Bethany lies just over the brow of the Mount of Olives outside Jerusalem, and Jesus visited Jerusalem frequently, according to John's Gospel. Jesus found that Mary, Martha, and Lazarus offered the nearest thing to a home for Him during His ministry that He knew.

The death of Lazarus was devastating to his sisters and to Jesus for many reasons. It meant losing the means of support for Mary and Martha as well as losing one of the family circle. For Jesus, it was the loss of a friend He loved. John, the only Gospel writer to include this episode, records Jesus' display of grief. John also inserts details such as Lazarus's body being entombed for four days to emphasize that he really had died. The Christian faith never ignores the reality of death.

The raising of Lazarus was another sign of who Jesus is. John recounts the story not to portray Jesus as a sensational stunt worker who can resuscitate a dead man but to be a sign that Jesus is the Resurrection and the Life. The mighty announcement, "I am the Resurrection and the Life" is the picture; the raising of Lazarus is the frame.

With this dramatic sign and saying, the narrative leading to the final days of Jesus' earthly life quickens. Jesus is suddenly so famous that He cannot be ignored by anyone. His career is moving toward the climax of the Cross and the Resurrection. His words spoken to two grieving sisters about being the Resurrection and the Life will soon be acted out in His own life on Calvary and in the garden tomb.

NOTES ON THE PRINTED TEXT

I. *When Martha heard that Jesus was coming, she went and met him, while Mary sat in the house:* Martha was the doer, the busy one. Martha took the initiative. Martha ran the household. It is typical of Martha to rush out of the village to greet Jesus, and also typical of her sister Mary to sit passively inside the house.

"Lord if you had been here, my brother would not have died": Again, true to her nature, Martha speaks her mind. In fact, she doesn't even exchange a greeting, but gets to the point immediately. Her words are both a mild scolding and an expression of faith in Jesus. She feels certain that Jesus' presence earlier would have changed the outcome of Lazarus's illness, and chides Jesus for not arriving earlier.

II. *Jesus said to her, "Your brother will rise again:"* Jesus' words sound to Martha like typical words of condolence. To Martha, the vague hope of a final resurrection of the dead offered no real comfort. "Rise again? When? That's so remote and far away," Martha thinks.

Martha numbly acknowledges what she takes to be a commonplace bit of piety that people say at funerals. Talk about an eventual resurrection apart from Jesus is in the category of "churchspeak"—throwaway words which may sound pretty but have little meaning. Martha interprets Jesus' promise about the resurrection as pious froth.

III. *"I am the resurrection and the life; he who believes on me, though he die, yet shall he live, and whoever lives and believes in me shall never die":* Jesus' words jar Martha. He tells her that she won't have to wait until some distant day for the resurrection. He Himself is the Source of new life. He asserts that He is stronger even than death! He pledges His word to Martha that if she or anyone trusts in Him personally, that person need have no terrors of dying or separation from loved ones! Death no longer has the final say, Jesus asserts. He does! The future hope of resurrection is a present reality through association with Him.

"Do you believe this?": All of Jesus' claims to be the Resurrection and Life are mere words unless Martha believes this herself. The same is true for each of us. "Do *you* believe this?" Jesus continues to ask. Do *you* believe this as you stand at the grave of one whom you love and have shared so deeply of life? Do *you* believe this as you become increasingly aware of your own impending death? Do *you* believe this as you contemplate the apparent futility to all human existence because of what seems to be a march toward the oblivion of the grave for everything?

She said to him, "Yes, Lord, I believe that you are the Christ, the Son of God, he who is coming into the world": Martha's hopes are centered on the person of Jesus. Therefore, she is given hope. She finds comfort. Because of Jesus, she has faith again, in spite of the terrible loss she has experienced.

Our hopes rest on Jesus. Not on philosophical arguments for the immortality of the soul. Not on quasiscientific evidence of life after death. Not on the silliness of seances and spiritualism. But on Jesus. When we can affirm with our hearts and minds as well as our mouths that He is the Christ, the Son of God, we discover that He is eternal life!

IV. Jesus illustrated His claims of being the Resurrection and the Life by raising Lazarus. He went out to the tomb. John the Gospel writer indicates that Lazarus was dead and not in a coma, by stating that he had been dead four days. Popular Jewish lore held that the spirit of the deceased lingered over the corpse for three days and then departed. Lazarus's body had been put in the tomb four days earlier.

Jewish burials took place the day of death. The corpse was never embalmed but wrapped in a sheet and a towel wound around the head. In that part of the world, the body was placed in a low tomb carved out of the soft limestone on which several niches were hollowed out on each side and the back for laying dead bodies. The entrance was usually a low hole big enough to crawl through with a body, but small enough to be able to be closed off with a stone slab to keep out animals.

Martha shudders at the prospect of approaching the tomb because of the odor of a decomposing corpse. Jesus reminds her of His words promising her that He is the Resurrection. He orders the slab sealing the entrance to the tomb to be pushed aside. He utters a prayer of thanks as if Lazarus has already been wakened again to life.

"I know that thou hearest me always, but I have said this on account of the people standing by, that they may believe that thou didst send me": Jesus did not have to ask for extra power from God. He already had it. He spoke these words out loud in order for the bystanders to understand that the source of His power was the Father. Jesus never descended to the realm of sensationalist. He would not play up His powers. He will not have those watching Him go away thinking of Him as merely an exceptionally good wonder-worker. He reminds everyone that God has sent Him.

"Lazarus, come out": Jesus speaks Lazarus's own name, and calls him forth from death. Jesus asserts His mastery over the grimmest power of the world—death! He knows His friends by name, and He assures us that He will also call us forth from the tomb at the time God deems right.

SUGGESTIONS TO TEACHERS

This great Scripture passage hardly needs a teacher and lesson plan for a class. Furthermore, the subject of death, especially the death of someone close, is one that your class will want to discuss. Your one problem may be in keeping the discussion on the main theme of Jesus as the Resurrection and the Life and not letting the conversation meander off into side issues.

Set the scene for your class. Lazarus, Mary, and Martha were Jesus' adopted family, the group where He felt most at home. They frequently welcomed Him, and Jesus felt close to them. Lazarus's death was a shattering loss to his sisters and to Jesus.

1. *CARES.* Caring means risk-taking. Jesus was willing to take risks to express His care. In the case of Mary and Martha, it meant Jesus had to travel to Judea again—going into the lion's mouth where enemies were wanting to seize Him. Jesus consistently accepted the cost of caring. He went to Bethany to comfort two grieving sisters. Later, He went to Calvary to bring life to dying humankind. Stress in your lesson the extent of Jesus Christ's love for others. Use the episode of His going to Mary and Martha at great cost and danger to illustrate the concern God has for each of us.

2. *CRIES.* The shortest verse in the Bible is John 11:35: "Jesus wept." But what significance! God has feelings! Here is the Lord who cries with us. This will offer you an opportunity to talk about showing feelings during times of personal loss. It can also open the discussion on funerals and grief.

3. *CONFRONTS.* Jesus takes death seriously. He confronts its awesome finality. He faces the sense of futility which dying can give to human existence. The Christian Gospel never smears chocolate coating of cute sayings or shallow philosophy over death. Instead, Jesus stands up to all the terrible qualities of death with Mary and Martha. He realizes, for example, that they have lost their breadwinner. He knows the desolation of parting. In your lesson, you can permit any of the terrors which death holds to be expressed, because Jesus recognized these. At the same time, Jesus vanquished these!

4. *CONQUERS.* Although death is called "the final enemy" in the New Testament, Jesus Christ is the Final Victor! Your lesson must above all pound home the mighty claim of Jesus as the Resurrection and the Life. Talk with your class exactly what this means to you, from your own experience, and encourage the class to relate what it means.

TOPIC FOR ADULTS
THE RESURRECTION AND THE LIFE

The Church Window. "Have you ever read something over and over without being really aware of its meaning? Every Sunday for three years, I sat in our choir facing a large stained-glass window that portrayed Christ at the tomb, with Mary standing near awe-stricken and afraid. Underneath were the words, 'Because I live, ye shall live also.'

"Then, suddenly, I was told I must undergo a major operation. The few days before the operation were a severe strain on my husband and two children. My fourteen-year-old son was quiet, but visibly concerned. My daughter of four thought only of how she would miss me.

"On the evening of the day I learned about the operation, our minister came to our home. He prayed with us and for us, as a family. Two days later was Sunday. Should I attend church?

"We all went, as usual, even though I was to enter the hospital the next day. I retained my composure during the service fairly well, until we sang a favorite hymn of mine.

> Oh, Love that will not let me go,
> I rest my weary Soul in Thee.

"A very dear friend stood beside me in the choir, and my husband directly behind me. I sang three stanzas through bravely; then I came to:

> Oh, Cross, that lifteth up my head,
> I dare not ask to fly from Thee.

"I stopped, my eyes overflowing. I could no longer read the words, and my voice broke. At that same moment the voice of my friend ceased also. At the close of the hymn, my husband placed a reassuring hand on my shoulder.

"When I was able to glance up again, I saw the window. Bright sun was shining through it; myriad colors played on the robes of Christ and Mary. Most vivid of all was the face of Christ. There was the real story of the 'Cross that lifteth up my head.' 'He is speaking to me,' I thought, 'saying, *"Because I live—ye shall live also."* ' Christ became alive and real to me at that moment. My composure was regained; my faltering faith was restored, and all my *fear* was removed.

"The operation was a success. I was returned to my thankful family. Everyone attributed my quick recovery to my courageous spirit. But I knew it was because I found faith enough to believe that I had heard Christ speak to me, through that blessed church window, saying, 'Because I live—ye shall live also!' "—Evelyn Weeks Taylor, *Sunday Digest,* August 24, 1952. Reprinted from *Sunday Digest,* © 1952 David C. Cook Publishing Co., Elgin, IL 60120. Used by permission.

Ideas and Details. Will Rogers, the late, great American humorist, was once invited to meet with a couple of top officials from the Navy. The conversation turned to methods to counteract the threat of submarines in the Atlantic. Will Rogers listened for a long time as the naval brass discoursed. Finally, the cowboy columnist turned to his audience and, with a deadpan face, said in mock seriousness, "Why, that problem is easy. Heat the Atlantic to 212 degrees, and the subs will pop up like boiling eggs!" The admirals sputtered, and began to ask Will Rogers how he could ever heat the ocean to the boiling point. Will drawled, "Waal, I get the ideas. You guys work out the details."

Sometimes, we think along these lines about our faith, especially when it comes to hope beyond this life. We may have the idea, and we may even think that God has some idea of something for us after we die. Through Jesus Christ, however, we know that God has not only got the idea but also worked out the details! He is the Resurrection and the Life, and any person who trusts Him will not be separated from Him even by dying!

Billions for Nothing. Theologian Emil Brunner wrote about death. We must face the fact that we can't stay in this world forever. Medical science has helped delay the day of death for many, but that doesn't change the situation at all. We still try to avoid thinking of death through our amusements and entertainment.

"That is how men do not like to think about death," said Brunner. "Americans have built a billion dollar industry to help them forget about death—the entertainment industry. This is a tremendous effort on the part of man to forget about death. But it doesn't succeed. Man pays billions for nothing."

Questions for Pupils on the Next Lesson. 1. Did Jesus realize that His death was inevitable and accept it? 2. What implications do Jesus' death and Resurrection have in your personal life? 3. How would you answer someone who is troubled over the apparent finality of death? 4. Is there any glory in death when a loved one must go through a long and intense time of pain? 5. Are you willing to die for any cause or purpose?

TOPIC FOR YOUTH
NEW LEASE ON LIFE

Can Afford to Wait. Thomas Carlyle, the Scottish philosopher-writer, once asked Bishop Wilberforce if he had a creed.

"Yes, I have," replied the Bishop, "but sometimes I am bewildered at the length of time it takes for right to triumph."

Carlyle, a dour Scot, pondered this for a few moments, then said, "Aye, if you have a creed, you can afford to wait."

We have a creed based on Jesus' assurance that He is the Resurrection and the Life. Therefore, even though we may not know all the reasons, proofs, or answers to our perplexing questions about death and the hereafter, we can afford to wait!

Resurrection in Mid-Pacific. "The Navy transport had 1,500 Marines on board who were being brought back to the United States from Japan for discharge. On the second day out a small group of them came to the chaplain and, to his intense surprise, asked him to lead them in a Bible study class each morning. Swallowing his amazement, the chaplain jumped at the chance.

"Toward the end of the trip the group read the eleventh chapter of John, which describes the raising of Lazarus from the dead. The chaplain suggested that the incident *dramatized* what Jesus said on that occasion: 'I am the resurrection, and the life: he that believeth in me, though he were dead, yet shall he live: and whosoever liveth and believeth in me shall never die.' More important even than the reanimation of a corpse in A.D. 30 was the question of whether or not that statement of Jesus was true in (what was then) A.D. 1946.

"He told them the story of Raskolnikov, a man in Dostoevski's *Crime and Punishment* who had killed his very self in the act of murdering another, but had in truth been brought back to life as these words of Jesus were read to him.

"There was a little discussion. A couple of questions were raised. But on the whole there was nothing to indicate to the chaplain that he had made his point particularly well.

"When the discussion was over, a Marine corporal followed the chaplain back to his cabin. After a few false starts, he got down to the point, 'Chaplain,' he said, 'I felt as though everything we read this morning was pointed right at me. I've been living in hell for the last six months, and for the first time I feel as though I'd gotten free.'

"As he talked, the story came out. He had just finished high school when he was called into the service. He had spent a long time in the occupation forces in Japan. He had gotten bored. Finally he had gone off one night with some friends and gotten into trouble. Serious trouble. Fortunately (so he thought) no one else knew about it. But *he* knew about it. And he was sure God knew about it. He felt guilty, terribly guilty. And each day the ship got nearer to San Francisco, his feeling increased that he had ruined his life and that he would never be able to face his family back home.

"But somehow that wasn't the end, after all. He kept repeating one idea, over and over again: 'Up until today, Chaplain, I've been a dead man. I have felt utterly condemned by myself, by my family (if they knew), and by God. *I've been dead,* but now, after reading about Jesus and Lazarus, I know that I am alive again. The forgiveness of God can reach out even to me. The resurrection Jesus was talking about is a real thing, after all, right now.'

"When the corporal left the cabin, it was clear that he still had a lot of problems to iron out, and that things wouldn't automatically be easy in this 'new life,' but as the chaplain watched him go, he knew that on that day, on that ship, in the middle of the Pacific Ocean, the miracle of resurrection had taken place. It was quite evident that Jesus' words *were* true: 'He that believeth in me, though he were dead, yet shall he live.' "—From *The Bible Speaks to You* by Robert McAfee Brown. Copyright, MCMLV, by W. L. Jenkins. Used by permission of The Westminster Press, Philadelphia, PA.

No New Lease on Life for Him. William Tecumseh Sherman, the ruthless Union General whose march through the South left a swath of destruction and misery, lost his son, William, at the Battle of Memphis. Desolate with grief and regret, Sherman never got over the blow. He wrote to his wife the words he often repeated to others, "Why was I not killed at Vicksburg? I will go on to the end, but feel the chief stay to my faltering heart is now gone." Although Sherman was a nominal Christian, he never apparently understood that Jesus Christ, the Resurrection and the Life, brings those in sorrow a new lease on life.

Questions for Pupils on the Next Lesson. 1. Does the international strife and danger of nuclear disaster make you more concerned about life and death? 2. Does your concern over your choice of vocation lead you to consider the meaning and purpose of life? 3. Are you curious about what happens after death? 4. Are there any causes you are willing to give your life for? 5. Does the finality of death trouble you?

LESSON XIII—FEBRUARY 24

THROUGH DEATH TO LIFE

Background Scripture: John 12
Devotional Reading: John 12:44–50

KING JAMES VERSION

JOHN 12 20 And there were certain Greeks among them that came up to worship at the feast:

21 The same came therefore to Philip, which was of Bethsaida of Galilee, and desired him, saying, Sir, we would see Jesus.

22 Philip cometh and telleth Andrew: and again Andrew and Philip tell Jesus.

23 And Jesus answered them, saying, The hour is come, that the Son of man should be glorified.

24 Verily, verily, I say unto you, Except a corn of wheat fall into the ground and die, it abideth alone: but if it die, it bringeth forth much fruit.

25 He that loveth his life shall lose it; and he that hateth his life in this world shall keep it unto life eternal.

26 If any man serve me, let him follow me; and where I am, there shall also my servant be: if any man serve me, him will *my* Father honour.

27 Now is my soul troubled; and what shall I say? Father, save me from this hour: but for this cause came I unto this hour.

28 Father, glorify thy name. Then came there a voice from heaven, *saying,* I have both glorified *it,* and will glorify *it* again.

29 The people therefore that stood by, and heard *it,* said that it thundered: others said, An angel spake to him.

30 Jesus answered and said, This voice came not because of me, but for your sakes.

31 Now is the judgment of this world: now shall the prince of this world be cast out.

32 And I, if I be lifted up from the earth, will draw all *men* unto me.

33 This he said, signifying what death he should die.

REVISED STANDARD VERSION

JOHN 12 20 Now among those who went up to worship at the feast were some Greeks. 21 So these came to Philip, who was from Bethsaida in Galilee, and said to him, "Sir, we wish to see Jesus." 22 Philip went and told Andrew; Andrew went with Philip and they told Jesus. 23 And Jesus answered them, "The hour has come for the Son of man to be glorified. 24 Truly, truly, I say to you, unless a grain of wheat falls into the earth and dies, it remains alone; but if it dies, it bears much fruit. 25 He who loves his life loses it, and he who hates his life in this world will keep it for eternal life. 26 If any one serves me, he must follow me; and where I am, there shall my servant be also; if any one serves me, the Father will honor him.

27 "Now is my soul troubled. And what shall I say, 'Father, save me from this hour'? No, for this purpose I have come to this hour. 28 Father, glorify thy name." Then a voice came from heaven, "I have glorified it, and I will glorify it again." 29 The crowd standing by heard it and said that it had thundered. Others said, "An angel has spoken to him." 30 Jesus answered, "This voice has come for your sake, not for mine. 31 Now is the judgment of this world, now shall the ruler of this world be cast out; 32 and I, when I am lifted up from the earth, will draw all men to myself." 33 He said this to show by what death he was to die.

KEY VERSE: I, when I am lifted up from the earth, will draw all men to myself.
John 12:32 (RSV).

HOME DAILY BIBLE READINGS

Feb.	18.	M.	*Mary Anointed Jesus.* John 12:1–8.
Feb.	19.	T.	*Riding on a Colt.* Mark 11:1–10.
Feb.	20.	W.	*Triumphant Entry.* John 12:9–19.
Feb.	21.	T.	*Greeks Seek Jesus.* John 12:20–26.
Feb.	22.	F.	*Believe in the Light.* John 12:27–36a.
Feb.	23.	S.	*People's Unbelief.* John 12:36b–43.
Feb.	24.	S.	*Judged by Jesus' Words.* John 12:44–50.

BACKGROUND

We are a little more than halfway through the Gospel of John but we are ready to start the last days of Jesus' life. At first, we think this is a strange way to write about the life of Jesus. Why is John giving so much space to the events from Palm Sunday through Easter, the span of a little more than a week?

We must remember that none of the Gospel writers had any interest in writing a biography of Jesus. They were men in a hurry to tell the astonishingly Good News that Jesus had died on a cross but was raised alive to them. As far as they were concerned, the main thing to write about was the way Jesus willingly laid down His life for others but was vindicated by being brought back to them again as the Risen, Living Lord.

The writer of the fourth Gospel was an eyewitness of many of the events of Jesus' final days of earthly ministry. The twelfth chapter of John is packed with his reminiscences. John was a good observer. He remembered the way those last days affected the bystanders, the authorities, the disciples, and, most of all, Jesus Himself.

The scene for this and the following chapters is Passover time in Jerusalem. Scholars estimate that huge influx of Passover pilgrims swelled the population of the city to as many as 2 million for this annual celebration. Such a number meant great excitement, just as a big crowd at a sporting event today generates enthusiasm. However, the enormous number of Jewish visitors to Jerusalem also meant a heightening of nationalist feelings. The Romans, realizing this, always beefed up their security forces at Passover time, and breathed a sigh of relief when the crowds dispersed without incident. Jerusalem was a powder keg in Jesus' time, and some hoped that Jesus would be the messianic leader to provide the spark of revolt.

The Jewish authorities had been uneasy about Jesus for a long time. Recent events, such as the reports of the raising of Lazarus, heightened their anxieties. They had been ready to arrest Him on several occasions, and were definitely keeping their eye on Him when He arrived in Jerusalem for this Passover.

NOTES ON THE PRINTED TEXT

Jesus mounts the final part of His campaign, and advances to Jerusalem for the last time. At this time, He knows that He will inaugurate His Kingdom through His sacrificial death.

Jerusalem is jammed with Passover pilgrims. Everyone living within several days' travel to Jerusalem tried to be in the great capital for Passover. Every Jew, living somewhere else, no matter how distant, tried to get to Jerusalem for Passover at least once during his lifetime.

I. *Now among those who went up to worship at the Feast were some Greeks:* Judaism was regarded as the highest and most spiritual religion at that time, and had attracted many inquirers. Although non-Jews, they tried to live pious and moral lives. They were called "God-fearers." Because they usually lived outside the area of Jerusalem and spoke Greek, they were referred to as "Greeks." This did not mean that they came from Greece, but merely that they were Greek-speaking Gentiles who had also come to Jerusalem to participate in the Passover celebration.

So these came to Philip: Philip is a Greek name. Perhaps this disciple had connections with Gentile God-fearers or came from such a background himself. In any case, he is approached by a contingent of Greek-speaking outsiders to arrange a meeting with Jesus. Philip, however, apparently is not quite sure how to handle their request and goes to Andrew, his friend and a man from the same town. Andrew, who always seems to be taking somebody to Jesus such as his brother, Simon Peter, or the boy with the loaves and fishes, takes Philip and the Greeks' request immediately to Jesus.

And Jesus answered them, "The hour has come for the Son of Man to be glorified": This seems at first to be a strange answer to the request. However, Jesus is acknowledging that the Gentiles are already starting to recognize Him, and is stating that this signals the start of the new age which will be brought about on the Cross. Jesus will be "glorified" as the Messiah by all kinds of persons after His sacrificial death. These "Greeks" are the first of what will be millions.

II. *"He who loves his life loses it, and he who hates his life in this world will keep it for eternal life. If anyone serves me, he must follow me":* Here is the great law for Christian living; namely, that a selfish regard for self-preservation brings doom, whereas service to others through self-sacrifice brings life on a plane with the Eternal. Jesus knows that for Him this will mean taking up a cross and accepting agony and disgrace. But He also is certain that His act of self-sacrifice will bring immense blessings. Any person who wants to be with Jesus, He declares, must be willing to live the same kind of life of disregard for his or her own selfish ambitions and follow Him to his or her own personal Calvary.

III. *"Now is my soul troubled. And what shall I say, 'Father, save me from this hour'? No, for this purpose I have come to this hour":* John points out that Jesus contemplates the kind of sacrifice He will have to make. Jesus was not a robot without personal feelings. He was as human as anyone as well as being as divine as God, and He had normal human uneasiness over accepting pain with which everyone has to deal. He knew that He could slip out of the city or could mute His message or take a lot of steps to save His own skin. But He also remembered His purpose in the Father's plans for the universe.

The crowd standing by heard it and said that it had thundered: In the Bible, God's voice was often described in terms of thunder. The bystanders heard the rumble of thunder, but Jesus heard the message of God's reassurance. His doubts were dispelled. His uneasiness was swept away. Encouraged afresh by the Father, Jesus accepts His imminent execution on the cross. But He also knows He will be vindicated and will rise victorious! "I, when I am lifted up from the earth, will draw all men to myself!" (12:33).

SUGGESTIONS TO TEACHERS

The last days of a famous person holds a certain fascination, especially if the person dies unexpectedly. If the famous person is also a martyr, the chances are great that something will be written about those final hours. For instance, the assassinations of Presidents Lincoln, Garfield, McKinley, and Kennedy have created a body of literature.

The closing days of Jesus' earthly ministry also brought forth written accounts after His death. However, there was an essential difference between, say, Plato writing about Socrates taking the hemlock, or Jim Bishop telling about Lincoln's approaching the fateful Friday at Ford's Theatre, and the Gospel writers. Plato and Jim Bishop were writing to satisfy the curiosity of the public. Not Matthew, Mark, Luke, or John. These authors wanted to share important news about God.

John's Gospel, from the start of chapter 12 to the end of chapter 21, could carry the subtitle, "From Death to Life." Your lesson for this Sunday starts this section dealing with Jesus' final days.

You will quickly notice that chapter 12 has so much material in it that you cannot hope to cover everything. Therefore, you will have to select certain portions. You may wish to organize your lesson as follows:

1. *VISION OF OPPORTUNITY.* Both Mary and Philip see possibilities to serve. Mary, realizing that Jesus' hours were numbered, anointed His feet with expensive ointment. She knew what no one else seemed to know: Jesus would soon die. She took advantage of the opportunity to show her love for Him. Philip seized the opportunity to take some Greek-speaking Jews to Andrew and then to Jesus. Remind your class members that they must always seize opportunities to serve Christ. One of the saddest phrases is, "If only I had. . . ."

2. *VALUE OF SACRIFICE.* Hold your class's attention on John 12:24–26 and Jesus' words of sacrificing for others as the key to real living. Note that Jesus speaks of following Him in serving. Jesus never asks more of us than He has already done. Through dying comes life!

3. *VOICE OF REASSURANCE.* John discloses Jesus' own inner struggles over accepting His call to go to His death for others. Nonetheless, God reaffirmed Jesus in His sense of mission. And Jesus showed that He was certain that He would be glorified in death. Devote plenty of time on Jesus' use of the crisis of the last week of His life for divine purposes.

TOPIC FOR ADULTS
THROUGH DEATH TO LIFE

Law of Self-Sacrifice. " 'Describe to me Brahma,' said a pupil to his guru.
"The sage was silent for a long time.
" 'Will you not tell me?' the pupil urged.
" 'You have received your answer,' replied the sage.
"Brahma was the Vast Silence. We are to lose ourselves and the universe in order to gain THIS. It is a vast negation of life. In trying to make God everything it makes him akin to nothing. It cheapens him.
". . . Self-sacrifice is the law of Christ's being—it is the law of my being, for selfishness spreads a pall of unhappiness and misery within while the heart sings as it bleeds and bears for others."—E. Stanley Jones, *Christ at the Roundtable.*

Your Type of Sacrifice? "Dear Lord, I want to serve you so badly! I'm literally burning with the fever. I've been on a vacation and I'm more ready than I've ever been. What I need now is an assignment. That's what I want to discuss with you. I've been offered the position of program chairperson for the women at the church, but I'm hoping you'll agree with me that it's not quite right. They need a teacher badly in the Junior Department of the Sunday School, but I know too many of the children. Wild bunch if I ever saw one (but it's no wonder, considering the homes they come from). I would love to help out in the nursery, but that would mean missing the worship service occasionally, and I know you would not want me to do that. Besides, my children are too old for the nursery. The woman next door can't drive. She needs help with the groceries and she needs company, but she never lets go once she gets hold of you.
"How about something different? No nursing homes, please; I can't stand some of what I see in those places.
"I know you'll think of something. I can hardly wait. With all my love, Ima Servant."—Cherokee Heights Baptist Church, Macon, Georgia.

Closing Comments Contrasted. "Do you think," said Byron to the doctor who attended him in his last illness—"do you think I care for life? I am heartily sick of it. Few men have lived faster than I have done. I have known pleasure under every form. I have drunk up all the nectar in the cup of life. It is time to throw the dregs away."
Contrast these words with Jesus' comments in John 12 as He contemplated His

death. Byron lived only for his own pleasure and thereby saw only death and dregs. Jesus Christ lived and died for others and thereby brought hope and harmony.

Questions for Pupils on the Next Lesson. 1. How did Jesus live a life of being a servant of others? 2. What forms of self-giving and self-sacrifice did you show through your life this past week? 3. Why do many people want to dominate others rather than to serve others? 4. Do you sometimes find that you struggle with the contradictions between your actions and your words? 5. Do you belong to a group in which you may both find and give love?

TOPIC FOR YOUTH
DYING TO LIVE

Living to Die or Dying to Live? Sandra Ilene West inherited enough money from her wealthy family to indulge every whim. The Oil Heiress died in 1977 at the age of thirty-seven in California. Her life was spent pampering herself. Her death continued the pattern. She was buried as she requested "in my lace nightgown . . . in my Ferrari, with the seat slanted comfortably," at the San Antonio cemetery where her husband is also buried. Several hundred awed spectators looked on as a gray-painted wooden crate, 6 ft. by 8 ft. by 17 ft., was lowered into the ground by a crane. To deter any grave robbers cum 1964 Ferrari buffs, the crate was covered with concrete.

Compare this person who seemed to live only to die with Jesus who died to live! Which for you?

Access to the Ruler. Early in the morning of July 9, 1982, an unemployed vagabond named Michael Fagan managed to scramble up a drainpipe of Buckingham Palace and creep into the bedroom of Queen Elizabeth II. He woke the startled monarch and talked to her for ten minutes before a servant finally arrived. This is the account in Fagan's words of what happened at Buckingham Palace, related by his sister, Marjorie Tomlin:

"When I stepped into the queen's room, I looked at her in bed and our eyes met . . . I didn't know if she was already awake or it was me who had disturbed her," he said.

Fagan said the queen "looked astonished" when she realized he was not a servant. He told her his name and said: "I'm sorry to be here like this but it's the only way I could get anyone to listen to me. I'm not here to hurt or hinder you. Please don't be afraid."

He said the queen was not nervous and told him: "Please carry on."

Fagan said: "I sat down on the edge of her bed and she pushed herself a bit further up on the pillows to listen."

Fagan said he told the queen he has four children and his wife had left him but he could not get any help from welfare workers to look after them.

"People like me are scraping the bottom of the barrel," he said.

The queen "seemed very sympathetic and genuinely interested in what I was saying," he said.

Because of Jesus Christ's sacrifice for us, we all have immediate access to our Supreme Ruler. We do not have to sneak in or worry about intruding on the Lord. We can discuss anything with this One. We can be certain that our God understands our woes. And we need not fear that we will be trespassing any time we come into His presence. He welcomes us. We know all this through the Person who died that we might live with God.

Stopped the Lethal Blow. There is a charming legend about St. Giles, the Patron Saint of Edinburgh. We're told that he used to travel all over Scotland in the company of a deer. It was his favourite pet. He, when speaking to the congregations, used his pet as an illustration. "As the deer panteth after the living brooks, so panteth my soul after thee, O God."

One day, as he was walking in the woods, from the corner of his eye he saw a bowman take aim at his deer. In desperation, he saw the arrow fly, and he ran to intercept it. So, he flung out his hand before the animal. The arrow pierced it completely, and went into the side of the deer.

Fortunately for the deer, he had taken the real impact of the arrow in his hand, and the pet was only slightly wounded.

That, if you please, is how God helps us. He stops the lethal blow!

Questions for Pupils on the Next Lesson. 1. What examples of people serving others have meant the most to you? 2. Why do some people sometimes misinterpret the meaning of serving others? 3. When is it most difficult for you to do what is right? 4. Do you find yourself wanting to dominate others or to serve them? 5. Do you belong to any group in which you may both give and receive caring?

MARCH—MAY 1985

JOHN: THE GOSPEL OF LIFE (CONTINUED)

LESSON I—MARCH 3

RELATIONSHIPS IN THE NEW LIFE

Background Scripture: John 13
Devotional Reading: John 15:11–17

KING JAMES VERSION

JOHN 13 Now before the feast of the passover, when Jesus knew that his hour was come
that he should depart out of this world unto the
Father, having loved his own which were in the
world, he loved them unto the end.

2 And supper being ended, the devil having
now put into the heart of Judas Iscariot, Simon's
son, to betray him;

3 Jesus knowing that the Father had given
all things into his hands, and that he was come
from God, and went to God;

4 He riseth from supper, and laid aside his
garments; and took a towel, and girded himself.

5 After that he poureth water into a basin,
and began to wash the disciples' feet, and to
wipe *them* with the towel wherewith he was
girded.

6 Then cometh he to Simon Peter: and Peter
saith unto him, Lord, dost thou wash my feet?

7 Jesus answered and said unto him, What I
do thou knowest not now; but thou shalt know
hereafter.

8 Peter saith unto him, Thou shalt never
wash my feet. Jesus answered him, If I wash
thee not, thou hast no part with me.

12 So after he had washed their feet, and had
taken his garments, and was set down again, he
said unto them, Know ye what I have done to
you?

13 Ye call me Master and Lord: and ye say
well; for *so* I am.

14 If I then, *your* Lord and Master, have
washed your feet; ye also ought to wash one
another's feet.

15 For I have given you an example, that ye
should do as I have done to you.

16 Verily, verily, I say unto you, The servant
is not greater than his lord; neither he that is
sent greater than he that sent him.

17 If ye know these things, happy are ye if ye
do them.

34 A new commandment I give unto you,
That ye love one another; as I have loved you,
that ye also love one another.

35 By this shall all *men* know that ye are my
disciples, if ye have love one to another.

REVISED STANDARD VERSION

JOHN 13 Now before the feast of the Passover, when Jesus knew that his hour had come
to depart out of this world to the Father, having
loved his own who were in the world, he loved
them to the end. 2 And during supper, when the
devil had already put it into the heart of Judas
Iscariot, Simon's son, to betray him, 3 Jesus,
knowing that the Father had given all things
into his hands, and that he had come from God
and was going to God, 4 rose from supper, laid
aside his garments, and girded himself with a
towel. 5 Then he poured water into a basin, and
began to wash the disciples' feet, and to wipe
them with the towel with which he was girded.
6 He came to Simon Peter; and Peter said to
him, "Lord, do you wash my feet?" 7 Jesus answered him, "What I am doing you do not know
now, but afterward you will understand." 8
Peter said to him, "You shall never wash my
feet." Jesus answered him, "If I do not wash
you, you have no part in me."

12 When he had washed their feet, and
taken his garments, and resumed his place, he
said to them, "Do you know what I have done to
you? 13 You call me Teacher and Lord; and you
are right, for so I am. 14 If I then, your Lord and
Teacher, have washed your feet, you also ought
to wash one another's feet. 15 For I have given
you an example, that you also should do as I
have done to you. 16 Truly, truly, I say to you, a
servant is not greater than his master; nor is he
who is sent greater than he who sent him. 17 If
you know these things, blessed are you if you do
them.

34 A new commandment I give to you, that
you love one another; even as I have loved you,
that you also love one another. 35 By this all
men will know that you are my disciples, if you
have love for one another."

KEY VERSE: A new commandment I give to you, that you love one another; even as I have loved you, that you also love one another. John 13:34 (RSV).

HOME DAILY BIBLE READINGS

Feb. 25. M. *Cleansed for Life Together.* John 13:1–11.
Feb. 26. T. *Serving One Another.* John 13:12–20.
Feb. 27. W. *A Betrayal of Intimacy.* John 13:21–30.
Feb. 28. T. *Love Gives Us Away.* John 13:31–35.
Mar. 1.   F. *A Fellowship of Life.* 1 John 1:1–10.
Mar. 2.   S. *The Vine and the Branches.* John 15:1–11.
Mar. 3.   S. *You Are My Friends.* John 15:12–17.

BACKGROUND

Matthew, Mark, and Luke have accounts of Jesus instituting the Lord's Supper in their accounts of the Upper Room events before Jesus' arrest. John does not. In its place, he tells about the foot-washing—an incident none of the earlier Gospel writers mention.

Why did Jesus wash His disciples' feet? John suggests several reasons. First, Jesus wanted to express His unswerving caring for these people. In addition, Jesus wished to bring them the cleansing awareness of God's forgiveness. John also makes it clear that Jesus insisted upon countering the contentiousness which had seeped into the disciple band. Earlier, they had argued among themselves about who was more important. Also, John was anxious to hold up Jesus as a model of humble service. Jesus' washing the disciples' feet was demonstrating in a compelling way how each disciple was to act toward others. He was showing love in action. The foot-washing is a preview of the final and greatest act of sacrificial love: the Cross.

It is almost impossible for people like us to comprehend what was involved in Jesus' washing the disciples' feet. Even with us, there is something distasteful about stooping and bathing someone else's feet. It was even more so in Jesus' time. For that reason, the task was relegated to the lowest flunky or slave in the household. The custom was to have the hapless person assigned the menial chore of washing the guest's feet meet the guests at the door, kneel down, remove the sandals of the guest, pour cool, fresh water from a large jug over the hot, tired, dirty feet with a basin under them to catch the water, then gently dry each foot with a clean towel. Since people wore flimsy sandals or went barefoot, the feet of the guests were usually caked with dust or mud and bits of dung and garbage from the streets and roads. Foot-washing was a decidedly unpleasant job. Therefore, it was considered degrading to do it for someone else. No self-respecting person would deign to lower himself or herself to the level of this kind of work.

In the case of Jesus and His disciples, who had no servant, Jesus shocks the group by performing this degrading chore in person.

NOTES ON THE PRINTED TEXT

John opens his account of the foot-washing by setting the scene for us. The Last Supper took place, John states, just prior to Passover, or Nisan 13 by the way Jewish calendars reckoned the date. Later, John records that Jesus died on Nisan 14, the date of Passover. The Last Supper, according to John's date, was not a Passover meal but a Kiddush or fellowship meal just before the actual Passover celebration.

Now before the feast of the Passover, when Jesus knew that his hour had come to depart out of this world to the Father, having loved his own who were in the world, he loved them to the end: Jesus realized that He would soon be seized and forced to go to His death. Nonetheless, His thoughts are not centered on His own problems or fears but on His disciples. He was aware that Judas had plotted to turn Him in to the authorities. He also knew what a shaky, squabbling collection of followers to whom He was entrusting His work. The words, "his hour," refer to His impending death. In spite of all these concerns, Jesus gave no whimper of self-pity. Instead, he continued to love those around that table.

. . . the devil had already put it into the heart of Judas Iscariot, Simon's son, to betray him: The words seem to indicate that although Judas had earlier taken some steps toward betraying Jesus, he had not yet followed through and could still stop the devil from working on him to turn traitor. Judas was slipping fast, but he had not carried out his terrible scheme at that point. John hints that Judas had not yet gone over the brink, although dangerously close.

. . . began to wash the disciples' feet: Jesus went around the circle, laying aside all pride and dignity to perform the most menial chore imaginable. John would have us understand that Jesus even washed Judas's feet.

Peter said to him, "Lord, do you wash my feet?" Jesus answered him, "What I am doing you do not know now, but afterward you will understand." Peter said, "You shall never wash my feet." Jesus answered him, "If I do not wash you, you have no part in me": Peter, ashamed that his Master and Superior was doing the foot-washing, pulled back his feet. Jesus insisted, knowing that Peter had to experience undeserved love and service before he could ever be expected to love and serve others.

. . . laid aside his garments . . . and taken . . . These verbs are the same words Jesus used in the Good Shepherd passages earlier to speak of His death and His Resurrection (*see* John 10:11, 15, 17).

"If I do not wash you, you have no part in me": John was pondering a deeper meaning to the foot-washing. Only when Peter is cleansed finally by Jesus' atoning death will he be able to be in genuine fellowship with Jesus. In other words, the action of foot-washing did more than scrub clean Peter's soles; it cleansed his soul!

"Do you know what I have done to you? You call me Teacher and Lord: and you are right, for so I am. If I then, your Lord and Teacher, have washed your feet, you also ought to wash one another's feet. For I have given you an example": Jesus offers His own action as a model for what is expected of every person who dares call Him "Teacher" and "Lord." Thomas a Kempis wrote a devotional classic in the fourteenth century called, "The Imitation of Christ" in which he prays that he may follow Jesus as a model. Every believer must imitate Jesus Christ by humbly serving others.

A servant is not greater than his master: If Jesus is our Master, and if He performs acts of sacrificial service for others, then we must do the same. As ones under His orders, we are not exempt from doing what He did.

"A new commandment I give you, that you love one another: even as I have loved you, that you also love one another": Jesus does not make a suggestion or drop a hint. He offers "a new commandment." He updates the decalogue delivered to Moses on Sinai. The eleventh and greatest of all is to practice a love which knows no bounds, makes no exceptions, looks for no rewards. Jesus Himself is both the model and the motive for this kind of sacrificial love for others.

"By this all men will know that you are my disciples, if you have love for one another": The only badge to identify a Christian is *agape* or Christian caring. The new life the crucified, risen Lord brings a believer empowers that person to have a caring relationship toward others, regardless of what happens or who the other persons may be!

SUGGESTIONS TO TEACHERS

"See how these Christians love one another!" astonished observers of the earliest Christians often remarked. Those outside the Christian Church commented most frequently on the way Christ's followers cared—genuinely cared—for each other. (By the way, do people outside the Church say this about your congregation?) Such concern for others puzzled people, and they wondered how Christians could love each other.

The reason, of course, was Jesus Christ. His supreme act of sacrificial love on the Cross motivated early believers and continues to inspire. His death and Resurrection meant—and still mean—a completely new life.

The lessons for today and the next several weeks examine various meanings of that new life. Today's lesson reflects on how Christians love each other, or, how those participating in the new life relate to each other.

1. *LESSON OF THE TOWEL.* You will probably find that those in your class will not appreciate immediately the way Jesus undertook such a menial chore as washing the disciples' feet. Take the necessary time to help the people in the class understand Jesus' willingness to serve by doing what we would call "flunky work." Remind the class that love means more than feelings; it means acting. Direct the discussion to Peter's shock at finding Jesus preparing to wash his feet. "You shall never wash my feet," the big fisherman proudly blurts (John 13:8). Point out the need for humility on Peter's part—and each believer's part. In fact, you must emphasize, a person must receive before he or she can give. One must be "washed" or forgiven before he or she can truly serve others!

2. *LOSS OF JUDAS.* Judas's defection never ceases to hold a fascination. If you are not careful, you may find that a disproportionate amount of your time in class can be spent on armchair-psychoanalysis of Judas. While this may be interesting, it is not necessarily profitable. Remind your class that Judas was once a trusted member of the Twelve chosen by Jesus. The lesson for everyone is that even one of the inner circle can fall away and end by betraying the Lord. Furthermore, every act of betrayal results in darkness. The little verse, "It was night" (13:30) refers also to the darkness in Judas's life at that hour.

3. *ELEVENTH COMMANDMENT.* Budget lots of lesson time for reflection on Jesus' command to love. Get below the surface meanings of the word *love*, and ask each one in the class to tell of examples of *agape*-caring in his or her own experience.

4. *LED TO A CROSS.* The prime thrust of this lesson must be Jesus' mighty display of love by laying down His life for others. Let the impact of the Cross on Peter and the other followers be felt by asking what those in your class would have done if in Peter's shoes. Above all, stress that following Jesus Christ means sacrificing for others. Ask what specific sacrifices for others each sees others in the class making. Reinforce those acts of Christian service. Challenge each person to deeper commitment to serving others sacrificially.

TOPIC FOR ADULTS
RELATIONSHIPS IN THE NEW LIFE

The Power of Love. Louis Lawes became the warden of the infamous correctional institution at Ossining, New York, better known as Sing Sing, and found the prisoners living in deplorable conditions. Lawes brought better conditions and became one of the great leaders in penal reform in the world. His wife Kathryn, however, was the person who touched the lives of the prisoners most deeply. She took her children to baseball and basketball games when the prisoners were playing, and insisted on sitting with the gangsters, murderers, rapists, and robbers. She won deep appreciation for her way of regarding each prisoner as a

human being. Kathyrn Lawes was killed in an automobile accident one day in
1937. The men of Sing Sing were stunned. The following day, Kathryn's body was
on display in a casket in a funeral home a quarter of a mile from the prison. When
the warden entered the prison that day, hundreds of convicts were congregated
at the entrance gates. Lawes knew what they wanted to do. "Men," he said, "I'm
going to trust you. I'm opening the gates. You can go to see her one last time."
Sing Sing's gates were opened. No prison count was taken. No guards were
posted. At lock-up time that night, every prisoner was back in Sing Sing. Love for
them had made those hardened criminals dependable for that day!

Hans's Hands. Around 1490, Albrecht Durer and a young man known now
only as Hans, were struggling artist friends. They were very poor and had to work
to support themselves while they studied. Work kept them from classes. Progress
was slow. Then one day Hans, the older of the two, insisted that Albrecht devote
all his time to study while he, Hans, worked to support them both. They agreed
that when Albrecht was successful he would in turn support Hans, who would
then learn to paint.

The bargain was struck. Albrecht went off to the cities of Europe to study
painting. He had more than talent, it was genius, as the world now knows. He was
soon successful and went back to keep his bargain with Hans. But Albrecht
quickly discovered the price his devoted friend had paid. For Hans worked at
manual labor, hard rough work, in order to support his friend. His slender, sensitive artist's hands had been ruined for life. Those stiff gnarled fingers could no
longer use the artist's brush in the delicate strokes necessary to painting. So Albrecht Durer, great artist and great soul, painted the hands of his friend, painted
them as he had so often seen them raised in prayer for their success.

Today, art galleries throughout the world exhibit Albrecht Durer's paintings
and etchings. But of them all, beautiful and famous as they are, none holds the
place in the hearts of the people as does Praying Hands, which tells its own eloquent story of love, labor, and sacrifice on the part of the subject, and of the love
and gratitude of the painter.

Kept by Spending. "We cannot save life by hoarding it. When a person tries to
be a miser with his health, he usually makes himself miserable. We develop our
physical and mental powers by spending them. Whoever tries to save his muscle
or his memory by not using them is sure to weaken them. The power of love or
sympathy is never exhausted by use. But these do shrivel by self-protection."—
Ralph W. Sockman, *Quote,* October 14, 1962.

Questions for Pupils on the Next Lesson. 1. How do you demonstrate your
commitment and love for Christ? 2. Does faithful discipleship exempt a believer
from suffering and hardship? 3. What values and actions challenge your assump-
tions? 4. Exactly what is the peace which Christ says He brings? 5. Whom do you
depend on most when you are lonely, afraid, or experiencing difficulties?

TOPIC FOR YOUTH
TRADEMARK OF NEW LIFE

More Than One Chance to Die. Columbia Pictures Television filmed Pulitzer
Prizewinner Bruce Catton's book, *The Blue and the Gray,* near Prairie Grove,
Arkansas. The book and the film trace the fortunes of two families, a Northern
and a Southern, through the Civil War era from 1859 to the assassination of President Lincoln in 1865. The Columbia Pictures's staff and producers wanted as authentic a setting for the backgrounds for the filming as possible. They found an
area in western Arkansas which had many Civil War houses and artifacts. Fort
Smith, Arkansas, has so many historically preserved streets and buildings from
the mid-nineteenth century that it was used for scenes from both Vicksburg and

Gettyburg in the movie. To the delight of people in the area, almost 3,000 extras were hired from that part of Arkansas. Ninety speaking parts were cast from local people.

One of those selected was an eighty-two-year-old woman named Lylah Jackson. Mrs. Jackson, who ordinarily worked as a cashier at the local Holiday Inn, was the oldest member of the cast. She announced proudly, "I get killed at Bull Run when my house explodes." Pondering her film debut, she added, "Most people my age get only one chance to die. I'm getting at least two."

Actually, any Christian gets many chances to "die"; any Christian gets to share life with others and die to pride and selfishness many times! The trademark of the new life Jesus Christ brings is sacrificial love—dying for others many times throughout life!

Trademark of Concern. A certain Christian survived the horrors of the Buchenwald death camp. He was deeply scarred physically and emotionally by the ordeal. When asked about himself, however, he said that his sufferings were nothing compared to the brokenheartedness he felt toward the young Nazis who served as guards at Buchenwald. This Christian could not hate; he could only weep in concern over the guilt and remorse which he felt would eventually plague these German youths. He did not show any concern for himself or for the four terrible years he had spent in the camp. He didn't express as deep a concern ever for the thousands of people who had suffered and died around him. He said that those who had suffered were with God. He worried most for those who had been the tormentors and prayed for them.

Love is like that. Christ makes us want to have even the worst enemy live as God's child.

Giving Without Expecting Anything in Return. "The difference between proselytizing and evangelism is the difference between browbeating and faith-sharing, between coercion and free choice, between demanding an answer and offering a possibility, between pressure and compassion, between self-serving labor and self-giving love (*agape*). What is needed, therefore, is a listening, caring stance. If the church wants to be understood, it must seek to understand. If the church really cares, it will give without expecting anything in return."—Richard S. Armstrong, *Service Evangelism,* Philadelphia: Westminster, 1979.

Questions for Pupils on the Next Lesson. 1. Do you ever experience a need to depend on someone? If so, to whom do you turn? Why? 2. Why do we need assurance that we need not go it alone? 3. Where do you find loyalty and dependability in others? 4. Why do you and others seem to feel a lack of interior peace in your lives?

LESSON II—MARCH 10

SUPPORT FOR THE NEW LIFE

Background Scripture: John 14–16
Devotional Reading: John 16:4–15

KING JAMES VERSION

JOHN 14   18 I will not leave you comfortless: I will come to you.

19 Yet a little while, and the world seeth me no more; but ye see me: because I live, ye shall live also.

20 At that day ye shall know that I *am* in my Father, and ye in me, and I in you.

21 He that hath my commandments, and keepeth them, he it is that loveth me: and he that loveth me shall be loved of my Father, and I will love him, and will manifest myself to him.

22 Judas saith unto him, not Iscariot, Lord, how is it that thou wilt manifest thyself unto us, and not unto the world?

23 Jesus answered and said unto him, If a man love me, he will keep my words: and my Father will love him, and we will come unto him, and make our abode with him.

24 He that loveth me not keepeth not my sayings: and the word which ye hear is not mine, but the Father's which sent me.

25 These things have I spoken unto you, being *yet* present with you.

26 But the Comforter, *which is* the Holy Ghost, whom the Father will send in my name, he shall teach you all things, and bring all things to your remembrance, whatsoever I have said unto you.

27 Peace I leave with you, my peace I give unto you: not as the world giveth, give I unto you. Let not your heart be troubled, neither let it be afraid.

16   32 Behold, the hour cometh, yea, is now come, that ye shall be scattered, every man to his own, and shall leave me alone: and yet I am not alone, because the Father is with me.

33 These things I have spoken unto you, that in me ye might have peace. In the world ye shall have tribulation: but be of good cheer; I have overcome the world.

REVISED STANDARD VERSION

JOHN 14   18 "I will not leave you desolate; I will come to you. 19 Yet a little while, and the world will see me no more, but you will see me; because I live, you will live also. 20 In that day you will know that I am in my Father, and you in me, and I in you. 21 He who has my commandments and keeps them, he it is who loves me; and he who loves me will be loved by my Father, and I will love him and manifest myself to him." 22 Judas (not Iscariot) said to him, "Lord, how is it that you will manifest yourself to us, and not to the world?" 23 Jesus answered him, "If a man loves me, he will keep my word, and my Father will love him, and we will come to him and make our home with him. 24 He who does not love me does not keep my words; and the word which you hear is not mine but the Father's who sent me.

25 "These things I have spoken to you, while I am still with you. 26 But the Counselor, the Holy Spirit, whom the Father will send in my name, he will teach you all things, and bring to your remembrance all that I have said to you. 27 Peace I leave with you; my peace I give to you; not as the world gives do I give to you. Let not your hearts be troubled, neither let them be afraid.

16   32 "The hour is coming, indeed it has come, when you will be scattered, every man to his home, and will leave me alone; yet I am not alone, for the Father is with me. 33 I have said this to you, that in me you may have peace. In the world you have tribulation; but be of good cheer, I have overcome the world."

KEY VERSE: I have said this to you, that in me you may have peace. In the world you have tribulation; but be of good cheer, I have overcome the world. John 16:33 (RSV).

HOME DAILY BIBLE READINGS

Mar.	4.	M.	*Only One Way.* John 13:36–14:7.
Mar.	5.	T.	*Jesus' Works and Our Works.* John 14:8–14.
Mar.	6.	W.	*I Will Still Be With You.* John 14:15–24.
Mar.	7.	T.	*The Gift of Peace.* John 14:25–31.
Mar.	8.	F.	*Enmity in the World.* John 15:18–27.
Mar.	9.	S.	*I Have Overcome the World.* John 16:25–33.
Mar.	10.	S.	*The Spirit Who Guides Us.* John 16:4–15.

BACKGROUND

Time was running out for Jesus. Judas had fled from the Upper Room to complete his dirty work. The Jerusalem police would soon round up Jesus and any sympathizers. An arrest was inevitable. The outcome of the trial, Jesus knew, would be a guilty verdict. And the disgrace and agony of being executed by being crucified would come quickly. Jesus was certain of what was going on.

However, He did not try a last minute escape. Nor did He consider a desperate compromise to save His hide and live to preach another day. Rather, He calmly and deliberately turned His attention to the eleven followers in that Upper Room. He knew that He had to stake everything on them.

What a pathetic lot they must have appeared to Jesus! What poor material to build His entire cause on! How could this ragtag crew of lower-class fishermen, seething with jealousies and shaky in faith, be entrusted to inaugurate the rule of Jesus as Messiah?

The Upper Room words of Jesus in John are sometimes called Jesus' Farewell Address. The section from John 13:31 through 17:26 is a series of Jesus' final discourses and prayers collected by John the Gospel writer. Sometimes, when we read the familiar words from John 14 about "in my Father's House are many mansions," we think that these were merely spoken for our comfort in times of sorrow such as at a funeral. The sections from John 14 through John 16 which are the focus of this lesson, we should remember, come from that last seminar Jesus held with His disciples before His arrest. These words were intended to instruct and equip the eleven followers—and us, also—to live the new life Jesus brings.

NOTES ON THE PRINTED TEXT

"I will not leave you desolate": The word in the Greek text here is *orphanoi*, and is obviously related to our word *orphans*. In other words, Jesus is reminding us that we will never be abandoned by or orphaned from God! In the case of the gathering in the Upper Room, He assures them that He will return to them. Neither they nor the world have seen the last of Him, He states.

Because I live, you will live also: Jesus promises His friends, huddling uneasily in that Upper Room, that He will not desert them but will appear to them as the Resurrected Lord. Furthermore, His presence with them will enable them to live with an awareness of the Eternal and a confidence that nothing will be able to separate them from Him. Neither here nor anywhere in the New Testament is there any idea that humans achieve immortality or have immortal souls, as in Greek philosophy. The focus is on the Resurrection of Jesus Christ. His presence as Risen Lord brings hope of an unbreakable relationship with believers.

In that day, you will know that I am in the Father, and you in me, and I in you: The phrase, "in that day," refers to the time of the Resurrection appearances, and also to that new glorious era which will come when believers will have an intimate personal relationship with Jesus Christ.

Lord, how is it that you will manifest yourself to us, and not to the world? The other Judas (*not* Judas Iscariot but Thaddaeus or Lebbaeus) in the disciple band feels that it would be much simpler if Jesus would dazzle the entire world, and not merely make some promises to the eleven anxious men, so that everyone would immediately recognize His claims. It's an appealing idea. Why not convince the skeptical masses with one whopper of a proof? Jesus, however, gently reminds the group that only the obedient, trusting follower will be able to discern His nearness. The experience of communing with the Living Christ is given only to the morally sensitive and responsible. *If a man loves me, he will keep my word and my Father will love him, and we will come to him and make our home with him.* Jesus' spiritual presence will be known to the faithful only.

But the Counselor, the Holy Spirit, whom the Father will send in my name: This is the second remark in this chapter about the Holy Spirit's coming to the disciples. Jesus announces that He will be seen, able to be heard and touched only for a relatively brief period. However, He also announces the Spirit's presence with those disciples. The word that Jesus chooses first for the Spirit is translated *Counselor.* The Greek word is the *Paraklete,* and means literally someone "called to one's side." It became the term for an attorney. It referred to the person a defendant called to his side to plead his case and to intercede on his behalf. In the Church, the word came to have deep significance because Christians knew that the Holy Spirit was constantly beside them, working tirelessly on their behalf. Here, Jesus solemnly states that the Father will send such an ever-present and all-powerful Counselor re-presenting the same divine grace and truth embodied in Jesus. The Spirit, operating in Jesus' name, will be God's own envoy, with authority to continue everything that Jesus has been doing while on earth.

He will teach you all things, and bring to your remembrance all that I have said to you: The Holy Spirit, Jesus announces, will perform two vital tasks. First, He will continue to instruct exactly as Jesus has been instructing His disciples. Second, He will recall Jesus and all that He has said and done to the minds of believers. How supremely important it is that the Spirit brings to your remembrance all that Jesus has said! We easily forget, sometimes by intention and sometimes by carelessness. But the Spirit is our Prompter who persistently nudges us to remember Jesus. He will not let us forget Jesus; He is the living reminder of Jesus for us.

Peace I leave with you; my peace I give to you not as the world gives do I give to you: Jesus leaves His own *shalom* or peace with the disciples. Peace means more than an absence of turmoil within or without. In the Scriptures, it always means a state of wholeness and harmony with God, with others, with the entire created orders of the universe as well as within one's self.

Let not your hearts be troubled, neither let them be afraid: Jesus also offers His legacy of confidence and security to His followers. In spite of His impending arrest and execution, Jesus exudes hope and calm.

Be of good cheer, I have overcome the world: What astonishing words from a man soon to die! But what joy for friends in that Upper Room and friends today!

SUGGESTIONS TO TEACHERS

Every pastor can recount stories of people who tell him, "I suppose I'm a backslider or something. Haven't been in church for years. But I professed my faith in Christ when I lived back home, and really got active in the church there. Then we seemed to move around so many times that I sort of got away from the Church. Somehow, nowadays, I find I've fallen away from a sense of closeness to the Lord."

The statistics of most mainline Protestant denominations tell this story in the column showing annual net loss in membership. Many church bodies are not providing support for the new life in Christ which members need. This is where you and today's lesson come in. Your lesson for this Sunday is not meant to turn around the statistical trends in church membership, but to point to support which Christians may have in their new life as Christians.

1. *THE COMMUNITY WITH CHRIST.* In John 14, Jesus uses the familiar image of a home. "The Father's House" means the loving concern of the God who remembers us the way a caring parent welcomes all of his or her children. There is a room at "home" for each of us. At the same time, remind the class members, this implies a family relationship with those others whom the Father welcomes. Devote enough time on the family aspect of the Church to get below the usual clichés. Ask if your congregation lives together as an extended family.

Probe for ways by which the relationships of those in your church can be strengthened to be more like brother-sister ties.

2. *THE CHRISTLIKE GOD.* Frequently, Christians are caught up in such speculative thinking about God's nature that they lose sight of Jesus' claims. And sometimes Christians question how Jesus can be both divine and human, and get into windy wrangling over Jesus' nature. This is where today's blunt words from Jesus' own lips as recorded in John 14 will prove helpful. Let your class members encounter Jesus' statements such as "I am the Way, the Truth, and the Life," and "He who has seen me has seen the Father." Ask members to state what these are *meant* to mean to them, according to John 14.

3. *THE CONDITION OF PETITION.* Believers' prayer lives must not be neglected. As teacher, channel the lesson into some conversation about the way Christians are to pray. The scriptural material (John 14–16) in today's lesson contains many arresting statements by Jesus, including "Whatever you ask in my name, I will do it" and "If you abide in me, and my words abide in you, ask whatever you will . . ." (15:7).

4. *THE COUNSEL OF THE SPIRIT.* Remind your class that Jesus promised the continuing direction and strength of the Spirit. No one in your class is abandoned or forgotten. The Spirit guides! And the Spirit empowers! "Because I live," Jesus assures each Christian, "you shall live also (14:19).

TOPIC FOR ADULTS
SUPPORT FOR THE NEW LIFE

"Gave Me That Faith Back." Maximilian Kolbe was a Franciscan friar in Poland who was an outspoken opponent of Nazism. He courageously cared for hundreds of Jewish refugees and was a marked man when the Germans invaded Poland in 1939. Shipped to Auschwitz, where Christian clergy were singled out for special brutality, Kolbe comforted others. He even shared his meager food rations with fellow prisoners. In July, 1941, the commandant at Auschwitz arbitrarily picked out ten men to be starved to death in reprisal for one inmate esaping from the camp. One of the ten pleaded for his wife and two children. Kolbe stepped forward and offered to take that prisoner's place. Marched to a basement cell, Kolbe survived for almost two weeks without food or water. All of his waking hours were spent consoling fellow victims with prayers. A prison guard finally killed him. Other survivors of Auschwitz recounted how Father Kolbe's words and kindness encouraged them to go on living. One such survivor is Sigmund Gorson. Gorson is the only Jewish survivor of Auschwitz who knew Kolbe. At that time, Gorson was a thirteen-year-old orphan. Gorson recalls, "He used to wipe away my tears. Because of the death of my parents, I had been asking, 'Where is God?' and had lost faith. Kolbe gave me that faith back. He was like an angel."

God sends His own comforter, exactly as Christ promised. He restores our faith. He wipes away our tears. A saint such as Maximilian Kolbe gives us faint hints of how God has acted and continues to act.

One Night I Had a Dream. "I dreamed I was walking along the beach with the Lord, and across the sky flashed scenes from my life. For each scene, I noticed two sets of footprints in the sand; one belonged to me, the other to the Lord. When the last scene of my life flashed before us, I looked back at the footsteps in the sand. I noticed that many times along the path of my life there was only one set of footprints. I also noticed that it happened at the very lowest and saddest times in my life. I questioned the Lord about it, 'Lord, You said that once I decided to follow You, You would walk with me all the way. But I have noticed that during the most troublesome times in my life, there is only one set of footprints. I don't understand why in the times when I needed You most, You would leave.'

The Lord replied, 'My precious child, I would never leave you during your times of trial and suffering. When you see only one set of footprints, it was then that I carried you.' "—Unknown.

Freely Breathe. "Perhaps the challenge of the gospel lies precisely in the invitation to accept a gift for which we can give nothing in return. For the gift is the life breath of God himself, the Spirit who is poured out on us through Jesus Christ. This life breath frees us from fear and gives us new room to live. A man who prayerfully goes about his life is constantly ready to receive the breath of God, and to let his life be renewed and expanded. The man who never prays, on the contrary, is like the child with asthma; because he is short of breath, the whole world shrivels up before him. He creeps in a corner gasping for air, and is virtually in agony. But the man who prays opens himself to God and can freely breathe again. He stands upright, stretches out his hands and comes out of his corner, free to boldly stride through the world because he can move about without fear.

"A man who prays is one who can once more breathe freely, who has the freedom to move where he wishes with no fears to haunt him."—Henri Nouwen, *With Open Hands.*

Questions for Pupils on the Next Lesson. 1. Why do we sometimes experience barriers and alienation that make us feel at odds with others, including those whom we love? 2. Is it possible for a Christian to experience joy and peace even in a hostile environment? 3. How is it possible to build lasting relationships and a sense of unity with others despite differences? 4. Have you ever had to forego popularity or to experience suffering rather than compromise with the truth as you understood it? 5. Why is unity a gift of God?

TOPIC FOR YOUTH
SOMEONE TO COUNT ON

Shipwrecked Soul. Florence Nightingale had a fierce self-will which drove her to incredible labors. Although she seemed to be the model of gentleness and tender compassion, she had no joy. It was not self-forgetting service, but the attainment of proud self-satisfaction.

In her diary, *Lady with the Lamp,* she wrote: "Am I the one who once stood on that Crimean height?—the 'Lady with the Lamp' shall stand. The lamp shows me only my utter shipwreck."

And what was the cruel rock on which her soul had been shipwrecked? It was the rock of self-willed pride in her devotion to duty.

Years later, after hard, bitter years of mourning, refusing to ask for forgiveness through stubborn pride, she finally wrote: "O Father, I submit. I resign myself, I accept with all my heart this stretching out of thine hand to save me."

Hold on to Me! There is a delightful story about a little boy from New Jersey who had never been into New York City. One day his father took him on a tour of Manhattan to see the sights. They walked up one street and down another with the boy holding his father's hand tightly as they moved through the city traffic. At last, at the point of exhaustion, the son said to his dad, "I've held on to you as long as I can; now you've got to hold on to me."

Stop Struggling to Be Saved. Old time shepherds in the Scottish highlands report that sheep sometimes must be rescued. Usually, these sheep wander off toward a steep cliff, and notice a grassy patch below. One will leap down and feed for a time on the sweet grass in that spot. However, it cannot climb back up the ten or twelve feet it has jumped down. This sheep bleats pitifully. The wise shepherd will not come down at once to rescue the sheep. He knows that if he jumps or climbs down that it will immediately move toward the edge of the precipice in panic and destroy itself. Therefore, the shepherd waits. When he sees that the sheep becomes too weak to stand, he will lower himself on a rope and pick up the helpless animal and carry it to safety. Only when the foolish sheep stops struggling and is at the point where it won't run away can it be rescued.

Our Good Shepherd Lord can help us only when we stop trying to save ourselves and learn that we must rely totally on Him. We may count on Him to rescue us when we acknowledge our helplessness and let Him be Lord!

Questions for Pupils on the Next Lesson. 1. Do you experience conflict or divisiveness in your family? 2. How does your faith help you in situations where there is disunity? 3. Do groups to which you belong experience struggle for unity? 4. Do you ever feel tensions between your own goals and the goals of a group to which you belong? 5. How does Jesus Christ bring unity within the Church?

LESSON III—MARCH 17

UNITY IN THE NEW LIFE

Background Scripture: John 17
Devotional Reading: John 16:17–24

KING JAMES VERSION

JOHN 17 These words spake Jesus, and lifted up his eyes to heaven, and said, Father, the hour is come; glorify thy Son, that thy Son also may glorify thee:

2 As thou hast given him power over all flesh, that he should give eternal life to as many as thou hast given him.

3 And this is life eternal, that they might know thee the only true God, and Jesus Christ, whom thou has sent.

4 I have glorified thee on the earth: I have finished the work which thou gavest me to do.

5 And now, O Father, glorify thou me with thine own self with the glory which I had with thee before the world was.

6 I have manifested thy name unto the men which thou gavest me out of the world: thine they were, and thou gavest them me; and they have kept thy word.

7 Now they have known that all things whatsoever thou has given me are of thee.

8 For I have given unto them the words which thou gavest me; and they have received *them*, and have known surely that I came out from thee, and they have believed that thou didst send me.

9 I pray for them: I pray not for the world, but for them which thou hast given me; for they are thine.

10 And all mine are thine, and thine are mine; and I am glorified in them.

11 And now I am no more in the world, but these are in the world, and I come to thee. Holy Father, keep through thine own name those whom thou has given me, that they may be one, as we *are.*

20 Neither pray I for these alone, but for them also which shall believe on me through their word;

21 That they all may be one; as thou, Father, *art* in me, and I in thee, that they also may be one in us: that the world may believe that thou has sent me.

REVISED STANDARD VERSION

JOHN 17 When Jesus had spoken these words, he lifted up his eyes to heaven and said, "Father, the hour has come; glorify thy Son that the Son may glorify thee, 2 since thou hast given him power over all flesh, to give eternal life to all whom thou hast given him. 3 And this is eternal life, that they know thee the only true God, and Jesus Christ whom thou hast sent. 4 I glorified thee on earth, having accomplished the work which thou gavest me to do; 5 and now, Father, glorify thou me in thy own presence with the glory which I had with thee before the world was made.

6 "I have manifested thy name to the men whom thou gavest me out of the world; thine they were, and thou gavest them to me, and they have kept thy word. 7 Now they know that everything that thou hast given me is from thee; 8 for I have given them the words which thou gavest me, and they have received them and know in truth that I came from thee; and they have believed that thou didst send me. 9 I am praying for them; I am not praying for the world but for those whom thou hast given me, for they are thine; 10 all mine are thine, and thine are mine, and I am glorified in them. 11 And now I am no more in the world, but they are in the world, and I am coming to thee. Holy Father, keep them in thy name, which thou hast given me, that they may be one, even as we are one.

20 "I do not pray for these only, but also for those who are to believe in me through their word, 21 that they may all be one; even as thou, Father, art in me, and I in thee, that they also may be in us, so that the world may believe that thou hast sent me."

KEY VERSE: *Holy Father, keep them in thy name, which thou hast given me, that they may be one, even as we are one.* John 17:11 (RSV).

HOME DAILY BIBLE READINGS

Mar.	11.	M.	*From Glory to Glory.* John 17:1–5.
Mar.	12.	T.	*My People, Thy People.* John 17:6–10.
Mar.	13.	W.	*Kept—and Commissioned.* John 17:11–19.
Mar.	14.	T.	*That All May Be One.* John 17:20–26.
Mar.	15.	F.	*One in the Spirit.* 1 Corinthians 12:4–13.

Mar.   16.   S.   *In Unity and Peace.* Ephesians 4:1–6.
Mar.   17.   S.   *We Will Meet Again.* John 16:17–24.

BACKGROUND

Just before leaving the Upper Room or shortly after arriving in the Garden of Gethsemane, Jesus prayed. That prayer made a profound impression on the disciples. In this prayer, Jesus prayed for Himself, for His followers, and for all disciples yet to come. The words and the tone reminded His hearers of the prayer which the High Priest always offered on the Day of Atonement worship. On this great sacred occasion, the High Priest consecrated himself, interceded on behalf of all the priests and Levites, and prayed earnestly for the entire people of Israel (*see* Leviticus 16). Jesus' prayer as recorded in John 17, therefore, is universally referred to as the great High Priestly Prayer.

The High Priestly Prayer of Jesus, carefully preserved by John the Gospel writer and no other, has three main parts. The first section (verses 1 through 5) deals with Jesus' own personal consecration. In these words, we hear Jesus entering the Holy of Holies. He assumes a living unity with the Almighty. No other person could utter these words. He commits His life as the complete offering and the perfect sacrifice for all time and for all people. Jesus prayed for Himself in these verses, but there is not the faintest hint of selfishness. The prayer about Himself discloses a serenity about taking the Cross which came from a knowledge that He was coming to the climax of His life and was fulfilling the plan of the Eternal One.

The second section of this great High Priestly Prayer is directed toward Jesus' disciples. He knew them better than they knew themselves. He was totally aware that they were weak, petty, self-centered, and undependable. Therefore, Jesus earnestly pleaded on their behalf for power and direction. John 17:6–19 shows Jesus consecrating these eleven followers.

The third petition in this High Priestly Prayer (17:20–26) is on our behalf and on behalf of all disciples who come after His days on earth. Early Christians, facing terrible reprisals for their faith, were heartened by the certainty that Jesus continued to pray for them. Think about your life for a moment. Consider what it means to remember that our Lord continues to pray for His Church!

NOTES ON THE PRINTED TEXT

Father, the hour has come: Note the use of the familiar word, *Father,* for God. Jesus not only taught that the Almighty through Him wants to be on intimate, family terms with us but also lived it Himself. All of Jesus' life was lived with an awareness of the Parent-God.

"The hour" refers to the long-awaited occasion of His sacrificial death for others. Jesus frequently used this expression, according to the number of times John's Gospel quotes it, and always meant by it the climax of His ministry when He would be put to death.

Thou hast given him power over all flesh, to give eternal life to all whom thou hast given him: Jesus remembers His commission, namely "to give eternal life to all," beginning with the disciples. He then elaborates in His prayer on what eternal life means: *"that they know thee the only true God."* By knowing Jesus, the disciples have come to an ever-deepening and continually-progressing relationship with the Eternal One. This friendship through Jesus puts their lives on a new level, a quality which knowing the Eternal brings to all of life.

And now, Father, glorify thou me in thy presence with the glory which I had with thee before the world began: The word *glorify* here may seem a bit disconcerting at first. Jesus, however, is not asking for applause. He is girding Himself to complete His work. The Greek word here is the same word from which our word *doxology* comes, and Jesus in communing with the Eternal asks that His coming death may be a great doxology, bringing praise and thanks to God.

Jesus next turns to consecrating His own disciples and interceding for them. First, He describes them. He calls them *"the men whom thou gavest me."* He next pictures them as the people they are meant to be: *"They have kept thy word."* Through His life and death, Jesus prays, these same followers now *"know that everything that thou hast given me is from thee."* Jesus confidently turns them over to the Almighty, stating to the Father that this nucleus of eleven frail humans knows the secret of the ages, namely *"the words which thou gavest me, and they have received them and know in truth that I came from thee; and they have believed that thou didst send me."*

I am praying for them: Jesus intercedes for them because they have been God's gift to Him during His earthly ministry. Now it is time to hand them back. Jesus and the Father have a reciprocal relationship. The disciples, overhearing this part of the prayer, must have been strengthened mightily at that moment to hear that they were commended to the keeping of God with such complete confidence on the part of Jesus. Although Jesus will no longer be in the world and the disciples will, they are sustained by the same concern that Jesus had for them while He was among them in the flesh. *"And now I am no more in the world, but they are in the world, and I am coming to thee. Holy Father, keep them in thy name."*

The third part of Jesus' great High Priestly Prayer embraces those who will come to know the truth about God through Jesus Christ beause of the disciples' words and works. This magnificent set of petitions centers on one basic theme: *"that they all may be one."*

Jesus fervently intercedes for followers in subsequent years down to our times, and for followers centuries in the future from our times. He prays for His Church universal. He prays for our unity in the Lord, that we may share together as one family of Jesus, just as the disciples shared together with Him during His days on earth among them. How does this unity come?

. . . that they all may be one; even as thou, Father, art in me, and I in thee that they also may be in us . . .: a personal relationship of mutual trust and caring because of the basic oneness of Jesus and the Father with believers brings about this unity. Jesus is not talking about structure or organization. He prays for unity. Nor is He praying for uniformity. He pleads for oneness in loving relationships. And the reason for this unity He prays for?

That the world may believe that thou hast sent me: The sense of Christians living together as a loving family, united in obedience and service to God in Christ, will convince people of the Good News more than anything else!

SUGGESTIONS TO TEACHERS

A European and a man from India were seated in the same railway compartment on a train in India. The Indian pulled out a copy of the New Testament and began to study it intently. The European man politely said to the other, "Excuse me, but you are a Christian, aren't you?"

Looking up briefly, the Indian with the New Testament replied, "No, I'm a Canadian Primitive Baptist." The story illustrates the way Western world denominations have sometimes exported their divisions, and also reflects the disunity among Christian believers. Your lesson for this Sunday faces these facts. More important, today's lesson discusses the unity among followers which Jesus Christ intends us to show.

Before you begin to prepare this lesson, reflect for a few minutes why you think you should be committed to a closer sense of unity among Christ's people. Is it merely for pragmatic reasons—such as the railroads have been forced to merge in order to survive? Or is it for theological reasons? You should clarify the purpose for unity in your own mind first because some in your class will almost certainly try to think of unity only in terms of "practical" reasons such as saving money by not competing as churches or denominations. Look carefully at John 17! Once you have a better sense of the biblical material and the words of Jesus in John 17, your lesson outline can develop along these lines:

1. *PRECONDITIONS FOR UNITY.* John 17 suggests two such preconditions. The first is an awareness of the unity already existing between the Creator-God and Jesus. Jesus emphasized this oneness, but not every Christian understands the meaning of that claim. The second precondition, Jesus announces, is an awareness of the unity He has with those who believe in Him. There is a oneness of purpose between the Risen Lord and His People. Both of these points mean serious consideration of who Jesus is. Put this matter to your class to discuss.

2. *PRAYER FOR UNITY.* Think what it means to have Jesus praying for us! And this is what He claims to do. He says that He prays for us whom God has given Him. "Keep them in thy name" (17:11) . . . "that they may be my joy" (17:13); "keep them from the evil one" (17:15); "sanctify them in the truth" (17:17). In addition, Jesus prays for those who will become His disciples through our sharing the Gospel! What a marvelous promise to know Jesus prays also for those hearing us teach or tell the Good News!

3. *PURPOSE OF UNITY.* The purpose of unity is "that the world may know that thou hast sent me and hast loved them (17:23); that the love with which thou hast loved me may be in them and I in them" (17:26). Do not slight this vital point in your lesson. You may get at this issue by probing for the reasons why members of your class think the church should be concerned about unity of Christians.

TOPIC FOR ADULTS
UNITY IN THE NEW LIFE

New Tune Brings Harmony. One time during the American Civil War, Union and Confederate forces were encamped on opposite sides of the Potomac River. The two armies could not cross to attack each other because there were no bridges or places to ford the river. In the evenings, the bands sometimes played, but always tried to drown one another out. Whenever the Northerners would start a patriotic tune, the Southerners would begin to play one of their Confederate songs. The effect would be discordant noise. Historians record that on one evening, one of the bands struck up "Home, Sweet Home." For once, the other band did not blare forth with another melody, but, instead, joined in. Soon soldiers from both armies joined in. By the end of the song, a great chorus of voices, both Northern and Southern, accompanied by the Union and Confederate Armies' bands, were singing, "There's no place like home."

Christ brings us the tune of love and hope through His own life which unites us. We all know that we belong to Him and therefore belong to one another. We all can join to raise our hearts and voices in praise to Him and concern for each other. Jesus Christ brings harmony out of our discord. With Him, we remember our true and real home is with God.

New Details From The Last Supper. The Apostles in Leonardo da Vinci's *Last Supper* were eating oranges and drinking from gold-rimmed glasses in a tapestried room. These details, unseen by the public for hundreds of years, have come to light as a result of painstaking restoration work on the fresco of Christ and His apostles that da Vinci painted on the wall of the refectory of the church of Santa Maria della Grazia in Milan, between 1494 and 1499. According to Carlo Bertilli, the city superintendent of artistic and historical heritage, slices of oranges now appearing on some of the apostles' pewter plates were not visible before. Another detail uncovered, he said, is what seemed like "dark doors" in the room turned out to be tapestries, not doors. Still another newly discovered feature: the Apostle Peter did not originally have a beard. The beard was added much later, Bertilli said. Restoration of the work, which had been deteriorating badly, was begun in 1979, using special solvents and microscopic analysis. The work has so far covered only a portion of the right side of the painting. Mr. Bertilli said he hoped the restoration project could be completed soon.

There are other details which some of us need to recover from the Upper Room, namely the words of Jesus about the unity we must have in the new life. Jesus prayed for and continues to pray for us, "that they all may be one." We have discovered new and previously-unnoticed portions of the great da Vinci fresco. Let us also discover the previously unnoticed details of the great prayer of Jesus at the Last Supper! Let us find the unity in the new life He brings!

"True Christians." On the Japanese island of Ikitsuki, a strange sect practices a strange ritual. The group numbers about 10,000 persons and is called *Kakure Kirishitan,* meaning crypto-Christians. The *Kakure Kirishitan* are members of a fossilized faith that has worship forms that are a blend of Buddhism, Shintoism, Christianity, and superstition and uses prayers which sound like garbled Latin. They are survivors of the once-strong Christian Church on Ikitsuki which was ruthlessly persecuted by warlord shoguns two and a half centuries ago. The *Kakure* developed elaborate ways of evading detection, mostly by praying before hidden altars on which bundles of cloth hid Christian statues or medallions. For over 250 years, their prayers and rituals were secretly handed on among illiterate peasants. The Latin slowly became distorted and the meaning forgotten. They have no Bible. They practice a baptism-like ceremony with water from the site of a seventeenth century martyrdom. They do not understand the meaning of the Trinity. They hold aloof from other Christians in Japan. When Pope John Paul II came to Japan, some of the sect's chief priests turned up to meet him, but emphasized that they came solely "to register the fact that we exist. We have no interest in joining his church. After all, we and nobody else are true Christians."

Without meaning to put down the *Kakure* leaders, we must note that being a Christian means recognizing the unity which new life in Christ brings. The *Kakure* and others of us who claim to be Christ's people must constantly remember that our Lord wills it for us to come into a relationship of recognizing that we are one family in faith.

Questions for Pupils on the Next Lesson. 1. What exactly is meant by Jesus' "kingdom"? 2. Why were Jesus' enemies so intent on destroying Him? 3. How do you explain Pilate's actions at the Trial of Jesus? 4. What is the ultimate source of all power and authority? 5. Do you have difficulty understanding the idea that someone would willingly suffer for you?

TOPIC FOR YOUTH
GETTING TOGETHER

Communion in Siaochang.
Situation: The Civil War between the Japanese and a united front of Chinese Nationals and Communists
Place: Siaochang, China (in the Great Northern Plain of Southern Hopei)
Time: 1937
One day a general of one of the Chinese armies, a man of wealth and power, arrived in Siaochang with his soldiers. As he was escorted around the hospital, his eyes filled with tears as he observed the great number of babies who were ill and starving. It was explained to him that because of the civil war, it was impossible

to obtain milk for these infants so they were being fed nothing more nourishing than local bean curd milk.

A few days later, a number of cases of tinned milk arrived at the hospital. The milk was a gift from the general, a man who had no use for religion and had become hardened at the sight of battlefield blood. No one ever knew for certain what had softened this hard man's heart. Perhaps, it was the sight of the starving babies, or perhaps it was because of the kind treatment he had received from the hospital staff. Eric Liddell had taught his staff at this hospital at his mission station to treat ALL people as children of God. To Liddell, there was neither Japanese nor Chinese, neither soldier nor civilian. All people were men and women for whom Christ had died.

The term *communion* literally means "to share or feel together." Communion was shared in Siaochang, China, on that day in 1937 between Chinese soldiers and a Scottish mission staff. They shared the same fears and hungers, and they shared the same care and concern over the small children. The two groups were able to identify with each other, and they were able to feel together through the sharing of tinned milk.

Communion is what some of us call the Lord's Supper. It reminds us of how much God was willing to share with us. He was willing to share His son with us. His total feeling or identification with us was shown through a broken body and spilled blood. All this for us!

Moreover, Eric Liddell, the same young man who won the 400 meter race in the Paris Olympics and has recently come to the public's eye through the film *Chariots of Fire,* showed us how to get together through his operation of his mission staff. All were the same. All were treated with the same Christlike love and kindness. All were children of God.

Hermit Christians. Soviet geologists, on a helicopter search for iron ore in Siberia's remote Abakan River basin, were startled to spot a lean-to settlement in the hilly forest far from the nearest charted town. Even more surprising were its inhabitants—seventy-nine-year-old Karp Osipovich Lykov and the two sons and two daughters he had raised to adulthood in fierce religious devotion and total isolation from Communist society. One of his daughters, seeing outsiders for the first time, burst into tearful prayer and cried, "Our sins! Our sins have brought us this!"

The strange encounter is described by Soviet journalist Vasily Peskov, who claims to have visited the hermits in their craggy mosquito-infested retreat in the Sayan hills above the Abakan River in 1981.

A 1980 article on the Lykovs, published in the newspaper *Sotsialisticheskaya Industria,* condemned the old man for raising his family outside the comforts and duties of civilization. It said that three years after their first contact with the geologists, in the fall of 1978, three of the Lykov children died: Savin, fifty-six, Natasha, forty-six, and Dmitry, forty.

Peskov, interviewed by telephone, said Soviet authorities have decided not to meddle further with the lonely lives of Lykov, now eighty-four, and his youngest daughter, Agatha, forty. The geologists gave the Lykovs their first taste of wheat bread, their first news of the outcome of the 1917 Bolshevik revolution, their first account of World War II.

The elder Lykov and his wife belong to an old believers' settlement, adherents of a sect that broke from the Russian Orthodox Church in the seventeenth century and have lived as voluntary outcasts since then. They were caught between the red and white armies during the 1917–21 civil war, but managed to slip upriver into the primeval forest. After the war, the area became a national preserve and most of the families moved closer to civilization. Lykov, however, reportedly fled farther upriver, settling along nameless streams.

A flintlock rifle he carried became useless, and his only ax also wore out. They survived on potatoes, nuts, and wild game, living in temperatures plummeting to minus 58 degrees Fahrenheit.

It may be possible for a few persons to continue in the wilderness without others for a time, but ultimately even sturdy Siberian peasants such as the Lykovs will perish. It is also as hard for Christians to survive as people of faith without others. Christ intends for us to get together as His family. He does not want us to be hermit believers. He brings us into a family relationship for our own survival. Just as the sect to which the Lykovs belonged has dwindled and died when it became fragmented, regardless of the fervor of adherents such as the Lykovs, so the Church, the community of the faith, will disappear if we refuse to get together. Recognize, therefore, the unity in the new life Christ brings!

Divisiveness Through Hunger. The Food and Agriculture Organization of the United Nations and 262 private voluntary organizations, estimate that as many as 400 million to 500 million people suffer from poverty-induced malnutrition, particularly in the Third World.

When so many have-nots are suffering hunger, the human family is broken. What can we do to get together through sharing with those 400 million to 500 million brothers and sisters?

Questions for Pupils on the Next Lesson. 1. What exactly did Jesus mean by His "kingdom"? 2. If Jesus was so good, why did some want to kill Him? 3. How would you describe Pilate? 4. How do you explain someone willingly taking the blame and accepting punishment for you? 5. Why would anyone willingly sacrifice for another?

LESSON IV—MARCH 24

BROUGHT TO TRIAL

Background Scripture: John 18:1–19:16
Devotional Reading: John 18:1–10

KING JAMES VERSION

JOHN 18 33 Then Pilate entered into the judgment hall again, and called Jesus, and said unto him, Art thou the King of the Jews?

34 Jesus answered him, Sayest thou this thing of thyself, or did others tell it thee of me?

35 Pilate answered, Am I a Jew? Thine own nation and the chief priests have delivered thee unto me: what hast thou done?

36 Jesus answered, My kingdom is not of this world: if my kingdom were of this world, then would my servants fight, that I should not be delivered to the Jews: but now is my kingdom not from hence.

37 Pilate therefore said unto him, Art thou a king then? Jesus answered, Thou sayest that I am a king. To this end was I born, and for this cause came I into the world, that I should bear witness unto the truth. Every one that is of the truth heareth my voice.

19 6 When the chief priests therefore and officers saw him, they cried out, saying, Crucify *him*, crucify *him*. Pilate saith unto them, Take ye him, and crucify *him*: for I find no fault in him.

7 The Jews answered him, We have a law, and by our law he ought to die, because he made himself the Son of God.

8 When Pilate therefore heard that saying, he was the more afraid;

9 And went again into the judgment hall, and saith unto Jesus, Whence art thou? But Jesus gave him no answer.

10 Then saith Pilate unto him, Speakest thou not unto me? knowest thou not that I have power to crucify thee, and have power to release thee?

11 Jesus answered, Thou couldest have no power *at all* against me, except it were given thee from above: therefore he that delivered me unto thee hath the greater sin.

14 And it was the preparation of the passover, and about the sixth hour: and he saith unto the Jews, Behold your King!

15 But they cried out, Away with *him*, away with *him*, crucify him. Pilate saith unto them, Shall I crucify your King? The chief priests answered, We have no king but Caesar.

16 Then delivered he him therefore unto them to be crucified. And they took Jesus, and led *him* away.

REVISED STANDARD VERSION

JOHN 18 33 Pilate entered the praetorium again and called Jesus, and said to him, "Are you the King of the Jews?" 34 Jesus answered, "Do you say this of your own accord, or did others say it to you about me?" 35 Pilate answered, "Am I a Jew? Your own nation and the chief priests have handed you over to me; what have you done?" 36 Jesus answered, "My kingship is not of this world; if my kingship were of this world, my servants would fight, that I might not be handed over to the Jews; but my kingship is not from the world." 37 Pilate said to him, "So you are a king?" Jesus answered, "You say that I am a king. For this I was born, and for this I have come into the world, to bear witness to the truth. Every one who is of the truth hears my voice."

19 6 When the chief priests and the officers saw him, they cried out, "Crucify him, crucify him!" Pilate said to them, "Take him yourselves and crucify him, for I find no crime in him." 7 The Jews answered him, "We have a law, and by that law he ought to die, because he has made himself the Son of God." 8 When Pilate heard these words, he was the more afraid; 9 he entered the praetorium again and said to Jesus, "Where are you from?" But Jesus gave no answer. 10 Pilate therefore said to him, "You will not speak to me? Do you not know that I have power to release you, and power to crucify you?" 11 Jesus answered him, "You would have no power over me unless it had been given you from above; therefore he who delivered me to you has the greater sin."

14 Now it was the day of Preparation for the Passover; it was about the sixth hour. He said to the Jews, "Here is your King!" 15 They cried out, "Away with him, away with him, crucify him!" Pilate said to them, "Shall I crucify your King?" The chief priests answered, "We have no king but Caesar." 16 Then he handed him over to them to be crucified.

KEY VERSE: *You say that I am a king. For this I was born, and for this I have come into the world, to bear witness to the truth.* John 18:37 (RSV).

HOME DAILY BIBLE READINGS

Mar   18.   M.   *A Failure of Faith.* John 18:12–18, 25–27.
Mar.   19.   T.   *You Know the Answer.* John 18:19–24.
Mar.   20.   W.   *A Different Kingship.* John18:28–38.
Mar.   21.   T.   *Pilate on Trial.* John 19:1–11.
Mar.   22.   F.   *A Miscarriage of Justice.* John 19:12–16.
Mar.   23.   S.   *We Too Will Be Tried.* Matthew 10:16–25.
Mar.   24.   S.   *I Am the One.* John 18:1–11.

BACKGROUND

Exactly as Jesus had predicted, He was seized by the Temple authorities' police. Also as predicted, He watched Judas leading the squad sent to make the arrest. Jesus was hurried to the high priest's house for questioning by Annas, the father-in-law of Caiaphas, the high priest. This hearing was not a formal trial. In fact, it violated all the usual procedures for a court case for which the death penalty was asked.

The Gospel of John provides few details about Jesus' appearance before the high priestly party. Except for a few verses (18:19–24) giving a brief exchange between the high priest and Jesus, John doesn't tell us much about what went on at the hearing before the high priests. We know, however, that the high priest and his henchmen had made up their minds that Jesus had to be silenced for good. John alludes to the fact that Caiaphas, the high priest, had advised other Temple leaders that "it was expedient that one man should die for the people" (18:14) rather than to have the entire nation led to ruin.

One problem remained. The Temple leaders were not permitted to carry out an execution. They could sentence someone to die, but they would not put the culprit to death. The Romans reserved the right to inflict capital punishment. Therefore, the Temple rulers had to turn to the despised Roman occupation government to have those convicted of the death penalty actually killed. John doesn't explain all the legal fine points in his account of Jesus' arrest, trial, and appearance before Caiaphas and Pilate, but describes Jesus being taken at daybreak to Pilate.

Pilate, according to tradition, was a Roman army officer. He married Caesar Augustus's granddaughter in Rome and managed to get the rules waived so that he could bring his wife with him when he was appointed procurator of Judea in A.D. 26. He quickly made himself unpopular in Judea by trying to bring the Roman Imperial insignia of the eagle (a graven image, to sensitive Jews) into the sacred city of Jerusalem After a tense confrontation, Pilate had to back down. Later, Pilate raided the Temple treasury for funds to build a water system. When rioting broke out in protest, Pilate turned loose his tough legionnaires, killing a number of Jerusalem civilians. Pilate was officially reprimanded by the Emperor Tiberius for his high-handed conduct. He arrogantly triggered a third uproar, however, by decorating Jerusalem with Roman shields. Again, bloodshed followed and a scathing rebuke from the Emperor was sent to Pilate.

Pilate had been publically humiliated three times in the four years since his arrival in Judea. He was loathed by the Jews. His career was in jeopardy. He hated serving in the seething province of Judea, and made no effort at trying to understand the customs or tradition of the occupied people. This was the stubborn, uneasy man who was presented with the most momentous decision of his lifetime early one spring morning in Jerusalem: "Shall I crucify your King?" (19:15).

NOTES ON THE PRINTED TEXT

Although John shows many of the same details of Jesus' trial before Pilate that the other Gospel writers have in their accounts, John stresses the theological meanings. John's account of the Trial also takes us inside Pilate's private head-quarters as well as outside in the public hearing area. *Pilate entered the prae-torium again:* the scene here takes place in the headquarters and takes the form of a private interrogation away from the din and disorder of the crowd in the open-air courtyard of the big Fortress Antonia.

Are you the King of the Jews? Pilate tries to find out if Jesus, the prisoner, is guilty of sedition as charged. Pilate's task is to keep the lid on the tumultuous area. He knows the fierce determination of the Jewish people to be independent. Pilate also knows the Romans have had their troops tied down for years in the area, try-ing to quell a series of bloody revolts. Guerrilla bands and fanatic leaders have been fanning the underground independence movement. Pilate wants to find out what political plans Jesus has. The charge, "King of the Jews," means something different to the Temple leaders. To them, the words mean a person pretending to be the Messiah. To Pilate, it means a person threatening treason. The high priestly group realize this, but Pilate doesn't. Pilate finds himself facing someone accused of claiming to be a ruler rivalling the Emperor and wanting to overthrow Roman authority.

Jesus answered, *"My kingship is not of this world; if my kingship were of this world, my servants would fight, that I might not be handed over to the Jews; but my kingship is not from the world":* Jesus states clearly that He is indeed a King. However, He also clearly acknowledges that He has no political ambitions such as all other rulers have. His kingly authority, Jesus maintains, comes not from the usual sources in this world but from elsewhere.

"I have come into the world to bear witness to the truth. Everyone who is of the truth hears my voice": Unlike all other kings, Jesus refuses to throw His weight around or to promote His own personal regal power. He announces to the puz-zled Pilate that He comes to disclose the Almighty whose rule is the truth which is somewhat reflected in earthly kingdoms. Those who recognize the royal au-thority of Jesus' personification of the truth about God will acknowledge Him as the highest authority on earth.

Take him yourselves and crucify him: Pilate, exasperated with the shrieking crowds, yet refusing to accept responsibility as the representative of Rome, taunts the mob to carry out the sentence themselves. He knows, of course, that the crowd cannot do this, and infuriates them further.

But Jesus gave no answer: There are times when Jesus remains silent. When Pilate tries to continue a pointless cross-examination, with such questions as, "Where are you from?" (19:8), Jesus gives no answer. Sometimes, He will have nothing to say to us when we try to banter with Him.

"Do you not know that I have power to release you?" Jesus answered him, "You would have no power over me unless it had been given you from above": Jesus reminds Pilate of the Source of all authority. Pilate's authority is granted from God. Jesus tells Pilate to use his God-derived authority responsibly. However, He adds that Caiaphas's guilt is greater because that man, the high priest, is abusing his God-given authority to promote evil purposes.

"Shall I crucify your King?" The chief priests answered, "We have no king but Caesar": Pilate flings one last sarcastic jab at the religious rulers. They throw aside all restraint and decorum and scream a fateful phrase, "We have no king but Caesar." To John the Gospel writer, this signifies the utmost in degradation. The very leaders of the religious community have sold out. Instead of claiming that God alone is their King, they desert and shout that Caesar is king. The priestly rulers will stoop to anything to get Jesus nailed up; they even offer an ex-pression of loyalty to the divine emperor to have Jesus executed!

SUGGESTIONS TO TEACHERS

A woman watched a particularly well-presented dramatic reenactment of Jesus' trial in a Passion Play during Holy Week. Afterward, she remarked, "I had never realized it before, but now I see that it was not Jesus who was on trial. It was the others. Although He was the One who was formally charged, those involved in the trial were the ones who come out convicted and guilty."

The woman was correct. If you read the account of Jesus' trial in John 18 and 19, you will see the woman's point is well taken. Your lesson today should bring out the way that all of us are put on trial when charges are brought against Jesus.

You may find that the best way to develop today's lesson, in fact, is to take today's scriptural material and show how many of the key figures in Jesus' final days come across as "on trial" themselves! For starters, why not show how Judas, the High Priests, Peter, and Pilate seem to be on trial?

1. *VICTOR AND VICTIM* (Judas and Jesus). Judas thinks that he will be the victor and Jesus will be the victim when he cleverly arranges to cooperate with the Temple authorities for thirty pieces of silver. To his surprise, of course, Judas ends as the tragic victim, while Jesus continues as the triumphant Victor of both life and death. Try not to view the events of Judas's betrayal as merely a fascinating footnote of history. Instead, consider the Judas-side in each of us, who, like Judas, sometimes try to manipulate Jesus to fit our plans. Whenever we attempt to make Jesus the victim of our schemes, we bring ruin to ourselves!

2. *ACCUSERS AND ACCUSED* (Annas and Caiaphas, the High Priests, and Jesus). The High Priestly group assumes it will put Jesus on trial, but ends as the accused. In our times, we sometimes try to make Jesus answerable to us. Church School class people, like others, need to remember that we are accountable to Jesus!

3. *DEFENDER AND DEFECTOR* (Peter and Jesus). Peter brashly assumes that he will stand by Jesus through every crisis. He even recklessly slashes with his sword in a dramatic moment of confrontation with armed opponents. He discovers a few hours later that it is tougher to stand up against the withering jeers of ordinary folks. Have your class comment on how hard it often is to show commitment to Christ among those closest to you or to those with whom you associate.

4. *CONQUEROR AND COMPROMISER* (Pilate and Jesus). Here is the representative of the greatest power, the most able government, and the most enlightened legal system of the ancient world, yet unable and unwilling to face the truth about Jesus. Pilate equivocates in trying Jesus. The trial ends with Pilate being tried and convicted. Your class may find the ramifications of the encounter between army man and governmental authority Pilate, backed by the Emperor of Rome, and Jesus, backed only by the Father. Ask whose backing those in your class are most anxious to secure.

TOPIC FOR ADULTS
BROUGHT TO TRIAL

One of the Crowd. In a painting of the Crucifixion by the Dutch artist Rembrandt, attention immediately focuses on the cross and on Him who hangs there. Then your gaze falls on the crowd gathered around the cross. At the edge of the picture, at the very fringe of the crowd, one figure stands in the shadow. This is Rembrandt himself; Rembrandt helping to crucify Jesus.

Perhaps, Rembrandt recalled something we have forgotten. The Crucifixion is not simply a historical fact. It is a personal experience.

Passing Parade. A little country boy saw a poster announcing a circus coming to his county seat. He had never seen a circus. He counted the days. He saved his money. On the last night, he could hardly sleep because he was so excited. He was up at the crack of dawn. He stood along the street to watch the circus parade. He saw lions, tigers, and bears. He saw the beautiful horses, the tremendous elephants, the acrobats, the jugglers, the clowns, and the circus band. His eyes were large and glistening, and he was thrilled with it all. When it was over, he stepped out of the crowd, handed the last man in the parade his money and went back home. Not until years later did he discover he had never been to a circus and never been inside the big top. He had only watched the parade. Palm Sunday reminds us that there is more to Christianity than the brief emotional experience, more than the passing parade. The multitude missed the Cross of Good Friday and the Resurrection victory of Easter. They were interested for a few moments, but their response was nominal and negligent.

Costly Ransom. King Richard the Lionhearted of England took part in the First Crusade. He fell afoul of enemies when crossing Europe and was incarcerated in a castle in Austria. The story goes that his loyal servant, Blondel, set off to find his master, and to do so he wandered from castle to castle. He would stand beneath a castle turret and whistle a line of Richard's favorite song. Finally, from away up in a turret chamber, he heard the tune taken up and the song completed. Away back home to England he hurried and aroused the English people. They then raised sufficient money from their own pockets, rich and poor, aristocrat and peasant alike contributing whatever they could to ransom their royal master from bondage in prison. The ransoming was thus a costly business.

What such an idea could mean for the Lord God, who suffers to gain His loving purpose, is something that we must examine. God must let us human beings see His suffering and His pain. In His wisdom, God chose to reveal Himself to us, not in the realm of ideas or human thought, but in the realm of history and event. This means that even the pain that God Almighty suffered in ransoming His beloved became visible to our human eyes. This happened when men nailed the Lord Jesus Christ to the cross.

Questions for Pupils on the Next Lesson. 1. How does the biblical text make it clear that in death as well as in life Jesus associated with sinners? 2. How was the mission of Jesus completed on the Cross? 3. Would Jesus' death on the Cross be considered a success or a failure by our society's standards? 4. Are you able to identify with those who feel rejected?

TOPIC FOR YOUTH
TAKING THE BLAME

The Man in the Water. Air Florida Flight 90 to Tampa, a Boeing 737 with seventy-four passengers on board, rolled down the Washington's National Airport runway through the snow flurries. Something went wrong during the take-off on that icy January 20, 1982 afternoon. The plane slammed into the crowded Fourteenth Street bridge, smashing five cars and a truck, then skidded into the frozen Potomac River. Horrified spectators watched helplessly as the big aircraft sank beneath the ice floes. A handful of passengers bobbed to the surface, screaming for help. Rescue trucks, ambulances, and a Park Service helicopter quickly appeared. Six survivors were trying to cling to the part of the plane's tail protruding above the water. The helicopter maneuvered close to them, dangling a life preserver ring, and began ferrying the shivering passengers to the shore. The most memorable act of heroism was performed by one of the survivors who was among the group grasping the tail in the freezing water. He was a balding man in his early fifties. Each time the life ring was lowered from the chopper, he grabbed it and passed it along to another. The effect of the cold was too much, however;

after passing the ring to five others, he could not maintain his grip. By the time the helicopter made its next trip, he had slipped beneath the murky waters.

The nation never learned the identity of the balding hero in his fifties who passed the life preserver to five other survivors in order for them to be saved first. He was one of the seventy-four on board Flight 90 who perished. But his act of sacrifice caught the attention of everyone. The man in the water became a symbol of the Christian who suffers for others. That act of self-giving in the Potomac reminded millions of the significance of Jesus giving His life for others, when He, too, could have saved Himself!

Skyre Thursday. In the North of England, the Thursday of Holy Week was often known as Skyre Thursday. The term comes from an old Norse word, *skira,* meaning "to purify." Further south in England, it was also known as Shere Thursday, a corruption of the same word. The idea was prevalent in the early British Church that the Thursday of Holy Week was a time to prepare for Easter by purifying oneself. This consisted not only of cutting one's hair and washing the head, but also of serving others through the practice of washing others' feet.

Foot-washing demands sacrificing one's dignity. It means considering others ahead of oneself. Although you may not be called upon literally to wash the feet of others, are you prepared to purify yourself by living a life for others, even as Jesus Christ has done for you?

With Open Hands. "Because of our faith in Christ and in humankind, we must apply our humble efforts to the construction of a more just and humane world. And I want to declare emphatically: Such a world is possible. To create this new society, we must present outstretched, friendly hands, without hatred, without rancor—even as we show great determination, never wavering in the defense of truth and justice. Because we know that seeds are not sown with clenched fists. To sow we must open our hands."—Adolfo Perez Esquivel in Oslo, Norway, December 10, 1980 upon receiving the Nobel Peace Prize.

Questions for Pupils on the Next Lesson. 1. Was there ever a time when Jesus was not concerned about other persons? 2. Why do Christians claim that Jesus completed His mission in life by dying on a cross? 3. Is death the end of everything? 4. Does sacrifice for others ever accomplish anything? 5. Do you feel that others are not particularly concerned about your needs?

LESSON V—MARCH 31

NAILED TO THE CROSS

Background Scripture: John 19:17–42
Devotional Reading: John 19:38–42

KING JAMES VERSION

JOHN 19   17 And he bearing his cross went forth into a place called *the place* of a skull, which is called in the Hebrew Golgotha:

18 Where they crucified him, and two others with him, on either side one, and Jesus in the midst.

19 And Pilate wrote a title, and put *it* on the cross. And the writing was, JESUS OF NAZARETH THE KING OF THE JEWS.

20 This title then read many of the Jews; for the place where Jesus was crucified was nigh to the city: and it was written in Hebrew, *and* Greek, *and* Latin.

21 Then said the chief priests of the Jews to Pilate, Write not, The King of the Jews; but that he said, I am King of the Jews.

22 Pilate answered, What I have written I have written.

23 Then the soldiers, when they had crucified Jesus, took his garments, and made four parts, to every soldier a part; and also *his* coat: now the coat was without seam, woven from the top throughout.

24 They said therefore among themselves, Let us not rend it, but cast lots for it, whose it shall be: that the scripture might be fulfilled, which saith, They parted my raiment among them, and for my vesture they did cast lots. These things therefore the soldiers did.

25 Now there stood by the cross of Jesus his mother, and his mother's sister, Mary the *wife* of Cleophas, and Mary Magdalene.

26 When Jesus therefore saw his mother, and the disciple standing by, whom he loved, he saith unto his mother, Woman, behold thy son!

27 Then saith he to the disciple, Behold thy mother! And from that hour that disciple took her unto his own *home.*

28 After this, Jesus knowing that all things were now accomplished, that the scripture might be fulfilled, saith, I thirst.

29 Now there was set a vessel full of vinegar: and they filled a sponge with vinegar, and put *it* upon hyssop, and put *it* to his mouth.

30 When Jesus therefore had received the vinegar, he said, It is finished: and he bowed his head, and gave up the ghost.

REVISED STANDARD VERSION

JOHN 19   17 So they took Jesus, and he went out, bearing his own cross, to the place called the place of a skull, which is called in Hebrew Golgotha. 18 There they crucified him, and with him two others, one on either side, and Jesus between them. 19 Pilate also wrote a title and put it on the cross; it read, "Jesus of Nazareth, the King of the Jews." 20 Many of the Jews read this title, for the place where Jesus was crucified was near the city; and it was written in Hebrew, in Latin, and in Greek. 21 The chief priests of the Jews then said to Pilate, "Do not write, 'The King of the Jews,' but, 'This man said, I am King of the Jews.' " 22 Pilate answered, "What I have written I have written."

23 When the soldiers had crucified Jesus they took his garments and made four parts, one for each soldier; also his tunic. But the tunic was without seam, woven from top to bottom; 24 so they said to one another, "Let us not tear it, but cast lots for it to see whose it shall be." This was to fulfil the scripture,

"They parted my garments among them,
and for my clothing they cast lots."

25. So the soldiers did this; but standing by the cross of Jesus were his mother, and his mother's sister, Mary the wife of Clopas, and Mary Magdalene. 26 When Jesus saw his mother, and the disciple whom he loved standing near, he said to his mother, "Woman, behold your son!" 27 Then he said to the disciple, "Behold your mother!" And from that hour the disciple took her to his own home.

28 After this Jesus, knowing that all was now finished, said (to fulfil the scripture), "I thirst." 29 A bowl full of vinegar stood there; so they put a sponge full of the vinegar on hyssop and held it to his mouth. 30 When Jesus had received the vinegar, he said, "It is finished"; and he bowed his head and gave up his spirit.

KEY VERSE: When Jesus had received the vinegar, he said, "It is finished"; and he bowed his head and gave up his spirit. John 19:30 (RSV).

HOME DAILY BIBLE READINGS

Mar.	25.	M.	*The King on the Cross.* John 19:17–22.
Mar.	26.	T.	*Old Ties End, New Begin.* John 19:23–27.
Mar.	27.	W.	*It Is Finished.* John 19:28–37.
Mar.	28.	T.	*Forsaken and Forgotten.* Psalms 22:1–11.
Mar.	29.	F.	*The Overwhelming Flood.* Psalms 69:1–15.
Mar.	30.	S.	*A Sacrifice of Love.* 1 John 4:7–12.
Mar.	31.	S.	*Laid to Rest.* John 19:38–42.

BACKGROUND

Putting a condemned man to death by nailing him to a cross beam on a pole, and letting him dangle in agony until he died, was devised in the Middle East by the Persians, used by the Phoenicians, and refined by the Carthaginians. The Romans took over the practice. However, punishment by crucifying a person was reserved for slaves and foreigners. No Roman citizen would be subjected to crucifixion. Crucifixion was the usual penalty for people other than citizens convicted of sedition or armed robbery.

The two aspects of death by crucifixion which made it seem so cruel were (1) the disgrace attached to dying on a cross; and (2) the pain involved.

The shame of being crucified cannot be completely comprehended by us in modern times. To the ancients, the practice was indescribably abhorrent. Commenting on how unthinkable a disgrace dying on a cross was, Cicero the great Roman orator once stated to the Senate, "It is a crime for a Roman citizen to be bound; it is a worse crime for him to be beaten; it is almost like murdering a parent to have him put to death; what am I to say if he is put to death on a cross? A wicked action by any word, for there is none fit to describe it."

The physical agony was also terrible. The idea was to prolong the victim's pain and make death as slow as possible. The crucified man was usually held by ropes to the upright post, and sometimes put astride a protruding peg. The arms were spread and a heavy spike hammered through each wrist on to the cross beam. The cross beam usually rested on the upright post, so that the execution device itself looked more like the letter *T.* Usually, a spike was also nailed through the feet or separate nails were hammered in just above the heels. The body was held completely immobile and subject to heat and cold, hunger and thirst, flies and insects, cramps and fatigue. Frequently, crucified men lasted several days before dying. Death finally came from exposure or suffocation from being unable to continue to push air in and out as a result of the arms stretched and the body's weight pulling on them.

This is the horrible finish which Jesus subjected Himself to endure on behalf of others.

NOTES ON THE PRINTED TEXT

Jesus knew all the gory details of a crucifixion. He had undoubtedly personally seen crucified men writhing and gasping. We are told, for example, that over 2,000 men and boys were put to death on crosses in a neighboring village to Nazareth during his boyhood. Galilee was a hotbed of rebellion, and Roman army patrols crucified revolutionaries frequently in Jesus' home territory. He had also certainly heard the horror stories of crucifixions told and retold in the villages. Jesus went to His own death knowing what it entailed. He was not duped into dying this way, nor was He under any illusions about the shame or the pain.

So they took Jesus, and he went out, bearing his own cross, to the place of a skull, which is called in Hebrew Golgotha: John makes no reference to Simon of Cyrene. All the Gospel writers agree that Jesus started out by carrying His cross. Actually, He was shouldering the heavy cross beam or piece on which the arms were spread and lashed. *Golgotha* means the execution place which looked bare and rounded as the top of a cranium. Our word *Calvary* comes from the Latin word *Calvaria* for the Hebrew term *Golgotha* meaning simply "the place of the Skull."

There they crucified him, and with him two others, one on either side, and Jesus between them: John also omits the conversation between Jesus and the two other condemned men which Luke includes. Furthermore, John says nothing about whether the other two were robbers as Matthew and Mark state, or criminals as Luke says. John, in fact, shows remarkable restraint and reticence. He refuses to sensationalize or harp on the grisly details, but merely announces quietly that "they crucified him."

Pilate also wrote a title and put in on the cross; it read, "Jesus of Nazareth, the King of the Jews." . . . *and it was written in Hebrew, in Latin, and in Greek:* Pilate has his last sarcastic jab at the Temple leaders. He knows that this inscription will infuriate them. Little does he realize the truth of the inscription! Putting the placard in the three languages was as common in those days as the signs in several languages in European railway stations today.

When the soldiers had crucified Jesus they took his garments and made four parts, one for each soldier: The execution squad was allowed to keep the cloth.ng and personal effects on the body of a crucified man.

But his tunic was without seam, woven from top to bottom; so they said to one another, "Let us not tear it, but cast lots for it to see whose it shall be": John is the only Gospel writer to mention the interesting detail of Jesus' seamless tunic and the soldiers' tossing to see who would get it. John adds the comment that Psalms 22:18—often referred to as "The Psalm of the Suffering Servant"—states that the suffering Servant would watch His malefactors divide His garments by casting lots. "They parted my garments among them and for my clothing they cast lots" reminded John of Jesus' suffering for others.

Standing by the cross of Jesus were his mother, and his mother's sister, Mary the wife of Clopas, and Mary Magdalene: John specifically adds that Jesus' mother, Mary, was one of the women who witnessed the Crucifixion. Other Gospel accounts leave her name out. John the Gospel writer also adds the beautiful and sensitive account of how Jesus gave Mary over to John's care, and gives John to Mary as a "son" to look after. The Gospel of John is the only one to record these words from the Cross.

After this Jesus, knowing that all was now finished, said (to fulfill the scripture), "I thirst": This saying also is to be found only in John's Gospel. John wishes to make the point that Jesus endured all the pain that a human could have known, including thirst. It was not a phantom hanging on that cross; it was not a superman. Perhaps the Gospel writer was trying to counteract some of the heresies that circulated later to the effect that Jesus was some sort of spiritual being who never really suffered.

A bowl of vinegar stood there; so they put a sponge full of the vinegar on hyssop and held it to his mouth: John's account also says nothing of Jesus being offered a drug to help dull his senses to the pain. The bowl of vinegar was simply the soldier's beverage, the ration of cheap sour wine to slake thirst.

"It is finished": Jesus died with a shout of victory on His lips. The words mean, "It is accomplished!" They are the triumphant cry of the One who carried out His mission successfully, not the whimper of one quitting in defeat.

He bowed his head and gave up his spirit: The words mean that Jesus gave back His life to the Father.

SUGGESTIONS TO TEACHERS

The Cross of Jesus. How do you teach a lesson on an event of such monumental significance? Even John Milton, the great poet, who planned a sequel to his poem celebrating Jesus Christ's birth, found he could not pen the promised follow-up on the subject of Jesus Christ's death. The subject proved to be too great to be expressed in verses. You may think that if Milton couldn't say it, how can you? Remember, however, that you are not an artist crafting immortal lines, but a teacher pointing people to Jesus' sacrifice. Sticking to the Scripture for this lesson, you will find your lesson taking on content and significance for yourself and the class.

1. *STIGMA.* Your class must be helped to understand the almost indescribable disgrace attached to crucifixions in Jesus' day. There is nothing quite similar in our society. The electric chair, the gallows, the executioner's rifle, the guillotine—none of these have the terrible stigma connected with them that a cross did. Jesus, however, accepted this form of unspeakably disgraceful death (reserved always for the lowest kind of scum of criminals). He willingly bore the cross—for others.

2. *SIGN.* Have the students in your group note that the sign over Jesus' head on the cross had words *King of the Jews* in Latin, Greek, and Hebrew. Although it was intended as a pun by those who put it there, and resented by the leaders of His own people, the sign truly describes Jesus to the world of laws (Latin), of philosophy and thought (Greek), and religion (Hebrew).

3. *SOLDIERS.* Without spending an undue amount of time on the execution squad, you may wish to point out the callous disregard of the soldiers. Relate how these Roman G.I.'s were more concerned about Jesus' garments than Jesus' person.

4. *SOLICITUDE.* Take sufficient time to reflect on Jesus' concern for Mary His mother and John the disciple. How remarkable that Jesus, in spite of personal agony and loneliness, continues to care for others! Notice that His care always takes very practical forms. Here, Jesus gives John to Mary as a new "son" and Mary to John as a new "mother." The Lord's care is often mediated through other persons, and He often calls us to be mediators of that care!

5. *SAYINGS.* Deathbed statements of famous people in popular thinking are thought to have profound meaning, but in actuality are often shallow sayings not worth repeating. Not so with Jesus, however. Your class must examine the phrases, "I thirst" and "It is finished" in John 19. Insist that those in your class ponder what both of these sayings mean to them.

6. *SECRET.* This passage in John 19 also discloses some secret followers: Joseph of Arimathea and Nicodemus. Your class can profitably discuss the great risk these two took when they asked for Jesus' body. The class also may reflect on the sad fact that these two had hesitated in going public with their faith until it was too late. While Jesus was alive, they had held back. Will "too late" be the case with those in your class?

TOPIC FOR ADULTS
NAILED TO THE CROSS

Wisdom From the Fool. In an Austrian town, the center section of the town was targeted for urban renewal. Some tottering buildings were to be torn down, and several tiny, winding streets and the town square were to be ripped up. A new civic center complete with adequate parking areas and good traffic flow was planned. The bulldozers moved in and began clearing the area. The modern mechanical equipment, however, could not budge the big granite cross which earlier citizens had embedded in the center of the old town marketplace. The wrecking crew struggled unsuccessfully to dislodge the ancient cross which had stood for centuries. A large crowd gathered. The workmen attached cables and brought in a crane. They still couldn't pull the cross out of the ground. As the engineers and workmen took a break after their latest effort to wrest loose the cross and planned their next move, the town idiot began to dance up and down and laugh boisterously. "Ha, Ha, Ha! You can't dig it out," the fool cackled gleefully. "You'll never pull it out. It goes to the center of the world!"

Sometimes fool's words are not foolishness. In the case of the Austrian character, he spoke more truth than he—or his hearers—realized. The Cross of Jesus Christ does go to the very center of every person's world! The Cross goes to the core of all history. And it cannot be pulled out of life.

Redeemed From "King of Evil" for King of Kings. Most people associate Bali with a song from *South Pacific* and think of it only as a tropical island paradise. Few know that Christianity was introduced to Bali in 1931, the first baptism being on November 11, 1931. The Church grew very quickly until 1939. By this time, the government was concerned about its growth and the effects it was having in the Hindu culture. It was then decided to move all Christians to an area in West Bali in an attempt to suppress them. This area was at the base of Klatakan Mountain, a dense forest region. It was at that time uninhabited except by tigers and snakes, and worst of all was totally infested with malaria. The name of the region at that time was *Alas Rangda* which means "King of Evil." Men from the Christian community went out to the Alas Rangda and cut the forest down in the shape of a cross, and started to build a village. Three months later the men were joined by their families—thirty-nine families in all. God blessed them in their work and witness and now instead of Alas Rangda, the King of Glory reigns there. Blimbingsari, as the village is now known, has grown considerably and at present has a population of over a thousand consisting of 183 families. It has won the award for the best village in Bali for the past two years, and continues to grow in numbers. It is the largest Christian congregation in Bali.

The Christians in Blimbingsari point out the power of the Cross over the Alas Rangda. The act of the brave builders of the village in 1939 in clearing the King of Evil's forest in the shape of the cross symbolized their trust in the meaning of Christ's atoning death. They knew His mission was finished on the Cross, and they knew their mission had to be founded on the Cross.

Is your life, your church, your community based on the power of the Cross in order that the reign of evil may be arrested?

Loved Enough to Suffer. A Christian schoolmaster in Japan named Professor Neesima taught his boys the meaning of the Cross of Jesus Christ in a vivid way. Whenever any boy was caught doing an evil deed, Neesima ordered the guilty boy to take the cane from the wall of his office. However, Neesima did not strike the miscreant with that cane. Instead, he handed it to the boy. Neesima held out his hands and ordered the boy to strike him with the rod. There were never any stripes across the hands of any of Neesima's boys. But there were stripes across their hearts. They could never forget the schoolmaster who loved them so much that he insisted on suffering for them. When Neesima died, the old cane was placed upon the wall of his university with an inscription under it in memory of the teacher who cared so much for his students. It continues to be a sign of that inward pain of penitence that hurts far deeper and longer than physical punishment. The Cross punishes, but it punishes with a pain that purifies.

Questions for Pupils on the Next Lesson. 1. Do you sometimes grapple with the implications of death? 2. Why do so many people want assurances that there is a life after death? 3. Do you have difficulty believing what cannot be scientifically verified? 4. What was the earliest proclamation of the Resurrection? 5. Is Easter a report of Resurrection for you or an encounter with the Risen Lord?

TOPIC FOR YOUTH
MISSION ACCOMPLISHED

Safe, Sanitary, and Temporary. Fifty people from a small Baptist church watched silently in an Oakland, California, park one July afternoon in 1976 as the Rev. Willie Dicks had himself nailed to a cross. Dicks, a minister from San Carlos, had the cross propped under the shade of a tree. The thirty-seven-year-old minister also had a doctor give him a shot as a precaution against lockjaw and carefully washed his hands and the nails in disinfectant. "If you wonder why I'm taking all these precautions," he said, "Well, I'm not going up there to die. I'm going to come down in one piece." Dicks had himself comfortably supported by towels around his arms and a friend who held him around the waist. Carefully instructing another associate to put the nails into the fleshy part of his hands between the third and fourth fingers near the top of the palm in order not to injure his hands, Dicks cautioned the hammerer not to "miss the nail and hit my hand. I don't want no broken bones." There was little blood. Dicks, held by the towels and friends' grip, had his arms extended and secured by the careful nailing for a total of ten minutes. During that time, he made rambling comments about crime in modern society, saying that he was "disgusted that our senior citizens cannot walk the streets." Dicks cried out only when the nails were pulled out. Looking haggard, he walked to his pickup with his wife, Carole, and young son, and drove to a nearby hospital for a checkup.

Contrast the Oakland crucifixion of the Rev. Willie Dicks with the sacrifice on Calvary. Dicks's exhibition was concluded after about ten minutes of relatively pain-free discomfort, and had no lasting impact. It did not cost. Jesus Christ's suffering on Calvary concluded a life spent in sacrifice for others. He took no precautions, made no provisions for comfort, had no safeguards. But His mission accomplished new life for us!

Mission Accomplished. The residents of a French town named Sarreguemines, located near the German border, have deep appreciation for Major Robert Henderson Bennett, an American soldier who kept them alive during severe fighting in December 1944–April 1945. Major Bennett's heroic deeds provided the town with critically-needed supplies. He arrived in Sarreguemines on December 21, 1944, with eleven G.I.'s and two French liaison officers.

Three days later, on Christmas Eve, Nazi forces broke through American lines to the north and mounted a secondary attack on the American lines in the seven miles between Sarreguemines and the German border.

Instead of a sleigh and reindeer, Major Bennett prepared for his Christmas voyage by commandeering any vehicle he could get his hands on.

His convoy then braved heavy shelling and bombing and nearby infantry combat in search of food, water, and medical supplies desperately needed by Sarreguemines, which had become a gathering point for refugees.

Major Bennett was also credited with boosting the morale of residents by persuading them that the German threat was only temporary and that the Allies would win.

When the Germans retreated in January 1945, Major Bennett helped revitalize the town by restoring electricity and water and finding housing, supplies, and medical care for those in need.

"It was a city that was nearly destroyed. There was very little food, no electricity, no gas, no water, and housing was so bad that 2,800 people were living in a cave. He solved all those problems," the mayor of the town recalled. A few days later, Bennett was ambushed and killed by German soldiers. His mission of saving the town of Sarreguemines, however, was accomplished. In December 1981, the grateful villagers invited Bennett's widow, two sons and members of his outfit for a ceremony in which they renamed the town's main square after the American soldier.

Message of the Cross. A few years ago, a disgustingly sacrilegious film attempted to do a satire on the Crucifixion. The movie's producers thought it amusing to portray some people on crosses while tapping their feet to a lively melody and singing, "Look on the Bright Side of Life." Few thought it funny. Most were offended. Christians were insulted. The meaning of the Cross on Calvary is that Jesus Christ did not treat us flippantly. No cute dance steps to jazzy tunes to distract us. No cheap messages about looking on the bright side of anything. Rather, He fulfilled His mission of loving us to the utmost, even to the cost of laying down His life for us.

Questions for Pupils on the Next Lesson. 1. What do you do when you encounter disappointments that depress you? 2. What does the Easter message suggest to you in regard to God's care for you after you die? 3. Do you often have problems accepting what cannot be scientifically verified? 4. How did the Resurrection bring hope to despairing disciples? 5. Have you been made aware that Jesus Christ is alive?

LESSON VI—APRIL 7

RAISED FROM THE DEAD

Background Scripture: John 20:1–23
Devotional Reading: John 20:19–23

KING JAMES VERSION

JOHN 20 The first *day* of the week cometh Mary Magdalene early, when it was yet dark, unto the sepulchre, and seeth the stone taken away from the sepulchre.

2 Then she runneth, and cometh to Simon Peter, and to the other disciple, whom Jesus loved, and saith unto them, They have taken away the Lord out of the sepulchre, and we know not where they have laid him.

3 Peter therefore went forth, and that other disciple, and came to the sepulchre.

4 So they ran both together: and the other disciple did outrun Peter, and came first to the sepulchre.

5 And he stooping down, *and looking in,* saw the linen clothes lying; yet went he not in.

6 Then cometh Simon Peter following him, and went into the sepulchre, and seeth the linen clothes lie,

7 And the napkin, that was about his head, not lying with the linen clothes, but wrapped together in a place by itself.

8 Then went in also that other disciple, which came first to the sepulchre, and he saw, and believed.

9 For as yet they knew not the scripture, that he must rise again from the dead.

11 But Mary stood without at the sepulchre weeping: and as she wept, she stooped down, *and looked* into the sepulchre,

12 And seeth two angels in white sitting, the one at the head, and the other at the feet, where the body of Jesus had lain.

13 And they say unto her, Woman, why weepest thou? She saith unto them, Because they have taken away my Lord, and I know not where they have laid him.

14 And when she had thus said, she turned herself back, and saw Jesus standing, and knew not that it was Jesus.

15 Jesus saith unto her, Woman, why weepest thou? whom seekest thou? She, supposing him to be the gardener, saith unto him, Sir, if thou have borne him hence, tell me where thou hast laid him, and I will take him away.

16 Jesus saith unto her, Mary. She turned herself, and saith unto him, Rabboni; which is to say, Master.

18 Mary Magdalene came and told the disciples that she had seen the Lord, and *that* he had spoken these things unto her.

REVISED STANDARD VERSION

JOHN 20 Now on the first day of the week Mary Magdalene came to the tomb early, while it was still dark, and saw that the stone had been taken away from the tomb. 2 So she ran, and went to Simon Peter and the other disciple, the one whom Jesus loved, and said to them, "They have taken the Lord out of the tomb, and we do not know where they have laid him." 3 Peter then came out with the other disciple, and they went toward the tomb. 4 They both ran, but the other disciple outran Peter and reached the tomb first; 5 and stooping to look in, he saw the linen cloths lying there, but he did not go in. 6 Then Simon Peter came, following him, and he went into the tomb; he saw the linen cloths lying, 7 and the napkin, which had been on his head, not lying with the linen cloths but rolled up in a place by itself. 8 Then the other disciple, who reached the tomb first, also went in, and he saw and believed; 9 for as yet they did not know the scripture, that he must rise from the dead.

11 But Mary stood weeping outside the tomb, and as she wept she stooped to look into the tomb; 12 and she saw two angels in white, sitting where the body of Jesus had lain, one at the head and one at the feet. 13 They said to her, "Woman, why are you weeping?" She said to them, "Because they have taken away my Lord, and I do not know where they have laid him." 14 Saying this, she turned round and saw Jesus standing, but she did not know that it was Jesus. 15 Jesus said to her, "Woman, why are you weeping? Whom do you seek?" Supposing him to be the gardener, she said to him, "Sir, if you have carried him away, tell me where you have laid him, and I will take him away." 16 Jesus said to her, "Mary." She turned and said to him in Hebrew, "Rabboni!" (which means Teacher).

18 Mary Magdalene went and said to the disciples, "I have seen the Lord"; and she told them that he had said these things to her.

KEY VERSE: *Mary Magdalene went and said to the disciples, "I have seen the Lord."* John 20:18 (RSV).

HOME DAILY BIBLE READINGS

Apr.	1.	M.	*A Puzzling Absence.* John 20:1–10.
Apr.	2.	T.	*From Grief to Joy.* John 20:11–18.
Apr.	3.	W.	*Death Could Not Bind Him.* Acts 2:22–32.
Apr.	4.	T.	*Raised on the Third Day.* 1 Corinthians 15:1–11.
Apr.	5.	F.	*If Christ Were Not Raised.* 1 Corinthians 15:12–19.
Apr.	6.	S.	*The Resurrection Has Begun.* 1 Corinthians 15:20–29.
Apr.	7.	S.	*A Breath of Power.* John 20:19–23.

BACKGROUND

Crucified corpses usually hung on their crosses until they rotted and fell apart. Romans wanted to have crucifixions teach the natives the harsh lesson that it never paid to challenge the Emperor or his representatives. Consequently, Roman army men took a certain pleasure in allowing the gruesome sight of a cross and dead victim to stand for weeks in a public place.

Jewish rules, however, called for immediate burial. Deuteronomy specifies that a hanged man's "body shall not remain all night upon the tree, but you shall bury him the same day, for a hanged man is accursed by God; you shall not defile your land which the Lord your God gives you for an inheritance" (Deuteronomy 21:23). The Jewish leaders were anxious to make sure this part of the Law was kept after Jesus' death on the cross for two reasons: (1) the Sabbath was about to begin; and (2) the opening great Feast of Passover was about to start. They didn't want the holy city ritually defiled by the unburied, decaying bodies suspended from crosses. Therefore, they persuaded Pilate to have the execution squad finish off the men on the crosses on Golgotha so they could be hauled down and buried.

Burial in that part of the world nearly always meant depositing the body in tombs. These tombs were hewn out of the soft limestone. Usually low caverns with several niches or shelves for bodies on each side and in the rear, they were sealed with heavy stones to keep out animals and grave robbers. The Jews never embalmed their dead but merely washed the body and wrapped it in a clean sheet, and put a cloth around the head. To offset the unpleasant odor of decomposition, they placed fragrant spices around the corpse.

As every Gospel writer makes clear, Jesus was dead. He was not in a coma. His followers knew the clinical details of death, and were certain that He had died. Furthermore, they were not expecting a resurrection. They were convinced that everything was over for Jesus—and for themselves.

Then came the surprise encounter by the Risen, Living Lord!

NOTES ON THE PRINTED TEXT

The earliest witnesses to the Resurrection were women. They, of course, had no inkling that they would find the tomb empty or, later, meet Jesus raised from the dead. They were merely going out to the tomb to carry out some of the rites of mourning. It was customary to visit the tomb of a loved one for three days after burial. Popular notion held that the spirit of the departed person lingered for three days near the body. The women who were followers of Jesus could not come to the tomb on the day after His Crucifixion because it was the Sabbath, and were therefore prohibited from traveling. The earliest opportunity for the women to come to the tomb was after the Sabbath, or after dark on Saturday evening. Since it was hazardous to walk in the dark, the women had to wait to the time just before dawn on the first day of the week.

Now on the first day of the week, Mary Magdalene came to the tomb early, while it was still dark, and saw that the stone had been taken away from the tomb. So she ran, and went to Simon Peter and the other disciple, the one whom Jesus loved, and said to them, "They have taken the Lord out of the tomb and we do not know where they have laid him": Mary Magdalene approaches the tomb between 3:00 A.M. and 6:00 A.M. Finding the large cartwheel-size stone rolled to one side leads her to surmise that someone has broken into the tomb. Robbers often rifled tombs shortly after bodies were left. Mary perhaps wonders if some ghoulish criminals have dragged the body outside to strip it of anything valuable, or if Jesus' enemies have desecrated the tomb as a way of adding additional insult. The emotional strain has been terribly heavy during the past days. This additional shock impels her to hurry to Peter and John, two leaders in the disciple group, to tell them that Jesus' tomb is empty.

They both ran, but the other disciple outran Peter and reached the tomb first: John, "the beloved disciple," was probably younger and could run faster than Peter.

He saw the linen cloths lying, and the napkin which had been on his head, not lying with the linen cloths but rolled up in a place by itself: If the tomb had been molested by grave robbers, it would have been a shambles. Or, if some disciples had removed the body, they would have left the wrappings around the body and the head intact. John the Gospel writer states that the wrappings were tidily in place inside the tomb as if the body had slipped out of them. The napkin, according to the Greek words, lay "twirled up" somewhat like a turban and neatly placed in a separate place from the shroud, as if Jesus' body had passed out of the sheet and napkin, leaving them in the same position as when they had enclosed His physical form.

The two disciples discern that Jesus has been raised from the dead.

But Mary stood weeping outside the tomb, and as she wept she stopped to look into the tomb; and she saw two angels in white: Matthew reports one angel; Mark, a young man; while Luke states that there were two men inside the tomb. However, these differing details help us to understand the report of the Resurrection was not a made-up story by Jesus' followers. As any good attorney or judge knows, witnesses of an event will almost certainly have slightly different recollections of minor details but will agree on the central facts. All of the Gospel accounts are in accord that there was an announcement of the Resurrection from inside the tomb.

She turned around and saw Jesus standing, but she did not know that it was Jesus: Mary Magdalene was not expecting to meet the Risen Lord. When Jesus presented Himself, her eyes were so blurred with tears she could not tell it was He. In the dialogue which followed, she states that she assumed that He was a gardener. Mary's failure to recognize the Lord's presence is typical of all of us! We cannot believe He is alive!

Jesus said to her, "Mary": Jesus speaks to Mary by name. The familiar sound of His voice calling to her personally startles her into realizing that it is Jesus alive! The meaning of the Resurrection is also that Jesus knows us by name and speaks to us individually.

She turned and said to him in Hebrew, "Rabboni!" This is what some have called the greatest recognition scene in history. The word, *Rabboni* sums it up. It is an Aramaic word. It is a more powerful word than *rabbi*, and means "My Lord." For Jews, *Lord* was a term reserved for God. Mary Magdalene here offers the earliest confession of faith, the first expression about Jesus as the Divine One, raised from the dead!

SUGGESTIONS TO TEACHERS

A church choir director was explaining the music program in her church to a prospective choir member, and referred repeatedly to "our Easter routine." The singer heard the words "Easter routine" used so many times by the choir leader that he finally said, "Sounds as if you've got your Easter service down to a routine."

Unfortunately, for many church people, Easter has been reduced to an annual routine. You may have some like that in your class. You may even feel a little that way yourself if you've been teaching for several years. Remember, however, that Easter celebrates the Good News that Jesus Christ was raised from the dead and lives!

Examine the biblical passage from John 20 as if you are hearing the news of the Resurrection for the first time. Ask yourself how the original witnesses to the Resurrection must have felt. Listen afresh to the words of the Risen Lord. You may easily put together a great lesson with these points:

1. *MISINFORMED INDIVIDUALISTS.* Part of the reason the earliest followers of Jesus did not expect the Resurrection was that they "did not know the scripture" (John 20:9). Ignorance of the promise in the Bible still hampers people from appreciating the significance of the Resurrection. Stress the need to work diligently with the Scripture so that your people may know personally the assurance of new life through the Living Lord.

2. *MISTAKEN IDENTITY.* Dwell for a few minutes on the way Jesus was not recognized at first but was assumed to be the gardener. Remind the class that we still fail to recognize Jesus when He quietly presents Himself. Especially, we don't seem to notice Him as He makes Himself known through the lives of the hurting, the oppressed—"the least of these" His brothers and sisters. Take some time to discuss the way Jesus sometimes surprises His followers by introducing Himself through humans in need.

3. *MAGNIFICENT INSIGHT.* Mary Magdalene suddenly has a flash of recognition. "Rabboni!" she blurts (20:16). Many Christians have had unexpected moments where the Lord was extremely real and close. This may be a good time to share experiences of deep awareness of Christ's presence and goodness.

4. *MISSIONARY IMPULSE.* Times of heightened awareness of the reality of Jesus Christ, however, are never ends in themselves. They are always given to propel us to share the Good News of the Resurrection. Mary Magdalene understood this. She rushes back to where the others are sitting and shouts, "I have seen the Lord!" (20:18). Ask your class members if they have shared the Good News of Easter with others recently.

5. *MAGNANIMOUS INVOLVEMENT.* Easter means that Jesus Christ is deeply involved in our lives. He lives with us. Now we in turn are sent to others to bring His forgiving love to them. Have your class consider the way Peter and the other witnesses to the Resurrection realized that they were forgiven and therefore driven to share divine forgiveness with others.

TOPIC FOR ADULTS
RAISED FROM THE DEAD

When Empty Means Full. Let me rephrase and condense a "true story" Fr. Tom Bowers told Dr. Louie Crew: His classmates noted that eight-year-old Stephen's mental retardation was becoming even more manifest. Could they retain their love of him as they came to see his difference? In April, the Sunday School teacher asked all eight children in his class to hide within an empty L'eggs pantyhose container one small object that represented the new life in spring. Fearing that Stephen might not have caught on, and not wanting to embarrass him, the teacher had the children place all unlabeled containers on her desk so she could open them. The first had a tiny flower. "What a lovely sign of new life!" The donor could not help but erupt, "I brought that one!"

Next came a rock. That must be Stephen's, since rocks don't symbolize new life. But Billy shouted that his rock had moss on it and moss represented new life. The teacher agreed. A butterfly flew from the third container, and another child bragged that her choice was the best sign of all. The fourth L'eggs container was empty. "It has to be Stephen's," thought the teacher, reaching quickly for a fifth. But, "Please, don't skip mine," Stephen interjected. "But it's empty." "That's right," said Stephen, "the tomb was empty, and *that's* new life for everyone."

Later that summer Stephen's condition worsened and he died. At his funeral on his casket mourners found eight L'eggs pantyhose containers, now *all* empty. "In truth, in very truth, I tell you, a grain of wheat remains a solitary grain unless it falls into the ground and dies; but if it dies, it bears a rich harvest." Reprinted from *Context* (July 1, 1979) by permission of Claretian Publications, 221 West Madison, Chicago, IL 60606.

Those Empty Years. "Malcolm Muggeridge was one of England's brightest success stories. He began his career as a university lecturer, then moved into journalism, becoming the editor of *Punch* and eventually a famous television personality. Gradually the fruits of success turned sour, and as he evaluated his life he found that it amounted to little of real value.

"The turning point came a few years ago when he went with a camera team to film on location the story of Jesus for the British Broadcasting Company. One day he and a friend were walking the six-mile journey between Jerusalem and Emmaus. They pondered the events of Jesus' death just as Cleopas and a friend had done two thousand years ago. And the same thing happened to the modern travelers. Muggeridge said that he was aware of 'a third presence.' After that experience, he was convinced that Jesus is alive today.

"He wrote in his autobiography: 'Somehow I missed you. You called me and I didn't answer. Oh, those empty years, those empty words, that empty passion.'"—Alan Walker, "Call the Witnesses," *The New Pulpit Digest,* March–April 1976.

What Easter Means. "Dr. George Buttrick rightly notes that 'mere immortality is not the Easter message.' Many religions and philosophies, past and present, entertain the notion of a life after death. The types of future existence vary from the somewhat materialistic concepts offered by the ancient Scandinavians with their Valhalla, to the idea of re-absorption of the individual soul with the eternal Soul which is God—as some oriental religions hold.

"The central meaning of Easter is that the seemingly unconquerable power of evil is broken. 'God's war with man's evil has been fought and won in love. There is a power, now available, the presence of the Risen Lord, stronger than the bondage of all our sins.'

"While the assurance of resurrection does indeed provide comfort and hope for those who are close to the end of life's journey, its central meaning lies in our confidence that the power of the Risen Lord can be a reality to us in our daily lives as we encounter temptation in all of its manifest forms.

"The Apostle Paul prays that his friends at Ephesus may know the fullest blessings of Christian faith, reminding them that the power, which is at work in all who believe, is the very same power which God used when He raised Christ from the dead. Our celebration of Easter is joyful in the degree to which we are relying daily on that power to help us to overcome the fears, the anxieties, the hostilities and all the other negative forces of life which prevent us from enjoying the Heavenly Father's greatest gift."—Charles P. Robshaw, Bulletin, East Liberty Presbyterian Church, Pittsburgh, March 26, 1978.

Questions for Pupils on the Next Lesson. 1. Why do we sometimes have difficulty acting consistently with our professed values? 2. What are the hardest long-term commitments you have to make? 3. Is it wrong to have doubts? 4. Why was the Gospel according to John written, according to the Scripture in this lesson? 5. How would you write your personal confession of faith in one or two sentences?

TOPIC FOR YOUTH
EYEWITNESS NEWS

The Resurrection Is Sufficient. "A researcher and professor of theology at Loyola University, the Rev. Francis L. Filas, says he has new evidence to support a claim that the Shroud of Turin was Christ's burial cloth.

"The shroud is an ancient burial cloth about 14′ by 3½′ which has been kept in a cathedral at Turin, Italy, since 1578. The cloth bears an outline of a man with what appears to be blood stains about the figure's head, hands, and feet.

"According to Filas, what *National Geographic* (June, 1980) reported as buttons over the eyes of the figure are really coins minted during the reign of Pontius Pilate between A.D. 30–32.

" 'I don't see any hole in the evidence,' he said. 'I think that this is as good a test of authenticity as we could hope for.'

"Poor Filas! He should know better. He should know that literally thousands c f people were crucified and buried in simple linen shrouds. It's absurd to believe that two coins of Pilate's time represent irrefutable evidence that Jesus lived, died, and was buried in this shroud.

"Still, some rather naive people like Filas, will accept this evidence as proof of Jesus' existence. In all likelihood, these people who see the shroud as proof of Jesus' death and burial are like the women on Easter morning who came to memorialize a fallen friend, to pay their respects at the graveside, to carry out the necessary funeral rites, and then to depart. But Jesus was and is alive!

"God acted to raise Jesus, and our belief is that He has acted for us as well. Through Christ's rising from the dead, each of us is promised life after death. We don't need to gather evidence to support Jesus' resurrection. We need no proof of authenticity of Jesus existence or of life after death. The announcement that God resurrected Jesus is sufficient. Rejoice! He lives! He lives for us!"—John Barker, *West Sunbury Newsletter,* April 1, 1981.

Orthodox Easter. In the Easter tradition as in Russian Orthodox churches, Easter is the great feast of the year. Even in Moscow, church buildings which are normally empty museums maintained by the state as relics of the past, are thronged with enormous crowds on Easter eve.

In front of the ikonastasis (screen of icons) on Easter eve worship services is a casket. Covering the casket is an embroidery outlining the figure of Jesus lying dead. All icons are draped in black. The music and liturgy emphasize the mourning. At midnight, all leave their building and circle the church three times. This symbolizes the women coming to the tomb to search for the body. The Patriarch knocks at the door three times. The music and liturgy continues:

> "He is not here. He is risen from the dead.
> He has trampled down death by death, and on
> those in the tomb bestows life.
> Alleluia! Alleluia!"
> Then, with a great shout: "HE IS RISEN!!"

The crowds respond, "HE IS RISEN INDEED." The kiss of peace is shared on each cheek. Inside the church, the shrouds have been removed. A happy, quick-beat music is heard. Everyone immediately goes from the announcement to the table or altar for a meal. There is nothing funereal, but all is celebratory. The reality of life over death sets everyone's feet a tapping. None is allowed to kneel between Easter and Pentecost. For the next 50 days, the greetings everywhere are, "Christ is risen" and "He is risen indeed" as a reply. The people having fasted for forty days (no meat, dairy products) adjourn to homes for great Easter feasts, carrying home baskets of food brought to church to be blessed. And they always try to take home a stranger as a guest, with the idea that the stranger symbolizes or represents Christ.

Evita's Encore. Several years ago, in 1971, a visitor was invited to dine with Juan Peron, the one-time President-Dictator of Argentina who had been packed off to Spain in exile. To the consternation of the visitor, those present at the table included not only Peron and his new wife, Isabel, but also the carefully embalmed body of his first wife Evita. The weird practice of placing Evita's corpse at the table was a nightly ritual. When Evita died of cancer in 1952, Peron instructed her physician to do the best embalming job possible. He took almost a year, and received a handsome sum for his efforts. Evita's body was put on display and seen by over 2 million in Buenos Aires. However, before Evita's body was placed in its tomb, Peron was forced from power and fled to Madrid. Evita's body in its casket meanwhile was stored in a large packing case in Argentinian government buildings and warehouses for many months. Somehow, it got shipped to West Germany, then to Rome, and finally to Milan, Italy, where it was buried in the Musocco Cemetery. Peron heard that Evita's final resting place was in that cemetery in 1971. He arranged to have the casket removed from its grave and shipped to him in Madrid. When he had the casket open, the seventy-four-year-old Peron broke into sobs, crying, "She is not dead, she is only sleeping!" Thanks to the excellent embalming job nineteen years earlier, Evita's body was preserved almost exactly as when the ex-dictator had last seen her. Peron insisted that her corpse be placed at the dining-room table each evening. When he was recalled to Argentina, he planned to bring Evita's body to Buenos Aires, but died in 1974 before carrying out this intention. Isabel, Peron's widow, however, arranged to have Evita's body flown from Spain and to lie in state beside Peron. Evita's remains were reinterred in 1976, and rest in an underground tomb in the Recoleta Cemetery in Buenos Aires.

Peron's hopes rested on the make-believe of the embalmer's art. He carried the pretense to a ridiculous extreme. Contrast this to the news of the Resurrection. Jesus Christ is with us. He is not propped up in a coffin beside our tables, He is not a corpse whom we try to convince ourselves "is only sleeping." He lives! He enlivens us! He brings new life to the world!

Questions for Pupils on the Next Lesson. 1. Have you an uneasy sense that it's wrong to have religious doubts? 2 How did Jesus handle Thomas and his doubts? 3. Why is it so difficult to trust Jesus Christ? 4. Does your faith in Jesus Christ have to have proofs? 5. In one sentence, how would you describe who Jesus Christ is to you?

LESSON VII—APRIL 14

ACKNOWLEDGED AS LORD

Background Scripture: John 20:24–21:25
Devotional Reading: John 21:1–14

KING JAMES VERSION

JOHN 20 26 And after eight days again his disciples were within, and Thomas with them: *then* came Jesus, the doors being shut, and stood in the midst, and said, Peace *be* unto you.

27 Then saith he to Thomas, Reach hither thy finger, and behold my hands; and reach hither thy hand, and thrust *it* into my side; and be not faithless, but believing.

28 And Thomas answered and said unto him, My Lord and my God.

21 15 So when they had dined, Jesus saith to Simon Peter, Simon *son* of Jonas, lovest thou me more than these? He saith unto him, Yea, Lord; thou knowest that I love thee. He saith unto him, Feed my lambs.

16 He saith to him again the second time, Simon, *son* of Jonas, lovest thou me? He saith unto him, Yea, Lord; thou knowest that I love thee. He saith unto him, Feed my sheep.

17 He saith unto him the third time, Simon, *son* of Jonas, lovest thou me? Peter was grieved because he said unto him the third time, Lovest thou me? And he said unto him, Lord, thou knowest all things; thou knowest that I love thee. Jesus saith unto him, Feed my sheep.

18 Verily, verily, I say unto thee, When thou wast young, thou girdedst thyself, and walkedst whither thou wouldest; but when thou shalt be old, thou shalt stretch forth thy hands, and another shall gird thee, and carry *thee* whither thou wouldest not.

19 This spake he, signifying by what death he should glorify God. And when he had spoken this, he saith unto him, Follow me.

20 Then Peter, turning about, seeth the disciple whom Jesus loved following; which also leaned on his breast at supper, and said, Lord, which is he that betrayeth thee?

21 Peter seeing him saith to Jesus, Lord, and what *shall* this man *do?*

22 Jesus saith unto him, If I will that he tarry till I come, what *is that* to thee? follow thou me.

20 31 But these are written, that ye might believe that Jesus is the Christ, the Son of God; and that believing ye might have life through his name.

REVISED STANDARD VERSION

JOHN 20 26 Eight days later, his disciples were again in the house, and Thomas was with them. The doors were shut, but Jesus came and stood among them, and said, "Peace be with you." 27 Then he said to Thomas, "Put your finger here, and see my hands; and put out your hand, and place it in my side; do not be faithless, but believing." 28 Thomas answered him, "My Lord and my God!"

21 15 When they had finished breakfast, Jesus said to Simon Peter, "Simon, son of John, do you love me more than these?" He said to him, "Yes, Lord; you know that I love you." He said to him, "Feed my lambs." 16 A second time he said to him, "Simon, son of John, do you love me?" He said to him, "Yes, Lord; you know that I love you." He said to him, "Tend my sheep." 17 He said to him the third time, "Simon, son of John, do you love me?" Peter was grieved because he said to him the third time, "Do you love me?" And he said to him, "Lord, you know everything; you know that I love you." Jesus said to him, "Feed my sheep. 18 Truly, truly, I say to you, when you were young, you girded yourself and walked where you would; but when you are old, you will stretch out your hands, and another will gird you and carry you where you do not wish to go." 19 (This is said to show by what death he was to glorify God.) And after this he said to him, "Follow me."

20 Peter turned and saw following them the disciple whom Jesus loved, who had lain close to his breast at the supper and had said, "Lord, who is it that is going to betray you?" 21 When Peter saw him, he said to Jesus, "Lord, what about this man?" 22 Jesus said to him, "If it is my will that he remain until I come, what is that to you? Follow me!"

20 31 but these are written that you may believe that Jesus is the Christ, the Son of God, and that believing you may have life in his name.

KEY VERSE: These are written that you may believe that Jesus is the Christ, the Son of God, and that believing you may have life in his name. John 20:31 (RSV).

HOME DAILY BIBLE READINGS

Apr.	*8.*	*M.*	*Believing and Seeing.* John 20:24–31.
Apr.	*9.*	*T.*	*Their Eyes Were Opened.* Luke 24:28–32.
Apr.	*10.*	*W.*	*Beyond Illusion.* Luke 24:33–43.
Apr.	*11.*	*T.*	*You Are My Witnesses.* Luke 24:44–53.
Apr.	*12.*	*F.*	*Make Disciples of All Nations.* Matthew 28:16–20.
Apr.	*13.*	*S.*	*It Is the Lord.* John 21:1–14.
Apr.	*14.*	*S.*	*Feed My Sheep.* John 21:15–25.

BACKGROUND

Periodically, someone writes a book or an article claiming to show that the Resurrection of Jesus was a hoax or a hallucination. There is no need to get upset by these sensationalist authors. People have been trying to "explain away" the report of Jesus being raised alive since the earliest days after the Crucifixion.

Hoax? The New Testament mentions that enemies of the earliest believers tried to spread the report that Jesus was alive by hiding the body.

Hallucination? Some first-century and second-century A.D. people had such an aversion to anything material and nonspiritual that they practically reduced the Resurrection to a spook story.

The writer of the Fourth Gospel refutes both of these mistaken ideas. First, he emphasizes repeatedly how the disciples themselves had no idea that Jesus would actually be raised from the grave by telling the story from their own accounts. In these, the disciples don't come across as heroes but as scared and shaken people who were not expecting to see Jesus alive again. They had no time to plan a elaborate bit of fakery. Furthermore, a hoax, since it is a lie, is inevitably morally weakening. Often, too, one lie leads to another. In the case of the Resurrection, Jesus' disciples were strengthened by the news He was alive, not weakened. In addition, they reported seeing Jesus alive for a brief time then stated that He appeared no more after a few weeks.

The Gospel of John also makes sure that readers know that the Risen Lord was not a wraith, but one who could hold out nail-pierced hands, prepare fish for breakfast, and eat food. In other words, John the Gospel writer wanted to make certain that his readers take seriously his reports that early followers acknowledged Jesus as raised from the dead only after having misgivings themselves about the Resurrection stories.

NOTES ON THE PRINTED TEXT

John the Gospel writer skillfully portrays the struggle in faith two of Jesus' followers had before being able to acknowledge Jesus as Risen Lord. Thomas and Peter are covered in detail to help readers understand the claims of Jesus and the response expected.

I. *Eight days later, his disciples were again in the house, and Thomas was with them:* Why wasn't Thomas in the Upper Room with the rest of the disciples on the Easter night when Jesus first presented Himself? Was he so disillusioned by the Crucifixion that he thought it was useless to meet with the others? Or, was he so frightened that he and the others would be scooped up by the authorities, tortured and perhaps executed as Jesus had been? For whatever reason, Thomas was not expecting ever to see Jesus again, and was not present at the first appearance of the Risen Lord to the disciple band. He scoffed at the reports when disciples told him that they had seen the Lord alive. He demanded irrefutable proof by personally touching the nail holes in Jesus' hands before he could accept such an impossible story as true. Thomas was afraid to take the risk of faith. He had been hurt and let down by the terrible ending to Jesus, and didn't want to get his hopes built up only to be dashed again. He reluctantly agreed to meet with the disciples the following week.

But Jesus came and stood among them, and said, "Peace be with you." Then He said to Thomas, "Put your finger here, and see my hands, and put out your hand, and place it in my side; do not be faithless, but believing": Jesus quietly appears in the Upper Room, and gives the familiar greeting, *"Shalom"* or "Peace." Then He turns His attention to the skeptic who had demanded tangible proof. Challenging Thomas to touch the nail-pierced hands and the spear-punctured side, Jesus reproaches Thomas for believing his doubts instead of doubting those doubts.

Thomas answered him, "My Lord and my God." Thomas springs from the depths of doubt to the heights of faith and he states one of the earliest Christian creeds. Every person who takes Jesus seriously must ultimately make this affirmation. Jesus is both Messiah and God. Furthermore, each believer must acknowledge that Jesus is *"my* Lord and *my* God."

II. Shifting to the scene on the Sea of Galilee, the Gospel writer describes the Risen Lord appearing to a group of seven disciples who had returned to their fishing. The focus, however, is on Peter. Peter had denied Jesus three times. Jesus realizes the sense of guilt and failure Peter had been carrying.

"Simon, son of John, do you love me ... ?" Jesus searchingly asks the question not once but three times to nullify Peter's triple denial. Jesus is not trying to put down Peter or to make him more miserable, He is reinstating Peter as an apostle. He also knows Peter's weaknesses. Three years earlier, he had called Peter on that same lake, and here Peter was back at his old life again. The repeated question, "Do you love me more than these" (the nets, the boat, the freedom, the income) is to cement Peter's loyalty once again, this time for good.

The exchange between Jesus and Peter uses two Greek words for *love.* One means "to care" and the other means "to be a friend." Another way of translating the conversation could be, "Peter, do you care about me?" Peter: "You know I am your friend." Jesus, asking a second time: "But do you care about me?" Peter: "You know I am your friend." Jesus: "Are you my friend?" Peter: "You know everything; you know I am your friend."

"Feed my lambs ... Tend my sheep ... Feed my sheep." Peter is to be a shepherd of Jesus' flock. If Peter means to be Jesus' friend, he is to do Jesus' work of caring about the helpless, leaderless ones which Jesus entrusts to Peter's care.

". . . you will stretch out your hands": John the Gospel writer hints that Peter will be crucified also. Jesus' words here also mean that in Peter's younger days, he was free to go as he pleased. Now, however, he is like an old man having to be helped and led. Peter from this point on is not free to do as he wishes because he will be helped and led by Jesus Christ—to a death of sacrifice!

"What about this man?": The Gospel writer wants to clear up a misunderstanding. A rumor being passed around had it that the Beloved Disciple would survive until Jesus' coming again. John's Gospel account makes it clear that Jesus was not predicting any such thing about the Beloved Disciple, but telling Peter bluntly that it was none of his business if some other follower should happen to go on serving longer than he should serve on earth. Peter's prime concern, Jesus makes clear, is to be a faithful shepherd. Jesus in these lines is also telling us not to busy ourselves in the future of other Christians, but to tend to our own tasks of serving!

SUGGESTIONS TO TEACHERS

Sometimes we think that the earliest believers in the Risen Lord were a bit gullible—folks who had few problems in acknowledging that Jesus had indeed been raised from the dead. We even envy them. "If only I had lived then, faith would have come easily," we say.

Today's lesson takes a hard look at the people in Jesus' circle of followers at the time the Easter news broke. You and your class will quickly discover that these disciples were not gullible or easily swayed. To the contrary, some of them resisted the evidence and announcements. Others didn't seem to be able to let the incredible news sink in. It was obviously not easy for them to acknowledge Jesus as Lord.

And it is not easy for us, either!

This is why today's lesson is so important.

Therefore, work seriously with the background Scripture and look at some of these issues:

1. *SCOFFER'S CRITICISM.* Start by holding up Thomas as a case history in skepticism. Thomas, the original "Show me!" believer, the prototype "man from Missouri" Christian, scoffs at the reports that Jesus had been raised and was alive. After all, why shouldn't he? Wouldn't we if we had been there and heard such impossible news? You may find it profitable for at least some in your class to take some time to talk about handling doubts. Remember, there is a streak of Thomas the skeptic in each person!

2. *SAVIOR'S COMING.* The words, "Jesus came and stood among them" (20:26) and, "Peace ..." should be pondered. Jesus quietly but insistently presents Himself always. Often, we fail to take notice of Him. Remind your class that He always comes bringing His *Shalom.* And *Peace* is more than a greeting, more than an absence of conflict. In the Bible, it always means a harmony and wholeness.

3. *SKEPTIC'S CONFESSION.* Have your class consider Thomas's statement of faith, "My Lord and my God!" (20:28). Tell your people what they have heard before but need to hear again, namely that every Christian must daily restate allegiance to Jesus Christ as his or her Lord and God.

4. *SIMON'S CONVERSION.* Conversion is not a once-and-done-with matter. It is daily. Simon Peter's story is an account of many conversions or occasions of turning again toward the Lord. The Resurrection appearance to Peter while fishing was still another conversion experience. Ask if your class members are aware of their need for daily conversions!

5. *SCRIPTURE'S CONTENTION.* The Bible contends that Jesus did so much that "the world itself could not contain the books that would be written" (21:25). What is He doing in the lives of your class? Are their lives "books" for the world to "read" about what Jesus does?

TOPIC FOR ADULTS
ACKNOWLEDGED AS LORD

Special Use. Mr. and Mrs. Roberto Cadei operate the Cross Hands Hotel in a rural area of southwestern England. The Cadeis bought the sixteenth century, stone-built coaching stop on the Bath-Cirencester Road in the Cotswolds a few years ago, and operate the fifteen-room hotel and dining room with their two teen-daughters and a small staff. Late one Sunday in December, 1981, an unexpected blizzard hit with such ferocity that Mr. and Mrs. Cadei figured that no additional guests would appear. They were preparing to lock up for the day when the first of a stream of people appeared who had been forced to abandon their cars. Eventually, there were over 100 in the lounge and dining room. All rooms except one were taken. Mr. Cadei was busy trying to arrange for food for the influx of guests when a distinguished-looking gentleman arrived and explained to him that Queen Elizabeth was outside. Like dozens of others, the Queen and her party had become snowbound. Mr. Cadei rose to the occasion. Grabbing a shovel, he cleared a path to the one remaining place, Room 15, which could be reached only by an outside set of steps. Mr. Cadei's sovereign spent the rest of the afternoon and most of the night at the Cross Hands in Room 15 or in the Cadeis's private apartment for tea and dinner. "I must have been the only woman who ever received the Queen in the old blue jeans and sweatshirt," confessed Mrs. Cadei. The Cadeis were deeply touched by the graciousness of Queen Elizabeth, and feel a profound attachment to her as their monarch. Today, the crockery and cutlery used by the Queen are carefully preserved in a separate box and kept in a place of honor in the Cadeis's bedroom. They have set apart what the Queen had touched.

The disciples of Jesus were just as profoundly affected by the unexpected appearances of Jesus in their midst after the Crucifixion. The encounter in the Upper Room changed Thomas in particular. Thomas and the other followers were touched so deeply by the presence of the Risen Lord in their midst that they set themselves apart for special service. They knew that their lives could no longer be used in the ways they once had. Because the Risen Lord had touched their lives, they knew everything they owned had a special purpose as Christ's!

He Conquers! On the Eucharistic wafer used in the Greek Church, a Cross is stamped. In the four angles formed by the Cross, the letters *IC, XC, NI,* and *KA* are stamped. The letters stand for *Jesus* (*IC* are the Greek letters for the abbreviation of Jesus), *Christ* (*XC* for Christos) *conquers* (*NIKA* is Greek for "Jesus Christ Conquers!").

The Communion wafer or loaf always states implicitly that Jesus Christ must be acknowledged as Lord. However, do you acknowledge that Jesus Christ conquers as you leave worship and go into the world? Do you live as evidence that Jesus is conqueror? In a sense, acknowledging Him as Lord means having *IC, XC,* and *NIKA* engraved on your heart, hands, and tongue so that others may realize that Jesus is your Lord and your God!

New Scale of Values. Sixteen men survived seventy days in the Andes Mountains in the winter of 1972. The ordeal began October 13, 1972 when a chartered Uruguayan Air Force Fairchild F-227 crashed while carrying the Old Christian Rugby Club to Chile. Seventeen of the forty-five people aboard died at once, and others perished of injuries or of exposure and starvation amid the lifeless, snow-covered peaks.

"My life is divided into before-the-crash and after-the-crash," said the bearded and robust Gustavo Zerbino, manager at a Montevideo chemical company and at twenty-nine still an active rugby club player.

Zerbino said he and the others—most were barely twenty when they were rescued—feel "total tranquility."

"The mountains drastically changed our scale of values. We lit fires with money in the Andes. Money may help attain goals, but it is not a goal in itself."

Sometimes it takes a tragedy or dramatic experience to give us a proper scale of values. In the case of the Andean survivors, it was the ordeal in the cold before their rescue. In the case of us who have known Jesus Christ, it is the awareness that He is Lord. Acknowledging Jesus as Lord means a changed scale of values. Money, time, personal goals, and everything else, have a different purpose and meaning since the Resurrection.

Questions for Pupils on the Next Lesson. 1. Why did Job regret that he was born? 2. Should God be held responsible for human suffering? 3. How can you best comfort someone who has experienced sorrow or hardship? 4. Does suffering pose a threat to your values? 5. Do only the wicked suffer?

TOPIC FOR YOUTH
A QUESTIONING FAITH

New Garden. When work was begun on the great Cathedral of St. John the Divine in New York in 1896, workmen preparing the site for excavating for the foundation came upon a spring. They looked upon the spring as a nuisance. Some cursed it as an impediment to proceeding with the building. Engineers, annoyed with the spring, finally had its bubbling flow diverted into a sewer. Nobody seemed to remember the fresh waters that once issued from that spring. Construction on the magnificent edifice in Morningside Heights in New York ground to a halt at the outbreak of World War II because of scarcity of money, materials, and manpower. Forty years later, building was resumed on what will be the largest cathedral in the world. Workmen excavating an area near the structure were surprised to come upon the ancient spring, with its flow turned into a sewer. They reported their find to the Cathedral authorities. The Dean of the Cathedral had the old spring uncovered and ordered a garden built around it. The fresh water trickling from the pipe no longer is wasted in the flow of a hidden sewer, but brings green and growth and beauty to that part of the concrete-filled expanses of the city. It is literally water of life for the verdant plants and flowers in that lovely cathedral garden, and it reminds everyone of the Lord who is The Water of Life!

Sometimes we don't recognize the evidence of Christ's power or presence. We doubt His goodness and nearness, and we divert what He gives to wasteful ends. We allow ourselves to live negatively, and see Him, like the workmen saw the spring, merely as an obstacle to our plans. He brings life! His refreshing Presence as Risen Lord can make a garden in the slum of our lives!

Real hero. Penn State's great 1982 football team was spearheaded by a deeply Christian junior from North Canton, Ohio, named Todd Blackledge. His superb passing and expert running made him the toast of thousands. Fans and sportswriters heaped praises on Blackledge. He was Penn State's hero. Some said he was the greatest quarterback Coach Joe Paterno had ever coached. After a nail-biting sixty-five-yard drive with quarterback Blackledge hitting receivers with two-minute drill confidence and capped with a touchdown pass in the last four seconds of the game with second-ranked Nebraska, Penn State won 27–24. Fans were nearly delirious. The locker room was a scene of electrified excitement and celebration after the game. Reporters sought out Todd Blackledge. They found him calmly applying ice packs on a sore arm and leg and ignoring the pandemonium elsewhere. He was the hero, but he was seemingly oblivious to that. Blackledge has his own hero. "I thought of my favorite Bible verse," Blackledge quietly told the crowd of sportswriters interviewing him, "I can do all things through Christ and His strength." Blackledge has made the journey beyond doubt to faith! He acknowledges who is the real hero in life: Jesus Christ. Do you?

Best Friend. Hetty Green was a penny-pinching miser who inherited a fortune in stocks and securities and made millions of dollars more through shrewd trading and investing. Known as "The Witch of Wall Street," Hetty Green distrusted everyone. She dressed herself in cast-off rags from Bowery mission clothing barrels and ate stale leftovers in her unheated slum flat. She spent almost her entire life trying to remain unrecognized. Her only associate was a fierce mongrel dog. The dog had the unfortunate habit of sometimes biting the few acquaintances who tried to befriend Hetty. One of these friends finally had enough of the ferocious dog and scolded Hetty, "Hetty, that dog just bit me again. You've got to get rid of him."

Hetty Green answered immediately, "He loves me. He doesn't know how rich I am."

Poor woman, she felt she was accepted for who she was only by a mongrel. But isn't this like others, also? In fact, don't you sometimes feel that no one loves you for yourself? Remember, however, that the Risen Jesus Christ comes to you in love, accepting you for the person you are, not for what you do or what you own! Acknowledge Him as your Lord!

Questions for Pupils on the Next Lesson. 1. Why did Job regret the day he was born? 2. How do you handle setbacks, hurts, and sorrows? 3. Do you think that God deliberately sends suffering to punish people? 4. Have others comforted you when you have been sad or depressed? 5. How can you be a true friend to others who are going through times of suffering?

STUDIES IN WISDOM LITERATURE

LESSON VIII–APRIL 21

FAITH ENCOUNTERS SUFFERING

Background Scripture: Job 1–4
Devotional Reading: Job 1:13–22

KING JAMES VERSION

JOB 3 2. And Job spake, and said,
3. Let the day perish wherein I was born, and the night *in which* it was said, There is a man child conceived.

20 Wherefore is light given to him that is in misery, and life unto the bitter *in* soul;
21. Which long for death, but it *cometh* not; and dig for it more than for hid treasures;
22 Which rejoice exceedingly, *and* are glad, when they can find the grave?
23 *Why is light given* to a man whose way is hid, and whom God hath hedged in?
24 For my sighing cometh before I eat, and my roarings are poured out like the waters.
25 For the thing which I greatly feared is come upon me, and that which I was afraid of is come unto me.
26 I was not in safety, neither had I rest, neither was I quiet; yet trouble came.
4 Then Eliphaz the Temanite answered and said,
2 *If* we assay to commune with thee, wilt thou be grieved? but who can withhold himself from speaking?
3 Behold, thou hast instructed many, and thou hast strengthened the weak hands.
4 Thy words have upholden him that was falling, and thou hast strengthened the feeble knees.
5 But now it is come upon thee, and thou faintest; it toucheth thee, and thou art troubled.
6 *Is* not *this* thy fear, thy confidence, thy hope, and the uprightness of thy ways?
7 Remember, I pray thee, who *ever* perished, being innocent? or where were the righteous cut off?

REVISED STANDARD VERSION

JOB 3 2 And Job said:
3 "Let the day perish wherein I was born. and the night which said,
'A man-child is conceived.'

20 "Why is light given to him that is in misery,
and life to the bitter in soul,
21 who long for death, but it comes not,
and dig for it more than for hid treasures;
22 who rejoice exceedingly,
and are glad, when they find the grave?
23 Why is light given to a man whose way is hid,
whom God has hedged in?
24 For my sighing comes as my bread, and my groanings are poured out like water.
25 For the thing that I fear comes upon me,
and what I dread befalls me.
26 I am not at ease, nor am I quiet;
I have no rest; but trouble comes."
4 Then Eliphaz the Temanite answered:
2 'If one ventures a word with you, will you be offended?
Yet who can keep from speaking?
3 Behold, you have instructed many,
and you have strengthened the weak hands.
4 Your words have upheld him who was stumbling,
and you have made firm the feeble knees.
5 But now it has come to you, and you are impatient;
it touches you, and you are dismayed.
6 Is not your fear of God your confidence,
and the integrity of your ways your hope?
7 "Think now, who that was innocent ever perished?
Or where were the upright cut off?"

KEY VERSE: *"Let the day perish wherein I was born, and the night which said, 'A man-child is conceived.'"* Job 3:3 (RSV).

HOME DAILY BIBLE READINGS

Apr.   15.   M.   *Why Is Job Good?* Job 1:1–12.
Apr.   16.   T.   *Job Passes a Test.* Job 1:13–21.
Apr.   17.   W.   *Job's Lament.* Job 3:1–10.
Apr.   18.   T.   *A Sense of Being Abandoned.* Job 19:1–12.
Apr.   19.   F.   *A Cry for Help.* Psalms 28:1–9.
Apr.   20.   S.   *Thy Will Be Done.* Matthew 26:36–46.
Apr.   21.   S.   *Suffering for Christ's Sake.* 2 Corinthians 6:1–10.

BACKGROUND

With this lesson, we start a six-study series dealing with Wisdom Literature in the Old Testament. These lessons will be drawn from the books of Job, Ecclesiastes, and Proverbs.

First, we need to clear up what we mean by "Wisdom Literature." To us, wisdom is merely a set of axioms boiling down the meaning of certain philosophies. Therefore, we may think of the books of Wisdom in the Bible the same way we look at Ben Franklin's *Poor Richard's Almanac* or Lord Chesterfield's letters to his son. We dismiss the sayings in these Old Testament books as merely another group of pithy sayings or bits of advice.

In the Old Testament, however, Wisdom Literature was an important strand, and stands alongside the prophetic and the priestly traditions or "schools" of writings. And what did the Hebrews mean by *Wisdom?* It was to look at human experiences and to reflect on what these experiences meant in the light of God. Or, as O. S. Rankin puts it, "Wisdom is the ability to assess truly the values of life" (*Israel's Wisdom Literature*). The Hebrew word (*hochmah*) for Wisdom basically means right living or obedience to the Lord, enabling a person to face all the vicissitudes of life.

The first three lessons of this series are taken from the Book of Job. These portray a good man's struggle to understand the meaning of suffering. They show Job wrestling with the problems raised by suffering and trying to maintain his faith in spite of his questions, doubts, and deep pain.

The story of Job was undoubtedly passed around by Hebrew storytellers for many years before someone wrote down the plot around the time of King David, and others added the dialogues between the questioning Job and his three advisers perhaps in the sixth or fifth centuries B.C. Much of the book is in poetry form, and takes its place with the greatest literature as well as the deepest thinking of the Hebrew Scriptures.

NOTES ON THE PRINTED TEXT

We have a saying in English about "the patience of Job." A quick look at today's background Scripture will show you, however, that Job was not very patient. Job grew angry with God because of the suffering God seemed to permit him to experience.

That is part of the appeal of the Book of Job. It is intensely human. The story of a good person having to endure undeserved pain and heartache gets down to the basic issues of life. If God is all He is supposed to be, why does an innocent man lose his children and his property in a series of catastrophes? Why does a good person come down with excruciating and repulsive illness so that even his wife tells him to pack in his faith? Why do the crooks seem to get away with flaunting God?

Job is not patient. Nor is he pious. In fact, he has the honesty to complain to God and others about the injustices he receives. These injustices seem worse because Job is not an old man. Fourteen times in the Book of Job, Job describes himself as a strong and vigorous person. In the face of the series of calamaties which have killed his children, taken his wealth, ruined his health, and wrecked his reputation, Job turns into an angry man. "Let the day perish wherein I was born, and the night which said, 'A man-child is conceived.' " These are the words of a person so miserable that he regrets he was ever conceived and survived.

The Bible never blinks at the tough questions. Job puts into words the question of a person so wracked with doubts about God's presence or purposes in the midst of so much evil that he screams to God that he wishes he had never been born! Don't ever think that the Bible is a collection of sweet stories on lavender paper with a delicate whiff of perfume. The Bible faces the gutsy issues!

Job's soliloquy in these verses describes a person who is ready to quit on life and settle for death. Human existence seems to be so hopeless that non-being is preferable, Job is saying. Yet Job cannot shake off the sense of God in his life. But it is not God the Friend; it is God the Enemy that Job cries to.

"Why is light given to him that is in misery, and life to the bitter in soul, who long for death, but it comes not . . . who rejoice exceedingly and are glad when they find the grave?" Job roars and rages in his misery, asking why God doesn't finish him off and be done with it instead of subjecting him to a living death. Job wonders about the intentions of the Creator and accuses Him of deliberately sending evil upon a human.

". . . whom God has hedged in": Job compares himself to powerful wild animals caught with no possible way of escaping.

"I am not at ease, nor am I quiet; I have no rest; but trouble comes": It is more than physical pain which wracks Job. It is also the mental anguish. In fact the Hebrew word translated as *trouble* in verse 26 is the same word to refer to the rumbling of thunder and also means "raging." Job's tormented condition astonishes everyone.

Then Eliphaz the Temanite answered: Here comes the first of Job's three "friends" or comforters. Eliphaz is the oldest. He is the most attractive of the trio. He sincerely tries to comfort Job. In many ways, he is somewhat like Job once was before the calamities struck. Eliphaz has neat little theological "answers." Basically, Eliphaz believes that Job ought to realize that God can find some fault with everybody and recognize that God is offended by something that Job has done. Although courteous and fatherly, Eliphaz sounds like a preacher mouthing commonplace religious trivia. He seems to bring his fingertips together, smile piously, and intone, "Now, my boy, if I were you, I'd own up and come clean before God. Then you'll find that everything will turn out nicely."

Behold, you have instructed many, and you have strengthened the weak hands. Your words have upheld him who was stumbling: Eliphaz refers to the way Job once helped many people who were in trouble. Obviously Job was once deeply respected for his upright life and practical care.

Is not your fear of God your confidence and the integrity of your ways your hope?: These words from Old Eliphaz are platitudes. They really don't say anything to Job or to anyone suffering as he is. Furthermore, they show that Eliphaz is not empathizing much with Job, but merely applying religious maxims about "having faith."

SUGGESTIONS TO TEACHERS

A couple active in their church wanted children and prayed for years. Finally, it seemed, their prayers were answered and they were blessed with a beautiful little boy. The boy is now five years old, and their only child. Last month, the youngster was diagnosed as having a rapidly-progressing form of leukemia.

A tornado roars through a Texas town, completely destroying the recently-dedicated church which members have sacrificed valiantly to build.

A young missionary doctor and his wife, eager to serve humanity in Christ's name, are killed in a bus accident two weeks after they arrive at their overseas assignment.

Questions follow. People of faith find themselves bewildered and asking deep questions about God, about life, about their faith, about themselves.

Everyone in your class has had to ponder some of these questions at some time or other. And every person will have to think about these questions again.

Today's lesson and the two following face these questions. Sometimes, it may appear that church people dodge the tough questions. In these lessons, however, you and your class are facing them head-on.

1. *DOES PAIN COME TO GOOD PEOPLE?* Job's story, the basis for these lessons, answers *Yes.* Even "the blameless and upright," as Job is described, suffer. Faith in God does not mean being exempted from pain and disasters. Take some time to let this point sink in among your class members.

2. *CAN PEOPLE HELP?* It depends. Some don't or can't, such as Job's friends. Have your class look at each of them and their windy speeches. These three "friends" offer slick solutions to Job's problems, when Job actually needs a fellow-sufferer or empathetic friend to sit with him. Talk with your people about the best ways to minister to those experiencing grief or hurts.

3. *IS PROTEST ALL RIGHT?* Don't try to mute Job's protests to God. And don't try to pretend that sufferers don't feel like cursing God and the day they were born in these times. Remind your people that God prefers an honest shriek of anger and anguish toward Him to fake piety and pretended acceptance.

4. *IS PUNISHMENT THE REASON?* Job's story opens the question whether suffering is sent by God to punish us. Many still believe it is. Although this will be discussed in subsequent lessons, you may start to work with it in this lesson.

There is, of course, no snappy answer, but there is the Cross and its message to guide you and your people.

TOPIC FOR ADULTS
FAITH ENCOUNTERS SUFFERING

Things We Don't Deserve. "The late Jack Benny once remarked, on accepting an award, 'I don't deserve this, but I have arthritis and I don't deserve that either.'

"Perhaps we can turn this clever observation around and say, 'I don't deserve this difficulty, but I have many blessings for which to be grateful and I don't deserve them either.'

"We can often say, 'I don't deserve this adversity, but neither do I deserve the priceless gift of life.'

"All of us can say, 'Probably I don't deserve this bitter disappointment, but neither do I deserve the wonderful friends that always stand by me when I need them the most.'

"Each of us can say at one time or another, 'Surely I don't deserve this sorrow, this valley of despair, or this tribulation, but neither do I deserve God's comforting assurance, His compassionate love, or His constant companionship.'

"Many times you and I can say, 'I don't deserve this financial reverse, this rotten luck, or these unpleasant circumstances, but neither do I deserve such a wonderful family, such a great country, or such glorious freedom.'

"Let's learn to be thankful for everything—even the undesirable things we don't deserve . . . and especially the beautiful things we don't deserve."—William Arthur Ward, *Quote*, September 15, 1982.

Faith Encounters Suffering. The Rev. James H. Costen is a black minister who currently serves as the dean of the Johnson C. Smith Seminary in Atlanta, Georgia. A few years ago, while serving in a church in another town, Dr. Costen and his family were startled to discover that rowdies from the Ku Klux Klan had planted a cross on the lawn outside, and set it afire. It was the middle of the night, but the Costens got their children up and dressed them and took them outside to the blaze in the front yard. The hooded K.K.K. men had fled, but the Costens sensed the hatred symbolized in the burning embers. Deeply faithful Christians, the Costens also felt suffering for the Klan members who had made the midnight raid. James Costen most of all wanted to help his children not to hate in return for the hate shown them by the Klan. Dr. Costen did an inspired act. Walking into the kitchen of his house, he found a package of marshmallows and some roasting forks. He handed them to his youngsters, and turned the experience of suffering into a marshmallow roast for his family and the neighbors who had gathered.

This is the way Christians react to experiences of hurt and ostracism! They use the embers of hate and suffering to celebrate Christ's faithfulness.

Life's Value. "The value of life depends not on what happens to us, but on what we make of it, or rather on what we allow God to lead us to make of it. Life is coming to know God in himself and in others, and letting his love for us and for others work through in our lives. It is by this and by nothing else that we can measure either 'value' or 'happiness' in human beings. This growth in holiness, in love for God and for his world, has nothing to do with our physical or mental capacities: the quality of our life depends upon our moral nature."—Michael Keeling, *Morals in a Free Society*, SCM Press, London.

Questions for Pupils on the Next Lesson. 1. Why do we usually try to find reasons for our suffering? 2. Is all suffering caused by wickedness? 3. Do prosperity and success usually lead people to honor God? 4. How do you characterize each of Job's friends who come to console him? 5. Is it fair of God to permit human suffering?

TOPIC FOR YOUTH
WHY ME?

Make Today Count. When Orville Kelly of Burlington, Iowa, heard the doctor's diagnosis after having a tumor removed from his armpit on June 15, 1973, his world collapsed. Kelly was told he had malignant cancer of the lymph glands in an advanced state and that the cancer could be treated but not cured. Orville Kelly went home asking, "Why me?" and feeling full of self-pity and depression. He sulked silently and refused to share his real feelings with his wife Wanda and tried to keep the report of his cancer from his children. Family relationships grew strained. When he concluded that his cancer undoubtedly began when he was exposed to nuclear fallout during A-bomb testing on a Pacific atoll where he was stationed for a year as a sergeant in the army, Kelly grew angrier. Nevertheless, he began a long series of chemotherapy treatments at the University of Iowa Hospital in Iowa City. During this time, he began through his faith to realize that his spiritual and emotional problems were destroying him more than the cancer. He decided he would try to cope by helping others to try to cope.

Kelly, a former newspaper reporter, wrote an article for his local paper to describe how it was to live with cancer. To his surprise, the telephone started ringing nearly nonstop. Kelly proposed to the callers that they get together. In January, 1974, eighteen Burlington people met. They decided to share ideas and problems associated with cancer. They adopted the name, "Make Today Count." Within five years, "Make Today Count" mushroomed to over 200 chapters in the United States, Canada, and Australia.

Orville Kelly could have allowed himself to have been consumed by feelings of being sorry for himself and angry at others and God. Instead, he learned Christ's grace is present. He says, "There are three major therapies for the treatment of cancer: surgery, chemotherapy, and radiotherapy. But there's a fourth therapy which is just as important: tender, loving care. What cancer victims look for is someone to reach out, hold their hands, squeeze their arms. Someone who'll look them in the eye. Someone who cares."

Why Me? Why Not Others? In his poem, *On His Blindness*, John Milton wrote from experience when he said, "They also serve who only stand and wait." From young manhood, Milton dreamed of writing a Christian epic that would make England preeminent in literature. But his numerous involvements kept him from undertaking his masterpiece. Then, in the prime of his life, he became blind. He felt like asking, "Why me?"

The poet felt isolated from the world and as though he were being passed by. But during this time he wrote *Paradise Lost*, acclaimed as one of the world's greatest pieces of literature. So Milton's supreme effort for God and England was accomplished while he was "standing and waiting," rather than during the very active life he had lived before.

Some change or circumstance may cause you to ask why me? And to feel that you are only standing and waiting in your *service* for God, while others, running to and fro, appear to be accomplishing much more for Him. When tempted to compare yourself with others, remember that though "thousands at his bidding speed, and post o'er land and ocean without rest: they also serve who only stand and wait."

Fire-Bombing to Faith. "I always felt that God has a plan and purpose for one's life and you have to pray to find it. God works through people in history to bring about justice," says Coretta Scott King. But it was after she and her first child were alone in their home in 1956 when the house was fire-bombed that she found her faith forged. After the initial anger and hurt and fears, she knew she would have to have a commitment to the Lord which matched her husband's, Martin Luther King, Jr. Coretta Scott King was shaken by the danger of the fire-bombing, and recalls, "I had to do some deep soul-searching about my commitment to the struggle. I knew I would have to be as committed as my husband." Then and there, in earnest prayer, cradling her child outside their blasted bedroom, she made her commitment, "prepared for whatever might take place.

"It ultimately did," she adds of the 1968 assassination of King.

"In faith, you turn to the source in times of stress and there'll always be direction," says Coretta Scott King. "It may not be what you asked for, but it's what God wants you to do."

Questions for Pupils on the Next Lesson. 1. Do you sometimes feel that some adults try to minimize the intensity of your suffering? 2. Why is it often hard to cope with the emotions you feel in the midst of suffering? 3. Does anyone seem to understand you when you experience suffering? 4. Is all suffering caused by human wickedness, either your own or someone else's? 5. Do you ever ask why God permits suffering?

LESSON IX—APRIL 28

FAITH WRESTLES WITH SUFFERING

Background Scripture: Job 20, 21
Devotional Reading: Job 23:1–13

KING JAMES VERSION

JOB 20 Then answered Zophar the Naamathite, and said,

2 Therefore do my thoughts cause me to answer, and for *this* I make haste.

3 I have heard the check of my reproach, and the spirit of my understanding causeth me to answer.

4 Knowest thou *not* this of old, since man was placed upon earth,

5 That the triumphing of the wicked *is* short, and the joy of the hypocrite *but* for a moment?

21 But Job answered and said,

2 Hear diligently my speech, and let this be your consolations.

3 Suffer me that I may speak; and after that I have spoken, mock on.

4 As for me, *is* my complaint to man? and if *it were so*, why should not my spirit be troubled?

5 Mark me, and be astonished, and lay *your* hand upon *your* mouth.

6 Even when I remember I am afraid, and trembling taketh hold on my flesh.

7 Wherefore do the wicked live, become old, yea, are mighty in power?

8 Their seed is established in their sight with them, and their offspring before their eyes.

9 Their houses *are* safe from fear, neither *is* the rod of God upon them.

14 Therefore they say unto God, Depart from us; for we desire not the knowledge of thy ways.

15 What *is* the Almighty, that we should serve him? and what profit should we have, if we pray unto him?

16 Lo, their good *is* not in their hand: the counsel of the wicked is far from me.

REVISED STANDARD VERSION

JOB 20 Then Zophar the Naamathite answered:

2 "Therefore my thoughts answer me, because of my haste within me.

3 I hear censure which insults me, and out of my understanding a spirit answers me.

4 Do you not know this from of old, since man was placed upon earth,

5 that the exulting of the wicked is short, and the joy of the godless but for a moment?"

21 Then Job answered:

2 "Listen carefully to my words, and let this be your consolation.

3 Bear with me, and I will speak, and after I have spoken, mock on.

4 As for me, is my complaint against man? Why should I not be impatient?

5 Look at me, and be appalled, and lay your hand upon your mouth.

6 When I think of it I am dismayed, and shuddering seizes my flesh.

7 Why do the wicked live, reach old age, and grow mighty in power?

8 Their children are established in their presence, and their offspring before their eyes.

9 Their houses are safe from fear, and no rod of God is upon them.

14 They say to God, 'Depart from us! We do not desire the knowledge of thy ways.

15 What is the Almighty, that we should serve him? And what profit do we get if we pray to him?'

16 Behold, is not their prosperity in their hand? The counsel of the wicked is far from me."

KEY VERSE: *Why do the wicked live, reach old age, and grow mighty in power?* Job 21:7 (RSV)

HOME DAILY BIBLE READINGS

Apr.	22.	M.	*How Long, O Lord?* Psalms 6.
Apr.	23.	T.	*A Cry of Despair.* Psalms 38:1–11.
Apr.	24.	W.	*God's Steadfast Love.* Psalms 90:1–4, 9–17.
Apr.	25.	T.	*God Helps the Sufferer.* Psalms 103:1–14.
Apr.	26.	F.	*Whence Comes My Help?* Psalms 121.
Apr.	27.	S.	*Waiting for the Lord.* Psalms 130.
Apr.	28.	S.	*Let Your Heart Take Courage.* Psalms 27.

BACKGROUND

How does a person understand the riddle of existence? How does a human come to terms with the presence of suffering in life?

The Book of Job raises these profound questions through the great drama of a good man enduring a series of catastrophes. Job could have won the approval of the community by accepting his lot without a murmur or by acknowledging some wrongdoing. But he refused. Although Job was a godly man, he would not put on a religious charade. He was a man of integrity.

His first reaction was despair. The irony of the human situation made him question everything. He rejected his "simple faith" in a nice genial deity. He insisted that he had done nothing to merit the suffering which had come to him. Job even reached the point where he gave up on life and on himself; he wished for death. He doubted God's intentions for humans.

Much of the drama of Job comes from the conversations of Job with his three would-be comforters, Eliphaz, Bildad, and Zophar. These three offer windy sermons which fail to give Job any realistic appraisal of his situation or any warmth of human caring. They are champions of traditional or conventional theology, and not easily moved by facts. They are convinced that Job is stubborn as well as sinful. Their speeches merely spur Job to protest his innocence. They also provoke Job into confronting his relationship with God.

There are three rounds of debate between Eliphaz, Bildad, and Zophar, the friends, and Job. In the scriptural material for today's lesson, we hear the end of the second cycle of talks between the friends and Job. The three friends are less sympathetic than in the first series of speeches. They persist in dogmatically asserting their pat beliefs about sin and suffering. There is a perceptible movement from sympathy to suspicion, and from suspicion to condemnation in their remarks to Job. They feel angry because Job has not "confessed."

Job himself is not as bothered by the bitterness of his friends. He has begun to understand that God is still Friend and not Enemy by chapter 20. Job in chapters 20 and 21 is freed to seek an answer to the fact that prosperity and righteousness do not always go together, and that wickedness is not always punished. He begins to understand that there is no clear-cut system of rewards for the good and punishments for the evil.

NOTES ON THE PRINTED TEXT

Of all the three would-be "comforters," Zophar is the least attractive. At least Eliphaz and Bildad try to be consoling. Zophar, however, wraps himself in self-righteousness and harshly tells off Job in each of his three speeches. Even his name in Hebrew can mean "sharp nail" or "twittering bird" or "goatlike jumper."

Zophar the Naamathite: This friend came from Naamah, situated in northwestern Arabia.

I hear censure which insults me: Job has been unreceptive to all the advice and urgings of Eliphaz and Bildad throughout their second series of speeches to Job. Zophar is irritated. He thinks, "What's wrong with this stubborn Job? Why won't he listen? Here we are, trying to help him and he rejects everything we say. If he insults us like this, I'll insult him in return."

Do you not know this from old, since man was placed upon earth, that the exulting of the wicked is short and the joy of the godless but for a moment? Zophar actually has nothing new to say that has not already been said earlier except that he says it more forcibly than the others. His entire speech in chapter 20 is a shrill rerun of the other two speeches. Zophar comes across as the angry shouter who is dogmatic because he is insecure. And he has not tried to listen to Job at all! He does not begin to understand what Job is asking. Zophar never realizes that Job is wrestling with the deep question of why suffering comes to innocent people. All Zophar can do is bellow aphorisms about God always settling the score with the bad people. Making it unmistakably clear that Job is one of those bad people because of his troubles, Zophar offers no help or answers to Job.

Then Job answered: *"Listen carefully to my words, and let this be your consolation. Bear with me, and I will speak, and after I have spoken, mock on:* Job realizes that none of his friends have begun to grasp what he is experiencing, but pleads with them to try to understand. If they would only shut up and listen for a while, he'd try to tell them what bothers him, then let them resume their mocking if they insist.

As for me, is my complaint against man? Job states that his quarrel is not with his friends but with God! Job wants to "have it out" with the Lord! If Eliphaz, Bildad, and Zophar could only comprehend this, Job says, then perhaps they'd let up on their accusations.

Look at me, and be appalled, and lay your hand upon your mouth. When I think about it I am dismayed, and shuddering seizes my flesh: Job warns his three friends to brace themselves for a real blockbuster of a statement. They haven't heard anything so far as shocking as what he is going to tell them now.

Why do the wicked live, reach old age, and grow mighty in power? Their children are established in their presence, and their offspring before their eyes. Their houses are safe from fear, and no rod of God is upon them: Here is Job's question that no one has taken seriously. "Why do the wicked live?" Why do evil people get away with murder? Job spells out the human scene: rotten, godless persons enjoying a long and prosperous life, surrounded by family and unconcerned about God or punishment. Why? Job asks how Zophar can talk about the "joy of the godless (being) but for a moment"? All human experience points to exactly the opposite conclusion, namely that bad people often seem to have everything going for them in this world. It's especially galling to Job, who has lost all of his children and misses the joy of family gatherings, to see evil people having the happiness of sons, daughters, and grandchildren nearby.

Job continues to state how notoriously evil people in the community sing and dance their way through life, grow fat and rich, romp with their little ones, and even mock God! It's one thing to have an easy time of it in life. But it's another matter to sneer at the Almighty as these wicked are doing.

"They say to God, 'Depart from us! We do not desire the knowledge of thy ways. What is the Almighty that we should serve him? And what profit do we get if we pray to him?' ": What's the point of living a responsible life before God, Job asks, when these evildoers are flaunting their wickedness and insulting God? What's the use of praying and trusting in God's goodness in the light of the way so many wealthy, successful and happy people go out of their way to offend God? It apparently does not pay to be religious!

Job, the man of faith, wrestles with the inescapable facts that frequently good people experience terrible suffering and despicable people have any easy time of it. Job finds there is no simple answer to this theological problem. We Christians are finally driven to look at the person of Jesus on the Cross. In this good man suffering, we gain the understanding that Job—and everyone who wrestles with suffering—seeks.

SUGGESTIONS TO TEACHERS

"Why?"
Job shakes his fist toward heaven and demands of God, "Why?" So does every person who has lost a loved one, who has experienced an undeserved setback, who has throbbed with pain.

These lessons on faith and suffering get deep inside a person to the aching areas of human experience. Some in your class may find the topic too sensitive to talk about. Others may dismiss the subject with simplistic "answers." Between the grim and glib, others may simply be confused. Everyone, however, asks the question, *"Why?"* when suffering comes. Start your lesson by assuring everyone that it is perfectly okay to raise the question, "Why?" Remind the class that Jesus on the Cross asked the same question.

1. *"WHY SHOULD I NOT BE IMPATIENT?"* (Job 21:4). Job hears one comforter, Zophar, tell him that suffering means that God is balancing His books and Job has obviously been guilty of a lot of secret sins. Job impatiently tries to tell Zophar that he has nothing to confess. This part of your lesson should go into the issue of whether God pays back people for sinning by sending suffering. Job insists that the righteous also suffer.

2. *"WHY DO THE WICKED LIVE, REACH OLD AGE, AND GROW MIGHTY IN POWER?"* (Job 21:7). In this question, you and your class must face up to the question of whether or not there is any justice in the universe. Read the eloquent and poignant way Job puts this question to God (*see* 21:7–16). Why do the evil people seem to be able to get away with flaunting God and all morality? Through this part of the discussion as well as throughout the entire lesson, you will find that you will not necessarily come up with pat reasons. But don't worry about it. The best thing you can do is to keep pointing your people to the Cross. On Calvary, the mystery of evil and suffering is answered not by slick solutions but by the sacrificing Savior. God is involved in our hurting. And love is poured out!

3. *WHY DO SOME CLAIM THAT A DAY OF RECKONING WILL COME TO A LATER GENERATION?* (*see* 21:19–20). Shouldn't each person be responsible for his own sins? You will also want to have your class wrestle with the problem of personal responsibility and the accompanying issue of social and long-term effects of our sinning. Job, told that he is paying for his ancestors' sins, claims that each person should be held accountable.

4. *WHY BOTHER?* Job wonders what is the point of life since both the prosperous and the paupers alike end up in the grave. You are undoubtedly aware that many—especially among the young—are saying this in these times. Discuss this weighty question in your class by asking for what each person is living.

TOPIC FOR ADULTS
FAITH WRESTLES WITH SUFFERING

When a Five-Year-Old Wrestled With Suffering. " 'Your father's dead,' he said.
"It was like an accusation that my father had done something vile and criminal, and I came to my father's defense.
" 'He is not,' I said.
"But, of course, they didn't know the situation. I started to explain. He was sick. In the hospital. My mother was bringing him home right now. . . .
" 'He's dead,' Kenneth said.
"His assurance slid an icicle into my heart.
" 'He is not either!' " I shouted.
" 'He is too,' Ruth Lee said. 'They want you to come home right away.'
"I started running up the road screaming, 'He is not!'
"It was a weak argument. They had the evidence and gave it to me as I hurried home crying, 'He is not. . . . He is not. . . . He is not. . . .'
"I was certain before I got there that he was.
"And I was right. Arriving at the hospital that morning, my mother was told he had died at 4 A.M. in 'acute diabetic coma.' He was thirty-three years old.

"When I came running home, my mother was still not back from Frederick, but the women had descended on our house, as women there did in such times, and were already busy with the ritual housecleaning and cooking that was Morrisonville's instinctual response to death. With a thousand tasks to do, they had no time to handle a howling five-year-old; I was sent to the opposite end of town, to Bessie Scott's house.

"Poor Bessie Scott. All afternoon she listened, patiently as a saint, while I sat in her kitchen and cried myself out. For the first time, I thought seriously about God. Between sobs, I told Bessie that if God could do things like this to people, then God was hateful and I had no more use for Him.

"Bessie told me about the peace of heaven and the joy of being among the angels and the happiness of my father, who was already there. This argument failed to quiet my rage.

" 'God loves us all just like His own children,' Bessie said.

" 'If God loves me, why did He make my father die?'

"Bessie said I would understand someday, but she was only partly right. That afternoon, though I couldn't have phrased it this way then, I decided God was a lot less interested in people than anybody in Morrisonville was willing to admit. That day, I decided God was not entirely to be trusted.

"After that, I never cried again with any real conviction, nor expected much of anyone's God except indifference, nor loved deeply without fearing it would cost me dearly in pain. At the age of five, I had become a skeptic and began to sense that any happiness coming my way might be the prelude to some grim cosmic joke."—Russell Baker, "Memoir of a Small Town Boyhood," New York Times Magazine, September 12, 1982. © 1982 by the New York Times Company. Reprinted by permission.

The God Who Wrestles With Suffering With Us. "Jesus Christ stood at the center of life. God and man met in him. As the *Son of man,* mankind suffered in him; and as Son of God, God suffered in him. In this synthesis of suffering the lower life is raised by the higher life taking on itself the burdens and suffering and sins of the lower.

"But the Hindu and the Moslem find here a difficulty. A leading Mohammedan college principal put it this way: 'A God who would stoop and suffer is not perfect.' And a Hindu put it this way: 'If Brahma would suffer, he would be unhappy; and if he were unhappy, he would be imperfect; and if he were imperfect, he would not be God.' This is the crux of the Non-Christian difficulty. Is it not based on a superficial view of life? For the most miserable people are those who are self-centered and who refuse to do anything for others at a cost to themselves. The most joyous people on earth are those who are helping others through self-sacrifice. 'There is nothing so absolutely blessed as to suffer well.' A God who would sit apart from the tragedy of life and would refuse to bear the pains of his children upon his own heart would be a God miserable and unhappy. He would know nothing of the joy of redemption at cost."—E. Stanley Jones, *Christ at the Round Table.*

Friends Who Comfort. Job's friends never comforted him because they never took his wrestling with suffering seriously. They did not try to listen. They did not pray with him or cry with him.

In the midst of the civil rights strife in the '60s, a young minister in a small Southern town was being castigated by several of his elders for his stand on racial integration.

The argument was stopped cold when the oldest member of the church board spoke up. "You are not going to talk about our minister in this fashion. I do not agree with all he says and advocates, but I know this: I would have lost my mind the night my wife died if that young man of God had not been there to walk the floor with me all night, praying or keeping silent as I indicated the need." The pastor stayed several years longer.

Questions for Pupils on the Next Lesson. 1. What happened to Job when he tried to exalt himself at God's expense? 2. Why is it so hard to acknowledge God's supremacy? 3. Why do some people abandon their value system in the face of suffering? 4. How do you try to deal creatively with personal suffering? 5. How may personal experience of God through Jesus Christ change your attitude toward suffering?

TOPIC FOR YOUTH
HOW DID THIS HAPPEN?

Whose Fault? The little blonde girl born to Benjamin and Diana Chappell in Summerhill, Pennsylvania, in 1980 was normal in every way except for her skin. Her name is Shawna Chappell.

Shawna was born with "an alligator hide" for skin, the victim of a rare disease that leaves thick, crusty scales over most of the body. Doctors predict the incurable illness will worsen with age. Shawna suffers from one of the rarest forms of ichthyosis, more commonly known as fish-skin disease because of the skin's dry, rough, and scaly surface. She waddles so her scaly scarred legs won't touch, crumbling her skin and exposing sensitive flesh. She touches with her fingers but not with her crusty hands. She's never known what it's like to hug or be hugged.

The bright-eyed little blonde's condition has deteriorated. Although the disease itself is not fatal, victims are susceptible to life-threatening infections because of the frequently exposed flesh.

Shawna has been given a stronger antibiotic to fight infection, and she must exercise daily in hopes of developing arches in her feet.

Worst of all, however, the scabby patches of sores have spread—they now partially cover her palms and feet, further limiting her movement.

The Chappells have received many letters. Some contained medical suggestions—none of which helped when tried. Some contained money to help with Shawna's bills.

Not all the mail has been kind, however.

"Some people got kind of rude as if we were the fault that this happened to Shawna. Like as if we did something evil," Mrs. Chappell said.

The Chappells are trying to cope with the heavy expenses of caring for their daughter, and also handle the negative comments of those who tell them that it's their fault that Shawna suffers from fish-skin disease. Diana and Ben Chappell sometimes find it hard when people call or write that they are being punished or that they must have done something evil.

God, however, loves little Shawna and her Daddy and Mommy and assures them through Jesus Christ that He never sends torture to *anyone!*

Act of Nature. "I remember the day after a tornado had hit Cleveland, Ohio, that I was riding with a funeral director to a committal service and he beamed as he said, 'God certainly got people's attention yesterday when he sent that tornado into Cleveland. That will get them back on their knees.' One of the tragedies in that tornado was a tiny baby in a carriage caught up in the churning tornado's tail and never seen again. Insurance companies say that when an earthquake takes place that such an event is 'an act of God.' I say that such a statement is taking the name of God in vain. Better to say that it was 'an act of nature.' "—W. E. Goist.

Surviving Suffering. During World War II, Ernest Gordon was captured by the Japanese Army and spent three years as a Prisoner of War working on the infamous "Death Railway" through northern Thailand. Thousands of Allied prisoners perished from disease and exhaustion. The suffering around them made many men lose the will to live. Gordon describes the experience:

"Dying was easy. When our desires are thwarted and life becomes too much for us, it is easy to reject life and the pain it brings, easier to die than to live. It is an easy thing to adopt a philosophy of despair: to say, 'I mean nothing; there is nothing; nothing matters; I live only to die.'

"Those who decided they had no further reason for living, pulled down the shades and quietly expired. I knew a man who had amoebic dysentery. Compared to the rest of us, he was in good condition. But he convinced himself that he could not possibly survive and he did not. An Allied naval lieutenant reached the point where he could no longer endure his misery and tried to commit suicide. He did not succeed in his attempt, but died shortly afterward with nothing wrong with him; he died from failure of his will to live."—From p. 63 in *Through the Valley of the Kwai* by Ernest Gordon. Copyright © 1962 by Ernest Gordon. By permission of Harper & Row, Publishers, Inc.

In the midst of suffering, however, the Living Christ gives despairing people new hope! Gordon himself and others learned this.

Questions for Pupils on the Next Lesson. 1. How did Job's own personal experience with God change his outlook toward suffering? 2. Why did Job in spite of undeserved suffering refuse to abandon his trust in God? 3. Do you sometimes experience difficulty in living with unanswered questions about suffering? 4. How do you react to the popular or simplistic answers some people offer to those who are suffering?

LESSON X—MAY 5

FAITH IN SPITE OF SUFFERING

Background Scripture: Job 40:1–42:6
Devotional Reading: Job 34:10–28

KING JAMES VERSION

JOB 40 Moreover the LORD answered Job, and said,

2 Shall he that contendeth with the Almighty instruct *him?* he that reproveth God, let him answer it.

3 Then Job answered the LORD, and said,

4 Behold, I am vile; what shall I answer thee? I will lay mine hand upon my mouth.

5 Once have I spoken; but I will not answer; yea, twice; but I will proceed no further.

6 Then answered the LORD unto Job out of the whirlwind, and said,

7 Gird up thy loins now like a man: I will demand of thee, and declare thou unto me.

8 Wilt thou also disannul my judgment? wilt thou condemn me, that thou mayest be righteous?

9 Hast thou an arm like God? or canst thou thunder with a voice like him?

42 Then Job answered the LORD, and said,

2 I know that thou canst do every *thing*, and *that* no thought can be withholden from thee.

3 Who *is* he that hideth counsel without knowledge? therefore have I uttered that I understood not; things too wonderful for me, which I knew not.

4 Hear, I beseech thee, and I will speak: I will demand of thee, and declare thou unto me.

5 I have heard of thee by the hearing of the ear: but now mine eye seeth thee.

6 Wherefore I abhor *myself*, and repent in dust and ashes.

REVISED STANDARD VERSION

JOB 40 And the LORD said to Job:

2 "Shall a faultfinder contend with the Almighty?
He who argues with God, let him answer it."

3 Then Job answered the LORD:

4 "Behold, I am of small account; what shall I answer thee?
I lay my hand on my mouth.

5 I have spoken once, and I will not answer; twice, but I will proceed no further."

6 Then the LORD answered Job out of the whirlwind:

7 "Gird up your loins like a man;
I will question you, and you declare to me.

8 Will you even put me in the wrong?
Will you condemn me that you may be justified?

9 Have you an arm like God,
and can you thunder with a voice like his?

42 Then Job answered the LORD:

2 "I know that thou canst do all things.
and that no purpose of thine can be thwarted.

3 'Who is this that hides counsel without knowledge?'
Therefore I have uttered what I did not understand,
things too wonderful for me, which I did not know.

4 'Hear, and I will speak;
I will question you, and you declare to me.'

5 I had heard of thee by the hearing of the ear,
but now my eye sees thee;

6 therefore I despise myself,
and repent in dust and ashes."

KEY VERSE: *I had heard of thee by the hearing of the ear, but now my eye sees thee.* Job 42:5 (RSV).

HOME DAILY BIBLE READINGS

Apr.	29.	M.	*Remembering Better Days.* Job 29:1–13.
Apr.	30.	T.	*Encounter With God.* Job 40:1–14.
May	1.	W.	*A Change of Attitude.* Job 42:1–6.
May	2.	T.	*God Answers Prayer.* Matthew 7:7–12.
May	3.	F.	*God's Concern for Us.* Luke 15:11–24.
May	4.	S.	*Seek Heavenly Things.* Colossians 3:1–4.
May	5.	S.	*A Vision of the Future.* Revelation 21:1–4; 22:1–5.

BACKGROUND

Job's problem is not so much philosophizing abstractly about why bad things happen to good people—it is more of a demand to know what life is all about. About the time the anonymous poet was writing the drama of the dialogues in the Book of Job, the world of the people of Judea had crumbled. Many were asking the meaning of life with God. At the end of the upheaval, many scattered Hebrews abandoned their faith. The dark riddle of human existence led to despair.

The author, borrowing a case history of ancient literature showing the shock of adversity striking a good person, tries to scrutinize the human situation at its worst. Job protests against stuffy orthodoxy and revolts against institutionalized religion in his exchanges with the three "comforters."

The author holds off until near the end of the book to disclose his purpose: the divinity of God and the humanity of a human, or the relationship between the Lord who is truly God and a man who is truly human.

Job is an "essential man." He has correct relationships at the start with God, with family, with others. He is pious. He is respected. He has achieved success and acquired wealth. The perfect man who can bless God becomes a person who disintegrates to the point of cursing his own life. He suffers. Bereft of everything including love, destitute, isolated and ostracized, estranged even from God, Job nevertheless cannot quite dismiss God from his world. His agony and residual sense of the Divine make him veer between denial and affirmation, doubt and certainty, revolt and acceptance, struggle against God and acceptance of God, flight from the Lord and turning toward the Lord.

Job finally comes to realize that when he tries to justify his ways, it leads him to condemn God's ways. A human trespasses the limits of his or her own humanity whenever he or she presumes to judge God's character. Nevertheless, God does not condemn Job or any human! More extraordinary, God never censures Job for his theological errors or puts down Job for his questions. Our God is not ever an Olympian Zeus. And Job is not a Prometheus.

NOTES ON THE PRINTED TEXT

Job has doubted the righteousness of God, yet at the same time he has recognized that righteousness since he has made claims on it. Yet Job persists in condemning God and reducing God to human size in his effort to justify himself. He thinks of divine justice not in relation to God and the world but to himself. In other words, Job makes the mistake of imagining that the universe centers on Job rather than on God!

Chapter 40 opens God's second discourse to Job.

And the Lord said to Job: "Shall a faultfinder contend with the Almighty?" God reminds Job that Job is not God's equal. But God is doing more than putting Job in his place for daring to try to question God's providence. God is urging Job to turn away from himself and to start to see that God is involved in all the mystery of the universe. God wants Job to behold the revelation of God's wisdom and power, but, more important, also to behold the revelation of God's love.

Then Job answered the Lord: "Behold, I am of small account; what shall I answer thee?": The word in Hebrew means literally "I am light or insignificant." Job is beginning to recognize his proper place in the universe. He is becoming aware of his foolishness in judging God.

"I lay my hand on my mouth. I have spoken once, and I will not answer; twice, but I will proceed no further": Job finally realizes that it is time for him to remain silent. But God renews the challenge.

Then God answered Job out of the whirlwind: "Gird up your loins like a man: I will question you, and you declare to me. Will you even put me in the wrong?

Will you condemn me that you may be justified?" Job's silence is not deemed sufficient. Job still does not see in the irony of human existence the irony of God's love! God insists that He does not disclose Himself to humans in order to offer excuses for Himself. In fact, God will not discuss the mystery of human suffering. He offers no explanations. He does not need to justify Himself. The heart of the Book of Job's message is that humans are justified by their faithfulness to God.

Then Job answered the Lord: "I know that thou canst do all things, and no purpose of thine can be thwarted. 'Who is this that hides counsel without knowledge?'": Job acknowledges God's great power. He also recognizes God's great wisdom. God has a purpose threading throughout all human affairs. Life is not a random series of sick jokes. Job repeats the words, "Who is this that darkens counsel without knowledge?" which God had directed at him earlier (38:2) and acknowledges that God deserves to ask this question. Job confesses his rash words have not helped him to understand God's ways.

"Hear, and I will speak; I will question you and you declare to me": Job repeats this question which God had put to him earlier on two occasions (38:3 and 40:7). He humbly says he cannot accept God's challenge because he is ignorant and has been presumptuous. He had come to challenge and complain but now realizes how puny and silly he has been.

I had heard of thee by the hearing of the ear, but now my eye sees thee: Formerly, Job's belief had been by hearsay. It had been intellectual stuff only. His knowledge of God was secondhand. Therefore, it had been confused and defective. Based on hearsay, it had not been helpful or satisfying. Now, however, Job's new-found sense of God's presence means he has a faith based on experience. Job has progressed from what may be called "the mediacy of belief" to the "immediacy of faith."

Job now no longer needs to scream his questions at others or at God. He recognizes that God is not putting questions to him. Life finds fulfillment when a person is not so much aware of his ultimate concern as he is the concern of the Ultimate. The orphan discovers the heart of the Father. God's lonely person is welcomed into a relationship with the Lord. The derelict in the universe learns he has a home.

Job never solves the riddle of human suffering. God fails to give neat "answers." Job never learns why he suffers but his ignorance does not torture him. He does not need to know. He has the Lord. And that is enough!

SUGGESTIONS TO TEACHERS

One of the greatest teachers I have known was a woman whose formal education had stopped in the tenth grade, but whose learning the meaning of faith continued through a long, difficult life. She knew disappointment; she never had been able to finish high school or go on to college. She knew grief; she lost a son in World War II and her husband in a railroad accident shortly before the war. She knew hardship; she and her children barely made ends meet and went without luxuries. She knew pain; she contracted a crippling form of arthritis hunching over a sewing machine too many hours each night to earn extra income. But she also knew what real faith is. As she put it, "Faith always goes with the words *'In spite of.'"* She was saying that she continued to trust the Lord *in spite of* her disappointments, in spite of her grief, in spite of her hardships, in spite of her pain.

Can you? How about the members of your class?

This is the fundamental question of today's lesson. Can we believe in spite of whatever may happen to us? And this is what Job finally comes to understand about faith. He trusts God in spite of . . . *anything!* Look again at Job 40–42, then trace Job's growth in faith.

1. *FROM DOUBT TO TRUST.* Job finally comes to the place where he can honor God again. "I know," Job humbly states, "thou canst do all things and no purpose of thine can be thwarted" (42:1,2). What a magnificent prayer! Are your class members able to say this to the Lord in the midst of suffering?

2. *FROM PRIDE TO HUMILITY.* "I have uttered what I did not understand, things too wonderful for me, which I did not know" (42:3), Job confesses to God. Note that throughout this soliloquy, Job in effect is on his knees. Only then is he receiving insights into the meaning of his suffering. Only when he adopts an "In spite of" form of trust does Job discover that God has been with him all along! Assist your people to understand this by suggesting that each person tell another the roughest experience he or she ever went through but how, looking back on it, he or she now realizes God was also present.

3. *FROM HEARSAY TO CERTAINTY.* When the "In spite of" quality of faith is present, a firsthand knowledge of God grows. Job finally quietly acknowledges to the Lord, "I had heard of thee by the hearing of the ear, but now my eye sees thee" (42:5). Nudge your class to a deeper understanding of this by sharing something of your own faith journey. As teacher, you have had occasions even in the times of tears and hurts when you moved from a religion of hearsay to personal certainty.

4. *FROM ARROGANCE TO REPENTANCE.* Job's story ends with Job accepting humbly and gratefully the presence of the Lord and repenting for his previous arrogance. So also must conclude the story of every believer!

TOPIC FOR ADULTS
FAITH IN SPITE OF SUFFERING

To God the Companion. God answered Job. But not the way Job expected . . . or wanted. God lets Job know that He is still God. God makes certain that Job understands that he is not God's equal, and that Job is still a human.

God primarily lets Job know that he is not alone. God is there, too. God does not give answers to Job. He gives Job His Presence.

Now Job is content. God being what Job knows Him to be, Job can trust that God will arrange a solution for anything. Job, calm and satisfied with knowing God is present, speaks, "I had heard of thee by the hearing of my ear; now my eye hath seen thee!" (42:5). Job has moved from a hearsay understanding of God to a personal awareness of The Presence.

Alfred North Whitehead, the English philosopher-theologian, experienced the same pilgrimage when he came to terms with the loss of his eighteen-year-old son, Eric, in action in France in March, 1918. "It runs through three stages, if it evolves to its final satisfaction," Whitehead wrote later; "It is the transition from God the void to God the enemy, and from God the enemy to God the companion."

Job made the transition from God the void to God the enemy, and from God the enemy to God the companion. With The Companion, Job had everything and everyone.

Job's questions had not been answered by God. But Job didn't mind. Job's pain continued. The enigma of existence remained. But back of the enigma and in the midst of the pain, in the depths of his heart, Job sensed the evident presence and stunning might of the Lord. Job, the tortured questioner, could leave his unresolved doubts and unanswered problems, and was firmer in his faith than his narrowly orthodox friends.

Crippled Confidence. Some bystanders watched a one-legged veteran painfully drag himself up the steps to a chapel. As the cripple clumsily worked himself toward the door, one onlooker cynically commented, "What's he expect—that God will grow him a new leg?"

Overhearing, the man without a leg turned and replied, "He always gives me enough to get along with the one I have."

Job learned this about God.

And so may we!

God has identified with us. He drew near, face to face, with all of us through that unique Personality of the Cross and the empty tomb. Through Jesus Christ, God does not give us answers to our jillion angry questions. He does not offer explanations. He does not deliver doctrines. He does not pose solutions. He gives us better. He presents Himself!

Ministry of Presence. We present-day Jobs also are promised God's sufficiency. We, too, discover that He gives more than answers to our whimpering "Why?". He shares His life with us. And, in turn, He means for us to represent His presence to each other and to those who are afflicted in any way.

A hopelessly ill woman, twisted and shrivelled from years of suffering from deterioration of her spine, sentenced to a bed in an enormous ward of a state institution for incurables, sometimes had a visitor from her church. Other patients scoffed. "What's your church friend say to you that's so great, Martha?" one sneered one afternoon after the visitor left.

"Oh, nothing. Nothing at all, really," replied Martha from her bed; "She just comes, and she sits with me, and sometimes she cries with me."

The world around us does not need more advice. Or "answers." Or "solutions." Or "explanations." We don't have much in the way of advice or answers or solutions or explanations anyhow. Besides, everyone has heard enough.

We can give our presence. We can make incarnate now the concern which God has directed toward us. Without presuming to be God's proxy, we can provide God's kind of care. Through our nearness, others may make the Job-transition from God the void or God the enemy to God the Companion!

Questions for Pupils on the Next Lesson. 1. Who is the ultimate judge of people's attitudes and actions? 2. What is the best way to find meaning and purpose in life, according to Ecclesiastes? 3. How would you characterize the value system of our society? 4. What were some of the sources of satisfaction in life that Ecclesiastes tried and found inadequate? 5. Where do you find the greatest fulfillment in life?

TOPIC FOR YOUTH
WHERE DO I GO FROM HERE?

The Suffering One. The letterhead of a society purporting to study all the religions of mankind carries representations of the leaders of the major faiths. Across the top of each sheet of the official stationery is a picture of each founder, each in a characteristic pose. Some are teaching. Some are orating. Some are meditating, some praying. Some are studying. Only One is suffering. Only One is sacrificing His life.

Only One discloses completely what Job painfully surmised: God is present. God did not clear His throat and propound a weighty and witty philosophical discourse on the problem of evil and suffering. Through the suffering and risen Christ, He communicates Self!

Christians: Extraordinary People. "For Christians are not differentiated from other people by country, language, or customs; you see, they do not live in cities of their own, or speak some strange dialect, or have some peculiar lifestyle.

"This teaching of theirs has not been contrived by the invention and speculation of inquisitive men; nor are they propagating mere human teaching as some people do. They live in both Greek and foreign cities, wherever chance has put them. They follow local customs in clothing, food, and the other aspects of life. But at the same time they demonstrate to us the wonderful and certainly unusual form of their own citizenship.

"They live in their own native lands, but as aliens; as citizens, they share all things with others; but like aliens, suffer all things. Every foreign country is to them as their native country, and every native land as a foreign country.

"They marry and have children just like every one else; but they do not kill unwanted babies. They offer a shared table, but not a shared bed. They are at present 'in the flesh' but they do not live 'according to the flesh.' They are passing their days on earth, but are citizens of heaven. They obey the appointed laws, and go beyond the laws in their own lives.

"They love everyone, but are persecuted by all. They are unknown and condemned; they are put to death and gain life. They are poor and yet make many rich. They are short of everything and yet have plenty of all things. They are dishonored and yet gain glory through dishonor.

"Their names are blackened and yet they are cleared. They are mocked and bless in return. They are treated outrageously and behave respectfully to others. When they do good, they are punished as evildoers; when punished, they rejoice as if being given new life. They are attacked by Jews as aliens, and are persecuted by Greeks; yet those who hate them cannot give any reason for their hostility.

"To put it simply— the soul is to the body as Christians are to the world. The soul is spread through all parts of the body and Christians through all the cities of the world. The soul is in the body but is not of the body; Christians are in the world but not of the world."—From an anonymous *Letter to Diognetus,* possibly dating from the second century.

Where Do I Go From Here? Here are a few one-liners which may give some clues:

"There comes a time when we must make friends with God, or we shall have no friend at all."—Eugene O'Neill.

"Our real business is business with God."—John Calvin.

"God's mercy is an odd sort of mercy; it sometimes looks like a punishment."—Graham Greene.

Questions for Pupils on the Next Lesson. 1. What, according to Ecclesiastes, is the most fulfilling way of living? 2. What were some of the ways that Ecclesiastes sought meaning and satisfaction in life? 3. What do you think is the clue to finding purpose and significance to your life? 4. Who is the final judge of your attitudes and actions? 5. Why is our value system of affluent living ultimately empty and useless?

LESSON XI—MAY 12

COPING WITH FUTILITY

Background Scripture: Ecclesiastes 1:1–2:11; 12
Devotional Reading: Ecclesiastes 7:1–13

KING JAMES VERSION

ECCLESIASTES 2 I said in mine heart, Go to now, I will prove thee with mirth; therefore enjoy pleasure: and, behold, this also *is* vanity.

2 I said of laughter, *It is* mad; and of mirth, What doeth it?

3 I sought in mine heart to give myself unto wine, yet acquainting mine heart with wisdom; and to lay hold on folly, till I might see what *was* that good for the sons of men, which they should do under the heaven all the days of their life.

4 I made me great works; I builded me houses; I planted me vineyards:

5 I made me gardens and orchards, and I planted trees in them of all *kind of* fruits:

6 I made me pools of water, to water therewith the wood that bringeth forth trees;

7 I got *me* servants and maidens, and had servants born in my house; also I had great possessions of great and small cattle above all that were in Jerusalem before me:

8 I gathered me also silver and gold, and the peculiar treasure of kings and of the provinces: I gat me men singers and women singers, and the delights of the sons of men, *as* musical instruments, and that of all sorts.

9 So I was great, and increased more than all that were before me in Jerusalem: also my wisdom remained with me.

10 And whatsoever mine eyes desired I kept not from them, I withheld not my heart from any joy; for my heart rejoiced in all my labour: and this was my portion of all my labour.

11 Then I looked on all the works that my hands had wrought, and on the labour that I had laboured to do: and, behold, all *was* vanity and vexation of spirit, and *there was* no profit under the sun.

12 13 Let us hear the conclusion of the whole matter: Fear God, and keep his commandments: for this *is* the whole *duty* of man.

14 For God shall bring every work into judgment, with every secret thing, whether *it be* good, or whether *it be* evil.

REVISED STANDARD VERSION

ECCLESIASTES 2 I said to myself, "Come now, I will make a test of pleasure; enjoy yourself." But behold, this also was vanity. 2 I said of laughter, "It is mad," and of pleasure, "What use is it?" 3 I searched with my mind how to cheer my body with wine—my mind still guiding me with wisdom—and how to lay hold on folly, till I might see what was good for the sons of men to do under heaven during the few days of their life. 4 I made great works; I built houses and planted vineyards for myself; 5 I made myself gardens and parks, and planted in them all kinds of fruit trees. 6 I made myself pools from which to water the forest of growing trees. 7 I bought male and female slaves, and had slaves who were born in my house; I had also great possessions of herds and flocks, more than any who had been before me in Jerusalem. 8 I also gathered for myself silver and gold and the treasure of kings and provinces; I got singers, both men and women, and many concubines, man's delight.

9 So I became great and surpassed all who were before me in Jerusalem; also my wisdom remained with me. 10 And whatever my eyes desired I did not keep from them; I kept my heart from no pleasure, for my heart found pleasure in all my toil, and this was my reward for all my toil. 11 Then I considered all that my hands had done and the toil I had spent in doing it, and behold, all was vanity and a striving after wind, and there was nothing to be gained under the sun.

12 13 The end of the matter; all has been heard. Fear God, and keep his commandments; for this is the whole duty of man. 14 For God will bring every deed into judgment, with every secret thing, whether good or evil.

KEY VERSE: *Fear God, and keep his commandments; for this is the whole duty of man.* Ecclesiastes 12:13 (RSV).

HOME DAILY BIBLE READINGS

May	6.	M.	*A Sense of Futility.* Ecclesiastes 1:1–11.
May	7.	T.	*No Pleasure in Riches.* Ecclesiastes 2:1–11.
May	8.	W.	*Enjoyment in Work.* Ecclesiastes 2:18–26.
May	9.	T.	*A Time for Everything.* Ecclesiastes 3:1–13.

May 10. *F.*   *Wisdom Is Better Than Might.* Ecclesiastes 9:9–16.
May 11. *S.*   *Advice for Good Living.* Ecclesiastes 11.
May 12. *S.*   *Reverence and Obedience.* Ecclesiastes 12.

BACKGROUND

Ecclesiastes is the Latin translation of a Greek rendering for a Hebrew word, *Koheleth,* meaning literally "one who speaks in an assembly." In other words, the title of the book stands for "preacher," not for a particular human's name. But what a preacher!

He probably lived around the third century B.C. at a time when Judaism had ossified into "religion." Many of his contemporaries were saying something like this: "We are wise and good people, therefore we must be godly people. We scrupulously observe the rules and follow the rituals of our religion, therefore we are of the Lord."

"Ecclesiastes" or *Koheleth* or, as we will call him, the Preacher, was a lot wiser than these so-called wise people. Gathering his students around him, the Preacher said in so many words, "So wise and good? So what? But we'll all die anyhow. Godly? But how godly?" He was a gadfly to the Establishment. His critiques of the popular goals and ideals such as making money and having a good time were devastating. Many dismissed him as a crank and a cynic. After all, who wants someone telling the country-club set that "all is vanity and a striving after wind" (1:14)?

Many modern readers also dismiss the Preacher as a pessimist when they first hear his words. Some even ask how this writer, apparently so bitter and disappointed with life, could have had his words included in the Bible. Careful reading, however, will show that this ancient skeptic is speaking about the vanity and foolishness of humans and facing the cold, harsh realities of human existence in the light of God's ultimate control over everything. The tough-minded Preacher is a healthy antidote to the frothy, aphoristic "Mary Poppins" religion of his time—or any time. He scorns the rationalizations, the shallow answers, the self-justifications, the cute sayings, the collections of regulations that some people try to label *faith.* With ruthless candor, the Preacher sweeps away the platitudes and piety and points to the deepest truth about life and the mystery of God.

NOTES ON THE PRINTED TEXT

The Preacher takes his readers through a search for satisfaction in life in chapters 1:12 through 11:6. All of the ideals which people hold up as "good" are examined, including knowledge, pleasure, rule-book religion, accomplishments, and various combinations of these. The popular proofs and sayings of each of these sources of satisfaction are carefully spelled out. In each case, however, regardless of how appealing each may be, it is shown to end in failure. The Preacher ruthlessly and methodically shows that any of these, if pursued as the clue to ultimate meaning in life, will end in a sense of futility.

I said to myself, "Come now, I will make a test of pleasure": The Preacher turns his attention toward pleasure as the source of deepest satisfaction for living. He announces he will "make a test" or experiment with having a good time. The verses that follow almost read like a catalogue of varieties of pleasure. Some are sensual. Some are subtle. Some are not regarded as "evil" in themselves. In fact, some of these categories of pleasure are superrefined forms of selfishness that often are paraded as virtues. Other kinds of pleasure noted in the Preacher's list are examples of plain, old-fashioned hedonism.

". . . a test of pleasure: Enjoy yourself": Here is the bottom line for this ideal for life. "Enjoy yourself." Self-gratification, the Preacher says, is what this notion is all about, regardless of the name it may take. "Enjoy yourself!" Sounds as if it's

from a 1985 magazine ad, doesn't it? Or from a pop-psychology lecturer. Whether 250 B.C. or the last part of the twentieth century A.D., the words purr with appeal!

But behold, this also was vanity. I said of laughter, "It is mad," and of pleasure, "What use is it?": The Preacher warns that even the unrestrained pleasure seeking of a king with Solomon's wealth and power may provide enjoyment for the moment but will have no lasting value.

I made great works: I built houses and planted vineyards for myself: The key words here are "for myself." There is nothing inherently wrong with building or planting, but when it is merely for one's own pleasure, it eventually becomes an obsession. And ultimately, such selfishness is destructive.

Building and planting "for myself" are, of course, an attempt to find security in things and in achievements.

I made myself gardens and parks, and planted in them all kinds of fruit trees: The Hebrew word here for *parks* is the cognate for our English word *paradise*. It comes from the Persians, who were masters at the art of laying out magnificent estates of incredible beauty and splendor. Obviously, only a fabulously rich person could afford such luxury. Such idyllic layouts require a huge outlay of money and the constant attention of an enormous retinue of gardeners, repairmen, and other staff for their upkeep. However, these paradises brought their owners the satisfaction of being able to point to proof of their wealth and success. Other people would admire those magnificent estates and congratulate the builders for achieving so much.

I had also great possessions of herds and flocks, more than any who had been before me in Jerusalem. I also gathered for myself silver and gold and the treasure of kings and provinces: The Preacher lets his imagination run free, and supposes that he is richer than Solomon and can satisfy every whim that money can buy.

I got ... concubines, man's delight: Under the topic of "Pleasure," the Preacher examines sexual gratification as the prime source of meaning in life. The "new morality," of course, is as old as the Bible. People then as people now, the Preacher knew, try to degrade what God intends to be the pleasures of marital relationships into selfish sexual exploitation. Our eroticized culture, excusing the extramarital affair and "sleeping around," and pretending liberation from "repressive Judeo-Christian culture values," will eventually come to the dreary conclusion of Ecclesiastes that this, too, is vanity.

The end of the matter; all has been heard. Fear God, and keep his commandments; for this is the whole duty of man: Life lived merely for its own sake is not worthwhile. The Preacher states that the foundation for personal character and the key to satisfaction in life come from reverence and obedience to God. The highest human achievements will result in failure and futility unless they are subordinated to the demands of law and duty to others. Wholeness for every human comes from realizing this divine plan for each.

SUGGESTIONS TO TEACHERS

Life's but a walking shadow, a poor player
That struts and frets his hour upon the stage
And then is heard no more: it is a tale
Told by an idiot, full of sound and fury,
Signifying nothing.—*Macbeth*, Act V.

Shakespeare stated it memorably in his great tragedy, and many of the lyrics of popular songs in our time repeat the theme. From *Macbeth* to the Beatles to last night's hit number, sensitive people, looking for life's meaning, conclude that all is futile. The same miasma of despair creeps into the thinking of many church folks.

Your lesson this Sunday is intended to help those in your class to cope with despair. You probably do not fully appreciate what a struggle some of your class members are having at this time. Therefore, your ministry through this lesson may have deeper impact than you suspect!

The background Scripture from Ecclesiastes may turn you off because of its apparent pessimism when you first read it. However, a careful second reading should point up the realistic view of life that the "Preacher" had. Further, it should disclose the sense of purpose to living he discovers through his faith. Here is the antidote to futility which your class members need to hear!

1. *THE POINTLESSNESS OF THE GODLESS LIFE.* The preacher-author of Ecclesiastes insists that human existence apart from the Lord is a dreary cycle leading nowhere. The person who lives unmindful of God is forced into an empty, ephemeral existence. You can find examples of those who are bored with life or tired of living from almost every daily paper or weekly magazine. Comment on the need which these had for a sense of God's presence and purpose.

2. *THE PALLIATIVES FOR MEANING IN LIFE.* Ecclesiastes offers as complete a list as any one of ways by which people think they can squeeze meaning into their existences. Have your class members pick out as many as possible from that list: Learning, Pleasure, Work, Possessions, Fame are a few. Note that none of these are necessarily evil *per se.* It's that none of these can adequately replace God in one's life.

3. *THE PURPOSE OF THE GOD-CENTERED LIFE.* Life is brief, and death comes soon, according to Ecclesiastes. Therefore, "Fear God, keep his commandments; this is the whole duty of man" (12:13). Allow time for your people to reflect on the brevity of life and the responsibility of humans as the only way to live on the plane of eternity. Introduce Jesus' words of promising "eternal life" to those who trust Him and obey Him.

TOPIC FOR ADULTS
COPING WITH FUTILITY

Bored to Death. A few years ago, George Sanders apparently had everything to live for. He was rich. He was famous, having won an Academy Award. He was superbly educated in England. His career, spanning three decades, included singing and acting. But he took a plane to Castelldefels, Spain, and checked into an expensive resort hotel for a vacation. His body was found after he had taken an overdose of sleeping pills. Beside it, carefully written, was a suicide note. The note read: "I am leaving because I am bored."

George Sanders was literally bored to death. Although his case is extreme, Sanders sounds somewhat like Ecclesiastes. The writer would have understood George Sanders. This strange little book doesn't quite seem to belong in the Bible because it seems so cynical and pessimistic.

The writer knew how jaded life could become. The final thing that could be said was that existence is such a boring thing. Is there anything really new? Anything really meaningful or lasting? Wearily, Ecclesiastes sighs and shakes his head. Ultimately, life is boring, no matter what you do, he concludes.

That big emptiness he tries to fill with various means. Maybe pleasure, he thinks. So he tries hobbies. He buys a vacation home. He takes cruises. He collects expensive trinkets. He joins clubs and groups. But the harder he strains after fun, the more boring it all becomes.

The Pantry of Your Soul. "A cooking school director, speaking on 'Putting the Lure in Leftovers,' said every good cook was forced to take what was left from yesterday's meal and try to make it appetizing today. In a real sense, we are forced to do this in life ... take what yesterday did to us and see what we can make out of it today. We have to concern ourselves with the remnants of life. ... We are forced many times to build on waste places, to reclaim what has been lost, to use what has been left. Who of us has not faced the pantry of his soul, found little, but what he found took and tried to put a lure in it?"—Wallace Fridy, *A Light Unto My Faith*, Abingdon Press.

The Most Beautiful Thing. "The most beautiful thing we can experience is the mysterious. It is the source of all true art and science. He to whom this emotion is a stranger, who can no longer pause to wonder and stand rapt in awe, is as good as dead: his eyes are closed.

"This insight into the mystery of life, coupled though it be with fear, has also given rise to religion. To know that what is impenetrable to us really exists, manifesting itself as the highest wisdom and the most radiant beauty which our dull faculties can comprehend only in their most primitive form—this knowledge, this feeling, is at the center of true religiousness."—Albert   Einstein quoted in *New Frontiers in Living*, by Howard Whitman, 1960.

Questions for Pupils on the Next Lesson. 1. How is true wealth measured? 2. What is the key to happiness in life? 3. How does the book of Proverbs describe wisdom? 4. What are the differences between society's definition of wisdom and the Bible's definition? 5. What is meant in Scripture by the phrase "the fear of the Lord"?

TOPIC FOR YOUTH
WHY AM I HERE, ANYWAY?

Better Than Miss Universe. Linda Light, former Miss Kansas and airline stewardess, now in a wheelchair as a victim of multiple sclerosis, but a junior in college and teaching in elementary school: "*Life* was good as a beauty queen, even if I didn't win the Miss Universe title, but I sure like it better as it is now. It was fun and exciting before, but I certainly wasn't very useful or productive."

Hours for What? According to a recent survey, the average man in his lifetime spends twenty years working. He spends another twenty years sleeping, sixteen years playing, five years just waiting. In a lifetime, the average man spends 8,760 hours telephoning, the equivalent of one full year.

How are you spending God's gift of time allotted to you? Why are you here, anyway? Are you merely waiting for the hours, days, and years to pass? Are you simply frittering away those precious daily rations of time? Or, do you realize that there is an alternative to the sense of futility which many seem to feel? Do you accept gratefully each new allotment of minutes as God's gracious opportunity to serve?

Dullsville? A recent Gallup Poll of those interviewed asked them to answer whether they thought life was dull, routine, or exciting. Of those who responded, 51 percent reported that they thought life is dull. Sixty percent of those who were over fifty years of age stated that they felt life was dull. Seventy percent of all those interviewed confessed that they were bored with their jobs. How do you answer these kinds of questions? Have you learned the meaning of life starts with your relationship with Jesus Christ?

Questions for Pupils on the Next Lesson. 1. How would you define real wisdom? 2. What is the definition of wisdom in the book of Proverbs? 3. What is wisdom, according to our materialistic and fun-loving society? 4. What is meant in the Bible by the words, "the fear of the Lord is the beginning of wisdom"?

LESSON XII—MAY 19

THE VALUE OF WISDOM

Background Scripture: Proverbs 3:13–18; 8:1–21
Devotional Reading: Proverbs 2:1–15

KING JAMES VERSION

PROVERBS 3 13 Happy *is* the man *that* findeth wisdom, and the man *that* getteth understanding:

14 For the merchandise of it *is* better than the merchandise of silver, and the gain thereof than fine gold.

15 She *is* more precious than rubies: and all the things thou canst desire are not to be compared unto her.

16 Length of days *is* in her right hand; *and in* her left hand riches and honour.

17 Her ways *are* ways of pleasantness, and all her paths *are* peace.

18 She *is* a tree of life to them that lay hold upon her; and happy *is every one* that retaineth her.

8 6 Hear; for I will speak of excellent things; and the opening of my lips *shall be* right things.

7 For my mouth shall speak truth; and wickedness *is* an abomination to my lips.

8 All the words of my mouth *are* in righteousness; *there is* nothing froward or perverse in them.

9 They *are* all plain to him that understandeth, and right to them that find knowledge.

10 Receive my instruction, and not silver; and knowledge rather than choice gold.

11 For wisdom *is* better than rubies; and all the things that may be desired are not to be compared to it.

REVISED STANDARD VERSION

PROVERBS 3 13 Happy is the man who finds wisdom,
and the man who gets understanding,

14 for the gain from it is better than gain from silver
and its profit better than gold.

15 She is more precious than jewels,
and nothing you desire can compare with her.

16 Long life is in her right hand;
in her left hand are riches and honor.

17 Her ways are ways of pleasantness,
and all her paths are peace.

18 She is a tree of life to those who lay hold of her;
those who hold her fast are called happy.

8 6 Hear, for I will speak noble things,
and from my lips will come what is right;

7 for my mouth will utter truth;
wickedness is an abomination to my lips.

8 All the words of my mouth are righteous;
there is nothing twisted or crooked in them.

9 They are all straight to him who understands
and right to those who find knowledge.

10 Take my instruction instead of silver,
and knowledge rather than choice gold;

11 for wisdom is better than jewels, and all that you may desire cannot compare with her.

KEY VERSE: *For wisdom is better than jewels, and all that you may desire cannot compare with her.* Proverbs 8:11 (RSV).

HOME DAILY BIBLE READINGS

May	13.	M.	*Warning Against Temptation.* Proverbs 1:7–19.
May	14.	T.	*The Appeal of Wisdom.* Proverbs 1:20–33.
May	15.	W.	*The Key to Happiness.* Proverbs 3:5–18.
May	16.	T.	*Diligence and Purity.* Proverbs 6:6–19.
May	17.	F.	*Wisdom Is Timeless.* Proverbs 8:22–31.
May	18.	S.	*The House of Wisdom.* Proverbs 9:1–12.
May	19.	S.	*Maxims for Living.* Proverbs 10:1–12.

BACKGROUND

The Hebrew Bible is divided into three parts. They are known as "The Law," "The Prophets," and "The Writings." The "Law," or *Torah,* is the basic and authoritative body of sacred Scripture for Judaism and consists of the first five books of the Bible. "The Prophets" consists of the messages of great spokesmen for God following the "Prophetic" interpretation of Israel's story in the section from Joshua through 2 Kings. "The Law" and "The Prophets" are written from the priestly and the prophetic points of view. The third grouping in the Hebrew Bible, "The Writings," reflect the thinking of the wise men more than that of the priest or the prophet. Three of the books in "The Writings," Job, Ecclesiastes, and Proverbs, which we have been studying, are part of a type of writing called "Wisdom Literature." The writings of these wise men represent a kind of "third force" in the Old Testament.

The Wisdom Literature writers, unlike the priests and the prophets, say very little about institutional religion. They don't comment about Israel and its inhabitants being a "chosen people." These wise men talk about humans as individuals out of their own experience. They were primarily concerned about the practical questions and concerns which a sensitive, thinking person would reflect upon. They were anxious to impart "Wisdom."

"Wisdom" to them meant a quality and principle to living, or as R.B.Y. Scott states, "The trained ability to live in equilibrium with the moral order of the world . . . moral understanding . . . the capacity to consider profounder problems of human life and destiny."

The book of Proverbs was such a manual or source book for wisdom about living in a moral universe before God. It was designed to instruct both the young people and the older generation. The first nine chapters, from which the scriptural material for today's lesson comes, are a kind of introductory section extolling the value of Wisdom.

Wisdom is taken so seriously and held in such honor by the writers of Wisdom Literature that they personified it. Therefore, frequently in Proverbs, you will find Wisdom referred to as a woman bringing nourishment to her children!

NOTES ON THE PRINTED TEXT

Happy is the man who finds wisdom . . . : The writer of the book of Proverbs was also a gifted poet. Proverbs 3:13–18 is a lovely Hebrew poem describing the joy and contentment which association with Wisdom brings. The opening line, "Happy is the man who finds wisdom . . . ." is expanded in the following lines of the poem. Throughout this poem, Wisdom is spoken of in a way that a man might speak of a woman with whom he is in love. The word in Hebrew for "Wisdom" (*hochmah*) is a feminine gender noun, and used in Proverbs in the way one would talk about a charming lady.

Remember, however, that the writer of Proverbs is not speaking of Wisdom in the way we ordinarily use it. Wisdom has to do with living responsibly before God in a moral universe. The writer emphasizes that when we understand our place and our duty in God's universe, we walk with Wisdom and she provides purpose and satisfaction.

She is more precious than jewels: Literally, Wisdom is more valuable than magnificent and costly necklaces made from rubies or pearls or coral. The writer of Proverbs raises the important question of what is most valuable to a person. Some persons, of course, immediately answer, "Money! Possessions!" Wisdom, however, is so much more valuable than a portfolio of blue-chip stocks or a present from Tiffany's.

Long life is in her right hand; in her left hand are riches and honor: Wisdom here is thought of in terms of a woman holding priceless gifts in her hands. In her right hand, she holds the expensive treasure of a long and healthy life; in the left, she holds the gift of recognition and encouragement from others. While these may seem to be materialistic gifts, the writer knows human nature well enough to know that we all need these to some degree, and also knows divine nature well enough to know that God wants us to have contentment and joy during our lives.

Her ways are ways of pleasantness, and all her paths are peace: Walking with Wisdom means being led to a sense of being free from anxiety. The wise man or woman is not a worrier. He or she, aware of God's overarching plan and goodness, has a sense that life is good and has a harmony to it.

She is a tree of life to those who lay hold of her; those who hold her fast are called happy: The expression "tree of life" is a traditional Hebrew term for health and a long life. References in Genesis 2:9 and 3:22, Ezekiel 47:12, and Revelation 2:7 and 22:2 also depict Wisdom as a magnificent fruit tree bringing healing and vitality.

Hear, for I will speak noble things and from my lips will come what is right; for my mouth shall utter truth: In chapter 8, Wisdom is shown as a winsome woman moving throughout a group. She will not seclude herself in some hard-to-reach place, or hide or avoid people. She calls to everyone to listen to her words. She appeals to her hearers to take her seriously not because they can do something for her but because she can do so much for them. She will show people what is right. She will tell them what is truth. Lady Wisdom's appealing speech in chapter 8 of Proverbs is a plea to take her seriously if people really want to know how to live with integrity.

Wickedness is an abomination to my lips. All the words of my mouth are righteous; there is nothing twisted or crooked in them: Wisdom will never deceive. Wisdom will not stretch the truth. The person who heeds Wisdom will not shade the meaning of words for the sake of expediency. Wisdom insists on honesty in all speech.

SUGGESTIONS TO TEACHERS

It is important that your class members understand what the Bible means by *wisdom*. Why not open today's lesson by distributing pencil and paper and having each person write a definition of *wisdom* according to the Scriptures. If the class seems to be having difficulty coming up with words to tell what wisdom is, suggest looking at the background Scripture from Proverbs in today's lesson. As the teacher, you will want to clarify your own thinking about wisdom beforehand. You already know that the Bible does not think of wisdom merely in terms of "book-larnin' " or "savvy" from experience. Rather, Proverbs and the other pieces of Wisdom Literature offered guidance for living by suggesting the rules of the moral order under God, and exploring the meaning of life within God's universe.

Today's lesson makes it clear that wisdom in the scriptural tradition has several spin-off's and many facets. Here are some:

1. *SATISFACTION FROM WISDOM.* As long as your people have those pencils and papers, encourage them to write down as many of the benefits of wisdom as they can find in the background Scripture. Some of these, you will hope, are happiness, a long life, riches, honor, peace, and satisfaction. These must not be taken in a crass sense in which God "pays off" the wise person in material ways. Rather, the man or woman who has God's kind of wisdom will have a sense of joy, will be wealthy in spiritual matters, will be honored by the Lord. Remind your class that when a person lives faithfully and obediently as Christ's person, he or she is given a wisdom which no other will have.

2. *SOURCE OF PROPER CONDUCT.* Dwell for a time in your lesson on the sense of confusion in regard to morals and values, goals and means which seems to pervade our culture. Undoubtedly, persons in your class will have examples to offer of how people aren't certain how to make decisions or whether to live by traditional Jewish-Christian morality. The "wise" man or woman, however, will

be guided on behavior. That person, you may assure your class, will find proper conduct.

3. *SUPERIORITY OF WISDOM.* The writer of Proverbs relates the value of wisdom to material wealth in 8:10,11. Here is a place for some helpful thinking—especially in our culture where money is so important. The truly wealthy person is the wise person, according to Proverbs. A healthy bank balance and a bulging investment portfolio are not the sources of security or joy. In the face of the materialistic, consumer-society your people live in, how do they react to these words?

4. *SIGN OF WISDOM.* Humility, goodness, discretion, counsel, insight, and strength are the evidence of wisdom in a person's life, according to Proverbs 8:13,14. How obvious are these traits in your life as teacher? How prevalent are they in your students' lives?

TOPIC FOR ADULTS
THE VALUE OF WISDOM

Standing in the Wings. In the novel, *The Bridge of San Luis Rey*, Thornton Wilder describes a patient, kindly musician who works hard to bring out the potential talent in a young protegé. The young singer had musical gifts, but was also temperamental. She had been a popular entertainer in a small town, and had little ambition except applause. She was satisfied to be mediocre and catered to the wishes of her uncultured audiences. The musical director saw the possibilities with her voice and persisted in raising her sights. He tried to encourage her to move beyond silly ballads and to learn to use her gifts more effectively. She continued to give programs, however, that appealed to the crowds. Savoring the applause even though she had given a disappointing performance, she would always encounter her musician-teacher in the wings. She had to face his loving criticism. She knew that he demanded her highest.

Wisdom is recognizing that the Lord stands in the wings always, demanding our best. Wisdom is heeding the loving criticism of God, not seeking the brief applause of the crowd. Wisdom, in short, is living as God's own person, tuned to His wishes and committed to His will.

Talking to God Tonight. The tiny cabin in East Tennessee had no electricity or running water. The old mountain woman lived on a small pension and the produce from her garden. Her hands were gnarled and back bent from years of heavy physical labor. The plain, hand-hewn pine table, three ancient chairs, a cot, and a shelf for supplies were the only furnishings. A big, well-worn Bible was the only book, and rested on the pine table.

"Does it help you?" asked the reporter interviewing her.

"Yep. Sure does," chirped the woman. "Whenever I start to do anything wrong, I jes' says to myself, 'You're goin' to be talkin' to God tonight.' And that keeps me from doin' it."

Wisdom is recalling that we live each hour accountable to God. Wealth, possessions, power, and accomplishments—all the world's values and goals—mean little when we wisely remember, as the old mountain woman did, that we're going to be talking to God every night. That's wisdom!

The Other Preachers. "Even a cursory review of contemporary media leads to an inescapable conclusion. Many advertisements are attempting to sell far more than just a product. In order to convert the public into an army of efficient, loyal consumers, they are peddling a whole way of life. Granted most ads are merely after our dollars; but some are after bigger game—our souls.

"If a set of values is being systematically taught via the media, it is hardly a minor academic matter. The average man spends many hours per day watching television, attending movies, and leafing through periodicals. Vance Packard estimated, as far back as 1960, that the average man is exposed to over 1,500 selling messages a day. In time, such massive repetition is bound to have its effect.

"Contrast this onslaught with the efforts of the average clergyman. He has only limited media aid to supplement his twenty-minute weekly sermon or Sunday-School lesson. It's hardly a fair fight.

"Also, contrast the message patterns. At the risk of oversimplifying, the clergyman is largely recommending service, humility, and self-denial. There is little ambiguity in such passages as these:

" 'If any man would come after me, let him deny himself . . .' Matthew 16:24.

" 'Make no provision for the flesh, to gratify its desires.' Romans 13:14.

" 'Take heed and beware of all convetousness: for a man's life does not consist in the abundance of his possessions.' Luke 12:15.

" '. . . do not be anxious about your life, what you shall eat or what you shall drink, nor about your body, what you shall put on.' Matthew 6:25.

"Now, note the shift involved in the phraseology of some recent magazine ads.

" 'Go where you want, do what you wish. Never let anything hold you back from enjoyment.'

" 'If you have a taste for elegance, indulge it.'

" 'Pamper yourself.'

" '. . . the gourmet's delight.'

" '. . . When it comes to money, we are all of the same religion.'

" '. . . success today is measured by the dollar sign.'

" 'Dive into the daily whirl designed for pleasure-bent playboys and play-mates.'

" 'Be good to yourself this (Christmas) Season.'

" 'Easter is a new pair of shoes.'

"Such ads are hardly preaching self-denial. Clearly they are recommending a spiritually deadly blend of materialism and hedonism which strikes at the very heart of biblical teachings."—Benjamin A. Ramsey, "The Other Preachers," *Southern Cross*, August 1974.

Questions for Pupils on the Next Lesson. 1. Do you agree that an attitude of reverent obedience to God is the foundation for wisdom? Why or why not? 2. What are the demands of the Bible's kind of wisdom? 3. Are there limits to human wisdom? 4. What are the chief causes of frustration and destruction in human life? 5. Are knowledge and wisdom one and the same?

TOPIC FOR YOUTH
WEALTH IN WISDOM

Real Success. "One of the important things that religion does for life is to put the emphasis on the proper values. According to the thinking of much of the world, men succeed or fail almost in direct proportion to the amount of money that they accumulate. If a man can pay his way into the exclusive clubs of his city, if he can operate an expensive automobile and keep a fine house, if he stands out as one who has battled with the world of commerce and has come out victorious—he is characterized a success, and almost instinctively the rest of the community regards him with honor. And it may be perfectly true that he is a great success in life. But, if he is, it is despite the fact that he has accumulated money, not because of it. If he is really successful, that fact would be evident whether he had a dollar in the bank or not."—Blanche Thompson Richardson, "Sense—Not Dollars Counts!" *Wesleyan Advocate*, August 24, 1970; *Quote*, October 11, 1970.

Wisdom Leading to Wealth. Where is your real wealth? In possessions? Or in being wise enough to know what is important in life? Mrs. Fritz Kreisler could have sought after more money, more headlines, and more parties. One day, a New York socialite commented to Mrs. Kreisler that she didn't seem to get a kick out of social life among the rich in New York. Mrs. Kreisler answered, "No, I don't really. I get more of a kick out of feeding poor children. I get my kicks in a different way."

What a way to get kicks! That's what the Bible means by wisdom. And that's real wealth!

Danced to the Wrong Tune. Some of the most money-loving, pleasure-obsessed people ever to live were the citizens of the city-state named Sybaris in ancient Greece. They thought that the purpose of living was wealth and fun. And they managed to get lots of both. But in the end it was their undoing. These wealthy and "wise" Sybarites, the envy of nearly everyone else, became so luxury-loving that they took to spending their time on such pleasures as dancing horses. They also arrogantly went to war in 510 B.C. with the city-state of Crotona. The Sybarites confidently told themselves and everyone else that they had bought the finest weapons and hired the strongest soldiers. They lost disastrously, however. How? Simple. The Croton men shrewdly played the tunes to which the Sybarite horses had been trained to dance and threw the Sybarite defenders into helpless confusion. The Crotona army advanced as the Sybarites's horses danced, and slaughtered the soldiers of Sybaris. Sybaris was so completely ransacked, burned, and destroyed that it disappeared from history in one short day. In fact, when others tried to start a colony on the site of Sybaris sixty-five years later, they could hardly find a trace of what had once been the richest, proudest city in ancient Greece!

Questions for Pupils on the Next Lesson. 1. What is the source of real wisdom? 2. What causes most human destruction and frustration? 3. Why is the way of the fool, according to the Scriptures, so attractive? 4. What do you do when you are faced with a variety of choices on how to live your life? 5. Who are some persons you know or have heard of who have learned the kind of wisdom which is described in Proverbs?

LESSON XIII—MAY 26

TWO WAYS OF LIFE

Background Scripture: Proverbs 1:7–19; 3:5–8; 14:1–12
Devotional Reading: Proverbs 6:1–15

KING JAMES VERSION

PROVERBS 1 7 The fear of the LORD *is* the beginning of knowledge; *but* fools despise wisdom and instruction.

3 5 Trust in the LORD with all thine heart; and lean not unto thine own understanding.

6 In all thy ways acknowledge him, and he shall direct thy paths.

7 Be not wise in thine own eyes: fear the LORD, and depart from evil.

8 It shall be health to thy navel, and marrow to thy bones.

14 Every wise woman buildeth her house: but the foolish plucketh it down with her hands.

2 He that walketh in his uprightness feareth the LORD: but *he that is* perverse in his ways despiseth him.

3 In the mouth of the foolish *is* a rod of pride: but the lips of the wise shall preserve them.

4 Where no oxen *are*, the crib *is* clean; but much increase *is* by the strength of the ox.

5 A faithful witness will not lie: but a false witness will utter lies.

6 A scorner seeketh wisdom, and *findeth it* not: but knowledge *is* easy unto him that understandeth.

7 Go from the presence of a foolish man, when thou perceivest not *in him* the lips of knowledge.

8 The wisdom of the prudent *is* to understand his way: but the folly of fools *is* deceit.

9 Fools make a mock at sin: but among the righteous *there is* favour.

10 The heart knoweth his own bitterness; and a stranger doth not intermeddle with his joy.

11 The house of the wicked shall be overthrown: but the tabernacle of the upright shall flourish.

12 There is a way which seemeth right unto a man; but the end thereof *are* the ways of death.

REVISED STANDARD VERSION

PROVERBS 1 7 The fear of the LORD is the beginning of knowledge;
fools despise wisdom and instruction.

3 5 Trust in the LORD with all your heart, and do not rely on your own insight.

6 In all your ways acknowledge him, and he will make straight your paths.

7 Be not wise in your own eyes; fear the LORD, and turn away from evil.

8 It will be healing to your flesh and refreshment to your bones.

14 Wisdom builds her house, but folly with her own hands tears it down.

2 He who walks in uprightness fears the LORD,
but he who is devious in his ways despises him.

3 The talk of a fool is a rod for his back,
but the lips of the wise will preserve them.

4 Where there are no oxen, there is no grain;
but abundant crops come by the strength of the ox.

5 A faithful witness does not lie,
but a false witness breathes out lies.

6 A scoffer seeks wisdom in vain,
but knowledge is easy for a man of understanding.

7 Leave the presence of a fool,
for there you do not meet words of knowledge.

8 The wisdom of a prudent man is to discern his way,
but the folly of fools is deceiving.

9 God scorns the wicked,
but the upright enjoy his favor.

10 The heart knows its own bitterness,
and no stranger shares its joy.

11 The house of the wicked will be destroyed,
but the tent of the upright will flourish.

12 There is a way which seems right to a man,
but its end is the way to death.

KEY VERSE: *The fear of the Lord is the beginning of knowledge; fools despise wisdom and instruction.* Proverbs 1:7 (RSV).

HOME DAILY BIBLE READINGS

May 20. M. *The Righteous and the Wicked.* Proverbs 11:1–10.
May 21. T. *The Right Use of Speech.* Proverbs 12:18–28.

May 22. W. *Honor Thy Father.* Proverbs 13:1–11.
May 23. T. *Give Heed to Wisdom.* Proverbs 13:12–25.
May 24. F. *Gentle Words.* Proverbs 15:1–10.
May 25. S. *Praise for a Good Woman.* Proverbs 31:10–22.
May 26. S. *The Fruit of Her Hands.* Proverbs 31:23–31.

BACKGROUND

For people in the Middle East, a proverb held an important place. Every business deal had to be closed with an appropriate proverb. Every court case was clinched by the lawyer who could quote the best proverb. People in that part of the world, especially in Bible times, liked a teacher best when he could state proverbs. We are used to speakers giving an introduction, developing two or three points in a logical, coherent outline, and closing with a summary of his main points. Oriental sages worked differently. They said little but watched much, and delivered their comments in a pithy sentence or two that said it all in a witty way.

Someone has described a proverb as follows: "The wisdom of many, but the wit of one." This is what each proverb in the Bible's collection is like. Some of the proverbs bring a smile. All of them are memorable ways of expressing an important point. Each proverb has one self-evident truth in it.

The Hebrews particularly enjoyed proverbs which set two ideas in sharp contrast to one another. They also liked the speaker who could put one idea in two keenly contrasting ways. Therefore, many of the proverbs in the Old Testament book of Proverbs pointedly describe two cleverly-worded comparisons. Some of these will appear in the scriptural material in today's lesson, and hold up the wise person who takes Wisdom seriously as opposed to the fool who turns away from Wisdom.

Proverbs are not exactly in fashion in our times, but up till a century ago, the book of Proverbs was probably the most-quoted, the best-known, and the best-liked book in the Bible. Our great-grandparents learned to write by copying verses from Proverbs into notebooks, memorized selections from Proverbs in classrooms, and stitched sayings from Proverbs on to samplers hung on thousands of dining room walls. Modern readers may still find wisdom through these sayings which have been preserved for over 2,500 years!

NOTES ON THE PRINTED TEXT

Proverbs emphasizes that Wisdom is godliness and folly is sin. Many of the sayings or proverbs in this collection delight in juxtaposing the wise person and Wisdom against the fool and folly, or responsibility to God versus refusal to accept that responsibility.

The fear of the Lord is the beginning of knowledge; fools despise wisdom and instruction: Here the contrast is put starkly. The wise person knows the Lord as the Source of all Wisdom. The fool rejects God's wisdom.

The *fear* of the Lord causes some persons uneasiness. They mistakenly imagine that this means cringing like a frightened pup before a cruel master. In the Bible, remember that the *fear* of the Lord means a reverence for God. Unless that perspective of respect toward God is present, a person will try to reverence himself. Put another way, respect or awe or reverence for the Lord means remembering one's place as creature before the Creator. This brings a right relationship between a person and the Lord. Being right with God is to become right in all the problems of life.

The *fear* of the Lord also carries connotations of holding His plans in such high regard that one will bend every effort to promote God's work and cooperate to carry out His intentions. The reverse is also true: reverencing God means opposing evil.

The phrase, "The fear of the Lord is the beginning of knowledge," could be the motto and summary of the entire book of Proverbs. *Beginning* in the Hebrew text means both "starting point" and also "chief part." In other words, reverence for the Lord is both the starting point for being a wise person and also the main part of wisdom!

Fools despise wisdom and instruction: The root of the Hebrew word for *fool* here has to do with being dull and thick. The fool, despising God's wisdom, becomes thick and dull by trying to live without taking God into account. Eventually, he becomes hopelessly insensitive to the Lord and morally corrupt.

Trust in the Lord with all your heart, and do not rely on your own insight: Reliance on any except God brings disappointment and disaster. God and only God is the Source of all Wisdom. Human intelligence constantly challenges God's Wisdom, however. We like to rely on our own insights. Or we waffle when it comes to trusting in divine Wisdom, and try to have it both ways. Our own plans become so important that we can find excuses for not relying on the Lord's plans. Therefore, the writer of this proverb advises trusting God wholeheartedly.

In all your ways acknowledge him, and he will make straight your paths: The word to be emphasized here is *all*. Faith means taking God with utmost seriousness and living in conscious obedience in *every* thing you do! This is the case not only in Judaism but in Christianity, too.

When that type of total surrender to the divine Will occurs in your life, you discover that God is directing your life. God shows you the path you should follow when you center on Him in all of your decisions and lifestyle.

It will be a healing to your flesh and refreshment to your bones. God brings fresh life to the person living daily in an attitude of humility and trust. The word translated here as *refreshment* comes from the Hebrew verb root having to do with drinking at a cool, clear spring after a long hot walk.

Wisdom builds her house, but folly with her own hands tears it down. As in the previous lesson, Wisdom is personified as a woman. Here, folly is also given human characteristics as a nasty, destructive shrew.

The talk of a fool is a rod for his back, but the lips of the wise will preserve them: Literally, the verse says that in the mouth of a fool is a stick for his pride. The picture is that of a branch or large twig shooting forth from the ungodly person's mouth.

The wisdom of a prudent man is to discern his way, but the folly of fools is deceiving. Here is another of these delightful antitheses which hearers of proverbs enjoyed. The question asked is: Discernment or Deceit—which way for you? God's Wisdom, given to the person living wholeheartedly obediently, brings a sense of leading for the future. On the other hand, refusing to live such a life of obedience inevitably means self-deceit and confusion.

SUGGESTIONS TO TEACHERS

Most of us resist sharp *Either-Or* choices. We don't like having to decide on the basis of, "Do this and you'll be doomed; do that and you'll be saved." Consequently, we play intellectual games and tell each other that we must consider everything in shades of gray instead of Right vs. Wrong, Good vs. Evil.

As you know, however, the Bible insists on presenting stark choices. Jesus had the disconcerting habit of offering two paths, one to life, the other to destruction (Matthew 7:13, 14), two ways of life. He was continuing a long tradition within the Bible. Proverbs gives many earlier challenges of choosing the right way.

Your lesson is meant to encourage your students to face the fact that as Christians they must make tough choices every day, and that these choices are alternatives between two ways of life.

1. *CLAIM.* Move into the lesson by having your class examine the verse, "The fear of the Lord is the beginning of knowledge" (Proverbs 1:7). Have the members delve into what the writer of Proverbs means by the *fear* of the Lord, and by *knowledge. Fear,* of course, here has to do with respecting God. And *knowledge* has the same idea as *wisdom* in the biblical sense of the word. The real question to be discussed, therefore, is how much each man or woman in your class demonstrates a sincere respect for the Lord?

2. *CAUTION.* Turn the class's attention to 1:8–19—a long catalogue of "foolish" folks. It includes the people hatching plots of violence, the unjust, those who deprive others or seize others' things, the greedy, the cruel, the persons who show a flagrant disregard for others' rights or others' lives, the grab-and-get-rich-quick schemers. By Jesus' tough standards, you will note that all of us are indicated in every category. What person has not wished someone who has crossed him to "drop dead!" Everyone has a streak of greed and cruelty.

3. *CONDITION.* Those who trust the Lord and acknowledge Him as Lord instead of promoting themselves will have the proper sense of perspective in life. These folks will be able to choose the right path. This brings up what may be the toughest choice of all: *Which shall be Lord—Jesus or me?* Like it or not, this is the basic issue. And it must be answered daily!

4. *CONTRAST.* The possibilities that result from that basic choice are almost endless: Strength or weakness? Building or destroying? Truth or lies? The way of wisdom or the way of wickedness: Impress on those in your class that every choice always has long-term ramifications, for good or for evil.

TOPIC FOR ADULTS
TWO WAYS OF LIFE

Costly Ambition. No man ever aspired to the Presidency of the United States more than Daniel Webster. His burning ambition and unscrupulous efforts to wangle the nomination, however, alienated many. Webster was acknowledged as an intelligent, clever lawyer. However, he lacked the kind of wisdom for which the Bible calls. His arrogance in thinking he was so wise cost him the Presidency on two different occasions! It is ironic that he could have achieved his goal and fulfilled his dreams had he practiced wisdom in the scriptural sense. It happened that Webster was offered the Vice-Presidential nomination when William Henry Harrison was running for the Presidency. Webster petulantly refused, stating that he had no intention of being buried before he was dead. Shortly after taking office, however, Harrison died. The Vice-President succeeded him. A few years later, again Webster was asked to run as Vice-President. Once again, Webster demanded that he be named as candidate for President. When told that he could have the Vice-Presidency, Webster in his "wisdom" bitterly renounced the offer. Astonishingly, once again the President—Zachary Taylor—died. The Vice-President was inducted into the office. Had Webster had a higher type of wisdom, he could have achieved his desire and taken office as the nation's President on two occasions! Webster might have been brilliant in many ways, but his ruthless ambition and pride made him a fool on two critical occasions.

The Way of a Foolish Person. A certain business man in England learned too late in life what real wisdom is. He picked out his tombstone shortly before he died, and prepared the inscription he wanted carved. The words he chose to have inscribed on the tombstone were: BORN (here he had his name chiseled) A HUMAN BEING; DIED (date) A WHOLESALE GROCER.

Someone asked him to explain the meaning of the odd epitaph. The man answered, "I was so busy selling groceries I did not have time to get married and have a family. There was a whole area of life crowded out by the grocery business. I was so busy selling groceries I didn't have time for the drama, for lectures, for concerts, or for reading. I was so busy selling groceries I did not have time for community service—religious, social, or political. All these areas of life were pushed out. I was successful. But I was so busy making a living I never had time to live." (Clyde E. Wildmer, *a Treasury of Sermon Illustrations*, edited by Chas L. Wallis, (Abingdon Press)).

Lotus Land People. Do not be easily discouraged in your search for a satisfying life. Some people sit down too soon. They remind us of the Lotus Eaters, people told about in Homer's *Odyssey*, who lay lazily on their beach eating a fruit which caused them to lose all interest in work and all desire to reach their native country. The worst thing in life is not to fail, but not to try to succeed; to live in the gray twilight that knows neither brightness nor shadow, neither victory nor defeat.

Questions for Pupils on the Next Lesson. 1. How did the Prophet Amos characterize the six nations that bordered Israel and Judah? 2. Why did Amos condemn Judah? 3. Why did Amos condemn Israel? 4. What did Amos say happens to immoral nations? 5. What causes war, and what brings peace?

TOPIC FOR YOUTH
A BETTER WAY TO LIVE

Marching to Which Tune? The scene was the dining room of a cruise ship. An American and a man from the Middle East shared a table. One evening, the ship's orchestra broke into the tune, "The Parade of the Wooden Soldiers." The Arab politely pushed back his chair and stood solemnly at attention. The American was puzzled and asked why his table-partner had gotten to his feet. The Arab politely replied, "Why, I thought it was your national anthem." He was not kidding. He was wrong, of course, but in a sense he was right. How many of us in actuality live as if we are part of a lockstep march of toy soldiers, rigidly conforming to what others demand of us. The national anthem almost could be "The March of the Wooden Soldiers" from the way so many of us choose to conform to the values of our society. We, however, march to Christ's own tune, and acknowledge that there is another way to live. We may be called fools by some in the world, but we prefer to live by God's own kind of wisdom!

Wisdom at a Party. God's kind of wisdom means acting in a way that helps others. Sometimes, it means making decisions which may not be easy. A young man attended a party where there was a lot of drinking. Suddenly, realizing that if he didn't do something quickly he would be the only one not drinking, he spoke out clearly, "Make mine tomato juice." Eight or ten others followed suit, young people who would not have dared to be different by themselves. It wasn't that they found pleasure in drinking; it was that they were afraid not to drink. Caught in a pattern, they were no longer strong enough to stand on their own feet and express their own moral judgment.

What Kind of Music? Benny Goodman, the jazz musician and clarinet virtuoso, was once interviewed. "Mr. Goodman," asked the reporter, "How do you manage to remain popular after three decades?" "Simple," replied Benny. "We play the music people like to hear." While this may be a key for success in the entertainment world, it is not the way Christ's people conduct themselves. We do not merely play what others may want to hear; we do not blithely conform to others' opinions. We do not go along with popular values. We do not give in to society's pressures. We belong to Jesus Christ. We sense that we are called to a different way from the throng around us. Therefore, we tune our lives by the wisdom of the Lord, which we find in the Scriptures.

Questions for Pupils on the Next Lesson.   1. Who was Amos the Prophet? 2. In what kind of society was he living? 3. Why did Amos condemn his nation, Israel, and Judah? 4. Does God still judge all nations? 5. How would God judge the way poor people are being exploited today?

JUNE—AUGUST 1985

THE MINOR PROPHETS

LESSON I—JUNE 2

WHY JUDGMENT COMES TO HUMANITY

Background Scripture: Amos 1:1–2:8
Devotional Reading: Amos 2:9–16

KING JAMES VERSION

AMOS 1 The words of Amos, who was among the herdmen of Tekoa, which he saw concerning Israel in the days of Uzziah king of Judah, and in the days of Jeroboam the son of Joash king of Israel, two years before the earthquake.

3 Thus saith the LORD; For three transgressions of Damascus, and for four, I will not turn away *the punishment* thereof; because they have threshed Gilead with threshing instruments of iron:
4 But I will send a fire into the house of Hazael, which shall devour the palaces of Benhadad.

11 Thus saith the LORD; For three transgressions of Edom, and for four, I will not turn away *the punishment* thereof; because he did pursue his brother with the sword, and did cast off all pity, and his anger did tear perpetually, and he kept his wrath for ever:
12 But I will send a fire upon Teman, which shall devour the palaces of Bozrah.

2 6 Thus saith the LORD; For three transgressions of Israel, and for four, I will not turn away *the punishment* thereof; because they sold the righteous for silver, and the poor for a pair of shoes;
7 That pant after the dust of the earth on the head of the poor, and turn aside the way of the meek: and a man and his father will go in unto the *same* maid, to profane my holy name:
8 And they lay *themselves* down upon clothes laid to pledge by every altar, and they drink the wine of the condemned *in* the house of their god.

REVISED STANDARD VERSION

AMOS 1 The words of Amos, who was among the shepherds of Tekoa, which he saw concerning Israel in the days of Uzziah king of Judah and in the days of Jeroboam the son of Joash, king of Israel, two years before the earthquake.
3 Thus says the LORD:
"For three transgressions of Damascus, and for four, I will not revoke the punishment;
because they have threshed Gilead with threshing sledges of iron.
4 So I will send a fire upon the house of Hazael,
and it shall devour the strongholds of Ben-hadad."

11 Thus says the LORD:
"For three transgressions of Edom, and for four, I will not revoke the punishment;
because he pursued his brother with the sword,
and cast off all pity,
and his anger tore perpetually,
and he kept his wrath for ever.
12 So I will send a fire upon Teman,
and it shall devour the strongholds of Bozrah."

2 6 Thus says the LORD:
"For three transgressions of Israel, and for four, I will not revoke the punishment;
because they sell the righteous for silver, and the needy for a pair of shoes—
7 they that trample the head of the poor into the dust of the earth,
and turn aside the way of the afflicted;
a man and his father go in to the same maiden,
so that my holy name is profaned;
8 they lay themselves down beside every altar
upon garments taken in pledge;
and in the house of their God they drink the wine of those who have been fined.

KEY VERSE: Behold, the eyes of the Lord God are upon the sinful kingdom, and I will destroy it from the surface of the ground. Amos 9:8 (RSV).

HOME DAILY BIBLE READINGS

May   27.   M.   *A Shepherd's Warning.* Amos 1:1,2.
May   28.   T.   *Called to Courage.* Amos 7:10–17.
May   29.   W.   *Transgression and Punishment.* Amos 1:3–10.
May   30.   T.   *The Nations Judged.* Amos 1:11–2:3.
May   31.   F.   *God's People Condemned.* Amos 2:4–9.
June   1.   S.   *Grace Without Gratitude.* Amos 2:10–16.
June   2.   S.   *Pride a Problem.* Amos 6:11–14.

BACKGROUND

You already are aware that the Jewish people divided the Scriptures into three sections: *The Torah,* consisting of the first five books of our Bible, *The Writings,* and *The Prophets.* Our past six lessons dealt with some of *The Writings,* particularly sections known as "Wisdom Literature" in Job, Ecclesiastes, and Proverbs. Our next thirteen lessons will come from *The Prophets.*

The Hebrew Bible divides *The Prophets* into two groups. These are: the "Former Prophets" consisting of four scrolls describing Jewish history—Joshua, Judges, 1 and 2 Samuel, and 1 and 2 Kings; and the "Latter Prophets." The "Latter Prophets" also includes four scrolls. These are Isaiah, Jeremiah, Ezekiel, and a scroll called "The Twelve." This group of twelve shorter "books" were often called the "minor" prophets. It does not mean that these twelve were less important. It simply means that they were briefer.

Each of "The Twelve" was and is significant. However, our lessons for this quarter will look only at the words of Amos, Micah, Hosea, Habakkuk, Zechariah, and Malachi.

Our lessons throughout the month of June will address the issue of God's Judgment and Righteousness, and will stress that *doing* justice is an essential element of faith. Our first three lessons in this series come from the powerful pronouncements of Amos.

Who was Amos? Why did he speak? He came from a village in Judah but preached in the northern kingdom of Israel about 750 B.C. He found Israel lolling in luxury but parading its piety. Amos soon discovered, however, that the prosperity of the nation was enjoyed only by the rich. Furthermore, the wealth came from exploiting the poor. The religion, moreover, was mostly for show. Although Israel looked powerful and secure, Amos fearlessly predicted that the rampant injustice, immorality, and oppression would bring ruin. Amos, like all of the Lord's prophets, found that his words cost him dearly!

NOTES ON THE PRINTED TEXT

The words of Amos, who was among the shepherds of Tekoa. . . . Amos, the third of the minor prophets, was one of the greatest prophets. He was rooted in history at a definite time, 786–742 B.C., *in the days of Uzziah king of Judah and in the days of Jeroboam the son of Joash, king of Israel, two years before the earthquake.* Although a country boy experienced in sheep herding, sycamore-tree dressing, and farming, God called Amos to be His spokesperson.

Amos came from a town south of Bethlehem called Tekoa, which means "the alarm trumpet." He left his work in Judah and went north to Bethel in Israel to sound the alarm of God's impending judgment. He first condemned Israel's neighbors for their sins.

Thus says the Lord: "For three transgressions of Damascus, and for four, I will not revoke the punishment." Amos began his condemnation with Damascus, the capital city of Aram, which was northeast of Israel. Damascus's numerous transgressions had provoked the Lord. Its cruel treatment in its military campaign against Gilead was illustrated. These victors of Damascus had *threshed Gilead with threshing sledges of iron.* They had dragged iron sledges used in threshing the grain over the bodies of conquered Gilead crushing them like dust on a threshing floor. Fire would be the instrument of God's punishment against Damascus and *the house of Hazael.*

Thus says the Lord: "For three transgressions of Edom, and for four, I will not revoke the punishment." Israel's southeast neighbor, Edom, had been hostile against its brothers. Traditional friendships had been discarded. *"He pursued his brother with the sword, and cast off all pity."* Amos pictured Edom's raid of Israel as being like an angry animal that guarded and perpetually tore at its prey. Fire would be used to destroy the fortified cities of Teman and Bozrah, symbols of Edom's strength.

Although international in his perspective, Amos's most blistering and lengthy attack was reserved for Israel. *Thus says the Lord: "For three transgressions of Israel, and for four, I will not revoke the punishment."* Amos enumerated upon Israel's sins. *"They sell the righteous for silver, and the needy for a pair of shoes."* Amos attacked the unjust courts which were utilized by the influential to bind the innocent over as slaves for small debts. The creditors *"trample the heads of the poor into the dust of the earth"* and *"lay themselves down beside every altar upon garments taken in pledge."* Amos blasted the rich who feasted on the profits exploited from the poor and needy and acquired through the corrupt judicial system. *"A man and his father go in to the same maiden, so that my holy name is profaned."* Amos condemned the promiscuity of the Israelites as well as the excesses that took place in the house of God when *"they drink the wine of those who have been fined."* All were crimes against God that were witnessed by Amos. Justice, an expression of Israel's commitment of God, had been ignored. God would judge and punish ALL the sinful nations.

SUGGESTIONS TO TEACHERS

"Minor Prophets" probably suggests that these writings are insignificant compared to others. The first thing you will have to deal with in your class is this title, "Minor Prophets." Point out to your class that these twelve were not Farm League material or second-rate stuff. The term arose only because of the brevity of their material in the Hebrew canon.

When your class meets Amos, it will quickly discover there is nothing "minor" about him. It will soon learn what a major personality he is. And Amos's topics continue to be major issues in every nation!

1. *PERCEIVING.* Amos perceived what was happening in the world. Not many people do. Most drift through life without understanding what is really going on in the nation or in the community. Amos, anchored in his knowledge of God, described what he saw in Israel in the heady days of prosperity in the eighth century B.C. Everyone else thought that everything was fine. Amos knew differently. The inhumanity and greed in Israel and surrounding nations flaunted God's intentions. Amos, typical of all who are conscious of God's purposes, became a perceptive person. His "visions" told how God holds even the most rich and powerful people and countries accountable. Talk with your class how the church and its members are meant to have Amos's kind of perceptivity in these times.

2. *PROPHESYING.* Amos frequently prefaces his remarks with, "Thus says the Lord." This is prophecy. He frequently follows with vivid ways of telling his hearers what God has in mind. For example in the scriptural material in this les-

son, Amos boxes the compass, starting in the northeast with Damascus, going to the west to Gaza, moving to the north to Tyre, and swinging to the southeast to Edom, then east to Ammon and southeast to Moab, reminding all nations that they must heed God by living responsibly. You should ask your class who, if any, speak for God today. Ask further what God would want His prophets to say to the world in these times. What issues, in the opinion of your class, would Amos hammer on if he were to visit our nation?

3. *PUNISHING.* Sometimes, we try to domesticate God; we think of the Lord as a dottering great-aunt, blandly overlooking the shenanigans of the kids downstairs. The notion of God punishing anyone is regarded as faintly unseemly. We dismiss talk about God judging humanity as a relic from medieval days. Remind your class of Amos's words about God dealing with disobedient nations and recalcitrant rulers. Have those in your class mull over the meaning of some of the passages in which Amos insists that a day of reckoning will come to those who persist in neglecting justice.

4. *PROFANING.* Make certain that you have lots of time in your lesson period for a good airing of Amos's comments on what real worship is all about. Rejecting the law of the Lord and not keeping His statutes, and accepting injustice, oppression, immorality are idol worship of the grossest kind. Talk with your people how our values and actions sometimes take the Lord's name in vain!

TOPIC FOR ADULTS
WHY JUDGMENT COMES TO HUMANITY

Community With a Conscience. "A church or synagogue that rouses its members from lethargy and sensitizes them to the social dimensions of their faith does not become thereby a welfare agency or a spiritual Red Cross. The role of religious leaders in this decisive area is precisely the formation of a community with a conscience, one that does not withhold compassion by pleading complexity. Such a community will recognize that, because we are all brothers and sisters to everyone else, we all stand under a common judgment. 'Will we ever achieve justice in Athens?' The wise Greek who was asked this question replied: 'We will achieve justice when those who are not injured are as indignant as those who are.' "—From *Religion and the American Dream: The Search for Freedom Under God*, by Christopher F. Mooney, S.J. Copyright © 1977 Christopher F. Mooney. Used by permission of The Westminster Press, Philadelphia, PA.

God's Time. The prophet is one who sees what God has in mind. Usually, he is out of step with others. Often, he experiences defeat and disappointment. For instance, in the British Parliament in 1866, William Gladstone saw that reforms would have to come in the way members of Parliament were elected. At that time, working-class people were regarded as too stupid and irresponsible to vote. Gladstone and Lord Russell realized that such elitism fostered class feelings and bitterness. They worked to introduce a bill reforming the election procedures. Gladstone was vilified by the opposition, many of whom accused him of deserting his party and his class. Nevertheless, Gladstone staunchly supported Lord Russell's Reform Bill. "You cannot fight against the future," he stated. "Time is on our side. The great social forces that move on in their might and majesty . . . are marshalled on our side." Referring to those for whom the Bill was intended to provide the franchise, the stalwart Christian statesman said, "The persons to whom their remarks apply are our fellow subjects, our fellow Christians, our own flesh and blood." The Reform Bill was defeated that year. Gladstone, however, was proved correct. He was the realist; he knew what God intended. Eventually, the right to vote was extended to laborers as well as lords.

Venetians First. Venice was once one of the wealthiest states in the world. Five hundred years ago, this beautiful and proud city of Italy ruled vast areas. As it grew richer, its faith in God seemed to decline. The Venetians continued, however, to make use of Christian trappings in all governmental and business dealings. It consoled the lower classes with parades and religious processions. Venetian merchants sold arms and slaves to all comers. In some cases, for a price, these wealthy citizens even gave military intelligence to Muslims at war with neighboring Christians. Nothing, not even the possibility of excommunication, allowed their Christian faith ever to interfere with business or war. In fact, the Venetians adopted the motto, *Siamo Veneziani, poi Christiani:* "We are Venetians; after that we are Christians."

God brings judgment on any community or individual which takes such a motto openly or privately! Only when we are Christians before we are anything else can we stand before the Lord! Civil religion, however, tries to put God second.

Questions for Pupils on the Next Lesson. 1. Must genuine worship necessarily include acts of justice? 2. How are nations judged, according to Amos? 3. Why does wealth interfere with faithfulness to God? 4. Does a religious pedigree, such as being a Christian or a church member or an adherent to a certain denomination, guarantee God's favor? 5. Is God still the Lord and Judge of history?

TOPIC FOR YOUTH
REASON FOR JUDGMENT

Blunt Questioning. God is never impressed by our excuses, our evasions, our cover-up for acting unjustly toward others.

George Meany, the American labor leader, was rarely without a colorful comment or penetrating question. Meany also was profoundly opposed to sham. Once, in 1955, when the French were continuing their colonialism in Tunisia in North Africa, Meany was invited to the French Embassy in Washington. Meany listened for a long time to a series of experts from France who enumerated reasons why Tunisia was better off under French rule. Finally, the speakers turned to Meany and asked if he had any questions.

"Just one," rumbled George Meany. "When are you fellows going to quit kicking the Tunisians around?"

This is the way God operates. He is not impressed by our expert opinions, but gets down to basics at once on the matter of whether or not we are kicking any others around in any way whatsoever. If we are, this is the reason for His judgment.

DEW Line for Judgment. Stretching for many thousands of miles across the northern part of the entire continent of North America is a series of sensitive devices to pick up first indications of a possible enemy missile attack. It is called the Defense Early Warning Line, or DEW Line. It signals emergency centers in the United States and Canada to prepare immediately to take steps to prevent destruction.

God's Word also provides a DEW Line for us in our living. The Scriptures, containing the Covenant and Commandments and the Christ, are divine provision for our welfare. By disregarding basic requirements of justice to others, we stand in danger of being destroyed. The prophets and Jesus have issued early warnings to us that we are disobeying God's signals. Will we heed these before it is too late?

Reason for Judgment? "To an ever increasing extent, productive wealth and control are concentrated in fewer and fewer hands. On income, for example, the top 20 percent of the population receives 41 percent of all income, eight times as much as the bottom 20 percent. In fact, statistics will show that the top 20 percent of the population receives more income than the bottom 60 percent combined. Or, going further, the bottom half of the U.S. population receives the same total amount of income as the richest 10 percent."—*Commonweal*, February 28, 1975; *Quote*, April 6, 1975.

Questions for Pupils on the Next Lesson. 1. What are the most glaring examples of injustice in our society in these times? 2. Is it possible to be a "good Christian" yet not be concerned about justice issues? 3. Why does Amos insist that it is impossible to worship without remembering the poor? 4. How are nations judged, according to Amos? 5. Does God play favorites with any group?

LESSON II—JUNE 9

WHAT GOD DESIRES

Background Scripture: Amos 4–5
Devotional Reading: Amos 5:4–13

KING JAMES VERSION

AMOS 4   Hear this word, ye kine of Bashan that *are* in the mountain of Samaria, which oppress the poor, which crush the needy, which say to their masters, Bring, and let us drink.

5   14 Seek good, and not evil, that ye may live: and so the LORD, the God of hosts, shall be with you, as ye have spoken.

15 Hate the evil, and love the good, and establish judgment in the gate: it may be that the LORD God of hosts will be gracious unto the remnant of Joseph.

21 I hate, I despise your feast days, and I will not smell in your solemn assemblies.

22 Though ye offer me burnt offerings and your meat offerings, I will not accept *them;* neither will I regard the peace offerings of your fat beasts.

23 Take thou away from me the noise of thy songs; for I will not hear the melody of thy viols.

24 But let judgment run down as waters, and righteousness as a mighty stream.

REVISED STANDARD VERSION

AMOS 4 "Hear this word, you cows of Bashan,
who are in the mountain of Samaria,
who oppress the poor, who crush the needy,
who say to their husbands, 'Bring, that we may drink!'

5   14 "Seek good and not evil, that you may live;
and so the LORD, the God of hosts, will be with you, as you have said.

15 Hate evil, and love good, and establish justice in the gate;
it may be that the LORD, the God of hosts, will be gracious to the remnant of Joseph.

21 "I hate, I despise your feasts,
and I take no delight in your solemn assemblies.

22 Even though you offer me your burnt offerings and cereal offerings,
I will not accept them,
and the peace offerings of your fatted beasts
I will not look upon.

23 Take away from me the noise of your songs;
to the melody of your harps I will not listen.

24 But let justice roll down like waters,
and righteousness like an everflowing stream."

KEY VERSE: *Seek good and not evil, that you may live; and so the Lord, the God of hosts, will be with you.* Amos 5:14 (RSV).

HOME DAILY BIBLE READINGS

June	3.	M.	Revealing Questions. Amos 3:1–11.
June	4.	T.	The Poor Oppressed. Amos 4:1–5.
June	5.	W.	Opportunities for Repentance. Amos 4:6–13.
June	6.	T.	God Knows Our Deeds. Amos 5:6–13.
June	7.	F.	Seek Good, Not Evil. Amos 5:14, 15.
June	8.	S.	Justice Required. Amos 5:21–27.
June	9.	S.	Danger in Security. Amos 6:1–8.

BACKGROUND

Amos thought of himself as an ordinary lay person. He earned his living by shepherding. He had no formal training as a prophet. He carried no priestly credentials. He could point to no illustrious family tree of Hebrew leaders and inherited no religious title. He left us only one sermon—the "Book of Amos"—but it is a blockbuster! (That sermon, incidentally, is in poetry, not prose, showing that Amos was not a rough rube!)

Palestine in the time of Amos was caught in the throes of an industrial revolution. People were moving from the ancestral family farms to the cities. Manufacturing was replacing shepherding. Some people were making fortunes. Many others, however, were living in grinding poverty. Unscrupulous people were exploiting the poor, charging them outrageous interest rates or hiring them for starvation wages.

The city of Bethel was a luxury-loving cathedral city which appreciated fine wool. Amos, bringing his wool to sell in Bethel, was incensed at the conditions. He noticed the elaborate ceremonies in the royal shrine, but he also observed the superstition and self-satisfaction which permeated worship in Bethel.

Bethel was situated on the great North-South trade route running along the ridge of western Palestine. Most of the commercial traffic between Africa and Asia Minor traveled on that highway and passed through Bethel. Amos heard the international news as well as the national news in Bethel as he listened to reports from travelers. Amos pondered the meaning of those firsthand reports from the great cities of the Middle East, Africa, and Asia. Most of all, Amos listened to God's evaluations of those reports!

NOTES ON THE PRINTED TEXT

George Plagens, a reporter for the *Cleveland Press*, reviewed the church services in his area. Using a restaurant-type rating scale (with three stars at the top for excellence), he evaluated worship in various congregations according to music, sermons, and friendliness.

Amos the prophet had a somewhat different set of criteria, but he also evaluated Israel's worship. Israel received no stars. Amos reported that God was disappointed particularly with the spiritual life of the affluent women of Samaria. Pointing to the contrast between the dress of the rich, trendy Samarian women and the threadbare rags worn by the suffering peasantry, Amos denounced the piety and worship of the wealthy leading women. *"Hear this word, you cows of Bashan, who are in the mountains of Samaria, who oppress the poor, who crush the needy, who say to their husbands, 'Bring, that we may drink.'"*

The Law of Moses provided that every person in Israel had to be provided with basic needs to survive, especially food and shelter. Amos knew that the Law was being ignored. Furthermore, the wealth of the rich was accumulating at the expense of the poor. The fashionable finery of the Samarian uppercrust meant that less-fortunate fellow Israelites were being exploited and oppressed. Amos warned that the Lord would be as harsh on luxury-loving worshipers in Samaria as the Assyrians were on their prisoners whom they bound together by fish hooks (Amos 4:2).

Amos's words are a stinging reminder to God's pampered people in every era. When we fret over styles and comforts while most of the rest of humanity suffers from improper drinking water, insufficient protein, and inadequate housing, God is most displeased. Amos also warns us not to allow our wealth to interfere with our faithfulness to God and to others. Faithfulness must include acts of justice to all. Justice, in its fullest biblical sense, is what the Lord desires.

For the third time (*see* Amos 5:4 and 5:6), Amos calls upon his listeners to seek the Lord that they might live. For Amos, life meant living in God's grace and favor. Amos offers instructions to his people on how to live. Simply, God commands the people to *seek good, and not evil, that you may live.* Israel is to be actively devoted to the doing of justice. Justice is to be shown in all actions. It is to be love shown through deeds.

Establish justice in the gate. The city gate was the courtroom in Amos's day. The court or the gate was also notoriously corrupt. Although the poor were to be protected, the needy helped, and the orphaned and widowed dealt with justly, the gate neglected and ignored them. Amos promised that only if justice prevailed would God be gracious with Israel, *the remnant of Joseph.*

I hate, I despise your feasts, and I take no delight in your solemn assemblies. Amos would have rated Israel's worship life poorly. God was disgusted with its worship (*solemn assemblies*) and nauseated by its music (*the noise of your songs*). Amos implied that the people's worship only reflected their luxury and the priests' corruption. God loathed the religious shows that were being played out in Israel's shrines and worship services. *Even though you offer me your burnt offerings and cereal offerings, I will not accept them, and the peace offerings of your fatted beasts I will not look upon.*

What did God desire? *Let justice roll down like waters, and righteousness like an overflowing stream.* God commands His people to be just and righteous. Let justice roll from you like the flood waters after a winter's rains. Let righteousness flow from you like an ever-flowing stream that continuously flows even during a summer's drought. God desires that we be righteous and just at all times and to all people!

SUGGESTIONS TO TEACHERS

Exactly what do you think God desires of your congregation? Of your denomination? Of the Church? Of your community? Of our nation?

To get your lesson underway this morning, try passing out slips of paper and pencils and asking each person in your class to answer at least some of those questions in two or three sentences. Insist that the answers be specific and not airy generalities. Give the class a time limit of five minutes to work on those questions.

After the class has struggled with what God desires of us today, ask it to study Amos's answers for his time, as shown in today's Scripture material. Some of Amos's points can be summarized as follows:

1. *RITUAL WITH RIGHTEOUSNESS.* Without getting bogged down in fruitless discussions about the sacrifical system in the Jewish Temple, remind your people that God calls on us to give over our time, energies, possessions—ourselves—to His service. Amos's biting sarcasm about the elaborate but empty forms of ritual in the Bethel shrine apply everywhere. This may well be a time to talk together about what Jesus Christ wants of us in worship both on Sundays and in our daily lives.

2. *HUMILITY IN HARDSHIP.* Amos pointed out that people often are unable to use hard times as a lesson. His people, Amos emphasized, needed to remember in all circumstances that they belonged to the Lord. His words of warning could well be chiselled on the walls of your classroom. " 'You were as a brand plucked out of the burning yet you did not return to me,' says the Lord" (4:11). How do those in your class use the rough times in which Christ has stood by them?

3. *COMMITMENT WITH CONCERN.* Commitment to God must be accompanied by concern for brothers and sisters. "Seek good, not evil, that you may live. . . . Establish justice in the gate," (5:14, 15) admonishes Amos. Concern for others is demonstrated by doing justice. Devote plenty of today's lesson to thinking with your class about areas where Christians must "establish justice in the gate" or work actively in the larger community to relieve those who are oppressed. Consider together who in particular are being forced to suffer injustice in your community. An ethnic group? A minority? The elderly and retired? Youth? Women? What can your church do to sensitize others to their plight? What can you do to ameliorate their hurts and to change things?

4. *SACRIFICE WITH SERVICE.* Giving is needed in every church, but service

is also a form of giving. In fact, some buy their way out of service by simply handing out some money. On the other hand, some stingily withhold their money under the pretense that they are doing so much service. Think with your class how both money and service must be shared. Discuss the ways Christians sometimes try to delude themselves (and God) when it comes to giving and serving.

TOPIC FOR ADULTS
WHAT GOD DESIRES

Feeding the Squirrels. Foreign correspondents in Berlin during the lean days of World War II commented about the way the city's inhabitants shared their precious bread rations to feed the squirrels in the city parks on Sunday mornings. In fact, people frequently expressed concern for the welfare of the squirrels. No one, however, commented about the disappearance of Jewish neighbors, or about the barbarities in Poland or the atrocities in Holland. No Berliner seemed to feel particularly upset about the Hitler cult. On the other hand, every citizen on the streets seemed to the foreign visitor to be decent, cultured people. The population never seemed to see anything morally wrong with Nazi cruelty. The Berlin folks felt sorriest for the squirrels. Their tenderness to the cute little animals in the parks moved them to write letters to the papers on their behalf and to share food with them. They prided themselves on being people of dignity, loving classical music, family gatherings, and caring for helpless wildlife.

At least one foreign correspondent, shaken at the way the Berliners were preoccupied with feeding the squirrels while neglecting justice toward the Jews, pondered at the way humans seemed to be able to make minor sacrifices for minor matters while forgetting major issues. God insists that we be more than pleasant, respectable people. He desires that we do more than be moved occasionally to petty charity such as feeding the squirrels while refusing to be involved with the shrieking examples of injustice around us.

Are we smugly content to go on feeding the squirrels, or will we respond to God's call to heed the helpless?

"He Is—Everything!" Arturo Toscanini, the great conductor, was renowned for being an exacting and sometimes tyrannical leader of his orchestras during rehearsals. Once, he practiced the *Ninth Symphony* by Beethoven with a symphony orchestra. He demanded repeated renditions by each section of the orchestra. First, the woodwinds, then the strings, next the brass, and so on, rehearsed separately. Finally, the entire orchestra at full concert strength went over and over the mighty piece of music. At last, the orchestra was rehearsed to Toscanini's satisfaction. The concert was magnificent. After the performance, the first violinist whispered to the second, "If he scolds us after that, I will jump up and push him off his platform." But the great Toscanini did not scold. He stood silently. His hands were outstretched. His deep eyes burned with an inner fire, showing a light of great rapture throughout his face. A sense of contentment seemed to enfold him. After a long silence, he spoke.

"Who am I? Who is Toscanini? Who are you? I am nobody. You are nobody." The crowded hall remained hushed. The master stood with arms still extended. The multitude waited in awed silence. Then, with the light upon his countenance of a prophet who has had a vision, Toscanini whispered, "Beethoven is *everything—everything!*"

Who are we? Do our plans matter? God is everything ... *everything!* This is the beginning of understanding what God desires us to understand.

What God Desires. "Americans are hampered in responding to the need for massive social action on a world scale because of our country's all-pervasive emphasis on private rights and interests. National well-being has come to be identified with a very individualistic understanding of the pursuit of happiness, quite unlike that of the Founders. As a result, most Americans today are not very much interested in the common good of the larger world community, some even insisting that the promise of a better life be fulfilled at home first, no matter what the international consequences. This is a peculiarly American form of blindness, and because it is rooted in societal reality it can be healed only by some societal change. Eventually government will have to act to ensure more equal access to economic wealth and cultural resources. But in the meantime the people of our country must be sensitized to what their religions say about committing oneself to institutions serving the needs of a more and more integrated human family. The great resource here is the original Judeo-Christian tradition which placed the community at the center of the people's awareness and presented individual life as a participation in the larger life of the community. Religious leaders in America must ask themselves to what extent they have appropriated this original tradition. To what extent have they allowed it to correct their inherited perception of society conditioned by the American preoccupation with private rights and interests?"—From *Religion and the American Dream: The Search for Freedom Under God,* by Christopher F. Mooney, S.J. Copyright © 1977 Christopher F. Mooney. Used by permission of The Westminster Press, Philadelphia, PA.

Questions for Pupils on the Next Lesson. 1. What examples can you think of in which people have claimed that God was on their side? 2. Is there any judgment apart from human judgment? 3. Do you view the future with pessimism, or with hope? Why? 4. What did the prophets usually mean by the phrase, "the Day of the Lord"? 5. Why do prophets claim that oppressing the unfortunate is acting violently toward them?

TOPIC FOR YOUTH
HATE EVIL AND LOVE GOOD

Record Sermon. The longest sermon on record lasted ninety-seven hours. It was preached in November, 1982 in Detroit by the Rev. M. Gregory Gentry. The Rev. Gentry set out to preach a 100-hour fund-raising "preach-a-thon" at 8:55 A.M. on Sunday, November 13, 1982, but was forced to quit at 9:47 A.M. Thursday by a split tongue and exhaustion. He topped the previous record of a ninety-three-hour sermon set by the Rev. Donald Thomas in Brooklyn, N.Y., in 1978, and felt pleased that he raised $10,318.86 for his church.

The minor prophets did not have long sermons, but they said so much. The Rev. Gentry and the Rev. Thomas might have sermonized for nearly five days, but did not seem to say much. No one commented on their messages. Everyone speaks of Amos's words.

The minor prophets such as Amos spoke of what God desires and summed it up in terse lines about hating evil and loving good. What would your sermon be if you had to preach on the topic of what God desires?

The Proper Subject. There is an ancient church in the town of Ystad, Sweden, which is undistinguished in every way except for a life-size, lifelike figure on a cross hanging on the pillar directly opposite the pulpit. The six-foot crucified figure even has human hair matted under a crown of real thorns, and confronts the preacher more than the congregation. Visitors are perplexed by the strange arrangement and the disproportionately large crucifix.

It seems that King Charles XII visited the church in 1716. The pastor was carried away by the presence of the ruler in the congregation on that Sunday, and set aside his text and substituted an ardent eulogy of the king. Charles was unmoved, and said nothing. Several months later, a large gift arrived at the church. It was the large, life-sized, realistically-carved figure of the crucified Lord. With it were instructions from Charles XII: "This is to hang on the pillar opposite the Pulpit, so that all who stand there will be reminded of their proper subject."

We must focus on the proper subject. Then we will hate evil and do good!

More Than Talk. William Brandon, Governor of Alabama, once was touring the grounds of the State Mental Hospital at Tuscaloosa and encountered a patient painting a barn. "Who are you?" demanded the patient.

Somewhat surprised, Brandon answered, "I am the governor of this great State." Thinking little of what he was saying, he added, "And I would like to help you in any way I can."

"Okay. Grab a brush."

God wants more than talk. He calls us to a "grab a brush" type of faith. Our worship, our creeds and our pronouncements are empty until they are backed with lives showing that we turn from evil to doing good!   *from GOD*

Questions for Pupils on the Next Lesson. 1. Have you ever experienced judgment in any form? If so, How? 2. How do you view the future? 3. What does the Prophet Amos mean by the words, "the Day of the Lord"? 4. What would the Prophet Amos have to say, in your opinion, to our nation at this time?

Classroom.

Amos job-
rotten
forecaster
turn
this clout
→ a group
Tx - ask others
orders →
resolute
situation.

LESSON III—JUNE 16

THE DAY OF THE LORD

Background Scripture: Amos 3:13–15; 5:18–20; 6:1–7; 8:7–12
Devotional Reading: Amos 7:1–9

KING JAMES VERSION

AMOS 5   18 Woe unto you that desire the day of the LORD! to what end *is* it for you? the day of the LORD *is* darkness, and not light.

19 As if a man did flee from a lion, and a bear met him; or went into the house, and leaned his hand on the wall, and a serpent bit him.

20 *Shall* not the day of the LORD *be* darkness, and not light? even very dark, and no brightness in it?

8   7 The LORD hath sworn by the excellency of Jacob, Surely I will never forget any of their works.

8 Shall not the land tremble for this, and every one mourn that dwelleth therein? and it shall rise up wholly as a flood; and it shall be cast out and drowned, as *by* the flood of Egypt.

9 And it shall come to pass in that day, saith the Lord GOD, that I will cause the sun to go down at noon, and I will darken the earth in the clear day:

10 And I will turn your feasts into mourning, and all your songs into lamentation; and I will bring up sackcloth upon all loins, and baldness upon every head; and I will make it as the mourning of an only *son*, and the end thereof as a bitter day.

11 Behold, the days come, saith the Lord GOD, that I will send a famine in the land, not a famine of bread, nor a thirst for water, but of hearing the words of the LORD:

12 And they shall wander from sea to sea, and from the north even to the east, they shall run to and fro to seek the word of the LORD, and shall not find *it*.

REVISED STANDARD VERSION

AMOS 5   18 Woe to you who desire the day of the LORD!
Why would you have the day of the LORD?
It is darkness, and not light;
19 as if a man fled from a lion,
and a bear met him;
or went into the house and leaned with his hand against the wall,
and a serpent bit him.
20 Is not the day of the LORD darkness, and not light,
and gloom with no brightness in it?

8   7 The LORD has sworn by the pride of Jacob:
"Surely I will never forget any of their deeds.
8 Shall not the land tremble on this account.
and every one mourn who dwells in it,
and all of it rise like the Nile,
and be tossed about and sink again, like the Nile of Egypt?"
9 "And on that day," says the Lord GOD,
"I will make the sun go down at noon,
and darken the earth in broad daylight.
10 I will turn your feasts into mourning,
and all your songs into lamentation;
I will bring sackcloth upon all loins,
and baldness on every head;
I will make it like the mourning for an only son,
and the end of it like a bitter day.
11 "Behold, the days are coming," says the Lord GOD,
"when I will send a famine on the land;
not a famine of bread, nor a thirst for water,
but of hearing the words of the LORD.
12 They shall wander from sea to sea, and from north to east;
they shall run to and fro, to seek the word of the LORD,
but they shall not find it."

KEY VERSE: *Woe to those who are at ease in Zion, and those who feel secure on the mountain of Samaria. Amos 6:1 (RSV).*

HOME DAILY BIBLE READINGS

June   10.   M.   *A Day of Punishment.* Amos 3:13–15.
June   11.   T.   *Darkness, Not Light.* Amos 5:18–20.
June   12.   W.   *Visions of Destruction.* Amos 7:1–9.
June   13.   T.   *The Needy Mistreated.* Amos 8:1–6.

June   14.   F.   *A Famine of the Word.* Amos 8:7–12.
June   15.   S.   *Sin Not Tolerated.* Amos 9:5–8.
June   16.   S.   *Restoration Still Possible.* Amos 9:11–15.

BACKGROUND

Certain phrases come to have a certain meaning to certain people. "Full-time Christian Service," for example, used to stand for being a pastor or a missionary. Then some bright soul pointed out that every Christian is in full-time service, not merely part-time, for Jesus Christ. And that slogan became a bit jarring to sensitive ears, especially of laypersons serving with just as much commitment as any clergy type.

"The day of the Lord" was a set of buzz-words for the Hebrew people for many generations. The phrase was the popular way of describing the day of light and vindication for Israel. The notion which everybody took for granted was that the Lord would intervene. Mr. and Mrs. Average Israelite assumed that "Day of the Lord" referred to times in the past when God had saved the nation from her enemies, such as in the days of the Pharaoh in Egypt, or in the days of the Judges. A future "Day of the Lord"? Most people were confident that it would be a glorious celebration when God would intervene in history, exonerate His chosen nation, and decisively punish all foreign powers which opposed Him.

You can imagine the shock and anger when Amos took this slogan, "The Day of the Lord," and turned its meaning around and made it apply to Israel! Instead of the Day of the Lord being a day of light and vindication for the nation, it would be a time of darkness and misfortune for Israel. The Lord's Coming, Amos bluntly stated, would not bring salvation for Israel, but rather judgment. Amos's audience, needless to say, did not take warmly to this idea. It was fine to speak of God's judgment meaning disaster for someone else, but not acceptable to talk of that time of reckoning and punishment for Israel! Amos, however, insisted on "telling it like it is" from God's standpoint. Sometimes God's prophets have the unpopular assignment of stating unpleasant truths.

Amos added a footnote to his dire warning. He announced that the Lord would save and deliver a remnant of Israelite people who remained faithful to Him. This idea of the remnant faithful to the Lord was remembered by later prophets, especially in the dark days when Jerusalem was captured and its people marched off to exile in Babylon.

NOTES ON THE PRINTED TEXT

Ancient Israel looked forward to the "Day of the Lord" as much as many people today look with anticipation toward the Second Coming. For the people of Israel, the "Day of the Lord" meant not only a time of judgment and disaster for the enemies of the Lord but a time of deliverance and salvation for those who were faithful to the Lord. Israel confidently called on God to intervene on its behalf, expecting that the "Day of the Lord" would bring them security. However, in a dramatic speech, Amos dashed the hopes of those who were looking forward to God's Coming as providing deliverance. Instead, Amos took this fundamental belief and turned it against them.

Woe to you who desire the day of the Lord! cried Amos with a wail of grief used over the dead. Israel's piety and confidence were misplaced. Instead of escaping the great calamity that the Lord would bring (a time when the lights would fail and great thick clouds of darkness would exist) and finding salvation for itself, Israel would find death. God's Coming would bring no security for Israel's people. *It is darkness and not light; as if a man fled from a lion, and a bear met him; or went into the house and leaned with his hand against the wall, and a serpent bit him.* Remembering his rural background, Amos compared Israel's death to a man who escaped a lion only to be killed by a bear and to a man who thought he was safe within his home only to be bitten by a snake. In both metaphors, the theme was the same. Israel would escape only to die.

Sadly, the same "God is with us" attitude of ancient Israel is reflected today. "One nation under God" our children pledge. "In God we trust" our currency reads. We picture ourselves as a decent, righteous, and well-scrubbed Christian country bearing God's seal of approval. Given our failings to help the world's victims of injustice and given our greed and crushing of the world's poor, hungry, naked, and needy, would not Amos's message be the same to us?

The Lord has sworn by the pride of Jacob: "Surely I will never forget any of their deeds." The outwardly religious merchants plotted ways to make sure the poor would pay more for the necessities of life such as food and cheated the poor by using false balances. Recent excavations at Tirzah show two eighth century weights, one for buying and one for selling (Amos 8:5), confirming that cheating and exploitation was a common practice in Amos's time.

I will bring sackcloth upon all loins, and baldness on every head. There would not be any joyful music and happy festivals. Instead, there would be only funeral dirges, mourning clothes and shaved heads. The only worship that would be heard would be the mourning of the funeral services.

If the arrogant nation still had not comprehended Amos's drastic interpretation of the "Day of the Lord," it now heard more doom. Amos announced a famine and drought such as Israel had never endured. *". . . not a famine of bread nor a thirst for water, but of hearing the word of the Lord."* God's mercy and help would be absent! From the Dead Sea to the Mediterranean Sea, from Dan to Bethel, the people would seek the Word of the Lord but would not hear nor find it. Israel would want the God they had ignored with the desperation of a starving, parched dry people, but they would not find Him.

SUGGESTIONS TO TEACHERS

Some in your class may be tuned out and turned off by this scriptural material from Amos because they think it is all doom and gloom. Others may be interested in the lurid details of Amos's dire warnings because they are absorbed by reckless talk about an imminent end of the world and time of judgment. This is why it's so important for you as teacher to know what's meant by the biblical phrase, "The Day of the Lord." The Background and Notes on the Printed Text are especially important for you for this lesson.

1. *REMNANT RESCUED.* Start with Amos's point about the remnant. Don't be put off by the way Amos described the remnant in terms of a piece of a carcass snatched from the jaws of marauding beasts. This is a typical colorful Middle Eastern metaphor. The message, however, is universal. God saves a remnant to continue to carry out His purposes. Without getting into involved development of the theme of the Remnant throughout the Bible, you should hit on the notion that Christians are such a remnant for God. The Church is intended to serve as the chosen remnant of the faithful. Take enough time to develop the implications of this for your class. Ask such questions as what does it mean to be a minority opinion when it comes to morals and values in a society given to pleasure and violence?

2. *RICHES REPUDIATED.* Amos fearlessly denounced the wealthy for their indolence and indifference. He saw the widening gap between have's and have-not's. The prophet knew that when have-not's are allowed to go hungry while the have's exploit them to indulge in luxuries, a showdown is inevitable. Amos's words still carry a sting when he describes the contrast between the hovels of the poor and the ostentatious summer residences of the rich. With Amos's words in

mind, turn your class's attention to the plight of the hungry and refugees in our world. Use the statistics showing the gap between rich and poor. What would Amos have to say to the class if he were to appear?

3. *RECKONING REMEMBERED.* This point in the lesson may be the best time to get a handle on the term, "The Day of the Lord." Amos points out that those looking for a vindication of their own ways will be surprised when the Lord comes. Furthermore, Amos warns those imagining that they will be free from responsibility when the Lord's Day comes. The point to stress in this part of the lesson is that God turns no blind eye to those indulging in luxury at the expense of the hungry, the homeless. When the wealthy and the powerful trample upon others, they are sowing seeds of violence! God's ways are not secret or hidden; He insists upon justice. He introduces occasions of reckoning in history when oppression is allowed to go unchecked.

TOPIC FOR ADULTS
THE DAY OF THE LORD

The Cost of Irresponsibility. Early Friday morning, October 21, 1966, an enormous avalanche of coal slag crashed down a steep mountainside and buried a school and a row of miners' cottages in the Welsh village of Aberfan. One hundred forty-six youngsters between the ages of seven and eleven—almost the entire generation of children of the tiny village—perished.

For years, the coal "typ" or tip had been piling up above Aberfan. Typical of hundreds of coal villages in Wales, the monstrous heap of slag and waste on the mountainside had been growing for over a century. In spite of warnings by uneasy miners and the Coal Board, the menacing, 800-foot-high black, oozing Everest was ignored. Finally, weakened by days of rain, the deadly mass roared down the slope, engulfing the bleak village and its school.

Our years of carelessness and complacency eventually catch up with us. Our children sometimes pay the price of our lack of concern. Irresponsibility costs. "The Day of the Lord" inevitably comes to our communities if we fail to show concern.

At Ease in Chicago. The Day of the Lord catches many by surprise because it comes in unusual ways. But God's judgment is inevitable.

In 1923, a very important meeting was held at the Edgewater Beach Hotel in Chicago. Attending this meeting were nine of the world's most successful financiers. Those present were:

The President of the largest independent steel company
The President of the largest utility company
The President of the largest gas company
The greatest wheat speculator
The President of the New York Stock Exchange
A Member of the President's Cabinet
The greatest bear in Wall Street
The head of the world's greatest monopoly
The President of the Bank of International Settlements

Certainly we must admit that here were gathered a group of the world's most successful men. At least, men who had found the secret of making money. Twenty-five years later, let's see where these men were.

The President of the largest independent steel company, Charles Schwab, died bankrupt and lived on borrowed money for five years before his death.

The President of the utility, Samuel Insull, died a fugitive from justice and penniless in a foreign land.

The President of the Gas Company, A. Howard Hopkins, went insane.

The greatest wheat speculator, Arthur Cutten, died abroad insolvent.

The President of the New York Stock Exchange, Richard Whitney, served a long term in Sing Sing prison.

The member of the President's Cabinet, Albert Fall, was pardoned from prison so he could die at home.

The greatest "bear" on Wall Street, Jesse Livermore, died a suicide.

The head of the greatest monopoly, Ivar Krueger, died a suicide.

The President of the Bank of International Settlement, Leon Fraser, died a suicide.

Serious Business Now! The Prophet Amos thundered that the Lord brings judgment on each nation this very day, and that God will not be put off. Amos called for obedience at once before it would be too late.

There is a striking story that comes to us from the ancient history of the East, when one of the rulers of Thebes was sitting at a banquet. He was enjoying himself hugely. He did not want to be disturbed because he was enjoying the food, the drinks, and the entertainment. When one of his servants came to him and handed him a scroll with the whisper: "This comes from a friend who says it's serious business and you should read it at once," he laughed, drunkenly, and pushed him aside with the words: "Serious business tomorrow." But the message which he pushed aside brought word of conspirators within the palace who that very night poisoned him.

Questions for Pupils on the Next Lesson. 1. Who was Micah and what did he preach? 2. What is the difference between charity and justice? 3. What does it mean to "walk humbly with God"? 4. What were the injustices in Micah's day? 5. What are the problems of trying to "do justice" in our times?

TOPIC FOR YOUTH
THE DAY OF RECKONING

Loved His Cadillac. Amos the prophet warned that a day of reckoning must come to those who put their love of luxury and possessions ahead of other matters. People scoffed at him. But his message is valid.

A few years ago, a man in Niles, Michigan, named Fred Marshall won $200,000.00 in the Michigan Lottery. He promptly went out and bought the fanciest, most luxurious automobile he could find as soon as he received the first installment of his winnings. Six months later, however, he was found dead.

The police ruled that the death of Fred B. Marshall, fifty-five years old, was accidental. Officials said he died of carbon monoxide poisoning. Mr. Marshall's death was discovered shortly after noon Saturday when his wife noticed the garage door open part way, the police said. Officers said they found Mr. Marshall with one foot out of the car as if he had been trying to get out. The garage was filled with exhaust fumes, but the car was not running though the ignition switch was on, the police said.

Mr. Marshall's oldest daughter, said her father often spent hours in the new Cadillac—he "loved it so much"—listening to the tape deck or watching the auto's color television. The car also was equipped with a bar and refrigerator.

Kid's Reaction. The minister was describing judgment day: "Thunder will roar. Flames will shoot from the heavens. Floods, storms, earthquakes will devastate the world." The little boy, excited with the prospect of seeing such a dramatic sight, turned to his mother. "Mom," he whispered, "will I get out of school?"

We smile. However, like that little boy, we often take lightly the words of Amos and the prophets. All we can often think about is whether we'll get a holiday, or have some fun, or see some excitement. God calls us to accountability each day.

Telltales. In the old days of railroads, there used to be telltales posted on the railroad right-of-way in strategic places. What were telltales? They were merely strips of lightweight canvas or rope hanging from the arm of a pole. These strips dangled over the tracks to warn someone riding on the top of a railroad car that the train was approaching a bridge or tunnel. When the strips of cloth or rope brushed over you, you knew that you had to get down immediately. You were in danger. If you didn't duck quickly, you would be knocked off the top of the railroad car and probably killed.

God sends His "telltales." Through the words of the prophets like Amos, He warns us of dangers approaching our community and nation. Unless we take steps soon, Amos insists to the people of the old Israel and to us, the "new Israel"—the Church—we can be in serious trouble.

Questions for Pupils on the Next Lesson. 1. What exactly does it mean to oppress someone? Can you give some examples? 2. What does Micah mean when he calls for people to "do justice" and to "walk humbly" with God? 3. Why is it so hard to think of injustices which you do to others, but so easy to identify injustices done to you? 4. What are the most glaring examples of injustice in our nation at this time? 5. Why is the Christian Church always under such close scrutiny by God?

LESSON IV—JUNE 23

THE LORD'S COMPLAINT

Background Scripture: Micah 3; 6
Devotional Reading: Micah 2:5–13

KING JAMES VERSION	REVISED STANDARD VERSION
MICAH 6 Hear ye now what the LORD saith; Arise, contend thou before the mountains, and let the hills hear thy voice.	MICAH 6 Hear what the LORD says; Arise, plead your case before the mountains, and let the hills hear your voice.

KING JAMES VERSION

MICAH 6 Hear ye now what the LORD saith; Arise, contend thou before the mountains, and let the hills hear thy voice.

2 Hear ye, O mountains, the LORD's controversy, and ye strong foundations of the earth: for the LORD hath a controversy with his people, and he will plead with Israel.

3 O my people, what have I done unto thee? and wherein have I wearied thee? testify against me.

4 For I brought thee up out of the land of Egypt, and redeemed thee out of the house of servants; and I sent before thee Moses, Aaron, and Miriam.

5 O my people, remember now what Balak king of Moab consulted, and what Balaam the son of Beor answered him from Shittim unto Gilgal; that ye may know the righteousness of the LORD.

6 Wherewith shall I come before the LORD, *and* bow myself before the high God? shall I come before him with burnt offerings, with calves of a year old?

7 Will the LORD be pleased with thousands of rams, *or* with ten thousands of rivers of oil? shall I give my firstborn *for* my transgression, the fruit of my body *for* the sin of my soul?

8 He hath shewed thee, O man, what *is* good; and what doth the LORD require of thee, but to do justly, and to love mercy, and to walk humbly with thy God?

REVISED STANDARD VERSION

MICAH 6 Hear what the LORD says; Arise, plead your case before the mountains, and let the hills hear your voice.

2 Hear, you mountains, the controversy of the LORD, and you enduring foundations of the earth; for the LORD has a controversy with his people, and he will contend with Israel.

3 "O my people, what have I done to you? In what have I wearied you? Answer me!

4 For I brought you up from the land of Egypt, and redeemed you from the house of bondage; and I sent before you Moses, Aaron, and Miriam.

5 O my people, remember what Balak king of Moab devised, and what Balaam the Son of Beor answered him, and what happened from Shittim to Gilgal, that you may know the saving acts of the LORD."

6 "With what shall I come before the LORD, and bow myself before God on high? Shall I come before him with burnt offerings, with calves a year old?

7 Will the LORD be pleased with thousands of rams, with ten thousands of rivers of oil? Shall I give my first-born for my transgression, the fruit of my body for the sin of my soul?"

8 He has showed you, O man, what is good; and what does the LORD require of you but to do justice, and to love kindness, and to walk humbly with your God?

KEY VERSE: *He has showed you, O man, what is good; and what does the Lord require of you but to do justice, and to love kindness, and to walk humbly with your God?* Micah 6:8 (RSV).

HOME DAILY BIBLE READINGS

June	17.	M.	*The Lord's Lament.* Micah 1:1–9.
June	18.	T.	*Woe to the Wicked.* Micah 2:1–5.
June	19.	W.	*Preachers Speak Lies.* Micah 2:6–11.
June	20.	T.	*Rulers Prevent Justice.* Micah 3:1–4.
June	21.	F.	*Prophets Lead Astray.* Micah 3:5–12.

June   22.   S.   *God Leads His Cause.* Micah 6:1–8.
June   23.   S.   *Corruption Will Be Punished.* Micah 6:9–16.

BACKGROUND

For many years, the economy of Israel and Judah had been based on agriculture. The traditional Law assumed an agrarian society and made provisions for the poor always to have enough to eat and a place to live. That food might have been the leftovers after harvest and the place to live might have been a mud hut, but at least everyone got by. When drought or plague or invasion came, everyone suffered alike. There was no well-to-do class, and there was no lower class. Everyone was pretty much on the same social footing and same economic level.

In the eighth century B.C., about the time of the prophets Micah and Isaiah, a great shift took place. The manufacturing age started in Israel and Judah. Mass production, using assembly line techniques amazingly similar to modern ones, became commonplace. Certain cities became one-industry towns. Peasant farmers flocked into the towns to work in the new industries. Sweatshop conditions quickly appeared. A surplus of labor drove down wages to a starvation level. A few people quickly became wealthy. These new rich people leased or bought farm land at low prices and began to control the food supply for the nation. Within a few years, a large number of desperately poor people was found in the nation—people who had no land, no savings, no jobs. This group of poverty-level people was either exploited or ignored by the establishment. The old Hebrew Law of Moses could not help the urban poor. And neither the religious nor governmental leaders seemed to care.

Enter Micah.

He was from a little town named Moresheth and knew the plight of the country folk who had migrated to the cities. He also had lived next to the great international highway, and therefore had a wider view than most of political movements in western Asia, especially Assyria, and their effect on Judah. For thirty years, Micah brought this global perspective to bear as he watched the degeneration of his own people under some of the worst rulers in Judah's history. His writings, taking only seven chapters, reveal the critical political events taking place in the world as the Assyrians threatened everyone, and the domestic problems in Judah as religion and morals became increasingly corrupt.

NOTES ON THE PRINTED TEXT

Micah, the straight-forward, no-nonsense prophet from Judah, preached against many of the same abuses as Amos. The corrupt courts, the greedy priests, and the depraved rulers were all condemned. Most importantly, Micah prophesied against the people's belief that nothing bad would ever happen to them because they were God's chosen people. Micah bluntly told them otherwise. *Hear what the Lord says,* Micah stated.

Micah pictures a courtroom scene. God summons Israel into court to plead its case. God commands Israel to argue its grievance against the Lord. The mountains, hills, and the very foundations of the earth are to witness the litigation between God and His people. God introduces the subject of the controversy. *O my people, what have I done to you?* Protesting His innocence, He continues, *In what have I wearied you?* Then God summarizes Israel's argument. Israel's patience is thinning. It is exhausted and devoid of hope. It is no longer obedient and holds God responsible for all of its problems. God, however, refuses to take the blame. He demands evidence. *Answer me!* He commands. In His rebuttal, He recounts Israel's history, a history in which He has long been involved. *For I brought you up from the land of Egypt, and redeemed you from the house of bondage; and I sent before you Moses, Aaron, and Miriam.* He asks Israel to remember *the saving acts of the Lord.* He then rests His case. In seeking settlement, God, through His Prophet Micah, calls for a return of faith and a knowledge of the Lord.

Such an overwhelming verdict against Israel could produce only a sense of guilt and sin. So Israel anxiously inquired what sacrifice could it offer to atone for its sins and appease God. How could Israel repair the relationship? What could it do to become acceptable again to the Lord? Micah asked rhetorically, *With what shall I come before the Lord, and bow myself before God on high?* Were burnt offerings or year-old calves enough? Would a thousand rams or innumerable jars of oil suffice? The desperation of the people was seen in the final offer of *my first-born for my transgression, the fruit of my body for the sin of my soul?* Did God want a human sacrifice as an atonement for Israel's sins and transgressions?

What does the Lord require? "You know what the Lord requires of you," Micah said. *Do justice.* As always, this was the essential element of faith that dominated the messages of Amos, Hosea, and Micah. In everything you do, Micah said, do it as God would do. Live according to God's will. Show it in your deeds. *Love kindness.* Be kind, merciful, and give your attention to others. Be gracious to others as God has been gracious to you. *Walk humbly with your God.* Yield to God. Offer yourself as the only sacrifice which God desires.

Micah's words have spanned the gulf of time. Calling these words a "timeless admonition," former President Jimmy Carter read them in his Inaugural Address. Do you practice justice, love kindness, and walk humbly with your God, or will the Lord complain about you, too?

SUGGESTIONS TO TEACHERS

In Medieval times, Eastern European Jews sometimes presented a play at Pass-over time in the Spring in which charges were brought against God. The shocking notion in these dramas was that God could be put on trial.

The idea that God is in the dock has not died. How often we think that when we accuse God and demand that He explain His actions. We frequently have the distorted notion that the Almighty stands accountable to us.

The Prophet Micah had to deal with this point of view. He disturbed many of his hearers by insisting that it is always the other way around. God has a case against His people! Here is where your lesson starts for this week.

1. *WHEN GOD PREFERS SILENCE.* Sometimes, however, God has nothing to say to certain people. Micah knows that God has no answers to those who hate good and love evil. Jesus also knew this: He remained silent on several occasions, such as when the wastrel Herod flippantly tried to interview Him. You may use this as an opening to discuss some of the reasons why prayer may seem empty and pointless. One of the most obvious but least-remembered reasons is that the Lord can really not communicate with those who have tuned Him out so completely by their persistent wrongdoing.

2. *WHEN GOD PRESSES CHARGES.* Micah lets the people of Judah know that the Lord has a case against them. Micah lays out the bill of particulars. Have those in your class list as many of the charges as they can find in Micah. These charges include such serious offenses as permitting injustice and bribery in the courts, oppressing the helpless poor, and ignoring the needy. Micah states that God indicts even the religious people. Micah has harsh words for false prophets who, having no insights or vision from the Lord, promise a phony security and peace. He also accuses the priests and religious leaders of practicing a flashy piety that lacks any passion for God and the hurting people. You as teacher must bring all of these concerns into the 1985 world by putting Micah's comments before your people. Are Micah's charges valid today?

3. *WHEN GOD PLEADS FOR SERVICE.* An entire lesson can be developed around Micah 6:8. Don't neglect this magnificent verse. Ask what God requires of us, His community of the faith, in these times.

4. *WHEN GOD PRONOUNCES SENTENCE.* Note Micah's vivid words about those who disobey God: "You shall eat, but not be satisfied, and there shall be hunger in your inward parts . . . you shall sow and not reap" (6:14, 15). Because of apostasy from the Lord, Judah will be destroyed, disgraced, and desolate. Not pretty words, but Micah assures his listeners that their turning from the Lord will inevitably have dire consequences. Without trying to sound morbid or harsh, move the class discussion to a consideration of destructive policies and practices in both the Church and the society in the latter part of the twentieth century. End on the positive note, however, of reiterating what Christ dreams we will be!

TOPIC FOR ADULTS
THE LORD'S COMPLAINT

Line Twenty-Five Times Around the World. "Suppose as you sat down to dinner, the doorbell rang, you opened the door, and then before you, ragged and disease-ravaged, stood the world's hungry in a single line, each begging for a crust of bread. How far do you think that line would reach? Beginning at your door, the line would continue out of sight, over continent and ocean, around the world—25,000 miles—and return to the place it started; and it would do this circling the globe not once, not five times, but twenty-five times, with no one in the line but hungry, suffering humanity."—Excerpted from Hunger Office booklet, 1268 Interchurch Center, 475 Riverside Drive, N.Y. 10027.

Difference Between Charity and Justice. ". . . we as Christians need to learn the difference between charity and justice.

"What is charity? Charity is full of pleasure. It gives us a good feeling. We can point to our individual acts of giving. We are in charge when we give charity. We decide when, how much and to whom or what we will give. We can impose our own limits. We are like the mother on the TV ad for Twinkies, who says, 'I decide when my family gets snacks and what kind.' We dish out little favors, the Twinkie donations, and wait for the, 'Thanks, Mom, you're really great.'

"What is justice? In the biblical sense, justice means to fulfill the demands of a relationship. It is righteousness in its deepest sense. Justice means to start filling a need and to keep on filling that need as long as necessary.

"All we have to do is look at the Old and New Testaments to see God's continued presence in the lives of His people as He fulfills their needs. That supreme example tells us how long we should go on fulfilling needs.

"Charity says that I bring in a can of corn for the church food basket. It goes to someone I do not know, someone whose need I only vaguely understand. But justice may say to me that, while a can of corn is marginally helpful, it does not go very far when the family of five that received it has nothing else for dinner that night. Justice tells me that the need was for dinner for five, not just a single can of vegetables that I so generously donated. Justice goes on to say that if this family had nothing else for dinner that night, it is probably true that the next night this family still had nothing else. Justice says that once I know the need, I am responsible for responding to it.

"Charity vs. justice. Charity is easy. Justice asks all kinds of questions that I don't want to hear. Questions that I know the answers to, but I am so rooted in planning my charity my way that I want to put my hands to my ears to shut out those answers. Justice makes me squirm, clear down to my toes and back up to my heart and my head."—Excerpted from article by Betsy Humphreys, "What is Needed," *Presbyterian Outlook,* November 1, 1982.

Cost of Unemployment. "For every 1 percent increase in unemployment there is a 3.4 percent increase in admissions for psychiatric treatment, a 4.1 percent increase in suicides, a 5.7 percent increase in homicides, a 1.9 percent increase in deaths from stress-related illnesses such as cardiovascular disease and a 4 percent increase in state prison admissions. Rising unemployment also correlates closely with increased divorce and desertion, alcoholism, malnutrition and rising infant mortalty rates."—Tim Atwater in "Reaganomics and Beyond: A Working Paper." Available from Interreligious Taskforce on US Food Policy, 110 Maryland Avenue, NE, Washington, DC 20002.

Questions for Pupils on the Next Lesson. 1. Why is it that our relationship with God also has an effect on our relationships with one another? 2. What happens to people's actions when they lack trust in God? 3. What were some of the examples of crime, dishonesty, and conspiracy stalking the land which Micah described? 4. Do you see many signs of hope in these times? On what do you base your answer? 5. How does God deliver people from unbelief and destructive consequences?

TOPIC FOR YOUTH
WHAT GOD REALLY WANTS

Now March! When Donatello, the great sculptor of the figure of Saint George on the facade of the Church of Saint Michael, had finished his work, all Florence waited for the prince of sculptors, Michelangelo, to come out and look it over. He found the pose to be perfect, the marble eye shining with light, the foot ready to step forth. At last, after a long pause, he said, "Now march!" It seemed ready, but it remained a thing of stone.

Is not this the way it sometimes is with our faith and with the Church? Everything looks poised for action, but seems to remain a thing of stone. God wants more than an appearance of religion. He commands us to march!

God's Reason. Stan Wisniski had been a heavy drinker. He lost his job and was unemployed for over a year and a half. He was finally able to put his life in order through Alcoholics Anonymous. Wisniski found a new job as a custodian at a college in Allentown, Pennsylvania. A few months later, he noticed an article in the newspaper describing the plight of Allentown's "street people." One of those pictured was Bill Smith, a man Stan Wisniski remembered that he had worked with for fifteen years at a clothing manufacturing company. Stan Wisniski was shocked to read that his former associate had lost his job, his room, and been forced to sleep in doorways, and cadge meals.

"God put me here for a reason," says Stan Wisniski. "Maybe it was to help someone else."

Stan Wisniski immediately began combing the back alleys of the center city in search of Smith, whom he had not seen for three years. Though time and a bout with the bottle had altered Smith's appearance, Stan recognized the gaunt, underfed associate among a group of men seeking refuge at a rescue mission. Stan Wisniski insisted on taking Bill Smith to his own one-bedroom apartment.

Stan has introduced Bill to Alcoholics Anonymous as well as providing a home. He helped Bill Smith to get back on public assistance after he had been denied it for not having a permanent address, had him fitted with a new pair of eyeglasses to replace the ones broken when he was beaten and robbed when he was living on the street. Stan Wisniski is even talking to Smith of looking for a job. Although Bill Smith is frightened to go far from the house, Stan reassures him, "It's all right, Bill, you have a home now."

This is the kind of service which God wants of each of us!

A World That's Up in Arms. Our world in a recent year spends more than $600 billion on military expenditures. Twenty-five million people currently serve in regular armies, backed up three-to-one by reserves, paramilitary forces, and necessary civilians. The international trade in conventional arms now tops $35 billion each year, proliferating sophisticated weapons of war into the most remote and least developed areas of the world. An uncontrolled build-up of nuclear weapons now provides an explosive force equal to three and a half tons of TNT for every living person on this planet at this time.

All of this is being done while one person in seven in the United States lives below the poverty level, and the infant mortality rate in Russia is twice the average for other countries.

In the face of these facts, what does God really want?

Questions for Pupils on the Next Lesson. 1. What happens to human relationships when people don't trust enough in God? 2. Can God deliver the nations of this world from destructive tendencies today? 3. What are the effects when humans refuse to trust each other? 4. What effect do your values have on your attitudes and relationships?

LESSON V—JUNE 30

THE HARVEST OF UNBELIEF

Background Scripture: Micah 7
Devotional Reading: Micah 7:14–20

KING JAMES VERSION

MICAH 7   Woe is me! for I am as when they have gathered the summer fruits, as the grapegleanings of the vintage: *there is* no cluster to eat: my soul desired the first ripe fruit.

2 The good *man* is perished out of the earth; and *there is* none upright among men: they all lie in wait for blood; they hunt every man his brother with a net.

3 That they may do evil with both hands earnestly, the prince asketh, and the judge *asketh* for a reward; and the great *man,* he uttereth his mischievous desire: so they wrap it up.

4 The best of them *is* as a brier: the most upright *is sharper* than a thorn hedge: the day of thy watchmen *and* thy visitation cometh; now shall be their perplexity.

5 Trust ye not in a friend, put ye not confidence in a guide: keep the doors of thy mouth from her that lieth in thy bosom.

6 For the son dishonoreth the father, the daughter riseth up against her mother, the daughter in law against her mother in law; a man's enemies *are* the men of his own house.

7 Therefore I will look unto the LORD; I will wait for the God of my salvation: my God will hear me.

REVISED STANDARD VERSION

MICAH 7   Woe is me! For I have become as
  when the summer fruit has been gathered,
    as when the vintage has been gleaned:
  there is no cluster to eat,
    no first-ripe fig which my soul desires.
2 The godly man has perished from the earth,
    and there is none upright among men;
  they all lie in wait for blood,
    and each hunts his brother with a net.
3 Their hands are upon what is evil, to do it diligently;
    the prince and the judge ask for a bribe,
  and the great man utters the evil desire of his soul;
    thus they weave it together.
4 The best of them is like a brier,
    the most upright of them a thorn hedge.
  The day of their watchmen, of their punishment, has come;
    now their confusion is at hand.
5 Put no trust in a neighbor,
    have no confidence in a friend;
  guard the doors of your mouth
    from her who lies in your bosom;
6 for the son treats the father with contempt,
    the daughter rises up against her mother,
  the daughter-in-law against her mother-in-law;
    a man's enemies are the men of his own house.
7 But as for me, I will look to the LORD,
  I will wait for the God of my salvation;
  my God will hear me.

KEY VERSE: *But as for me, I will look to the Lord, I will wait for the God of my salvation; my God will hear me.* Micah 7:7 (RSV).

HOME DAILY BIBLE READINGS

June   24.   M.   *God's Continued Intention.* Micah 2:12,13.
June   25.   T.   *The Peaceable Kingdom.* Micah 4:1–5.
June   26.   W.   *Salvation in Suffering.* Micah 4:9–13.
June   27.   T.   *Deliverance Will Come.* Micah 5:1–4.
June   28.   F.   *False Worship Uprooted.* Micah 5:10–15.
June   29.   S.   *Wait for the Lord.* Micah 7:1–9.
June   30.   S.   *God Ever Faithful.* Micah 7:14–20.

BACKGROUND

Micah lived during a time of international tensions and upheaval. In the eighth century B.C., the mighty Assyrians were on the march. Their armies seemed invincible. They either gobbled up smaller nations by conquest, usually with terrible slaughter followed by deportations, or forced them into submission by threatening to overrun them. Everyone had heard about the Assyrians's atrocities.

Micah and Isaiah both lived in Judah during the reign of King Hezekiah who had to deal with the Assyrian threats. They received the firsthand reports of the way the Assyrians besieged Samaria, capital of Israel, to the north. Micah and his contemporaries shuddered when news came of Samaria's fall and Israel's destruction. They knew that it would not be long before the Assyrian juggernaut would head south toward Jerusalem. It took the Assyrian king ten years to move against Jerusalem, but he finally moved his war machine into position to subdue Judah. Miraculously, Jerusalem was delivered. The Assyrians became enmeshed in a long campaign on the coastal plain against the other world superpower, Egypt, and left Judah alone for the time being.

The people of Judah smugly assumed that God was playing favorites and was seeing to it that Jerusalem would be unscathed. Looking down from their hilltops, they felt secure. Assyria and Egypt could slug it out, but Judah would always be preserved, they told each other. Folks in Judah congratulated themselves that they were God's own chosen people who would always be exempt from disaster.

Micah saw things differently because he had insight into the way God works in history. He warned that the Assyrians would overrun the country of Judah right up to the gates of Jerusalem. More startling, Micah stated that Judah's eventual collapse would come because of internal flaws. The real weakness of the nation, Micah warned, was from the way the political, business, and religious leaders connived to perpetuate economic injustice. Judah's threat was from within. No matter how religious the people of Judah claimed to be, Micah announced, rampant greed made them practicing unbelievers. And their unbelief would eventually reap a terrible harvest!

NOTES ON THE PRINTED TEXT

Nearly every newspaper carries an inspirational self-help column. Invariably, the writer attempts to demonstrate that you need not be defeated by anything; that you can have peace of mind, improved health, and a never-ceasing flow of energy. The standard themes are basic. Love yourself and do not try to change society.

What a contrast to Micah's way of thinking! As he looked at the evil around him, he cried, *Woe is me.* His anguish was depicted through a picture of a very hungry and very frustrated harvester in the midst of his stripped vineyards and bare fig trees. *There is no cluster to eat, no first-ripe fig which my soul desires.*

Micah's despairing metaphor became even more apparent as he looked out at those around him. He saw corruption everywhere. Like a harvester who saw nothing good to eat anywhere, Micah did not see a good or faithful man around anywhere. *The godly man has perished from the earth, and there is none upright among man.* Micah showed his sense of total defeat as he described the crime, the violence, and the dishonesty that he saw around him. Micah felt that everyone was lying in ambush to shed blood. The very leaders on which justice, law, and order depended were corrupt. The things they did best and with great diligence were evil things. *The prince* (an official) *and the judge ask for a bribe, and the great man utters the evil desire of his soul.*

This love of self infuriated Micah. Far from wanting to cope or learning to live with that problem as the self-help people preached, Micah wanted change. He realized that anyone who wanted justice from the leaders was caught in a thicket of intrigue and greed ("briers" and "thorns"). Micah announced God's intervention and punishment of the guilty. *The day of their watchmen, of their punishment, has come.*

Micah next turned his attention to the ordinary people of the land. Again, he decried the faithlessness he saw. *Put no trust in a neighbor, have no confidence in a friend.* Lamenting the lack of trust within the community and among family members, including husbands and wives, Micah cried, *a man's enemies are the men of his own house.*

But as for me, I will look to the Lord, I will wait for the God of my salvation; my God will hear me. Micah looked with confidence to God. Having vented his anger and frustration, Micah waited for God's salvation. Even when it appeared that there was no hope, God was present. God could be trusted. *My God will hear me.* No self-care or positive thinking for Micah! No pep talks! Nothing would defeat him. Micah could wait for the Lord with confidence and faith.

What about us? How confidently and faithfully can we wait? Have we not been promised in Romans 8:38,39 there is nothing that will separate us from the love of God!

SUGGESTIONS TO TEACHERS

What happens when nearly everyone in a community refuses to trust God and show concern for others? Micah gives a grim picture of what it's like. His own country of Judah was rich but degenerate, comfortable but corrupt—and headed for ruin.

In ancient Israel and Judah, even the poorest person would expect to find a few leftovers to pick up after the grain or grapes had been gathered. It was the Hebrew Law that some gleanings be left on the vines and on the fields so that the stranger or widow or orphan would be able to harvest something to survive. Micah, using the image of the Lord coming to His vineyard, would expect to find a few pickings of faithful people but finds none. The question for your class to address is what kind of harvest could the Lord expect from the community of the faith in these days? How similar is God's community in our times to His community of Judah in Micah's times?

1. *CONFUSION.* Micah insists that the community which persists in turning away from serving the Lord will find itself confused. When God's own people become separated from Him, they will experience alienation and loneliness within themselves. Part of the harvest of unbelief is a state of confusion within the group. Micah tells Judah that the reason for its state of uncertainty of purpose and its lack of direction lies in its lack of commitment to the Lord. Without allowing the entire lesson period to be spent on a negative bent of "what's wrong with the Church," take a few minutes to allow your class to point out examples of confusion which it detects in the local or national church. Ask whether those in your class agree with Micah's analysis of the cause of such confusion.

2. *CORRUPTION.* Any newspaper carries examples of leaders in government, business, labor, education, and other segments of society indicted for dishonest acts. Take a look at Micah's "newsclippings" from Judah in the eighth century B.C. in Micah 7. Have your class observe the comparisons between then and now.

3. *CONTEMPT.* Micah alleges that part of the harvest of unbelief is the breakdown of neighborliness. Contempt replaces concern. Neighbors change from being advocates of one another to adversaries. What is going on among those who live on the streets where your class members reside? How can building trust in the Lord lead to building trust among neighbors?

4. *COLLAPSE.* Finally, Micah paints a terrible picture of the collapse of faith

leading to the collapse of the family. With all the sociological studies being made of the rapidly-developing new configurations of human relationships, the fact emerges that people must have some kind of family, either real or contrived. The only enduring central cell of any human community is the family, and, if this is preserved, the larger community may survive. Micah warns, however, that the health of the family depends on belief. Give enough time to discussing the crucial importance of having Christ-centered families among those in your class.

TOPIC FOR ADULTS
THE HARVEST OF UNBELIEF

National Security. The code room of the communications systems for the C.I.A.'s "spy" satellites has been carefully designed to prevent any unfriendly foreign agent from breaking in to steal secrets. This code room is called the "black vault." It is hard to imagine a more elaborate system of security to guard knowledge inside that room from the Soviet Union. Cocooned on three sides by special penetration proof layers of concrete and on the fourth side by a thick Mosler Safe door, like the ones banks use to guard their cash, the "black vault" was considered impenetrable. Only eight people were allowed to enter the "black vault" and each of them had been carefully screened. Before entering it, they had to pass through three guard checkpoints, closed circuit TV monitors, and dozens of guards. Yet materials from the "black vault" got into the hands of Soviet agents.

How?

A bright, sensitive young man named Christopher Boyce, who had never had any trouble with the law and whose father was a career F.B.I. man, was in charge of the code room. He and a friend named Andrew Daulton Lee decided to conspire against their government, and for two years photographed secret material from the "black vault" early in the morning and late at night, then passed on the negatives to Soviet operatives in Mexico City.

In spite of all the precautions and in spite of steel and concrete around the code room, the moral deterioration of Boyce and Lee allowed national secrets to be taken to an unfriendly nation. It is a reminder again that our real security is based on people. People, in turn, are reliable only when they behave morally. And they act morally only when they live in trust and obedience before the Lord. Christopher Boyce and Andrew Lee had brains, background—everything, it seems—except that sense of morality resting on faith! The harvest of their unbelief has cost their countrymen dearly.

Noticing the Figures. A few years ago, *Reader's Digest* featured a picture puzzle in which the reader was to find many figures of people and animals cleverly hidden in a picture from an old Currier and Ives collection. At first glance, no one would notice anything unusual in the picture. The figures of the humans and animals were so skillfully drawn into the lithographs that they could not be easily detected. Only by careful scrutiny and after long study could any viewer pick out the figures hidden in the drawings. The reader had to observe the scene patiently and look diligently to find the figures.

A prophet is one who finds the figures hidden in the scene which others don't notice. As a Christian, you are called to be one who, like Micah and the prophets, notices what most people miss when looking at a picture of life. You are to study and find carefully what may be missed: the human figures which are ignored, overlooked, and forgotten in our society. Micah did this. You must do this. In a sense, this is what living in the world with the eyes of faith is all about. This is seeking and finding the lost. This is belief in action. If you do not see the outcasts, you help reap a harvest of unbelief!

Harvest of Unbelief. John Ehrlichman says vanity and pride prevented him from pleading guilty in the Watergate cover-up and saving his family the agony of a trial. He thinks now he should have "quietly gone to jail and moved along."

Ehrlichman says now he thinks at times that he might have deflected the course of history by persuading or forcing Richard Nixon to come clean early.

"But I do know," he writes, "that I should have realized and admitted my own guilt much earlier."

Ehrlichman was forced by Nixon to resign his job as the President's No. 2 man at the height of the Watergate scandal in 1973. At a trial the following year, after the Nixon resignation, he was convicted along with Nixon's chief aide, H. R. Haldeman and former Atty. Gen. John N. Mitchell of taking part in the Watergate cover-up.

Ehrlichman says that when Nixon declined to come clean with the American people, "I did what I had been doing for nearly five years: I fell into step with his decision rather than to chart my own course by my own ethical compass."

He concludes: "I intend never again to abdicate the moral judgments I am called upon to make. I hope I succeed. Nothing I've learned is more important to me."

Questions for Pupils on the Next Lesson. 1. Who was Hosea and what kind of a woman was his wife, Gomer? 2. What do the names of Hosea's children symbolize? 3. What insights into God's nature did Hosea get from his personal domestic problems? 4. How can a person offer and receive forgiveness for deep hurts? 5. Where does a person begin again after life has been seriously disrupted?

TOPIC FOR YOUTH
YOUR VALUES ARE SHOWING

Wrecked the Car. John Z. DeLorean's rise to success and power was the fulfillment of the American dream. DeLorean seized the invalid Pontiac division of General Motors and pumped it back to life. He was cheered as the wonder man in Detroit. His personal flamboyance brought headlines. He married and divorced the beautiful daughter of an All-American football hero, dated movie stars, wedded a world-famous fashion model. Everything about John Z. DeLorean—clothes, hair style, hobbies, women, car designs—flashed style and success. Folks in Detroit cheered when he told G.M. corporate officials that the world wanted a snazzy, fuel-efficient car. When he didn't think the men around the boardroom table were listening to him, DeLorean cockily told the officials that the auto industry would not survive without his suggestions. He broke from G.M. and announced grandiose plans to build a sporty automobile using little gasoline suitable for the common person. It was to be called, of course, the DeLorean. Although critics complained that DeLorean was a hotshot who used other people's ideas and cash, DeLorean put together his automobile empire with a Hollywood touch. The hard-nosed founder of the DeLorean corporation had no values except greed, success, and pleasure, but no one seemed to mind except those who got hurt by him or who crossed him. But when banks began to be among those who were going to get hurt because of shaky financial arrangements, John Z. DeLorean learned he would have to come up with a lot of quick cash in October, 1982. DeLorean laughed. No rules ever bound him. Fast money? Easy. The sacks of dollars, however, came from sacks of cocaine sold in Los Angeles in a sordid deal with the underworld. DeLorean was busted when the F.B.I. found the dope in his car. His dreams crashed with his arrest. The DeLorean car company folded. John Z. DeLorean apparently had the wrong kind of values. Ultimately, in God's scheme of this world, a person's values show. For the one-time wonder boy of the car industry, those values brought ruin.

Rethinking Values. "The arms race is awesome and the church is pussyfooting.

If we can kill the enemy six times in what we call 'overkill' and the enemy suddenly can overkill eight times—our mentality at the moment is to raise the overkill ten times. And here is an illustration that graphically motivates rethinking our situation.

"A football game is about to be played. The stadium is full. Before the kickoff, the announcer states that underneath the field is a heavy charge of explosives that will destroy everyone present. The first team to score will detonate the explosives. The gates are locked. No one can escape. This would require a rethinking of the whole game. So the world must rethink or the survivors will envy the dead."—W. E. Goist.

Choosing Values. "If we choose to eat so much that we make ourselves sick, who is to blame? If we choose to drive our cars so fast that we cannot control them, who is to blame? If we have failed to learn how to live, whom shall we blame? God? Oh, no not anybody. We hurt ourselves through the bad use of this great power that God gave us ... THE POWER TO CHOOSE."—J. Martin Kohe, *Your Greatest Power*, The Ralston Publishing Co.

Questions for Pupils on the Next Lesson. 1. How would you describe Hosea's marriage? 2. What is the meaning of the strange names of Hosea's children? 3. Why did Hosea try to win back Gomer? 4. What lessons did Hosea learn about God's mercy from his marriage? 5. Why is it so hard to forgive when you have been deeply hurt?

LESSON VI—JULY 7

THE LORD'S CONSTANT LOVE

Background Scripture: Hosea 1–3
Devotional Reading: Hosea 4:15–5:7

KING JAMES VERSION

HOSEA 1 2 The beginning of the word of the LORD by Hosea. And the LORD said to Hosea, Go, take unto thee a wife of whoredoms and children of whoredoms: for the land hath committed great whoredom, *departing* from the LORD.

3 So he went and took Gomer the daughter of Diblaim; which conceived, and bare him a son.

4 And the LORD said unto him, Call his name Jezreel; for yet a little *while*, and I will avenge the blood of Jezreel upon the house of Jehu, and will cause to cease the kingdom of the house of Israel.

5 And it shall come to pass at that day, that I will break the bow of Israel in the valley of Jezreel.

6 And she conceived again, and bare a daughter. And *God* said unto him, Call her name Lo-ruhamah: for I will no more have mercy upon the house of Israel; but I will utterly take them away.

7 But I will have mercy upon the house of Judah, and will save them by the LORD their God, and will not save them by bow, nor by sword, nor by battle, by horses, nor by horsemen.

8 Now when she had weaned Lo-ruhamah, she conceived, and bare a son.

9 Then said *God*, Call his name Lo-ammi: for ye *are* not my people, and I will not be your *God*.

3 Then said the LORD unto me, Go yet, love a woman beloved of *her* friend, yet an adulteress, according to the love of the LORD toward the children of Israel, who look to other gods, and love flagons of wine.

2 So I bought her to me for fifteen *pieces* of silver, and *for* a homer of barley, and a half homer of barley:

3 And I said unto her, Thou shalt abide for me many days; thou shalt not play the harlot, and thou shalt not be for *another* man: so *will* I also *be* for thee.

4 For the children of Israel shall abide many days without a king, and without a prince, and without a sacrifice, and without an image, and without an ephod, and *without* teraphim:

5 Afterward shall the children of Israel return, and seek the LORD their God, and David their king; and shall fear the LORD and his goodness in the latter days.

REVISED STANDARD VERSION

HOSEA 1 2 When the LORD first spoke through Hosea, the LORD said to Hosea, "Go, take to yourself a wife of harlotry and have children of harlotry, for the land commits great harlotry by forsaking the LORD." 3 So he went and took Gomer the daughter of Diblaim, and she conceived and bore him a son.

4 And the LORD said to him, "Call his name Jezreel; for yet a little while, and I will punish the house of Jehu for the blood of Jezreel, and I will put an end to the kingdom of the house of Israel. 5 And on that day, I will break the bow of Israel in the valley of Jezreel."

6 She conceived again and bore a daughter. And the LORD said to him, "Call her name Not pitied, for I will no more have pity on the house of Israel, to forgive them at all. 7 But I will have pity on the house of Judah, and I will deliver them by the LORD their God; I will not deliver them by bow, nor by sword, nor by war, nor by horses, nor by horsemen."

8 When she had weaned Not pitied, she conceived and bore a son. 9 And the LORD said, "Call his name Not my people, for you are not my people and I am not your God."

3 And the LORD said to me, "Go again, love a woman who is beloved of a paramour and is an adulteress; even as the LORD loves the people of Israel, though they turn to other gods and love cakes of raisins." 2 So I bought her for fifteen shekels of silver and a homer and a lethech of barley. 3 And I said to her, "You must dwell as mine for many days; you shall not play the harlot, or belong to another man; so will I also be to you." 4 For the children of Israel shall dwell many days without king or prince, without sacrifice or pillar, without ephod or teraphim. 5 Afterward the children of Israel shall return and seek the LORD their God, and David their king; and they shall come in fear to the LORD and to his goodness in the latter days.

KEY VERSE: ". . . I will betroth you to me in righteousness and in justice, in steadfast love, and in mercy." Hosea 2:19 (RSV).

HOME DAILY BIBLE READINGS

July	1.	M.	*Significant Names.* Hosea 1:1–11.
July	2.	T.	*God's Love Spurned.* Hosea 2:1–9.
July	3.	W.	*The Truth Will Surface.* Hosea 2:10–13.
July	4.	T.	*Living Together in Love.* Hosea 2:14–23.
July	5.	F.	*Love Dramatized.* Hosea 3:1–5.
July	6.	S.	*Unfaithful in Love.* Hosea 9:1–4.
July	7.	S.	*Unfaithfulness Rebuked.* Hosea 9:10–17.

BACKGROUND

Hosea was the last great prophet in the northern kingdom of Israel during its final years. The setting for his life and his writings is the Israel of about 750 B.C. to about 734 B.C. When Hosea started his powerful ministry, Amos had already been preaching. Amos, the southerner from Judah, was an outsider, but Hosea, born and raised in Israel, was an insider. Amos had confronted the smug, prosperous Israel in a temporary lull of peace. Hosea spoke during the tumultuous period when the awesome Assyrian war machine was on the move again after that lull. Hosea sensed that time was running out for his beloved nation. He predicted Israel's doom with a certainty and definiteness that even Amos had not been able to do.

That doom came when the Assyrian forces swept through Syria and Israel in 733–732 B.C. The Assyrians seemed invincible. They captured Damascus in 732 B.C. and took most of the leading cities. The Assyrian invaders swiftly carried off large segments of the conquered populations to distant parts of their empire, and settled those they had uprooted from other conquests in Israel and Syria. The most feared and most hated warriors in the ancient world, the Assyrians had a well-deserved reputation for being cruel and ruthless.

Israel did not collapse immediately, but went through a final spasm of near anarchy. Four Israelite kings were assassinated in a period of fifteen years. The capital of Israel, Samaria, held out against the Assyrian siege for a time, but finally fell in 721 B.C.

Israel, in spite of the pleas of the prophets, could not seem to bring herself to leave her degenerate ways. In fact, the moral condition of the community seemed to decline more rapidly than the political situation.

Hosea presents his own personal story as a painful and poignant description of Israel. The first three chapters of his writings relate how his beloved wife, Gomer, is unfaithful. She bears three children to her other lovers and leaves Hosea. Hosea insists on bringing her back and publicly welcomes her again as his wife in spite of the humiliation and hurt he has endured. Hosea dramatically states that Israel's faithlessness to God is like Gomer's infidelity. Just as Hosea's wife deserted him to have adulterous affairs, Israel has ignored her vows to the Lord and prostituted herself with other gods. Hosea predicts disaster for Israel. But he also announces that the Lord's love continues, and that God would persist in His attempts to win back Israel in order to restore the relationship.

NOTES ON THE PRINTED TEXT

Go, take to yourself a wife of harlotry and have children of harlotry. Prophets occasionally acted in unusual or symbolic ways. Hosea married Gomer, a prostitute. Gomer was the *daughter of Diblaim. Diblaim* translated also meant fig cake. Gomer could probably have been had cheaply—for a few fig cakes.

And the Lord said to him, "Call his name Jezreel." Gomer conceived and bore a son. By God's command, the newborn son became a part of the prophetic symbolism begun by the marriage of Hosea and Gomer.

Jezreel was the name of the town and valley between Samaria and Galilee and was known as a place where a great deal of violence and bloodshed had occurred at the hands of the kings of Israel. Hosea announced the impending doom when the nation of Israel would be called to task. *The bow of Israel* (military might) would be broken on that famous plain of Jezreel.

She conceived again and bore a daughter. Dramatic symbolism continued through the use of the name of Hosea's newborn daughter, called "Not Pitied." Literally, her name meant "not cared for" as if she was a child that had been abandoned by her parents. In this name, Hosea showed that the nation of Israel would be left without God's care, like an abandoned child.

And the Lord said, "Call his name Not my people, for you are not my people and I am not your God." Two to three years later, the average weaning time of a child, Gomer gave birth to another boy. Hosea's name for the boy—also symbolic—was "Not My People." This child's name symbolized a death sentence for Israel. The name announced God's abandonment of the Israelites as His people. No longer could they expect God to protect and provide for them.

And the Lord said to me, "Go again, love a woman who is beloved of a paramour and is an adulteress. What happened after the birth of the third child will never be known. Probably the immoral Gomer deserted Hosea. Hosea was commanded to go again and love the unfaithful woman who had given herself to another man. Originally, Hosea was to take Gomer as a wife, but now he was ordered to court her again and to take her back as his wife. The symbolism was obvious. God, through His love, would find a way to reunite Himself and Israel though His people had turned away from Him and offered their love to Baals.

Hosea bought back Gomer. After purchase, Hosea told Gomer what she must do. *You must dwell as mine for many days; you shall not play the harlot, or belong to another man; so will I also be with you.* He could not command her love or offer his love without her involvement. Gomer must live with Hosea within their marriage covenant and have no other men but Hosea. With these stipulations stated, Hosea waited *many days* for Gomer to return his love. This symbolism was interpreted in verses 4 and 5 when "for many days" Israel would live without leadership ("king or prince"), without any offensive sacrificial cults ("sacrifice or pillar"), and without any way of knowing God's will ("ephod or teraphim"). *Afterward the children of Israel shall return and seek the Lord their God, and David their king; and they shall come in fear to the Lord and to his goodness in the latter days.* However, God tempered His judgment with love. Despite Israel's unfaithfulness, God still loved His people. Eventually, Israel, like a woman who has turned from sin and returned to her husband, would return and seek the Lord.

SUGGESTIONS TO TEACHERS

"Don't talk to me of love—Show me!" These words from a popular song a few years ago could also be the theme song for today's lesson.

But there is more. Although God's people may wail for the Lord to show His love, the Good News is that He has done more than talk to us of His love. He has shown us—especially through the sacrificial love of Jesus Christ toward us.

That kind of "Show me!" love was prefigured in Hosea, the subject of this lesson. Some think that Hosea's message of the Lord's constant Love is the high-water mark of the Old Testament. Although Hosea is classified with the Minor Prophets, neither the man nor his message is to be dismissed as of minimal importance. Through the anguish of forgiving love for his wife, Hosea offers a glimpse of the costly kind of love God shows toward Israel. Throughout this lesson, you will also want to allude often to the love poured out on Calvary for us.

1. *HALLOWING A HARLOT.* Hosea's own marriage provides the backdrop for his understanding of God's constant love, and introduces your class to the topic of how God shows us His love through Jesus Christ. The details of the story of Gomer, Hosea's faithless wife, must be told to your class. As teacher, you are not trying to titillate or entertain like a gossip columnist. Instead, you are using this episode in the way Hosea himself wanted it used: to illustrate Israel's faithlessness. Israel, in fact, had been like a promiscuous woman, "forsaking the Lord," to whom she was bound through mutual promise-making. But Hosea cared for Gomer. The point the prophet makes is also the one you are making to your class, namely that the Lord loves His people even though they turn away from Him like a wife turned prostitute. God loves the unlovable!

2. *HURTING A HUSBAND.* A shallow slogan popular a few years back proclaimed that, "Love is never having to say you're sorry." The implication in this saying is that you never really do anything for which you have to be sorry. Christians know that this is simply not true. We *do* things we are sorry for; we *say* things for which we are sorry. We hurt others. We hurt God. The Gomer story has such meaning because of the way she hurt Hosea so deeply, yet is still loved. At this point in your lesson, shift the focus to the Crucifixion and the way we humans hurt God by executing Jesus. Ask how our faithfulness as ones bound to God is shown in our times. In what ways do we turn away from God as His Church?

3. *HUNTING THE HEINOUS.* The Bible never glosses over our human faithlessness toward the Lord. Like Hosea saying, "Therefore I will speak tenderly to her" (2:14) and wooing back Gomer so that she will say, "My husband" (2:16) and being wed to this hurtful, faithless woman simply because he loves her and not because she is so nice, God seeks us in love. He loves us, unworthy though we are of His love! In the face of such caring depicted in Hosea's words and portrayed in Christ's life and death, we can only say, "Love so amazing, so divine, demands my life, my soul, my all!"

TOPIC FOR ADULTS
THE LORD'S CONSTANT LOVE

The God Who Does Not Hang Up Jawbones. "If a translator is to communicate God's word in a relevant manner, there must be a constant awareness of local indigenous expressions, even if they may be incredibly strange to those who are not familiar with the culture. For example, in the language of one tribe in the Baiyer River area of New Guinea, the only way to talk about God's forgiveness is to say, 'God does not hang up jawbones against us,' an idiom that reflects a common practice among those former headhunters. People who had lost a member of the family in an enemy raid would rescue the body, remove the jaw, cut away the meat and then hang up the jawbone on the doorpost as a reminder that sometime within the next month, year, or even generation, someone in the family must kill a member of the enemy tribe or clan. But when such persons become Christians, the most significant ceremony is one in which they take down the jawbones and burn them to indicate that since they have experienced the forgiveness of God, who 'does not hang up jawbones,' they likewise have forgiven others. . . ."—Eugene A. Nida, "Why So Many Bible Translations?" in *The Word of God: A Guide to English Versions of the Bible,* Edited by Lloyd R. Bailey, Richmond: John Knox Press, 1982.

No Way to Love a Woman. New York (AP). "The author of the best-selling book *How to Make Love to a Woman* pleaded guilty to punching his former girlfriend in the face. 'We got into a heated argument and for one second I lost control,' Michael Morgenstern said of the incident in which he hit his former girlfriend, twenty-two-year-old fashion model Ethel Marie Parks. The guilty plea was entered after Morgenstern agreed to a $30,000 settlement of a civil lawsuit Miss Parks had filed against him.

"Morgenstern's book, which was on the *New York Times* best-seller list for several months, urges men to take the lead in relationships and show sensitivity toward women.

"The incident occurred August 5, 1981, the day after Miss Parks moved out of the apartment she had shared with Morgenstern on Manhattan's East Side. Morgenstern said he had intended to discuss their relationship when he went to the apartment where Miss Parks was staying. The author was accused in a court complaint of punching the model 'once in the mouth, fracturing one of the bones in her upper jaw, and breaking a tooth.' "

Only an awareness of God's constant love enables a person to love a partner in marriage. All the good intentions on showing sensitivity and all the good advice on sexual relationships mean little without keeping a covenant relationship in marriage with the Lord who declares His constancy and caring.

Royalty Recollects. King George IV once wanted to receive Holy Communion, and sent for his bishop to administer it.

The messenger loitered along the way, and as a result, considerable time elapsed before the bishop arrived.

When the bishop's delay was explained, the angry King fired the messenger from his service.

Then, turning to the bishop, the King said, "Now, my bishop, if you please, we will proceed."

The bishop, with great mildness but at the same time with firmness, refused to serve communion while any irritation or anger toward a fellow creature remained in the mind of the King. George IV, suddenly recollecting himself, said, "Bishop, you are right!"

He then sent for the offending person, and he forgave him and restored him to favor.

Questions for Pupils on the Next Lesson. 1. What are God's basic moral requirements for a stable society? 2. How does God deal with us to encourage us to return to Him? 3. What exactly does it mean to be repentant? 4. Why is it that persons who are aware of their own faults are generally patient with others? 5. How do you handle personal guilt and failure in human relationships?

TOPIC FOR YOUTH
GOD LOVES THE UNFAITHFUL

"What Is Forgiveness?" "Cathy Meyers, a therapist at Great Oaks, a center for handicapped children in Silver Springs, Maryland, asked this question of her nine- to fifteen-year-old students. These are some of the answers they gave her:

" 'It's when my mother screams at me and says she hates me for being a burden, but it's okay, because I know she really loves me, and she's just feeling sad.'

" 'It's when other kids laugh at me and make fun of me because I can't walk . . . and instead of being mad, it makes me want to ask God to make them feel good inside, so they don't have to laugh at less fortunate people to make them feel good.'

" 'Forgiveness? I think it's wanting happiness for someone who once hurt you very badly.'

" 'It's letting go and moving on . . . and being able to laugh at the things that were once breaking your heart.' "—*Faith at Work* magazine: February, 1979.

No More Guilt to Carry Around. "John Erwin is chaplain at Chicago's Cook County Jail. He survived many orphanages, foster homes, and juvenile centers as a child. At the age of twenty-two he came in contact with Dave Pitman through mutual interest in trombone. For a year, Dave and his wife, Rozzie, took a special interest in John without putting any evangelistic pressure on him.

"John said of the Pitmans: 'They knew nothing of my scattered past. If they knew all the garbage I hauled around inside, they'd surely feel degraded in my presence. I tried to explain to them the great loneliness I had had for as long as I could remember and how mixed-up I felt. I told them . . . about the guilt I carried with me.'

"The Pitmans shared from the Bible how life could be changed. He prayed, asking Christ for forgiveness. John remembered, 'When I stood up, I saw tears streaming down Rozzie's cheeks. She hugged me while Dave just stood there beaming. "Your sins are forgiven, John." Dave kept saying, "You don't have to carry that guilt anymore." ' "—John R. Erwin, *The Man Who Keeps Going to Jail:* Cook.

God Loves the Unfaithful. It was a dismal, familiar story of a man in his late forties on long business trips to the Orient who was unfaithful to his wife. Perhaps Jim was trying to justify himself, but he told Helen, his American wife, that he was tired of being married to her and was in love with Haruka, a pretty young Japanese girl. Jim divorced Helen after twenty-five years of marriage, and moved out to be "free." His company continued to send him to the Far East on business. He picked up the affair with the woman in Japan each time he visited Tokyo. When Haruka sent word that she was pregnant, Jim felt twinges of guilt and uneasiness. He cabled some money. During the next few years, Jim continued to visit Haruka and their baby daughter, Jasmine, and give them a small allowance. Suddenly, one day back in Chicago, Jim was taken violently ill. The doctors examined him and discovered he had a rapidly-spreading form of cancer. In spite of surgery and chemotherapy, Jim quickly grew weak and realized that he would not live more than a few months. Friends told Helen, Jim's ex-wife. Helen had gone through the stages of hurt and anger when Jim had left, but still remembered that she was a Christian. One day, Helen appeared at Jim's bedside in the hospital. She and Jim tried to talk, but it was difficult. Finally Jim broke down and cried, asking for Helen's forgiveness. Helen groped for words. "Is there anything . . . I can do?" she found herself asking.

"It's Haruka and Jasmine," Jim whispered. "I've used up nearly all my money on this sickness, and I don't know what will happen to them. All my insurance is still being left to you."

Helen couldn't answer. She left Jim's hospital room and struggled in prayer for several days. A few days before Jim died, she wrote to Haruka and Jasmine, inviting them to come to Chicago to live with her. A month after the funeral, a moving scene took place at O'Hare International Airport as a fragile Japanese girl and frightened child were taken into the arms of Helen and welcomed as family. Helen now has made a home for them, and thanks God for the way she has learned to appreciate His undeserved mercy.

Questions for Pupils on the Next Lesson. 1. What does it mean to "show repentance?" 2. What are God's moral requirements for a stable society? 3. What persons and influences are shaping your basic moral values? 4. How do you handle guilt?

LESSON VII—JULY 14

A CALL FOR TRUE REPENTANCE

Background Scripture: Hosea 4–6
Devotional Reading: Hosea 7:1–7

KING JAMES VERSION

HOSEA 4   Hear the word of the LORD, ye children of Israel: for the LORD hath a controversy with the inhabitants of the land, because *there is* no truth, nor mercy, nor knowledge of God in the land.

2 By swearing, and lying, and killing, and stealing, and committing adultery, they break out, and blood toucheth blood.

5   15 I will go *and* return to my place till they acknowledge their offense, and seek my face: in their affliction they will seek me early.

6   Come, and let us return unto the LORD: for he hath torn, and he will heal us; he hath smitten, and he will bind us up.

2 After two days will he revive us: in the third day he will raise us up, and we shall live in his sight.

3 Then shall we know, *if* we follow on to know the LORD: his going forth is prepared as the morning; and he shall come unto us as the rain, as the latter *and* former rain unto the earth.

4 O Ephraim, what shall I do unto thee? O Judah, what shall I do unto thee? for your goodness *is* as a morning cloud, and as the early dew it goeth away.

5 Therefore have I hewed *them* by the prophets; I have slain them by the words of my mouth: and thy judgments *are as* the light *that* goeth forth.

6 For I desired mercy and not sacrifice; and the knowledge of God more than burnt offerings.

REVISED STANDARD VERSION

HOSEA 4   Hear the word of the LORD, O people of Israel;
for the LORD has a controversy with the inhabitants of the land.
There is no faithfulness or kindness,
and no knowledge of God in the land;
2 there is swearing, lying, killing, stealing,
and committing adultery;
they break all bounds and murder follows murder.

5   15 I will return again to my place,
until they acknowledge their guilt and seek my face,
and in their distress they seek me, saying,
6 "Come, let us return to the LORD;
for he has torn, that he may heal us;
he has stricken, and he will bind us up.
2 After two days he will revive us;
on the third day he will raise us up,
that we may live before him.
3 Let us know, let us press on to know the LORD;
his going forth is sure as the dawn;
he will come to us as the showers,
as the spring rains that water the earth."
4 What shall I do with you, O Ephraim?
What shall I do with you, O Judah?
Your love is like a morning cloud,
like the dew that goes early away.
5 Therefore I have hewn them by the prophets,
I have slain them by the words of my mouth,
and my judgment goes forth as the light.
6 For I desire steadfast love and not sacrifice,
the knowledge of God, rather than burnt offerings.

KEY VERSE: *For I desire steadfast love and not sacrifice, the knowledge of God, rather than burnt offerings.* Hosea 6:6 (RSV).

HOME DAILY BIBLE READINGS

July	8.	M.	God's Controversy. Hosea 4:1–3.
July	9.	T.	Unfaithful Priests. Hosea 4:4–10.
July	10.	W.	Unfaithful People. Hosea 4:12–14.
July	11.	T.	Apostasy Condemned. Hosea 5:5–12.
July	12.	F.	Repentance Called For. Hosea 6:1–6.
July	13.	S.	Rejection Has Its Consequences. Hosea 8:1–8.
July	14.	S.	When Hearts Are False. Hosea 10:1–6.

BACKGROUND

Hosea was a brokenhearted husband whose wife insisted on living like a Canaanite temple prostitute. Her debauchery typified the way Israel had become morally and spiritually degenerate in the eighth century B.C.

Hosea lamented the way that God's own people, Israel, had abandoned the Lord and taken up the Canaanite religion. Canaanite cults had popular appeal. A mishmash of superstition, sex orgies, and sacred rites, Baal worship practices had competed for the attention of the Israelites from the earliest days. The horde of gods represented various forces of nature and natural processes, such as sun and moon, the changing seasons, the fertility of livestock and birth of young, trees, springs and fire, and so on. The ceremonies associated with these *Baalim* (plural of *Baal*, the Canaanite "master") were often cruel and degrading. Sometimes, Canaanite religion sank to encouraging child sacrifice. Usually, it involved sexual debauchery. Male and female prostitutes consorted with cult worshipers in the sacred groves or the high places of the cities. These cult practices were a constant temptation to Israelite farmers when their crops weren't growing well or their sheep or goats weren't reproducing normally. Hosea, like all of the Lord's prophets, warned his people against participating in these heathen rites.

Hosea aimed much of his prophesying against Israel's leaders. He was dismayed at the way the kings, princes, and priests not only acquiesced in the wrongdoing but often encouraged the evil practices by participating themselves. Their example caused the rank-and-file of the people to go along with Canaanite idolatry. In spite of his calls to repentance, Hosea saw the national leaders ignoring him and stubbornly continuing their immoral ways. He reserved his toughest words, however, for the priests. Knowing that these were intended to teach the people of Israel about the covenanting God, Hosea was incensed at the way they neglected their calling. He takes these religious leaders to task for changing worship from honoring the Lord to seeking to manipulate Him for their own interests. Nonetheless, Hosea patiently and repeatedly calls for repentance on the part of everyone!

NOTES ON THE PRINTED TEXT

Breach of contract is a legal term denoting a violation of a legal obligation. Hosea argues that there has been a breach of contract between God and His people. In a courtroom type drama, Hosea convenes the trial with a summons to all Israel: *Hear the word of the Lord, O people of Israel.* In the case of God versus the people of Israel, the covenant, the contract between God and His people, has been breached. The charge: *There is no faithfulness or kindness, and no knowledge of God in the land.* Israel has violated the first and second commandments. The people are guilty of worshiping other gods, notably Baal, and of failing to demonstrate love and kindness toward their fellow Israelites. They no longer know God or the requirements of their covenant with Him. They are guilty of a breach of contract and will be judged.

Hosea cites specific examples of guilt. *There is swearing.* More than profanity, Israel is guilty of using God's name for the wrong reasons—a violation of the third commandment (Exodus 20:7). *There is lying,* particularly within the judicial system. This is a transgression of the ninth commandment (Exodus 20:16). Killing, stealing, committing adultery are also prohibited in the commandments (Exodus 20:13,15,14). Israelites are violating all of these laws, and tramping on the rights of their fellow citizens. The people of Israel love neither God nor each other.

The verdict: God will depart. *I will return again to my place, until they acknowledge their guilt and seek my face, and in their distress they seek me.* Israel's sin has separated it from God. The people of Israel next acknowledge their guilt and seek God.

The people glibly respond, singing *Come, let us return to the Lord* and *let us press on to know the Lord.* They think they may come to the Lord without repenting. *After two days he will receive us; on the third day he will raise us up.* They want their restoration to take place quickly and painlessly. They express no guilt. Rather, they assume that all will be well. The Israelites are not aware of their sin. The mention of God coming *as the showers, as the spring rains that water the earth* refers to fertility signs controlled by Baal. This insincere repentance is not acceptable.

The Lord had done everything possible for His people. What can He do now? *What shall I do with you, O Ephraim? What shall I do with you, O Judah? Your love is like a morning cloud, like the dew that goes early away.* Israel's love of God seems to evaporate as quickly as the heavy morning dew disappears into the dry, dusty earth. This is why the prophets have been sent to speak judgment. *Therefore I have hewn them by the prophets.* Hosea, like the other prophets, reminds us that God will judge those who do not demonstrate true repentance. Loyalty to God and pure worship, not sacrifices and burnt offerings, will show knowledge of God and demonstrate true repentance.

SUGGESTIONS TO TEACHERS

A fifteen-year-old girl attending a summer church conference found herself deeply moved by the closing service which stressed personal commitment to Jesus Christ. She lighted her candle and stood reverently. With the others, she repeated a prayer stating that she repented of her sins and offered her life to Jesus. For two months after her return home, she faithfully prayed and read her Bible. By mid-October, however, she confessed to her Church School teacher after class one Sunday that she couldn't understand why she no longer seemed to feel very close to Jesus Christ.

"Did you really mean it when you said you repented of the way you'd been living?" asked the teacher, knowing the girl's reputation for cheating on school tests and doing some occasional shoplifting.

"Oh, sure, I told God I was sorry."

"But have you repented? Have you turned around and started in the other direction?"

"I thought it was enough to say I was sorry," the girl answered. "Do you mean I have to change things?"

Repentance means more than saying you're sorry. God wants more than apologies. Repentance means heading in a new direction. Repentance is leaving the past ways and living the Christ way.

Your lesson this Sunday is designed to drive home that point. The biblical material from Hosea lends itself well to show your class God's call for true repentance. Here are some of the points which emerge:

1. *INDICTMENT.* Hosea presents a bill of particulars against Israel. Your people in your class could well consider what kind of list the Lord would prepare against His people in your church and your town.

2. *IMPLICATION.* Hosea also submits God's list of sinners. Your class should note that everyone is implicated—Israel, Judah, Ephraim—all the states—and all the leaders—priests, civic leaders, and ordinary citizens alike. Is this not also true in these times?

3. *INVITATION.* "Come, let us return to the Lord," Hosea pleads (6:1). Remind your class that God has not withdrawn this gracious invitation, but through Jesus Christ continues to issue this welcome to His presence!

4. *INSIGHT.* God's love, Hosea knows from personal experience, continues toward us. God cares! Here is an opportunity to point out that there is not a difference between the "God of the Old Testament" and "the God of the New Testament." The one Lord has loved us from the beginning!

5. *IMPETUS.* The emphasis in this lesson is that God's idea of repentance is "steadfast love, not sacrifice" (6:6). A "knowledge of God rather than burnt offerings" is what the Lord desires as evidence of true repentance.

TOPIC FOR ADULTS
GOD'S PATIENCE AND HUMAN SIN

Weaponry Outstrips Wisdom. Jane's Weapons Systems, the authoritative survey on its subject matter, says in its 1982–83 edition, "War in space is now a practical matter." To say the least, that practicality is terrifying. Editor Ronald T. Pretty described aircraft-launched, antisatellite (or ASAT) as the latest developments in the U.S. and Soviet military arsenals. He said the U.S. MX system, together with its protective system, and the new laser and particle-beam weapons being developed are "potentially destabilizing in the longer term." He also noted that the United States and the Soviet Union no longer have a monopoly on high-technology weapons. Israel, Japan, Taiwan, and South Africa, he wrote, have new missile systems. "National frontiers are seldom proof against the seepage of weapons technology for long," he added.

And then he made the understatement of the year: "It is a matter of regret that ... the impressive progress in modern weapons technology we have recorded ... has not been matched by a comparable growth in wisdom or expertise of those responsible for (its) application."

We humans seem to be slow learners. Our human sin continues to try God's patience. His call for true repentance is issued constantly. When will we listen and respond?

Repentant Judge. Sir Francis Bacon, one of the great statesmen and best legal minds in England, held offices under Queen Elizabeth I and King James I. He eventually became King James's Lord Chancellor. However, like many others in his time, Bacon accepted gifts from litigants in his court. Bacon vigorously denied that these gifts influenced his decisions in any way, and, in fact, in several cases ruled against the giver. Parliament in 1621 was in angry revolt against King James and decided to strike at the King by deposing Bacon for irregularities. Bacon was convicted of accepting gifts, fined a ruinous amount, forbidden ever to hold any public office or sit in Parliament, and sentenced to the Tower. The King had Bacon released after four days and remitted the impossibly large fine, and the chastened ex-Chancellor retired to his home in disgrace to write. After his death, written in a private cypher, a biographer found a statement by Francis Bacon which showed his repentance. "I was the justest judge that was in England these fifty years, but it was the justest censure in Parliament that was these 200 years." Bacon was a great enough man to recognize that he should not have accepted the gifts, and that it was right of Parliament to protect the society from venality by public officials.

God's Patience and Human Foolishness. Several years ago, a group of amateur explorers driving through Death Valley, California, discovered the skeleton of a man who had died on the drifting dunes of the desert. Clutched in his bony hand was a chunk of mica whose pyrites, resembling gold, had deceived him. He had mistaken the yellow streaks in this rock for gold. On a scrap of paper under the skeleton were written the words, "Died rich." He had thought he was rich, but starved to death, lost and alone. Such is the deceitfulness of riches. If we have nothing more than money, we are poor indeed.

Our human foolishness leads us to greed and deceit. God patiently calls us to repentance. In some cases, we think the most important part of living is to clutch and clasp our possessions rather than to care and serve our neighbors. In the case of the Death Valley victim and of any person who ignores God's call, all that is left is literally, "Fool's Gold."

Questions for Pupils on the Next Lesson. 1. Does God offer hope with His judgment, or only doom? 2. What are some of the modern forms of idolatry? 3. What did Hosea say when things looked hopelessly bleak? 4. Does God ever give up on His people? 5. Do you ever despair of life?

TOPIC FOR YOUTH
GOD WAITS FOR YOU

No Messages From Flying Saucers. Certain that a flying saucer would wait for them to give them messages in the snowy, frozen wilderness of northeastern Minnesota in November, 1982, Gerald Flach and LaVerne Landis drove from St. Paul. They waited in their car for more than four weeks, eating vitamins and drinking water from nearby Leon Lake at the end of the remote Gunflint Trail. Flach, thirty-eight, had become obsessed with UFOs, and had told friends that he had been receiving messages through LaVerne Landis from "some higher power." The last "message" directed them to go to the end of the Gunflint Trail to await further messages from a waiting UFO. A month later, Flach was found semi-conscious by a passing motorist. He was rushed to the hospital and found to be suffering from starvation, dehydration, and hypothermia (lowering of the body temperature). Rescue squad workers found Landis, forty-eight, dead in the front seat of the car several hundred yards off the road. An autopsy determined that she had died of a combination of starvation, dehydration and hypothermia.

Tragically, Flach and Landis apparently never understood that God waits for each of us each day. They placed their trust not in the Lord who has come to our planet earth in the person of Jesus but in illusionary stuff from science fiction.

God waits for you. You don't have to bother with "secret messages" or mysterious extraterrestrial visitations. You may encounter Him in the person of Jesus Christ right where you are!

Lord of All. A group of Christians in a large university welcomed a newcomer who joined the Bible study group. The students encouraged the young man to take part in the events of the gathering, to read his Bible daily, to pray regularly, and to grow in the faith. After several weeks, the newcomer made a commitment to Jesus Christ as his personal Lord and Savior. He enthusiastically participated in the program of the church group. He asked to be baptized. However, he also said that he was "into meditation." Frequently, he talked about his mantra and asked why he couldn't also practice TM. The other students pointed out that he didn't need Transcendental Meditation because Jesus was Lord of all. The young man insisted he could be both a good Christian and a good follower of Mahareshi. However, he began to miss the Wednesday evening Bible Study sessions, and he gradually gave up his associations with the other Christians. Although the members of the Christian fellowship repeatedly tried to befriend him and invite him back, the young man seemed to have repudiated his connection with the Christian faith.

God, however, waits for this student. He patiently waits for each of us to return to Him. He also waits for you! Furthermore, God calls each of us to an exclusive and uncompromising allegiance to Christ. Only when we commit ourselves wholeheartedly to Him will we discover the meaning of His steadfast love in our lives!

"What's the Angle?" "This is the true story of a man who lived in a city in Pennsylvania. He was an executive who operated a manufacturing plant during

the day and acted also as a detective on the police force of his city. By night he tracked down criminals and by day he employed ex-convicts in his business.

"Let us call one of the ex-convicts Mr. Employee and his employer Mr. Boss.

"Mr. Employee became suspicious when Mr. Boss offered him a job, because it was Mr. Boss who was responsible for Mr. Employee's conviction and jail sentence. Mr. Employee thought, 'There must be an angle to this. What is the catch?'

"Mr. Employee thought everybody had an angle, some easy and perhaps shady way of taking advantage of others, some quick method of getting what one wanted. But Mr. Boss assured Mr. Employee that he had no unworthy motive. He merely wanted to give a penitent wrong-doer a chance to make good.

"Mr. Employee did not believe Mr. Boss. He decided to take advantage of his position to rob the office safe before Mr. Boss could take advantage of him. Mr. Boss suspected that Mr. Employee was up to no good and was waiting, gun in hand, when the would-be burglar came into the office. Confronted by Mr. Boss, Mr. Employee was in a quandary. Mr. Boss had already removed thousands of dollars from the safe and piled them on the desk. Mr. Employee was told he was free to walk out with the money, with the warning, however, that he would surely be caught and sent to jail again. On the other hand, Mr. Employee was free to walk out of the office without the money, and nothing further would be said or done about the matter.

"That made Mr. Employee all the more suspicious. What possible motive could his boss have for acting so unorthodxly? He asked the boss whether he really meant what he said. The employer assured his employee that he was acting in good faith. 'In fact,' said he, 'if you stay in my employ for several months longer and in that time find that I do have an unworthy angle, or am taking advantage of you, you can have all this money, and double the amount.'

"That seemed good enough to Mr. Employee. He remained in the employ of his benefactor and learned that his boss had only one motive, to help a man redeem his life.

"It is not difficult to imagine Jesus using a situation like that as the basis of a parable. God is like a detective-businessman who does not let wrong-doing go unnoticed. He keeps after the wrong-doer, trying to convince him of the error of his ways, indeed, offering forgiveness before the wrong-doer ever has a chance to say he is sorry."—Joseph Mohr, *The Weekender*, Call-Chronicle Newspapers, Allentown, Pennsylvania, October 30, 1982.

Questions for Pupils on the Next Lesson. 1. Have you ever felt that you were living without any hope for the future? 2. Do you think that God will ever give up on you? 3. How are you determining the direction your life will take in the years to come? 4. Are there any "catches" to God's love?

LESSON VIII—JULY 21

WHERE THERE'S LOVE, THERE'S HOPE

Background Scripture: Hosea 11, 14
Devotional Reading: Hosea 11:5–8; 14:5–9

KING JAMES VERSION

HOSEA 11 When Israel *was* a child, then I loved him, and called my son out of Egypt.

2 *As* they called them, so they went from them: they sacrificed unto Baalim, and burned incense to graven images.

3 I taught Ephraim also to go, taking them by their arms; but they knew not that I healed them.

4 I drew them with cords of a man, with bands of love: and I was to them as they that take off the yoke on their jaws, and I laid meat unto them.

8 How shall I give thee up, Ephraim? *how* shall I deliver thee, Israel? how shall I make thee as Admah? *how* shall I set thee as Zeboim? mine heart is turned within me, my repentings are kindled together.

14 O Israel, return unto the LORD thy God; for thou hast fallen by thine iniquity.

2 Take with you words, and turn to the LORD: say unto him, Take away all iniquity, and receive *us* graciously: so will we render the calves of our lips.

3 Asshur shall not save us; we will not ride upon horses: neither will we say any more to the work of our hands, *Ye are* our gods: for in thee the fatherless findeth mercy.

4 I will heal their backsliding, I will love them freely: for mine anger is turned away from him.

REVISED STANDARD VERSION

HOSEA 11 When Israel was a child, I loved him,
and out of Egypt I called my son.

2 The more I called them,
the more they went from me;
they kept sacrificing to the Baals,
and burning incense to idols.

3 Yet it was I who taught Ephraim to walk,
I took them up in my arms;
but they did not know that I healed them.

4 I led them with cords of compassion
with the bands of love,
and I became to them as one
who eases the yoke on their jaws,
and I bent down to them and fed them.

8 How can I give you up, O Ephraim!
How can I hand you over, O Israel!
How can I make you like Admah!
How can I treat you like Zeboiim!
My heart recoils within me,
my compassion grows warm and tender.

14 Return, O Israel, to the LORD your God,
for you have stumbled because of your iniquity.

2 Take with you words
and return to the LORD;
say to him,
"Take away all iniquity;
accept that which is good
and we will render
the fruit of our lips.

3 Assyria shall not save us,
we will not ride upon horses;
and we will say no more, 'Our God,'
to the work of our hands.
In thee the orphan finds mercy."

4 I will heal their faithlessness;
I will love them freely,
for my anger has turned from them.

KEY VERSE: *I will heal their faithlessness; I will love them freely, for my anger has turned from them.* Hosea 14:4 (RSV).

HOME DAILY BIBLE READINGS

July	15.	M.	*Time to Seek the Lord.* Hosea 10:11, 12.
July	16.	T.	*God the Faithful Healer.* Hosea 14:4–9.
July	17.	W.	*Hold Fast to Love.* Hosea 12:1–6.
July	18.	T.	*God the Only Savior.* Hosea 13:1–6.
July	19.	F.	*Led With Cords of Compassion.* Hosea 11:1–9.
July	20.	S.	*Entreated to Return.* Hosea 14:1–3.
July	21.	S.	*The Way of Love.* 1 Corinthians 13:4–13.

BACKGROUND

Hosea was a family man. He tells us of his intense love for his wife-turned-harlot. He also discloses that they had three children (1:4, 6, 9). Hosea as a parent knew the trials of raising youngsters. But he also acknowledges the deep loving concern he feels toward his little ones. As any parent will admit, the love of a mother or father has both a tender side and a tough side. Hosea reveals that he understands this.

However, he uses his personal domestic recollections to talk about God's ways with His own child, Israel. No one had ever portrayed the Almighty, Eternal Creator in terms of a parent training a little one. Hosea knows from personal experience how exasperating a young child can be. He also knows how a willful small child can try the patience of the kindest mother or father. Applying these insights to God's ways with Israel, the "little one" the Lord has cherished and nourished and taught, Hosea relates that God must have the same sense of pain and hope and love. Chapters 11 and 14 reveal God has the same feelings which a parent has. At the same time, Hosea represents the Lord as saying, "I am God and not man" (11:9). Hosea never scales down the majestic divine personality to mere human size.

Hosea comes closer than any other Old Testament figure, however, in attributing feelings to God. Hosea dares state that God suffers. Hosea, who could never remain apathetic in the face of his wife's infidelity or his children's waywardness, senses that God also knows sorrow and feels hurts. In the words of this eighth century B.C. prophet, we come closer to the mystery of God's suffering at the Cross than at any other point in the Old Testament.

NOTES ON THE PRINTED TEXT

When Israel was a child, I loved him, and out of Egypt I called my son. Hosea depicted God as a divine father with an abiding love for His son, Israel. As a father, God summoned Israel out of Egypt. He rescued the inexperienced boy and began his training. However, the child proved to be a disobedient son who *kept sacrificing to the Baals, and burning incense to idols.* Yet God did not give up. As a loving father who taught his boy to walk, carried him when he was tired, healed him when he was injured, disciplined him with compassion and love, so the Lord cared for Israel.

How can I give you up, O Ephraim! How can I hand you over, O Israel. Israel had been rebellious and deserved punishment. (Deuteronomy 21:18–21 declared that a rebellious son was to be stoned to death.) Yet the Lord could not give up on His child. *How can I make you like Admah! How can I treat you like Zeboiim!* Admah and Zeboiim were two cities at the southern end of the Dead Sea that were destroyed along with Sodom and Gomorrah for their wickedness. *My heart recoils within me* at the thought of an equal fate for Israel. Instead, God demonstrated His fatherly patience and forgiveness.

Return, O Israel, to the Lord your God, for you have stumbled because of your iniquity. Israel has turned its back on God, the Father. Now it must return to the Lord and confess its sin in penitence. If it does this, God will forgive and restore it to Himself. *Take your words, and return to the Lord.* The Lord, unlike the Baals who require animal sacrifices, desires words of penitence. He asks that Israel acknowledge Him as the only God. He pleads to Israel, *Take away all iniquity; accept that which is good and we will render the fruit of our lips.*

Until now, Israel has relied more on international agreements (especially with Assyria) than in the Lord and has trusted more in military power (*ride upon horses* refers to war chariots) than in God. It has relied more in idols (gods made by *the work of our hands*) than in the Eternal. Israel (*"the orphan"*) must learn to turn to God, the forgiving Father.

I will heal their faithlessness; I will love them freely. . . . God responds as a loving parent to His child. He forgives when Israel repents. God pours out His love freely. God announces that His healing already has begun, *for my anger has turned away from them.*

SUGGESTIONS TO TEACHERS

Have you ever tried to take an independent-minded two-year-old on a walk? Have you ever tried to spoon dinner into the mouth of a cranky youngster?

Start this lesson by asking people to tell of exasperating times they have had in looking after a small child who is determined to have its own way. Everyone has some firsthand recollection of trying to feed or walk a toddler which has a mind of its own and seems determined to disregard the oldster's intentions.

Next, apply these experiences the same way the Prophet Hosea does—to Israel, and to God's community in these times. And encourage your class members to imagine the feelings which God holds toward His "child." Have the class members use the Bible selections from Hosea to illustrate the way God acts. Remember, this lesson is essential about the Lord and His caring. You and the class will find these issues emerging:

1. *THE MATERNAL GOD.* The picture is touching—God stooping over and taking the tiny hands of a baby just learning to take its first uncertain steps; God gently picking up the little one who has clumsily tumbled and fallen; God quietly taking the child in strong, protective arms; God patiently nursing and feeding a youngster too small to provide for itself. Here are maternal images of the Lord. Since so many of our images of God in the past have been supposedly "masculine" traits (such as strength and power), it is vital to understand that God also has "feminine" characteristics, or that God is both paternal and maternal!

2. *THE MOURNING GOD.* Ask your class if God can cry. Discuss whether or not the Lord has feelings. Then point to passages such as, "How can I give you up . . . how can I hand you over . . . my compassion grows warm and tender" (11:8). God, you must make clear, anguishes over His children. The God of the Bible is not the detached, disinterested deity of Eastern religions. Our God suffers. You will find you will bring in the suffering of God at the Crucifixion of Jesus with great effect in this lesson.

3. *THE MOVING GOD.* God acts. He is not motionless. Nor helpless. He returns His people to their rightful place with Him. He brings back the wayward and idolatrous. He heals the faithless. Ask how God is "in action" in these times.

4. *THE MINDFUL GOD.* Stress the report of Hosea that the Lord knows what is going on. Hosea insists that God is not forgetful or disinterested, but involves Himself with His people because He loves them as a good parent loves his or her own child. Conclude the lesson with the thrust that where there is this kind of love, there is always hope! This is the supreme lesson of the amazing love shown on Calvary!

TOPIC FOR ADULTS
WHERE THERE'S LOVE, THERE'S HOPE

Love Brings Hope. "Tex" was a truck driver with a big heart and a lot of faith. When he saw one of his buddies, Jerry, start to drink heavily, Tex tried to talk to him about what he was doing to himself and his family and, more important, what the Lord could do for anyone. Jerry shook his head. Tex told Jerry that he'd keep praying for him. Jerry laughed cynically. But Tex meant it. He kept trying to convince Jerry that God had other plans for his life. He pleaded with Jerry to quit drinking.

One day, Tex followed him into a bar and persuaded Jerry to come out with him without starting to drink. When they got outside the door, suddenly Jerry turned to Tex and poured forth a torrent of abuse. He paused for breath and angrily shouted, "Dammit, Tex, when are you going to leave me alone?" Tex smiled and answered, "I won't. Not while we're both still above ground." Jerry looked stunned. He lowered his eyes. Tears started to flow down his grizzled cheeks. That was the turning point.

Later, Jerry told his wife, "If I'm worth that to any man, I guess I'm worth something yet. I'll lay off the booze, and give life another try."

What's Your View? There is a report that a king many years ago who called his Prime Minister stated, "I have been looking out the window for the past few days and I observe that the country is in serious trouble."

"Begging your pardon, your majesty," replied the Prime Minister, "but that is not a window—it's a mirror!"

If we are seeing only our own images, we will never have hope. We will be confronted with bleak news. But God's mercy through Jesus Christ brings hope! If we look on Him, we get a different perspective about the world and the future! Let us look not at the mirrors of self-concern but through the windows of faith.

Source of Hope. John Wesley had always thought he was a perfect Christian until he journeyed to the colonies. One day in the course of his voyage across the Atlantic in a sailing ship, a fierce storm came up. The ship tossed and shuddered. Huge waves broke over the decks, sending cascades of icy salt water down through the corridors and lower decks. The wind shrieked through the rigging, ripping sails. Even the crew had anxious expressions, trying to work the ship. Most of the passengers shivered and screamed in terror every time the ship plunged into a deep trough, or listed far to one side before righting herself. The only people who did not seem to be frightened, Wesley noticed, were a small group of Moravian missionaries. Finally the storm slacked off. "Were you not afraid?" Wesley asked one of the Moravians, remembering how terrified he had been of dying during the storm.

"Afraid?" replied the Moravian. "Why should I be afraid? I know Christ." Then, looking at John Wesley with disarming frankness, he asked, "Brother Wesley, do *you* know Christ?"

Wesley realized that for the first time in his life that he really did not know Jesus Christ personally, and therefore lived in fear and hopelessness. Later, he did come to know Christ personally. From that day on, Wesley lived with serene confidence and hope!

Questions for Pupils on the Next Lesson. 1. Why was Jonah so reluctant to preach God's message to Nineveh? 2. Why did Jonah get angry when the Ninevites repented and God forgave them? 3. How did God use a plant to teach Jonah about love? 4. Is God's freedom to love ever limited by our feelings and expectations?

TOPIC FOR YOUTH
RESPONDING TO GOD'S LOVE

New Identity and Hope. Until December 11, 1982, Joe, a teenager, did not legally exist. He was unable to hear or speak, and he had spent nineteen years as a nameless nomad. He does not know anything about his background. His only clue to his identity is a vague memory of being abandoned in a mountain cabin when he was a small child. His age has been estimated by doctors to be nineteen years. He spent the years of childhood and adolescence sleeping under bushes, in doorways, and in cars, of walking, being hungry and sick. He was never able to find steady work because he did not have a birth certificate necessary to obtain a Social Security card. A newspaper article about Joe brought in a few donations that helped him to rent a room in Los Angeles and learn to live indoors. The money ran out a few months later, but a kindly woman named Virginia McKinney decided to welcome him to her own home. Later, Mrs. McKinney petitioned the court to adopt Joe, give him an identity and a name. The Judge of the Los Angeles Superior Court legally conferred a birth certificate (arbitrarily selected as April 1, 1963) and announced that the orphan without a name or home is now Joe McKinney.

God's love is like that for you. You may feel you have no real identity and exist without hope. But in the person of Jesus Christ, God has sought you out and welcomed you as one He cares about and wants you to be with Him. When there's this kind of love, there is always hope for you!

Saw Potential Worth. After World War I, factories sprang up around Jamaica Bay in New York City. Industrial wastes and sewage were dumped into the waters. Later, the area became a garbage dump. Birds and fish disappeared. Pollution ruined the site. Experts looking at that part of New York shook their heads, realizing Jamaica Bay had become an ecological disaster area. After World War II, however, Herbert Johnson insisted that there were possibilities in the foul-smelling dump. Johnson gathered and planted grasses, trees, and shrubs, and had two dikes built to create two ponds of fresh water. Today, the onetime dump is the lovely Gateway National Recreation area, and its wildlife refuge is home to over 300 species of birds! Just as Johnson saw the potential worth in a hopeless dump, Jesus sees the potential worth of each individual!

Reason for Response. Headmaster Boynton of Deerfield Academy built his institution into one of the great preparatory schools of the country. His students went on to make their marks in the leading universities and subsequently to outstanding careers in every profession. Deerfield alumni became noted for their achievements. A disproportionately high number were elected to great honors and won fame. Finally, someone decided to interview Boynton, asking for his philosophy of education. It was actually quite simple, explained Boynton. He explained that his philosophy of education was "constant confrontation with greatness."

When we encounter the love of God through Jesus Christ, we experience an even greater confrontation with greatness. We can never be the same. We know that we must respond!

Have you responded to God's love by living a life exhibiting hope?

Questions for Pupils on the Next Lesson. 1. Why didn't Jonah want to go to Nineveh? 2. What happened to Jonah when he tried to run away from his responsibilities? 3. How did God use a gourd vine to teach Jonah about love? 4. What are some of the prejudices you and your friends sometimes show? 5. How do you know that God's love includes all kinds of persons?

LESSON IX—JULY 28

GOD'S INCLUSIVE LOVE

Background Scripture: Jonah
Devotional Reading: Jonah 3

KING JAMES VERSION

JONAH 4 But it displeased Jonah exceedingly, and he was very angry.

2 And he prayed unto the LORD, and said, I pray thee, O LORD, *was* not this my saying, when I was yet in my country? Therefore I fled before unto Tarshish; for I knew that thou *art* a gracious God, and merciful, slow to anger, and of great kindness, and repentest thee of the evil.

3 Therefore now, O LORD, take, I beseech thee, my life from me; for *it is* better for me to die than to live.

4 Then said the LORD, Doest thou well to be angry?

5 So Jonah went out of the city and sat on the east side of the city, and there made him a booth, and sat under it in the shadow, till he might see what would become of the city.

6 And the LORD God prepared a gourd, and made *it* to come up over Jonah, that it might be a shadow over his head, to deliver him from his grief. So Jonah was exceeding glad of the gourd.

7 But God prepared a worm when the morning rose the next day, and it smote the gourd that it withered.

8 And it came to pass, when the sun did arise, that God prepared a vehement east wind; and the sun beat upon the head of Jonah, that he fainted, and wished in himself to die and said, *It is* better for me to die than to live.

9 And God said to Jonah, Doest thou well to be angry for the gourd? And he said, I do well to be angry, *even* unto death.

10 Then said the LORD, Thou hast had pity on the gourd, for the which thou hast not laboured, neither madest it grow; which came up in a night, and perished in a night:

11 And should not I spare Nineveh, that great city, wherein are more than sixscore thousand persons that cannot discern between their right hand and their left hand; and *also* much cattle?

REVISED STANDARD VERSION

JONAH 4 But it displeased Jonah exceedingly, and he was angry. 2 And he prayed to the LORD and said, "I pray thee, LORD, is not this what I said when I was yet in my country? That is why I made haste to flee to Tarshish; for I knew that thou art a gracious God and merciful, slow to anger, and abounding in steadfast love, and repentest of evil. 3 Therefore now, O LORD, take my life from me, I beseech thee, for it is better for me to die than to live." 4 And the LORD said, "Do you do well to be angry?" 5 Then Jonah went out of the city and sat to the east of the city, and made a booth for himself there. He sat under it in the shade, till he should see what would become of the city.

6 And the LORD God appointed a plant, and made it come up over Jonah, that it might be a shade over his head, to save him from his discomfort. So Jonah was exceedingly glad because of the plant. 7 But when dawn came up the next day, God appointed a worm which attacked the plant, so that it withered. 8 When the sun rose, God appointed a sultry east wind, and the sun beat upon the head of Jonah so that he was faint; and he asked that he might die, and said, "It is better for me to die than to live." 9 But God said to Jonah, "Do you do well to be angry for the plant?" And he said, "I do well to be angry, angry enough to die." 10 And the LORD said, "You pity the plant, for which you did not labor, nor did you make it grow, which came into being in a night, and perished in a night. 11 And should not I pity Nineveh, that great city, in which there are more than a hundred and twenty thousand persons who do not know their right hand from their left, and also much cattle?"

KEY VERSE: The Lord . . . is forbearing toward you, not wishing that any should perish, but that all should reach repentance. 2 Peter 3:9 (RSV).

HOME DAILY BIBLE READINGS

July 22. M. *Fleeing From God's Presence.* Jonah 1:1–16.
July 23. T. *Prayer in Distress.* Jonah 1:17–2:10.
July 24. W. *Proclamation and Repentance.* Jonah 3:1–5.

July 25. *T.* *Turning From Evil.* Jonah 3:6–10.
July 26. *F.* *A Pouting Prophet.* Jonah 4:1–5.
July 27. *S.* *A Parable on Pity.* Jonah 4:6–11.
July 28. *S.* *The Sign of Jonah.* Matthew 12:38–41.

BACKGROUND

When people hear of Jonah, they usually think only of the story of a man being gulped up by a great fish. Actually, only three of the forty-eight verses in the book have to do with the fish incident. The important thing about this important little book is not a curious tale of a person being swallowed and emerging alive from a fish after three days but the inclusive love of God. The Book of Jonah illustrates the concern of the Lord even toward hated enemies, and the missionary destiny of God's people.

In the case of ancient Israel, the most hated enemies were the Assyrians. Swarming out of their magnificent capital of Nineveh, located on the east bank of the Tigris River (across from the modern city of Mosul, Iraq), the Assyrian armies dominated the world scene for two centuries. They conquered nearly everyone in the Middle East. They were feared by everyone. Their inscriptions and firsthand reports describe their terrible brutality, such as cutting off the heads of conquered warriors and civilians and heaping them in huge pyramids in front of the walls of captured cities and stripping the skins from corpses and covering the walls with these. Nineveh finally fell in 612 B.C., but the memory of the Assyrian horrors remained for centuries.

A prophet named Jonah is named in 2 Kings 14:25. He lived in the early part of the eighth century B.C. He was probably an eyewitness to the Assyrian invasion under Shalmanesser III. Doubtless many of his relatives were slain or taken prisoner and deported. All the grain and food supplies for the following year were carried off.

Whether the book is to be read as actual history or as a parable (reputable scholars may be found holding either position), the object of the account is Jonah's reluctance to preach God's message to the loathed citizens of Nineveh. Jonah reflects the narrow, bitter attitude of Israel toward its enemy. Through this story, God warns the people of Israel that such an attitude means rejecting Him, the God of their fathers. Denying divine mercy to anyone, including the Assyrians, is repudiating the God of Abraham, Isaac, and Jacob, the God of the Covenant, who is merciful and gracious to all who turn to Him.

NOTES ON THE PRINTED TEXT

But it displeased Jonah exceedingly, and he was angry. On a very prominent sign, posted on the door of the Lambda-Xi-Alpha fraternity on Main Street in Slippery Rock, Pennsylvania, the following inscription was found: "Non-Brothers Please Knock." Jonah shared the same feelings of exclusivism. God was the God of the Jews. Jonah could not understand God's interest in non-brothers. Moreover, Jonah did not want anything to do with that interest and concern, especially if it was for the Ninevites. That attitude lay behind the events of the first three chapters of the Book of Jonah.

The Word of the Lord came to Jonah telling him to go to Nineveh and preach against its wickedness. Nineveh was the capital of Assyria. Archeology has revealed a truly "great city." The walls of Nineveh were seventy-five feet high, double brick, thirty-two feet thick, and protected by fifteen gates with a moat seventy-five feet wide. Many of its buildings were decorated with glazed polychrome tiles whose colors are still vivid, especially the deep blues. Including the suburbs, Nineveh covered fifteen miles from one side to the other, a good "three days" journey to walk through. Furthermore, Jonah knew the Assyrians.

He had heard of their cruelty and torture, their scorched earth policy and slave taking. Why would God be concerned with the Assyrians? Go to Nineveh? Who needed Nineveh, Jonah thought.

So Jonah fled to Joppa to take the slow boat to Tarshish, a city in Spain, about as far away from Nineveh as Jonah could get. However, Jonah learned the hard way that it was impossible to flee from God's presence. The result of Jonah's efforts to flee comprised chapters one and two of Jonah. A storm arose and lots were drawn; Jonah was cast overboard and swallowed by a great fish. Having proved to be indigestible, Jonah was vomited up on a beach and a second time commanded to go to Nineveh. This time Jonah went.

His city-wide crusade in Nineveh was short. He preached only a one-sentence sermon. "Yet forty days, and Nineveh shall be overthrown" (Jonah 3:4). Jonah was delighted to offer this message because he hated these people. However, to Jonah's dismay, Nineveh immediately repented. The Ninevites covered themselves in sackcloth, sat in ashes, and fasted—all signs of repentance. The population cried out to the Lord who immediately suspended His sentence of death. The Lord was delighted, but Jonah was furious. Jonah wanted to keep Israel's God exclusively for Israel.

I knew that thou art a gracious God and merciful, slow to anger, and abounding in steadfast love. Jonah had long suspected that God would forgive Nineveh. Remembering God's overflowing grace, Jonah sensed that God's love included all people, even non-Jews. In fact, Jonah's reluctance to go originally to Nineveh was based on this knowledge of God and his own feelings of exclusivism.

Therefore now, O Lord, take my life from me, I beseech thee, for it is better for me to die than to live. Miffed at God's inclusive love, Jonah pouted under a shrub. Feeling that God had betrayed him, Jonah wanted to die. Rather than participate in the fraternity of humankind, Jonah chose Jonah.

Sitting to the east of the city, Jonah enjoyed the cool, lush shade of the leafy shrub. However, on the next day, a worm attacked the shrub, causing it to wither. The sun beat mercilessly on Jonah's head making him a candidate for heat exhaustion. Jonah again was angry. *Do you do well to be angry for the plant?* God demanded of Jonah. *You pity the plant for which you did not labor, nor did you make it grow, which came into being in a night, and perished in a night?* In one verse came the whole message of the story of Jonah. While Jonah grieved over the loss of a shrub, God was concerned for over 120,000 Ninevites, men and women. Through a plant, God taught Jonah and us about His all-inclusive love. All brothers and sisters may enter the door of the Kingdom.

Jonah's story is our story. His "descendants" are numerous. Go to Nineveh? Go to Lebanon? El Salvador? Bedford-Stuyvesant? Do we understand there's a wideness in God's mercy? We spend too much time on the fish and not enough on God! Maybe that's why we want, "Non-Brothers Please Knock" signs!

SUGGESTIONS TO TEACHERS

Your first assignment in teaching this lesson will be to get your class to see that Jonah is much, much more than a curious story of fish that swallows man for three days. You may as well start off by stating that you don't propose spending any time on this relatively minor part of the Book of Jonah. Tell your people that the point of the book is God's inclusive love for everyone, and that is what you'll be discussing.

The little Book of Jonah could actually serve as the basis for a number of important lessons for your class. When you read through the book (as you must!) you will find several significant subthemes under the main topic of the Lord's compassion.

1. *DISOBEDIENT PROPHET.* Jonah, the prophet, is commanded by God to preach to the people of Nineveh. Jonah, however, refuses and flees toward Tarshish by ship. The writer is trying to make the point that God's people have a missionary mandate. Israel, if it was true to its calling, was commissioned to be a light to the Gentiles. Today, we as God's people are called to evangelize everywhere. Our task is the same as Jonah's: to go to the peoples of the Ninevehs in our age. Talk with your class where God intends His message to be heard in these times. Especially discuss the call of the Church to be a mission-minded people. Is your congregation zealous for missions? How obedient is your class to the Lord's Great Commission?

2. *DETERMINED GOD.* Point out to your students that God insists on bringing Jonah back to his task. (This is the purpose of the fish spitting out Jonah.) God intends that His work be completed; He wills that His mercy be shown to all peoples. He will not let you or your class or your church alone until you act responsibly and obediently as His missionary people!

3. *DESPONDENT PREACHER.* Jonah, the reluctant preacher, finally goes to Nineveh and grudgingly tells God's message of His inclusive love couched in terms of a call to repent. Jonah, however, is astonished to find the people of Nineveh repenting! He sulks because God relents from destroying Nineveh and accepts the Ninevites. Is not this the way we sometimes are with carrying out God's orders? We don't expect much. We often don't want much to happen, we don't want to change our ideas. We sometimes accuse God. We much prefer denouncing our enemies to granting them Good News. We would rather be prophets of doom than agents of hope. We want to see wrongdoers get their just punishment, and we have little interest in promoting divine deliverance.

4. *DIDACTIC DEITY.* God used a gourd plant as an object lesson for His peevish prophet. When Jonah gets worked up over the death of his plant, God levels His blast at Jonah: "You pity the plant . . . and should not I pity Nineveh . . . ?" (4:10, 11). God sometimes has to bring us up short to teach us that His mercy extends to those we despise. This may be a suitable time to think with your class whether or not the Lord also loves Russian Communists, homosexuals, welfare chiselers, muggers, rapists, and murderers.

TOPIC FOR ADULTS
GOD'S INCLUSIVE LOVE

Left Foot Only. A small town in Tennessee had a place of worship with a sign in front: LEFT FOOT BAPTIST CHURCH. A student had passed it many times and had often wondered about the meaning of the name of the church. Finally, one day, waiting for his bus, the student asked someone in the town about the significance of the unusual name for the church.

It seems that there had been a split in the local congregation which practiced foot-washing. The break occurred over which foot should be washed first. The group insisting on the left foot taking precedence finally withdrew to organize its own church, and named its congregation accordingly!

How frequently we forget that God's love is inclusive! We have a constant tendency to be like Jonah, to try to keep God's grace for folks who agree with us, especially who try to emphasize minor matters such as which foot is to be washed first. Christ calls to a greater vision. He intends us to be missionaries to all others to share the Good News of God's care.

The God Who Will Never Write Us Off. "Look, I see the scum," growled the prison official to his minister. "Where I work, I have to deal with the worst. Guys who would pull a knife on their grandmother for a nickel. I mean it literally! Murderers. Rapists. You name it, I see them every day. And I'm convinced you just have to write off characters like these. In fact, although I belong to your church, I feel that God just has to write off these people. You know, a business has to write off bad debts. Or a store writes off spoiled or damaged stuff. Or a plant takes a write-off on something defective. Well, it's the same way with God. These guys are too rotten. Some people are like that. We may as well face the facts and write them off."

This correctional officer in a large county prison reflected the attitude that Jonah held. Both the prison official and the prophet try to tell the Lord to write off certain people. For the correctional officer, it's the inmates of his jail. For Jonah, it was the inhabitants of Nineveh. Both were convinced that God would have to regard a certain group of people as hopelessly beyond God's caring.

Neither the county prison staff member nor the Old Testament missionary could understand that with God the notion of "write-offs" applies to everyone. God could find reasons to write off each of us! His problem with you and me is the same as the correctional officer and Jonah thought that He had with jail-house prisoners and Ninevites. But God will not write us off! He cares! We know this through Jesus Christ. Therefore, we continue to show an inclusive love to *everyone!*

The Spirit of a True Missionary. Betty Stam was one of those added to a long list of missionary martyrs when she was killed by Chinese bandits during the unrest in China during the 1930s. Betty Stam was the opposite of Jonah. She recognized God's inclusive love for all, including Chinese people. She committed herself wholeheartedly to Jesus Christ. Nine years before she met death, she wrote these words in her diary: "Lord, I give up my own purposes and plans, all my desires, hopes, ambitions whether they are fleshly or soulish. I accept Thy will for my life. I give myself, my life, my all utterly to Thee to be Thine forever. I hand over to Thee for Thy keeping all my friendships and my love. All the people whom I love are to take second place in my heart. Work out Thy whole will in my life at any cost, now and forever."

Questions for Pupils on the Next Lesson. 1. What was happening in the world at the time Habakkuk lived and wrote? 2. If God is always actively involved in the world, why do His ways often seem to be a mystery? 3. How can a person be faithful to God and rejoice when times are terribly bad? 4. Exactly what does it mean to speak of "living by faith"? 5. Are doubts necessarily a sign of unbelief?

TOPIC FOR YOUTH
GOD'S LOVE IS FOR EVERYONE

"I Have Great Love and Regard for You." Son of a famous British Admiral, young William Penn seemed to his parents and the English Establishment to be a rogue upstart when he got interested in the group of Christians known as Quakers. By 1666, Penn laid aside his sword and formally united with the Quakers. He determined to find freedom for his fellow Quakers, and negotiated with King Charles II to secure a large grant of land in the colonies, in 1681 to settle a debt owed his father by the crown. Penn's woods, or Pennsylvania, attracted hundreds of persecuted Quakers. Philadelphia, meaning "City of Brotherly Love," was laid out in 1682, and, at Penn's insistence, his colony extended religious and political freedom to all comers. Penn was exceptionally considerate of the native Americans or the Indian population, and always dealt fairly with them. As a devout Christian, William Penn was convinced that God's love is for everyone. Therefore, he never persecuted or cheated them. He said to the Indians, "I have great

love and regard toward you, and I desire to win and gain your love and friendship, by a kind, just, and peaceable life: . . . and if in anything any shall offend you or your people, you shall have a full and speedy satisfaction for the same."

China: A Classic Case for Missions. "If anyone wants a classic case history to demonstrate the validity of 'foreign missions,' it is now available in spades. It is the Christian community in the People's Republic of China.

"Take the concept of the 'church' into the laboratory. Postulate that the 'church' is a human organization, but with mysterious transcendent qualities that make for its survival in some form through anything the political structures could exert. Then try to destroy it. Take away its property, resources, finances. Remove the financial security of the professional leadership, as well as the prestige, and even the permission to function at all, scatter the flock, banish the core group, eliminate the books, forbid the songs, prohibit gatherings, punish those who speak of it even within the family.

"The communists seized control of the country in 1949 and in 1958 began the policies of public disapproval and bureaucratic control of the Christian churches. In 1966, the onslaught of the 'Cultural Revolution' brought on the decade of total repression, as per the laboratory paradigm.

"The result? The profound drama of death and resurrection! Today, the Christian community is strong and growing, completely free of foreign control, influence or finance. The Protestant part is a single body, known as the 'Three-Self Movement,' and the Roman Catholics are restoring the pastoral and sacramental ministries without a reliance on or accountability to Rome. It is estimated that each week sees more than a million people in attendance at public worship. Both experiences we had were in crowded churches with adamant worshipers, fervent preachers and a warm and loving fellowship.

"But on our recent trip to China it was in the interviews that we heard the words of gratitude and reflections of life-changing friendships that caused us to appreciate the missionary. For all the criticisms by historians of heavy-handed Western culture being impressed as God's own viewpoint, and the denominational divisiveness, and the exploitation by over-directive churchmen, *there is a basic authenticity that has survived.* It has been refined in the crucible, more purifying than we can ever imagine. And the end product is a church ready to serve its Lord, well aware of the cost."—Wesley C. Baker, *Presbyterian Outlook,* November 1, 1982.

Two Lines. God's love is for everyone. How do we show it is inclusive? Well, partly by our lifestyles. And partly by our sharing. Here is the contrast between us who have so much and those who have so little.

A line forms. Fifty plus people are waiting to buy ice cream . . . banana-coffee, chocolate-cinnamon, pineapple-ripple . . . at $1.60 for a large scoop or $2.00 for a "mix-in" such as M&M's or pulverized Oreos which are "expertly kneaded into the very flesh" of the scooped ice cream.

The picture is true. American's love of ice cream has gone beyond the plain old chocolate variety to elaborate $7.00 a quart hand-packed ice cream. It is a 1.6 billion dollar a year industry which produces 829,798,000 gallons of ice cream, and Americans consume more of it than any other country in the world.

Consider also that anyone in that line eating plain vanilla will consume 267 calories which will take them 87.6 minutes to burn off if playing a game of golf or 210 minutes if they loaf.

Now, picture another line. Fifty plus people are waiting for the rice, split beans, and milk that will be given to them. They are part of the most vulnerable of the world's hungry . . . infants, pregnant lactating women, widows, and the elderly. Most of the food, however, that is distributed is payment for labor contributed to community self-help projects.

This picture is equally true. More than 500 million people are still malnourished. We as a nation spend more on ice cream (almost double) than we do to feed the world's hungry. One ice-cream cone has more calories than many of the world's hungry eat in a single day.

Questions for Pupils on the Next Lesson. 1. What was going on in the world which caused Habakkuk to write as he did? 2. Why does God who is good allow people to suffer? 3. How is it possible to be faithful to God in the midst of bad times? 4. What is the value of daily prayer? 5. In the midst of difficulties, are you able to find something to rejoice about?

LESSON X—AUGUST 4

FAITH IN THE MIDST OF DESPAIR

Background Scripture: Habakkuk
Devotional Reading: Habakkuk

KING JAMES VERSION

HABAKKUK 1 The burden which Habakkuk the prophet did see.

2 O LORD, how long shall I cry, and thou wilt not hear! *even* cry out unto thee *of* violence, and thou wilt not save!

3 Why dost thou shew me iniquity, and cause *me* to behold grievance? for spoiling and violence *are* before me: and there *are that* raise up strife and contention.

4 Therefore the law is slacked, and judgment doth never go forth: for the wicked doth compass about the righteous; therefore wrong judgment proceedeth.

2 2 And the LORD answered me, and said, Write the vision, and make *it* plain upon tables, that he may run that readeth it.

3 For the vision *is* yet for an appointed time, but at the end it shall speak, and not lie: though it tarry, wait for it; because it will surely come, it will not tarry.

4 Behold, his soul *which* is lifted up is not upright in him: but the just shall live by his faith.

3 17 Although the fig tree shall not blossom, neither *shall* fruit *be* in the vines; the labour of the olive shall fail, and the fields shall yield no meat; the flock shall be cut off from the fold, and *there shall be* no herd in the stalls:

18 Yet I will rejoice in the LORD, I will joy in the God of my salvation.

19 The LORD God *is* my strength, and he will make my feet like hinds' *feet*, and he will make me to walk upon mine high places. To the chief singer on my stringed instruments.

REVISED STANDARD VERSION

HABAKKUK 1 The oracle of God which Habakkuk the prophet saw.

2 O LORD, how long shall I cry for help, and thou wilt not hear?
Or cry to thee "Violence!" and thou wilt not save?

3 Why dost thou make me see wrongs and look upon trouble?
Destruction and violence are before me; strife and contention arise.

4 So the law is slacked and justice never goes forth.
For the wicked surround the righteous, so justice goes forth perverted.

2 2 And the LORD answered me:
"Write the vision;
make it plain upon tablets, so he may run who reads it.

3 For still the vision awaits its time; it hastens to the end—it will not lie.
If it seem slow, wait for it; it will surely come, it will not delay.

4 Behold, he whose soul is not upright in him shall fail,
but the righteous shall live by his faith.

3 17 Though the fig tree do not blossom, nor fruit be on the vines,
the produce of the olive fail and the fields yield no food,
the flock be cut off from the fold and there be no herd in the stalls,

18 yet I will rejoice in the LORD, I will joy in the God of my salvation.

19 GOD, the Lord, is my strength;
he makes my feet like hinds' feet,
he makes me tread upon my high places.
To the choirmaster: with stringed instruments.

KEY VERSE: *The righteous shall live by his faith.* Habakkuk 2:4 (RSV).

HOME DAILY BIBLE READINGS

July 29. M. *God Works Among the Nations.* Habakkuk 1:1–5.
July 30. T. *The Righteous Live by Faith.* Habakkuk 2:1–4.
July 31. W. *Woe to the Unjust.* Habakkuk. 2:9–17.
Aug. 1. T. *Prayer for Mercy in Judgment.* Habakkuk 3:1–6.
Aug. 2. F. *Strength in the Cause of Salvation.* Habakkuk 3:9–13.
Aug. 3. S. *Rejoice in the Lord.* Habakkuk 3:17–19.
Aug. 4. S. *Faith Makes Endurance Possible.* Hebrews 10:36–39.

BACKGROUND

"Lord, if You govern this world, why do You permit such terrible wickedness? Can't you hear me, Lord? You claim that You are holy and powerful, but You do

nothing about the immoral conditions in Jerusalem. And why are You silent when the Babylonians act so cruelly against others?" These in essence were Habakkuk's problems with God.

Habakkuk lived near the end of the seventh century B.C. in the southern kingdom of Judah. The northern kingdom of Israel had been wiped out by the Assyrians a century earlier. But Judah had not learned any lessons. It seemed to become more corrupt. King Jehoiakim's reign in Judah, starting about 608 B.C., made matters worse. Like his contemporary Jeremiah (whose encounters with the nasty Jehoiakim are recorded in Jeremiah 36), Habakkuk had to speak to a nation threatened from within by moral decay. He was heartbroken and perplexed. How could God permit such rampant evil and injustice to go unpunished?

Judah was also threatened from without. By the time Habakkuk began to prophesy, the mighty Assyrian empire had been overrun by the Babylonians. But the new world superpower had also designs on the smaller nations and wanted to force them to pay tribute money. The Babylonians turned out to be almost as crafty and cruel as the Assyrians. To the dismay of the prophets, King Jehoiakim decided to play the game of devious politics instead of relying on the Lord. Habakkuk and Jeremiah and the handful of God-fearing people in Jerusalem knew that Jehoiakim's clever attempts to play off Egypt against Babylon and switching sides by making and breaking treaties with these power-hungry neighbors could only end in disaster for the nation. Habakkuk, however, was shaken by the violence of the Babylonian forces against innocent people. He anguished over the way God seemed silent and indifferent in the face of what was happening on the international scene.

We know no details of this prophet's personal life. We know that he must have lived during one of the most unsettling periods of history since he lived in the days immediately preceding the destruction of Jerusalem and the great Temple. Much of his writings are a dialogue with God, asking God to answer him. The Lord did answer Habakkuk. God in effect told Habakkuk that He was at work in history, and would act in His own good time. Furthermore, Habakkuk learned the startling news that the Babylonians would be the Lord's agents of judgment against Jerusalem. Meanwhile, Habakkuk discovers, those who are righteous will live because they are faithful to God! This great insight—known in Christian parlance as "justification by faith"—is one of Habakkuk's great contributions!

NOTES ON THE PRINTED TEXT

Judah had long been on a collision course with Babylon, and now it was under attack (1:7–9). However, unlike the other prophets who spoke for God, Habakkuk spoke to God. He expressed in a song of lamentation the thoughts that were on his mind as well as the people's. *O Lord, how long shall I cry for help, and thou wilt not hear? Or cry to thee 'Violence!' and thou wilt not save?* Habakkuk saw before him violence and destruction on a vast scale. In Judah there was strife, contention, and corrupt morals. Among the prophet's own people justice could not be found, only wrongdoing. *For the wicked surround the righteous, so justice goes forth perverted.*

Habakkuk's complaint is nothing new. Modern day Habakkuks ask the same questions. *Why dost thou make me to see wrongs and look upon trouble?* Why do the good suffer? Why do the evil prosper? Why does God not teach the evil not to disregard Him? How long will the Lord ignore these injustices?

God answered Habakkuk that Babylon was the nation appointed by God to punish the corrupt Jewish people (1:5–11). Once again, Habakkuk complained. *Thou who are of purer eyes than to behold evil and canst look on wrong, why dost thou look on faithless men, and art silent when the wicked swallows up the man more righteous than he?* How could God let a ruthless and tyrannical people like the Babylonians so mercilessly swallow up the people of Judah, hook them, and drag them off in nets? This seeming cruelty on God's part mystified Habakkuk.

I will take my stand to watch, and station myself on the tower. Full of questions, Habakkuk watched the approach of the mighty Babylonians from a watchtower. It was a blitzkrieg invasion that had not been halted. All the fortresses had been reduced to ruin. One of the last cities to fall just before Jerusalem was Lachish, southwest of Jerusalem. In the city gate of Lachish beneath what were once watchtowers, excavators have found a series of letters written on pottery describing the last moments of Azekah, the sister fortress of Lachish that guarded the southern approaches to Jerusalem. "We can no longer see the signal fires of Lachish," one of the letters stated. Lachish was soon reduced to a fiery ruin. Like the sentries of Lachish, Habakkuk took his stand on the watchtower to see how God would answer his complaint.

God finally responded to Habakkuk. *Write the vison; make it plain upon tablets, so he may run who reads it.* Then the Lord told Habakkuk to wait patiently. Even if it seemed slow, judgment was definitely coming. For the answer to be written on the tablet was *Behold, he whose soul is not upright in him shall fail, but the righteous shall live by his faith.* It was a two-part answer. The first part answered Habakkuk's complaints about the Babylonians being God's instrument of punishment. Those who were not upright, honest, or morally straight would fail. The arrogantly proud who trusted in themselves alone would die. Ultimately, the Babylonians would be destroyed. However, the second part answered Habakkuk's questions about Judah by saying that those who kept their faith in God would survive. Be faithful and trust in God!

Habakkuk listened. Facing obvious starvation, thirst, and the threat of slavery, or exile, Habakkuk rejoiced with a psalm. He sang! In spite of the fig tree's destruction, the lack of fruit on the vines, and scorched fields devoid of crops or cattle, Habakkuk exalted with: *yet I will rejoice in the Lord, I will joy in the God of my salvation. God the Lord is my strength.* Now, hope and confidence rang in his words. Now, there was faith in the midst of despair. Though city gates would be destroyed, the walls breached, and the cities conquered, Habakkuk's strength and trust were now in the Lord. God would not fail.

Habakkuk's theme of encouragement to the righteous to remain faithful (2:4) was echoed by Paul in Romans 1:17 and Galatians 3:11. Moreover, the writer of Hebrews 10:37, 38 also called on his readers to hold fast to their faith even in the presence of difficult situations. Living by faith and rejoicing even in the worst of times was the summons of Habakkuk and these others to all God's people.

SUGGESTIONS TO TEACHERS

"How do you cope when there seems to be no hope for better things to come?" asked a Detroit machinist who has been out of work for two years and about to lose his home. "Without hope, I can't cope," he added in an unintentional rhyme.

Hoping and coping go together. But how can a person find hope when the economic conditions are bleak, or personal tragedy has struck? This is the topic of your lesson for this Sunday.

You will be working with one of the most influential yet least-read books in the Bible: *Habakkuk.* You and your class will discover that this prophet who lived in the midst of one of the most unsettling times for Judah and the world helps people in every age find faith in the midst of despair.

1. *TIME OF WAILING.* Habakkuk speaks of nearly every person when he cries, "How long shall I cry for help?" (1:2). Violence, injustice, and oppression are rampant. The prophet uses an image of lawless, cruel rulers "fishing" for

human victims, devouring people with impunity. These vivid metaphors should help you to get your lesson off on a fast start by introducing the question, "Why does God apparently allow people to get away with evil and hurt good people?" Habakkuk struggled with this question. Your people struggle with it, too. Permit your class members to air their private misgivings about divine justice in the universe and bring out their secret questions about God's plans.

2. *TIME OF WAITING.* Habakkuk has to learn a difficult lesson, namely that the Lord has His own schedule. Sometimes we must wait. God, however, will not fail. Meanwhile, "the righteous will live by his faith" (2:4). Here is that magnificent doctrine which brought hope to a despairing Saul of Tarsus! This is the basis of Saul's (later Paul, the Apostle's) mighty announcement, "He who through faith is righteous shall live!" (Romans 1:17 and Galatians 3:11). Justification by faith is the name of this great bedrock belief. Martin Luther reclaimed it and brought new life to the Church in the sixteenth century, and John Wesley discovered it applied to him and others in the eighteenth century. Do you and your class members realize the significance of these words in the twentieth century?

3. *TIME OF WAKING.* Habakkuk says that when we have God, we have enough. In fact, with the Lord, regardless of the surroundings or circumstances, we should rejoice! We are given strength and certainty for the present and for the future. Use lots of the lesson period to examine all the meaning of Habakkuk 3:17–19. Press the point that God may be trusted, and therefore we have hope!

TOPIC FOR ADULTS
FAITH IN THE MIDST OF DESPAIR

Blitz Blessing. In the midst of the Battle of Britain, in which London was hit with bombs night after night in the autumn of 1941, it seemed as if the city was a gigantic inferno from the fires and explosions. Thousands of Londoners were forced to seek shelter from the air raids in the London underground or subways. In fact, many civilians had to carry bedding and suitcases and sleep on subway station platforms nearly every night after the sirens started. One night, a little girl was heard to start her bedtime prayers beside her little makeshift bedroll in the Kings Cross station in the following way: "God bless Mummy and Daddy, God bless my aunties and uncles and cousins. And take good care of Yourself, for without You, we've had it. Amen."

Habakkuk would have understood that kind of prayer. Without God, we have "had it." But with the Lord, we can cope with sleepless nights, damaged homes and demolished dreams, bombs, losses and death! With God, we have enough!

God's Arm of This Sparrow. Ethel Waters, whose trademark was the song, "His Eye Is on the Sparrow," was one of the most beloved and talented singers in show business. Her success came out of the most unlikely beginnings. She was born to a mother who was an unmarried girl of only twelve, and hardly knew her father. She grew up fast in the tough slums, and was street-wise by the time she was a toddler. She earned her first money by running errands for the prostitutes in her neighborhood. She knew the language of the gutter with her first spoken words. Her grandmother tried to raise her to know something other than the world of pimps, pushers, and prostitutes, but it seemed hopeless. Ethel Waters broke into the entertainment world when she was seventeen, but she already carried the scars from being consigned to a girlhood in the gutters. She was a fighter. The public was not altogether pleased at that time with black entertainers succeeding. The racial slurs and prejudice made her bitter. She once explained to an interviewer why she wore the rings she had on both hands, "I had two diamond rings on my hands: one for decoration, and one for emergencies—both offensive and defensive work." Ethel Waters's life was an epoch of hurts and struggle, but she finally was encountered by Jesus Christ. Her faith in the Lord saved her from destroying herself in her times of despair. She became aware that through all of the trials of her life, this same Lord was standing with her in love. Her rendition of the old black spiritual, "His Eye Is on the Sparrow," was more than a trademark in her later years; it was a testimony from her heart about the hope God gave her. With twinkling eyes and an enormous smile, Ethel Waters would announce, "I know God's arm is around this big fat sparrow. And I know He cares for you, too!"

Do you know this?

Open Hands for Sowing. When Adolfo Perez Esquivel received the Nobel Peace Prize in Oslo, Norway, in 1980, he was quoted thus: "Because of our faith in Christ and in humankind, we must apply our humble efforts to the construction of a more just and humane world. And I want to declare emphatically: Such a world is possible. To create this new society, we must present outstretched, friendly hands, without hatred, without rancor—even as we show great determination, never wavering in the defense of truth and justice. Because we know that seeds are not sown with clenched fists. To sow we must open our hands."

To sow we must open our hands . . . and our ears and eyes. We must be willing to hear people with our hearts as well as our minds. Mr. Esquivel was speaking of peace and justice . . . the justice of having an adequate meal and a roof over head, and the opportunity to work. Things most of us take for granted, but are in jeopardy to thousands of people in our own community. Have we heard them? And, having heard, have we opened our hands to them?

Questions for Pupils on the Next Lesson. 1. Who were the "exiles" to whom Zechariah was speaking? 2. How can God's people rejoice in a hostile environment? 3. Do you ever feel that what you do has little effect on community and world affairs? 4. What are some of the lessons of history that you have learned from your study of the Scriptures? 5. What were some of the times in your life when you were so preoccupied with relatively minor personal problems that you failed to recognize the "big events" in life?

TOPIC FOR YOUTH
FAITH IN THE MIDST OF DOUBT

Night Shift. Episcopal Bishop Will Scarlett was deeply involved in a long, bitter strike at Ford in Detroit some years ago. Feelings were running high on both sides, and violence had broken out causing injuries and death. Scarlett had driven himself to the point of physical and emotional exhaustion to try to mediate between the two opposing sides. The outlook looked hopeless. His efforts had seemed futile. One night, the bishop tried to go to sleep after he had gone to bed but tossed restlessly. He felt himself tense after a gruelling eighteen hours of meetings, and tense about the morrow. He heard the clock strike the hours, and angrily wished for rest. Then, just after 3:00 A.M., it seemed that a voice spoke to the sleepless churchman, "Go to sleep now, Scarlett. I'll take over the rest of the night." Scarlett learned the lesson of faith in the lonely darkness of those early A.M. hours. God could be trusted with the night time as well as with the waking hours. Bishop Scarlett found faith in the midst of his doubts!

What Can a Little Person Like Me Do? A Quaker named Joseph Hoag was talking to an audience in London in 1812, calling for people who would make the Christian decision. A man in the crowd called out: "Well, Stranger, if all the world were of your mind, I would turn and follow after!" To this Hoag quickly replied: "So thou hast a mind to be the last man in the world of good. I have a mind to be first." Have we "a mind to be first," in stepping out of the parade and trying to be different from what we are, more like Christ, more useful to Him?

So you see, there is a great deal that "a little person like me" can do. Enough of us little persons can cause a spiritual conflagration in this neighborhood, and city, and state, and nation that will be seen from very far, if we are faithful and pray that the Holy Spirit light and fan the flames.

Harvest Hopes. A farmer wrote a letter to the editor of a newspaper: "Dear Mr. Editor, I want to tell you something. All of my neighbors go to church, and all of my neighbors observe Sunday. They won't do anything on Sunday. I plowed my fields on Sunday, I cultivated my fields on Sunday. I sowed my fields on Sunday, and I harvested them on Sunday. Mr. Editor, at the end of the season, at the end of the harvest, I did better than any of my neighbors who observed Sunday and went to church. Mr. Editor, how do you explain that?"

The editor's brief answer was: "God doesn't make up His final account in October."

Questions for Pupils on the Next Lesson. 1. Why did God tell Zechariah to challenge the exiles in Babylon to return to Jerusalem? 2. Have you ever tried to be joyful about God in an unfriendly setting? 3. Is there a lot of security in your relationship with your friends? 4. In your sense of loneliness, are you open to seeking God's presence? 5. Why do you sometimes feel insecure?

LESSON XI—AUGUST 11

GOD WILL NOT FORSAKE HIS OWN

Background Scripture: Zechariah 1:1–6; 2:1–12; 8
Devotional Reading: Zechariah 8:9–19

KING JAMES VERSION

ZECHARIAH 2 I lifted up mine eyes again, and looked, and behold a man with a measuring line in his hand.

2 Then said I, Whither goest thou? And he said unto me, To measure Jerusalem, to see what *is* the breadth thereof, and what *is* the length thereof.

3 And, behold, the angel that talked with me went forth, and another angel went out to meet him,

4 And said unto him, Run, speak to this young man, saying, Jerusalem shall be inhabited *as* towns without walls for the multitude of men and cattle therein:

5 For I, saith the LORD, will be unto her a wall of fire round about, and will be the glory in the midst of her.

6 Ho, ho, *come forth*, and flee from the land of the north, saith the LORD: for I have spread you abroad as the four winds of the heaven, saith the LORD.

7 Deliver thyself, O Zion, that dwellest *with* the daughter of Babylon.

8 For thus saith the LORD of hosts; After the glory hath he sent me unto the nations which spoiled you: for he that toucheth you, toucheth the apple of his eye.

9 For, behold, I will shake mine hand upon them, and they shall be a spoil to their servants: and ye shall know that the LORD of hosts hath sent me.

10 Sing and rejoice, O daughter of Zion: for, lo, I come, and I will dwell in the midst of thee, saith the LORD.

11 And many nations shall be joined to the LORD in that day, and shall be my people: and I will dwell in the midst of thee, and thou shalt know that the LORD of hosts hath sent me unto thee.

12 And the LORD shall inherit Judah his portion in the holy land, and shall choose Jerusalem again.

REVISED STANDARD VERSION

ZECHARIAH 2 And I lifted my eyes and saw, and behold, a man with a measuring line in his hand! 2 Then I said, "Where are you going?" And he said to me, "To measure Jerusalem, to see what is its breadth and what is its length." 3 And behold, the angel who talked with me came forward, and another angel came forward to meet him, 4 and said to him, "Run, say to that young man, 'Jerusalem shall be inhabited as villages without walls, because of the multitude of men and cattle in it. 5 For I will be in her a wall of fire round about, says the LORD, and I will be the glory within her.' "

6 Ho! ho! Flee from the land of the north, says the LORD; for I have spread you abroad as the four winds of the heavens, says the LORD. 7 Ho! Escape to Zion, you who dwell with the daughter of Babylon. 8 For thus said the LORD of hosts, after his glory sent me to the nations who plundered you, for he who touches you touches the apple of his eye: 9 "Behold, I will shake my hand over them, and they shall become plunder for those who served them. Then you will know that the LORD of hosts has sent me. 10 Sing and rejoice, O daughter of Zion; for lo, I come and I will dwell in the midst of you, says the LORD. 11 And many nations shall join themselves to the LORD in that day, and shall be my people; and I will dwell in the midst of you, and you shall know that the LORD of hosts has sent me to you. 12 And the LORD will inherit Judah as his portion in the holy land, and will again choose Jerusalem."

KEY VERSE: They shall be my people and I will be their God, in faithfulness and righteousness. Zechariah 8:8 (RSV).

HOME DAILY BIBLE READINGS

Aug. 5. M. *Learn From the Past.* Zechariah 1:1–6.
Aug. 6. T. *The Man With a Measuring Line.* Zechariah 2:1–12.
Aug. 7. W. *Iniquity Taken Away.* Zechariah 3:1–5.
Aug. 8. T. *Restoration Promised Jerusalem.* Zechariah 8:1–8.
Aug. 9. F. *A Remnant Will Be Saved.* Zechariah 8:9–13.

Aug. 10. S. *The Great Homecoming.* Zechariah 10:6–12.
Aug. 11. S. *The Triumph of a Humble King.* Zechariah 9:9–13.

BACKGROUND

We have been studying some of the Minor Prophets. The writings of these twelve great men of faith make up a scroll in the Hebrew canon, and cover a period of over 200 years in the history of Israel and Judah. We have already seen how Israel, the northern kingdom, was overrun by the Assyrians in 721 B.C. We also have learned that Judah, the southern realm, fell to the Babylonians, and Jerusalem and the great Temple were destroyed.

Most of the leading people in Jerusalem and Judah were marched off as captives to Babylon. From 586 to 536 B.C., they lived in exile. Suddenly, international events changed the course of their lives again. The Persians conquered the Babylonians. The rulers of the new world empire decided to allow many persons displaced by the Babylonians to return to their original homes. This meant that the survivors and their children and grandchildren uprooted from Jerusalem could go back to the holy city.

After fifty years, however, it was harder than most realized to pick up the pieces of living in Jerusalem. For one thing, the once-magnificent city had been in ruins for a half-century, and it was disheartening for a relatively small group to try to rebuild on the rubble. Another problem was the local squatters and descendants of those who had never left the area. Many of these had intermarried with Canaanites and become indifferent in their worship practices. These people were suspicious, even hostile, to the returnees from exile in Babylon. Those returning from exile also had to contend with opposition from crooked or malicious local officials.

Zechariah prophesied from 520 to 518 B.C. His words are mostly in the form of a series of visions. These visions were to inspire those returning to Jerusalem to persist in (1) rebuilding the Temple, and (2) living as a purified community. Zechariah had a zeal for worship in the rebuilt Jerusalem Temple. He also joined with other leaders in urging greater effort to live consciously as a people untainted with the vices of the surrounding population.

NOTES ON THE PRINTED TEXT

Zechariah, the son of Berechiah, son of Iddo, was a young priest who prophesied for only two years, 520–518 B.C. The core of the Book of Zechariah, the eleventh in the series of twelve short prophetic books, is the eight visions received by Zechariah during a single night. Like Haggai, a contemporary, Zechariah was concerned with the rebuilding of the Temple at Jerusalem in 520 B.C. Unlike Haggai, however, Zechariah's visions covered a wide range of topics. These visions were drawn upon by later writers such as John in his Revelation.

In this the third vision, Zechariah: *lifted my eyes and saw, and behold, a man with a measuring line in his hand* preparing to measure Jerusalem. Zechariah began to talk with him but was interrupted by an angel who declared that *Jerusalem shall be inhabited as villages without walls, because of the multitude of men and cattle in it.* The vision referred to the majority of the people who felt that it was necessary in the interests of national defense to first rebuild the walls of Jerusalem. They wanted to see Jerusalem restored but were intent on constructing the city first and God's Temple second. It was against these people and these thoughts that the prophets Haggai and Zechariah prophesied. In Zechariah's vision, the angel informed his audience that the Jerusalem of the future could not possibly have any walls because of the multitudes of people and cattle. Unlimited growth would make walls obsolete before they were even completed.

Moreover, God Himself would dwell with the people and be its protector as *a wall of fire round about.*

Flee from the land of the north, says the Lord ... Escape to Zion, you who dwell with the daughter of Babylon. Zechariah challenged the exiles in Babylon to return to the holy land and reestablish Jerusalem. They must return to Jerusalem for here God would again dwell in their midst. *Sing and rejoice, O daughter of Zion; for lo, I come and I will dwell in the midst of you, says the Lord.* For the fainthearted, those who lacked courage and faith, Zechariah offered God's own promise when He said *he who touches you touches the apple of his* (God's) *eye.* Those who had plundered Judah would themselves be plundered. Zechariah was anxious for the exiles to return. In fact, he took it for granted that they would respond to the summons.

Why was Zechariah anxious for the exiles to return? Zechariah believed that the Messianic Age was about to begin. The rebuilding of the Temple was only the beginning of the new age. The faithful had to return to God's holy hill and prepare for the coming of the new age, an age when *many nations shall join themselves to the Lord in that day, and shall be my people; and I will dwell in the midst of you.* It would be an age when God's glory would fill the Temple. It would be an age when all people, not just Jews, would come to God as His people. They would come to God's Temple in Jerusalem. Judah was God's special possession, and Jerusalem was the city that He loved most of all. So, the rebuilding of the Temple had to continue as quickly as possible for *the Lord will inherit Judah as his portion in the holy land, and will again choose Jerusalem.*

And it happened! Zechariah's preaching had effect. The nation stirred itself. More exiles returned, perhaps due to the revolt and the fighting that erupted in Babylon. Darius I assumed the throne, work on the Temple continued, and in 515 B.C. the Temple was rededicated. However, even the shouts of joy, songs, huge amounts of animal sacrifices could not conceal the disappointment. A Temple stood, but it was rather commonplace. It certainly lacked the splendor of Solomon's Temple that some of the aged exiles could recall but which had been destroyed seventy-two years earlier. Nonetheless, in spite of the disillusionment, this Temple stood for over 350 years until Herod the Great built the magnificent Temple in Jerusalem whose foundations still can be seen today.

Zechariah's name means "God remembers." In spite of the terrible difficulties in rebuilding a Temple, city, and country in a hostile world, Zechariah was challenged to recall that God had remembered His people. Zechariah's name was an announcement of the fact that God had remembered. God was dealing with Israel to accomplish His purposes. It was an announcement that demanded a faithful response. It was an announcement that assured Jerusalem of God's presence for God would not forsake His own.

SUGGESTIONS TO TEACHERS

Several years ago, a community in the Southern mountains experienced such a series of setbacks in farming that they began to feel sorry for themselves. They even renamed their little town. The new name? It was "Pity Me." The name reflected the attitude of the townsfolk living there. "Even God has forsaken us," moaned one old lady when asked about the town's name change. Not surprisingly, her words and the title of "Pity Me" portrayed such a defeatist outlook that eventually people moved away and the community died.

Your community has some folks who have a "Pity Me" mentality. In fact, nearly every person has times when he or she muses that God has seemed to have forsaken the world, or forgotten him or her.

The lesson for today is important because it answers the "Pity Me" crowd. State it at the outset: God will not forsake His own!

The scriptural material from a little-read book in the Old Testament—*Zechariah*—offers help to everyone in your class to appreciate God's faithfulness.

1. *PLEA FOR REPENTANCE.* Zechariah calls for his people to remember that the Lord calls, "Return to Me." He reminds them that they and their parents have been refusing to heed the Lord, but God wants them to have the joy of a right relationship with Him. This offers you as teacher a time to discuss the continuing need for repentance on the part of every Christian and each congregation. Christ still calls us to turn around toward Him.

2. *PROMISE OF RETURN.* Zechariah's vision of the measuring line shows the confidence of a person of faith. Zechariah trusts God, therefore, he is certain that God will provide a future when there does not seem to be any possibility for a new beginning. Draw out those in your class on what hopes they have for the future. Are they cynical? Do they have expectations of God?

3. *PREDICTION OF REALIZATION.* God triumphs! Devote enough of the lesson to Zechariah 2:6–12 for the class to appropriate the hopeful message into their own existences. Each Christian should be able to affirm a mighty "Amen" to Zechariah's statement, "Then you will know that the Lord Almighty sent me" (2:9).

4. *PROPOSAL FOR A REMNANT.* Save lots of lesson time for this important theme of the remnant. Have your people learn that the Church today should consider itself such a remnant people. The remnant people are God's, and have a special relationship to Him. Furthermore, God's remnant is meant, like Judah in Zechariah's day, to be "a blessing" to others. Is your congregation aware of its task of being a blessing? In a world that imagines itself forsaken by God, your congregation and your class members have a task to be the special group bringing new hope because of God!

TOPIC FOR ADULTS
GOD WILL NOT FORSAKE HIS OWN

Clinging to the Wreckage. "John Mortimer writes detective stories about Rumpole of the Bailey, and adapted *Brideshead Revisited* for television. He recently wrote his autobiography, called *Clinging to the Wreckage.* When asked where the title comes from, he tells how he was once talking to a yachtsman about his chosen sport and the man told him he had never learned to swim. Why not? 'Because,' said the yachtsman, 'When you're in a spot of trouble, if you can swim you try to strike out for shore. You invariably drown. As I can't swim, I cling to the wreckage and they send a helicopter out for me. . . . If you ever find yourself in trouble, cling to the wreckage.' "—*Publishers Weekly,* November 5, 1982.

Zechariah was one who clung to the wreckage when he and his people were in exile in Babylon. He was confident that eventually God would rescue them from the despair and distance they were experiencing. With the Lord, Zechariah knew there was a future. He clung to the wreckage, trusting that the helicopter would come!

In the lives of each of us, there will be occasions when we must cling to the wreckage, waiting in confidence that God will come. Through Jesus Christ, He assures us that He comes!

Hoping It Might Be So. Thomas Hardy, the English writer, once penned a poem called "The Oxen." It is a series of verses recalling a legend of the Norfolk country folk that at midnight on Christmas Eve, all oxen are said to kneel in their stalls in memory of the birth of Jesus in the stable at Bethlehem. Hardy himself was a religious skeptic. However, the poem concludes with the poet stating if someone told him that in a remote farm the animals were kneeling that very night and asked him to come, "I should go with him in the gloom, hoping it might be so."

So strong is the desire to hope that there may be some assurance that God has not forsaken us but chooses to dwell with us, Hardy and millions reveal a wistful longing. The faith of Zechariah that God will not forsake His own was vindicated in the life of Jesus Christ. Through the Gospel, we know it's more than "hoping it might be so."

Rescued. During the Civil War, Lieutenant James M. Wells of the Eighth Michigan Cavalry was captured on September 26, 1863, carried off to Richmond, and put in Jubley Prison.

After incredible efforts, he and 109 fellow prisoners escaped by a tunnel they dug. On February 9, 1863, Wells and a companion, McCain, traveled by night, hiding during the day and going without food, sleep, and warm clothes for four nights. On the fifth night, exhausted, weak, in a stupor from cold and lack of food, they stumbled out in a freezing rain and gave themselves up to a detachment of cavalry. To their surprise, it turned out to be the Eleventh Pennsylvania Cavalry, which had been sent out as a rescuing party.

There are times when we feel that the situation is hopeless and that we have no alternative but to quit. Many of Zechariah's people felt that way. Wells and McClain finally reached that conclusion. These two escaped prisoners-of-war, however, were surprised to find they had been remembered and sought. In our case, we discover in life that God knows our plight and provides His own way of delivering us through Jesus Christ!

Questions for Pupils on the Next Lesson. 1. What was the disaster which compelled Joel to preach for God? 2. Is the coming day of the Lord, according to Joel, a time of God's judgment or an example of God's redemptive purpose, or both? 3. What new possibilities do you see God opening up for your life? 4. How may we use calamities in our lives? 5. Where can we find the strength to start over when life crumbles about us?

TOPIC FOR YOUTH
NEVER ALONE

Presence of the Emperor. One of his generals once stated that the appearance of Napoleon on the field of battle was the equivalent to a reinforcement of forty thousand men. This reputation stood him in good stead during the campaign which culminated in the great victory of Austerlitz. By some mistake, Napoleon had allowed his advance guard to be cut off and hemmed in by the Austrian forces. Taking a sudden resolution, he traveled rapidly through the night and arrived in the French camp just as the troops had awakened to the hopelessness of their predicament and were preparing to surrender. But the moment they saw him, the whole situation changed as if by magic. Though the numbers against them were more than ten to one, every soldier suddenly became inspired with the conviction that the enemy was already beaten, and when the envoys arrived from the opposite side to demand their instant capitulation they laughed in their faces. The dismay of the Austrian officers was extreme, too, when, instead of the dispirited handful of men they had expected to greet they were ushered into the presence of Napoleon himself. Instead of coming to dictating terms to a beaten foe, they were sent back to tell their own commander that unless they themselves surrendered without delay they would be annihilated. As a matter of fact the Austrians did surrender without striking a blow.

Just at the time when we think we are most alone and desperate, we will discover that our Emperor, the Living Christ, stands with us. We may feel outnumbered and overwhelmed. We may assume we have nothing to hope for or future to expect. With the Lord, however, we become victors. We know we are not forgotten. We can live with confidence!

Don't Give Up on the World! Martin Marty, the witty writer and astute Lutheran scholar who teaches Church History at the University of Chicago, commented about the temptations Christians are having in these times to love the spiritual but hate the material realities of life. He warned against the attitude he finds in Hal Lindsey's *The Late, Great Planet Earth* and claims that Lindsey "gave up on the world before God did." Whether or not Hal Lindsey means to imply this, there are Christians who seem to say or think this. Don't give up on the world! God hasn't. He has promised He will never forsake His own! You are never alone.

Martin Marty's comments made at General Assembly Breakfast, UPCUSA, Monday, June 28, 1982, at Hartford, Connecticut, were called, "A Not-Quite-Clear Slate for Today."

Lonely but Not Alone. A tragic story came to light a couple of years ago when a state trooper in Alaska cut open a tent and found the body of Carl McCunn. McCunn had himself flown into a wilderness area to a nameless valley 225 miles northeast of Fairbanks with 500 rolls of film, cameras, firearms, and 1,400 pounds of provisions, but without plans to be picked up again. His diary, starting in March, 1981, began with recording the wonders of the end of winter, the emergence of spring and fascination with the natural beauty around him. By early August, his supplies were dwindling, and his concern was growing as temperatures began dropping and rains were starting. He was soon spending most of his time searching for food. Meanwhile, concerned friends asked the Alaska State Police to check on McCunn. Trooper David Hamilton flew over McCunn's camp, but later testified he saw McCunn waving a red bag. When he circled, McCunn waved in a casual way and walked away and watched the plane fly by, then walked back to his tent. In his diary, however, McCunn recorded how at first he was elated about sighting the plane, but later realized he had given the wrong signal to the pilot. "Turns out that's the signal (or very similar)," he wrote, "for ALL OK . . . DO NOT WAIT!" In November, McCunn ran completely out of food. The wasted body of the thirty-five-year-old loner was found four months later by Alaska Troopers.

McCunn in his loneliness and despair waved away his rescuers. He casually offered the wrong signal and consigned himself to additional loneliness and despair.

Is not this the way you and I sometimes act toward God? We sulk that we are deserted, but wave Him aside when He draws near. We think that we can manage alone, but end in despair. All the time, however, God merely wants some signal from us that we will receive Him!

Questions for Pupils on the Next Lesson. 1. What was the terrible catastrophe which prompted the Prophet Joel to preach and write? 2. Have you ever experienced any sense of God's Spirit being poured out on you? 3. Why do so many youth think there is no hope for the future? 4. What can a person do when life crumbles around him or her? 5. Do you wonder why trouble comes to people?

LESSON XII—AUGUST 18

JUDGMENT, REPENTANCE, AND HOPE

Background Scripture: Joel
Devotional Reading: Joel 2:14–17; 3:14–16

KING JAMES VERSION

JOEL 1 14 Sanctify ye a fast, call a solemn assembly, gather the elders *and* all the inhabitants of the land *into* the house of the LORD your God, and cry unto the LORD.

15 Alas for that day! for the day of the LORD *is* at hand, and as a destruction from the Almighty shall it come.

16 Is not the meat cut off before our eyes, *yea*, joy and gladness from the house of our God?

2 12 Therefore also now, saith the LORD, turn ye *even* to me with all your heart, and with fasting, and with weeping, and with mourning:

13 And rend your heart, and not your garments, and turn unto the LORD your God: for he *is* gracious and merciful, slow to anger, and of great kindness, and repenteth him of the evil.

26 And ye shall eat in plenty, and be satisfied, and praise the name of the LORD your God, that halth dealt wondrously with you: and my people shall never be ashamed.

27 And ye shall know that I *am* in the midst of Israel, and *that* I *am* the LORD your God, and none else; and my people shall never be ashamed.

28 And it shall come to pass afterward, *that* I will pour out my spirit upon all flesh; and your sons and your daughters shall prophesy, your old men shall dream dreams, your young men shall see visions:

29 And also upon the servants and upon the handmaidens in those days will I pour out my spirit.

REVISED STANDARD VERSION

JOEL 1 14 Sanctify a fast,
call a solemn assembly.
Gather the elders
and all the inhabitants of the land
to the house of the LORD your God;
and cry to the LORD.

15 Alas for the day!
For the day of the LORD is near,
and as destruction from the Almighty it comes.

16 Is not the food cut off
before our eyes,
joy and gladness
from the house of our God?

2 12 "Yet even now," says the LORD,
"return to me with all your heart,
with fasting, with weeping, and with mourning;

13 and rend your hearts and not your garments."
Return to the LORD, your God,
for he is gracious and merciful,
slow to anger, and abounding in steadfast love,
and repents of evil.

26 "You shall eat in plenty and be satisfied,
and praise the name of the LORD your God,
who has dealt wondrously with you.
And my people shall never again be put to shame.

27 You shall know that I am in the midst of Israel,
and that I, the LORD, am your God and there is none else.
And my people shall never again be put to shame.

28 And it shall come to pass afterward,
that I will pour out my spirit on all flesh;
your sons and your daughters shall prophesy,
your old men shall dream dreams,
and your young men shall see visions.

29 Even upon the menservants and maidservants
in those days, I will pour out my spirit."

KEY VERSE: But the Lord is a refuge to his people, a stronghold to the people of Israel. Joel 3:16 (RSV).

HOME DAILY BIBLE READINGS

Aug. 12. M. *A Plague of Locusts.* Joel 1:1–12.
Aug. 13. T. *A Solemn Assembly.* Joel 1:13–20.

Aug. 14. W. *A Day of Darkness.* Joel 2:1–11.
Aug. 15. T. *Repentance and Return.* Joel 2:12–17.
Aug. 16. F. *The Lord Has Pity.* Joel 2:18–27.
Aug. 17. S. *Judgment and Deliverance.* Joel 3:13–21.
Aug. 18. S. *God's Spirit Poured Out.* Acts 2:16–21.

BACKGROUND

There were at least twelve people in the Old Testament who were named Joel. This prophet, the son of Pethuel, is not mentioned anywhere else. His name means "Yahweh is God," and he found himself called to remind his fellow countrymen that Yahweh alone is the Lord, especially in times of difficulty.

We have to do a bit of detective work in placing Joel in history, but from his writings we can be reasonably sure that he lived in Judah after the Persians came to power (539 B.C.) and the Babylonians were defeated. The remnant of the population of Jerusalem carried off to exile in Babylonia was allowed to return and to rebuild the Temple in Jerusalem. Joel's writings show that he knew all about the rebuilt Temple and the reestablished priesthood. In fact, Joel seems to have been involved in the ceremonies of the Temple.

Joel was driven to prophesy, however, when a severe plague of locusts devastated the area, followed by a prolonged drought, followed by a critical food shortage. It may be difficult for us to appreciate how serious these crises were for Joel and his countrymen. Eyewitness accounts of locust plagues in the Middle East in fairly recent times describe the ways the enormous clouds of insects will suddenly appear and ravage an area, literally devouring every bit of vegetation. Denuded of all leaves and grass and grain, the earth becomes parched. Wells dry up. Livestock weakens and dies. Eventually, as stocks of food and supplies of water give out, the humans begin to suffer. Famine and starvation result. These were the conditions prompting Joel to write.

Through these disasters, Joel sees signs that the Day of the Lord will come, a time when God will settle accounts with those who flaunt Him and refuse to obey Him. Joel calls for repentance. He also assures his contemporaries that God will give a new blessing to His people by sending His Spirit upon all, young and old, men and women alike. Five hundred years later, Acts 2 tells how Peter reports that Joel's words came to pass at Pentecost.

NOTES ON THE PRINTED TEXT

The exiles returned and built the Temple. They felt that was sufficient. "Go to church once a week, visit God's sanctuary, but live as you please," was the attitude of these returning exiles. They slipped into immorality and hypocrisy. Nothing seemed to motivate them to live as God's people. Nothing short of catastrophe!

Catastrophe came. A huge locust invasion swept over the land, and everything was eaten up—even the bark on the fig trees! Without food, the animals died. There was no oil, wine, or grain. There were no cereal offerings or drink offerings made in the Temple because there was nothing to sacrifice! Sound impossible? In June of 1978, thirty-three separate locust swarms, each numbering in the hundreds of millions and each covering a range of five to forty square miles, devastated Ethiopia and Somalia. They swept clean over 100 square miles overnight. Famine and drought was the result. The same was true in ancient Israel. So terrible was the devastation that Joel, son of Pethuel, feared that the Day of the Lord was near. Judgment was at hand! He urged the priests to proclaim a day of fasting. *Sanctify a fast, call a solemn assembly.* Fasting was a sign of penitence, so Joel, in his call, was summoning Jerusalem to repent. *Gather the elders and all the inhabitants of the land to the house of the Lord your God; and cry to the Lord,* he urged the priests. Not satisfied with simply one call for repentance, Joel again raised the cry.

Joel's second call for repentance was more explicit. Sounding a bit like an old-time evangelist, Joel pleaded, *Yet even now, says the Lord, return to me with all your heart, with fasting, with weeping, and with mourning.* Ancient man believed that the heart was the central all important organ. It was the center of people's physical, intellectual, moral, and emotional lives. It expressed the total person. The Lord called for each person to return totally to Him. The people were to give themselves completely to God. Repentance called for a change in their moral and spiritual lives as well. *Rend your hearts* meant to get rid of all the wicked and perverted ideas carried within. With a "broken and contrite heart" (Psalms 51:17), return to the Lord. This return should be expressed outwardly with the usual signs of repentance: fasting, weeping, and mourning.

They could return to the Lord in hope. No matter how terrible the Day of the Lord was supposed to be, God would redeem His people. *Return to the Lord, your God, for he is gracious and merciful, slow to anger, and abounding in steadfast love.* God's characteristics were spelled out by Joel. Graciousness, mercy, patience, and love were all part of God's vocabulary. If they had not been, the warning (as terrible and devastating as the locust plague had been) would have been worse! Perhaps there would have been no warning at all!

Joel's preaching had effect. The people listened. The Lord promised the removal of the locusts and a restoration of the fertility of the land. The drought would end with the abundant rainfalls. The threshing floors would be full of grain and the vats would overflow with wine and oil. The pastures, fig trees, and vines would all produce abundant harvests. *You shall know that I am in the midst of Israel, and that I, the Lord, am your God and there is none else.* Only God could promise that His people would *never again be put to shame.*

After all these blessings had been given, Joel confidently predicted still more blessings. Joel promised the gift of God's spirit. *And it shall come to pass afterward, that I will pour out my spirit on all flesh.* At some point in the future, God's spirit would be poured out! On the prophets only? No! On the priests only? No! On men only? No! On EVERYONE! *Your sons and your daughters shall prophesy, your old men shall dream dreams, and your young men shall see visions.* Everyone would have the gift of prophecy. Everyone would know God. Previously, only the priests and a few prophets whom God called could know and speak for God. They had the gift of prophecy. They were the recipients of dreams and visions. Now, everyone would know God. Everyone would know His will. All of this was made possible by His spirit.

Out of this terrible destruction and judgment, Joel looked towards a new age. The future outpouring of the Spirit would create a new human community. Joel lived with hope and expectation!

SUGGESTIONS TO TEACHERS

Chances are no one in your class will ever go hungry because of a locust plague. In fact, chances are that no one will even *see* a real, honest-to-goodness locust plague. At least not the kind they have in the Middle East and Africa, where hundreds of square miles are devastated and the entire crop devoured. But there are other kinds of terrible events which come which seem to kill off hope. And this is the place to start your lesson. Begin by having your class members describe times when their lives seemed eaten up by misfortune or setbacks. Call these occasions "Locust Plague" Days in My Life.

1. *DAY OF THE LOCUST.* As each shares his or her experiences of suffering or hardship brought on by events beyond human control, compare it to Joel's de-

scription of the hopelessness felt after the total ruin of the locust attack in Judea. Encourage those in your class especially to describe their feelings when the "locust plague" occurred in their lives. Did they question God? Were they angry at the Lord? Did they feel God had deserted them? Were they able to deal with the mixture of emotions, including rage, guilt, anxiety, depression, they probably experienced?

2. *DAY OF THE LORD.* This lesson is not meant simply to be a time to share dreary old horror stories. It is intended to move on to a discussion in the light of God's Word to Joel of how the Lord's people may use disasters for positive purposes. Joel suggests that, among other things, locust plagues may serve as a reminder to remember God. In fact, he even intimates that the plague in his time was an opportunity to recall that God always brings a time of reckoning for each person and for every nation. Without implying that God maliciously sends plagues as a way of telling us to shape up, you as teacher may help your students realize that locust days can be occasions to recall how dependent each person is upon the Lord.

3. *DAY OF LEARNING.* Joel offers a helpful way of understanding what real repentance is (2:12, 13). "Rend your hearts, not your garments," he instructs his fellow countrymen. Think for a few minutes what form of "rending hearts" you and those in your church should follow. What about tearing yourselves away from some of the interests your hearts are fixed on, such as violence on television, exploitation of women, reliance on firepower and build-up of weapons systems as national policy?

4. *DAY OF LIFE.* Take plenty of lesson time on Joel 2:26–29. Here is the promise of renewal, the anticipation of Pentecost. God assures His people that He effects a new creation. Just as at the first creation, the Lord breathed His spirit into the nostrils of Adam, so He will instill new breath of life into His followers! Note that this includes both females and males, youths as well as older persons. How is the Lord drenching your congregation with His Spirit? Or, do most of those in your church feel "out of breath" or act as if they have been little touched with the Holy Spirit? Remind your class that God continues to pour out Spirit on His faithful people. Every new day is meant to be, in a sense, a new celebration of Pentecost!

TOPIC FOR ADULTS
LOOK BEYOND JUDGMENT

Hope Is Not Optimism. "Optimism tends to minimize the tragic sense of life or foster belief that the remedy for life's ills is simple. According to Gabriel Marcel, optimism is possible as a constant attitude only when people take a position that isolates them from the real evils and obstacles of the world.

"The hoping person is fully aware of the harshness and losses of life. In order to hope, one must have had experiences of fearing, doubting, or despairing. Hope is generated out of a tragic sense of life; it is painfully realistic about life and the obstacles to fulfillment, within and without. The Christian believer cannot simply focus attention on the positive in life, since there is a cross at the heart of Christian faith preceding any resurrection. For the devout Jew, there is the remembrance of the painful exile, out of which deliverance comes. Unless a person passes through a "valley of the shadow of death," can genuine hope be born? With this understanding we can appreciate anew St. Paul's insistence that everyone lives by hope. Hope is the sense of possibility; in despair and trouble, it is the sense of a way out and a destiny that is going somewhere, even if not to the specific place one had in mind."—From pp. 50–51 in *Finding Hope Again: A Pastor's Guide* by Roy W. Fairchild. Copyright © 1980 by Roy W. Fairchild. By permission of Harper & Row, Publishers, Inc.

Hero at the Intersection. A transformer fire knocked out power to the 6 million people of Quebec province in December of 1982, cutting off light and heat in freezing temperatures, stopping the Montreal subway, and forcing thousands of businesses to shut down.

The power failure was traced to an explosion and fire at one of the utility's main power transformers, at St. Jean Chrysostome, near Quebec City. The fire was extinguished after about ninety minutes.

Power was restored to some areas of the 600,000 square-mile province by mid-afternoon, but most of Montreal remained blacked out as darkness fell.

The blackout, the most widespread in Quebec since a province-wide failure in August 1975, brought the subway system to an immediate halt. Most trains were able to reach stations under emergency generator power, however, and discharged their passengers before shutting down.

Thousands of Montrealers turned to the surface transit system, but many buses were caught in huge traffic jams that developed when traffic lights failed. People waited in block-long queues for buses.

Firemen were dispatched across the city of 2 million to evacuate people trapped in elevators. In Montreal and elsewhere, many major office buildings were shut down and workers were sent home early, further snarling traffic.

At the scene of one of the worst traffic jams in one of Montreal's busiest and most congested intersections, nothing could move, and anger and confusion were mounting. Finally, a nameless civilian jumped into the midst of the hopeless tangle and sorted out the mess with hand signals. Buses and cars began to move again, thanks to this willing volunteer who took the initiative in the midst of disaster.

Against the background of calamity, you and I are called to work to straighten out the mess. We are called to look beyond judgment and to see the possibilities God is presenting us in our world. Be a hero at the intersection instead of cursing the blackout!

God's Own Time. A party of American tourists was visiting the Royal Observatory in Greenwich, England, where Greenwich Mean Time, by which all the clocks of the world are set, is established through exact measurement by sensitive and precise instruments. One old farmer listened as the guide described the way the delicate mechanisms worked and heard the guide state, "This device is the clock from which all the world takes its time." The old gentleman deliberately drew out his big, gold pocket watch and carefully examined it. Interrupting the guide, he drawled, "Wait a minute, young feller. Let me tell you something. That there timepiece of yours is pretty near four minutes fast!"

God has His own time. We cannot tell Him whether it's too early or too late for anything. We must let Him be the arbiter of all time. Sometimes, we interpret human events as the end of all time for us or for the world. We are not called to pronounce the time of final judgment but to help the world look beyond judgment. Even when disasters strike, great and terrible though they are, we must not impose our sense of time on God.

Questions for Pupils on the Next Lesson. 1. What was going on in the lives of God's people when Malachi came on the scene? 2. How do you answer someone who claims that God has left him or her? 3. Does our consumer-oriented society encourage Christian people to forsake their moral and religious commitment? 4. Why do so many folks long for "the good old days"? 5. Why do misplaced values almost inevitably lead to estrangement in personal relationships?

TOPIC FOR YOUTH
A LOOK BEYOND JUDGMENT

Judgment, Repentance, and Hope. "Soaring divorce and crime rates, the mounting death toll of slaughtered unborn, sexual mores so permissive as to be perverted are but the most visible manifestations of our decadence.

"The fact is, we are a nation overrun by hordes of little tin gods all made in our own image, their charge led by the crown prince of self riding his shiny golden calf. Our various sins spring from one common cause: we do precisely what we want to do, answering only to the whims of our desires.

"Many Christians keep one eye anxiously cocked on the skies, watching dolefully for signs of God's wrath—perhaps drought or earthquakes or plague. Maybe the locusts of Exodus have become the medflies of the eighties. Or perhaps Mount Saint Helens is merely a preliminary rumbling of things to come.

"We tense as each crisis flashes across our TV screens. Then, when the medflies are sprayed into momentary extinction, or the volcano is quiet, we breathe easily again. But deep inside, I suspect, we all know we deserve God's judgment. A perfect God cannot tolerate flagrant disobedience; we must be living on borrowed time.

"So our churches fill up with more and more people professing to be born again while the sins that so grieve and offend Almighty God continue. And no matter how much incense we may burn in the shadow of stained glass windows, its scent is overwhelmed by the stench of our sin. Religion is supposed to cure our ills, yet the more religious we are, the more those sinful conditions worsen. Why?

"The answer to that seeming paradox may give us a clue: Could it be that judgment is already upon us? Instead of balls of fire hurled down from above or visitations of plagues and boils, perhaps God is simply allowing us to wallow helplessly in the mire of our sin.

"The hope for our society today is not in clichés and slick religious slogans. Nor will it come by droning 2 Chronicles 7:14 until it becomes some sort of liturgical chant. Only by radical repentance, and the deepest hunger for God's justice and righteousness, can we be saved from our judgment.

"It is better to have locusts or famine than the sentence of being gradually swallowed up unawares in the cesspool of our own greed and lust and hate.

"To starve to death has some degree of dignity—it is the result of exterior forces. But to die a slow and dull-eyed death of excess, even as we cram more sweets into our drooling mouths, is the ultimate debasement. Yet we continue to inflame our passions, swollen and gluttonous, gorging ourselves and sleeping it off.

"With broken and contrite hearts, let us pray that there is still time for God to spare us from ourselves."—Charles W. Colson, *"Christianity Today,* August 6, 1982.

The Face in the Bathroom Mirror. "We are all of us judged every day. We are judged by the face that looks back at us from the bathroom mirror. We are judged by the faces of the people we love and by the faces and lives of our children and by our dreams. Each day finds us at the junction of many roads, and we are judged as much by the roads we have not taken as by the roads we have.

"The New Testament proclaims that at some unforeseeable time in the future God will ring down the final curtain on history, and there will come a Day on which all our days and all the judgments upon us and all our judgments upon each other will themselves be judged. The judge will be Christ. In other words, the one who judges us most finally will be the one who loves us most fully.

"Romantic love is blind to everything except what is lovable and lovely, but Christ's love sees us with terrible clarity and sees us whole. Christ's love so wishes our joy that it is ruthless against everything in us that diminishes our joy. The worst sentence Love can pass is that we behold the suffering which Love has endured for our sake, and that is also our acquittal. The justice and mercy of the judge are ultimately one."—From p. 48 in *Wishful Thinking* by Frederick W. Buechner. Copyright © 1973 by Frederick Buechner. By permission of Harper & Row, Publishers , Inc.

Looking Beyond Judgment. As unemployment and cuts in government aid forced more people to seek more emergency help in recent years, many have merely shaken their heads and said that the situation was a judgment on the economic situation or on the capitalist system or on the unions or on the corporation stockholders or on American workers. A church member named Lynne Hill in Vancouver, Washington, however, looked beyond judgment. During the recession of 1974 when unemployment in her area hit 20 percent, Hill proposed gathering a group of church members to can food for the area's hungry. At first, everyone was skeptical. Few people volunteered the first year. Nevertheless, inspired by Lynne Hill, fruits and vegetables were purchased on sale and canned in the church kitchen. That year, 739 cans of food were processed, costing an average of 11 cents a can. The cans of fruit and vegetables were dedicated at a Sunday morning church service at the Columbia Presbyterian Church and distributed through FISH (Friends in Service to Humanity), an agency helping the area's hungry. By 1983, requests had grown so greatly that two other churches were helping Lynne Hill's congregation, and over 3,000 cans of fruit and vegetables were prepared in the church kitchens by volunteers. A local can manufacturer donates the 16-ounce tins, and many local farmers and markets give or offer mark-down prices on fresh items. In other cases, volunteers pick or harvest at local gardens and orchards to get free vegetables and fruits. In the steaming church kitchens five times each fall, busy crews of volunteers peel, slice, cook, fill tins, seal them, load canners, check the timing, unload, mark and pack in morning and afternoon "canning bees."

"It helps immensely," says FISH President Velma Lair; "It's a wonderful project."

Questions for Pupils on the Next Lesson. 1. Have you ever felt that God has deserted you? 2. What circumstances motivated Malachi to speak and write to his people? 3. What concrete ways could your church show that it truly keeps its word with God? 4. In what ways do you show others that you are a Christian?

LESSON XIII—AUGUST 25

PREPARE FOR GOD'S RETURN

Background Scripture: Malachi
Devotional Reading: Malachi 1:6–14

KING JAMES VERSION

MALACHI 3 Behold, I will send my messenger, and he shall prepare the way before me: and the LORD, whom ye seek, shall suddenly come to his temple, even the messenger of the covenant, whom ye delight in: behold, he shall come, saith the LORD of hosts.

2 But who may abide the day of his coming? and who shall stand when he appeareth? for he *is* like a refiner's fire, and like fullers' soap:

3 And he shall sit *as* a refiner and purifier of silver: and he shall purify the sons of Levi, and purge them as gold and silver, that they may offer unto the LORD an offering in righteousness.

4 Then shall the offering of Judah and Jerusalem be pleasant unto the LORD, as in the days of old, and as in former years.

6 For I *am* the LORD, I change not; therefore ye sons of Jacob are not consumed.

7 Even from the days of your fathers ye are gone away from mine ordinances, and have not kept *them.* Return unto me, and I will return unto you, saith the LORD of hosts. But ye said, Wherein shall we return?

8 Will a man rob God? Yet ye have robbed me. But ye say, Wherein have we robbed thee? In tithes and offerings.

9 Ye *are* cursed with a curse: for ye have robbed me, *even* this whole nation.

10 Bring ye all the tithes into the storehouse, that there may be meat in mine house, and prove me now herewith, saith the LORD of hosts, if I will not open you the windows of heaven, and pour you out a blessing, that *there shall* not *be room* enough *to receive it.*

11 And I will rebuke the devourer for your sakes, and he shall not destroy the fruits of your ground; neither shall your vine cast her fruit before the time in the field, saith the LORD of hosts.

12 And all nations shall call you blessed: for ye shall be a delightsome land, saith the LORD of hosts.

REVISED STANDARD VERSION

MALACHI 3 "Behold, I send my messenger to prepare the way before me, and the Lord whom you seek will suddenly come to his temple; the messenger of the covenant in whom you delight, behold, he is coming, says the LORD of hosts. 2 But who can endure the day of his coming, and who can stand when he appears?

"For he is like a refiner's fire and like fullers' soap; 3 he will sit as a refiner and purifier of silver, and he will purify the sons of Levi and refine them like gold and silver, till they present right offerings to the LORD. 4 Then the offering of Judah and Jerusalem will be pleasing to the LORD as in the days of old and as in former years.

6 "For I the LORD do not change; therefore you, O sons of Jacob, are not consumed. 7 From the days of your fathers you have turned aside from my statutes and have not kept them. Return to me, and I will return to you, says the LORD of hosts. But you say, 'How shall we return?' 8 Will man rob God? Yet you are robbing me. But you say, 'How are we robbing thee?' In your tithes and offerings. 9 You are cursed with a curse, for you are robbing me; the whole nation of you. 10 Bring the full tithes into the storehouse, that there may be food in my house; and thereby put me to the test, says the LORD of hosts, if I will not open the windows of heaven for you and pour down for you an overflowing blessing. 11 I will rebuke the devourer for you, so that it will not destroy the fruits of your soil; and your vine in the field shall not fail to bear, says the LORD of hosts. 12 Then all nations will call you blessed, for you will be a land of delight, says the LORD of hosts."

KEY VERSE: *But for you who fear my name the sun of righteousness shall rise, with healing in its wings.* Malachi 4:2 (RSV).

HOME DAILY BIBLE READINGS

Aug. 19. M. *God to Be Honored.* Malachi 1:6–12.
Aug. 20. T. *Being a Faithful Priest.* Malachi 2:4–9.
Aug. 21. W. *Refined and Purified.* Malachi 3:1–5.
Aug. 22. T. *When People Rob God.* Malachi 3:6–12.
Aug. 23. F. *God's Special Possession.* Malachi 3:13–18.

Aug. 24. S. *The Sun of Righteousness*. Malachi 4:1–6.
Aug. 25. S. *Preparing the Way*. Luke 1:8–17.

BACKGROUND

When those returning from exile in Babylonia to Judah started to rebuild Jerusalem, they had high hopes. They planned to construct a Utopia. After all, they were the divinely-preserved remnant of the faithful. God had miraculously delivered them from exile for a purpose. They set about with vigor and vision to fulfill that purpose. They rebuilt the Temple. They separated themselves into a super-pure community. Led by Ezra and Nehemiah, this community, the nucleus of Judaism, around 500 B.C. to 450 B.C. entered a covenant relationship with the Lord. The people promised to worship properly and regularly, and to give proportionately and faithfully.

Alas, performance never came up to the promise. Utopia in Jerusalem turned out to be just another collection of selfish, stubborn people. At least that's the way Malachi and other sensitive spirits saw things.

Malachi means roughly "my messenger." Although we know almost nothing about the person, we do know that this prophet considered himself a special messenger for God. Malachi's understanding of God's message for his times was that the Jerusalem people in 450 B.C. had grown lax and indifferent to God, and were in danger of spiritual death.

The people in defense said in effect that life was harsh and wearying. Exhausted from trying to survive and rebuild the Temple, they could not see that keeping the faith brought many positive results. Occasionally the rains did not come and the crops failed, food was scarce and hunger prevailed. In spite of the great dreams of rebuilding the Temple a few years earlier, the people began to feel a sense of depression and cynicism. What was the point of scrupulously keeping the worship practices in the Temple? Even the priests and other spiritual leaders felt discouraged.

Malachi preaching in an age of discouragement brought God's message of both judgment and hope. He is the perfect bridge between the Old Testament and the New, the old covenant and the new. The Lord will come, Malachi promised, purifying His people and proclaiming His covenant.

NOTES ON THE PRINTED TEXT

Behold, I send my messenger to prepare the way before me and the Lord whom you seek will suddenly come to his temple. "He is coming!" said Malachi. However, a messenger of the Lord would come first. This harbinger would prepare the way for God's return to the Temple, but what a return it would be!

For he is like a refiner's fire and like fullers' soap, Malachi warned. Malachi makes a promise as well as a threat. Fire, along with water, was one of the elements of purification. In the purification process, fire burned away the impure and worthless and left only the durable and pure. The heat tempered and purified the material during the refining process. These same qualities were found in fullers' soap, a cleansing agent used to bleach wool. Both similes exemplified how the Lord would cleanse the people of their evil. The forerunner of the Lord would come to purify the Temple and the priests, the *sons of Levi.* Only then, *as in the days of old,* would worship and *the offering of Judah and Jerusalem be pleasing to the Lord.* Malachi pleaded for worshipers to have dignity and sincere hearts. He stated that not only the priests would be purified but also the people!

I the Lord do not change. God had been faithful. The people had not been faithful. God had kept His covenant; the people had not kept their covenant. *You have turned aside from my statutes and have not kept them.* Judgment was at hand. *Return to me.* Repent! Return to God! Literally, Malachi said, "Turn around and retrace your steps." This turnabout had to show itself in deeds. The people's actions as well as words had to speak. How could they show evidence of their return to God? They should stop robbing God by withholding their tithes and special offerings that were used to support the Temple. (*See* Leviticus 27:30 and Numbers 18:21.) Drought, insects, and crop failures had caused hard times. The people of the nation were using these difficulties as excuses for not paying their tithes. "Hard times," they argued. However, Malachi charged that if the nation expected God to bless it, it would have to present evidence of its spiritual return to the Lord and His covenant through its worship, tithing, and offering. *Bring the full tithes into the storehouse . . . and put me to the test* says the Lord. *See if I will not open the windows of heaven for you and pour down for you an overwhelming blessing* (rain). If the nation returned, God would bless the nation. If the nation returned, the blessing would be in the form of God's presence. God loved His people. Those who loved Him would experience His blessing. Those who did not love Him would perish.

Malachi was more than a name. His name meant "My messenger." The message remains for us. Many of us are lethargic. Many of us have lost the spiritual intensity experienced years ago. The initial loyalty that we felt and confessed when we joined the church has waned. We have robbed God of our presence in church and our presents to Him. Malachi's message speaks to us who are in need of purification. *Return to me, and I will return to you.*

SUGGESTIONS TO TEACHERS

Malachi is probably just a name to some in your class. To others, it isn't even that, because they won't even know it is the title of the last book in the Old Testament. Even to regular churchgoers and serious readers of the Bible, *Malachi* doesn't receive much attention. You are therefore introducing a portion of Scripture to most of the people in your class today.

Bridge the gap between the time of the Prophet Malachi and this Sunday by pointing out the parallels between the setting both then and now. Malachi's contemporaries wondered if it was any use to expect anything in life, especially from God. So do many today.

1. *THE PRACTICE OF MINISTRY.* By ministry, you must remind your class members, you mean everyone, not just clergy types. All of God's people are "called" to "full-time service." That emphatically means that each member of God's community is a leader, and that each has responsibilities. Unfortunately, in Malachi's time, many leaders neglected their responsibilities. Malachi called them to keep faith with God and with others. Bring this into the orbit of those in your class by pointing out that each person present also must be faithful to God and others in God's community. Discuss what it means to be "full of faith" toward the Lord and toward brothers and sisters.

2. *THE PERMANENCE OF MARRIAGE.* Malachi pleads for those who are married to remember that marriage vows are for keeps. Unlike the Hollywood screen starlet whose marriage vows were altered from "as long as we both shall live" to "as long as we both shall be happy," God's people take marriage commitments seriously. Malachi's frank comments on the destructive dimensions of divorce need to be heard by Church members today.

3. *THE PROMISE OF THE MESSENGER.* God's people, like others in the society during difficult days, feel uncertain and alone. Malachi assures his hearers and readers that God's special messenger will come. His arrival will be like a re-

fining fire. A new era will follow. To those still living in the B.C. era, this announcement in Malachi's time offered hope and called for preparation. In these times, many have not understood what Christ's coming means. They are still living in a "B.C." time. As teacher, stress that those in your class may have new hope and also must prepare for Christ's arrival in their lives.

4. *THE PRETENSIONS OF YOUR MONEY.* Malachi's words about possessions and money need to be reread by believers. In our culture, "BUY! OWN! GET!" are more than imperative verbs. They are accepted as a creed because they are taken so seriously by us and our friends. Depending upon the time available, you may find it helpful to clip out advertisements from a few recent issues of popular magazines to illustrate this point. Only the Lord offers security, not things!

TOPIC FOR ADULTS
A VISION OF HOPE

God's Message Spreading. Recently a 1,010 page volume was published entitled the *World Christian Encyclopedia* compiled over the last fourteen years by the Reverend Dr. David B. Barrett. He traveled through 212 countries and territories and had a team of 21 editors and 500 local experts in various countries working with him. The encyclopedia reveals that despite the decline of Western Christianity during the present century, Christianity is becoming the first truly universal religion in world history, within indigenous outposts in all nations and among many inaccessible tribes where vital Bible translation is booming and church broadcasts reach 990 million people a month. Some 6,850 of the 8,990 ethnic or linguistic groups on earth by now have been penetrated to some extent by the Gospel. Thus, though the Christian proportion of the world population is declining, mainly in the main line Protestant sector, "The outreach, impact and influence of Christianity have risen spectacularly."

The Lord's Pigs. Malachi brought a vision of hope to his people, but he also gave them a reminder that keeping the covenant with God meant honesty in their offerings. Malachi's message has to be repeated frequently. The story is told about a country pastor talking to one of his church members one day about his giving.

"Brother Brown, if you had fifty head of cattle, would you give them to the Lord?"

"Yep," replied Brown eagerly, "That I would do."

"If you had fifty head of sheep," continued the minister. "would you give half of them to the Lord?"

"You know I would, Reverend."

"Well, if you had two pigs, would you give one of them to the Lord?"

"Aw now, Reverend," answered Brown, "that's an unfair question; you happen to know I have two pigs."

Who Owns Your Town? Midland, Pennsylvania, is a dusty mill town on the Ohio River west of Pittsburgh. In 1982, the Crucible specialty steel mill shut down, leaving most of the working people in the town without jobs and the town without its main tax payer. Unemployment skyrocketed. Municipal services were jeopardized because the town had no money. Townsfolk were startled to hear of a strange offer from an Arab oil billionaire to the town. Sheik Mohammed al-Fassi proposed a gift of $3 million to Midland. However, there was a catch to the Sheik's offer: he would give the hard-pressed town $3 million if all of Midland's 2,200 registered voters pledged to not support President Reagan in 1984! The folks in Midland had mixed feelings whether to consider the Sheik Mohammed al-Fassi's proposed gift.

Who owns your town? Does anyone purchase your vote? Are you willing to sell out to the highest bidder?

Do you realize that the Lord is the ultimate owner and ruler of your life, your property, your community, your vote? Malachi offers a vision of hope to all who recognize the claims and covenant of God.

Questions for Pupils on the Next Lesson. 1. How do you resolve the struggle in your life to find clear direction for living? 2. What is meant when the Bible speaks of Jesus Christ as "the image of the invisible God?" (Colossians 1:15). 3. What are some of the modern heresies which compete with Christ? 4. How does Jesus Christ enable you to overcome broken human relationships?

TOPIC FOR YOUTH
A VISION OF HOPE

Music From Another Room. Malcolm Muggeridge, the British journalist, was known for his acid tongue and biting satires for many years. He wrote for leading English newspapers and served as editor of *Punch,* a magazine famed for its witty comments on the British Establishment. Muggeridge, however, became a Christian. Although he had been a scoffer and skeptic for years, he confessed that he was miserable and depressed. For Muggeridge, the gift of faith came as a result of his disbelief in the pomp and powers of this world's princes, presidents, and prime ministers, and his deep sense of alienation. While working one night in the news room of *The Evening Standard* in the midst of an acute period of depression, he was deeply moved by the sound of a sung hymn breaking through the cacophony of the newspaper's babble. He was never quite the same again. Although it was many years before he finally confessed his faith in Jesus Christ, he acknowledged that the music from another room reminded him that "the things I really love in life are worship, sincerity, love."

Malachi's vision of hope was "music from another room," the song by God that in the midst of the babble and confusion He cares for us and calls to us.

Have you heard the "music from another room" in your life? Have you been made aware of the things you should really love in life? Have you allowed Christ's own vision of hope to come to you?

Smothered by His Own Junk. A man was found dead in a rambling old New York house. He was a victim of his own plan to catch the robbers who might someday come into his house. He was a quaint, odd little fellow, a recluse. Nobody ever saw him or knew what he was or how he lived. One day he tripped over a wire which he had strung in a hallway in his house and that let fall a whole mountain of junk. Police found him smothered to death under this pile of old newspapers, umbrella handles, clothing boxes and broken flower pots!

Out of the Weeds. Christopher Columbus on his famous voyage found his party was entangled in the thick weeds of the Sargasso Sea in the midst of the Ocean to the west of the Canary Islands. As far as the eye could see, the surface was thickly covered with weeds. The situation looked hopeless. The weeds seemed impossible to penetrate. Columbus's sailors, grumbling that the weeds were a sign of God's displeasure, rebelliously said that Columbus was impiously trying to penetrate the Lord's secrets and demanded to turn around and go home. Columbus himself worried that the weeds were hiding dangerous rocks which could wreck his fragile vessels. Strong in his faith of finding the land on the other side, however, he insisted on pressing on. He commanded his helmsman to steer westward, ordered crewmen to take soundings carefully and regularly. In a few days, the ships sailed clear of the entangling weeds and into the broad ocean. Columbus's vision of a Western shore eventually brought them into touch with the New World, in spite of obstacles and fears.

In the same way, Malachi's vision of hope inspired his people to prepare for the new age. Their hope in God's promise has been fulfilled in Jesus Christ. How appropriate that Malachi's writings with this vision be the link between the two covenants, the Old Testament and the New!

Questions for Pupils on the Next Lesson. 1. What is the foundation for your life? 2. If someone should ask you what God is like, how would you answer? 3. Why do some youth experiment with a variety of cults, religions, and philosophies? 4. What is ultimate and real in life? 5. What does it mean to come to "fullness of life" in Jesus Christ?